DEDICATION

To my precious wife, Carrie, you are my best friend and greatest supporter. I could not have done this without you doing all you do for me and for our family.

CONTENTS

PREFACE

The goal of this book is to get people to read the Bible. Many followers of Jesus are not spending the time needed to be healthy disciples through study and meditation on the Bible. Those who know the Word of God can know the will of God and walk in the way of Jesus. This is the great need of our day.

The reading plan for each day listed at the top corner of each page is the "M'Cheyne Reading Plan" developed by Robert Murry M'Cheyne (1813-1843). He was twenty-nine when he went to be with the Lord. He left behind a great legacy of faith and a wonderful tool for reading the Bible. This plan allows for a person to read the Psalms and New Testament twice a year and the Old Testament once a year.

While reading all four chapters is preferred, those reading this devotion can limit themselves to reading one chapter a day. The underlined chapter is the one being written about. If a choice must be made between reading the devotion or the chapter of the Bible, please read the Bible.

The intent of the book is to help readers gain an overall understanding of the Bible by using a central theme to guide the reading. The theme of the book is hope. *Hope is the confident realization that good is occurring and the confident expectation that good is going to come.* That is the simple definition being used throughout this volume.

.

Genesis 1; Matthew 1; Ezra 1; Acts 1

There is nothing quite like a new beginning to inspire hope. In the heart of a fresh start there is hope. Hope helps our perspective, our attitude, and our capacity to serve in ways that bless others. Those who believe that positive outcomes are achievable will often act on them inspired with hope. Hope can change the world. Those who believe in the God of the Bible live with hope.

The first chapter of the Bible explains the beginning of the universe. This beginning helps us understand God, our world, and ourselves. We discover beauty and majesty in the creation of God. We find an order to life that promotes structures for well-being and sanity. The creation narrative of Genesis 1 is poetic. It celebrates God's power and explains the uniqueness of humanity.

The world was made in perfect harmony by God, who existed before there was time, space, and matter. There has never been a time when God did not exist. God created everything out of nothing. Many who cannot accept the viability of the God of the Bible have sought to develop explanations for the universe and its beginning that do not allow for the mystery of the supernatural. They often struggle to offer a durable answer to "why" for creation and human dignity.

Whenever someone dies, whenever an evil takes place, or whenever there is conflict of any kind, there is something inside of the human heart that says, "No! This is not how it is supposed to be." That instinct is right. God made us to relate rightly to God, to self, and to the world in perfect harmony. To be at peace with God, with ourselves, and with others creates harmony or shalom, the Hebrew word for peace. It is only in Christ that harmony in this life is possible again. Christ is the hope of humanity.

God made human beings in His image, which provides humanity with a special responsibility. All of God's creation is precious and important, but human life is the most sacred. Human lives resemble God and have been given charge of caring for all God has made. Human beings have a unique sex: male or female. Together, the first man and woman were called to create and care for other image-bearers and fill the earth with them. Each generation was to have children and raise them in a world that was in harmony under God. The animals were to be overseen and the fruit of the land was to be food. It was paradise.

While the world we live in today is not paradise, it certainly holds some of the original beauty God designed. This beauty points us to God and is one of the ways we can perceive who He is and delight in Him (Romans 1:20). The power that enabled God to make what was nothing into something gives hope to those who choose to believe in the One God sent who proclaimed that He would make all things new (Revelation 21:5).

What once was is no more, but it will be again. God designed a perfect world. Although we spoiled it with sin, Jesus has come to rescue us. Are you living with the hope of knowing that God is good? Do you trust in His power to redeem? Are you looking forward to a new heaven and earth? Those who believe in the God of the Bible live with hope.

Genesis 2; Matthew 2; Ezra 2; Acts 2

Hope has a name. His name is Jesus. He was conceived by the Holy Spirit and born of the Virgin Mary. He is God. He has always been God. He will always be God. He lived a holy life. In love He died to pay for the sins of the world. He was raised three days after His death and is alive today. After proving He was alive, He ascended into heaven. He is now at the right hand of God and will one day return for His church and establish His Kingdom on earth. It will be the new heaven. Those who have faith in Jesus live with hope.

The birth of Jesus was the beginning of the fulfillment of the promise of God to bring salvation to the world. His entrance was met with two different responses that are revealed in Matthew 2. The responses of the Magi and Herod are still the responses that Jesus gets today. Some come and worship and adore Him, while others reject Him and seek to remove Him from having influence.

The wise men, the Magi, came from the East to worship the One who was promised (v.2-12). There was a cosmological phenomenon that guided them. This star led them to Bethlehem, where they brought their gifts, which communicated their belief in Him. They gave gold, which pointed to the majesty of this child who was the King of Kings and Lord of Lords. They brought frankincense, which spoke to the divinity of this child who would be the mediator through whom the prayers of God's people would enter into the throne room of God. They brought myrrh, which spoke to the humanity of this child who was the suffering servant who would die for the sins of the world. This Jesus, who was born in Bethlehem, which means "house of bread," is the bread of life. All those who receive Him by grace through faith become children of God. The children of God are heirs of the Almighty and the benefactors of His providence.

Herod did not bother to go and see this One whom the prophets spoke of and that was promised from the beginning. Thinking he could trick the wise men, he sent them to Bethlehem and then had his soldiers follow afterward. Those soldiers slaughtered every male child under the age of two in that unsuspecting city (v.16-18). How horrific! What a reminder of the need for the Savior. The world is still plagued by the likes of Herod who refuse to submit to the true King of Kings.

By divine intervention Mary and Joseph escaped to Egypt (v.13-15). This was not a coincidence. This was providence. The Old Testament promised that the Messiah would be born in Bethlehem (Micah 5:2), be called a Nazarene (Matthew 2:19-23), and come out of Egypt (Hosea 11:1). God always provides for His plans, and the resources given by the Magi would have been a great help in getting this poor couple out of Israel to where God wanted them in Egypt. There is often more to God and His plan than we can understand.

Those who pursue Jesus, as the Magi did, will discover the faithfulness and providence of God. Have you trusted God with your life by repenting of self-sufficiency and believing in the saving sufficiency of Jesus? Those who have faith in Jesus and trust God to provide live with hope.

Genesis 3; Matthew 3; Ezra 3; Acts 3

The most important thing a person can have in life and death is the assurance that they have a right standing with God. Before anything can be sought from God or done for God, a person must be made whole in a holy relationship with God. This is not something a human being can produce. It is something that is experienced by grace through faith in Christ alone. A right relationship with God gives a heart hope.

When the Israelites returned from the Babylonian captivity, one of the first things they did was to construct an altar and establish the sacrificial system (Ezra 3:2-3). They did this according to the Law of Moses (Leviticus 3:1-17). This system of animal sacrifice pictured the coming of the Lamb of God, Jesus Christ, who would take away the sin of the world (John 1:29). The Old Testament believers and those who lived before the death, burial, and resurrection of Jesus were saved by looking forward to the atoning sacrifice of Jesus. Today, on the other side of the resurrection, we look back to the redemptive work of Jesus in order to be saved.

Having established a right relationship with God, these believers began to live in obedience to God by keeping the appointed feasts and festivals (v.4-6). They were faithful to do the will of God, according to the Word of God, having been blessed with leaders who taught and led them to know the Bible. It is through God's Holy Word that His people are able to do what God commands, to be transformed, and to be renewed in their thinking. God's people need the Word of God in order to know the will of God so they can be obedient in the way of God.

Once these Israelites were made righteous by the blood sacrifice and were living obediently to the commands of God, they were ready to do the will of God. They were sent to build the temple but were afraid of the peoples around them (v.3). The Lord had already given them provisions through Cyrus (v.7). By faith they would have to trust and obey God and hope in His protection. Faith is the way of Christ in the world.

When they laid the foundation, there were instruments played and there was great singing and shouting. This was a good thing because, while there were some who were rejoicing, others were weeping (v.12-13). This temple was not nearly as big as the temple that Solomon had built and that had been destroyed. Many saw this new construction as a failure, rather than a success. It is always a mistake to make spiritual comparisons. Each life has a purpose and God always provides for His purpose. Some could only see what had been and not what was being gained. God often works in small things to accomplish His big plan.

When we live in a position of righteousness by grace through faith in Jesus and we practice the faith we possess. Pride and despair are the result of human comparisons. As we focus on Jesus, our faith will grow along with our hope (Hebrews 12:1-3). Are you living with hope today or are you discouraged because your circumstances are not like those you are wrongly comparing yourself to? Those who trust and obey Jesus by faith live with hope.

5

Genesis 4; Matthew 4; Ezra 4; Acts 4

When we see God for who He says He is, we fear Him. We live in awe of His love, grace, power, and purity. Those who love Him will trust and obey Him no matter what. Fear of God inspires faithful saints who live with hope.

In Acts 2, Peter and John were serving out of their fear of God and were filled with hope. Having healed a man, Peter and John entered Solomon's Portico. Peter began to boldly preach the Gospel. Around five thousand men came to saving faith. The Jewish authorities were alerted and annoyed by these two disciples faithfully proclaiming the truth of the resurrection of Jesus. Not knowing what else to do, the authorities arrested Peter and John. Faithful, effective ministry is often costly to the minister. Difficulty should never be a deterrent but needs to be an encouragement. Ministers should make it their goal that at their death the devils of hell say, "I'm glad that one is gone."

The next day, when the rulers, elders, and the high priest with all of his entourage gathered in Jerusalem, Peter and John, along with the man who had been healed, were brought into their midst. This was surely meant to intimidate Peter and John, but it did not work. When God's people fear God, they cannot and will not fear man (Psalm 118:6-9). Peter and John were two uneducated men standing up to the religious establishment by proclaiming truth. The religious leaders recognized that these two had been with Jesus (v.13). When we spend time with Jesus, we experience significant changes. Spiritual transformation is not a result of simply being in a building or in a study. True spiritual transformation is the result of being in the presence of the living Christ.

These two fishermen refused to back down. They made it clear where they stood in terms of their faith. Where they stood was in opposition to these religious leaders, who denied that Jesus is Lord (v.19-22). Peter and John believed in Jesus Christ. They believed He was the Son of God. They believed He died for their sin. They believed He was resurrected and alive. They believed He was coming again. The result of their faith ignited the faith of others. Believers are like dry straw. If one catches fire, it is not unusual for others to catch fire as well.

The church began to pray. They asked God to make them bold and to be allowed to join God in the miraculous work He was doing (v.29-30). When God's people are faithful to pray, share, and trust God, the results are often significant. When this church dared to ask God for great things and believed and shared their hope in Jesus, the place where they were gathered shook and the love of God was made manifest in their community. Generosity and compassion are the outcomes of a community being changed by the power of Jesus and the hope He gives.

Until Jesus returns, there will always be opposition to the Christian faith. Those who believe must tell the truth and trust in God. In so doing they will have hope. Do you have this hope? Do you live in fear of God or of man? Are you becoming more like Jesus? Those who are in awe of God live with hope.

Genesis 5; Matthew 5; Ezra 5; Acts 5

When people come to know their purpose, it is liberating. It thrusts them into a direction. It compels them. Being busy is not a blessing. Being intentional is. When people are able to pursue a purpose with passion, believing God is with them and for them, their life is filled with hope.

In Genesis 5, we find God giving clarity as to the sexual identity of His image bearers. People are made either male or female. Their sexual designation gives a unique perspective and provides a pathway that enables each man and woman to pursue his or her destiny. The sex of each person places them in a specific role that enables them to do the special things and be the special people God designed them to do and be.

In our fallen world, where there is brokenness because of sin, not every boy that is born biologically a boy has the same feelings or sense of himself as other boys. The same is true of girls. There are some who struggle with their sexual identity because of biological issues and some for other reasons. There are also some who are tempted with same-sex attraction. God's grace is sufficient to provide the hope necessary to find peace through obedience to God's design in any circumstance. Those who struggle with sexual identity and same-sex attraction need the love, compassion, prayer, and the care of Christ followers. It is among God's people that they can and must find solace. They may never be able to experience Biblical marriage or have a family of their own, but that does not make God's design wrong. Those who live with confusion concerning their sexual identity and have same-sex attraction need the healing hope of Christ expressed and experienced through the redeemed people of God.

Having established the uniqueness of each sex, God provided a genealogy from Adam to Noah (v.3-32). The consistent refrain throughout the chapter concerning each man was that he fathered an eldest son "and had other sons and daughters... and he died." There are two important things to see in this consistent statement. First, each eldest son was given the responsibility of taking on the family mantle and perpetuating it, but the worth of the others was in no way diminished. The other sons and daughters were just as important in the eyes of God, but the eldest son was given a specific role. Second, each man died. This is the consequence of the fall. God made people to live, but because of the fall, death has now become a sad reality. The New Testament gives more clarity concerning death. It is not an end, but a beginning. Every person will face judgment for the life they lived and spend an eternity with the consequences of their actions (Hebrews 9:27).

Life is filled with challenges and then we die. God is to be thanked because He has not abandoned us. God offers salvation through Jesus to all who repent and believe in Him. No matter what sex we are, what challenges we have, or what role we play in our family and world, God has a plan for us. His love is real and His Gospel is powerful. Can you trust God's plan for how He made you, where He has put you, and what He has gifted and called you to do? Those who know their purpose in Christ and pursue it with passion live with hope.

7

Genesis 6; Matthew 6; Ezra 6; Acts 6

There is great hope found, when we release the details and outcomes of our life into God's capable hands. As long as we are holding on to our lives and trying to control what others do and what ultimately happens to us and those we love, we will always be plagued with anxiety. We will look for the approval of people and the comfort of circumstances rather than God. We will look to build our own earthly, temporal, empty kingdom rather than the Kingdom of God. We will have to settle for empty religion rather than a dynamic relationship with God. We will have to settle for the best of this dying and soon-to-be destroyed world rather than receiving God's best in this life and in the world to come. Those who trust in Jesus live with hope.

Matthew 6 contains the middle section of the Sermon on the Mount. The chapter ends with an explanation of anxiety, its causes and complications. When we try to be our own god, the result is always anxious feelings. The one true God does not want us to concern ourselves with what we have now or with what we will have in the future. God does not want us to fret over what is happening in our lives in any given moment. God wants us to trust Him and His love and His goodness and His purpose in every moment of our lives.

Our trust and devotion to God's provision is seen in our generosity or the lack thereof. The Christian who claims to love God but does not give financially in both faithful and sacrificial ways is revealing a lack of faith in God. When we know that everything we have that is good comes from God, we will gladly give to God's work and to others in need. If, however, we think that everything we have comes from us, we will only give in as much as it pleases us. We must never mistake the root of the fruit of our resources. God is the origin of every good thing.

Generosity will only be as real as our prayer life. Jesus taught how His disciples are to pray. Prayer is to begin by acknowledging God, then speak to motive, and end by asking for needs to be met. Why we pray is crucial. If our motive is for selfish gain, we can know we are not asking according to God's will. When we ask so that God's will can be done on earth, as it is in heaven, we can know we are praying rightly.

Thinking rightly about God provides a unique freedom. When we believe in Jesus and entrust Him with our lives, we don't live for the approval of people. We are free to pursue God's approval and blessing. Being in pursuit of God will lead us to fast and pray. We fast to remind ourselves of what Jesus said to Satan in Matthew 4:4, during His time of temptation, "Man shall not live by bread alone, but by every word that comes from the mouth of God."

The goal of giving, praying, and fasting is so that we can invest in eternal things. Do you live an anxious life? Are you a generous person with your time, energy, and money? Are you seeking God in prayer and confidently making your requests known to Him? Those who trust in Jesus live with hope.

Genesis 7; Matthew 7; Ezra 7; Acts 7

Hope inspires prayer. When we are hopeful, we are prayerful. Prayer provides clarity concerning the will of God, and this clarity motivates belief and the pursuit of noble causes. Praying people look for God's provision and seek it expectantly. Those who look to God in prayer live with hope.

Ezra was a hopeful man who was not afraid to ask God and others for big things in order to accomplish God's purpose. He was a priest, but he was also a leader. He was a man who believed in himself, in his God, and in his calling (Ezra 7:1-9). He had hope in the Word of God and was willing to risk his life in order to make God's Word known to the new settlers in Israel, who had left Babylon to build the temple and a new nation (v.10-26). He was clearly loved by God and given a special blessing in order to accomplish the task God had ordained for him (v.27-28).

Regardless of where we are born or what family we are born into, we have to make choices that determine the direction of our life. Ezra had clearly sought the Lord and gained the Lord's favor. Through his trust and obedience, Ezra was able to discern the will of God and the resources needed for the work God had for him. From Artaxerxes king of Persia, Ezra asked for and was given the letters of recommendation needed to venture to Jerusalem. He was also given the power to exercise authority over the people there (v.7-26). He was also given the supplies and people to accomplish God's purpose (v.6).

Armed with faith in himself, in God, and in his calling, he set out to do a hard thing. Ezra had hope in God and he was passionate to see that others obtain it too. In order to make this hope known, Ezra did three things. He learned the Law of the Lord, he lived it, and he let others know about it (v.10). Becoming an expert in the law took years, but Ezra was faithful. Obeying the law required discipline and a delight in the Lord. Telling others took courage, but when a person is confident in God, there is never a reason to fear anything else. Disciples of Jesus are faithful learners that obey God's Word and share God's truth with others.

The ability to overcome the fear of the very real threats and obstacles that were before him required Ezra to be certain of God's love for him. The love Ezra had from God was not something he could earn. It was given to him by grace. He received God's love through his personal faith. Ezra's confidence in God's love led him to pray. God answered Ezra in love and moved the heart of Artaxerxes to provide for the temple in Jerusalem. The King of Heaven's involvement made the king's counselors and mighty officers kindly disposed toward Ezra. God also caused leading men from Israel to leave what had become a comfortable place in Persia to start over in desolated Jerusalem.

We rarely grow in safe places. Those who are willing to trust God and pray will see God do great things. It is in the difficult times that we pray. With each answer to prayer our faith grows. Is your prayer life strong? Is God providing for His purpose in your life? Those who look to God in prayer live with hope.

Genesis 8; Matthew 8; Ezra 8; <u>Acts 8</u>

Hope will lead us to obey God. When we obey, we will see God at work, which produces even greater hope within us. Hope produces obedience, which produces greater hope. Each step of obedience inspires greater trust in God and the fruit of trusting God is a changed life. That change will inspire hope. Obedience to God leads to a life of hope.

Like the early church, the church today has not always been faithful to make disciples in all the earth. When we do not obey, God has a way of helping us out. Sometimes, God will allow us to suffer in order to get us to obey. We see in Acts 8 how God allowed the early church to face horrible persecution (v.1-3). In response to this persecution, the church scattered with the Gospel to the places where God had called them to go.

Philip went to Samaria (v.4-25). This was step two of the Gospel movement God had commanded the church to fulfill in Acts 1:8. Philip performed many miracles, and the people were attentive and able to believe. The Holy Spirit had not come upon them, so Peter and John were sent for, and after the apostles prayed for the people, the Holy Spirit came down and a revival broke out. Revival comes through the power of God and the obedience of His people.

In the midst of this great revival, God called Philip to go on a mission trip (v.26-40). We must never let our hope be found in any given circumstance. Philip, filled with hope, obeyed God and left the excitement of Samaria to go to a desert place. The distinction is striking. He went from an urban awakening to a winding road in the middle of nowhere. A sign that our faith is in Christ alone is that we will gladly give up what is comfortable and enjoyable in order to expand the Kingdom of God, as God commands us to. God provides what we long for and could never get on our own, when we are willing to obey Him.

On this road in the middle of nowhere, Philip found an important man looking for hope. Having been commanded by the Spirit to approach him, Philip ran up to his chariot and asked him about what he was reading. The man invited him along for a ride and beginning with the text he was reading in Isaiah, Philip explained the Gospel to him. This man repented of his sin and believed in Jesus Christ and wanted to be baptized immediately. Philip had obviously done more than invite this man to convert. He had explained what it meant to be a baptized believer who walks in humble obedience to Christ. Jesus calls His people to make disciples of Jesus and not just halfhearted converts. Philip was supernaturally carried away to Azotus, which was about forty miles away, and the man went on his way rejoicing. God always has a next step for His disciples.

Because Philip hoped in Christ and not in his circumstances, he was willing to leave the excitement of Samaria and go to a desert place to serve God. He had a hope that enabled him to obey. His obedience led to greater hope. This is what happens to those who hope in God and obey Him no matter what. Do you trust God? Are you obeying His command to make disciples? It is in obedience that hope is experienced.

Genesis 9–10; Matthew 9; Ezra 9; Acts 9

In His grace, God provides new beginnings. A fresh start with God gives hope to our hearts and drives us to pursue and recover the harmony that humanity once enjoyed with God. God gives a fresh start to those who become followers of Jesus. Those who receive new life in Christ live with hope in the harmony that grace gives.

After God had destroyed the earth with the flood, He provided a new beginning. Genesis 9 tells of the new beginning God gave to the human race after the flood. Genesis 10 reveals how humanity filled the earth, as God commanded, and lists the many nations that came to be. Both chapters reveal humanity's ongoing challenge.

The fact that there were prohibitions and consequences given by God, after the flood, points to the reality that, while God was gracious to give humanity a new beginning, the curse of sin was and is still active (v.1-7). The Lord would have been justified in completely destroying the human race, but instead, He saved a remnant by grace. These saved people continued to struggle with sin. So it is with those who are in Christ now. God has given new life to all who believe. That life provides a right standing with God in grace. There is now harmony with God, but we still live in a fallen world and will struggle with sin. Life is not yet perfect.

After the flood, God made a covenant that He would never again destroy the earth with a flood (v.8-17). This is a wonderful promise. While humanity did and has since deserved destruction, God has been and has continued to be gracious to preserve life on the planet. This covenant is both similar to and different from the new covenant made in Christ Jesus. It is similar in that it is a lasting covenant. It is different in that it is a covenant of common grace. It is made with all of creation. The covenant of Christ is a covenant of special grace.

After the common grace covenant was established and the family of Noah had left the confines of the ark, the first thing the Bible records was Noah getting drunk and one of his sons, Canaan, shaming him (v.18-29). This resulted in the cursing of Canaan and division within the human family. This is the way of the world now. There are broken relationships that are caused by broken people. Foolishness leads to sin, which causes more devastating consequences. And yet the world goes on with children being born to produce more children. The population of the planet grew and now grows (Genesis 10). The more people there are, the more sin there is. Thankfully, where sin abounds, grace abounds all the more (Romans 5:20).

There are many problems on our broken planet, but the main problem is sin. Thankfully, Jesus has come to give a fresh start with a new covenant. Jesus died to pay the penalty for sin and was buried in a tomb from which He was resurrected. Jesus can bring harmony to a life. Have you received that new life from Jesus by faith? Have you had that fresh start? Are you fighting against the temptations? Those who receive new life in Christ live with hope in the harmony that grace gives.

Genesis 11; Matthew 10; Ezra 10; Acts 10

The follower of Jesus can answer the most important questions of humanity. Why do I do what I do? Why do I think the way I think? Why do I feel the way I feel? The answers have to do with Jesus. Those who live on mission for Jesus with the right perspective and attitude live with hope.

In Mathew 10, Jesus commanded the disciples to go on a mission trip. He did not send them out with some over-the-top motivational speech about how much fun, success, and comfort they would have on their journey. He told them of the realities of being rejected, persecuted, and having to deal with family strife because of their calling. He pointed to the fact that, in the end of it all, there would be a reward that would come to those who were found faithful. This gave them hope. It is the hope of all followers of Christ.

Given the difficulty and sacrifices these men had to make, the question must have crossed each of their minds a few times along the way, "Why am I doing this?" They were sent to the "lost sheep of the house of Israel" (v.6) to tell them that, "the Kingdom of Heaven is at hand" (v.7). They were going to perform miracles, as they made their proclamation (v.8), but they were not to receive contributions in order to acquire wealth (v.8-10). They were also not to take items that would allow them to depend upon themselves. Instead, they would have to depend on God every step of the way (v.10-13). They were told that if the people they went to would not receive them or their message, they were to shake it off and leave for the next town to continue the work they were called to do (v.14-15). They did what they did because they had hope in their message and in the One who sent them. This is the mindset of all followers of Christ.

Jesus made it clear that this would not be an easy journey and that they would not always be well received (v.16-33). The reason for the persecution was because of the nature of the world. Their thinking needed to be right about this, so Jesus helped them understand that they were engaging in a spiritual battle. In this battle, there would be those who would want to harm them, but Jesus assured them they need not fear because they were under the care of God (v.28-33). God was sending them into enemy territory to rescue those who were perishing. This was dangerous work (v.34-39). This is the work of all followers of Christ.

Although their task was difficult and the obstacles were intense, these men had every reason to feel upbeat and confident. Jesus assured them of their value to God (v.29-31). Jesus prepared them to see many who would believe and acknowledge that Jesus is the Christ (v.40-42). These new believers would be rewarded not only for their faith, but for their kindness to the disciples. These men would see what redeemed lives look like. Faith and generosity are attributes of all followers of Christ.

God calls His disciples to live on mission for Him. God is at work in the world through His disciples. Are you living on mission for God? Are you seeing lives transformed by Jesus? Those who live on mission for Christ live with hope.

Genesis 12; Matthew 11; <u>Nehemiah 1</u>; Acts 11

God is at work in the world and is moving His people to be burdened for specific spiritual purposes. The fact that a heart that was once dead to God and lost in sin can be stirred to join God in what He is doing in the world is a tremendous miracle. Those who can sense God's leading and gladly obey Him live with hope.

In Nehemiah 1, we see how God stirred the heart of an influential man to accomplish a purpose that had eternal implications. Nehemiah was in exile in Babylon serving as the King's cupbearer (v.11). This was a place of great trust and importance. He had access to the most powerful man on earth at that time. As an exiled Jew, God had providentially put Nehemiah where he needed to be in order to be able to do what God wanted him to do.

The fact that Nehemiah's heart would be broken for the city of Jerusalem is amazing considering the fact that Nehemiah had so many good things going in his own life (v.1-4). There is no doubt that Nehemiah lived well. He had a successful career. He did not appear to be in any financial, political, or spiritual trouble. He basically had everything a person could want in terms of comfort, power, and prestige. It did not make sense from a human perspective for him to be concerned with a place he had never seen. Those walls had been destroyed for over 100 years. But God stirred his heart. When God stirs the heart of a person for His purpose, it does not always make worldly sense.

The prayer method of Nehemiah is worthy of replicating (v.4-10). He began his prayer with praise. He acknowledged the character and attributes of God. He prayed day and night. He confessed sin. The prayer was based on the truth of God's Word. It was in God's Word that he found the confidence to seek the blessing that was promised. He prayed for what he believed was the will of God. God's will is always revealed and is consistent with God's Word. He prayed in community. Nehemiah asked God to hear his prayer and the prayers of his fellow servants who feared God's name. The prayer concluded with Nehemiah asking for a blessing. Nehemiah asked God to give success to what he was about to do and for mercy. Those who pray in humble confidence pray with repentant and expectant hearts.

Nehemiah was about to go before the king and to risk his own life for the cause of God's work in the world. What God calls us to do is rarely easy and often requires sacrifice. It is in our dependence on God and not in our strength and creativity that God gets the glory. Trusting in God gives God's people great peace. The children of God can always know that the victory is dependent on God's power and not their strength.

It is a marvelous thing to join God in His work. When God stirs a heart to pursue a purpose that demands sacrifice, the right response is obedient faith that glorifies God. What is God stirring you to do for His glory? What are you faithfully praying for? Do not be afraid to ask God to do great things through your life. He is a great God. Those who can sense God's leading and gladly choose to trust and obey Him live with hope.

Genesis 13; Matthew 12; Nehemiah 2; Acts 12

The world is not as it should be, but it is not as bad as it could be. God has graciously chosen to intervene in the world. Yes, tyrants and sickness and injustice are rampant in our world, but so is God's power. Those who are willing to turn to Him in prayer will find that God is at work with a wonderful plan. Those who join God in what He is doing in the world live with hope.

In Acts 12, the power of God is on display. King Herod, who gained power by manipulating people, killed James, the brother of John, and imprisoned Peter (v.1-4). Herod's political skill was impressive, but his pride led to his death (v.20-23). Despite him and because of the power of God, the message of the Gospel continued to spread and the number of disciples grew (v.24).

When Peter had been arrested, the church began to pray (v.5). The night before Peter was to be executed by Herod, Peter was bound by chains between two sleeping soldiers. There were also soldiers guarding the entrance to the prison (v.6). Peter was stuck and it would have taken a large armed mob to have freed him, but God's people were praying. That night, seemingly at the last moment, an angel showed up and freed Peter. The angel gave Peter step by step instructions for how to get out (v.7-9). There are times, when we go through difficult days and we cannot see a way out. In those moments we can look to God and simply trust and obey Him. He will hear our prayers and take us step by step through our challenge.

Once Peter was freed, he immediately headed for the house where the church was praying (v.10-12). A miracle had just happened. Peter was free. And yet, when he went to the place where the people were praying, the people praying did not believe it was actually Peter who was outside the door. (v.13-16). Once Peter was finally inside, he explained what God had done and then he left town (v.17) The soldiers who were in charge of him were put to death the next day (v.18-19). God's people must be ready to receive God's provision in response to their prayers.

We live in a very serious world. We have a very serious spiritual enemy (1 Peter 5:8). Through every challenge, God's people can turn to God for help. When we pray, we must pray specifically, so that we can know when God has answered our prayer. We must pray and believe that He will answer our prayer (James 1:6-8). The acronym P.U.S.H. has served me well over the years as it pertains to prayer. We must: Pray Until Something Happens! We must pray and believe God has the power to answer our prayer and then wait patiently as we continue to pray. As we wait and pray in faith, we must look expectantly for the hand of God to provide.

God is at work in the world. There are many enemies seeking to undermine the work of Christ. It is crucial that God's people pray specifically and expectantly. What are you praying specifically for today? Are you consistent in your prayers and confident of God's will and God's power to work? Are others joining you in what you are praying for? God is at work in the world and those who join Him, through prayer and obedience, live with hope.

Genesis 14; Matthew 13; Nehemiah 3; Acts 13

The Bible explains what was, what is, and what is to come. The Bible is not a collection of stories or sayings. It is a single story with four distinct parts: creation, fall, rescue, and restoration. It is the story of a King who created a world, where his loyal subjects could live with Him in harmony. Instead of being loyal, His people committed treason. This treason or sin created a fallen world and caused death. Rather than allow His subjects to remain hostage to the consequences of their sin, the King chose to rescue them. Jesus came to save sinners. Jesus now reigns in and through His people and is at work through them to save others and will one day return and make a new heaven and earth. This restoration will bring about harmony again. Those who believe in Jesus live with hope in the story of God.

The story of God: creation, fall, rescue, and restoration, is explained over and over in many different ways throughout the Bible. One example is in Genesis 14.

Lot, the son of Abram's brother, was taken hostage (v.1-12). Rather than remain loyal to his uncle and serve him in love, Lot had chosen to take his family and place his trust in the people of Sodom. Lot chose a life on his own and a purpose apart from that of his uncle. This is what happened to the human race. Rather than trust in the goodness of God and remain under His leadership, humanity chose a life and purpose apart from God.

Abram could have shrugged off the situation and rightly said, "Lot chose to go his own way and now he must suffer the consequence of his decision." Instead of turning away, Abram pursued Lot to save him. Abram took his fighting men to defeat Lot's oppressors. At great sacrifice and in the face of great danger, Abram defeated those who had taken Lot captive. Abram set Lot free (v.13-16). This is what God did. God could have rightly said, "Humans chose to go their own way and must now suffer the consequences of sin." Instead of turning away, God chose to come and save us by defeating sin and death with the cross and His resurrection.

The salvific expedition that Abram pulled off was miraculous. It was the work of the God Most High and this fact was celebrated by Melchizedek, the mysterious king who was also a priest (v.19-20). What a strange meeting this was (v.17). Abram stood in the King's Valley between a holy man, the king of Salem, and a dirty man, the king of Sodom. The holy man, Melchizedek, brought praise to God. He, like Jesus, was a prophet, a priest, and a king. As a prophet, he proclaimed the truth that God saved. He also served as a priest of God and at the same time was the king of Salem. The dirty man, the king of Sodom, came to steal praise for himself. Rather than honor God, he tried to make a deal with Abram. Abram refused to rob God of glory. Instead, Abram remained faithful to God (v.21-24). Until the Lord returns, God's saved people are to live to glorify Him and reject the way of the world.

When we look to God for salvation, we bring God glory. Are you part of God's redemptive story? Those who trust in Jesus live with hope.

Genesis 15; Matthew 14; Nehemiah 4; Acts 14

The world rages against God. This is why there is so little peace on earth and why people seek to find solace in pleasure, popularity, possessions, and power. When the temporary things they are trusting are threatened, they attack whoever or whatever is threatening them. This is the way of the world, but those who trust in God have an eternal hope.

In Matthew 14, there is a striking difference seen between a person with eternal hope and a person with temporary hope. Jesus revealed how to live with eternal hope.

John the Baptist had eternal hope, even though he had a hard life and powerful enemies (v.2-4). There were moments when John's faith in Christ was challenged, but he remained faithful to Jesus. Herod the Tetrarch, who was a weak and insecure leader, had married his half-brother's wife, and John called him out for his sin. Herod, like all fallen people, had his identity wrapped up in a created thing he could not keep, his popularity and power. John was a threat to both of those and so Herod had John arrested and later killed (v.5-12). It might have appeared at that time that Herod had it all and John had nothing. In reality, John had everything and Herod had nothing. John's momentary affliction was nothing compared to the weight of glory of his eternal reward. Herod's temporal comfort and authority was soon snuffed out and eternal death became Herod's infinite reality.

When Jesus heard of John's death, He sought to get away to a desolate place (v.13). Jesus was fully God and fully man. His humanity was on display here. He sought to find comfort and strength in time alone with God the Father, but was confronted with the needs of people. He chose to serve them (v.14-21). He fed the hungry and taught His disciples to trust in God. Eternal hope is found not in the comfort of circumstances, but in faithfulness to God. What Jesus needed in that moment of sadness was not isolation, but investment in ministry. Having fulfilled His purpose for that moment, Jesus sent the crowds away and the disciples to the other side of the lake (v.23-23). Loving others and giving hope is one of the ways that followers of Christ are renewed with eternal hope.

Once He was done being renewed in prayer, Jesus walked to His disciples on water. It was another miracle. The disciples were in awe (v.24-27). Walking on water did not seem to be a big deal to Jesus. The truth is that all things are small things to God. Feeding a multitude, walking on water, and finding solace in a sad time are not big things to God. God is mighty! He gives hope in death, provisions in times of need, and power to do the extraordinary. To receive what God gives requires faith. Peter was able to join Jesus in walking on water, as he had faith. He only sank when he lost focus on Jesus and His power (v.28-33). Having crossed over the water and started a new day, the ministry began again (v.34-36).

There are always needs in our broken world. God is always there to provide. Do you trust God? Is your hope temporal or eternal? Those who trust in God have eternal hope.

Genesis 16; Matthew 15; Nehemiah 5; Acts 15

Justice inspires hope. Injustice produces frustration. When people choose to do what is best for others, it brings about strong feelings of appreciation and confidence. When there is a culture of corruption, there is usually disappointment and discouragement, which leads to doubt and disengagement. Those who live like Jesus live with hope and share it with others.

In Nehemiah 5, the leaders were doing what was unjust. In wisdom, Nehemiah led the people to repent and honor God. It was a picture of the leadership of Jesus.

The people were supposed to be working together to accomplish the purpose of God by providing a wall that would protect the city of Jerusalem. The poor people of the community were making sacrifices. Meanwhile, the leaders were extracting from them their very means to make a living (v.1-5). Their sons would soon join their daughters in becoming slaves, as a result of their poverty. In those days, when people could not pay their bills, their lives were given in exchange. God's people must always be helping each other and not taking advantage of one another.

Nehemiah got angry, but rather than just rant and rave at the leaders, he took some time to collect his thoughts and determine his words (v.6-7). There is nothing wrong with being angry when there is injustice. Saying the right thing the wrong way makes the right thing being said wrong. When we speak, we must speak of it with a Christ-honoring attitude or the message will have no authority and will lose its meaning.

The response to Nehemiah's words of rebuke was silence and then repentance (v.8-12). Because the wrong was public, Nehemiah had them commit to making the reparations public. Nehemiah called down a curse as a consequence to any that did not keep their oath (v.13). Sin is serious. Before there can be true forgiveness, there must be genuine repentance.

The best leaders are those who do not ask people to do what they say, but who can challenge others to do what they do. Nehemiah was an exceptional leader. His example was not only just, but also gracious. From the first day, when he had become their governor, he never took advantage of the opportunities that were rightly his (v.14-18). Because of his generosity, Nehemiah was able to ask God to do good for him. The confidence to request a blessing from God comes from a faithful heart.

Nehemiah's leadership is like the leadership of Jesus Christ. There never has been and never will be a leader like Jesus. Nehemiah sought to serve the people. Jesus came to serve and to give His life as a ransom for sin (Mark 10:45). Nehemiah's way of life matched his words. Jesus lived a holy life in love. Nehemiah paid a price to lead the people. Jesus paid the debt for sin. All who have faith in Jesus and follow Him are saved.

Nehemiah gave the people hope by providing justice, truth, and grace. Are you living a just life? Are you helping the cause of Christ or hurting it by your lack of compassion and generosity? Those who live like Jesus live with hope.

Genesis 17; Matthew 16; Nehemiah 6; Acts 16

God is in control and is working out a perfect plan. Those who trust in Jesus are able to join in God's work. It takes faith to obey Jesus. Those who trust and obey Jesus live in and give others hope.

In Acts 16, we see how Timothy became a part of Paul's missionary team (v.1-5). At some point, Timothy repented of his sin and believed on Christ for salvation. His family background provided him with a unique capacity to connect with those Paul was called to minister to. His mom was Jewish and his dad was Greek. Paul was called to reach the Greeks with the Gospel, but he often began by going to the synagogue and explaining to the Jews how Jesus is the Messiah. Both his background and reputation made Timothy a great candidate for leadership in Paul's ministry. In order to go with him, Timothy had to be circumcised. Timothy complied with this demand because it served the purpose of God. Leadership demands sacrifice.

Paul had planned to go to Asia with the Gospel, but God provided him with another calling. He was to go to Macedonia and preach the Gospel there (v.6-10). God guides His people to where He wants them. Having arrived in Philippi, they went to a place of prayer outside of the city (v.11-14). Lydia, a businesswoman from Thyatira, became a believer when "The Lord opened her heart to pay attention to what was said by Paul" (v.14). This was the beginning of the Philippian church.

The next person to be impacted by Paul and his mission team was a psychic slave. Paul released her from this demon, which got him arrested (v.15-24). While in jail, Paul and Silas were singing and praying and an earthquake occurred, opening their prison doors. Paul did not leave the prison. Unlike Peter's situation (Acts 12:7-10) when the angel told him to leave, Paul received no such instruction. So he stayed put, along with the other prisoners. When the jailer saw that the jail had been opened, Paul announced that they were all still there and that he should not harm himself. This jailer and his family believed and became a part of the church at Philippi (v.25-34).

The next morning the magistrates announced that Paul was free to go, but wanting to protect the integrity of the ministry of the church among the Gentiles, Paul announced his Roman citizenship and demanded that the magistrates publicly recognize his innocence. It was against the law for a Roman citizen to be scourged or imprisoned without a formal hearing. Paul used his citizenship to force these magistrates to publicly apologize and to walk him out of the city (v.35-40). This would protect the Philippian church and possibly other churches in Roman cities in the years to come. This public spectacle was both out of love for the church and also a means to protect the church.

God's plan can often seem strange to us. Paul went west rather than east and planted a church with a businesswoman, a demon-possessed woman, and a jailer. By choosing to trust and obey, Paul and his team accomplished God's purpose. Are you trusting and obeying God? Are you fulfilling God's purpose for your life? Those who trust Jesus see God at work and live with hope.

Genesis 18; Matthew 17; Nehemiah 7; Acts 17

God's children will not always understand or agree with God's will. We cannot know what God knows. All any disciple of Jesus can do is to trust God and to obey Jesus. Those who trust and obey Jesus live in God's will. The concern of a disciple of Jesus is to honor God, to pray, and to trust God's decisions. Those who live in the wisdom and goodness of God live with hope.

Abraham was a man who lived an obedient life. In Genesis 18, we find him living about twenty miles southwest of Jerusalem in a tent surrounded by a large grove of trees in a place called Mamre. God met with him, as Abraham honored God (v.1-5). God reveals Himself and His plans to those who honor Him.

After the meal, the Lord announced that about a year from then Sarah would have a son. When she heard the news, she laughed. Who could blame her? This was ridiculous! And yet it was true. And it is true that God often does ridiculously wonderful things according to His will and the promise of His Word. After an awkward exchange involving Sarah lying about laughing, the Lord made it clear that Abraham and Sarah would have a son (v.6-15). After years of obedient wandering, God was going to keep His promise. God's timing is perfect. His people can count on Him.

The mood changed when God informed Abraham that Sodom was to be destroyed (v.16-21). God wanted Abraham and his progeny to understand the seriousness of sin and the justice of God. The Lord explained that He would "go down and see" (v.21) the sin of this city. It is not as though God was not already aware of what was taking place. He is God. The Lord was making it clear that His actions are never flippant. When God makes His decisions, He does so with full knowledge of the facts. God is always right in what He does.

Abraham could not imagine such justice being necessary, and he entreated the Lord to withhold this judgment in light of the perceived good that Abraham imagined was there (v.22-23). The exchange that followed provides a picture of how prayer works (v.24-32). Abraham asked the Lord to do something, according to what God had revealed about Himself. Abraham knew that the destruction of the righteous would be counter to God's will. God was not angry with Abraham for his repeated request that this people not be destroyed. When our hearts reveal genuine love and faith, God delights in His children making requests of Him.

After the exchange was over, Abraham went home (v.33). This is the way of prayer. Having sought God, according to truth with love, a child of God can leave their requests to the will of God. We need not worry. We can simply trust that God is just and good.

The hope of the children of God is not that they will always get what they want, but that God will always do what is best. Sarah had given up on having a child of her own, but God was faithful to His promise. Abraham did not know Sodom's outcome, but having asked with hope and trusted in God's character, Abraham left the matter to God. Do you trust and obey God in all things? Are you pursuing God and praying for His will? Obedient disciples live with hope.

Genesis 19; Matthew 18; Nehemiah 8; Acts 18

For those who follow Jesus and live for His glory, the challenge is not simply to get through life, but to thrive in Christ. This task is made difficult because, even though we have new life in Christ, we still have to deal with the flesh, the world, and the Devil. We must always battle against these three foes. It is in pursuing Christ's plan that God's children live with hope.

Matthew 18 provides God's plan for how a follower of Jesus can live with hope in this fallen world. A disciple of Jesus needs humility, a faith community, and the ability to make peace.

Humility is crucial for a follower of Jesus. The disciples were known to argue about who was the greatest from time to time. According to Jesus, the greatest is the one who is humble like a child (v.1-4). Humble disciples of Jesus will care for other believers. They will serve God by loving His people. Any who cause God's children to sin will face judgment (v.5-6). The person through whom temptation comes is in trouble with God (v.7). Sin is serious (v.8-9). Humility is the first step in holiness.

Church involvement is crucial for a follower of Jesus. It is vital that God's people stay together and near the Good Shepherd (John 10:11, 14). The Lord cares about His sheep. The people of God are to recognize the value of every single soul in God's family and if any wanders from the faith, those who are faithful are to join God in calling them back to faith and to involvement in the local church (v.10-14).

Peacemaking is crucial for a follower of Jesus. The best way to destroy any organization is to divide it. The Devil delights in seeing God's people tear each other down. There will always be conflict in life. Every person on the planet right now is either coming out of conflict, in the midst of conflict, or about to get into a conflict. Jesus provides a step by step process for how to make peace (v.15-17). The Lord provides not only the means for peace, but how to handle those who will not make peace (v.18-20).

Forgiveness is crucial for a follower of Jesus. In light of the teaching on peacemaking, Peter asked the number of times he should forgive. The typical expectation in Judaism was three times. Peter said he was ready to forgive up to seven times (v.21). Jesus told him that he was not to keep count and simply forgive over and over (v.22). Jesus provided an illustration that showed why (23-34). The reason we are to forgive others is because we have been forgiven so much. God became flesh and died for our sin so we can be forgiven. Those who receive this mercy and grace are to give that same mercy and grace to others. Those who do not forgive others are not in a right relationship with the Lord (v.35). A lack of forgiveness reveals a lack of relationship with God.

Jesus has won the battle for our souls, but the flesh, the world, and the Devil conspire against us. The one who walks in the path of grace will do so by faith in Jesus. Are you humbly serving God? Are you involved in a local church? Are you a peacemaker who forgives? Obedient disciples of Jesus live with hope.

Genesis 20; Matthew 19; Nehemiah 9; Acts 19

We will either view God as a thief, who seeks to rob us of the life we want, or as a Father, who wants the very best for us. The sin nature in humanity does not trust God and will often perceive God as keeping us from the good we want. Those who trust God and have been adopted into the family of God perceive God as a loving Father (Galatians 4:4-7). Those who know God as Father, through the grace of Jesus Christ, live with hope.

In Nehemiah 9, the children of God were gathering for worship, during a season of covenant renewal. God had blessed them and now they were consecrating themselves to God. This recommitment took place in the context of worship. The people had assembled themselves (v.1), separated themselves (v.3), submitted themselves (v.4-37), and were ready to commit themselves to God (v.38). This is what the children of God regularly do. In His grace and for His glory, God calls His people to assemble together for times of worship. It is crucial that God's people come together regularly to stir one another up, to encourage one another, and to remember the Lord is soon returning. (Hebrews 10:24–25). This gathering is not a taker of time, but a blessing in time. Worship points us beyond time to the Father.

When the church gathers for God's purpose, it is a sacred moment. There needs to be a specific time, a specific place, and a specific plan for the church gathering. This time is to be prayed for and prepared for by the leaders for the glory of God. The prayer proclaimed by the priests was prepared by them in advance and was not extemporaneous (v.6-37). It was prepared in advance so that it could be jointly offered to God. The time of prayer seemed to be the centerpiece of the six-hour worship service. While the prayer itself was presented by the priests, it is clear that it was meant to be a congregational prayer. The people submitted themselves to the truth of the prayer as the priests provided it. The people also submitted the prayer to God by agreeing to it and affirming the words in their hearts and minds. In worship, the public prayer of one is the shared prayer of all.

Having walked through the history of the children of Abraham and been reminded of the mercy and grace of God that was offered over and over again, the people made a covenant with God. In light of their sin and the sin of their fathers, the people agreed in writing to submit to the law of God. The covenant was sealed with the names of their leaders (v.38). This was a serious commitment. The people were giving their lives to God and choosing to trust in Him. Under the new covenant, the children of God are now able to give their lives to Jesus Christ. It is in trusting Jesus that God becomes a person's Father.

Living under the authority of God the Father is a blessing. When God is our Father, life makes sense. Christ provides this life. Are you gathering with a church family each week to worship the Father? Are you living under Jesus Christ by grace through faith? Are you obeying the covenant of Christ by loving God and others? The blessing of God comes to those who trust Him as Father. Hope is found in His grace.

Genesis 21; Matthew 20; Nehemiah 10; Acts 20

There is little that is more important to a church, an organization, or a nation than its leadership. Gifted, Godly leadership gives hope.

In Acts 20, Paul was preparing leaders. He was preparing the Ephesian elders for the important task of caring for that congregation without the benefit of his presence or participation. From his first days of faith, when Ananias was used by God to return his sight, to the days of being with Barnabas, until his last days, when he was comforted by missionaries like Epaphroditus of the Philippian church (Philippians 4:18), Paul always had good, Godly leadership praying for him and serving alongside of him. This was true on his journey back to Jerusalem (v.1-6). Leaders must choose their associates wisely.

While leadership is certainly a gift of God, it is also developed. Paul was a leader of leaders and was used by God to identify, to train, and to deploy people into leadership. Much of the training Paul provided was like the training Jesus gave His disciples. He taught by his way of life and with his words. The best leaders are authentic and have a life that matches their teaching and expectations of others.

Paul was in a hurry to get back to Jerusalem by Pentecost (v.16), but also knew he would probably not have another opportunity to train these people again, and so he taught late into the night in Troas. While he was teaching, a young man named Eutychus, who was sitting near the window, fell into a deep sleep and then fell from the third-story window and died (v.7-9). Paul raised him from the dead, which was a great comfort to the church (v.10-15). What an understatement! Eutychus was not wise. When a leader is tired, it is always best for that leader to go and get rest, even if it means missing something important. Leaders that are tired will often make serious mistakes.

It was for strategic purposes that Paul met with the Ephesian elders in Miletus. Wise leaders must schedule their time well and be intentional about where they go in order to maximize their influence. Paul reminded the elders of what he had done while with them (v.18-22). He explained what he was about to do (v.23-25). He made clear his good relational standing with them all (v.26-27). This is what leaders do. Leaders speak of what was, what is, and what will be, while keeping a clear conscience at all times. The challenge Paul gave to the elders is one that all leaders need. He told them to lead their own lives well and then to focus on those under their care (v.28). Leaders must look after themselves and those who follow them (v.29-35). When it is time for a leader to leave, it should be sad. Sadness is sometimes a sweet blessing (v.36-38).

God has chosen to have His church led by imperfect people. The church must follow those God raises up to lead. Pray they have wisdom. It is a wise leader who seeks to give and get accountability, prayer, and support. Are you praying for your leadership? Are you honoring your leaders by following them and helping them accomplish God's work? Are you making life difficult for your leadership? Those who lead well and those who are led well live with great hope.

Genesis 22; Matthew 21; Nehemiah 11; Acts 21

Trials build our faith and teach us to trust God. Once a trial is over and the faith lessons are learned, we are made stronger and are more effective for Kingdom service. A life with a growing faith in Jesus and a deep trust of God is filled with hope.

In Genesis 22, Abraham faced a trial. Abraham was a dad. His son was healthy. The man was finally at peace and getting a glimpse of God's plan working out. But God's plan was not just to work through Abraham. God's plan was to work in Abraham.

In this happy moment in Abraham's life, God showed up and told Abraham to sacrifice his son, his only son, whom he loved (v.1-2). The next verse is shocking. "So Abraham rose early in the morning, saddled his donkey, and took two of his young men with him, and his son Isaac. And he cut the wood for the burnt offering and arose and went to the place of which God had told him." Was something left out of the story? Maybe it was. The Bible does not contain every single detail of each event. But it appears that what it says is exactly what happened. Abraham did not argue with God. Abraham did not delay in obedience. Abraham did not run from God. It says that Abraham got everything ready to do what God had told him to do.

He traveled three days to Moriah. This is believed to be Jerusalem. The hill he journeyed to is believed to be the place where Solomon's Temple later stood and where sacrifices were made. When he saw the place, Abraham told his men to stay put (v.4-5). He and Isaac went on alone. There would be none to restrain Abraham. There would be none that Isaac could look to for help. Isaac had to carry the wood to the place where his life was to be sacrificed and Abraham took the knife and fire (v.6). When Isaac asked about the animal for sacrifice, Abraham said, "God will provide for himself the lamb for a burnt offering, my son" (v.7-8).

The rest of the event must have been like a blur to Abraham. The altar is set. The boy is laid on it. Abraham takes the knife to kill his son and then a miracle happens. An angel of the Lord commands that he stop. Abraham is commended for his faith. A sacrifice is made, but it is a ram that God provides (v.9-13). Abraham names the place "The Lord will provide" (v.14). Abraham and Isaac return home (v.15-19). Later on, Abraham receives word that his brother, Nahor, has been blessed with many children (v.20-24). Was this information meant to be the next test of faith to see if Abraham would be content? We don't know.

What we do know is that years later in that same area, the Father came to sacrifice his Son. Jesus carried the wood that he would die on. He too was left alone. His servants did not follow with Him to give Him comfort. His father also held in His hand the wrath that would be poured out and would kill His Son. This time the Father's hand was not restrained. Jesus died to save sinners. Do you have faith in Jesus? Are you fulfilling your calling and growing in faith? A life with a growing faith in Jesus and a deep trust of God is filled with hope.

Genesis 23; Matthew 22; Nehemiah 12; Acts 22

When life gets complicated, we can lose sight of the Gospel and become discouraged. When we see life from the perspective of Jesus, the things of this world do not overwhelm us and the things of heaven inspire us. It is crucial to see life through the lens of Jesus. A simple life in Jesus is a hopeful life.

In Matthew 22, Jesus spoke to things that can complicate life. If the Devil cannot get us to live in sin, he will settle for the next best thing and will work to keep our lives complicated. Complicated lives are easily manipulated, confused, and disturbed.

Busyness complicates life. In the parable of the wedding feast there are two sets of people (v.1-14). There is one set of people who are aware of the wedding feast but are busy. The other set of people are those who know little or nothing of God but are supernaturally drawn to Him. They come to His house not knowing why. Some are good and some are bad humanly speaking. All who get dressed in righteousness remain. Those not dressed in holiness are removed to an eternal life of weeping. A life simply lived in pursuit of Jesus has hope.

Politics complicate life. When Jesus was questioned about paying taxes, He knew it was a political ploy (v.15-22). The religious leaders were trying to get Jesus either into trouble with the Jews, who hated Rome, or with Rome. Jesus saw their motives and made a profound statement on responsibility. We are to do what is right by the human institutions we are under and associated with and ultimately and always to God. People who trust in God and focus on fulfilling their responsibilities to Him have hope.

Doctrinal heresy complicates life. God has revealed what is to come (v.23-33). The resurrection is the hope of all who believe. This world is not the home of the saints of God. When Jesus returns and the earth is restored and the Lord is reigning in His righteous eternal Kingdom, then there will be peace. God's law is to love (v.34-40). The love of God revealed in Jesus Christ is not like limited human love. The love of God is pure. It is unconditional. God's love is to be received and then given back to God and also to others. The Son of God is the object of saving faith (v.41-46). Jesus Christ is the Son of God who has come to save sinners. He is the promise God kept. In the Old Testament, God made the promise over and over again and in many different ways that Jesus would come through the line of David and establish an eternal Kingdom. Jesus has come. While God is certainly mysterious, He has also made clear what can be known (Deuteronomy 29:29). Those who hold to what is true and refuse to accept what is false live with hope.

The person who is able to see life on this fallen planet for what it is and look beyond the brokenness and to the future of the coming of Christ will live a simple life by faith in Jesus and embrace and share His love. Is your life complicated with worldly things? Have you lost sight of Jesus and His call to love? Can you discern your natural inclinations and temptations that tend to complicate your life? A life simply lived in Jesus is filled with hope.

Genesis 24; Matthew 23; Nehemiah 13; Acts 23

Ambiguity kills confidence. The person who obeys God's clear expectations can always go forward with confidence, knowing that they are living under God's authority and doing His will. A confident person has hope.

Faithful saints live lives that are distinct and different and defined by holiness through dedication to God. In Nehemiah 13, the clear calling of God is made known concerning what God expects from His people. They were to be homogenous in their racial uniqueness (v.1-3). God was restarting His plan through them and it was crucial that they be uniquely Israelite.

While Nehemiah was away, the people strayed (v.4-5). When Nehemiah returned (v.6-7), he confidently did what needed to be done and removed the evil from among the people and cleansed the temple for God's use alone (v.8-9). Godlessness sought to contaminate the community of faith by rotting it from the inside out. This is a typical strategy of evil. Nehemiah discovered that the priests and singers were forced to find other means to support themselves and were unable to carry out their ministry functions (v.9). With a clear vision, Nehemiah went and spoke to the leaders about their lack of responsibility, which was leading to the disobedience of the people. He corrected them verbally and then held them accountable forcibly so that the city was able to function and live in obedience to the Word of God (v.10-31).

What Nehemiah did is exactly what Godly leaders do. They seek to know the will of God based upon the Word of God and demand obedience to the way of God. Leaders must live and call others to this faithfulness. There is no guarantee that everyone will agree with the decisions of the leader. The situation may even require that influential people be removed from the community. Leaders must confidently do what God commands.

What is true of a community of faith is also often true of an individual believer. Each believer must confidently discipline his or her life so that it is lived according to God's Word. Children of God will always be tempted to be disobedient to God. Seemingly small sins, like letting something live in a space that is meant for God, will lead to greater sin. Rather than gathering for worship with the church, a believer may be tempted to sleep in or participate in some form of recreation. Rather than giving financially to the work of God, a believer may be tempted to spend resources on other things. Rather than obey God's Word, a believer may be tempted to listen to the words and ideas of the culture and tolerate sin in their life and relationships. God's will is that His Word be obeyed.

Jerusalem was in a sad spiritual state. Your life or church or ministry may fall into a similar rut. If it does, act with confidence according to God's Word. Is God's Word the ultimate authority in your life? Do you have the confidence to trust and obey God in order to make the hard decisions concerning sin? Are you allowing little things to contaminate your life? Those who live confidently in Christ and obey His Word live with hope.

Genesis 25; Matthew 24; Esther 1; Acts 24

God is sovereign over all things and He is always at work to accomplish His purpose. God has determined to do and is doing in the world in every situation what is best. Knowing that all things are working toward an ultimate good makes it possible for God's people to live with hope.

In Acts 24, there are three kinds of people presented. Each type of person is represented by the motivation that guides their decision making. Within each person there is hope, but the kind of hope each has is radically different.

Paul was a Christian missionary. He believed that Jesus Christ was God. He believed that God the Father loved Him and had sent His Son, Jesus Christ, to die and be raised to atone for His sin in order to make Him into a new person. He believed in the Holy Spirit and trusted in His power to be at work in His life to overcome the sinful desires that remained at work in his flesh. Because of his faith, Paul was compelled to tell the truth and live with a clear conscience. Even though he had been wrongly accused, imprisoned, and threatened, he was not angry or vindictive. He saw every circumstance as an opportunity to share the Gospel. He had eternal hope.

Tertullus and Felix were secularists. These men believed in man-made systems and served them for their own advancement. Their hope was in their comfort, which was produced by power, popularity, pleasure, and possessions. Telling a lie or accepting a bribe was completely acceptable behavior for them, although they would never want anyone to know that. By gaining power, they protected themselves. By gaining popularity, they celebrated themselves. By gaining pleasure, they accommodated themselves. By gaining possessions, they justified themselves. They had hope in what they had, how they felt, how others perceived them, and what they were able to make others do. Their hope was temporary.

Ananias and the elders were religious professionals. These men believed they could get what they wanted through religious power plays and manipulation. They sought power, popularity, pleasure, and possessions, but they would never have wanted their true desires to be exposed. They wanted to appear to be serving God and the needs of others, even though by doing so, they were actually serving themselves. Their hope was temporary.

People who pursue temporary things as an ultimate goal will often do horrible things to get what they want. They will lie, manipulate, and hurt others. They will justify their actions and seek to appear to be serving the greater good of others. God's people have an eternal living hope that motivates them. Because they love God, they obey and serve Him. The truth is always their friend. They are free to be who they really are and express the fact of who they serve. This transparent life sets them free. God is their refuge and strength.

We all must choose what we will pursue with our one and only life. God has offered His Son to be our hope in life and death. Do you trust in the power and goodness of God to provide for you? Is it your desire to honor Jesus with your life? Is your hope eternal? Those who live for Jesus live with hope.

Genesis 26; Matthew 25; Esther 2; Acts 25

Everyone has issues, problems, and difficulties. Those who trust in God are able to see their lives from the vantage of God's purpose, provision, and power. The blessings of Jesus Christ give His disciples hope.

Isaac and Rebekah trusted God. How they responded in Genesis 26 to their calling, challenges, and hurts shows God's people how to live by faith. There will be good and better days for God's people. Believers don't really have bad days because even in the worst of times, God is with them.

The life of a believer begins and is sustained by trusting God. The Lord spoke to Isaac in times of want (v.1-5) and in times of plenty (v.22-25). Although Isaac's circumstances changed, God never did. God is always the same (Hebrews 13:8). His ultimate plan does not change either. God was with Isaac in the famine and did not want him to do what his father Abraham had done when he went through a famine (Genesis 12:10). God does not always call us to do what is seemingly practical. Instead, God calls us to trust Him. Isaac was told by God what to do and to trust in the faithfulness of God. The Lord's blessing of provision is always found through obedience.

Just because God's people are faithful does not mean there will be no tough days for them. God knows that in order for our faith to grow, we must face trials of many kinds (James 1:2-5). Isaac obeyed God and the Lord provided, but Isaac still faced difficulties. He was forced to live in a foreign land where the beauty of his wife threatened his life (v.6-21). To protect himself, Isaac lied. Lies often seem practical, but they are dangerous. Abimelech spoke truth to Isaac when he told of the danger Isaac's lie might have led to (v.10). The child of God is free to be honest and simply trust God.

The mission of God must never be lost in the midst of making a living. Isaac was to be the blessing to the world God promised Abraham his progeny would be (Genesis 12:1-3). The presence of Godly people brings common grace, the general kindness of God. Abimelech was wise to seek a covenant with Isaac (v.26-33), and Isaac was right to bless Abimelech with peace. This is always to be the response of God's people. We are sojourners in a foreign land. Our home is heaven, but while we are here on earth we are to be God's blessing.

Obedience to God and provision from God will not protect us from being hurt. It is often the tender heart that gets hurt the worst, but even so, we must not let our hearts become hard. Isaac and Rebekah were faithful to God, but they still had their hearts broken by a wayward son (v.34-35). Each person must choose their own path. Parents must instruct their children but realize they cannot control them.

In every season and circumstance God is good. God is with His people. There will be good days and better days. Do you truly trust God? Is your faith seen in your day-to-day actions? Do you live with confidence in the plan, provision, and power of God? In Christ, the redeemed are blessed to live in the will of God and experience hope in good and tough times.

Genesis 27; Matthew 26; Esther 3; Acts 26

A crisis of faith is often accompanied with pain, difficult circumstances, and sometimes, what seems like silence from heaven. There have been many people who have lost their hope when life did not turn out the way they thought it would. The good news is that despite our lack of faithfulness, God is always faithful. God's faithfulness is the hope of all who believe.

At the end of Jesus' life, described in Matthew 26, the means of salvation revealed an ongoing reminder of what salvation provided, and two men are found entering into a crisis of faith. These three events help us know the hope we have in the grace of God, but also how that hope can be missed if there is a lack of genuine faith.

Jesus made clear the means of salvation He would provide. The Passover celebration was in two days (v.2). The Passover was an annual celebration that reminded the Israelites of God's salvation from the Egyptians. On the night the Passover occurred, Israel was commanded to sacrifice a lamb, to take the blood of the lamb and paint the doorposts of their homes, and to eat the lamb with bitter herbs and unleavened bread (Exodus 12:3-7). That night, the Lord came and on any house where there was no blood, the firstborn of that house was killed (Exodus 12:23). Where there was the sign of faith, the blood of the lamb, the Lord passed over that house and none were killed. Jesus is the ultimate Lamb of God, who was killed to save all who repent of sin and believe in Him for salvation.

For over a thousand years God's people had been celebrating the Passover feast. The night before Jesus gave His life as the atoning sacrifice for sin, the Passover meal was being celebrated. On that night, Jesus created the Lord's Supper (v.26-29). Like the Passover meal, this meal would be a reminder to God's people of the means of salvation God provided. The bread is the reminder that God became flesh and that His body was broken and given. The wine is the reminder that Jesus' blood was shed, which paid for the sin of all who believe.

In this midst of that unforgettable night, Judas and Peter entered into a crisis of faith. Judas was a thief who wanted to use Jesus to get what he wanted out of life. He did not like money being "wasted" on others (v.6-16). He betrayed Jesus, just as Jesus said he would (v.25). That same night, Peter denied Jesus three times (v.69-75). Jesus had told him to stay awake and pray, but Peter was tired (v.36-46). He did not pray, but he did attempt to protect Jesus with force (v.47-56). Rather than pray and die, Peter wanted to fight and live in his power. God calls us to live by faith in Jesus.

Jesus came to save sinners. God will give grace to any who will repent and believe in Jesus. Times of crisis will come and faith will be tested. Those with genuine faith will find hope in the faithfulness of God. Have you trusted Jesus to save you from your sin? Have you gone through a crisis of faith and found God faithful to see you through? Are you willing to trust and obey God no matter the cost? God is always faithful. God's faithfulness is the hope of all who believe.

Genesis 28; Matthew 27; Esther 4; Acts 27

Every challenge we face is known by God and is meant for good. God's children can know that we probably will not walk away from this world unscathed. There will be battle scars for those who fight the good fight of faith. The good news is that the battle is won in Christ. Those who trust Jesus in a faith family have hope.

During the Babylonian exile, God's people faced many faith challenges. In Esther 4, it appeared that the evil one was finally going to be able to destroy the Jews and defeat God's eternal plan to bring salvation through them. This chapter shows us what we should do in tough times of desperate need. We should never focus on the problem but always look past the problem to God. We should always pray and never panic. We should never allow ourselves to be victims of circumstance. We should always team up with God's people and never isolate ourselves physically, emotionally, or spiritually.

When word got out that Haman had gotten permission to wipe out the Jews, Mordecai panicked. He protested by going to the king's gate in sackcloth. Tearing clothes, wearing sackcloth, and sitting in ashes were ways of showing grief. This was fine and well at home, but this would be seen as a blatant show of disrespect. Esther sending him clothes was protective (v.4). Rather than simply responding emotionally, Mordecai responded faithfully and wisely in prayer. Having prayed, civil disobedience may have been the wise choice, but it appears that, once reason had set in, a better plan was revealed.

The plan involved Esther. Mordecai became convinced of God's faithfulness and that the Jews would survive (v.14). It was Esther's responsibility and opportunity to stand for God by going before the king. This was dangerous. She knew that unless the king was willing to accept her unannounced visit, she would be killed (v.11). Mordecai made it clear that this was a time for her to stand for God and trust in His power to provide and not a time for her to be a victim of circumstance. His now famous words in v.14 were, "And who knows whether you have not come to the kingdom for such a time as this?" Her response revealed her faith. God's people are called to do hard things.

She requested that Mordecai gather the people for prayer on her behalf (v.15). One of the great blessings of being a member of God's family is the emotional and spiritual support the church gives. Knowing that she was doing God's will with the support of God's people would inspire Esther with the physical strength she needed to take her stand. The worst thing a child of God can do in a difficult moment is to become isolated from other believers. God's people must come together in tough times. It is in community that hope is found, as God's people express their commitment to Christ and one another.

There will always be challenges. These moments are never a surprise to God. They are allowed by God so He can be honored by the faith of His people and so the faith of His people can grow. Are you ready for your tough moment? Do you have the confidence to pray, the faith to act, and a church to lean on in tough times? Those who trust in Jesus in a faith family have hope.

Genesis 29; Matthew 28; Esther 5; Acts 28

The hope of God's people is not found in the circumstances of life, but in the promises of God. If things are good, we might wrongly think God is pleased with us, even though we may be living in disobedience to God. If things are bad, we might doubt God. Living in God's sovereign care gives hope.

In Acts 28, the Apostle Paul was dealing with the difficult life of a missionary. Having survived a shipwreck on his way to Rome, Paul suffered in a way that could have caused him to doubt God. Suffering, humanly impossible challenges, and false accusations can rob us of confidence in God. As bad as those things are, the one thing that seems to crush the heart of a child of God more than anything else is conflict. So many individual believers and congregations have been destroyed by conflict. Paul faced all of these and more and maintained his faith. We would do well to learn from him.

While Paul was in Malta, he faced potential death and had false accusations made about him (v.1-6). Having barely survived a major boating disaster, once settled on land, Paul faced even more difficulty when he was bitten by a deadly snake. This led the locals to determine that he must have been a bad person. The accusation was a strong one. Paul shook off the snake and by the mercy of God, he did not die. The locals then claimed he was a god. As God's children, we should never assume that we won't get bitten by snakes, hit by cars, or become sick with disease. We live in a fallen world and those things happen here. When bad things happen, we must trust who God says He is and who He says we are. The world may say you are a terrible person or that you are a god. Both are lies. Focus on Jesus and do not allow suffering and wrong accusations to derail your faith.

Paul also faced a situation beyond his natural ability to solve (v.7-10). Paul and his companions were being cared for by the chief man of the island and his father was sick. There was nothing Paul could do for him in his human ability, but Paul prayed and God healed the man's father and many others. God will often put His children in positions where there is nothing they can do in their own strength. Praying releases needs and results into God's hands. That is where all things belong.

After finally making it to Rome, Paul was given the opportunity to preach the Gospel (v.23-28). The Jews in Rome had not been contacted by the Jerusalem authorities, and although they had heard bad things about Christianity, they wanted Paul to explain his faith to them (v.17-22). Paul was faithful in proclaiming the Gospel (v.23). Some believed and some did not, which created conflict (v.24-25). Rather than being discouraged by the conflict, Paul kept his focus on God's command for him to make disciples (v.30-31). God's people must be led by their calling to share their hope and not be derailed with conflict.

The life of faith is not easy. What circumstances might tempt you to lose hope? Are you willing to be faithful no matter what? Hope is found in the heart that trusts God.

Genesis 30; Mark 1; Esther 6; Romans 1

When we seek to accomplish God's plan in our own power for our own glory, we make a terrible mess of things. Not only do we hurt ourselves and sometimes other people, but we dishonor God in the process because we look to created things and our own strength to find meaning in life rather than to God. Those who trust in God live with hope.

In Genesis 30, God was fulfilling His promise to Abraham (Genesis 12:1-3), but the people He was working through were going about God's will in the wrong way. When we trust in ourselves rather than God, we end up living in either pride or despair. Pride comes if we succeed. Despair comes if we fail. God does not want us to live with pride or despair. The evil one wants that! God wants us to live with confidence. Confidence comes when we live by faith in what God wants and by faith in what God can do.

Rachel wanted a good thing. She wanted to have children, like her sister. The problem was that she had made that longing into an ultimate thing or what some would call an idol. An idol is anything other than God that we depend on to define us or satisfy us. Rather than praying together and seeking God's provision and direction, Jacob and Rachel became frustrated with one another (v.1-2). Idolatry always leads to discontentment and frustration.

In her desperation, Rachel offered her servant to her husband, as a surrogate (v.3-8). Rather than trusting in God, Rachel and Jacob chose to live in the way of their world. In the Ancient Near East this custom of giving a servant to a husband to act as a surrogate on the wife's behalf was not unusual. This was not the plan of God. The acceptance of bigamy and now surrogacy reveals the sinfulness and brokenness of this "chosen" family. Doing things God's way leads to God's provision.

The result of their sin is not surprising. Rather than having peace and joy, there was strife driven by pride and the desire for power. These sisters were in clear competition with one another (v.9-24). The goal was to win by having the most children. Because having children was the goal, rather than honoring God, the means justified the ends. Rachel and Leah both gave their servants to Jacob to have sex with him. They also bartered with each other. In exchange for Rachel's son's mandrakes, Leah received an extra night with Jacob, which produced another son and more strife (v.14-17). If God's glory is not the goal, conflict will always arise. In the midst of all of this idolatry, adultery, and strife, God was still at work. God's grace is truly amazing.

In the midst of strife in his home, Jacob continued to have strife with his father-in-law (v.35-43) Because of God's gracious plan, Jacob enjoyed the Lord's provision. It is not because of Jacob's worthiness. It was by grace Jacob was blessed. It is by God's grace that any sinner is blessed.

There is none that deserves God's blessings. God is gracious and works out His plans for His glory and our good. Is there anything you are trusting in rather than God? If so, it is an idol. Stop seeking to live for that person or thing and choose to trust God. Those who trust in God live with hope.

Genesis 31; Mark 2; Esther 7; Romans 2

There is nothing like seeing God accomplish what only God can do. It happens all over the world every second of every day, and yet many never get a glimpse of His hand at work. God is at work in the world, and those who believe in Jesus and join Him in His Kingdom purpose experience hope.

There are forces at work that will cause us to doubt, disagree with, and even reject the work of God that is taking place all around us. Those who believe will see what God is doing. Many will never see because they do not believe. It is hard to overcome the ways of the world, the desires of the flesh, and the lies of the Devil. In Mark 2 there are several examples of how God works in the world.

There was a group of four men who believed in the power of God, and they brought their friend to Jesus (v.1-12). Many came that day to hear Jesus but did not believe He was God. Those four friends believed. They could not get their sick friend in front of Jesus because of the dense crowds. Instead of giving up, these men got creative and did what they had to do in order to get their friend to Jesus. It was their faith that enabled this man to be transformed. Some there did not believe Jesus was God and objected to Him granting forgiveness. To prove His divinity, Jesus healed the man. God was at work in the world and those four men believed it.

Levi was a tax collector, which made him a terrible person in the eyes of the people. And yet Levi believed in Jesus. Jesus called him to follow Him (v.13-17). Levi left his life of wealth and sin. It was not enough that he believed. Levi wanted others to know Jesus, and so he invited his friends to a party with Jesus. The religious leaders objected to Jesus associating with Levi and his friends. In their minds Jesus was becoming like them in sin. They could not perceive or understand Jesus' purpose. He came among sinners to save sinners, making them righteous. "For our sake he made him to be sin who knew no sin, so that in him we might become the righteousness of God" (2 Corinthians 5:21). This is the Gospel of God!

Many people today believe in Jesus, and they are experiencing new life and what it means to truly rest in God. Jesus taught that a new day had come (v.18-28). It was not a day to pursue righteousness by works, but by trusting in the grace of God. This grace is like new wine. It cannot go into an old system of religion. The grace of God comes through faith. It is a life supernaturally given through His Spirit. This life leads to rest. Those who want to earn their salvation and create a life of comfort through their own activity will never rest. Jesus is God and He came to give what every soul longs for.

God is at work in the world giving new life through His death, burial, and resurrection. Have you received forgiveness of your sin? Are you joining God in His work in the world by sharing the Gospel of God? Are you resting in the power and peace of God? Those who believe in Jesus and join Him in His Kingdom purpose experience hope.

Genesis 32; Mark 3; Esther 8; Romans 3

The greatest victory is the one that was almost lost. And so it is with hope. The greatest hope is the hope that almost failed. It is the hope that came when it appeared lost. Those who trust in God's power and plan live with hope.

In Esther 8, God saved the day. The Jewish people were on the verge of extinction. The plan of God seemed to be thwarted, but then the miracle happened. In the midst of impending death there was life. Haman was inspired by the enemy of God to kill God's people (Esther 3:8-11). This is the same evil that inspired the king of Egypt to kill the sons of Israel (Exodus 1:15-16). Just as God protected Moses and then raised him up to save God's people, so God protected Esther and raised her up to be used to save God's people.

Instead of Mordecai and the Jews being killed, Haman and those who sought to kill the Jews were killed (Esther 7:10; 8:10-11). Rather than dying, Mordecai was honored and his name was made great. The weak defeated the strong. The servant was used to save the people and was honored for his actions. This is the story of the Gospel.

Jesus was saved from King Herod who murdered all of the male sons in Bethlehem (Matthew 2:16-28). Salvation in Christ was not by political might, but by His humble service. Unlike Moses, Mordecai, and Esther, Jesus had to die. He was like the Paschal Lamb that was provided to save the children of Israel (Exodus 12:21-23). Jesus died to pay for the sin of the people. To His disciples it appeared that Jesus had failed and the movement Jesus had led was over. When it seemed hope was lost, Jesus was raised from the dead. He was honored like Mordecai. He was not left for dead by God. Jesus was and is now honored forever. He is clothed in righteousness. He is at the right hand of God.

But the story is not yet done. The enemies of the Jews were destroyed in the days of Esther (v. 9-17). One day, the enemies of Jesus will be destroyed. The resurrection of Jesus was not the end. There is another task still left to be done. There is a glorious day coming, when the enemies of God will be completely vanquished. What a stirring picture Revelation 19:20–21 provides. "And the beast was captured, and with it the false prophet who in its presence had done the signs by which he deceived those who had received the mark of the beast and those who worshiped its image. These two were thrown alive into the lake of fire that burns with sulfur. And the rest were slain by the sword..." Once the enemies of God are destroyed, the eternal reign of Jesus will begin. There will be no more death for God's people. There will be no tears or pain. It will be paradise restored.

The ultimate victory is the victory of Jesus over sin and death. Those who believe in Jesus have eternal hope in Him. It was a hope almost lost. It is a hope that sustains us in life and gives us confidence in the face of death. Is Jesus your hope? Are you experiencing His victory in your life today? Those who trust in God's power and plan live with hope.

Genesis 33; Mark 4; Esther 9–10; Romans 4

Peace with God is fundamental to all of God's blessings. Once we have peace with God, we gain peace within, which frees us to pursue peace with others and God's plan for our lives. The root of peace is Christ and the fruit of Christ is hope.

Peace with God is not something that can be earned. In Romans 4 we learn that peace with God comes through faith and not by deeds. This redeeming faith does not result in passivity, but in a Gospel-driven activity that pursues God's plan, according to His promise. In this section of Scripture, Paul makes a very important point about salvation. He describes how salvation is gained, what salvation is, and what it ultimately does in a person's life.

Salvation is gained by faith alone. There is nothing a sinful fallen creature can do to recover their own righteous standing before God. God made humanity in His image to live as overseers of His world. After the fall, the human race became cursed. Under the curse, life became hard and the future bleak. As sinful creatures, humanity was separated from God. In His grace God provided the means for salvation – Jesus Christ. Abraham simply believed God's promise and trusted His life into God's hands and was saved. It was not because he had performed a religious duty. Abraham was saved by faith (v.1-3).

A righteous standing with God is what salvation is. In verses 7-8, Paul quotes Psalm 32:1-2. The salvation of God provides a double cure. To be saved is to be forgiven. It is to have the just demands of the law satisfied. But it is more than that. Salvation is not only having forgiveness, but also being covered in the righteousness of God. When God sees a saint, He sees the righteousness of Jesus Christ. A Christian is not only forgiven, but is made holy by grace.

Those who are forgiven and given a righteous standing before God are able to trust God's promises, which results in a life of obedience. Abraham did not always have perfect belief, but his belief grew over time (v.20). Even though he was old and Sarah was beyond childbearing years, Abraham kept his faith and lived a life of obedience to God (v.19, 21). When we believe and trust God, we obey God. We obey God because we have hope in His promises. As children of God, we may not always get what we want. We may have to go through many trials, carry many crosses, and endure many thorns, but through it all, we can rejoice in our salvation. We can hold on to God's promises. We can see beyond our limitations and the circumstances of the world and look to God in faith. This faith enables us to be transformed by God. Having been given a new life in Christ, we are free to live in obedience to God and enjoy His blessings.

Abraham had peace with God through faith. So it is with all of God's children. The Lord has a plan for us all. That plan can only be fulfilled when we have peace with God, peace within, and peace with others. With a right standing with God, we have the confidence to live in obedience to God and accomplish His purpose. Do you have saving faith? Are you fulfilling your divine purpose? The redeemed fulfill God's purpose and live with hope.

Genesis 34; Mark 5; Job 1; Romans 5

This world is not the home of the redeemed of God. We are just passing through. Our existence in this broken world is as bad as it gets for God's children. For those who do not know Jesus, this world is as good as it gets. It is crucial that God's people be wise in this world and trust that in God's time there will be justice and restoration. The coming of Christ is our hope.

In Genesis 34, the brokenness of this world is on full display. The sin seen in these verses will not exist in the world that is to come. When Jesus returns, there will be no sexual sin, no deceit, no killing, and no consequences for sin because there will be no sin.

All the terrible things that happened in this chapter: the rape, the lies, the murder, the enslavement, and the cause for potentially more death and pain, took place because of the selfishness of a single man (v.2). His actions led to the suffering and death of many. He had a deceived heart and a distorted mind. Lust led him to rape the daughter of Jacob. He claimed to love her (v.3). Love does not hurt and humiliate another. His desire to marry her did not justify his actions. Humans work hard to justify behavior, even the vilest of actions. Excuses do not override the serious consequences of sin.

Hamor, the father of the rapist, approached Abraham at a time when Abraham had no option but to hold his tongue. His sons were away tending to the livestock (v.5-6). When Jacob's sons heard what had happened, they headed home to intervene (v.7). No doubt they had developed a plan for revenge in route. Their response to Hamor was both practical and treacherous (v.8-19). The men on both sides acted selfishly. Seeing the opportunity to obtain Jacob's wealth, the men of Hamor's city submitted to the request of Jacob's sons that they be circumcised (v.20-24).

While all the men were sore, Simeon and Levi, Dinah's brothers, did the unthinkable. They killed all the men of the city (v.25-26). They took the women and children of the city and made them slaves. They also confiscated all the animals and possessions of the people (v.27-29). Regrettably, they felt completely justified in doing it (v.31). This is what sin does. It produces more sin and suffering. In light of all of this death and misery, Jacob's only concern seemed to be that he and his family were in danger because others might hear of what happened and believe themselves justified in attacking them (v.30). He was right to worry. Sin always costs more than we want to pay, takes us further than we wanted to go, and gives us less than it promised it would.

This tragedy is a picture of what is happening in our broken world. Sin is everywhere creating brokenness and suffering. Those who are hurt will act out in their brokenness and hurt others. Our world is in desperate need of a savior. The children of God can trust Jesus to redeem us and guide us. Only Jesus can save us and change us.

Jesus is coming soon! Are you hoping in Him? Are you praying for Christ's return? Are you living in light of the second coming of Jesus? Those who desire the coming of Christ live with hope.

Genesis 35–36; Mark 6; Job 2; Romans 6

Jesus not only sympathizes with us, but He can also guide us through the different challenges we face. Having become like us, God understands us and the difficulties we face living in a fallen world. Those who live as Christ through the complexities of worldly conflicts live with hope.

In Mark 6, Jesus was confronted with the real life issues almost everyone struggles through. He had to deal with the frustrations that come with having family and friends. He had to remain focused and accomplish the task for which He was sent and prepare those who would lead the church, once He ascended. He had to deal with tough situations as He cared for the needs of others.

While family and friends can be a source of great comfort and strength, they can also be a source of pain and discouragement. The people of Jesus' hometown doubted Him, and it appears that His siblings (there are four males named in verse 3) did not show much faith in Him either. Whether or not this was frustrating and disappointing, we do not know. Their lack of faith did have an impact (v.5-6). Our experience of God will only go as far as our faith.

Having dealt with the frustrations of being home, Jesus sent out the twelve on a mission trip (v.7-13). God trains and then releases His followers to serve. Through the work of the disciples, people were healed and life transformation took place. The disciples had seen situations with little fruitfulness and some with much fruitfulness. They were prepared to face both. In life there will be disappointments and success. Our faith must be driven by our confidence in Jesus and not by others' responses.

The disciples' success reached Herod, which created fear in the tyrant because he thought John the Baptist, whom he had killed, had come back from the dead (v.14-29). There was some momentum in Jesus' ministry at this point. Word was getting out. Miracles were happening, like the feeding of the five thousand (v.30-44). In the midst of the excitement, Jesus took a prayer break and then caught up with the disciples by walking on water (v.45-52). The disciples revealed they still had much to learn at this point. Despite having been a part of performing miracles and been able to see the miracles of Jesus, "they did not understand" (v.52). Success in ministry is not always proof of spiritual maturity.

Jesus' family, friends, and His disciples had doubts. What an emotional and spiritual battle Jesus had to constantly face, and yet He kept going. The ministry continued (v.53-56). Lives were changed. Jesus did not get overly excited or overly discouraged. He maintained His focus.

In an active life there will almost always be frustrations, responsibilities, and needs to be met. Because Jesus is with us through the power of the Holy Spirit, we can be encouraged. The Lord is among His disciples. God's children can know God has been where they are and can guide them through every problem, opportunity, and challenge they face in life. Are you seeking Jesus and relying on Him through the trials, storms, successes, and ordinary moments of your life? Those who follow Jesus and trust in Him live with hope.

Genesis 37; Mark 7; Job 3; Romans 7

It is easy to get discouraged. The person who knows Jesus has every reason not to. Biblical math is strange to those who live without faith in Jesus, but the math is right: Jesus + Nothing = Everything. This mathematical fact is what gives hope. Those who have faith in Jesus have hope.

Job was a man of great hope because he had a great God. In every generation and in every lifetime there are times of suffering, loss, and pain. This is because we live in a fallen world. The only way to never suffer or feel the pain of loss is to never love or choose to care about anything. The stoics and some eastern religions offer that as a means of escaping suffering, but the cost is too great. To cease to love or to avoid pursuing a purpose worth caring about causes a person to lose their humanity. To be human is to care. Having been made in the image of God and given the responsibility to govern and multiply, the human race is compelled to live with affections and desires that drive us to seek to accomplish important things with our lives with important people in our lives.

Job suffered great loss. He lost his children. He lost his possessions. He lost his influence. He did have some gains, but they made life worse. He gained an unhappy wife. He gained counselors who were not helpful (Job 2:9-13). It is no surprise that he believed it would have been better if he had never lived. Job still had hope. Job's speech in Job 3 reminds us that this world is not as it should be, that what God allows is always best, and that God is never far away from those who love Him.

Job did not want to live the life he had. Not everyone is completely satisfied with the life they have. The good news is that this world is not as it should be and our pain tells us so. This gives us hope. The fact that we are miserable means that this world with its suffering and sorrow is not what we were meant for. If it was, we would not mind it. The fact that we know things are bad only means we know we were made for a place where things are good. Our desire is for a world without pain. We long for a life filled with love and peace. These desires point us to the reality that God has more than what this world can offer.

God in His grace wants us to know that things on this fallen rock cannot satisfy our eternal longing. In His grace God allows us to see how weak and broken this world is. He draws our attention beyond it to Himself. We must never think that our desires are too strong. We often settle for worldly things rather than pursue God's perfection. It is not wrong to long for perfect love, perfect health, perfect relationships, and perfect peace. Only a good, powerful, perfect God who lives outside this world, but chose to enter it, can give us what we want.

The hope of the world is Jesus. The suffering in the world points us to our need for what only Jesus can give. Is Jesus your hope? Do you trust His plan for your life even if it includes suffering? Those with faith in Jesus live with hope.

Genesis 38; Mark 8; Job 4; <u>Romans 8</u>

We cannot know peace until we rest in a sound and settled relationship with God. It is only through faith in Christ that a person can gain peace with God and peace within. When we are relationally right with God and ourselves, we can pursue peace with other people. A life that has peace with God comes from humble confidence in God's grace. God's forgiveness makes it possible to forgive others. Those who live with peace live with hope.

In Romans 8, an outline of what is needed to live a life filled with peace is given. It begins with a right relationship with God that shapes our identity. Once we know who we are, we are free to live in proper relationships with everything and everyone else in the world. The result is humble confidence.

Knowing there is no condemnation for those who are in Christ Jesus is the fundamental source of confidence needed to pursue God. Through the atoning work of Jesus Christ, a Christian is freed from the penalty of sin. What we could not do for ourselves, God did. In the flesh we could not earn our pardon, but in Christ, God has provided it. Those who live in God's grace live in His Spirit and no longer serve the desires of the flesh, but are guided to be Godly by the power and outworking of the Holy Spirit (v.1-11).

The presence of the Holy Spirit in those who trust Jesus enables them to know they are children of God. We are able to speak of the Almighty as Daddy. As we live in the Spirit and go to war against our carnal desires, we will suffer. The more we suffer in obedience, the more confident we become in our identity as the children of God. This holy standing in God's family provides a sense of self that delights our hearts (v.12-17).

Those who delight in the love of God and the grace He gives will find it possible to trust God's plan in every circumstance. We know that God is in control of all things, and so, when we suffer, we are neither surprised nor despondent. The good news for the beloved child of God that is called according to God's purpose is that everything works together for good. God is at work to seek and to sanctify His children. The children join in that work in anticipation of the coming glory (v.18-30).

Knowing that life may be hard, but is always under the sovereign care of God, a child of God is freed to fight the good fight of faith. Jesus is the ultimate victor. Because nothing will separate us from the love of God in Christ Jesus, we can always live with peace (v.31-39). In Christ the redeemed are humble because they know it is by grace they are saved. They are also confident because they know it is by grace they are saved. A humble, confident person is hopeful and helpful.

If we do not have peace with God, peace within, and peace with others, we cannot have hope. This peace is found only in Christ. In Jesus there is no condemnation. There is life. There is love. There is power. There is eternal peace. Is Jesus your hope? Do you live with a humble confidence in Jesus? Are you living in the power of the Holy Spirit? Through peace with God, followers of Jesus live with hope.

Genesis 39; Mark 9; Job 5; Romans 9

God's goal is to bring glory to Himself by raising up a people for Himself who love Him, worship Him, and gladly serve Him. How God accomplishes that end is at times mysterious. The hope of the faithful is not that we understand everything happening to us and in our world, but that we can trust the One who holds the whole world in His hands. Every day with God in His grace serving His purpose is filled with hope.

In Genesis 39, we find Joseph in the midst of bad circumstances. He had received a vision from God that he was to rule over his family, but he was sold into slavery by his brothers. He found himself in the house of a wealthy Egyptian named Potiphar, who trusted him. Although forced to live in a foreign land as a slave, God was with Joseph. God's divine favor provided Joseph with a place to serve with plentiful resources, a good set of managerial skills, and the trust of his master (v.1-6).

We can never know all of the pieces that are at play in the grand design of God. All Joseph knew was that he had been given a vision, was betrayed by his brothers, and was stuck as a slave. God knew that a famine was coming (Genesis 41:53–56). God knew and had told Abraham that Israel would be slaves in Egypt for four hundred years (Genesis 15:13). God knew Moses would be raised up to lead God's people out of Egypt into the land promised to Abraham, picturing the salvation that was to come through Jesus Christ (Exodus).

When Potiphar's wife pursued Joseph to have an affair, Joseph gave two reasons for rejecting her. One was his master's goodness to him and the other was his God (v.8-9). Just because God's people do the right things does not mean that life will be easy. Many times faithfulness leads to difficulty. Joseph was faithful to his boss and His God, but he still ended up in jail (v.10-20). This was part of God's plan. It was in prison that Joseph would meet servants of the Pharaoh and one of them would help him gain entrance into Pharaoh's service.

In prison Joseph continued to be a hardworking, trustworthy man. He stood out as he used his God-given abilities and as he served with integrity. God blessed Joseph even in prison (v.21-23). Something is said of Joseph in verse 21 and verse 23 that changes everything in a person's life. In both verses it says, "The Lord was with Joseph." The Lord, Yahweh, was with Him. The covenant name for God was used to speak of the One who was with Joseph. The God who promises to save and who saves His people was with Joseph. There is nothing greater or more important that can be said of a life than that. The person who trusts in the Lord can live with confidence in the providential care of God. The presence of God provides power and hope.

We may never know all the details of what or why something happened or is happening the way it is in our lives. What we can know is that God has a plan and the power to accomplish what is best. Do you trust God in difficult times? What drives you to work hard: God's glory or self-preservation? Those who trust in Jesus and live to bring Him glory have hope.

Genesis 40; Mark 10; Job 6; Romans 10

The great battle between self-autonomy and divine subjugation is constant. We each choose to pursue our own way or we submit ourselves to the rule of Jesus. Those who live under God's sovereign care live with hope.

In Mark 10, these choices are on full display. We see what the battle for control looks like. Through questions about divorce, the encouragement of childlikeness, the issue of wealth, the death of Jesus, the hunger for power, and the trust of a beggar, we can see how the human heart struggles to surrender to King Jesus. Through these unique interactions, we see the choice we all must make: trust Jesus or self.

When asked about divorce, Jesus offered a compelling and clear position. Jesus said the provision of divorce was not the desire or will of God, but it was allowed because of the hardheartedness of the people (v.1-5). The will of God is that a man will leave his family and be married to a woman and the two will become one until death parts them. God commands us to be faithful to His will and not our own personal always-changing desires (v.6-12).

The means by which a person can live under the authority of God is by being childlike (v.13-16). God does not desire or intend us to be the authority of our lives. God expects us to come to Him as little children who are dependent, trustworthy, thankful, and in need of being disciplined.

One of the things that will often keep us from living in childlike dependency on God is wealth. The rich young man who approached Jesus had a sense of his need for salvation. He knew what few do, that money can't buy what the soul needs. Jesus invited him to give up on his self-dependency. The young man refused. He chose to trust in money rather than Jesus (v.17-31).

The only way to eternal life is through death. Jesus had to give His righteous life for us so that we could give our old sinful life to Him (2 Corinthians 5:21). Jesus died to pay for our sin and was raised to prove His power to save (v.32-34). Those who will be saved must die to the life they had and be born again (John 3:1-18). Salvation is subjugation to Jesus and the reception of His remedy for sin and death.

James and John were faithful followers of Jesus, but they still struggled to give up their own ambition. They wanted to be in authority directly under Jesus (v.35-37). They had not learned that real power comes in weakness, personal sacrifice, and service to others. They later learned that to be true. Both died living for the cause of Christ, just as Jesus said they would (v.38-45).

When a person is truly living in submission to the authority of Jesus, it will appear reckless in the eyes of the world. It may appear irresponsible, but it is the wisest thing anyone can do. Blind Bartimaeus humbled himself and screamed for Jesus (v.46-49). When Jesus called him, Bartimaeus threw off his cloak (v.50), the thing he used to catch the money people would give him. Some might say this was reckless and irresponsible. He simply trusted Jesus (v.52).

We all must choose whether we will trust in ourselves or God. Are you submitted to Jesus? Those who live under Jesus' authority live with hope.

Genesis 41; Mark 11; Job 7; Romans 11

In the worst moments of life, when sorrow and pain are overwhelming, the child of God still has hope. Those who trust God in all circumstances find hope in the faithfulness and goodness of God.

Job's situation was sad. This man's experience allows us to see the real pain of life, the will of God, and the brokenness that is caused by sin. Job lost every physical thing that mattered to him. He was in anguish in heart, body, and soul. His transparency is refreshing. He was not putting on a smile and pretending that life was as it should be. He spoke from the depth of his pain and in so doing allows us to see something of ourselves, of God's will, and of the brokenness of our world.

The God that Job spoke of in response to Eliphaz is the One Job perceived to be looking on (v.8) and it was to this God that Job spoke to (v.12-21). This is the God who is all-knowing and powerful. Job could not escape this God. This God was just and always right. Job's problem was that he had no concept of the righteous suffering. We must always remember that God is doing more than we can see. Job had no idea that God was using his life for an eternal purpose. Our suffering is not always because of sin. Sometimes it is because of our righteousness.

The one thing that comforted Job was that his life was brief on this earth. Life is a breath (v.7-10). In his suffering, Job found death a comfort. The hope of all God's children is that this broken world is not our home. This world is as bad as it gets for God's people. The life we will have in heaven will be glorious.

Job seemed to understand that a big part of the reason for his predicament was that his life was, and all human life is, a big deal to God (v.17-21). Job felt God was focusing in on him. That fact that God makes much of man is not so mysterious. As God's image bearers and caretakers of creation, we have a big role to play in God's eternal purpose. This world is under sin. God hates sin but has a plan.

The suffering of Job was terrible but not eternal. We do not know how long Job suffered, but we know that it was a number of days that could be counted. His suffering was of body, mind, and soul. It was intense but not infinite. Job still had friends and some light, although his friends were not much comfort and the light was dim. In hell there are no friends and there is no light. It is eternal suffering. Job's suffering was nothing compared to that of those who are in hell. The children of God can endure anything in life knowing our eternal home is a place of peace and rest.

No matter what a child of God may go through, we can always be confident that God not only sees us and understands our pain, but He also cares for us. We can know God has a plan for our pain. We can also know we have eternal hope. Can you see your suffering in light of God's eternal plan? Do you find comfort in the hope of heaven? Those who trust God's plan in all circumstances live with hope.

Genesis 41; Mark 11; Job 7; Romans 11

In the worst moments of life, when sorrow and pain are overwhelming, the child of God still has hope. Those who trust God in all circumstances find hope in the faithfulness and goodness of God.

Job's situation was sad. This man's experience allows us to see the real pain of life, the will of God, and the brokenness that is caused by sin. Job lost every physical thing that mattered to him. He was in anguish in heart, body, and soul. His transparency is refreshing. He was not putting on a smile and pretending that life was as it should be. He spoke from the depth of his pain and in so doing allows us to see something of ourselves, of God's will, and of the brokenness of our world.

The God that Job spoke of in response to Eliphaz is the One Job perceived to be looking on (v.8) and it was to this God that Job spoke to (v.12-21). This is the God who is all-knowing and powerful. Job could not escape this God. This God was just and always right. Job's problem was that he had no concept of the righteous suffering. We must always remember that God is doing more than we can see. Job had no idea that God was using his life for an eternal purpose. Our suffering is not always because of sin. Sometimes it is because of our righteousness.

The one thing that comforted Job was that his life was brief on this earth. Life is a breath (v.7-10). In his suffering, Job found death a comfort. The hope of all God's children is that this broken world is not our home. This world is as bad as it gets for God's people. The life we will have in heaven will be glorious.

Job seemed to understand that a big part of the reason for his predicament was that his life was, and all human life is, a big deal to God (v.17-21). Job felt God was focusing in on him. That fact that God makes much of man is not so mysterious. As God's image bearers and caretakers of creation, we have a big role to play in God's eternal purpose. This world is under sin. God hates sin but has a plan.

The suffering of Job was terrible but not eternal. We do not know how long Job suffered, but we know that it was a number of days that could be counted. His suffering was of body, mind, and soul. It was intense but not infinite. Job still had friends and some light, although his friends were not much comfort and the light was dim. In hell there are no friends and there is no light. It is eternal suffering. Job's suffering was nothing compared to that of those who are in hell. The children of God can endure anything in life knowing our eternal home is a place of peace and rest.

No matter what a child of God may go through, we can always be confident that God not only sees us and understands our pain, but He also cares for us. We can know God has a plan for our pain. We can also know we have eternal hope. Can you see your suffering in light of God's eternal plan? Do you find comfort in the hope of heaven? Those who trust God's plan in all circumstances live with hope.

Genesis 43; Mark 13; Job 9; Romans 13

As limited beings, we can never know the ultimate drama that is being played out in and around and through our lives. Those who love Jesus have the assurance that we are called according to His purpose and are confident that God is working everything for good (Romans 8:28). Those who believe that every moment of their life makes sense to God and is going in the direction He has planned live with hope.

In Genesis 43, we see the grand drama of God playing out. This family had no clue as to what was really going on and could not begin to fathom the way that God was at work. God was fulfilling His ultimate plan through His particular plan for Joseph's life. His brothers were in a bind and their dad was mad at them because they had mentioned to "this man in Egypt" they had another brother, Benjamin, dad's new favorite. Pretending not to know them, Joseph demanded that they bring the other brother, his little brother Benjamin, with them. Jacob did not want Benjamin to go down to Egypt. Simeon had been held back and taken prisoner on their last visit because Joseph made it appear they were spies. Joseph had also placed their money back into their bags and made it look as though they had not paid for the food they had received (Genesis 42). Jacob was afraid that he would lose Benjamin just as he had lost Simeon (v.1-7). The stress was intense for the entire family.

The brothers really had no choice. They had to go and get food, and they had to take Benjamin with them to do it. To appease his father, Judah said he would take complete responsibility for his brother. He told his dad if he did not return with Benjamin, he would be held accountable forever for his failure (v.8-10). It was obvious that Jacob did not have confidence in Judah's pledge of protection, but he also knew that they must have food. He agreed to allow them to take Benjamin, but he had the boys take double the money, and he prepared a gift for the man to show respect and to hopefully appease him (v.11-13). Jacob showed faith in God. He spoke of his hope that God would have mercy on them and allow them to return along with Simeon and Benjamin (v.14).

Once the brothers got down to Egypt with Benjamin things were different. The man whom they still did not recognize as Joseph, the one they had sold into slavery, showed kindness to them. They were taken to his house and were seated according to their ages. The portion of food Benjamin was given was five times that of the others (v.15-34). These brothers had no idea what was happening. None of them knew God was doing even more than they could comprehend and was providing for His eternal plan to save the world.

We can never know all of the reasons for the things that happen in our lives. We experience success and delight and go through conflict with complications and pain, but God knows why. God has a plan for everything that happens. Do you trust God with your life in all its difficulty and success? Are you willing to step out in faith and rest in God's ability to work all things for good? Those who trust God and His plan and power have hope.

Genesis 44; Mark 14; Job 10; Romans 14

The Christian life is not easy. There will always be various trials and hardships, and the Lord has a purpose for every single one of them. We may be surprised by the intensity of the difficulties we face on our journey to heaven, but we should never be surprised that there are difficulties. Those who keep going forward in faith in Christ can struggle and still have hope.

In Mark 14, we see several of the basic struggles that all believers go through. Like our Lord and the twelve disciples, we will have to deal with evil conspiracies, misaligned motives, betrayal, unusual assignments, painful reminders, and frustrating friends.

The chapter begins (v.1-2) and ends (v.53-65) with evil conspiracies. Those who stand in opposition to God will always be forced to cover up and conceal their plans. God's purpose is pure and right and altogether good. While God's weapons are love and truth, the enemies of God use deceit and destruction. The Lord has the power to use their plans for His purpose.

When Jesus was anointed with a costly ointment (v.3-9), there were some disciples who were indignant and complained that this was a waste. Jesus made it clear this woman had done what was good. There is nothing greater we can do than to honor and glorify Jesus. The opportunity to bless the Lord is to be taken seriously with generosity.

Because of the nature of humanity and the chaos of this world, it is easy to get confused and intimidated. Judas lost perspective and Peter lost his nerve. Judas came to the conclusion that Jesus was wrong. Peter came to the conclusion that Jesus was not worthy of his life and devotion. It is easy for pride or fear to set in and cause anyone to betray and turn against God, as Judas did (v.10-11.43-50) and as Peter did (v.66-72). The Lord warns us of this danger throughout Scripture, as He did Judas (v.17-21) and Peter (v.26-32). It is a wise believer who fights to avoid a failing faith.

There are times when a child of God will not understand what God is doing or why, but in those moments we must simply obey. Jesus sent two of the disciples on a seemingly secret mission with strange instructions (v.12-16). God does not expect us to comprehend all He is doing. God expects us to trust Him.

The Lord's Supper reminds us of the broken body and shed blood of Christ that was necessary for our atonement (v.22-25). It is also a reminder of how God works. He chooses something ordinary, like a piece of bread, and He takes it, blesses it, breaks it, and then gives it so others can be blessed (v.22). Like the disciples on the night of Jesus' betrayal (v.32-42), we all fail. God's grace is sufficient to save and restore us as we repent and believe.

Jesus raised up and put to good use fallen men with imperfect motives and unfaithful attitudes. He is still doing that today. We must not get discouraged with ourselves or others. There is hope in the plan and grace of God. Do you trust in God's grace and power? Are you frustrated or discouraged with your failures and the failures of others? Although we all struggle, we can keep going forward in Christ with hope.

Genesis 45; Mark 15; Job 11; Romans 15

We are all capable of being deceived, but those who seek to honor God and live by faith in His goodness are more apt to see past the lies of the world, the flesh, and the Devil. We do not need the compliments of humanity, the pleasure of an easy life, or the sense of being in control to have hope. Those who can trust the Almighty and His purposes can always live with hope.

Job was a man with confident faith. He had a faith that said, "Though he slay me, I will hope in him;" (Job 13:15). In Job 11, he was being attacked by his so-called friend, Zophar, who was serving the purpose of the Devil by trying to rob God of glory by convincing Job of a lie. The Devil had told God that the only reason Job worshipped God was because God had given Job what he wanted (Job 1:9-12). In his attack on Job, Zophar used a similar line of reasoning to explain Job's suffering. Zophar wrongly thought only good things happen to those who are faithful to God. What Zophar did not know was that Job was living faithfully to God.

Job's faith allowed him to trust in the goodness of God. What was happening to Job was not because of his sin but because Job was a righteous man. Zophar insisted that Job was in sin and that he was being punished for the wrong he had done (v.1-12). That was a lie and we know it because we know the heavenly side of this story that is explained in the first few chapters of the book. God uses suffering and pain for good. We need only look at the cross to understand that.

What Zophar says about those with true faith is true (v.13-20). There is a great blessing that comes to those who prepare their heart and give it to God (v.13a), who stretch out their hands to God in prayer (v.13b), who repent of sin and refuse to live in sin (v.14a), and who refuse to allow sin in their home (v.14b). Those who live this way can look to heaven with confidence (v.15a), can live with the security of a believer (v.15b), can look past misery (v.16), can live through darkness (v.17), will know there is hope (v.18), and will not be afraid of others (v.19). The wicked that do not trust in God have no hope (v.20).

Job did not understand God's plan and wanted to be free of the burden that had been placed on him. Job had not sinned. Like Jesus, Job was suffering for sin he had not committed in order to bring glory and honor to God. Jesus did not sin, and yet He suffered. He suffered for the purpose of God. Jesus knew why He suffered. Job did not know why he was suffering, and yet he was still faithful. That is great faith!

God allows suffering for His glory. Could God use you this way? Would you remain faithful if you had to suffer for being righteous in order to bring God glory? Like Jesus, Job was willing to look beyond his own will and trust God and His will, when there was no earthly reason to do so. The kind of faith that Job exhibited is worthy of our study and pursuit. Those who can trust God as Job did can live through anything with hope.

Genesis 46; Mark 16; Job 12; Romans 16

When a child of God is living and doing what God commands, there is a great blessing that comes to both the child and those who see the child's faith in action. Those who trust and obey God live with and give others hope.

In Romans 16, Paul praised a number of believers, warned and encouraged others, and glorified God for the way God blessed His saints according to His purpose. Those who are blessed to believe in Jesus Christ are given a glorious life that is used by God to inspire others and honor God. There are many obstacles that a believer must negotiate, but even those are there for an ultimate good that brings glory to God.

In the first two paragraphs of the chapter, Paul pointed to certain people and called out specific qualities that all believers would do well to seek to have. He commended Phoebe for being generous (v.1-2). Those who give financially play a vital role in the Kingdom of God. Prisca and Aquila were honored for their faith and willingness to risk their lives for the cause of Christ (v.3-5a). Epaenetus was remembered and celebrated for being the first convert to Christ in Asia (v.5b). Mary was honored for working hard for the church (v.6). Andronicus and Junia were known by the apostles and appreciated as those who suffered for the cause of Christ (v.7). Paul listed a number of people and recognized them for being those who believed and who served the Lord faithfully (v.8-15). These were purveyors of hope. We would all do well to seek to do as they did.

Paul changed his approach abruptly in verse 19 to tell the people what they were to avoid. He told them to avoid those who cause divisions and discourage faithfulness. These kinds of people are emotionally and spiritually immature. Those who seek to gain approval by causing others to be unsettled or hurt need to be avoided. Also, those who teach false doctrine need to be avoided. Divisive people and those who teach what is contrary to the truth can kill a church. What is needed is faithful obedience (v.20), which comes from confidence in the coming destruction of Satan. Until then, the people of God are to remain in the grace of God and to honor those who serve the Lord. They are to greet them with grateful hearts (v.20b-23).

The result of God's people being faithful and encouraging one another through acts of faith and obedience will be glory to God. Paul finished this chapter and this letter with a great doxology pointing out the greatness of God the Father (v.25-27). The Father is worthy of this glory because He is the all-wise God who is to be praised through Jesus Christ. It is only through Jesus that the Father can be known, and when the Father is known through the Son, He is always glorified.

Paul pointed out the legacy of many first-century believers who served well as an example to us. We all leave a legacy. What is yours? Is it a legacy that inspires hope? Is it a legacy that brings glory and praise to God? Is it a legacy built on the Gospel of Jesus Christ? Those who live by faith in Jesus and obey the Word of God honor God and experience a hope that inspires others.

Genesis 47; Luke 1:1–38; Job 13; 1 Corinthians 1

God is at work in the world accomplishing His purpose for all things. It is beyond the capacity of finite beings to ascertain the vastness of God and His plans. God's sovereignty is a mystery. Knowing that God reigns gives disciples of Jesus hope.

In Genesis 47, God's authority over small and sizable matters is revealed. Not only was God at work in Joseph's little family in a famine-plagued land in Palestine, but also in a nation that was supplying food for untold numbers of people. Through God's providential care, Joseph became the savior of Israel and many nations. Joseph was betrayed and taken captive. He lost his life in order to become God's means of salvation. His life is a picture of the Gospel.

Israel was given new life. This family was provided with a place to thrive. They were witnesses to the power of God (v.1-6, 27-28). The father of the one who provided salvation to all through his sacrificial leadership blessed the nation that loved and honored his son (v.7-12). The son built a kingdom of servants who had been given new life through him (v.13-26). The father called the son and his brothers to look to the promised land as their final hope (v.29-31). This is a picture of the Gospel.

Joseph showed grace to those who had sinned against him. This was God's plan from the very beginning. So it was with Christ. God chose Him before the foundation of the world to be the savior. Humanity betrayed Him, abandoned Him, and put Him to death and He loved them still. In love and according to God's plan, Jesus paid the penalty for our sin and now by faith we are saved and given new life in Him. It is through the Son that we are able to live and thrive in Godliness.

In providing for the Egyptian population, Joseph made the people subject to the Pharaoh. They ultimately surrendered their very lives to the service of Pharaoh. So it is with Christ. All who are saved give their lives to the service of the King of Kings. They gladly submit to Him in all things because of the life He has given to them.

Israel made his son Joseph promise to bury him in Palestine. This is the land of promise. This is where God said He would provide for the nation of Israel and through the family of Abraham provide blessings to the entire world (Genesis 12:1-3). Israel challenged his son and his brothers to look beyond the land they were living in and to remember that it was not their home. So it is with Christ. God has led us to live in this world today, but this world is not our home. Our home is in heaven and we are eagerly awaiting for our exodus from this fallen place and our escape into the promised land of heaven, where there is no sickness and death and where God will reign forever (Revelation 21).

There are millions of things happening in our lives and in the lives of every person on this planet. God is working in all things great and small to accomplish His purpose. We, like Joseph and Jesus, may not want to walk the road God has planned for us, but it leads to God's blessed purpose. Do you trust God's plan for your life? Living under the sovereign care of God gives hope.

Genesis 48; Luke 1:39–80; Job 14; 1 Corinthians 2

There are no such things as accidents or coincidences with God. When we look at the world through a Biblical lens, we see that human beings are free and responsible to choose, but God is sovereign and accomplishes His will. Those who trust in God live with great hope in the plans of God.

In Luke 1:39-80, the providence of God and responsibility of humanity is on full display. Elizabeth and Mary are both experiencing miraculous pregnancies and enjoying the divine favor of God. Elizabeth was by this time an older woman, and yet she was able to conceive a son. Mary was a virgin and yet pregnant with a son. Elizabeth and her husband created life in the biological way of a husband and wife. Mary's conception was by the Holy Spirit. Both women were aware they were part of a bigger plan and gave God honor.

Mary made a visit to her relative Elizabeth and upon greeting her, the son in Elizabeth's womb leaped in response. What could this mean but that something supernatural was taking place, and even this unborn baby knew it. Elizabeth was filled with the Holy Spirit and provided praise to God, thanksgiving, and affirmation to Mary (v.39-45). She honored God by speaking of the blessing that Mary had received and that she was now receiving by being in Mary's presence. The affirmation received from Elizabeth must have been like a warm blanket on a cold night to Mary. Being pregnant and unmarried was not safe or acceptable for a woman.

These two statements of praise by Mary and Zechariah are significant. They both speak of the fulfillment of God's promise to bring the Savior into the world. Mary delights in God that she has found favor in His sight and has been allowed to be a part of God's mission (v.46-55). This mission was not an easy one. Mary's life would be in danger. The heartache she would experience over the years would be devastating. So much of what she would have wanted would not be possible. She would not enjoy a quiet life and see her oldest son live beyond her, marry, and have biological children. No, she would live with suspecting eyes all around and one day see her son killed mercilessly. It would be a life of sacrifice, but she thanked God for it.

Zechariah praised God for the fact that the Messiah was now coming into the world and his son would be the servant to go before the King of Kings and prepare the way (v.67-80). The horn of salvation promised to come through the line of David was entering into the world (1 Samuel 7:16). Zechariah praised God and prophesied over his own son. Again, this honor would demand sacrifice. John would live a hard life and die a terrible death. Despite the suffering that would come, Zechariah knew it was all a blessing.

Mary, Elizabeth, Zechariah, and John all had to make choices. They had to choose to do the things that God willed for their lives. God's sovereignty does not take away the necessity of the faithfulness or the great responsibility each person must bear in order to accomplish God's will. Do you delight to suffer for God's purpose? Do you give thanks for getting to participate in God's Kingdom cause? Those who choose to trust God and join in God's will have great hope.

Genesis 49; Luke 2; Job 15; 1 Corinthians 3

Those who can only have hope in God when He makes sense to them or when He gives them what they want have a limited hope. Those who can look beyond their suffering and deal with the difficult questions they have of God, and do so with their faith intact, are those who live with a living hope that will never fail.

Job was a man who was able to keep his faith even though there was seemingly no earthly reason to do so. His wife encouraged him to curse God and die (Job 2:9). Job had questions about things he did not understand, but he never stopped believing in the innate goodness of God. He wondered about the kind of God the one true God is, but Job never doubted in the perfection of God.

In Job 15, Job overcame a very strong temptation. God no longer fit into his safe and easy-to-define box. Rather than simply give up on God because God did not suit him, or to pretend to have a commitment to a man-made god he did not believe in, Job chose the narrow and difficult way. He chose to live by faith, deal with doubts, and pursue a relationship with God that was genuine. In so doing, he made a mess of the nicely defined theologies of his day, denied legalism, and caused his friends to have to struggle with the tragedies of life.

Job's so-called friends who turned into his prosecutors could not tolerate Job's defiance. If Job were right, then much of what they believed was wrong. They believed in a theology that said that God gives good things to good people and bad things to bad people. This, they assumed, is what kept the masses in check. Rather than allow these men to remain in bondage to a lie, God revealed truth through His servant who was righteous but suffered in order to show the world what kind of God He is. This is the Gospel!

Eliphaz told Job he was a dangerous fool (v.1-16). He told Job he was diminishing the fear of God and inspiring people to give up on meditating on God (v.4). Eliphaz was convinced that Job was deceived (v.5-6), had no authority to say what he said (v.7-13), and that Job was corrupt (v.14-16). Eliphaz's religion, like all religions of the world, taught a simple concept: God can be controlled through humanity's behavior. If a person was moral, then God was required to give that person good things and the wicked people must suffer for the bad things they did (v.20). While there are consequences to sin and righteousness, this theology makes no room for the Gospel.

The Gospel is the good news that even though all people have sinned and fall short of the glory of God (Romans 3:23), grace is offered through the sacrifice of Jesus (Romans 3:24-25). What we could not do for ourselves, God did. The righteous was punished so the unrighteous could be made right with God.

Job refused to believe and live under a lie. Do you think God owes you for your behavior? Is your concept of God one of only justice? What a terrifying thing it would be to have to appease God on our own. Those who trust in Jesus will not always have a comfortable life, but they will always have a blessed life. That is a life full of hope.

Genesis 50; Luke 3; Job 16–17; 1 Corinthians 4

Leadership at its best is servant leadership. Jesus Christ is the ultimate example of servant leadership. The Lord has called and equipped leaders for His church. Those who give and live under Christlike leadership live with hope.

The Apostle Paul was a good leader. He cared more about those he served than he did himself. His testimony is one of personal pain and sacrifice. At his calling to ministry the Lord made it clear that his work would be one that involved suffering (Acts 9:16). Paul said that it was granted to him and others to have the honor to get to suffer for Christ (Philippians 1:29). In 1 Corinthians 4, Paul reveals the heart of a servant leader. A servant leader understands God's calling (v.1-5), people's needs (v.6-15), and the importance of an effective challenge (16-20).

Paul understood that his calling to ministry was from God and he and those like him were supernaturally given the responsibility to steward the mystery of God – the Gospel (v.1). Stewardship is not ownership. The apostles and subsequent leaders of the church were not the owners of the Gospel of God. Leaders in the church are responsible to God to faithfully share the hope of glory (v.2-3). None are perfect (v.4). All are responsible. When the Lord Jesus Christ returns, He will bring judgment on all people, including the leaders of His church. At that time all will be revealed and rewards will be given (v.5). Until then, judgments need to be held in check with humble hearts and disciplined minds.

The people of Corinth were like all people. They needed good leaders. There is always a temptation among believers to go beyond what the Word of God teaches. Those who get outside of the bounds of the Bible will often become arrogant and will not be helpful to the cause of Christ (v.6-7). Paul sarcastically wrote of the Corinthians' blessings and reminded them that what they had received from Christ came at a great expense to him and those who have served them (v.8-13). His goal was not to shame the people, but to admonish them to be grateful to God and humble in their attitudes (v.14-15). God is glorified best by those who are grateful for the good things God has given to them by those who sacrificed for them.

Effective servant leaders are able to lead through modeling. Paul challenged the children of God in Corinth to imitate him (v.16). This was not a statement written in pride. This was the admonition of a spiritual dad who cared for those who had come to faith under his leadership. He was preparing them to receive another gift. Paul was sending Timothy to look after them (v.17). Paul planned to come soon as well and to deal with people causing problems (v.18-20). The announcement of his coming was a warning.

Jesus Christ is coming again! When He returns, perfect leadership will rule the world. Until then, Godly leaders will give oversight to the church. Are you a Godly servant leader? Are you humbly and gratefully following the leaders God has placed over you? Are you honoring God with your attitude and actions? Those who give and live under Christlike leadership live with hope.

Exodus 1; Luke 4; Job 18; 1 Corinthians 5

There is never a moment when God is caught by surprise. There is not a single atom or a single nanosecond that is not under the complete control of God. Believing in the power, goodness, and purpose of God gives God's people great hope.

The children of Israel were often plagued with painful circumstances. Some took place because of their sin, but sometimes they were the victims of evil. That was the situation in Exodus 1. God's people were slaves in Egypt. Having escaped a great famine four hundred years before, they were now being held captive by a regime in Egypt that had forgotten the good Joseph had done for them. God's people had become numerous and a threat to Egyptian power, and they were forced to be slave laborers (v.1-14).

What was happening during this time was a part of the ultimate plan of God presented in the Bible. The Bible is a single story with four parts: creation, fall, rescue, and restoration. God created the world in perfect harmony and placed His image bearers in a blessed land. Sin forced them out into a broken world, where they were slaves to sin and the consequences of the fall. God in His grace promised He would set His people free through a man who would reign forever. The rescuer who was promised, Jesus Christ of Nazareth, came in the midst of this bondage. At His birth the male children of the city where he was born were killed, but He escaped. Having been shaped by a desert wandering, Jesus emerged to save God's people. Having set them free, He is now leading His people to the promised land of heaven.

In Exodus 1, God's people were outside of the borders of the blessed land promised to Abraham. They were in bondage and victims of circumstance. God promised this would happen (Genesis 15:13-14), but God was about to send His rescuer, Moses. He would come out of a time of desert wandering to lead God's people to salvation and on into the promised land. At this point in the story, Moses is about to be born. Like Jesus, the male boys of his birth city were all killed (v.15-22), but he escaped to live and become the savior of God's people.

It is vital that God's people never forget that our individual lives are part of a larger story that is being lived out. The enemy of God gained control of the planet through humanity's treason, but God has not abandoned us or His world. Humanity now lives in an evil world, with a naturally evil nature, and is being pursued by an evil power. We are born captive to sin, but the Rescuer has miraculously come and Jesus will lead all who are willing into the promised land of heaven. This is grace! It is only by the grace of God that any are saved.

No matter what we are going through in life, we can know that God has a plan for us. God is never surprised. He has an ultimate plan for creation and a personal plan for every person. When we live in obedience to God, we maintain our hope and look forward with confidence to God's reward. Are you looking at your life from the broader picture of what God is doing in the world? Are you following Jesus to your divine destiny? Those with a Biblical perspective and faith in Jesus live with hope.

Exodus 2; Luke 5; Job 19; 1 Corinthians 6

God expects His children to trust Him. If a child of God must be in control of not only the effort, but also the outcome of life, then that child will live under constant stress and anxiety. The child who will simply trust and obey God will have hope.

In Luke 5, several reasons to trust God are given. He is the God who provides (v.1-11). He is the God who heals (v.12-16). He is the God who forgives (v.17-26). He is the God who cares (v.27-32). He is the God who renews (v.33-39).

It is easy for confident, capable people to get a false sense of their abilities. A mistake that many make is in thinking they have everything figured out. Peter probably thought he knew everything about fishing and what his life was going to be like. When Jesus provided a supernatural catch for Peter and his partners, Peter's eyes were opened to the reality of his inability to measure up to what God can do. In His grace, Jesus provided Peter a better way and gave him a life that God had destined him for: to be a fisher of men (v.10).

On this side of the fall there will always be pain and problems to deal with and overcome. Thankfully, God has the power to heal and there are times when God chooses to intervene miraculously. He has the power not only to heal bodies, but hearts, souls, and relationships. The leper Jesus healed gained far more than his physical health. Jesus told him to go and present himself to the priest (v.14). This act would open the door for the man to reenter the faith community of his day. Jesus gives people redemption and relationships.

Being restored to a right relationship with God is the greatest blessing a person can gain. God is a forgiving God. He takes traitors and is able to transform them into friends. The paralyzed man that was brought before Jesus received what he was not looking for and what he did not deserve. He and his friends were looking for a physical miracle. Jesus did more. He forgave the man of his sin and gave him a new life with God (v.20).

In a world where people live with fear and a compulsion for self-preservation, it is unusual to find people who genuinely care for others. God is a God who cares. Levi was a tax collector, and he and all of his friends were considered to be thieves and turncoats (v.27). God still cared about Levi and offered him a new life. Having received this new life with Christ, Levi introduced Jesus to his friends. Jesus cared about them too. Jesus can save anybody.

God has the power to give new life to those who trust in Him. That new life will not fit into old ways of living. It is like new wine. It cannot go into old wine skins (v.37). The miracle of grace is that it changes not only a person's standing with God, but their way of life in the world. It's all new!

We all are responsible for our lives, but by the grace of God, we can entrust ourselves to God's capable care. Who do you trust with your life? What is most important to you: control or faithfulness to God's purpose? Those who look to Jesus and rest in Him have hope.

Exodus 3; Luke 6; <u>Job 20</u>; 1 Corinthians 7

It is easy to praise God when life is convenient and troubles are few. How we respond when life is hard tells us a great deal about our true faith. Those who trust God in the storm live with hope.

Job believed that all of his suffering was under the gaze of and within the purpose of God (Job 19:1-22). He did not understand it and he did not want it to continue. And yet he maintained his confidence in God (Job 19:25), even in the face of discouraging friends who did not understand his faith, his life, or his God. In their ignorance and with a bad theological system, these so-called friends made Job's life worse. They did not want to believe what Job believed because it would make their performance-based theological system untenable.

In this fallen world, God allows the righteous to suffer so that the unrighteous can be made righteous (2 Corinthians 5:21) and so that the righteous can be sanctified and made strong through dependence upon God (2 Corinthians 12:7-10). Zophar's comments in Job 20 are not completely false in a general sense, but they are certainly not true of Job's specific situation. God's Gospel way is so unlike the way of the world.

God placed human beings on this planet with a divine purpose that still stands, but this planet is no longer the place God created. This fallen world is under a curse and filled with fallen people. These fallen people are easily insulted by the words of the righteous, as Zophar was (v.1-3). In this fallen world, comfort and happiness do not remain. Nothing, other than the divine blessings of grace and love remain (v.4-5). Sooner or later everyone, including those with resources, die (v.6-9). Each generation must deal with the pain of loss and the responsibility to carry on in the difficulties and struggles of this world (v.10-11). Although there are many good things to enjoy in this world, sooner or later evil corrupts what is good and spoils it (v.12-22). Not only will the natural consequences of evil fall upon all who live for the delights and comforts of this world, but then God will bring His judgment upon them. In the end, the unrighteous will be brought before God and completely exposed. Jesus told His disciples in Luke 12:2, "Nothing is covered up that will not be revealed, or hidden that will not be known." This loose description of hell is terrifying. There will be emotional distress under God's anger, the physical anguish of darkness and fire, and the mental torment of losing everything and having to exist forever as an enemy of the one true, good God (v.23-29).

Job listened to Zophar's speech and did not flinch. He knew that His "redeemer lived" (Job 19:25). Faith is so rich that no amount of suffering or pain can ever bankrupt it. Job did not have to worry about what comes of the wicked because he was not wicked. He was a righteous man by faith who was accomplishing God's purpose.

We may never know with certainty the reason for our suffering. What we can know for certain is that salvation in found in Christ. Those who trust in Him can endure suffering. Do you have steadfast faith in Jesus? Can you suffer and sustain your faith? Those who choose to trust in the Redeemer have hope.

Exodus 4; Luke 7; Job 21; 1 Corinthians 8

The way a person looks at and thinks about the world and their life in it will determine how they feel. Thoughts and feelings are crucial because they drive our actions. The person with a Biblical world-view has great hope.

The church at Corinth that Paul planted and later wrote multiple letters to was a mess. It was filled with people from varied backgrounds and points of view. It was at Corinth that Paul met Aquila and Priscilla, a Jewish Christian couple from Rome; Crispus, the synagogue ruler who came to believe in Jesus along with his entire family; Titius Justus, a God-fearing Greek; and a host of people from varying economic and social backgrounds. Some of those who came to know Christ and joined the church were influential political leaders and some were former cult prostitutes from the temple of Aphrodite, the goddess of love, which stood over the city of Corinth. It was quite a motley crew! Paul ministered there for a year and a half.

After Paul left, there were all kinds of problems in the church. He addressed these issues in letters to the church at Corinth. In 1 Corinthians 8, Paul addressed the issue of idols, pagan ritual, and church unity. Some in the church had no problem buying and eating meat sacrificed to idols, but some believed this meat was dishonoring to Jesus and should not be consumed. Paul provided a Biblical world-view from which the people could understand this issue and act appropriately.

He began by helping the church think correctly about idols and the one true God (v.1-6). Establishing their unity, Paul pointed to the fact that idols were man-made things and in reality there was only one true God (v.4-6) and they all knew Him.

Moving on from knowledge, Paul spoke to the people about their feelings. Those who knew the idols were of no consequence ate the meat, and it was almost a point of pride for them because they felt more Godly than those who would not eat it (v.7-8). Paul helped them understand that eating the meat might cause a former idol worshipper to fall back into idolatry and to be sensitive to weaker siblings (v.9-11). By eating meat offered to idols they were sinning against Christ by wounding the conscience of those who were weak in their faith (v.12). Given the circumstances, Paul provided a personal testimony that others should follow. Knowing that eating meat offered to idols would be emotionally difficult for others, Paul determined that he would not eat it (v.13). A Biblical world-view produces thoughts and feelings which lead to actions that unify the church and honor Christ.

We may not live in a world exactly like Corinth, but we do live in a world with man-made institutions and activities that cause people to stray from God. Are there things you do that might cause other believers to stumble into sin? Is there any sense of selfish pride in your heart? By encouraging other believers to live with a Biblical world-view we help each other maintain faithful lives to Christ. Thinking rightly about God, feeling rightly within, and acting consistently, according to a Biblically informed conscience, fuels hope.

Exodus 5; Luke 8; Job 22; 1 Corinthians 9

Satan is full of hate and violence and loves to devour and destroy any of God's image bearers, but the ones that get his attention and that he works hard to deter the most are the ones who are willing to stand and serve Christ. The good news is that the child of God who is living for God's glory gains an eternal blessing, which gives great hope.

When Moses and Aaron approached Pharaoh in Exodus 5, the Pharaoh responded, just as God said he would (Exodus 3:19; 4:21). He would not let the people go. If we could know all that God knows and do all that God could do, we would agree with everything God chooses. Moses and Aaron would have preferred an easier path, as we all would, but God's way in this world is a narrow, hard way (Matthew 7:14). It is also the way of great blessing and hope.

Moses and Aaron were serving God in God's name. Pharaoh wanted to be god and have people serve in his name. This contrast between Moses and Aaron and the Pharaoh is stark. Moses and Aaron said in Exodus 5:1, "Thus says the Lord, the God of Israel...'" Pharaoh orders the taskmasters and foremen over the Israelite slaves to say in Exodus 5:10, "Thus says Pharaoh...'" Those who serve the Lord speak and labor in His name and in His power. Those who do not live for the Lord speak and work in their own name and in their own power.

The battle got intense for Moses and Aaron. They were doing what God said, but instead of things getting better, things became significantly worse. Life was not only worse for the people, but dramatically worse for Moses and Aaron. Not only was Pharaoh against them, but the people turned against them (v.20-21). This is often how it feels to serve God. The best thing we can do is pray. That is what Moses and Aaron did (v.22-23).

The child of God who is serving the King of Heaven will often have to contend with spiritual oppression. It can come in any number of forms. The good news is that the children of God have the power of the Almighty at work in them, around them, and through them. Jesus said in John 16:33, "I have said these things to you, that in me you may have peace. In the world you will have tribulation. But take heart; I have overcome the world." God does not abandon His people to fight the enemy on our own. We can say as Nehemiah once said to the faithful of God in Nehemiah 4:20, "Our God will fight for us." It is a good and worthy goal to live to have the enemies of God to say of us at our death, "I am glad that one is gone!"

What is your goal in life? Is it to make your life as easy as possible or is it to make an eternal difference in the name of the Lord? Jesus said in Matthew 5:11–12, "Blessed are you when others revile you and persecute you and utter all kinds of evil against you falsely on my account. Rejoice and be glad, for your reward is great in heaven..." Is your reward in heaven great? Those who serve the Lord will face many trials and challenges, but their ultimate reward is great, which makes their hope great.

Exodus 6; Luke 9; Job 23; 1 Corinthians 10

For every good thing the Lord calls us to, there is a corresponding challenge. For every good thing God does through us, there is some form of opposition. For every truth we learn, there is a demanding step of obedience to take. For every powerful thing we learn the Lord can do, there is a measure of faith we must have. Those who trust and obey Jesus live with and grow in hope.

Many believers are tempted to think that the disciples who walked with Jesus during His earthly ministry really had it easy. The fact of the matter is that these men went through extreme difficulties. Those who have an enduring, living hope in their hearts through faith in Christ will be blessed, but that blessing will come with many toils and snares. In Luke 9, the challenges and blessings of being a disciple of Jesus are revealed.

The more the Lord gives us, the more that will be demanded. This should not surprise us. This is the way Jesus said it would be in Luke 12:48: "Everyone to whom much was given, of him much will be required, and from him to whom they entrusted much, they will demand the more." This should in no way deter us from asking for more of God or from God, but it does make us fully aware of what it is we are asking. When we ask God for more blessings, we are asking for more responsibility.

The first disciples of Jesus experienced amazing blessings and were exposed to supernatural truths. They were blessed to have spiritual power to serve God (v.1-6). The fact that Herod was perplexed by it is revealing (v.7-9). What an absolute joy it must have been to see Jesus feed the five thousand (v.10-17) and to know that Peter was correct in saying Jesus was "the Christ of God" (v.18-20). To hear Jesus must die must have been hard, but to know He would be raised, inspiring (v.21-22). Knowing their Lord's plan made their calling bearable. They too were called to deny themselves, take up their cross, and follow in the way of their Master (v.23-27). They saw Jesus transfigured and stand with Moses and Elijah and they heard the voice of God (v.28-36). Jesus healed a little boy and they learned it was possible by faith, the very faith they had been given (v.37-42). Jesus' plan was hard to understand. It was a mystery they were uniquely made aware of (v.43-45). Although called and trained by the Lord, this special circle of disciples that walked with Jesus was just part of God's plan. God always has an army (v.46-50). These leaders learned compassion (v.51-56). Jesus calls people to follow Him and to put aside all that cannot be kept in order to gain what can never be lost (v.57-62).

Knowing Jesus and being allowed to serve Him was a great honor for the first disciples. It was an honor that came with great demands. It is still an honor today that demands we be willing to pay the cost that comes with the calling. Are you willing to take responsibility for the blessings you are asking for and seeking from God? In order to enjoy the blessings of God, we must exercise faith and obey what we know. Those who are willing to grow in faith will face challenges. Those who have a growing faith have a growing hope.

Exodus 7; Luke 10; Job 24; 1 Corinthians 11

God truly is in control and His plan and timing are perfect. Those who humbly accept the plan and timing of God, no matter how painful their life may be at times, live with great hope.

Job was a man of great faith, but it is completely understandable why he asked the questions he asked in Job 24. It appears that Job was simply sharing what was in his heart. He longed for justice and could not understand why God allowed people who do evil things in the world to seemingly live without suffering. We know that Job had done nothing wrong, but was suffering for righteousness and for the glory of God. At the same time, Job was being chastised by his friends in and for his suffering. As Job looked out in the world and considered his own life and its immediate outcome, it seemed to him that things were not as they should be.

What Job asked makes sense from an earthly, finite perspective (v.1). From Job's vantage point it appeared that God was not dealing with evil and that those who have faith in Him were not seeing God's righteous judgment displayed. That is an accurate assessment of the world now, as we can see it. The description that Job laid out is spot on. He described the things that the wicked were doing (vv. 2–4, 9, 13–17, 21). These actions had very real consequences on very real victims (v.5–12). It appeared these evildoers faced no consequences for their actions. As far as Job could tell, his friends did not seem to be able to see what he saw. They talked as if the people of corruption were immediately dealt with and suffered immediate negative consequences (v.18–20). Job saw an apparent lack of fairness. It appeared to Job that there was no difference in terms of consequences between those who did what was evil and those who did what was good (v.21–25). He was right. The same is true today. Ultimate divine justice is still to come. The world is not as it should be.

What Job could not see and what we often do not see is the ultimate plan of God. Job could not know that through his suffering, God was bringing about victory. Through Job's faithfulness and sacrifice, others have come to know the truth and understand the greatness of God. That is the Gospel! Jesus Christ was given over to the evil one to suffer. His faithfulness provided the means by which people can know and be made right with God. In the end Job was blessed (Job 42:10-17). In the end Jesus was blessed (Philippians 2:9-11).

While Jesus had a sense of the ultimate purpose for his suffering, Job did not. Jesus knew He was from the Father and had come to give His life as the atoning sacrifice for sin. Job could not and did not know the reason for His suffering. We may never know the reason for our suffering on this side of heaven, but we can trust the one who knows all things. In the end, at the restoration (Revelation 21), all will be made right. Do you trust God's plan and God's timing? Do you look to God's Bible to define what is true or do you look to your own experiences and ideas? Those who simply trust God's plan and timing live with hope.

Exodus 8; Luke 11; Job 25–26; 1 Corinthians 12

Human beings are made to worship. God designed us to worship Him, but if we refuse to worship God, we will still worship something. What we worship defines us, inspires us, and guides us. Those who worship the One true God live with hope.

In 1 Corinthians 11 and 12, Paul wrote to the church about worship. While in chapter 11, Paul focused on the importance of being respectful of and loving toward one another by dressing modestly and receiving the Lord's Supper rightly. In Chapter 12, Paul gave attention to spiritual gifts and the importance of unity.

Chapter 12 begins with Paul pointing out the danger of idolatry. He started by speaking of spiritual gifts (v.1), but then shifted his attention to the recipients of God's gifts, God's people (v.2). The Holy Spirit is the source of God's gifts. Without Him a person will fall into idol worship. The absence of the one true God from a person's life does not keep them from worshipping. The absence of God from a person's life causes a person to worship the wrong things. It is only through the work of the Holy Spirit that a person is kept from believing and saying something heretical and destructive like "Jesus is accursed!" and enabled to say, "Jesus is Lord" (v.3).

The same Spirit that gives life to the soul and guidance in faith also gives gifts to use, services to perform, and activities to engage in (v.4-6). All of these are to be done for the benefit of the church – the body of Christ (v.7). The Holy Spirit unifies the work of each person, creating a powerful and beautiful interweaving of activity, which produces a healthy and dynamic church (v.8-11). Without the Spirit of God the people of God cannot serve the purpose of God and give glory and honor to God in worship.

The gifts are not intended for the person with the gift. The person with the gift is meant to use what God has given for the entire body. The Holy Spirit unifies the church and forms the people into an interdependent union (v.12-13). The church is like a physical body and each member is a specific part of it (v.14-20). Each role has a unique capacity for visibility and functionality. Each person must know their role and function within it without being jealous of another's role or being critical of their own. Each person is vital (v.21-26). God appoints each person to their role, according to His will. Disciples of Jesus are to seek not the applause of others, but to seek to contentedly fulfill the highest calling of all, to serve God with love for others (v.27-31).

It is the Spirit of God that enlivens, bestows gifts, and unifies God's people to worship Jesus. The worship that honors inspires each local church to live out the will of God. God's will is that His people worship Him and enjoy Him forever. Through faith, a redeemed person can live a life of God-honoring service, which makes their life meaningful. Is your life one that is united with a body of believers? Are you using the gifts God has given you to worship God? Those who worship God and serve His purpose have hope.

Exodus 9; Luke 12; Job 27; 1 Corinthians 13

God made humanity to live under His sovereign care. Even in this broken world, there is a way of life that is blessed (Psalm 1). Those willing to surrender to God and pursue His leadership will struggle in this world but will live with hope.

Moses was a man who learned the hard way. God called him to be the savior of His people. Seeking to provide deliverance to a Hebrew brother, Moses did not look to God. Instead, Moses took matters into his own hands and killed an Egyptian. Consequently, he had to flee to the desert. It was in the desert that God taught Moses to be a spiritual servant leader. When God called Moses to go back to Egypt to lead the Israelites to freedom, Pharaoh opposed him. In Exodus 9, Pharaoh is seen as a man with great power standing in opposition to God's purpose. Pharaoh fought with God and it cost him.

Pharaoh and the Egyptians seem to have had all of the power, good things, and a great future. It appeared that Moses and the Hebrews were weak, poor, and with no good options ahead of them. God allowed this circumstance for His purpose. God was fulfilling a promise (Genesis 15:13–14). The suffering of God's people in Egypt was a part of God's eternal plan. It was God's will to raise Pharaoh up to contend with Him in order that the world could know the greatness of the one true God (Exodus 9:16).

Today, there are many who appear to have the good life outside of the presence and direction of God. Know for certain, those who will not surrender to God will suffer for their sin. Like the Egyptians, they will have some power and some worldly blessings, but life will do what life in this fallen world always does. It will consume them in death. Meanwhile, God's people will be provided for and given God's providential care. God's people may not have the riches of the world, but they do have the riches of heaven, which are eternal. They may be seen as outsiders and experience persecution, just as the Israelites did, but God provides for His people, just as He did for Israel when they lived in Goshen. God's protective provision was given in Goshen (Exodus 9:26).

The calamities that the Egyptians faced and the security that the Hebrews enjoyed are a picture of the Gospel. The angel of death came and killed the firstborn of all of Egypt, while God's people were saved by the blood of a lamb. The Egyptians were drowned in the Red Sea, but the Hebrews walked on dry land. So too those who live without God, as their leader and redeemer, will die in sin and face the second death. God's children will enjoy rebirth and the eternal life of heaven. The unrighteous live under the curse of sin, while the righteous of God live under the blessing of God. God's righteous standing and blessing is found by grace through faith in Christ alone. It is the power of the Gospel that provides salvation.

Those who yield to Jesus and live under His grace and leadership are saved. Are you walking with God by grace through faith in Jesus? Is your life under God's direction or are you going your own way? Those who trust in God, like Moses and the Israelites, live and die with hope.

Exodus 10; Luke 13; Job 28; 1 Corinthians 14

We know intuitively that God made us to live in harmony and peace with other people, our environment, and God Himself. Our current conditions are not how God designed them. Those who look past the misery of this world and trust in Jesus live with hope.

Luke 13 begins with troubling events that occurred in the days of Jesus. There had been an attack on worshippers by the civil authorities (v.1). Why this took place is not clear. What is clear is this was a well-known and shocking tragedy. Another event that had occurred around that time was when the tower of Siloam fell and killed eighteen people (v.4). In response to both of these tragedies, Jesus made it clear that none who died were innocent and none who lived were superior to those who died. All will face judgment (vv.2-3, 5). We have all sinned. The only hope we have is to be made new by grace through faith in Jesus.

Those who believe in Jesus will live like it, and their way of life will reveal their faith. The parable of the fig tree communicates the fact that God expects His people to produce righteousness in their way of life (v.6-9). Those who are truly disciples of Jesus will cultivate grace and live in holiness. Those who do not produce spiritual fruit are not His people, and they will be judged by God.

Godly living is not a keeping of a list of rules. Godliness is love lived out in practical and ordinary ways. When we know and live in God's love, we love others and God the way He has loved us. This love results in holiness. When Jesus healed a woman who had suffered for eighteen years, the religious leaders were indignant (v.10-14). Jesus made it clear that their anger only showed their lack of true faith and love (v.15-17). Those who want to live by rules never experience the life of love God demands.

Those who live a life of love based upon the grace given to us by Jesus live for God's Kingdom. God's Kingdom of love is seemingly small, like a mustard seed or leaven (v.18-21), but it influences all that come in contact with it. The Kingdom is entered into by a narrow way, Jesus Christ (v.22-23). It is only through Christ that we can have our sin pardoned and be made righteous. All who believe in Jesus will be welcomed into heaven. Those who stand on their own will be removed from God's eternal home and left in darkness and despair for eternity (v.24-29). It does not matter how or when we come to Christ. It does not matter what our background or religious affiliations were. What matters is that we come to Christ and live for Him (v.30). God wants to save people from sin. He loves us and wants to lead us, but we must turn to Him, trust Him with our lives, and love Him, as He has loved us (v.31-35).

God loves all people, but only those who turn away from self-dependence and self-love will be saved by God's grace. We must trust Jesus. He has proven His love for us. Are you living a life that reveals the grace and love of Jesus in you? Do you act on the access you have to God through personal devotion? Those who abide in and share God's love live with hope.

Exodus 11:1–12:20; Luke 14; Job 29; 1 Corinthians 15

There is a tendency for human beings to look back and remember things as either far worse or far better than they actually were. What is always true is God is always with His people. His presence is not always felt in the same way, but God does not change and His promises are always true. Those who trust in God and believe in His goodness live with hope.

Job was struggling. Who could blame him? His children were killed. His wealth was taken. His health was gone. His faith was shaken. His friends were attacking him. His wife was despondent. When he looked in his past, he remembered better days. He had certainly seen better days. It appeared to him that God had abandoned him (v.5). He longed for the good old days when life was going the way he wanted it to go. He wanted to be happy again. He wanted it to feel like God was with him and for him (v.1-25). Job 29 is a personal reflection of Job's perception of what his life used to be like.

What Job could not see was he was truly blessed. His life was not as comfortable, but it was just as blessed as it ever was. We are all tempted, like Job, to judge our lives from an external vantage only. We look to see what we have, who thinks well of us, and how much we are enjoying life. If the sum total of our life is what we want, we tend to think that God is blessing us. If the life we are living is not what we want, we tend to see God as being against us. We often forget that God allows trials to increase our faith (James 1:2-4). The blessed person is not one who produces the fruits of righteousness in preferable seasons, but produces fruit in all seasons and does not wither under the heat of disappointment, discouragement, and danger (Psalm 1:3). The prosperity of a saint is more than bodily comfort.

God will often comfort the body to bless the soul. There are times of refreshment, when life is full of laughter, accomplishment, and fun. There are also times of refinement, when life is hard and faith is tested. In the time of ease, the child of God must learn to discipline the body through spiritual disciplines. When God allows suffering, the child of God must trust the Father's will. In difficult days we can know that God is forming us into the person He died for us to be. We are the clay. He is the potter. He knows what it is He wants us to be and what kind of service He has destined us for (Isaiah 64:8).

When we go through trials, we would do well to learn from Job. He held on to his faith and remained honest about his feelings. It was a tough battle and one that caused him great pain. We must also avoid his mistake of looking to his comforts as the only sign of God's blessing. No matter how good or bad things may be, we can always look to God in faith and trust His ultimate purpose. He is forming us into the image of Christ (Philippians 1:6). What kind of a time are you having in life right now? Is your faith growing? Those who trust in God in good and tough times live with hope.

Exodus 12:21–51; Luke 15; Job 30; 1 Corinthians 16

God made people to be connected with others. God may call us to specific times when we are not connected in rich relationships, but that is not God's typical plan. The person who is living in healthy relationships with other people has hope.

God is gracious to provide a means by which His people live in healthy relationships with other believers. This provision is the church. God promised to form a family of people adopted by His grace and called to gather for worship, to serve one another, and to love people in and of the world by helping them to personally know Jesus. 1 Corinthians 16 reveals many of the blessings that are available to those who participate in God's family.

One of the great blessings of the church is that believers are able to give financially to the work of God (v.1-4). God is at work all over the world. No single child of God has the capacity to be everywhere and do everything that needs to be done. Together, a church can be a support to others and enable them to be resourced as they fulfill God's purpose. In the days of Paul, there was a famine in Jerusalem. In order to provide for the needs of those believers, Paul took up an offering from the churches in the west to take back to Jerusalem. Through the mission efforts of those in Jerusalem, those in Corinth and other cities had heard the Gospel. Now they were being given the opportunity to care for those in Jerusalem who had cared for them. Generosity is meant to be a way of life for every Christian.

Another great blessing of the church is the blessing of servant leadership that is provided for believers (vv.5-12, 15-18). Everything rises and falls on leadership. Without leadership there is chaos. God purposefully raises up men and women to lead His church. He provides specific leaders in specific roles for His specific will. Those who are entrusted with leadership in the church understand they are servants. They do not influence others out of a need to be in control. Leaders in the church are called by God to serve the needs of others.

Another great blessing of the church is the instruction that is given to believers (v.13-14). The Bible is the source of all truth. In the Bible, God commands His people to live holy lives and reveals how that is possible in Jesus. The church was given the Bible by God to reveal who He is and what He is doing in the world. There are leaders who have the unique calling and gifting to study and then communicate the hope of Christ. When the Scripture is taught rightly, those enabled by the Spirit are blessed to understand the truth, apply it to their lives, and then share it with others. Those who teach refresh the church (v.15-18).

There is no concept in the New Testament of a believer who does not belong to a local church. Even those missionaries like Paul were sent by a local church. Disciples of Jesus must avoid allowing pride, hurt, or fear to keep them from being connected with other Christians. Are you fully engaged in a local church? The person who is in a healthy relationship with a local church is blessed and has hope.

Exodus 13; Luke 16; Job 31; 2 Corinthians 1

The follower of Christ is living in an in-between state of the already and the not yet. We are already forgiven of all of our sin. We already are alive to God by the power of the Holy Spirit. We are already in the Kingdom of God. The Kingdom of God has already come. And yet, we still battle with sin because we are still in the flesh, in a fallen world, and being pursued by an angry hoard of demons that want to destroy us. The child of God who can trust in the promises of God will live with hope.

Exodus 13 provides a means to understand the entire story of the Bible. The Bible is a single story with four parts: creation, fall, rescue, and restoration. Once God had passed over the people and brought judgment on all of Egypt by killing their firstborn, the children of Israel were freed. In this new life, they were to commemorate their salvation experience (v.1-2), they were to be set apart from the peoples of the earth (v.3-16), and they were to live by faith and grow in their trust of God in anticipation of their enemy being destroyed (v.17-22). This is what the story of the Bible is about.

The Israelites were told to consecrate the firstborn of their children and animals. God had saved the firstborn of Israel on the night of the Passover. Those who lived by faith in the grace given through the blood of the lamb were to remember and commemorate that salvation. Disciples of Jesus are commanded to do the same thing. They are commanded to commemorate their salvation through communion. The Passover Meal was an act of obedience that pointed back to Israel's salvation. Communion is an act of obedience that points back to the means of a believer's salvation.

The Israelites were ordered to live differently than the people who were inhabitants of Palestine. The practices of their faith were not salvific, but their way of life differentiated them from the people groups they were among so much so that it would be normal for their children to ask why they did the things they did. In response the parents were to point to the grace of God and His mighty hand of salvation. So it is with disciples of Jesus. Their way of life is to be different from the way of life of those who are lost in sin.

The Israelites were called to live by faith. God knew they had battles ahead and so He provided His presence and directed them in a pathway that would enable them to be trained to trust in Him. The people needed only to stay with God and follow His lead. In due time, God would destroy their enemies. Disciples of Jesus will fight battles with sin throughout their lives. Evil has not yet been vanquished, but one day God will destroy it completely. Until that time, God's people are to live by faith and follow Jesus.

The world is a dangerous place. God's children are saved and safe in God's care, so long as they follow and obey Him. Have you trusted in Jesus and been freed from sin? Do you celebrate that salvation by regularly receiving communion? Are you living by faith? The child of God who understands the dangers of this world and chooses to trust and follow Jesus will have hope.

Exodus 14; Luke 17; Job 32; 2 Corinthians 2

The Kingdom of God provides peace, joy, and life. The kingdom of self provides stress, discouragement, and death. All who are loyal subjects to King Jesus live with great hope.

There are many who claim to be subjects of the Kingdom of God, but not all truly are. It is vital that God's subjects live under God's rule. It is under God's rule that God's blessings flow. Luke 17 provides many ways disciples of Jesus can know they are true members of God's Kingdom and are living lives submitted to Jesus.

Those who are members of the Kingdom of God are at war with sin (v.1-4). Sin is either killing us or we are killing it. There is no in-between. Those who serve God in His Kingdom will be tempted, but will fight against that temptation and seek to limit its effects. God's people seek to be a help to those who sin in order that they overcome it. It is vital that God's people provide gracious correction to those who sin and always give personal forgiveness to those who sin against them.

Those who are members of the Kingdom of God live by faith (v.5-6) and gladly serve the King of Glory (v.7-10). Faith is a very small, but powerful thing. Those who have faith in God have access to the ultimate source of unlimited power in the universe. When we trust in God and count on what He can do rather than what we can do, we are depending on the One who with a word created all that there is out of nothing. God has the power to do anything that is according to His will. The person who knows and does the will of God is a citizen of God's Kingdom. When we serve Christ's cause by faith, we get to join God in accomplishing what is best.

Those who are members of the Kingdom of God are made clean and live with gratitude (v.11-19). Without being made righteous by Christ's atoning sacrifice, a person can never hope to enter into the Kingdom of God (2 Corinthians 5:21). By the grace of God, the blood of Jesus makes pure those who trust in Him and believe in His saving power. Those who experience God's redemption cannot help but be grateful. That gratitude is expressed in worship.

Those who are members of the Kingdom of God are waiting for the final installment of what God has determined for His creation (v.20-37). While it is true that the Kingdom of God has come, it is also true that there is still more to come. Right now, God is patiently pursuing people who are lost in darkness and calling them to repentance so they can be saved and made members of His Kingdom of light (2 Peter 3:9). Once all have heard and His people are accounted for, He will return (Mark 13:10) and make all things new (Revelation 21). Until that time, it is vital that God's servants attend to the truth of God's Word, pursue God's plan, and be prepared for God's judgment.

Those who live in the Kingdom of God live with hope in the healing power of Jesus and by faith join God in what He is doing in the world. Are you a servant in God's Kingdom living in obedience to King Jesus? Those who live in and for God's Kingdom live with hope and enjoy God's blessings.

Exodus 15; Luke 18; <u>Job 33</u>; 2 Corinthians 3

Life is not a theory. Life is lived in a real world with real challenges in the midst of a real spiritual war that has real consequences. There will always be pain and suffering in this world. Even the righteous will suffer, according to God's purpose. Those who have the ability to think rightly about God and live by faith in Him, no matter what the circumstances may be, live with hope.

In Job 33, Elihu got involved in the conversation with Job and his miserable counselors. He was pretty upset because Job was still not getting with their theological program. Job was sitting in an ash heap enduring sickness, loss, and an angry wife, but he still had his integrity and his faith. His faith was not without questions. Job was not proud. He was broken and confused. His friends were mad because they wanted Job to admit that what was happening to him was because he had sinned. Job knew this was not the case. The Bible is clear that all have sinned and fall short of the glory of God. Job was not claiming to be perfect. Job was claiming that he had sought the Lord and lived by faith in God's mercy but had been smitten, despite the fact that he had not turned from God. The life of Job reminds us of the reality of the Gospel. Job suffered because He was righteous. One day Jesus would come for God's glory and suffer for sin, even though He is the righteous God.

Elihu's speech was hostile. He began and ended his speech by telling Job to listen to him and to answer his theoretical concepts if Job could (vv. 1-7, 31-33). Elihu raised objections to Job's words and ideas about God. He dismissed Job's concerns (v.8-13). Elihu's real issue was that he believed God speaks, but people, like Job, do not listen and respond rightly (v.14-30). Elihu's intentions were not evil, but he was wrong. Elihu had no concept of a righteous person suffering for God's purpose. Those who trust more in man-made theories than the revealed Word of God will struggle in this fallen world to understand and honor God in all circumstances.

Humans suffer for many reasons. Some suffer as a natural consequence for their sin or the sin of others. Some suffer because God is using their pain to sanctify them or to grow their faith. God allows trials to strengthen our faith (James 1:2-4). Some suffer for a divine purpose. God's will was to allow His Son to suffer. Sometimes, God's plan may demand that His children suffer. We may never fully understand God's plan on this side of heaven, but we can always fully trust God's goodness and grace.

God is good no matter what. We live in a fallen world in fallen flesh in the midst of an evil that is powerful and persuasive. God is at work to redeem a people and will one day make all things right and good. Until the Lord returns, God's people will have to live and suffer by faith. Are you able to trust God in your suffering? Can you believe in the love of God when you do not feel loved? Those who can trust in the will of God and the goodness of God, even when there is no earthly reason to do so, will bring great glory to God and live with hope that does not fail.

Exodus 16; Luke 19; Job 34; 2 Corinthians 4

Trusting in the Lord to lead and provide through prayer is one of the most difficult aspects of the Christian life. When we believe in God's goodness, we are inspired to pray. Prayer is the means by which we communicate with God and are able to discern His will. When we pray specifically, we are able to see God's provision clearly. God always acts according to His Word. Those who pray trusting in the kindness and power of God live with hope.

If we are honest about our own faith journey, we would probably find that we are not much different than the people God called "stiff necked" (Exodus 32:9). Like the Israelites, we have all struggled to trust the goodness of God and rely on His provision. We, like Israel, often think that we know better than God or imagine that God has abandoned us. We might be tempted to be harsh in our criticism of Israel, considering the fact they had seen God do miraculous things like the plagues, the killing of Egypt's firstborn, and parting the Red Sea. We might think they have no excuse, but do we? We have the entire Bible that speaks of God's eternal plan in all of history. It could be argued that if anyone should be able to trust God, surely it would be the people who know the Messiah personally and are filled with the Spirit.

Every generation of God's family has failed to trust the Father perfectly. In His mercy, God's love does not fail. In Exodus 16 God's love is on display. He was dealing with people, like us, prone to wander and leave the God of love. The Israelites were on a physical and spiritual journey that would guide them into God's perfect plan. All of God's children are on a physical and a spiritual journey. God guides us all into His perfect plan.

God's plan is always to bring glory to Himself. The Israelites were not against that, but they were more concerned with the practical matters of their lives. They doubted God and spoke as if their old life in bondage to Egypt was better (v.1-3). Rather than pray to God for provision, they complained. God was still gracious to provide both "bread from heaven" and quail (v.4-30). God's provision came with instructions. They were to gather enough for each day, except the day before the Sabbath. On that day they were to get double so they could avoid work on the Sabbath and keep it as a holy day. Many did not trust in God, and yet, God was gracious and faithful. God always provides for His people. It may not be what we want, but it is always what we need. God calls us to trust in Him. We do not have to hoard resources. We can trust God and be generous with His provision. God provided the "manna" for Israel until they entered the land of promise (v.31-33).

Throughout their lives, God leads and guides His people. He meets needs in miraculous ways. He will meet our needs on our journey to heaven. As we make our way home, we must trust God. Do you trust in God's goodness and power to provide? Are you faithfully praying and seeking His blessing and direction? Are you giving to His work and living with contentment? Those who trust in God live with hope all the way home.

Exodus 17; Luke 20; Job 35; 2 Corinthians 5

The enemy of God works hard to distract and keep the saints from being inspired to obey Jesus. The strategy is simple: distract and destroy. The child of God who stays focused on the truth of God and lives by faith in God will enjoy the hope of God.

In Luke 20, Jesus taught some of the fundamental truths of the faith, while the enemy was at work to distract His followers and destroy their hope.

Jesus was preaching the "Gospel" and telling the people what He had come to do for them (v.1). We do not know the content of His discourse, but it was upsetting to the religious leaders who wanted to know by what authority Jesus was teaching (v.2). They could not refute His teaching and so they sought to distract Him and His hearers with questions they hoped would confound Jesus and confuse His followers. Jesus graciously offered a question that could have freed them. He asked by what authority John baptized (v.3). They chose to think politically rather than spiritually (v.4-6). They would not answer Him, so Jesus refused to answer them. Jesus then provided a story to help His hearers understand the Gospel He was preaching (v.9-18).

The religious leaders could not deny His power and appeal, so they tried to divide Jesus' supporters over politics (v.19-22). The enemy has often successfully used politics to divide God's people. They asked Jesus about paying taxes to Caesar. If Jesus said, "yes," His followers and the crowds might turn against Him. If He said, "no," the civil authorities would get involved in opposing Him. Jesus pointed to the power of God and the importance of human rule with a crafty statement that left his questioners silenced (v.23-26).

Like the devil, they kept looking for another opportune time to trip Him up (Luke 4:13). Again, the religious leaders attempted to create a conflict they hoped would distract Jesus' followers. This time it was about eschatology, end times doctrine (v.27-33). Again, Jesus overcame their deceit and, using the Word of God, pointed to the hope of His Gospel (v.34-40).

After their questions failed, Jesus asked a question about the authority of the Christ. Speaking of Psalm 110:1, Jesus affirmed that the Christ was clearly greater than King David (v.41-44). The religious leaders wanted and were looking for a leader like David. God had promised and sent someone greater than David. God Himself had come to save His people. This is the Gospel. After establishing the fact of the new covenant faith, Jesus warned His disciples about the snares of religion. Like the religious leaders of Jesus' day, religious powerbrokers today like to put on a good show by wearing unique garments, gaining places of authority, and using prayer to appear Godly (v. 45-47). They take advantage of people and use their authority as a means to gain things for themselves. The Gospel Jesus taught is built on loving sacrifice and grace.

Those who like to argue and have places of power create distractions. Are you aware of religious distractions that surround you? Do you have a personal knowledge and experience of the Gospel of Jesus? Those who trust in Jesus and avoid the distractions of nonsensical religious arguments live with hope.

Exodus 18; Luke 21; Job 36; 2 Corinthians 6

Like a broken clock that is correct twice a day, so are those who teach what is false and occasionally what is true. Neither can be trusted. The people who can identity what is true and denounce what is false have hope.

Job was surrounded by heretics. They were well-intentioned men who taught things that were partially true, but not completely true. They assumed they were good and God, being a good God, always and instantly rewarded those who are good. They did not understand they were far more sinful than they could know and God more gracious than they could imagine. The idea that God would cause a righteous man to suffer in order to accomplish His eternal purpose was a foreign concept to them.

Job knew he was not perfect, but he also knew he was a person who loved and sought God. There was no behavior in him that was not in others that would require him to suffer as he did. The so-called friends that surrounded Job during his suffering were of no help. Like the twelve disciples of Jesus, they wanted and expected God to act in ways that made sense to them and profited them. Job's counselors wanted a god that gave blessings to those who appeared good and cursed those who didn't. Their quid pro quo theology was heretical.

Thankfully, they, like their friend Elihu, in Job 36, revealed the signs of a heretic. Heretics typically reveal their wrong view of God by revealing their wrong view of themselves. Elihu was under the delusion that he was able to speak on behalf of God without error (v.1). The Bible is sufficient for understanding all things pertaining to life, faith, and the reality of God. God's word is inerrant, but God uses imperfect people to explain His Scripture. Those who teach God's Word will be tempted to think they speak without error, as Elihu believed (v.2). Anyone who thinks they teach God's Word perfectly is prideful and needs to be suspected of heresy.

Heretics often create categories that fit their preferences for how they prefer the world to be. Elihu believed God provided blessings to good people and pain to bad people (v.5-21). While it is true God blesses His people with many good things, it is also true that God allows suffering that serves His divine will. Those who do not provide space for God to work, as He wills in ways that are hard to understand, need to be suspected of heresy.

The chapter ends with a proclamation about the greatness of God (v.22-33). God is great in power and there is none like Him. He can be understood in the general revelation of His creation, but that general revelation does not give insight into the unique nature of God's ultimate will. God is a mysterious God who works in mysterious ways. Those who expect God to perform in this fallen world in ways that satisfy the expectations of fallen people need to be suspected of heresy.

On this side of the new heaven there will be mysteries and troubling realities. Those who make God more palatable to the sensibilities of sinners are dangerous. Are you taking the time to learn God's Word so you discern His will? Those who can discern truth live with hope.

Exodus 19; Luke 22; Job 37; 2 Corinthians 7

Life is hard, and those who dare to do something of significance in God's Kingdom will always feel at risk. God's will is that His people engage in ministry and put to use His blessings. Those who live on mission for God live with hope.

The Apostle Paul was a great missionary. The church at Corinth was one of the most challenging places Paul served. These precious people lived in a dark place during a dark time. They were surrounded by paganism, political enemies, and had personal problems that surfaced within their own ranks regularly. God used Paul to instruct, inform, and inspire this young church. In 2 Corinthians 7, the church was shown how to make the most of their lives in Christ and to produce hope personally, publicly, and privately.

The personal faith of each member of the Kingdom of God is meant to grow and develop over time. The Gospel enables believers to overcome sin and become more like Jesus. God has provided multiple blessings for His people (2 Corinthians 6:16-18). The Apostle Paul told the church to embrace these blessings and to use them for God's purpose. Although a child of God is eternally redeemed, pardoned, and made righteous through salvation in Jesus Christ, there are still obstacles to overcome. We must fight to free ourselves from the sin that so easily entangles us (Hebrews 12:1) By becoming more and more holy, we experience the purpose of our adoption into God's family (Ephesians 1:4).

The public faith of God's people is meant to inspire other believers. The command Paul gave to the people to "make room in your hearts for us" is a significant command (v.1). Life is very busy, conflict is inevitable, and the temptations to waste time on worldly engagements are very real. When God's people get busy with their own lives and the things that concern only them, they rarely make time for the church. When conflict arises, and it often will, it is important that God's people make peace with one another. When resources are plentiful and opportunities abound, it is easy to deprioritize the vital relationships within the church family. Every believer must work to choose to love and invest in God's people and His Kingdom purpose (vv.3-9, 12-16).

The private faith of each believer will involve dealing with grief. There is a big difference between "Godly grief" and "worldly grief" in terms of their cause and effect (v.10-11). Godly grief comes as a result of the awareness of sin. When a Christian comes into contact with sin, there is always grief. This grief leads to repentance (Galatians 6:1). Worldly grief comes from not having the temporary pleasures, popularity, possessions, and power of the world. This longing for that which does not last produces death because worldly things are not life giving. Grief is good when it is Godly.

The person who is personally seeking God's rule in their life, publicly living in and for others in God's Kingdom, and privately grieving over sin is blessed. Is your personal, public, and private life in line with Jesus? Those who seek Christ in this dark world have great hope.

Exodus 20; Luke 23; Job 38; 2 Corinthians 8

Once a person has come to saving faith in Jesus Christ, there is a freedom, a desire, and the power to obey Jesus. Obedience to Jesus comes from love. To know Jesus is to love Him and to love Him is to obey Him. The person who loves Jesus lives with hope.

The rescue of God given to all who believe in Jesus is pictured in the Exodus. In the Exodus the people were saved by the blood of a lamb, they passed through water and became identified publicly as God's people, and afterward, they headed toward home. Along the way, they were given the law, which provided them with the instructions for how to live rightly with God. This is the process of salvation: a person is saved by the blood of the lamb, baptized, and then begins the journey in life toward heaven. Along that narrow way, God's redeemed people learn to obey God and live with Him.

In Exodus 20, God provided specific commands for His people to obey. The first commandment is to honor who God is. His people are to have no other gods before Him (v.1-3). Human beings are made to worship, that is, to identify with and exalt something or someone that defines their being and purpose. In a fallen state, a human being will always be defined by a created thing. Only the eternal, holy God has the power and grace to sustain and give life to an eternal soul. It is only right that God be the object of our worship and the one who defines our being and purpose.

The people who have God first in their life and make Him the source of their being will be able to avoid worshipping a created thing (v.4-6) and using God's name inappropriately (v.7). They will rightly rest one day a week in order to put God first (v.8-11). Once a person's vertical relationship with God is right, the horizontal relationships will fall into place. The person who obeys the first four commandments will be empowered and inspired to obey the last six commandments (v.12-17). When we love God, we honor His created order and love other people.

The giving of the law came with manifestations of power. God often provided His Word through His servants and surrounded these moments of truth giving with signs of power. This was true of the moment when God gave the Ten Commandments. The power of God was revealed and it caused the people to be in awe of God and to desire a mediator to serve on their behalf (v.18-21). The altars the people were to erect and use were specifically spoken to by God (v.22-26). God commands people to come to Him on His terms, and He has clearly stated how we are to come to Him: by grace through faith in Christ alone.

In the Old Testament, God's people were saved by grace through faith by looking forward to the coming of Jesus. Those of us now living on the other side of the death, burial, and resurrection of Jesus Christ are saved by grace through faith looking back to the coming of Jesus. Are you living in a loving relationship with God by grace through faith in Jesus? Those who love and obey Jesus have hope.

Exodus 21; Luke 24; Job 39; 2 Corinthians 9

The resurrection was promised and fulfilled by Jesus. It was confirmed by eyewitnesses. This event provides the means for God's people to know God's power over sin and death. It inspires God's people to love, obey, and serve Jesus. Those who believe in the resurrection of Jesus live and die with hope.

Luke 24 provides insights into the resurrection of Jesus Christ. It reminds us that not only is this miracle a historical, verified fact, but it is fundamental to the story and purpose of God.

When the resurrection happened, the disciples struggled to believe it and understand it. The women who followed Jesus were the first to discover the tomb to be empty. John and Peter went after they had heard the testimony of the women and discovered their amazing words were true. They were all left in wonderment (v.1-12).

Soon after the resurrection, Cleopas and a friend, while journeying to Emmaus, were joined by Jesus. He coaxed them to tell Him of the events that had just occurred in Jerusalem. Cleopas and his friend shared in brief what happened and then revealed their lack of faith (v.21). Jesus was quick to point out their lack of faith (v.25-26) and then graciously explained how His death was a fulfillment of the Old Testament (v.27-28). What an amazing Bible study that must have been! This teaching by Jesus reminds us how important it is that we study the Old Testament and understand the Gospel of Jesus that it reveals so readily. God's Word has the power to make our hearts burn with delight (v.32).

Rather than keep their experience a secret, Cleopas and his friend did what any faithful disciple would do. They went back to where the other disciples were gathered and testified to how Jesus had met with them. While the disciples were gathered and talking about what had happened, Jesus showed up. He blessed them with peace (v.36-37) and then comforted them, instructed them, had fellowship with them, and commanded them (v. 38-48). This is what happens when God's people gather each week with their local church family. God blesses His gathered people with peace, love, hope, truth, and commands.

Having accomplished His purpose and prepared a motley crew to begin His church under the New Covenant, Jesus ascended into heaven. These eleven faithful men, along with several women, and Matthias, were blessed to be the forerunners of the greatest movement of God ever seen on the planet. Having seen Jesus lifted up to heaven, the disciples went back to Jerusalem to await the coming of the Holy Spirit, as promised by Jesus (John 16). They worshipped God with great joy and continually gathered at the temple, praising God for what He had done (v.50-53). This is a picture of what God's disciples are to be doing today. We are to gather and praise God with the local church we belong to, and from that gathering, we are to go into the world and make disciples.

God is at work in the world through His people. Are you living as a faithful disciple of Jesus? Do you belong to and participate in a local church? Are you making disciples as you go about your life? Those who love, obey, and serve the risen Christ live a life of hope.

Exodus 22; John 1; <u>Job 40</u>; 2 Corinthians 10

Like a child gladly submitting to the authority and care of a parent, the people of God can humbly and confidently submit to the Lord. The child of God who is humbled by the greatness of God and is confident in the grace and mercy of God lives with hope.

God finally gave Job the audience he requested, and Job discovered there was far more to the world, his life, and God than he could know. God is far greater than Job had perceived, and His goodness was far more than what Job deserved. After asking Job a selection of questions intended to put him in his place (Job 38-39), God gave him the opportunity to respond in Job 40.

God revealed Job's limitations to him. He also showed him his faults (v.1-2). Job was claiming to find fault with the Almighty. He was contending with the One who created all things and who sustains all things by His might, but Job showed wisdom. He repented. In repentance, he confessed his place before God and covered his mouth with his hands. He would speak no more (v.3-5). This is what a proper view of God will always do. It will cause a person to repent. Once God is seen for the God He is, human beings bow their knees to Him and gladly submit to the power and plan of the one true God. Grace produces repentance and faith.

God made the reality of His greatness and Job's limitations abundantly clear. He challenged Job to be the man he claimed he was and answer for his words (v.6-9). In His power, God spoke to Job and demanded that he explain how it was he could make himself appear in the right and the Almighty in the wrong. Job's pride was revealed in this statement. God sought to crush his pride so that he could live rightly under the authority and blessing of God. God alone is adorned with majesty and dignity and with glory and splendor (v.10). God alone is able to dole out justice with righteous anger and debase the proud (v.11). God alone is able to bring down the proud (v.12). God alone is able to rightly condemn and save (v.13-14).

Beyond those amazing things, God alone is able to subdue the mighty creatures of the world (v.15-24). The very creatures and the world that God has made are beyond the capacity of humans to control. Despite all of the technological advances of humanity, there are still so many things we cannot do. We are still subject to the laws and the rhythms of creation. It is a creation that God has made and that God rules over. He is the mighty God. He is righteous in all of His works. He blesses those who humble themselves and turn confidently to Him to find grace and mercy.

While none of us can earn the acceptance of God, God is gracious with us. He does not abandon us in our pride and sin. God in His grace reveals His greatness so that we can understand our need of Him. God in His grace reveals His purity and the righteousness of all His deeds so we will trust Him. Do you believe in the greatness and power of God? Do you believe in the goodness of God? Do you believe He loves you? The child of God who lives by faith has hope.

Exodus 23; John 2; Job 41; 2 Corinthians 11

God the Father is in the business of bringing glory to Himself by saving a people for His purpose. Those God saves by grace through faith in Christ alone are made heirs of the Kingdom of God and are adopted eternally into His family. The adopted children of God are given new lives with a new purpose. Those who live on God's mission in Christ live with hope.

One man who lived on God's mission in Christ was the Apostle Paul. His life was not easy. We should never confuse ease with hope by thinking they are the same. God's mission is challenging and painful, but it is also hopeful. The Apostle Paul saw many lives transformed in the city of Corinth while he was on mission there. The church at Corinth was filled with people who knew Jesus, but they were still people struggling in a fallen world and susceptible to sin. In his hope, Paul wrote to the church because he was concerned they were being deceived, as is seen by what Paul wrote in 2 Corinthians 11.

The church was being lied to by a group of people who claimed to have spiritual authority. In the first century, there were orators who made a living by traveling around and offering their teaching. Those who paid for their instruction would take great pride in the knowledge they gained from these instructors. Apparently, some of the professional speakers had come to Corinth and created a great deal of confusion. Paul loved this church. He was concerned they were being deceived, just as Eve had been in the Garden (v.1-3). The so-called gospel that these traveling teachers were offering was not the true Gospel that Paul taught. Paul's gift of communication was seen as inferior and so his message was considered by some to be of less importance. Paul condemned these false teachers and compared their work to that of Satan (v.4-15). Unlike these charlatans, Paul had come to give to and not to gain from the people. Like His Lord, Paul came to serve.

While the false teachers came with worldly credibility and expected worldly remuneration, Paul came with love and expected loyalty to His Lord. Paul's defense of his ministry was based upon the humiliation he had endured (v.16-23), the pain he had suffered (v.24-29), and the protection he had received (v.30-33). What a strange resume for a proud people to hear. The sarcasm of Paul in this chapter is rich as he speaks of their "wisdom" and "strength" and his "foolishness" and "weakness."

Paul's faith in the Gospel was revealed in his response to this attack by the evil one. He pointed to the power of God's Gospel for salvation. It is in Jesus that a person gains new life and a living hope. The way of the world is to appear powerful, to seek power, and to use power to get more power. The way of Jesus is to confess weakness, to pursue grace, and to find strength in Christ alone.

The Apostle Paul was living on God's mission in Christ. Are you living on God's mission in Christ? Are you embracing weakness in order to gain the strength that comes through the power of the Gospel? It is only when we give up on looking, feeling, and acting powerful that we are free to live simply by faith in Christ. It is in Christ alone we have hope.

Exodus 24; John 3; Job 42; 2 Corinthians 12

The way of humanity is destructive. It is the way of violence, hate, manipulation, and a slew of other destructive activities. The way of God is completely different. His is the way of sacrificial love, self-giving kindness, servant-hearted mercy, and life-giving peace. Those who know God and walk humbly and confidently in His ways live with hope.

In Exodus 24, God showed Israel His way. He allowed a representative, Moses, to come into His presence in order for the people to know and live under divine grace. This was part of the eternal plan of God. After the flood, the sons of Noah's descendants scattered, but God called a man from the line of Shem named Abraham and promised that through him all the nations of the world would be blessed (Genesis 12:1-3). From Abraham came Isaac and then Jacob. From Jacob came the nation of Israel. After being in bondage for over four hundred years, as foretold by God (Genesis 15:13), God raised up Moses to lead the people to fulfill God's plan.

In order to be God's people and dwell under His care, they would have to be redeemed. God provided redemption through a covenant, which pictured the final and fulfilling redemptive covenant of Jesus Christ. This redemption was an act of grace. It provided God's presence, a fellowship of saints, atoning sacrifice, and the means to be holy.

Only Moses was able to draw near to God (v.1-2). God established a covenant relationship with the people by covering their sin with a blood sacrifice that atoned for them and the instruments that would be used for them to continue in the grace of God (v.3-8). In the midst of applying the blood to the altar and the people, Moses read the covenant (v.7). Moses, Aaron and his sons, and the seventy elders actually saw God without dying (9-11). The people were made holy and the leaders were able to fellowship together with God. Moses and Joshua were called away temporarily into the presence of God on the mountain, leaving Aaron in charge (v.12-18). Despite being made righteous, the people still struggled with sin. This is a picture of what the church experiences today.

What Moses, the leaders, and the people could not fully comprehend was the fact that the grace that was being given to them was a picture of the grace that would one day be given to the New Testament church. God accomplished His eternal purpose through Abraham's line. Through the line of Abraham, people would gain access to God because of the atonement provided through Jesus Christ. This new covenant in His blood would one day save people from every tribe and tongue. This holy people would be consecrated and worship and fellowship in God's presence. Jesus would enter God's presence promising to return. Jesus would leave His bride, the church, to serve in the world on His behalf until He returned.

Through faith, we can receive the atoning sacrifice of Jesus and be made holy. We get to be among the redeemed of God. Are you living as a redeemed child of God? Are you representing God to the world? Those who are given the grace of God and live in God's way have hope.

Exodus 25; John 4; Proverbs 1; 2 Corinthians 13

There never has been and never will be another person like Jesus. He is unique. The person He is, what He did, and how He lived is the way of life that God calls all of His people to pursue. Those who pursue the life of Jesus are people with hope.

In the Gospels, there are several stories of Jesus interacting with hurting people. John 4 provides two of those unforgettable interactions. The way Jesus considered, listened to, responded to, and helped those people is a picture of what God's people can do today. We must understand how Jesus was a blessing. Considering the "woman at the well," we can learn to go where Jesus went, to love as Jesus loved, and to stand as Jesus stood (v.1-45). Looking at the official Jesus ministered to, we can learn how to care for those who do not have a genuine faith but want the benefits God can give (v.46-53).

When Jesus was in Samaria with His disciples, He was in enemy territory. There was a huge racial divide between the Jews and Samaritans. When Jesus led His gang of learners into that territory, they went into a place where they would not be wanted. Their presence there would be objectionable to their families and friends. Once there, Jesus stayed by Jacob's well while the disciples went to get food. Jesus went where people would typically go and where a conversation could take place. A woman came to draw water. When Jesus spoke to this woman, He was stepping way outside of social norms. Not only was she a Samaritan, but she was a *she* – a woman. Jesus showed His true love for her by speaking truthfully to her. He did not try to make her feel better about her sin, and He did not get into a religious debate, which she would have preferred. Instead, Jesus spoke honestly and directly to her with compassion and kindness. He offered her life, and having received it, she shared it with others. The disciples did not understand what He was doing, just as God's people often miss how God is at work today.

When Jesus took the time to speak to the official, He chose to give mercy. This man was not interested in knowing the one true God. This man needed a miracle and was desperate. He had heard about this Jesus, and so he took a shot. He got much more than he hoped for. That is what God does. He is able to do far more than any of us can think or imagine. God enabled this man to believe and Jesus restored his soul. This interaction is a reminder to the church that we must not prejudge those who come to the church. Many may come for the wrong reasons, but God can do more than what we can imagine.

The life of a believer in Jesus is meant to look like the life of Jesus. A disciple takes on the lifestyle of the one being followed. Are you following the example of Jesus and positioning yourself in public places to talk honestly with people about their life and offering them the living water of God? Are you investing in those whose motives are wrong but are looking for answers for life? When God's people choose to pursue the kind of life Jesus lived, they discover that God is at work, and they give and gain hope.

Exodus 26; John 5; <u>Proverbs 2</u>; Galatians 1

Wisdom is the ability to do what is best in any given circumstance. Wisdom is different than knowledge in that knowledge is just factual apprehension. Wisdom is active. It takes what can be known and then does what is right and good. Those who have wisdom live with hope.

In the book of Proverbs, the blessing and importance of wisdom is extolled. Those who exercise wisdom need not worry, even though life may be difficult. The wise person can know that as far as it was up to them, they did the right thing. When we do the right thing, we can trust that the outcome of our decisions will not end in regret. Doing the right thing will not always produce what we might want, but we can know that doing what is right will always align us with God's will.

In Proverbs 2, we read the God-inspired words of a father to his son. He expressed the importance of wisdom and pointed to the many blessings it would bring to his son's life. This good father provided a compelling "if-then" appeal to his son. He begins this long sentence by stating what the son should do (v.1-4) and then points to what the typical result will be. The son will enjoy God's divine protection (v.5-20). This divine provision will also lead to the ultimate blessing of God that all of the righteous receive (v.21-22).

The relational character of this chapter reveals the nature of the Gospel. All who will repent of their self-rule and ask God's forgiveness through faith in Christ will be given a new life. This new life is a life of a redeemed child of God. God's children are given many blessings. We receive God's love, God's Spirit, God's presence, and God's purpose. Because we are loved, God guides us in truth so that we can be wise in our decisions (Hebrews 12:7-11). The training and discipline required to be wise is not always pleasant, but the outcome is extremely beneficial. It is through the power of God's Spirit that God's children can enjoy God's presence and promises. Under the influence of the Holy Spirit and in the grace of Christ, God's children are able to wisely discern God's purpose and their unique place in God's eternal Kingdom.

The wisdom of God provides the blessing of His protection. Those who walk in the way of the Lord are able to avoid the many negative consequences that come from foolish choices (v.5-20). The way of wisdom provided by the Gospel leads to a life that will one day be received into heaven (v.21-22). This eschatological picture gives hope to those who believe. The wise person's life ends in the place where God dwells and evil is removed. In this land where all things are made new is the eternal home of God's children (Revelation 21-22).

It is only by receiving the grace of God through faith in Jesus Christ that wisdom can be found. While those outside of Christ may be able to make good choices, they do not have the life-giving love of the Spirit of God to govern them. Without faith it is impossible to please God and live wisely. Are you living by faith in Christ? Are you being wise? Are you living as a citizen of heaven? Those who trust in Christ and live in the wisdom of God live with hope.

Exodus 27; John 6; Proverbs 3; Galatians 2

The obedience that comes as a result of a deep, authentic love for Jesus is liberating. Those who seek to make a life on their own end up destroying it because of the strain and emptiness that sooner or later overcomes even the strongest. Disciples who trust and obey Jesus live with hope.

The Apostle Paul had a great love for Jesus. In Galatians 2, he shares some of his story and the challenges that he faced. The challenges all followers of Jesus face in this fallen world are similar to Paul's. After fourteen years of ministry, Paul and Barnabas went to Jerusalem and spent time with the leaders of the early church to explain the Gospel Paul was preaching to the Gentiles (v.1-3). Apparently, other Christian leaders were teaching the law must be obeyed before a person could be saved. Paul did not believe this, and he defended his Biblical faith (v.4-5). The leaders in Jerusalem agreed with the Gospel Paul preached. They gladly offered fellowship to Paul and Barnabas (v.6-9). The only stipulation that the Jerusalem leaders made of Paul and Barnabas in their ministry was they give care to the poor, which was something they had already been doing and were glad to continue to do.

The challenge of every church in every generation is the people within the church. They are saved by grace but are still in need of sanctification. There is not a perfect person in the church. That means there is not a perfect church on this planet. The Apostle Peter was a great leader and man of faith, but he was human and he made a mistake. Rather than being authentic in his faith concerning the Gentiles, he pretended he did not associate with Gentiles, when representatives from Jerusalem visited (v.11-12). Barnabas and some of the others joined Peter in this hypocrisy (v.13). Paul called them out for it (v.14). This is what faithful friends do for one another. Among authentic disciples of Jesus there is a healthy, loving accountability that exists. It is appreciated and celebrated by mature disciples. Those without accountability are often debilitated by sin.

Paul taught that salvation is by grace through faith and not by the dutiful works of human striving (v.15-18). The law was given to show us our need for grace. By understanding the law and the death it produces, we can die to the law in order to live to Christ (v.19). This is the testimony of Paul and of all genuinely redeemed people. Because of the Gospel, God's people are free to die to their old life. This is not a physical death. It is a spiritual death with physical consequences – obedience to God. The living, resurrected Christ abides and exists in His people by faith. None of us can overcome sin on our own. Christ had to die to pay the penalty for our sin and be raised to live in us so that we can love Him and obey Him out of delight and not mere duty.

The Christian life is based on the work of Jesus and not the merits of man. It is by faith we are saved, and that faith allows us to know and love Jesus. When we know and love Jesus, we obey Him. Are you living by faith in Jesus? Are you obeying Him out of a great love for Him? Those who live by grace through faith in Jesus live with hope.

MARCH 17

Exodus 28; John 7; Proverbs 4; Galatians 3

The power of the living God abiding in His people causes a transformation. The love of God that is received in Christ becomes the driving force of a Christian's existence. God's redemptive love changes who we are, how we live, and what we do. Those who are transformed by God's grace and love live with hope.

Exodus 28 is a chapter in a series of chapters that describes the way God intended His people to live and worship Him. Having rescued His people from Egyptian slavery and led them through the waters of the Red Sea, God began providing instructions for how they were to live with Him as they traveled to the Promised Land. This is a beautiful picture of the Gospel. This is what God is still doing today. He is saving a people for Himself by rescuing them from the slavery of sin. He has them pass through water in baptism to make a public proclamation of their salvation and then has them form into a faith community to worship and live for Him. The life of a disciple of Jesus exudes love. That love enables a truly redeemed person to love and obey God and to love and serve others.

Not only is each person among the redeemed of God given God's love, but each person is also provided with a unique and specific calling with corresponding gifts and abilities. God called Aaron's sons to serve the Lord as priests (v.1). God is still calling people to serve Him by serving His people. There are many different roles mentioned in the New Testament: pastor, elder, deacon, etc. There are also many other roles that do not have a specific title but are just as vital (Romans 12:3-7).

Through the generosity of His people, God was able to provide the garments the priests were to wear (v.2). These saints were able to provide a vital service that blessed the priests and enabled them to serve God and God's people. Every believer has a unique gift and role to play in a local church and in the Kingdom of God.

The garments and accessories of the priest reveal the unique purpose of God for His people (v.3-43). Every article along with its color and placement had a purpose. And so it is with each member of God's family. God forms and places each person exactly where He wants them (1 Corinthians 12:14-20). Each of us has a divine purpose. When we come to know God and discover who He is, we can understand our identity and the purpose God has made us to accomplish. We cannot truly know ourselves until we have come to truly know God. In knowing God we come to understand the ultimate questions in life: Why am I here? How did I get here? Where am I going? What am I supposed to do? Jesus provides the answers.

The formation of the Israelite priesthood presents a picture of the will of God. God is at work in the world to redeem a people who will live uniquely with a particular calling and a distinct purpose. Are you living a life of love that serves God and His purpose in the world with a sense of passion and with a clear reason? Those who know God are alive in Christ and live for Him with hope.

Exodus 29; John 8; Proverbs 5; Galatians 4

The truth is always a friend to those who have nothing to hide. It is the person who is duplicitous and scandalous that must deal in lies and half-truths and live with a fear of the truth. The truth does not intimidate an honest soul. Those who love and embrace truth live with hope.

In John 8, Jesus says a lot about Himself and truth. He explained that He is the light of the world (v.12). He is the means by which everything else can be seen. Jesus is not only the ultimate truth made flesh, but He is the light that is given so that all truth can be known. The religious leaders were blind. They were in darkness. They did not understand that Jesus was God (v.13). Jesus explained why He is the truth and why they could not understand Him (v.14-20). To believe in Jesus, a person must have God-given faith. Faith in Jesus gives sight.

Having explained who He is, what He does, and why the religious leaders did not understand or believe in Him, Jesus told of the future (v.21-28). The plan of God was to give His Son as the atoning sacrifice for sin. God's plan was and is for a worldwide movement to free people from the brokenness that is caused by the destruction of sin. God's plan was and is to set prisoners free from the power and punishment of sin. These religious leaders could not understand the message of the Father that was in the Son, even though He was right in front of them. Jesus was confident of the presence of the Father with Him (v.29). God abides with His people and is always with us (Hebrews 13:5).

There were some who believed in Jesus, and He instructed them in their faith (v.30-31). The same God who saves us is the God who remains with us to grow us in the truth of His Gospel. Jesus explained to those who believed that the truth is their liberator. They had thought that their genealogy was what redeemed them. The fact that they were descendants of Abraham could not save them. The only hope of salvation is Jesus (v.32-53). It was Jesus that Abraham longed to see. Now He was there. God came in flesh, but the people of His day could not understand Him. It takes faith to understand Jesus.

Jesus is God. He claimed to be God and they sought to kill Him for it (v.54-59). In order to believe and understand the hope of the Gospel, a person must have faith. Without faith it is impossible to know or please God (Hebrews 11:1, 6). Those who are blessed to have faith in the Gospel truth that God has come to die and be raised to save a people to the praise of His great name are liberated to understand reality. All others who cannot believe are deceived and live in the frustration of spiritual blindness.

The redeemed of God believe in God's grace, and they see everything else by His presence. When we choose to trust in Jesus, we honor God and we are set free. Are you living by faith in Jesus? Do you see your circumstances in the world by the light of Christ? Is Jesus alive in you and transforming your life? If you can believe and see by the light of God, you are free. This liberation gives hope.

Exodus 30; John 9; Proverbs 6; Galatians 5

We will always have to deal with problems. Those problems can create anxiety and frustration. Given the already treacherous terrain of this life, it is best we do all we can to reduce the possibility for problems. Those who live wisely can avoid so much misery. Wise people live with hope.

In Proverbs 6, a wise father provided his son with instructions for how to avoid some of the common mistakes that cause and create problems in life. There were three challenges that this father wanted his son to understand that had to do with finances, work ethic, and honoring others. In almost any bestselling book or popular movie these themes tend to surface. What causes problems in life is not a secret. These challenges are easy to identify, but not always easy to navigate.

When it comes to finances, it is wise to avoid being responsible for someone else's financial decisions (v.1-5). This is not a call to greed. This is a call to proper responsibility. It is unwise to take responsibility for that which we have no authority. To put resources we have earned and are to be provisions for our lives and families up as a security for someone else, who is not deemed capable of being trustworthy or having the capacity to care for their own decisions, is unwise. To be charitable is gracious and good. If a person has a need we can help with, we are commanded to help provide for their need (James 2:15-16). God calls us to be generous to others but not to encourage others to have a lack of personal responsibility.

When it comes to work ethic, it is wise to work hard when it is time to work and while there is work to be done (v.6-11). Work is one of the blessings of God. In the Garden, Adam was called to work. Work is not a result of the curse. The curse made work more difficult and frustrating (Genesis 3:17–19). It is easy to make an idol out of work. The way of life God commands and commends involves work for six days and then a day of rest. Both work and rest require faith and discipline.

When it comes to honoring others, it is wise to respect the rights and dignity of other people, especially as it pertains to their property and reputations (v.12-19) and also to their personal relationships (v.20-35). It is an evil thing to lie and to seek to cause harm to other people in any way. Those who devise schemes to gain an upper hand for personal profit are treacherous and hurt not only themselves, but society as a whole. Theft, deceit, and discord create distrust, panic, and hate. When people stop respecting and caring for others, but instead seek their own pleasure at the expense of others, there will always be negative results.

Living a blessed life filled with hope is not easy. There are many problems that can trip us up. Our natural tendency is to be lured into temptations and to act on carnal desires rather than obey God's Word. God has shown us a better way. Are you being wise in your dealings with other people? Do you discipline your thoughts and actions? The wise person who takes responsibility for their thoughts, feelings, and desires will be a blessing and live with hope.

Exodus 31; John 10; Proverbs 7; Galatians 6

God said that it was not good for man to be alone (Genesis 2:18). God lives in community. He is communal in His triune existence as one God in three persons. He is self-sufficient in His love and needs nothing beyond Himself. We need God in order to love rightly. Those who live in community with other believers and seek to share the love of God with a broken world live with hope.

In Galatians 6, Paul describes what it looks like to live in a loving community of redeemed people. Each member of the community has a responsibility to God to care for and seek the good of the others. In every community of faith, there will be challenges and blessings. These challenges exist because even though God has redeemed His people, each person is not perfect and is still struggling with sin. These blessings exist because God is at work in the lives of those He has redeemed and is faithfully providing for His people according to His promises.

In every community of faith there will always be saints that need to be restored. The restoration of a redeemed saint requires wisdom, humility, and confidence. The person who seeks to be used of God to restore another must be wise to see that they are not beyond being tempted with the sin that has confounded their sibling (v.1). The servant of the struggler must also be willing to humbly carry burdens that come along with being used by God to help another (v.2). In the confidence of Christ, a believer must be in the assured standing in their own faith to be of help to another (v.3-5). This is the will of God for all in Christ.

Every local church has gifted leaders who are called by God to teach His Word and equip the saints to do the work of the ministry (Ephesians 4:12). Those who live out this calling are to be cared for by those who receive the instruction from the leader (v.6). The giving of tithes and offerings is an investment with consequences (v.7-8). The people of the church are not just to give and grow in the truth, but are to do the good works the Word commands and not grow weary in doing the good God commands (v.9-10).

The guiding hope of every community of saints is the Gospel. There is no end to the distortions created by humanity that cause us to try to hope in things rather than Christ. The church at Galatia was struggling with a false gospel that taught that people must first be religious before they can be saved. This is not true (v.11-18). The only thing any person brings to their salvation is sin. By being so adamant about the centrality of the Gospel, Paul provided a protection for all who believe and a reminder to maintain sound doctrine.

Those who believe in the Gospel are formed by the Spirit of God into a community of believers. Within this community, God's love is revealed and His will is accomplished. Living in a community of saints is complicated, but God's Word shows us the way. Are you living faithfully in a local church? Are you dependable to the people and the leaders of the church? God calls all of His children to have a church home. Those who are active in a faith family live with great hope.

Exodus 32; John 11; Proverbs 8; Ephesians 1

We did not lose our sense of dominion and the ability to influence specific outcomes in the fall. The problem is we are sinful and live in a fallen world. We have the ability to use our influence for evil. Only those who gladly honor Jesus and live dependently under His leadership live with hope.

In Exodus 32, the capacity within humanity to do what is evil is on full display. Moses was on the mountain of God receiving instructions for what Israel was to do next. While he was there with God, the people were back at camp creating idols based on lies. They influenced Aaron to legitimize their godless scheme (v.1). The Israelites refused to live by faith in God, and instead had Aaron create a new salvation story that was a lie (v.2-4). The new religion was not void of the Lord (v.5). False Gospels rarely tell whole lies, but will use the name of God and maybe some other true words to give credibility to the deception. The false faith will encourage and enable sin in the end (v.6).

When God made Moses aware of what was going on, an interesting dialogue took place between Moses and God (v.7-14). God spoke of His intent to destroy the people and to pursue a new plan to make a nation through Moses. Moses' response gives a great example of servant leadership. Moses did not deny that the people deserved judgment but asked God to give them grace for His name's sake. Moses was jealous for God's name and did not want the Egyptians or any other nation to say God did not keep His promise. With the hope of the promise of God (Genesis 12:1-3), Moses interceded for the people.

When Christ came into the world, a similar thing was occurring. Israel had created a system of religion in the name of God, but it was not entirely true to the Word of God. The people were looking for a leader who would give them what they wanted. Just as Moses lectured Aaron, broke the tablets, destroyed the idols, raised an army that killed many people, and overcame the cult (v.15-29), so Christ preached to the religious leaders of His day, tore the veil at His resurrection, destroyed the temple, raised up the Romans to destroy the people who had rejected the Christ, and overcame sin and death.

Moses reminded the people of the seriousness of what they had done and spoke of his desire to be able to make atonement on their behalf (v.30). God was ready to destroy the people, but Moses offered his life in their place (v.31-32). What an example of servant leadership! God did not accept Moses' offer, but reaffirmed Moses' calling to lead the people to fulfill God's promise (v.33-35). The only worthy atonement God receives for sin is a blood sacrifice. God ultimately made that sacrifice Himself by dying on the cross. Those who are saved are saved by faith in Christ alone.

Everyone has influence. What we value and believe will determine our decisions and how we impact other people. Have you trusted in Christ? Are you living by faith in His love and sacrifice for your sin? It is easy to be deceived by religious leaders who deny the authority of God's Word and settle for idolatry. Those who look to Christ alone and seek to influence others with the Gospel live with hope.

Exodus 33; John 12; Proverbs 9; Ephesians 2

Christians, like all people, tend to like to find a point of comfort and reside in it. Disciples of Jesus are called to live a life that requires faith. Those who are willing to get beyond their personal preferences and seek the Lord in faithful ways live with hope.

Jesus had many interesting experiences. John 12 tells of a few of them. Each setting was unique and each experience had purpose. From these events we can see God's will for His followers. Disciples of Jesus are called to be generous, vulnerable, triumphant, and compassionate. By seeking the Lord in any and every situation of our life, God will allow us to know Him, love Him, obey Him, and enjoy Him forever.

God has been generous and He calls His people to be generous. Not only has He provided a planet and a system of life with family and friends that we can enjoy, but He has entered into the world we broke to give us eternal life through His sacrificial death. What Mary, the sibling of Lazarus and Martha, did was not strange in light of God's mercy and grace (v.1-8). It seemed strange to one who did not believe. To take a year's worth of wages to worship the Lord is a normal thing for a disciple of Jesus. God is worthy to receive every gift, service, and sacrifice we can offer. Those who give costly gifts to God should not be surprised when unbelievers criticize them for their faith.

Lazarus was a threat to the religious leaders of his day. They hated Jesus and wanted Him dead. Lazarus was an uncomfortable reality they also wanted gone (v.9-11). Jesus had raised Lazarus from the dead. This gave weight to His authority. The religious leaders were committed to killing not only the Son of God, but also this man who had miraculously been raised from death. The faithful should expect to be treated the way Jesus was treated by the world.

When Jesus entered Jerusalem on that Palm Sunday with shouts of praise from the crowds (v.12-19), the disciples had to have been excited. God is good to give us glimpses of the triumphant glory that is to come. These glimpses often happen when we least expect them, but when they do occur, they provide hope.

During the week, before Jesus died, a group of Greeks looking for the truth sought an audience with Jesus (v.20-26). The call to believe is a call to die to the life of the world and to live in the life of Jesus. This life is only possible because of the life, death, and resurrection of Jesus (v.27-36a). What God has done is simply amazing, but many will not accept it (v.36b-43). Jesus' claim was extravagant but true (44-50). Jesus came to bring salvation and eternal life through His death and resurrection.

The Christian life on this fallen planet is not comfortable. God did not enter into the world to make His children comfortable. God came to bring light into darkness. The darkness hates the light, but the light must shine no matter how much it is hated. Do you believe the Gospel of Jesus Christ? Are you generous like your Savior? Are you willing to be among those who are hated for Christ's sake? Are you sharing the Good News of who Jesus is and what He has done? Generous disciples of Jesus have hope.

Exodus 34; John 13; Proverbs 10; Ephesians 3

Everyone wants a good life filled with good things and good outcomes. The problem everyone faces is that it is not easy to do what is required in order to gain what is good. A good life comes as a result of a state of being the Bible calls being blessed. The blessed life is the best life. Those who do what leads to a blessed life live with hope.

Proverbs 10 provides direction for a blessed life. It presents two kinds of people: those who are wise and gain God's blessing and those who are foolish and don't. The blessed life is one that brings gladness. This is the life that is honest when dealing with others and that enjoys a righteous standing with God, which frees the soul from anguish. It is not a passive life. The life that enjoys God's blessing is one that works hard and makes the most of opportunities that come and go quickly.

What people do reveals their true character, but the words people use should never be dismissed. What we say says a lot about who we are. There is a strong contrast between the words of the righteous and the words of the wicked (v.6-32). This section of sayings has bookends that focus on the words that are from "the mouth" (v.6) and "the lips" (v.32). Those who say nothing can often conceal their lack of understanding, weaknesses, and brokenness. They can even be considered wise. Those who speak reveal their true identify, ideologies, and beliefs. The wise person knows how to use words effectively.

The challenge to take from this chapter is not to keep quiet, but to be the kind of person who has the right kind of heart that is able to say and do what is best. The righteous person makes their parents proud (v.1), avoids negative consequences (v.2-3), works hard at the right time (v.4-5), is remembered and respected (v.7), receives right instruction (v.8), has confidence (v.9), does and says what is beneficial to others (v.10-11), covers offenses with love (v.12), is affirmed (v.13), is a source of good information (v.14), is protected by wise financial stewardship (v.15), enjoys life and freedom from sin (v.16), seeks and says what is true (v.17-18), says only what is helpful (v.19-21), does what is right and honorable (v.22-24), does not fear difficulties, but fears the Lord (v.25-27), and possesses a joyful stability throughout life (v.28-32).

We cannot determine the circumstances of our lives, but we do determine how we think and act. Apart from God, we will never think rightly or choose what is best. The Lord is at work in the world. Those who seek to live in and for the glory of God are satisfied in life. Those who choose to live without God never get what they crave. That is the problem with sin. It never truly satisfies. It takes. It does not give. It appears profitable, but in the end, it always comes up short.

Jesus has come to bless the lives of those who believe in Him. This life is filled with the presence of God. That is what salvation ultimately is. To be saved is to be blessed to be in a right relationship with God. That relationship determines how we think, feel, and act. Are you living a life that trusts and loves God? If so, you will enjoy the blessings of God and be filled with hope.

Exodus 35; John 14; Proverbs 11; Ephesians 4

Whether spoken or assumed, every family has a set of values and a sense of purpose. How a family uses its resources, treats one another, and functions within the broader context of their community provides a clear picture of what a family is truly about. The family of God is the same way. Every local church has a specific personality, purpose, and set of priorities. God makes each church unique and works through that body for His eternal purpose. Those who are blessed to be members of a healthy local church live with hope.

In Ephesians 4, an explanation of what God wants to exist in each local church is given. Having provided the theological foundation for the faith of God's people in chapters 1-3, Paul gave commands that produce a healthy church. The expectations of the Father are simple. It is not a complex way of life, but it is a life that requires a firm faith in the Gospel and a great love for God and His people. This way of life is based on the Father's calling for His children (v.1-14), His desire for His children (v.15-16), and His design for His children (v.17-32).

It is a privilege to know God, and this privilege comes with a great responsibility. Every child of God is to live in a manner worthy of Christ's calling (v.1). A primary way believers live in a worthy manner is by helping sustain and strengthen the unity of the church (v.2-3). The universal church has one Spirit, one hope, one Lord, one faith, one baptism, and one Father who is over all (v.4-6). Having descended to earth to save His people, Jesus gives grace to each member of God's family and with it a calling to serve (7-11). Those in leadership are responsible to equip the saints to do the work of the ministry of the church (v.12). Every disciple is to fulfill their calling and to attain maturity in the faith (v.13-14).

When believers live out their calling in Christ, they grow into the person of Christ (v.15-16). A church that is growing in Christ-likeness will be one of the most loving places on the planet. A loving church will not be perfect, but they will be a blessing to God, to one another, and to the world.

Those without Christ are forced to live in the darkness of sin and are driven by selfish, fleshly desires (v.17-19). God's people are those who have come to know Christ and have been given new life in Him. The Christian life is a righteous and holy life recreated in the likeness of God (v.20-24). The influence of the Gospel will be evident in them to both believers and nonbelievers (v.25-32).

The Christian life is countercultural. The way of the world is the way of the evil one who lives out a selfish calling, a selfish desire, and a selfish plan. The way of God's family is a way of life that honors and emulates Christ. The Gospel that God has given will transform those who believe and create, through their love, a taste of heaven on earth. Are you a part of God's family by grace through faith in Jesus? Are you making God's family more unified, loving, and kind? The evil one seeks to persuade the faithful to be faithless. The faithful who accomplish God's purpose live with hope.

Exodus 36; John 15; Proverbs 12; Ephesians 5

A heart of generosity comes from a proper understanding of the Gospel. The Lord God has blessed us with every spiritual blessing though the grace of the Father, the atoning work of the Son, and the life-giving work of the Spirit (Ephesians 1). The right response to God's generosity is generosity to others.

Many of God's children struggle to be generous for many reasons. One, they do not understand the love of God, the power of God, or the purpose of God. Two, they do not appreciate the joy of giving and the pleasure derived from being a blessing. Three, they are not burdened by the depth of need in the world and the will of God to provide for the world through His people. It is wise to remember the words of the Lord Jesus, who said, "It is more blessed to give than to receive." (Acts 20:35) Those who remember and act in faith on the words of Jesus live with hope.

A beautiful picture of generosity is found in Exodus 36. The people, liberated from the bondage of Egypt, experienced the presence of God. God's presence was mediated through an edifice known as the tabernacle. Unlike the temple, this facility was mobile in order to serve the needs of God's mobile people, who were on their way to the land promised by God. This mobile facility pictured the means Jesus would offer to His redeemed people. It was a means by which sin could be atoned for, a means to call on God, a means to celebrate His grace, and a means to have access and fellowship with the Almighty and His redeemed people. The people were called to provide the materials for it.

In order to make the vision of this place a reality, individuals had to be generous with their resources. Those capable in construction and artistic design had to step forward and give their time and energy (v.1-2). The materials needed had to be provided by the people (v.3-4). The people were faithful to provide! A point came, when the construction team found that they had more than enough material to accomplish the work and no longer needed anything. They asked Moses to tell the people not to bring any more gifts (v.5-7). What joy they must have felt when they heard it proclaimed: "Dear people of God, Please stop bringing gifts for the Lord's work. We have more than enough!"

Having secured the needed materials, the craftsmen and laborers did their work (v.8-38). There is a lesson to be learned from their activity. These gifted people did not build what suited them. They built what God told them to build. Seeking God on our terms for our glory is sinful. When we live and worship God rightly, according to God's holy Word, we experience the benefit of God's divine presence. Pursing God on our terms and according to our whims dishonors God and destroys our fellowship with Him. The only way to rightly live and worship God is according to His commands.

Those who understand the grace and mercy of God are generous people. They choose to pursue God in ways that honor Him. It is through gratitude and faithful obedience that God is honored and life is blessed. Are you a generous person? Are you seeking to obey God's Word? Generous people obey God's Word and enjoy God's favor and live with hope.

Exodus 37; John 16; Proverbs 13; Ephesians 6

During His life on earth, Jesus was gracious to give His disciples a heads-up about what was about to happen. Jesus promised that, after His death, the Holy Spirit would enter into the world and into them. Those who are blessed with God's Spirit are able to live with hope.

In John 16, there are many words of hope for all disciples of Jesus for all time. It was here that Jesus announced that trouble would soon befall His faithful followers (v.1-4), that He would soon leave them (v.5-6), that "the Helper" – the Holy Spirit was coming (v.7-15), that they would see Jesus again and rejoice (v.16-24), and that He was going to overcome the world through His sacrificial victory (v.25-33). There are many mysteries associated with the Biblical faith, but there are also many clear facts that the saints of God are blessed to have and claim as their own. These truths sustain the faithful in the faith so that they can overcome the world through the victory of Jesus.

There is a battle waging in the world. The battle, though often unseen, is real. The temptation for disciples of Jesus to "fall away" is real, and it is an enticement that must be acknowledged in order to be avoided. When life gets hard and the world comes against us, rejecting the Lord, doubting Him, and joining those on the wide path that leads to destruction seems attractive. Jesus knew this and prepared His disciples to fight against this desire of the flesh.

The good news for God's people is that we have a secret weapon. Jesus promised that the Holy Spirit would come and bring conviction to our hearts. Those who are dead to God and unfeeling toward the destructiveness of sin can be given life by the Spirit and the freedom to repent and believe in Jesus (v.8-11). Jesus also promised that the Holy Spirit would teach and inspire His disciples (v.12-15). Those with apostolic authority would later be inspired to write the rest of the Word of God by the Spirit's inspiration (2 Timothy 3:16-17).

Jesus promised the disciples they would see Him again. Three days after His death, Jesus would be raised. The world would rejoice at His death, while the disciples lamented, but then the disciples' lament would turn into joy (v.20, 22). Jesus promised them they would be able to face the tribulation that was ahead because of the victory He was about to bring. His success over sin and death was their ticket and now our ticket to new life in Christ. It is a righteous life filled with the power of God.

The Christian life is a battle and the temptation to abandon the faith is real. Thankfully, the Holy Spirit came just as Jesus said He would. Through the Spirit of God, the Bible was given. Now, we who believe have not only the Holy Spirit alive in us to guide us into all truth, but we have the Word of God, which is God's true truth to those who believe. Are you living in the hope of the power of the Holy Spirit? Institutional religious practice is no replacement for the Helper who has come to bring us new life. The victory of Christ over the tribulation of the world is won. Are you living in that victory today? Those who live in the victory of Jesus in the power of the Spirit live with hope.

Exodus 38; John 17; <u>Proverbs 14</u>; Philippians 1

There is a natural order to life. While there are some who prosper in their sin, most people live with the appropriate consequences to their actions. Choosing to honor and please God allows us the comfort to know any negative outcomes in life are not a result of our pursuit of anything unadvisable, but because it is the will of God. God-honoring lives live with hope.

Proverbs 14 is an entire chapter of scenarios that describe the natural consequences of actions. The themes are varied, as are the titles given to the participants, but the overall picture is the same. The wise, the upright, the faithful, the understanding, the prudent, the good, the truthful, and the hardworking gain a good result for their attitude, faith, and knowledge. The foolish, the devious, the scoffer, the dishonest, the wicked, the simple, the quick-tempered, the lazy talker, and the envious people of the world gain negative results for their thoughts, words, and deeds. Generally speaking, life is better for those who are Godly.

Sprinkled throughout this Proverb there are a number of statements of fact that are not cause and effect in terms of personal choices. One idea is that an ox may make a mess, but that mess is worth dealing with because the ox is the one that plows the ground. This is an important thing to understand (v.4). Parents must understand that raising children is messy, but it is still a high calling and blessing to raise them. People are messy, but they are also gloriously productive, creative, and invigorating. Those who want to accomplish important things in life will have to deal with the messes that come with worthy pursuits.

Another truism is that life is meant to be shared (v.10, 12, 13). Those who do not share their lives with others have to bottle up their bitterness and keep it within. When they have joy, they have no one to celebrate it with. Those who do not submit and share their lives with God gain a destructive end. Those who laugh, even though their heart aches, and feign joy to hide their grief live with pain and misery that is multiplied. Inauthentic people have few real friends and experience little of the grace and goodness of God.

One more powerful axiom pertains to people who believe in the greatness and holiness of God. They will fear the Lord (v.27). That fear produces a pursuit of God that provides, through God's grace and mercy, a fountain of life. This life is supernaturally given and driven. Those who fear the Lord turn from sin to gain eternal life. The end result of a person of faith is salvation by grace through faith and a way of existence that enjoys the benefits of being under God's righteous and powerful care.

Our decisions come from a way of being, which determines our every move. It is vital to look behind our decisions to the identity and fundamental beliefs that inspire our actions. Those who humble themselves under God's mighty hand and seek His favor through faith in Jesus Christ enjoy a life and eternity of great blessing. What is your chosen way of life? Are you pursuing God's wise way by faith, or are you going your own foolish way that leads to death? The life that seeks to honor God is filled with hope.

Exodus 39; John 18; Proverbs 15; Philippians 2

While each member of God's family is a unique individual made for a specific purpose with particular gifts and abilities, there are shared qualities that all of God's children possess. These qualities serve as a bond that unites all of God's people. Those who serve peacefully and faithfully in God's family always have hope.

In Philippians 2, the blessed bond of God's people is explained and celebrated. The church at Philippi began supernaturally by the preaching of the Word and the movement of God's Spirit (Acts 16). The founding members of the church at Philippi could not have been more different. The first to believe was a wealthy woman in the textile industry. She was soon joined by a formerly demon-possessed slave. Finally, a jailer and his family became part of God's family there. These were saved by grace through faith by the same risen Lord and were made children of the most-high God. Their backgrounds, social status, education, and challenges in life could not have been more different, and yet they were united by an eternal bond.

The church at Philippi grew. Each one of these children of God experienced a supernatural encouragement they received from the risen Lord (v.1). This motley crew of Christians shared a loving mindset, which made Paul's joy complete (v.2). This Christlike mindset inspired each of them to serve others and to look out for one another's needs, just as Christ had cared for each of them (v.3-5). Christ emptied Himself. He clothed His divinity in humanity. His divinity was mediated through His humanity and He lived in flesh (v.6). He willingly suffered and died for the children of God. Because He was God, death could not hold Him. He is now raised and has the ultimate name, and all people will one day bow before Him humbly and acknowledge that He is Lord of all (v.7-11). Those who are in Christ are called to live a life of service to others in confident humility. They are confident in their identity, as children of God, and humbled by the fact it is by grace they are saved and sustained. In their assured faith each member of Christ's family serves others as Christ.

Being the church provided these dearly loved saints with great responsibility. Together, they were to obey the Lord and work out their salvation according to the will of God (v.12-13). They were to fulfill the Great Commission (Matthew 28:19-20) and live on mission in partnership with Paul. They had already sent Epaphroditus on a short-term mission trip and soon would be visited by Timothy. They would be responsible to care for Timothy's needs, heed his instructions, and follow his leadership (v.19-30). This is what every local church is to do: serve together, follow their God-given leaders, and give financially so others can be sent to share the Gospel and encourage God's work in the world.

The life of a believer is meant to be lived in the fellowship and love of a local church. Are you living out your calling in Christ in a local church? Are you serving, giving, and growing with other believers? Disciples of Jesus who live in the gracious bond of Christ with other members of their church live with hope.

Exodus 40; John 19; Proverbs 16; Philippians 3

God is a personal God. There is no greater blessing than to experience the living God in a personal and deeply meaningful way. This is God's will for His people. God has made Himself known and knowable. Those who live in the presence of God through His grace live with hope.

In Exodus 40, the tabernacle was completed and the furnishings set (v.1-11). The Aaronic line of priests had been positioned in their posts. They had been washed and made ceremonially ready (v.12). They had been given their uniforms for service and consecrated for their work (v.13-15). Moses had led the people to accomplish this work and had proven faithful to God's commands (v.16-32). What a satisfying moment this must have been in Moses' very difficult life. He was able to finish a vital job that God had given to him (v.33). Like the night of the Passover, the triumphal exit from Egypt, and the crossing of the Red Sea, this was a defining moment in the life of Moses and Israel. Moses could say of this divine assignment: it is finished! This completed project prepared the people for their life with God under the sacrificial system explained in Leviticus. All of the faith, sacrifice, and diligence of Moses and the people would now, finally, produce the outcome Moses had prayed for and that God had willed to accomplish. God would now dwell with His people.

The people certainly did not deserve this blessing. They had doubted and turned against God in many ways and at different times, but God was gracious. He could have rejected them and left them on their own to wander in the desert. Instead, God answered the prayer of Moses. As a good shepherd, Moses had interceded on behalf of the people in Exodus 32-34 and asked God to be with them and not abandon them. This is a powerful picture of the Gospel. God could have left us for dead and abandoned us in our sin, but instead, He sent a mediator who interceded for us, Jesus Christ.

Having built the tabernacle, according to God's specifications, prepared the priesthood, and provided the furnishings needed to relate rightly with God, the people saw the Lord come down and fill the place with His presence (v.34). It was so overwhelming Moses could not enter the tent (v.35). The presence of God was the means by which God's people would be guided. When the presence lifted, the people knew it was time to move to the next stop on their journey (v.36). When the presence was upon the place, the people knew they were to remain where they were (v.37). The people were able to see the manifestation of God and be led by Him (v.38).

The presence of God is the greatest blessing a person can experience. Without the presence of God, a soul and a community are left in sin and death. Those who know Jesus, the one the tabernacle pointed to, are able to live with God. This is the will and desire of God. The will of God has always been to be with His people. Jesus is alive and leading His people home.

Are you living in the presence of God? Is He alive in you? That only happens when we trust in Christ for forgiveness. His Spirit lives in those who believe. Those who live in the presence of God by grace live with hope.

Leviticus 1; John 20; Proverbs 17; Philippians 4

The resurrection of Jesus is one of the most powerful proofs of the truth of Christianity. It is a vital part of the redemptive story of God – the Bible. Those who believe that Jesus is God and that His life, death, and resurrection are the means for salvation live with hope.

John 20 offers eyewitness accounts of the day Jesus was raised from the dead. The events and conversations provide powerful insight into the majesty and sovereignty of God and the limited capacity of humanity. In this chapter we see the doubts of His disciples, the divinity of Jesus, the demand of God, and the depth of Scripture.

Even though the disciples had heard the sermons and seen the miracles of Jesus, they still doubted and had difficulty believing and understanding the resurrection. Rather than waiting with anticipation for the third day to come and racing to the tomb to celebrate, the disciples were hiding and grieving. The women went to the tomb, but their intention was to care for a dead body. It was only after hearing the words of the amazed women that John and Peter ran to the grave and found the evidence that made it obvious that Jesus was resurrected (v.1-10). Their reaction should be ours. Each day we should run to see the fulfilled promises of God and the answers to our prayers provided.

The conversation Jesus had with Mary points to the divinity of Jesus (v.11-18). Death could not hold Him. He was raised by the power of God. His death was to pay for sin. As God, He reentered into His earthly body. This body was to ascend soon. God's eternal plan was not yet finished. They would soon see Him leave again so the Helper could come (John 14).

Jesus later appeared to the other disciples (v.19-29). While it is significant to note the peace that was offered (v.19, 21, 26), the gift of the Holy Spirit that was given (v.22), and the proof of the bodily resurrection that was provided (v.27-29), it is important not to miss the demand Jesus made. He told them of their responsibility to live as a "sent" people and to tell of the forgiveness of God to the world (v.21-23). God demands the Gospel of God be shared by His disciples throughout the world (Acts 1:8).

God's Word is not a science book, history book, or geography book, although there are truths offered about all those topics. The Bible is, above all, a single story that tells of the plan of God to redeem a people for Himself by His grace and for His glory. The Bible does not tell everything that can be known about the world, God, and humanity. It would be too long if it did (v.30). The Bible has been given so that we can know the truth, believe the truth, and be saved by the truth of the Gospel – "that Jesus is the Christ, the Son of God" (v.31).

Do you believe that Jesus is God? Do you believe that Jesus was sent by God to save sinners by His life, death, and resurrection? Do you believe Jesus will return to make all things new and right? The story of the Bible is about God and His redemptive work in the world. Those who believe Jesus is God and trust the Word of God is the story of God's salvation live with hope.

Leviticus 2–3; John 21; Proverbs 18; Colossians 1

Human relationships can get complicating and exhausting. It is wise to keep life simple by being a person of peace who always seeks to live rightly in relation to others. Those who are free from strife can focus on having Godly attitudes, actions, and affections. Those with relational health live with hope.

Proverbs 18 provides a number of wise instructions for how to live appropriately with other people. We cannot determine how others will think, feel, or act, but we can choose our thoughts, feelings, and behaviors. Living appropriately with other people begins with thinking rightly. Thoughts determine feelings. Thoughts and feelings determine choices. This proverb provides practical insights for how to think, feel, and choose rightly.

The thoughts of a person drive everything else. While what we think about when we think about God is the most important thing about us, how we think about ourselves and other people in relation to God is significant. People who think they have nothing to learn from God or other people are not wise (v.2, 13, 15). What a person imagines about life and circumstances has a huge impact on the confidence of that person (v.11). It may be easier to believe one side of a story, especially our own side, but it is never wise or prudent (v.17). Mastering our own thoughts is the first step to living a blessed life.

What we think will drive what we feel. We cannot always control our feelings, but we can choose how we deal with our feelings. Those who live intimidated by others will often cause injustice (v.5). Feeling like we are in the know or needing to feel that we are in the know is a sure sign that we are insecure (v.8). Pride is dangerous. It almost always leads to bad results (v.12). It is vital that we protect our hearts and entrust them to Jesus and those we can truly trust because a broken heart is dangerous to others (v.14). Conflict is always confining. It robs us of emotional freedom (v.19), but those who are blessed with a marriage partner and good friends will enjoy the best blessings in life (v.22). Feelings must be fed with divine truth.

What we think and feel will drive what we do. The way to gain appropriate thoughts and feelings is by living by faith in the living God who loves us and has redeemed us to make us His people. His name, His character, and His grace are the means of our salvation and safety (v.10). The person who lives under the grace of God by faith in Jesus through the power of the Holy Spirit is inspired to live in accountable relationships (v.1), free of contempt (v.3), able to use appropriate words (v.4, 6-7, 20-21, 23), to work hard (v.9), to be generous (v.16), and to yield to objective decision makers (v.18). Those who do what is right live a blessed life.

Living by faith in Jesus allows us to see the world from a proper perspective. When we are thinking and feeling rightly, we make Godly choices. Do you know the love of Jesus? Do you have peace with others? Are your thoughts, feelings, and actions driven by God's truth, grace, and kindness? Obeying God enables us to live appropriately in relation to others, which gives us hope.

Leviticus 4; Psalms 1–2; Proverbs 19; Colossians 2

The Gospel has power. That power comes from the living God, who is at work sovereignly ruling over and sustaining creation. That power comes from the atoning work of Jesus. That power comes from the Holy Spirit, who gives life, conviction, and seals all who believe. Those who are established in the Gospel are able to spot the deceit of the darkness and live with hope.

We do not know the devilish attacks that the church at Colossae was dealing with, but we do know they caused Paul great concern. Inspired by the Holy Spirit, Paul wrote this letter to this church that he had never visited. Apparently while Paul was preaching in Ephesus, a man from Colossae, Epaphras, repented and believed the Gospel, then went back and shared the hope of the Gospel with his home town. By the grace of God, a church was established. Writing from prison, Paul instructed this church. Because this letter was inspired by the Spirit of God, all believers for all time are blessed with this holy, inerrant instruction. In Colossians 2, Paul instructs God's people in the attitude and mindset believers are to have toward the faith.

Believers are to have a firm faith (v.5b). Paul had given his life to ensure that the faith was delivered rightly in order that God's Kingdom of light might spread to the ends of the earth (v.1). He was not able to be with these people or see their faces, but he loved them and was concerned for them (v.5a). The goal of Paul was to call them to fidelity in the hope of the Gospel so that they gained full assurance in the knowledge of Jesus Christ (v.2). There is an eternal treasure of wisdom found in Christ (v.3). It is vital that the people of God pursue Christ and know the truth and avoid being dissuaded and deluded with concepts that seem acceptable on the surface, but are alien to sound doctrine.

Jesus is the only mediator between God and man. Being God, He was able to become man and to serve as the atoning sacrifice for all humanity (v.6-11). Those who believe in Christ are to profess Him publicly by identifying with Him in baptism (v.12). This symbolic act celebrates the new life Jesus makes possible through His death and resurrection (v.13-14). The saints' strong hope is that Christ has defeated darkness (v.15).

Christ came to set His people free. The children of God must work hard to continue in Christ and be His body (v.16-19). The way of Christ is a living way built on love and inspired by living hope. Human practices cannot overcome spiritual powers (v.20-23). Human practices breed pride. They have the appearance of wisdom, but true wisdom is simply trusting, loving, and obeying Jesus.

There will never be a day when we are not tempted to defy Christ and seek out our own means of self-sufficient salvation. This is the way of the world and the influence of darkness. God calls us to live by faith in Jesus Christ. Are you established and rooted in your faith? Can you defend it against the temptations of the world, which constantly calls us to trust in human wisdom rather than Christ? God gave His Son so that we can have life. Ritualistic religion leads to death. Those who live with an assured faith in the Gospel live with great hope.

Leviticus 5; Psalms 3–4; Proverbs 20; Colossians 3

The most important thing a person can learn about themselves is that there is no sin they commit that is inconsequential. All sin leads to death. It is God's grace that makes us aware of our sin by the work of the Holy Spirit. Those who are blessed to know the seriousness of sin and the saving grace of God live with hope.

The book of Leviticus rests in the middle of the Pentateuch, providing a hinge for the collection. While Genesis explains what went wrong and Exodus shows the way in which God redeemed His chosen people, the book of Leviticus reveals the grace and mercy of God. The world is not as it should be. Those who know the Bible understand why.

God has been gracious to the human race. We turned our backs on Him and committed treason against the righteous ruler of heaven and earth. In His divine mercy and for His glory, God chose to love us. He would have been completely justified in abandoning us in our sin. Instead, God has chosen to pursue us, to renew us with life eternal, and to transform us into what He created us to be.

Having been freed from the bondage of Egypt, been identified before the nations as the people of God, given the instructions for how to live in God's will, and provided the presence of God, the sojourning Israelites were ready to abide with their saving God. The great obstacle, which is the great obstacle of all humanity, was their sin. God is holy. In order to be with Him, they would have to be holy. In and of themselves they could not be. In order to be present with the people, God created a sacrificial system that would enable the people to be pardoned of their sin. God gave His law and loving presence to guide them through life. This is a picture of the Gospel. God dwelled with us. He atoned for sin so that we could be with Him, and He is now guiding all who believe in Him.

In order to rightly relate to God, sinners must be made saints. That's what Leviticus 5 is about. The Day of Atonement provided God's people with a year of redemption, just as the cross now provides a life of eternal redemption. In a right standing with God, God's people are able to repent of sin. The moment a child of God becomes aware of any sin in their life, they must immediately repent by going to the Forgiver of sins. Under the Old Covenant, the people had to go to the Tabernacle, where a priest would offer a sacrifice to make them holy (v.1-19). Under the New Covenant, God's people go to Jesus, the great High Priest, by faith, and are made holy.

Sin is serious. All sin leads to death and destruction. God is so good to care for us and provide the means by which we can be given a right standing with Him. The biggest consequence of sin is a broken relationship with God. We were made to live in God's presence. By grace we now can. God's presence will make us aware of sin. Are you aware of your sin? Are you daily seeking God and by faith turning from sin to live as a holy saint? Those who understand the seriousness of sin and look to Jesus for redemption have hope.

Leviticus 6; Psalms 5–6; Proverbs 21; Colossians 4

One of the great joys of the Christian life is the ability to be authentic with God. The Lord is omniscient and knows all things, but it is such a blessing for us, as His children, to be able to turn to Him with troubled or excited or bored hearts. Those who look to God for strength and affirmation live with hope.

The book of Psalms is not universally accessible. It is the prayer book for the saints of God. It is for the holy ones who by faith have been transformed from death to life. It is for the children of God who look to Him as Father. It is for those made alive and guided by the Holy Spirit. It is for those who trust in the atoning work of Jesus and the power of His resurrection. Those who trust in God need the book of Psalms.

Psalms 5-6 provide the proper beginning of a day for the child of God. Psalm 5 reminds us there is nothing more important we can do than to start the day looking to the provision of God (v.1-3). With holy expectations and hope we can present ourselves to God and look for His hand to provide. Disciples of Jesus are the children of the King of heaven. We can know that He hears us and cares for us because of His saving mercy.

The righteous know that the Lord hates sin and will not hear the prayers of the proud, but will in due course bring judgment on those who show no love or respect for God or other people (v.4-6). The redeemed of God are free to approach the throne of God with confidence and abide in His presence because of our righteous standing in Christ (v.7-8). The Devil is the father of lies. He used flattery in the Garden of Eden, and he still uses it today to deceive us (v.8-9). We can know that the enemies of truth will be judged (v.10), while the saints of God will take refuge in God's grace and experience the favor of God, which serves as a shield (v.11-12).

Psalm 6 calls us to turn to God in our trials and temptations. God's people will suffer spiritually, emotionally, and physically, as the Psalmist did (v.1-3). We live in a fallen world and physical death is never far away (v.4-5). There will be nights, when our pillows will be soaked with tears because of turmoil and grief (v.6-7). The good news for the people of God is that we never need go through our suffering alone. There will be a day when final victory is won (v.8-11). One glorious Day, all the workers of evil will be removed in judgment. The Lord will reign and God's people will be with Him forever (Revelation 21).

Disciples of Jesus live in the power of God's presence. Yes, the Christian life is filled with trials that grow our faith, crosses that allow us to fulfill our calling, and thorns that keep us humble and dependent upon God. We don't have to pretend. We can feel how we feel and be honest about it. We don't have to ignore our souls. We can turn to God. Are you turning to God? Do you entrust your life under God's sovereign care? Those who look to God and live by faith in the will and work of God honestly and authentically live with hope.

Leviticus 7; Psalms 7–8; Proverbs 22; 1 Thessalonians 1

Those who fear God and honor what He honors enjoy both eternal and temporal blessings. People who choose to live respectful of and grateful to God will make decisions from a God-fearing perspective and live with hope.

Proverbs 22 provides insight into the value God has placed on human life and the importance of human decisions. No matter what station or condition a person may be in, every person is of great value to the Maker (v.2). A good name is given to those who respect others and treat them well (v.1), who avoid destructive decisions (v.3), and who trust God enough to do what He commands in His Word (v.4).

It is a blessing to have a good name (v.1). God does not want us to make a name for ourselves, as those at the Tower of Babel did (Genesis 11:1-9). They did that out of conceit and pride. The consequence was destruction, which is always the result of pride (Proverbs 16:18). When we pursue a life that honors God and respects people, we will discover that our name is associated with being a blessing. That's what a good name truly is. It is a loving act to train and discipline a child. It blesses both the parent and the child (v.6, 11). Those who are blessed to see and gain good things and then share them with those in need are a blessing (v.9). Those who speak kindly to others from a pure heart are a blessing (v.11). Those who are kind to the poor bless them and, in the process, avoid God's condemnation (v.22-23). Those who honor God are blessed to be a blessing.

It is never wrong to do the right thing. It is right to avoid unnecessary negative outcomes in life. There are certain times when God calls us to do hard things that lead to pain and suffering (Luke 9:23), but it is wise to avoid making destructive decisions. The person who guards their eternal soul from sin avoids many thorns and snares (v.5). The person who is wise with their finances and has fair business dealings will avoid calamity (v.7-8, 16). It is easy to make excuses for why we should not do the right thing, but excuses lead to missed opportunities (v.13). Those who pursue wisdom and act on what is right avoid many mistakes (v.20-21). Refusing to take responsibility for others' decisions, respecting others' property, and doing honest good work is always right (v.26-29). Wise people avoid doing the wrong things.

Those who seek God's truth and live by it provide a benefit to themselves and others (v.12). They avoid adultery and the misery it creates (v.14). They enjoy an internal confidence by keeping God first (v.17-19). They form friendships with the right people (v.24-25).

Gaining a good name should never be our goal. The goal of wise people is to honor God and do what He commands out of a deep love for Him based on what He has done to redeem us, guide us with His Spirit, and train us in the truth of His Word. The result of a life leads to blessings. Do you have a good name in your home, community, church, and place of employment? Are you a blessing and benefit to others? Can others see the benefits of your faith in the world? Wise people who honor God and seek to be a blessing live with hope.

Leviticus 8; Psalm 9; Proverbs 23; 1 Thessalonians 2

There is nothing like having a clear conscience, a clear understanding of what we are supposed to be doing with our lives, a clear way of accomplishing our purpose, and a clear sense of God's presence to inspire us to live the lives God destined us to live. Life will always have challenges. There will always be a battle to fight. Those who are clear on who they are in Christ and what they are to do for God's glory live with hope.

Paul wrote to the church at Thessalonica to remind them of their divine calling and to comfort them with the truth. The church had been founded through sound teaching. Many Jews and Greeks came to faith. Some of them were very influential (Acts 17:1-4). Not wanting to give ground, the enemy attacked these new believers (v.5-9) and forced Paul to have to leave (v.10). And yet the church continued to thrive. As is often the case, the enemy sought to create disharmony and faithlessness with lies. In response, Paul wrote two letters to the church to help them walk in obedience to God.

In 1 Thessalonians 2, the church was reminded of what God had done and how God works to bring salvation to the world. Paul reminded them of the way he came and loved them. He pointed to the message of the Gospel and power of God and called them to live a life worthy of the grace they had been given. This is a message that every believer and local church needs to hear regularly. It is often easy to forget what we are supposed to be doing, why we do it, and how we are to do it.

Paul came to the Thessalonians in the power of the Gospel and with words of truth (v.1-6). He came with love and shared not only information, but his life and that of his friends (v.7-8). Rather than be a burden, Paul and his associates worked to care for their own needs and shared their hope compassionately (v.9-12). All of God's people are to be confident, loving, and respectable. This provides the proper foundation from which to live faithfully and fully in Christ.

After establishing credibility and seeing God's Word do the work it alone can do, the church was founded in the same manner as the other churches, through truth and tribulation (v.13-16). It was the church at Thessalonica's responsibility, as it is the responsibility of every church, to know that they were loved by the saints in other churches and to seek fellowship and a connection beyond their own congregation. God's people share a unique love with and for one another (v.17). Satan will often hinder personal interactions and engagements between God's people (v.18). Every believer and church must remember their high calling in Christ and live lives that look to the coming of Christ and to serve as a means of blessing in the family of faith (v.19-20).

Are you living your life with a clear conscience, calling, and commitment to God and feeling His pleasure in the way in which you live and serve Him? There are many ways to get distracted and deceived. We must work hard as individuals and collectively within our church family to avoid falling away from the truth. Those who keep the faith and live as faithful disciples of Jesus based on the hope of the Gospel in the power of the Spirit live with hope.

Leviticus 9; Psalm 10; Proverbs 24; 1 Thessalonians 3

If we ever get over what God has done for us in making us, loving us, providing atonement for our sin, and living in us and for us, we can know that we are off course and need to stop what we are doing and recover our sense of the magnificence, majesty, and mystery of God. Those who perceive the power of God in the Gospel and have a genuine passion and delight in Him live with hope.

In Leviticus 9, the people of God were receiving a front-row view of divine mercy. There is no doubt that these folks had seen God do great things for them. God had rescued them from the Egyptians, parted the Red Sea, guided them by a pillar of smoke and fire, and provided a law to live by, through Moses on Sinai. Now God was about to do something that would change the nature of His relationship with the people. Moses had been their mediator, but now He was passing the torch of spiritual leadership to Aaron and the priesthood. They had been engaged in a weeklong ordination process (Leviticus 8:33-36) and were now going to participate in the inaugural sacrificial rites on behalf of the people.

It is vital to note that Aaron had to offer a purification offering (v.7-11) and a burnt offering (v.12-14) for himself. Everyone was summoned to hear the instructions (v.1). Aaron was told what he must do (v.2) and then the people were told what they must do (v.3-5). The people acted in faith and responded to God's instructions by obeying His Word. While Aaron had to offer sacrifices for himself, there would soon come a priest who would not have to offer sacrifices for Himself in order to provide atonement for sin. Jesus would come in holiness and provide the ultimate sacrifice for sin (Heb. 9:11-14).

In order for there to be forgiveness, death had to come to one who had not committed sin. The people present at the first sacrificial offerings under the Levitical Law Code saw for themselves the seriousness of their sin. In order for their sin to be atoned for and their guilt removed, there had to be a purification offering (v.15) and a burnt offering (v.16) made on their behalf. And then, there was a fellowship offering that had to be made (v.18-21). It was then that the people could receive a blessing (v.22-23).

The sign of God's reception of the sin offering was miraculous. God showed His pleasure in their obedience by consuming the burnt offering with fire (v.24). This prefigured the reception of the ultimate offering that would one day be made. Jesus Christ would not simply die and waste away in a tomb. God received the Lord's body by raising Him from the dead. The people were able to know for certain that Jesus was the Lamb of God who took away the sins of the world by the authentication of the resurrection.

God has not left His people in sin. Through great sacrifice, God has given grace. This grace shows not only the goodness of God, but also His holiness. Are you living in awe of what God has done for you? Does it delight your heart to know that you are loved by God and in a right standing with Him? Those who genuinely appreciate the forgiveness and fellowship of God and view their lives through this lens live with hope.

Leviticus 10; Psalms 11–12; Proverbs 25; 1 Thessalonians 4

In a world filled with lies, it is not surprising that God's children get overwhelmed and want to flee and hide in a holy huddle or become cantankerous and long for what might be perceived as "the good old days." God's will is that His people recognize and follow His voice (John 10:27). In a world full of voices, the children of God must learn to ignore what is false and stay alert to what is true, honorable, just, pure, and lovely (Philippians 4:8). Those who know the truth and trust in Him live with hope.

Psalms 11-12 provide great insight into how to deal with all of the words that can overwhelm our hearts and minds. King David was in the midst of real world pressures and dealing with real troubles and trials. These difficulties had the capacity to produce either doubt or deeper faith. The same is true of all God's people. We will either mature through the challenges we face in life or our faith will fail and we will miss out on the blessings we are heirs to.

In order to overcome the lies presented to us, we must be able to identify them and then look past them to God. In Psalm 11, David is urged to flee, but God calls us to stand in faith. Whether these are ideas that David's imagination was creating or if David was actually surrounded by counselors saying these things, we do not know. What we do know is that David felt threatened (v.1-3). It was the voice of faith that saved him (v.4-8). The voice of faith knows that God is over all, He sees all, and He is at work to accomplish His sovereign will (v.4). The voice of faith knows that God tests the righteous with difficult circumstances in order to mature His saints (v.5). The voice of faith knows that God is just and will provide judgment in the proper portion at the proper time (v.6). The voice of faith knows that the righteous are loved by God and cared for by Him, and in God's time, the righteous will see Him (v.7).

In Psalm 12, David is urged to doubt. Doubt always springs from deception. Deceiving voices can sometimes seem to be right, and to an extent they do have some truth (v.1-2, 8). The right response to doubt is prayer. The righteous are to pray for the words of deception to be removed (v.3). Discernment is not always easy because the voice of dishonesty often speaks persuasively (v.4). God has promised that He will rise up and stand for those who are in need and trust in Him (v.5). The Lord has given pure truth that can be trusted and will guide us in paths of righteousness (v.6). The Lord's grace will persevere and guard His ransomed people from every evil (v.7).

There will always be deceptive voices, but through prayer and by holding to the promises of God, a child of God can prevail in faith. God calls us to listen to Him through the truth of His Word. If we listen with ears of faith in the discipline of prayer with confidence in the promises of God, we will prevail. Who has your ear and is driving your thoughts: God or worldly people and things? It is by faith we are saved and through prayer and faith in God's providential care that we live with hope.

Leviticus 11–12; Psalms 13–14; Proverbs 26; 1 Thessalonians 5

Given the natural inclination of humanity toward sin, it is difficult for people not to be foolish. God, in His grace, gives disciples of Jesus the ability to be wise. Those who can avoid being foolish and know how to rightly deal with those who are foolish are able to live with hope.

Proverbs 26 provides practical instruction for how to identify a fool, how to deal with a fool, and how to avoid being a fool. The best way to identify any person is to examine the outcome of their decisions, the way they make choices, and how they are treated by the people who know them.

Typically, fools are people who are living under negative consequences. There are times when people suffer for decisions they did not make. There are also times when God allows the just to suffer for His holy purpose. Foolish people cause problems for themselves and others. Fools are not honored for their words or deeds (v.1). They are often in conflict with other people because of the foolish things they have said (v.2). They are people that are consistently disciplined for their actions (v.3).

It is wise to learn how to deal correctly and effectively with foolish people so that their actions will not have a negative impact on your life. Do not be agreeable with a fool who is speaking inappropriately. A fool will often talk about things that should not be spoken of at a particular place or in a particular way. Never speak of foolish things or in foolish ways with a fool (v.4). Instead, be indignant toward a fool's words, which will make clear that their remarks are unfitting (v.5). Do not count on a fool to carry a message or to represent delicate situations (v.6, 9). Fools cannot handle important matters and so they should not be trusted with them (v.7). And do not honor or employ a foolish person. It is unproductive because they rarely succeed or learn from mistakes (v.8, 10-11).

While it is one thing to know how to identify and deal with a fool, it is another thing to be able to avoid becoming one. A few important axioms are given. Do not be lazy (v.13-15). Do not be arrogant (v.16). Do not get in the middle of other people's conflicts (v.17). Do not irritate people with practical jokes (v.18-19). Do not cause conflict (v.20-21). Do not gossip (v.22). Do not speak badly of others or harbor ill feelings for others (v.23-26). Do not cause harm to others with deeds or with words (v.27-28).

The best way to avoid foolishness is by being wise and investing in eternal things. The great missionary Jim Elliot is famous for saying, "He is no fool who gives what he cannot keep to gain what he cannot lose." A great way to avoid being foolish is by being generous, kind, gracious, hopeful and helpful. The person who seeks the welfare and good of others is a person who will be wise with resources, words, and energy.

It is not hard to be a foolish person. Avoiding foolishness and foolish people takes a great deal of effort. Are you doing all you can to avoid being foolish? Are you dealing correctly with foolish people? God in His grace gives blessings to those who are wise enough to trust in and live for Him. Those who avoid and overcome fools and foolishness have hope.

Leviticus 13; Psalms 15–16; Proverbs 27; 2 Thessalonians 1

A genuine compliment encourages the heart and steels the resolve. After a little league game, I saw a dad look into his son's eyes and tell him how proud he was of how the boy had played. In that moment the father gave his son something we all need: affirmation. Affirmation inspires. The person who is affirmed in their faith will often remain in the faith and live with hope.

In 2 Thessalonians 2, the Apostle Paul provided a strong affirmation to the believers. When giving affirmation to a person for their faith, there are several things to do. First, offer a blessing of grace and peace in Jesus Christ (v.1-2). Second, explain how their actions matter to you personally (v.3-4). Third, speak of their challenge and the victory or steps to victory they have taken to overcome their challenge (v.5-10). Finally, let them know how you will be praying for them (v.11-12).

The grace and peace of God is a glorious gift that has power. Those who live in the grace of God live with the ultimate acceptance. They have peace. Their sin has been paid in full by the blood of Jesus Christ. They have entered into eternal life by giving up their old life. They now have the heart of God in them by the power of the Holy Spirit. Throughout their lives and beyond death, they live with the power of the resurrection to strengthen them. The affirmation of this grace and peace is a glorious blessing.

There is no blessing like being a blessing. When God's people bless others, they are living out the original plan and purpose of God for His people (Genesis 12:1-3). To hear that their actions have in some way made it easier for another to believe, have made another's resolve to remain faithful more sure, or have given a way for another to go forward in their Kingdom work provides a powerful affirmation. While it is the work of Christ in them that is the cause for their own faithfulness, it is still their blessing because they acted in faith.

Trials do more than strengthen the faith of the one who has overcome through the power of Christ (James 1:3).
When others see and hear of the faith of another that has defeated darkness and overcome in the light of Christ, it is a great inspiration. Because "Jesus Christ is the same yesterday and today and forever" (Hebrews 13:8), God's people can know that what one saint was able to accomplish in Christ for the glory of God is possible for them too. Because the promise that "What is impossible with man is possible with God" (Luke 18:27) is true for all of God's people, seeing God do great things through one helps others.

Every person who has ever had to battle the darkness with light knows that it was through the power of prayer they were able to overcome. Our Lord, on the night of His betrayal, found the power to prevail through hours of prayer. Knowing that others are praying for us in specific ways is a great affirmation.

The life of a believer is often a blessing to others. Those who bless others need affirmation. Is your personal faith and life one that others can affirm? Who can you affirm for their faith? The person who is affirmed in their faith will live with hope.

Leviticus 14; Psalm 17; Proverbs 28; 2 Thessalonians 2

The Gospel is truly liberating. A disciple of Jesus is gloriously free. Those who are saved by grace through faith in Christ alone live a full life with many blessings and constant hope.

The plight of an Israelite living under the Old Covenant that was suffering from leprosy was tragic (Leviticus 13:45-46). This person was required to wear tattered clothes, live isolated from those who do not have the disease, and separated from the holy presence of God. When they were in public, they were to shout "Unclean!" to warn those of their condition. The infected parts of their body became numb and disfigured.

The tragedy of leprosy provides a powerful picture of what happens to a person suffering under the disease of sin. They may be able to wear nice clothes, but their soul is tattered and torn. They never experience the peace that comes from a personal relationship with God. Without God in their life, people are forced to find their identity in their looks, accomplishments, or connections – things that do not last. Without a solid sense of self found only in Christ, they feel isolated and incapable of deep connections with other people. Their way of life is outside of God's grace and their sin becomes so normal that their conscience becomes numb.

Just as God provided a means by which a person healed of leprosy could be readmitted to the Old Testament community (Leviticus 14:1-32), so also a saved person can be admitted into a local church family. It was a process that provided not only the leaders with the confidence to know that the person was healed, but also the community would be assured that this person was no longer infected with the disease.

This is a beautiful picture of the Gospel. A person who was once isolated and sick with sin is cleansed by grace through faith in Jesus. This cleansing is the result of Jesus dying for us (Hebrews 9:22). The life of Christ becomes alive in those who believe (Galatians 2:20). This life is a shared bond among believers and allows them to connect and form a body that is united in its many parts to serve God (1 Corinthians 12:12-27). Those who accept Christ are accepted into a local church, which allows the people to grow together in the grace and goodness of God (1 Peter 2:1-10).

The children of Israel who entered the land of Canaan were entering into a place that was infected with sin. These contaminated dwellings would need to be made holy (v.33-57). So also, the people of the New Covenant are sojourners in an unclean land. We are to keep our lives free from the contamination of sin and create communities that are pure and blessed with the glory of God (1 Peter 2:11-12). Like the Old Testaments saints, the New Testament saints are to be a people set apart.

Examine your life and see if there is anything unclean in the way you are thinking or living. If there is, repent of it by faith in the Gospel of Jesus. Are you right with God? Are you serving others? Are you being sanctified in Christ? Those who are seeking to serve God with other saints live with hope.

Leviticus 15; Psalm 18; Proverbs 29; 2 Thessalonians 3

There is no victory like a last-minute victory. Even better than that is a come-from-behind victory. When it appears all hope is lost and the opposing team has the upper hand, there is something sensational about a team that comes back and turns a defeat into a victory. God takes defeated and doomed people and intervenes to provide victory and life. Those who live in the victory of Christ live with hope.

King David lived through many horrific trials. One of the toughest battles was the one waged in his own mind concerning the goodness and the will of God. As a young boy, David was consecrated as the king of Israel (1 Samuel 16:13). His reign did not begin the day he was anointed. Before David became king, God had to train him to love, to live by faith, and to lead. This is what Psalm 18 is about.

David came to have a deep love for God. He did not always understand God. Like other Psalm writers, David was at times confused by God but was always able to trust in God's love. This love of God, when understood and appreciated, produces a love for God deep in the soul of a person. David believed God loved him and so he celebrated his love for God and acknowledged Him as his source of strength (v.1). Those who know God's love trust God's reason, even when it cannot be completely known or understood.

David came to have a deep faith in God. This was not a theoretical faith. This was a faith that was tested by the fires of life (v.2-30). David could point to God as his shield, provider, and protector because in life, David faced many trials and God saw him through each one. David believed the Word of God. Those who know the Scriptures and walk in the way of God grow to trust the Lord as their shield and refuge (v.30).

David came to be a great leader. The Lord trained him to fulfill God's calling on his life. By ancestry, David was a shepherd, but by divine calling he was a king. The Lord prepared David to accomplish his purpose (v.31-50). David's confidence was built by the victories God provided. David clearly understood that these victories were won by the Lord. It was grace.

While David was indeed a mighty and great king, there was another, who is greater, that would come. While David erred in his life, Jesus never did. He was surrounded by enemies from His birth to His death. It seemed Jesus had lost on the cross, but God provided the victory. His death brought life and His resurrection brought power. Now all who believe in Jesus can pray the prayer of David but with even greater confidence.

The God who worked in David is the same God who is at work in those who believe today. Today, God is raising up people, like David, to serve His purpose. They may not appear to be the natural choice, but God will train them. Are you living a life of love for God? Is your faith becoming stronger with each passing day and year? Are you fulfilling your divine destiny? This is the will of God for all of His children, not just kings. Christ has won the ultimate come-from-behind victory, and those who believe in Him will live with hope.

Leviticus 16; Psalm 19; Proverbs 30; 1 Timothy 1

Self-awareness is a great strength. The people who are able to truly define themselves in authentic and accurate terms are capable of seeing what others cannot see. Those who see themselves rightly are capable of seeing God for who He is. Through the lens of divine reality, people relate properly to reality and the brokenness of humanity and the dangers of this fallen planet. Those who can see and live in truth live with hope.

The words of Agur, who wrote Proverbs 30, provide encouragement to the dependent disciple of Jesus. Agur's wisdom is shown in his self-evaluation (v.1-4). He is worn out with life. Anyone who has truly lived and loved in this broken world will often become weary. Genuine love is a blessing and a burden. While it allows us to live out our divine Maker's intention, it also causes distress because everyone we can love is burdened and broken with sin. Those who know they do not know everything are wise. There is only One who truly knows all things, and those who know Him know truth.

The God of truth is always proven true, and those who take shelter under His mighty hand find they can endure the trials of life (v.5). God has not hidden Himself. As Psalm 18 clearly indicates, the creation is announcing His presence and power, and His Word reveals His character and mercy. Reality is like a theatrical performance. Creation is the stage. The Bible is the Story. The main character is the God-man who was promised, who came, who died and was raised, and who will come again. The Story that God has written is perfect and without error. To add anything to it is to desecrate it and demean the Author. The result will be a sharp rebuke and public disgrace (v.6).

The only prayer in Proverbs is found in v.7-9. This is the prayer of a wise person and worthy of repeating. It is a prayer that acknowledges the human condition, as well as the supremacy of God. He asks for two basic things. He asks that God make him honest and that his basic needs be provided for by God. With the truth and divine provision, he will always trust in God. This is a wise man!

Having established his sense of self and a right dependence upon God's Word and provision, he turns his attention to the facts of life and relationships (v.10-33). The overriding awareness of this wise sage is that the world is a terrible mess and that he and all others would do well not to add to the already existing issues of moral decay. Once we realize that the human condition is such that it produces conflict, injustice, laziness, selfishness, disrespect, and possesses a never satisfied appetite, it becomes easy to know what to avoid and what to pursue. There is a way in life that leads to destruction and one that leads to greater life, eternal life. Those who are wise have a humble gratitude for the strength of God that is fueling them.

We all have blind spots and need divine revelation. Do you understand your need for God? Are you wisely living dependent upon Him? Are you obeying God's Word? When we understand that we do not have the capacity to save ourselves and are able to trust Jesus to save us, we live with hope.

Leviticus 17; Psalms 20–21; Proverbs 31; 1 Timothy 2

While the faith of every person is extremely personal, it is also meant to be public. God is in the process of reaching the world with the Gospel. He has chosen to work through His people to accomplish this purpose. He has commanded us to go and make disciples (Matthew 28:19-20). Those who join God in His work in the world live with hope.

One of the men Paul mentored was Timothy. The book of the Bible we know as 1 Timothy was a letter by Paul to Timothy, who was serving as the pastor of the church at Ephesus at the time. This letter provides practical practices for how to lead a church and shepherd saints toward holiness. Paul was very aware of the church at Ephesus and its challenges and potential. In Chapter 2 Paul instructed the church in how it needed to bless society and shape its own internal culture.

A blessing the church provides society is prayer support. The church is to pray for everyone (v.1). There is not a person on this planet who does not need prayer. This can be private prayer, but it also needs to be public prayer. It is a kindness to ask a person how they can be best prayed for and then to actually pray for them then and there. Adding them to a private prayer list later is also helpful. Those in government are to be intentionally prayed for so that their decisions will lead to peace (v.2).

God's way is peaceful. War and conflict is a result of sin. Thankfully, Jesus came to defeat the power of sin to set humanity free from the bondage of hate, fear, and violence. God's will is for saints to share the Gospel so that others can know God's peace (v.3-6). Like Paul, we are all to profess the truth of the Gospel to the world and do all we can to let every tribe and tongue know the truth (v.7).A healthy church is a praying church that does not quarrel (v.8). Where there is peace and prayer, there is divine power at work.

God is to be the focus of the church. Women need to be mindful of their attire so that they do not draw attention away from God (v.9-10). Any attention they receive should be for services rendered to God, which brings glory to God. Men are to take responsibility for teaching and leading. In the Garden of Eden, it was the passivity of the man that led to sin. It is vital that men understand their responsibility to serve the church and to grow in grace so that they can be fit to teach and exercise authority in the church (v.11-14). Women are free to live under Godly male leadership and serve in their unique and blessed roles. They can serve in vital roles that men cannot and persevere in their salvation. This requires faith in Jesus, love for Jesus, holiness in Jesus, and self-control (v.15). God has made men and women with unique abilities that are meant to bless and bring God glory.

God has called the church to pray and to make disciples. The Lord has provided specific roles for men and women in that pursuit. All is to be done with peace and for the glory of God. Are you praying as God commands? Are you serving and creating peace and order in your church? Those who honor God and fulfill their calling are able to live with hope.

Leviticus 18; Psalm 22; Ecclesiastes 1; 1 Timothy 3

There is an umbrella of protection provided for those who are willing to come under God's grace and walk in His ways. This blessing does not mean that there will not be hard times. There will always be puddles and messy streets to negotiate, but these trials provide the means to grow in faith. Those who reside under God's grace, trust in His Way, and obey Him in love will live with hope.

There is often confusion concerning the law of God and how it applies to New Covenant Christians. Under the Old Covenant, there were three types of law: the moral law, the ceremonial law, and the civic law. The moral law pertains to all people for all time and comes with both blessings to those who obey and curses to those who disobey. These consequences are natural in the sense that they typically create conflict, pain, and suffering. They are also supernatural in that they produce the wrath of God, which is sometimes experienced in life, but always in death. The ceremonial laws have to do with the religious practices of the Israelite people under the Old Covenant, which pictured the coming of Christ. The civic law pertains to the nation of Israel under the rule of God. There is now no theocratic nation under God.

Leviticus 18 expounds God's moral law. God told His people to avoid living like worldly people (v.1-5). Their customs and religions led to death. He specifically spoke of the way of the Egyptians and Canaanites. In any generation there will be beliefs espoused by those outside of God's covenant community. They are to be rejected. God's statutes are to be attended to with great care so that His blessing and umbrella of protection can be enjoyed by His people.

The moral law of God pertaining to sexuality provided in detail in v.6-30 applies to all people for all time. Sexual attraction is not the issue. In a broken world, desires can become disconnected from divine intention. This happens not just with sexuality, but with all the good things God gives. The issue is action. The Canaanites were being judged for the abhorrent sinful sex activity and the murdering of their children (v.21-25). Sinful sex and the murdering of the innocent are normal activities celebrated in the U.S. God help us!

Those who ignore God's design and act according to their own sinful desires will face natural and divine consequences. The people of God are not only to discipline their desires, but to live for a greater motivation. God's people are not to simply say, "No!" to sinful desires, but are to say, "Yes!" to divine love.

The greatest blessing a person can enjoy is the presence of God in life and death. Those who come to God by faith in the redeeming love of Jesus enjoy much of what life was originally meant to be. It is a life filled with delight and purpose. It is a life that seeks more, while always being contented. It is a life that has a solid foundation and a divine source of identity. It is a life with an umbrella of protection from the deceit and destruction of the enemies of God. Are you living under the umbrella of God's grace? Are you obeying His law out of a faithful love for Jesus? Life will always have challenges, but those who live under God's law of love live with hope.

Leviticus 19; Psalms 23–24; Ecclesiastes 2; 1 Timothy 4

Jesus is the good shepherd (John 10:11, 14). What He does for His sheep is so gracious and kind. Who He is, as the good shepherd, is glorious and amazing. Those who know Jesus, as the shepherd of their soul and Lord of their life, are blessed beyond measure and have eternal hope.

Psalm 23 is one of the most well-known of all the Psalms. It provides a poignant and powerful picture of what the grace of Jesus provides to His redeemed people. While Psalm 24 is not as well-known, it provides a succinct and serious picture of the power of Jesus, as God.

Those saved by grace through faith in Christ alone are able to claim and to be claimed by Christ. They know and are known by Him. Psalm 23 speaks to the blessing that exists for those who believe. God provides for the fundamental needs of the soul (v.1). He provides the pasturelands of a local church and the celebratory waters of baptism, as a means to testify, obey, and grow in the hope of His handling (v.2-3). Life will always have tribulation (John 16:33), but because Jesus has overcome the world, His followers can live without fear (v.4). We are rarely comfortable, but always comforted. We are rarely powerful, but always strong in the Lord. In the midst of this spiritual battle, God provides the Lord's Supper to remind and assure His people of their standing and His provision (v.5). Life is filled with goodness and mercy and the hope of eternal life in heaven drives the hope of all who trust in Christ (v.6).

The good shepherd, Jesus, is unlike anyone else. Psalm 24 is a celebration of the greatness of Christ. Because He is the Maker, He is the true owner of the world and everything in it (v.1-2). It is Christ alone who was able, on His own merits, to enter into the holy of holies (v.3-4). He alone is worthy! He alone has a pure heart and clean hands. He is the holy one who lived as a man, but never sinned. All those who seek Him receive and experience His grace and His place with God (v.5). The Lord Jesus was raised, and after appearing to the disciples, He ascended into heaven (Acts 1). He is the King of glory (v.6). He is the one who conquered sin and death and now reigns as the King of heaven and earth (v.7). The doors of heaven opened to Him, and He is now receiving the praise He is due (v.8-10). All the angels of heaven and the saints of glory are celebrating Him and will do so forever and ever (Revelation 7:9-12).

Not only does a redeemed saint in Christ have the benefit of the presence of God and the blessing of being shepherded by Jesus, but because He is the King of glory, life in Him is one of infinite importance and power. God has not abandoned His people to figure out life on their own. The Lord has defeated the power of sin and death. He is now ruling and reigning in their lives. Is Jesus your shepherd? Are you living in the blessing of His grace and mercy and enjoying the benefits of His life? Do you worship and honor Him as the King of glory? Those who know Jesus, as the shepherd of their soul and King of their life, live with eternal hope.

Leviticus 20; Psalm 25; Ecclesiastes 3; 1 Timothy 5

God made all things to be in harmony, but sin entered the world and brought death and brokenness. Thankfully, God did not abandon us in this world. Those who can see God in the midst of the difficulties of life and discover the beauty of God's plan live with hope.

The book of Ecclesiastes is a glorious look at reality. With beautiful words and phrases this little book destroys the logic and basis for materialism, hedonism, and all forms of self-centeredness. Pleasure is a natural inclination of the human heart. God made us for paradise. It is no wonder that we want to feel the excitement, peace, fulfillment, and ecstasy in all of life at all times. This is found in God alone. Our fallen world cannot give us what we want. God has made us for Himself, and there's not satisfaction without Him.

In Ecclesiastes 3, the preacher provides a realistic understanding of time. While the human soul is eternal, the human experience on this fallen rock is limited. With sin came death. The winding down of life is now the norm. It is wise to accept the facts concerning life in our corrupted creation caused by human sin and seek to live for what is best, while there is time to do so.

In this life, there is a time for the matters of human life. In a poetic way the preacher lists the things that occur in life and compares them to their opposite (v.1-8). Each one must come to be. This never-ending cycle could lead to cynicism, but the child of God knows that God has a plan for those who love Him. There is meaning to it all in Christ. Everything has a purpose. God is causing all things to work for good for those who love Him and who have been called according to His purpose (Romans 8:28).

Work was never wrong. Work is good. God placed Adam in the Garden of Eden to work and said it was good (Genesis 2:15). The problem with work now is that it is made hard, as a consequence of sin (Genesis 3:19). Humanity must now sweat and toil to provide for their needs (v.9-14). Work will never provide the peace we desire. It is only when a person trusts God that they are free to pursue the purpose and calling God has for them and find peace in God's plan (Ephesians 2:10).

There is one certainty in life and that is death. Unless the Lord returns, every person currently alive will surely die. This is a result of the fall (Genesis 2:17). Because of the natural inclination toward sin in humanity, death is the result and justice is hard to maintain, but God is just and in time He will make all things right (v.16-17). This world is like a testing ground, and each person must determine the trajectory of their affections. Those who will only live for the things of this world will live and die with uncertainty and no eternal assurance (v.18-22).

The person who will trust in the grace of Jesus will live a life with great meaning and purpose. Are you living for Christ? Are you living for God's eternal purposes? Are you sure you are right with God and living for what is best? Those who understand reality through the lens of Jesus and pursue God's eternal rewards live with hope.

Leviticus 21; Psalms 26–27; Ecclesiastes 4; 1 Timothy 6

Perspective is a powerful thing. Everyone has a perspective. The real question is: what is my operating perspective and why? The way we view the world will determine our attitudes and feelings toward our circumstances, responsibilities, and other people. The person who is able to look at the world from an eternal perspective and know that God is pleased with their way of life lives with hope.

We are both the cause and the victims of our circumstances. While we cannot always choose what happens to us in life, we can always choose how we respond to or pursue certain paths in life. We learn in 1 Timothy 6 how important our perspective is and how it drives the decisions we make.

Paul told Timothy to command those who were bondservants to treat their masters with honor and respect (v.1-2a). Those who were bondservants were in their position because of a debt they owed. It was not a racist system. It was an economic system caused by financial mismanagement. Those who were under the authority of unbelievers were to treat them with respect so that the faith would not be tarnished. Those who were under believers were not to presume upon them. The same principles apply today in the labor force. Christians are to work for others as unto the Lord (Colossians 3:23).

Within the family of faith there will always be those who struggle to remain faithful to the Biblical faith. The ways people abandon the truth of Scripture are as varied as the people in the church. The reason for the disconnection from the truth is always pride (v.2b-5). Paul encouraged Timothy to remain content with the Lord's provision and to avoid being a slave to the need for more money (v.6-10).

Those who are willing to flee what is destructive and pursue what is pure succeed spiritually (v.11). Successful saints are those who are willing to fight daily for their faith. They embrace the life that Christ has called them to and that they confess to be their own (v.12). Those who keep the faith and sustain a good reputation for themselves and Christ are those who keep the commandment of Christ (v.13-4). His commandment is to love. They are also inspired by the greatness and goodness of God and are humbled by the knowledge that apart from Christ, they could never know and honor God (v.15-16). God's people who gain heaven's reward view their lives and resources as conduits of God's blessings to others (v.17-19). They see their lives as an investment for God that is meant to produce an eternal reward. Those who think otherwise abandon the faith and lose the blessing that Christ alone can give (v.20).

The only way that any person can live the life that God desires is through grace (v.21). Apart from God's grace we would not know the truth and we would be nothing more than slaves to the desires of the flesh. We would be self-centered and miserable. We would attempt to manipulate the truth of God and steal God's glory in order to build a name for ourselves. Do you have the right perspective on the truth, Christ, and money? The person who is able to look at the world from an eternal perspective lives with hope.

Leviticus 22; Psalms 28–29; Ecclesiastes 5; 2 Timothy 1

Humanity has no constant hope apart from Jesus. Jesus alone gives eternal living hope. Jesus provides all that satisfies the souls of humanity. Jesus makes us into all we were designed to be. The people who know Jesus and live by grace through faith in Him have a hope that does not disappoint.

In Leviticus 22, the limitation of humanity is displayed. God in His eternal grace had chosen Israel out of all the nations to be His people. They were not the best people, but graciously God chose them and commanded them to be His people. Despite being loved, being given clear commands, and being offered the divine means of grace to establish and maintain the Lord's presence among them, the people of God revolted against Him. Leviticus 22 points out the fact that the priests were prone to be made unclean (v.1-16), the people were prone to dishonor God (v.17-30), and the sanctification process of the people was inconsistent at best (v.31-33).

Now that Jesus has come, the world has the perfect priest. The priests in the Old Covenant were not perfect. Even if they were able to have their sin atoned for through their offerings, they continued to fall into temptation and sin. Jesus Christ is the perfect priest. He never sinned. There was never an atonement that had to be made for Him. He has overcome sin and death and now reigns in heaven ready to return. Jesus hears us and ministers to us perfectly.

Now that Jesus has come, the perfect promised sacrifice has been provided. The offerings of the Old Covenant had the capacity to be contaminated. The only offering God would accept was one without blemish. Jesus Christ is the perfect Lamb of God who takes away the sin of the world. God is loving and just. His love sent Jesus to die for us in our place and His death satisfied the just demands of God's law. The sacrifice of Jesus fully heals the hearts of those who believe. The indecency of Jesus' death makes us decent before God. Now those who believe are free to live in the presence of God without disgrace.

Now that Jesus has come, the world has the perfect power at work. The people of the Old Covenant could not keep the law of God. Jesus was able to keep the law perfectly. While saints may sin, Jesus' perfect record is applied to them. Not only are God's people legally made right, they are able to become more and more like Christ. This sanctification process is made possible by the power of the resurrected Christ living in and through His people by the Holy Spirit. This power is made perfect in human weakness. The more God's people rely on Jesus and His grace rather than on their will power, the more divine power they will experience. It is through the love and grace of Jesus that the divine power to obey God is made manifest in humanity.

Through the constant frustration and failures of the Israelites, God revealed the incapacity of humanity to save themselves. Now that Jesus has come and kept the law perfectly and died as the perfect substitute for His people, salvation is possible. The power to love and live for God is possible. Are you living as a satisfied child of God who has been pardoned of sin and set apart for holiness? Those who live in Christ live with hope.

Leviticus 23; Psalm 30; Ecclesiastes 6; 2 Timothy 2

Disciples of Jesus would do well to drink from the fountain of experiences of those who have gone before us on the "narrow way" that leads to eternal life. Christian biographies are a source of so much inspiration, information, and motivation to live for God. The Bible is filled with biographies. Those who learn from the saints of old are wise and will be encouraged with hope.

One saint worthy of stringent study is King David. He was the forgotten younger brother who was out keeping sheep when the prophet visited his dad, looking for the next king of Israel. He was the musician who became the warrior and hero of Israel. He was the accused usurper who was God's chosen ruler. He was the blessed king who committed adultery and murder. He was the busy father who ran a great kingdom but failed to run his home. He was the sinner who was loved by God and made righteous by grace.

In Psalm 30, David provided wisdom that he gleaned through the ups and downs of his personal journey. Centuries after David wrote this Psalm, it was used as the liturgical praise at the Hanukkah celebration, after the dedication of the Temple in 165 BC. It speaks of the miraculous provision of God (v.1-3), the merciful grace of God (v.4-10), and the majestic glory of God (v.11-12).

Prayer is both a personal and private part of the Christian life. Those who pray specifically and consistently see the provision of God that others miss. When we pray specifically, we are able to know when a prayer is answered. David survived persecution, health crises, and near-death experiences, but found God faithful to provide in practical and measurable ways as he prayed. When we see God provide, our faith grows stronger and our praise richer.

Humility and divine dependence are hallmarks of the Christian life. When David thought himself safe and secure, he got lazy and became sinful. God dealt with him for his sin. In that moment, when his own son turned against him and it seemed that death was imminent, David called out to God and God was gracious to him. Pride has a way of seeping into every believer's heart, and with pride comes a fall. God is gracious to those who trust in Him. Because of our sin and the brokenness of our world, there will be nights of weeping, but in God's grace and mercy there is a morning joy that rises.

Through the ups and downs of life, God's people grow and discover how great God truly is. Without the trials of temptation, we are inclined to be self-confident. It is through the grind of earthly sorrows that our confidence in God grows. The victorious Christian life comes with many failures. The wise believer looks to God and discovers how great He is and is able to proclaim to God with the saints of glory, "How great thou art!"

While the life of David is certainly worthy of study, the life we must never forget is the life of Jesus. His life is the foundation of hope. It was the joy set before Him that allowed Him to endure the cross (Hebrews 12:2). Are you looking to Jesus and learning from the saints who have gone before you? Is your story worth learning from? Those who learn from others and teach those who come behind them have an inspired and inspirational hope.

Leviticus 24; Psalm 31; Ecclesiastes 7; 2 Timothy 3

There is no doubt that life is often hard, but it is also true that God is good and those who know and trust God are able to experience both the bad and the good of life with hope. Disciples of Jesus can know that God is righteous, that His plan is perfect, and that His love is steadfast. Those under God always have hope.

Ecclesiastes 7 speaks to the wisdom of having an eternal perspective. Those who live for what is temporal must live in a temporary happiness that cannot and will not last. Those who live for what is eternal are able to see life for what it is and hope for what is greater.

Having a good name and knowing that death leads to heaven are consequences of a Godly life (v.1). Faithful saints need not worry about their reputations or their eternal resting place. Those who take life seriously will understand that this life is no laughing matter and will gain wisdom in knowing the world is a place of pain, but God is still good (v.2-6). This is the perspective of a wise saint.

A sound understanding of the greatness of God allows a person to see everything else properly. What God does cannot be undone (v.13). When a person comes to the conclusion that God is the one true God and all else is under Him, wisdom is attained. That kind of thinking will drive all other decisions (v.7-11) and there will be a protection in it and a security that gives confidence (v.12).

Life is not all bad and it is good to rejoice in good days (v.14). God allows both prosperity and poverty. Just because an evil person seems to have more enjoyment than the righteous, the person who is looking at life from the vantage of eternity will not lose hope. Appropriate choices are the result of a heart that fears God and trusts God's will to be done, including God's perfect timing for each person's death (v.15-18). There is a great strength in a life that trusts God (v.19). It is a balanced life that is secure in providence.

Those who pursue the will of God and trust in His grace will never live perfect lives on this side of heaven (v.20). Their sin and the sin of others will not surprise them (v.21-22). Rather than getting down or being hurt by others, the wise person looks to have faith in God's eternal plan. Relying on what we can know or what other people think is not always helpful (v.23-25). The best thing a person can do is to seek to know God, as He has revealed Himself, and to pursue what He made humanity to be (v.29). When we understand who God is, we will love Him. By loving Him, we will obey Him. In obeying Him, we will avoid the pain that comes from being lured into sin and the consequences that accompany disobedience (v. 26-28).

None of us is what we want to be, but by God's grace we can become better than what we would be on our own. Are you looking to God through salvation in Christ to be your anchor and strength? Can you mourn and weep at life's troubles, but maintain joy in the Lord? Those who can look to God by faith and trust in His steadfast love and plan will live and die with hope.

Leviticus 25; Psalm 32; Ecclesiastes 8; 2 Timothy 4

When God made the world, He said everything in it was good except for one thing: it was not good for man to be alone. Having been made in the image of God, human beings are made to be in relationships. Those who are blessed with Godly friendships live with hope.

The Apostle Paul had a dear friend in Timothy. Their bond was strong. Paul often referred to Timothy as his son. Timothy was Paul's trusted ally in the battle against the darkness. Paul depended on Timothy and Timothy looked to Paul for counsel and wisdom. In 2 Timothy 4, Paul wrote to Timothy to challenge him, encourage him, and to ask for his help.

Timothy was blessed to have a friend who would challenge him. Paul told Timothy to be ready to do his job of proclaiming the Gospel at any time (v.1-2). The only way Timothy could do that was by making sure he was in God's Word daily, prayed up, and focused on how God was at work in the world. That awareness and preparedness is what all believing buddies should challenge each other to do. Another thing Paul told Timothy to be ready for was the disinterest of some listeners (v.3-4). He went on to tell Timothy to focus on what Timothy could control and to focus on God's work (v.5). All of God's people need friends who will tell them what they need to hear.

Paul then encouraged Timothy with his own hope. Paul had a sense he would soon be martyred for the faith (v.6). There did not seem to be fear in his message. Paul sensed he was done with this life and was glad to be headed home to heaven. He believed he had served well (v.7) and was anticipating a reward in heaven (v.8). We give a great gift to our friends and family when we provide them the certainty that we know at death we will be in heaven.

Paul's last instructions are for Timothy to leave Ephesus and come see him for a final visit (v.9). Paul had experienced one of the great heartaches of the Christian faith. One who claimed to be of Christ had deserted the faith for earthly pleasure (v.10). This is a painful loss, but Paul had steadfast friends too (v.11). There were all kinds of ministries being accomplished by God's people, and their faithfulness was a great encouragement to Paul (v.12-13). There are enemies within the visible church and enemies of the world that God's people must always be aware of and avoid (v.14-15). The best defense is a good offense, and Paul encouraged Timothy with tasks to do that would accomplish God's will. Paul's last words were a blessing of grace (v.16-22).

Christian friends are a hallmark of a healthy Christian life. It is good to have friends who are not of the faith so the Gospel can be shared in a loving manner, but the Christian who is going to make a difference in the world will need fellow saints to stand with who will provide Biblical encouragement. Christian friendship is based upon a shared belief in sound doctrine, love in Christ, and God's grace. Do you have at least one Christian friend you can count on and who counts on you? Do you challenge, encourage, and help each other? Those with close Christian bonds live with hope.

Leviticus 26; Psalm 33; Ecclesiastes 9; Titus 1

The Lord is gracious and does not give us what we deserve. That is what mercy is. Those who believe in Jesus are freed from the power and the punishment of sin. Thank God! That does not mean we are free from all consequences of sin. Those who choose to live outside of God's design for humanity face negative consequences, but those who obey God and count on His mercy have hope.

God provides an explanation for how He works in the lives of people in Leviticus 26. Those who choose to pursue Him with a heart of love and a faith commitment to Jesus find God's blessings in many ways (v.1-13). Those who choose to go their own way in life and live apart from God will face the unfortunate consequences that accompany sin and the limitations of earthly comforts (v.14-46).

Wise people live in obedience to God. God's promises to His people apply to all who live by faith in Christ. Learning to appreciate the blessings God gives us is a crucial activity in the life of a disciple of Jesus. Without gratitude, we will focus on the negatives and difficulties of life. Those who live by faith can enjoy Christ and avoid building a life on idols (v.1). They can build their life on the one true God (v.2). Building a life on God brings blessings that are financial, emotional, inspirational, and deeply spiritual (v.3-13).

Unwise people are disobedient to God. Remember Galatians 6:7. "Do not be deceived: God is not mocked, for whatever one sows, that will he also reap." Those who choose to live in violation of God's law will face the consequences that come with their actions. There will be difficulties that are financial, relational, spiritual, and personal (v.14-39). When a disciple of Jesus experiences these negative actualities, it is vital that they repent (v.40-45). God is gracious to bless His people according to His promise. God keeps His promises!

While it is true that God blesses the righteous with good things, it can sometimes appear that it is the unrighteous who are blessed. The prophet Malachi complained in Malachi 3:15, "And now we call the arrogant blessed. Evildoers not only prosper but they put God to the test and they escape." God's people are blessed eternally and must look at life from an eternal perspective. Like the Psalmist we must pray, "Let me know how fleeting I am!" (Psalm 39:4).

The ultimate blessings of God will be experienced in the life that is to come. The greatest blessings of God will come when the new heaven and earth appear. Those who find comfort in the things of this world and live apart from Christ do not have the ultimate blessings found in salvation. Their comfort becomes a curse. Those in Christ are to learn contentment and see beyond temporal circumstances (Philippians 4:11-12).

Christians find their blessing in the person of Christ. Are you content in Christ? Are you living in obedience to His Word? Can God bless your lifestyle? Those who live in obedience to God by faith in Christ have hope.

Leviticus 27; Psalm 34; Ecclesiastes 10; Titus 2

God calls us to do the right things the right way. The person who is living for the right purpose the right way is truly blessed. Even when life is hard, Christians can be confident, when they are doing the right thing the right way. Those who do God's will God's way live with hope.

King David saw many difficult days. The Lord chose him to be king of Israel. The Lord gifted him with courage, strength, and faith. While in the process of being and becoming king, David faced many trials. He lived for many years in the already and not yet. He was already king of Israel, according to God and the anointing of Samuel, but there was a period of time when he was not recognized as king. During that time, Saul sought to kill David. So it is with all of God's children. We are already the children of God and blessed with every heavenly blessing, but it is also true that we have not yet arrived to where God designed us to be. There is more to be done before our full identity and hope are realized. There are battles to be won, trials to be overcome, and grace to be experienced.

In Psalm 34, David recounted the time recorded in 1 Samuel 21:10–14 when he fled from Saul and sought refuge with Achish, the king of Gath. Unfortunately, the Philistine people recognized David as the hero of Israel who had killed many of their people. To escape, David had to pretend to be mad. This Psalm is divided into two parts. David shares his testimony in verses 1-10 and then offers a succinct and significant teaching for God's people in verses 11-22.

David's testimony speaks of the greatness of God and of David's own weakness and meekness. Those who would have seen David in those days would have seen what appeared to be an amazingly gifted man. Not only was he a magnificent soldier, but he was loved by the masses and those with military might. Despite his appearance, David confessed that he was a poor man who was saved from his troubles by God alone (v.6).

Inspired by God's provision for him, David transitioned from testifier to teacher (v.11). His lesson was basic, but its implications are demanding. David was a man with great ability, but he knew he needed the Lord. The thing to do, according to David, is to take refuge in the Lord by trusting and obeying Him. Doing a thing is not hard. What is hard is figuring out the right thing to do. The difficult task of determining what is best is only possible by discerning God's Word.

We will all spend our lives doing things. The question we must answer is this: are we doing the right things the right way? It is not hard to do a task. What is hard is doing the task correctly. Regardless of what role we play in life, whether that of a king, salesperson, parent, spouse, friend, family, or public servant, there is a right way to do it and that is under Jesus. There is only one way that leads to life and that is the way of true faith in Christ. Are you living for and trusting in the Lord? Are your actions being driven by God's commands? Those who do God's will God's way live with hope.

Numbers 1; Psalm 35; Ecclesiastes 11; Titus 3

There will always be something to rob the heart of joy. It is incumbent upon all of God's people that we look to Jesus and see how He lived with joy, even as He endured the cross and shame (Hebrews 12:2). Jesus calls His disciples to live with the same joy. Those who can acknowledge difficulties, but choose to focus on the blessings, live with hope.

The writer of Ecclesiastes was clearly a thoughtful and profound person. Although he experienced the best things in life, his soul was still unsatisfied. This is what happens in our fallen world. The things of earth seem so great until we have them, and then we learn the hard way that God has made us for eternity. Until we rest in God's grace and find pleasure in God's love, we will live unsatisfied.

There is so much more to life than pleasure, popularity, possessions, and power. These earthly things will never satisfy the eternal soul because they are temporal. These things, in and of themselves, are not bad. If looked at rightly and used properly, all good things can be a blessing. In Ecclesiastes 11 the writer makes the point that there is nothing wrong with enjoying good things, so long as they do not cause us to sin. The resources we have are to be used wisely (v.1-4), the work we do is to be done well (v.5-6), and worldly pleasures are to be used according to God's commands (v.7-10).

The wasting of financial resources is unwise. Those with money would do well to follow the instructions of this wise rich man. First, give to the poor (v.1). Second, do not lump resources into one category. Instead, diversify investments and protect what wealth is available (v.2). Third, remember that money and other resources, like time, can only be used once (v.3). Fourth, avoid paralysis by analysis. Make the best decision possible, before opportunities are gone (v.4).

Resources are a result of hard work. Work is one of the great blessings in life. It allows people to use their abilities in rewarding ways. The outcomes of our labors are often beyond our capacity to compute. There are far more factors in our world than we can know or understand, but those who work hard consistently will typically see gain in some way (v.5-6).

There are many good things to enjoy in life and there is nothing wrong with enjoying what God has made, so long as God is honored in the enjoyment. While we are healthy, it is wise to enjoy we what can without offending God. The best way to enjoy anything is to do so by respecting God's law and pursuing what is pleasant within the parameters of God's design. Those who dishonor God with the good He provides will be judged (v.9). When life is lived for the glory of God according to the law of God in the love of God, there will always be the peace of God (v.10).

Life is full of both hard and happy things. We need not be bummed out by what is hard or disobedient because of what is happy. The question is: are you honoring God with what He has given to you? We all have to make choices with our life and resources. Those who honor God and seek to enjoy His blessings, according to His Word, live with hope.

Numbers 2; Psalm 36; Ecclesiastes 12; Philemon

While human beings make decisions and are responsible for every one of them, God is at work in the world accomplishing His purpose in all things. Those who trust God and His goodness and power live with hope. The book of Philemon is a powerful picture of the providence of God. It is a letter that was written by the Apostle Paul to a wealthy businessman in Colossae named Philemon. Paul was serving as a mediator and requesting that Philemon make peace with and receive back Onesimus, a former slave to Philemon, into his home. As God would have it, Onesimus met Paul while Paul was imprisoned, and Onesimus became a follower of Jesus. Having been made in a right relationship with God, Onesimus was responsible to be in right relational standing with everyone else (Romans 14:19).

Paul was not just requesting that Philemon accept Onesimus back into his home, but to accept Onesimus as his brother in Christ and to send Onesimus back to Paul as a missionary. Paul was asking Onesimus to do the right thing and go back, even though it may have cost him. Paul was also asking for Philemon to do the hard thing of giving forgiveness and looking forward to what God could do. Paul was asking Philemon to look at this situation with spiritual eyes and to think and act with a Kingdom-focused mindset.

Philemon was not just another Christian in Colossae. He was the property provider of the church. The church met in his home (v.1-3). Philemon was respected by the believers and Paul (v.4-7). Given Philemon's position of leadership, Paul could have demanded that Philemon do what Paul asked (v.8), but instead, Paul chose to make his request an appeal (v.9). Those in leadership of the church are often required to do what others can seemingly choose not to do. Christian leadership is servant leadership, and servant leadership is sacrificial. Paul requested that Philemon make peace with Onesimus and then allow Onesimus to return to Paul (v.10-14). It was the providence of God that allowed Onesimus' wrong decision to lead to his personal salvation (v.15-16). Now that Onesimus was a believer, Philemon was responsible to treat him as a brother in Christ, to forgive him, and bless him (v.17-22).

Paul made a huge request of Philemon. The world would see this action of Paul to be presumptuous and inappropriate. Paul knew it was an opportunity and a blessing for Philemon. We are never more like Jesus than when we are made uncomfortable and required to make sacrifices for the Kingdom of God.

In life we will often face difficult circumstances and be asked by God to do what would be considered an inconvenience by worldly standards. Giving forgiveness to someone who has wronged us is not easy. Giving up something we want so others can have what they need is challenging. Are you able to forgive people who have harmed you? Are you willing to make personal sacrifices for the growth and expansion of God's Kingdom? Do you see the demands of God to give and forgive as inconvenient or as an opportunity to be like Jesus? Those who trust God's providence and power are glad to give generously and will always have hope.

Numbers 3; Psalm 37; Song of Songs 1; Hebrews 1

Throughout life, we will always be in transition and forced to make decisions about the direction of our lives. The good news for God's children is that we can hold to certainties that are always true and that define our identity and purpose. Those who know whose they are and what it is they are supposed to do live with hope.

God provides a clear and compelling vision for life in Numbers 3. Those who live under the saving grace and authority of God must come to Him on His terms. Those who come to God will come because they have been called to Him by grace. Those who come to God will be given a specific role and purpose in His Kingdom.

God chose the tribe of Levi to serve as His priests. They were to serve the nation of Israel and function as mediators for the people. They alone were given access to the holy things of God, and they alone were permitted to serve in God's presence and provide the necessary sacrifices. They did what was necessary for the prayers of the people to be presented to God. The Levites were a picture of both the New Covenant church and Christ.

It is through Christ alone that a sinful human being can be made righteous and gain access to God. Any who attempt to approach God on their own merits or with their own religious practices will fail. Nadab the firstborn, and Abihu, the sons of Aaron, attempted to approach God with unauthorized fire and were killed for it (v.1-4). It is only through faith in the atoning sacrifice God prescribes that satisfies the just demands of His holy law that enables a person to approach God. God is holy, which makes Him dangerous to sinners. Any who come to Him must come by grace through faith in Jesus Christ.

Those who come rightly to God by faith in Christ alone in the new covenant of His blood are made members of the royal priesthood of God (1 Peter 2:9). By God's grace and for His glory, the Lord saves and then gifts each of His people to accomplish a specific purpose. As the Levite clans were each given a specific task to accomplish in service to God (v.5-39), so all of God's redeemed people in Christ are each gifted and given a specific destiny and divine purpose to accomplish in God's Kingdom.

Under the Old Covenant, the people had to pay a price for redemption. Rather than taking the firstborn among all of the people, the Levites became the substitute (v.40-51). Under the New Covenant of Christ, the price for redemption was paid by the blood of Jesus. God sent His only Son to be the substitutionary atonement for sinners. Now all who will repent of self-sufficiency and sin and simply trust that the life and death of Jesus provides the necessary means for salvation will be saved.

What God has offered to make a person holy and right before Him is merciful. Have you accepted the gift of God in Christ Jesus, or are you trying to make your own way in life? Are you willing to accept not only the salvation of God, but God's perfect plan for your life? The Lord has a purpose for each of His children. Those who live by faith and pursue God's purpose have hope.

Numbers 4; Psalm 38; Song of Songs 2; Hebrews 2

Finding forgiveness for sin is the most important thing a person will ever do. Without forgiveness there is no hope. While sin separates, grace unites. Those who gain forgiveness in Jesus are able to live with hope.

Forgiveness is found through repentance, which is a result of divine conviction. There are those who seek forgiveness because they are caught or because they want to minimize the severity of the consequences of their actions. They will often feign sorrow and ask for their indiscretions to be pardoned and their punishment minimized. True repentance comes from the heart and deeply desires to be made right with God. In Psalm 38, David revealed the process of forgiveness, the seriousness of sin, and the means of salvation.

Forgiveness begins with suffering (v.1-8). God is gracious and allows His children to suffer for sin, just as a good parent provides painful discipline to teach a child to avoid bad behavior. Suffering that accompanies sin gives a sinner a personal and powerful awareness of the significance of sin. Without pain people tend to make light of situations caused by sin. David experienced great pain because of his sin, which led him to look to God for grace. There was both a physical and emotional anguish within him.

What makes sin so serious is not just the personal pain it causes, but the relational brokenness it produces. David felt the separation that his sin had caused (v.9-14). Sin is deceptive. We often want to think that our sin will only harm *us*. The fact of the matter is this: sin always takes us further than we intended to go, costs us more than we wanted to pay, and gives us less than it promised. The cost is often shared by those we love and who love us the most.

The only way to gain freedom and healing from sin is by God's grace and mercy. God gives us what we do not deserve, which is grace, and withholds from us what we deserve, which is mercy. The only way to gain God's forgiveness is by looking to the Lord. David looked to the Lord, confessed his sin and genuine sorrow for what he had done, and trusted in God's promises (v.15-22). There is only one remedy for sin: Christ's redemption. Forgiveness is not simply overlooking sin. Sin demands justice. The means of salvation is the provision God made personally and practically when He took responsibility and suffered for our sin on the cross. Jesus died for our sin, but was raised and can now be looked to for life and hope.

Those who look to Jesus for salvation will not find justice withheld, but justice fulfilled. The just demands of the law have been met by Christ. David looked forward to Christ in faith and was saved, and we now look back to Jesus' death and resurrection by faith and are restored to a right standing with God. While there may be lingering natural consequences for sin, the relationship to God is made right through Jesus.

Sin is serious. Do you take your sin seriously? Are you looking to Christ to redeem and restore you? Without the forgiveness of God there is no hope. If we will confess our sin and by faith trust in Christ, we will discover the faithfulness of God to forgive us and cleanse us. Forgiven saints live with eternal hope.

Numbers 5; Psalm 39; Song of Songs 3; Hebrews 3

Godly marriages are meant to picture the Gospel. God has chosen to pursue, propose, and provide a way of life for His bride, the church. Those who enjoy a Godly marriage, which is pictured in the Gospel, live with hope.

Human beings are physical creatures, and the physical dynamic of a marriage relationship is crucial. The Song of Songs is an inspired poetic book intended to communicate the beautiful mystery of love between a husband and wife. The world would have us believe that physical intimacy is just a matter of touch. Song of Songs presents a broader and more compelling perspective on what it means for a husband and wife to experience the uniting of body, heart, and mind in marriage. Sex is to be confined within the context of marriage. Within that covenant, a man and a woman are free to trust, share, delight, and serve one another in Godly ways.

In Chapter 3, the bride-to-be was faced with a terrifying thought. She was frightened at the thought of being separated from the one she loved (v.1-3). One of the ways a person can be certain that the person they are considering for marriage is the one God has for them is to imagine being apart from that person and that thought causing them to be in anguish.

The young lady then imagined finding him. She pictured bringing him to her mother's home and calling upon her friends to hold her accountable to remain sexually pure in preparation for her marriage (v.4-5). A couple about to be married is truly blessed if they have trustworthy, Godly friends providing gracious accountability for them to help them remain sexually pure. Sex outside of marriage robs a couple of a great blessing.

Having provided Godly boundaries for their relationship, she imagined the day of her wedding (v.6-11). She was delighted. As young ladies picture their marriage day, they should be overwhelmed with delight and sense the dignity of the moment. By remaining sexually pure in their physical relationship, a couple getting married can look forward to their new life together knowing they have honored God in their pursuit of His plan.

Marriage is a picture of a Christian's relationship with Christ. The experience of this young woman resembles something of what a redeemed saint is to experience in Christ. The thought of being separated from Christ should terrify a believer. The idea that they would be disconnected from the redeemer and lover of their soul should produce tears and great fear. Being united to Christ and celebrating that dynamic union should provide great joy and elation. The second coming of Christ should produce excitement and anticipation. When Jesus comes for His bride, the people of God will finally and fully be with Him and they will live happily ever after.

Marriage is a gift from God. It blesses our personal and spiritual relationships. If you are married, are you delighting in your spouse? If you are not yet married, are you remaining sexually pure? Those who know Jesus are better prepared to experience a healthy marriage. A Christian marriage pictures the Gospel, and that unique love inspires hope.

Numbers 6; Psalms 40–41; Song of Songs 4; Hebrews 4

Living with confidence in God is crucial for all of God's children. There are plenty of obstacles to attaining the confidence that is freely available to all who believe in Jesus for salvation. The person who is able to trust God and His sovereign grace will rest in the hope of Jesus.

The writer of the book of Hebrews was faced with the daunting task of calling God's redeemed people to remain faithful to Him and confident in the provision of Christ in the midst of religious confusion and persecution. The original Jewish audience of this divinely inspired book of the Bible was in turmoil. They were looking to abandon their faith in Christ in favor of their former institutional systems based upon the Old Covenant. Inspired by the Spirit of God, the writer called these saints to realize the great gift they had been given in Christ and to understand that there is nothing to go back to. Chapter 4 is an explanation of how it is that Jesus Christ is truly the only option for redemption.

The chapter begins by showing the connection between the faithless who were saved out of Egypt and did not enter into God's rest and the original readers of Hebrews who were considering abandoning their personal faith in Jesus. Building on the argument established in chapter 3 and continuing to exposit Psalm 95, the writer called these Christians to maintain their personal faith in Christ. Those who came out of Egypt gave up on God and refused to believe in His provision and plan (v.1-3). Those who were called out of Egypt did not act in faith on what they had heard. They did not enter God's rest. God's rest comes to those who keep the faith.

The faith to be saved is based upon the finished work of Christ who died and was raised. Just as God rested on the seventh day, having established creation, so also a rest is now given for those who accept the finished work of Christ for salvation (v.4-7). This is a rest that already is, but is also still to come. The rest that Joshua led them to was not soul satisfying or eternal. The rest provided by Jesus was to come and now has come. The rest that has come is soul satisfying and eternal, but is not yet finalized (v.8-10). The coming of Christ will bring the final and full rest for God's people. God's people are those who have repented of sin and self-dependence for salvation and choose to trust only in Christ and His completed work for salvation.

Although salvation has come through Christ, faithful pursuit of this grace is still commanded (v.11). Disobedience is a real temptation, but the Word of God has the power to overcome the deceitfulness of the world, the flesh, and the Devil and dig down into the soul of God's people and free them to understand their own hearts and thoughts (v.12). The Lord is coming and judgment with Him (v.13). The righteous of God must remain faithful and avoid the errors of Israel.

It is easy enough to understand the plan of salvation. That plan of salvation must be received by faith personally and permanently. Do you trust in Christ alone to provide salvation? Are you living faithful to Christ? The person who is able to live by faith in the grace offered in Christ will always have hope.

Numbers 7; Psalms 42–43; Song of Songs 5; Hebrews 5

Coming to an understanding of God's Word takes work. God's people will always be in need of prayerful study in order to understand God's Word. Those who are willing to do the hard work of understanding and obeying God's Word live with hope.

One of the more challenging books to read in the Bible is the book of Numbers because of the amount of repetition it contains. Chapter 7 provides a repetitive explanation describing the days of the dedication of the Tabernacle. The gifts that were offered by each tribe were substantial. The purpose of the gifts was significant. The provisions for the sacrifices were necessary for the people to be in good standing with God. There is nothing inconsequential in this chapter. Although repetitive, the content is crucial and the importance of what took place should not be lost on the followers of Christ, who are called to be students of the Scriptures. What these leaders were doing may not seem to have a practical personal application or deeply devotional content for the lives of current readers, but the profound purpose of this time of dedication says something significant about God and His people.

This dedication says a great deal about God. It tells us that God is accessible to fallen, sinful people. God does not need humanity in order to be satisfied. He is God. In His three persons He is loved, praised, and honored. This dedication points to the fact that God is gracious and willing to be known by those who by nature would not seek to know Him. This dedication tells us that the means by which people have access to God requires an object of faith and an act of faith by people in order to know God rightly. The sacrificial system that was put in place through the construction of the Tabernacle and the ordering of the priesthood provided the objective means by which the people of God could be made right with God. In order for the people to know God and be right with Him, they had to have faith in God's provision. This dedication tells us that this God is holy. Only a blood sacrifice would provide atonement.

This dedication says a great deal about God's people. It tells us that they can have access to God. God revealed Himself to Moses, and through this Tabernacle, the people were given access to God. This dedication tells us that following God is not a matter of personal interest, but of personal obedience. This dedication tells us that God's people are to be led by Godly people and that God's people are expected to sacrifice for God's purpose. In response to the leadership of Moses and the Levites, the people had to make sacrifices that showed their faith in and love for God. Faith without sacrifice produces a shallow spiritual life. God calls and commands His people to make sacrifices. Those who give sacrificially are able to express their love to God in practical ways.

God is mysterious, but what He has revealed of Himself can be known and understood. Do you know God? Are you seeking to know Him more deeply through the study of His Word? By knowing and obeying God's Word a person lives with hope.

Numbers 8; <u>Psalm 44</u>; Song of Songs 6; Hebrews 6

In life, we will have difficult days, but we must never despair. Those who believe in Jesus and enjoy the saving faith provided by God never really have bad days. We have good days and better days, but in every circumstance we can be content because of what we know to be true. We know that God loves us, that God has a plan for what we are going through, that God is with us, and that God will work out His purpose in His time for the best outcome. Those who trust in God are able to live with hope.

There are times when we will be tempted to believe that God has forgotten us. The enemy will always be at work to deceive us and to lead us away from God. What makes this especially hard is the fact that God will often allow us to feel alone, but we are never alone. For His glory and according to His plan, God will allow His children to go through faith challenges. In those moments, Psalm 44 will serve as an encouragement. This Psalm teaches the steps to take when we are tempted to doubt God.

First, we must remember what God has done in the past to redeem, provide, and care for us (v.1-3). The Psalmist, joined by the entire nation, was able to speak of God's power that provided the victory that produced the nation that was then living in the Promised Land. They could not speak of their victory. It was not their victory. The victory was won by God's might.

Second, we must remember how we joined God in what He did to bring about His purpose (v.4-8). The life of faith is a life of activity. God's will is to bless the world through the work of His people. It is the faithful work of saints that accomplishes the will of God. All who have walked with God for any number of seasons can look back, as the Psalmist did, and remember times of activity, when they joined God in His work.

Third, we must remember that God brings redemption through suffering (v.9-22). Although these people had not broken the covenant made by God, they were being defeated by their foes (v.17). Obedience does not guarantee worldly success and comfort. It was only through Jesus' suffering that God's plan was accomplished. God's people will suffer in this world, but thankfully, this world is not our home.

Finally, we must remember that God must teach us to pray and through prayer train us to appreciate His blessings (v.23-26). Without desperate times that produce desperate prayers, we would tend to be spoiled children, thinking we deserved the good things God gives. It is often when the comforts of God are gone and we are made to feel alone that we learn to appreciate the kindness and mercy of God and the blessing of His presence. It is through prayer and authentic communication with God that we understand ourselves and God.

God is not happy about our suffering. He made us to live in paradise, but sin destroyed that pleasant place. Even though we must now live in the midst of suffering, we can live with confidence. God has not abandoned us. God has a plan for our trials and pain. Are you living confidently in the will of God? Those who trust in God are able to live with hope.

Numbers 9; Psalm 45; Song of Songs 7; Hebrews 7

God made us with physical bodies to honor Him. Human bodies are corrupted with sin, but they are still capable of providing pleasure to us and honor to God. Pleasure always has boundaries. A Godly gift used beyond its intended design is sin. Those who enjoy the pleasure of sex within the bounds of God's created purpose live with hope.

In Song of Songs 7 there are expressions and experiences intended to be enjoyed by a husband and wife, who are in the bonds of Biblical marriage. These poetic lines are filled with words that a husband and wife need to share with one another, experiences that model God's will for marriage, and attitudes that reflect God-honoring mutual delight. These words, experiences, and attitudes create what is known as romance. Romance is the ability to make a person feel as valuable as God already says he or she is. When a husband or wife is able to help the one they love to feel their value, they provide a blessing meant for marriage.

Physical intimacy is easy. Any healthy animal can have sex. God did not make human beings to simply act as animals. God made human beings to act according to His will, which will bring Him glory and great enjoyment to those He has made. When a man and woman love one another within the bounds of a marriage covenant, they have a freedom and a responsibility to express their love. When a husband speaks of the beauty of his wife to her, he provides her with what she needs and deserves from him (v.1-9). These words must be said about the right things, at the right time, and in the right way. Timely and touching words will create romance and appreciation (v.10-11).

Words are not enough to sustain romance. There must also be experiences with the appropriate attitude (v.12-13). It is a wise married couple that knows how to have fun and to experience romance. It is important that the activities that a husband and wife enjoy together are mutually edifying and are actualized with the right attitudes. When a husband and wife are grateful, joyful, and excited about his or her spouse, they create the right energy for a fun experience that produces romance.

This precious couple is picturing what the relationship with Christ and His bride is like. The church is the bride of Christ. Jesus loves His church (Ephesians 5:22-33). Under the covenant of grace, God's people are loved by Jesus and provide Him great honor and delight. One day this marriage will be consummated and Jesus will live happily ever after with His people (Revelation 19-22).

If you are married, it is crucial that you express your love, experience romance, and display a grateful attitude toward your spouse. A man making his wife feel as valuable as God already says she is and a wife doing the same for her husband honors God and makes a marriage romantic and enjoyable. For those who are married, are you experiencing romance? Christian, are you honoring Jesus and being faithful to Him and delighting in Him? Those who live faithfully to their marriage vows and to Christ live with hope.

Numbers 10; Psalms 46–47; Song of Songs 8; Hebrews 8

The confidence of a follower of Jesus is the solid, permanent, powerful, and fulfilled promise of God to save a people for His glory by being their personal savior and mediator. Those who hold to the promise God has made to save sinners will live with hope.

God promised He would save His people through His sacrifice (Genesis 3:15). He promised Abram that the whole world would be blessed through him and his family (Genesis 12:1-3). The rest of the Old Testament is an affirmation of this promise. Through the good times, when the people were faithful, and the bad times, when the people turned away, God's promise stood. In one of those bad times, God spoke through the prophet Jeremiah and renewed His promise. That promise in Jeremiah 31:31-34 is quoted in Hebrews 8. In this holy, inspired book of the Bible, God restates and explains how He has kept His promise and provided the only means of salvation through Jesus.

Jesus has established an eternal covenant by the power of His divine being (v.1-7). Jesus came and fulfilled what God promised in the Old Testament. Jesus is unlike the high priest of old. He is now seated at the right hand of God mediating on behalf of the people. His justifying work is done. It is finished. The atoning sacrifice made by the holy, infinite God has satisfied the just demands of God's law. Those who believe in Jesus now have direct access to God the Father. Those who are saved can approach God in the name of Jesus and know that He hears us, loves us, and is at work in us and for us.

This accomplished work of Jesus provided the means that fulfilled the promise of God (v.8-12). Now we, the people of God, have the presence of God in us. We are filled with the Spirit of God and the law is on our hearts. We are convicted and comforted by God. We know God. God knows us. What a thought! As God's people we are experiencing life in between the "already" and the "not yet." We know Christ now, but not as we will. In this in-between time, we hold on to the promise of God and live in light of His merciful grace. That merciful grace makes it possible for us to live rightly with God.

The new covenant of Christ makes the old covenant obsolete (v.13). What a shocking thought that must have been to those first-century Hebrews. There is nothing to go back to. Without Christ there is no life and no hope. Institutional religion built on human mediators cannot save. Only Jesus can save. Those Jesus saves are fully saved. There is no other way to God.

We human beings have a tendency to want to sidestep God and create our own means of salvation and rules for living. That was the reason humanity originally sinned. Those who choose to trust in human institutions and religious rituals have no hope. Do you trust completely in the finished work of Christ? Are you living by faith under the new covenant promise of God? Have you already experienced salvation? Are you looking forward to the final restoration, when Jesus returns? Those who trust in Jesus' finished salvific work live with hope.

Numbers 11; Psalm 48; Isaiah 1; Hebrews 9

An ungrateful heart is like poison. Not only does it sicken the soul of the thankless person, but it can influence others to be ungrateful as well. Once a person begins to question God's character, thankfulness disappears. Ingratitude typically causes hard-heartedness toward God and a disobedient life. Those who are able to appreciate the kindness of God and honor God for His grace and mercy live with hope.

The children of Israel that had been liberated from Egypt had every reason to be grateful to God. They had been in bondage for over four hundred years. Their prayers were heard by God and He provided a savior, Moses. Having had God's wrath "passover" them because of the blood of a lamb, crossed through the Red Sea, and given the law of God, they were ready to enter God's rest in the land of promise. They had been saved, baptized, and directed toward home, and yet they were unsatisfied.

In Numbers 11, the people complained against God and experienced the consequences for their actions. Moses' prayer recorded in the verse preceding this chapter in Exodus 10:35-36 would lead us to think that the people were happy and excited to be on their way home, but they were not happy. They were frustrated. Frustration is caused whenever reality does not meet expectations. The people clearly expected their lives to be easier, but the journey was hard and so they complained (v.1a). God's anger burned against them (v.1b). The people asked Moses to intervene, and he prayed and the plague by fire died out, but the people did not learn to appreciate what God was doing for them (v.2-3). The grace of God did not create grateful hearts in them.

A group of disgruntled leaders began to deceive the people and to lead them to be unjustly angry with God and Moses, and they roused the anger of God (v.4-15). Moses was frustrated and spoke to God about the burden that was his to bear, so God commanded Moses to gather seventy elders to help Moses lead the people and then God gave them the meat they asked for in abundance (v.16-32). The abundance of provision was not only an act of kindness, but a display of God's power. There is no record of thanks being given to God by the people. This ingratitude led to God's wrath being poured out on the people in the form of a plague (v.33-35).

These people had been given the salvation they had prayed for, the leaders they needed, the law, and the presence of God, but that was not enough for them. They wanted life to go the way they wanted it to, and when it didn't, they dishonored God and made what could have been a joyous occasion into a time of sorrow. If we are not careful, rather than giving God praise for His great grace and goodness, we will dishonor God with an ungrateful heart.

The only way to maintain a grateful heart is to focus on the kindness of God and His provision. Have you received salvation in Jesus? Are you walking by faith toward heaven with a grateful heart? Thankless hearts are faithless hearts. Those who appreciate God's goodness will focus on His grace and live with hope.

Numbers 12–13; Psalm 49; Isaiah 2; Hebrews 10

It may not often feel short, but life is short. Once we see our lives from the perspective of eternity, earthly things will not seem as important or as imposing. The person who is able to look at their life in any situation and remember that Jesus alone can satisfy their soul will live with hope.

In Psalm 49:5-6, the writer poses one of the all-time great questions: "Why should I fear?" Apparently, people had cheated the writer, and there were show-offs bragging about how much money they made, and he was tempted to be intimidated. There were some rich folks that were defining themselves by their resources that were making him feel he might have missed out on something. Having thought it through by studying a proverb, he came to specific conclusions about his own beliefs and poetically clarified his thoughts about life and what is truly most important (v.1-4).

His first point is straightforward and striking: no one cheats death (v.7-9). No one lives forever on this fallen rock orbiting the sun. It does not matter how smart or stupid a person may be. Everyone dies (v.10). Even the wealthy will one day reside in the ground that they once claimed to be theirs (v.11). The person with enviable pomp will lose all that was once owned because death does not receive our stuff with us. Our bodies are like those of animals. They die (v.12). It is just a matter of fact.

While all people die, not all people die the same way. There are those who will die who have not trusted in the grace of God and have squandered their lives pursuing what cannot save them and what they cannot keep (v.13-14). Those who die under the grace of God will be ransomed from the darkness of death and discover a new life in the light of God's presence when their life ends (v.15). Having lived by faith in the presence of God, the redeemed of God will die in the faith that saves them and welcomes them into God's presence.

The Psalm ends with a pointed and practical message for the redeemed of God: do not get caught up in keeping score like those who have no eternal hope. Rather than being afraid that something has been missed in life, if we were not able to gain riches, the wise look to what is gained eternally in God's grace (v.16-17). No one takes their stuff past death's door. The only things that last and that truly matter are the things that matter to God. Those who trust in wealth might think themselves blessed because they enjoy comfort briefly. Eternity will not be comfortable for them (v.18-19). People who have no real sense of the reality of God and the eternal matters of heaven and place their hope in earthly riches will die with a legacy of foolishness (v.20). With eternal souls made for love, people can only be satisfied by the eternal love of God in Jesus.

The world is full of good things to enjoy. There is nothing wrong with having resources and wealth. What is wrong is hoping in created things to satisfy the soul. What defines you as a person? What are you living for and looking to for happiness? Those who look beyond the things of earth and take the broader view of eternity in mind will make wise decisions and live with hope.

Numbers 14; Psalm 50; Isaiah 3–4; Hebrews 11

Everyone lives by faith. The questions that each person has to answer are: in whom or in what do I place my faith, and how will I live out my faith? God is at work to fulfill His eternal purpose in the lives of those who believe in Him. Those who trust in Jesus as the object of their faith live with hope.

The prophet Isaiah was tasked with a painful project. He was called by God to prophesy to a people who would not listen and could not see the error of their ways (Isaiah 6:9-10). The Israelites had been given a great blessing. The Lord chose them to fulfill His saving purpose for the world. God promised Abraham that the whole world would be blessed through His progeny (Genesis 12:1–3). God also promised David that his throne would be the means through which the world would receive salvation (2 Samuel 7:12–16). God provided this blessed people with land, leadership, and love. Rather than have faith in God and serve Him alone, as His grateful children, the people turned away from God. Instead of turning to God, they placed their faith in false gods. Their rebellion led to God's discipline.

The discipline God gives to His covenant people is different than the punishment He brings to those who are not His children. Isaiah 3-4 explains the horrific discipline that God unleashed on the children of Israel. The discipline God brought to His people was laced with hope. While Isaiah is not a prophecy of good tidings to the majority of the original readers, it is a message of hope to all who believe in Jesus. This divine message, through this faithful prophet, points to the fact that when we are faithless, God is faithful. He disciplines, but He does not abandon. The Lord works graciously to accomplish His plan and bring glory to Himself through those who have faith in Him.

The people in Isaiah's day were described as wealthy people with wanton eyes being led by liars and faithless leaders. The consequences of their actions would be desolation and deprivation (3:1–4:1). Their suffering would not only serve as a consequence to their sin, but also purify and pave the way for the few faithful left as a remnant to experience God's favor. God blesses obedient children who have faith in their good Father (v.10). Obedience is not the means, but the proof of faith in Jesus.

The salvation that Abraham, David, and the prophets were promised would finally come through "the branch of the Lord." This branch is the promised Messiah. Jesus Christ came but is coming again. When Jesus returns, there will be eternal blessings. The people of God will finally be fully holy. The filth of the fallen world will be forgotten as it passes away and gives way to the new heaven and new earth. The presence of the King of Kings and Lord of Lords will be a canopy that covers all and brings restoration to the world and to the faithful of God (4:2-6).

Only those who have faith in Jesus enjoy the confidence that comes with trusting in God's provision. Is Jesus Christ the object of your faith? Are you living in light of Christ's return? Are you enjoying the blessings that come through obeying God's Word? Those who believe in Jesus live with hope.

Numbers 15; Psalm 51; Isaiah 5; Hebrews 12

There is a powerful motivation that comes with being a part of a movement that has impacted the world and that has an inspiring history of heroes. For millennia men and woman have been joining God in the race of faith. Those who join this movement of Jesus Christ and run the race of faith not only follow in the footsteps of a multitude that now rests in eternal glory, but they live and die with hope.

Hebrews 11 is a listing of Old Testament heroes. Those examples are given as a model and an inspiration for all who seek to know and live for God. In Hebrews 12 the metaphor of a race provides inspiration to every generation of saints who choose to run the race of faith (v.1-2). The race requires dedication, devotion, and endurance. It will be difficult but not impossible. Christ came and for the joy set before Him, He endured the cross and provided the salvation promised by God. Now all who follow Him can run the race of faith.

Having Christ as our leader, we can face the hostility and sustain our stride (v.3-4). By looking to and trusting in Jesus, the faithful can run and not grow weary, as God promised (Isaiah 40:31). We will often be tempted to give up, but we can always find reasons to go forward in Christ.

Because of the challenges, discipline will be required. God calls us to discipline ourselves (1 Corinthians 9:27). When we refuse to discipline ourselves or when we are not capable of getting ourselves ready for the terrain that lies ahead, God steps in to provide for us what we need to be able to make it through the next stage of the journey. He is like a good father. He disciplines His children for their own good (v.5-11). It is never pleasant, but it is always necessary. God knows what is best for us. He knows what is coming our way.

It is vital that God's people trust the Lord in those times of discipline, but also take the initiative to continue to provide self-discipline. There are spiritual exercises that must be done that help us stay in the race (v. 12-17). We must strengthen our bodies to endure temptation and never bow to what our flesh wants or to what the world offers. We must choose the path that will not cause us to stumble. We must make peace and not allow roots of bitterness or footholds of sin to trip us up.

The blood of Jesus makes pure the souls of all who believe. Those who approach Him apart from the redeeming grace that is received by faith in Christ will be consumed by His holy judgment (v. 18-29). God is a consuming fire. He will not be mocked. He will not be patronized. He will not be deceived.

It is true that the race of faith is hard, but it is also true that it is a great privilege to get to run the race. There are a multitude of people who have gone before us. There is not much that any of us will go through that our predecessors have not had to endure. Our main model is Christ. Are you following Jesus? Are you running the race of faith? While comfort may seem appealing in the moment, those who choose to run the race of faith live and die with hope.

Numbers 16; Psalms 52–54; Isaiah 6; Hebrews 13

Pride is a poison to the soul. We humans have a strange capacity to think more of ourselves and less of others. We are often far more forgiving of ourselves than others. Pride always leads to failure. The person who is willing to submit to God and humbly serve Him will live with hope.

Moses was a humble servant. Sure, he made some big mistakes. He killed a man (Exodus 2:12) and then, many years later, he dishonored God in front of the assembly of God's people by striking a rock rather than speaking to it, as God had commanded (Numbers 20:11). He did both of these things because of pride. Although those were really bad things, he was generally a very humble guy. In Numbers 16, Moses' humility and dependency on God was demonstrated when a mob led by deceived men acted in pride.

Life was not turning out the way Korah and many of the people had thought it would. They were out of Egypt, but they were now wandering in the desert. The Lord was providing for their needs, but that was not enough for them. The leadership of Moses and Aaron became an issue of frustration. Korah, along with a large crowd of influential people, came to Moses and accused him of going too far with his authority and not recognizing that everyone else was just as holy as he and Aaron were(v.1-3). Moses' humble response of bowing did not affect them (v.4), but he did not react with pride. Moses was wise. He turned to the Lord and spoke the truth (v.5-11). Seeking God's face and speaking the truth will honor God and liberate leaders.

Not only did Moses have to deal with Korah and his mob, but he also had to deal with the son of Eliab. They blamed Moses for the people's desert wandering (v.12-14). This made Moses mad, but he turned to God with a clear conscience (v.15). A clear conscience provides great confidence.

Having opposed God by opposing God's leader, Korah and his companions were destroyed (v.16-40). The judgment of the Lord is a frightening thing. Seeing others destroyed for sin is not something saints should desire. These people were deceived. Their poor decisions led to their destruction. Every person is accountable to God. It is the work of the redeemed to seek to be ministers of reconciliation and to call all sinners to repentance in order that they might repent and enjoy peace with God and His will.

The day after Korah and his company of conspirators were destroyed, there was another riot. The people blamed Moses for the deaths of these "people of the Lord" (v.41). Like Korah's rebellion, this was not against Moses. This was an attack on God. This attack roused the wrath of God and the Lord unleashed a plague (v.42-45). Rather than sit idly by, Moses sought to provide salvation (v.46-50). This is what Jesus did for us. While we were in rebellion, Jesus came and atoned for our sin (Romans 5:8).

Every disciple of Jesus is to be a minister of reconciliation (2 Corinthians 5:11-21). We are to serve where God puts us. Are you serving God by being a humble follower and leader? Do you have a gracious heart toward sinners? Humble saints willing to serve God will live with hope.

Numbers 17–18; <u>Psalm 55</u>; Isaiah 7; James 1

Betrayal by a loved one or friend is one of the worst experiences in life. Something deep in us is hurt when someone we trust turns against us. There will always be conflicts and disagreements over issues and decisions. That is just how life is. Betrayal is not disagreeing. Betrayal is pretending to be for someone or to care for someone when actually acting in ways and speaking in ways that are detrimental or harmful to that person. Those who trust in the Lord always have a faithful friend in Him and will live with hope.

The Bible provides many examples of how to live in the midst of betrayal. Jesus, the Son of God, was betrayed by a dear friend. Paul, the great missionary and apostle, was betrayed by some who had once claimed to be Christians. David, the poet king, was betrayed by Saul and many others. Learning to deal wisely with betrayal is an unfortunate necessity. Psalm 55 provides insight into how we can survive it.

An instinct some may have is to simply flee from the situation. That is what David, the writer of Psalm 55, wanted to do (v.1-8). David prayed and talked about his problem and admitted to God that he would prefer to run away. Running away from a problem is never wise. Once we start running, we won't stop. Running away may occur differently for different people. The problem with running away is that no matter where you go, the world is still broken and you are still you.

Rather than run from his enemies, David turned to God for help. In turning to God he laid out his situation and asked for divine intervention (v.9-21). By speaking of the works done by those who had betrayed him, David made a case for justice. Justice is a double-edged sword. It is always wise to make sure that the justice we are seeking for others is also the justice we can live by and be held accountable to. David had a heart for God and was able to ask for justice because he was not guilty of the acts he claimed his enemies had perpetrated against him.

David had apparently done nothing wrong. He was living out his divine responsibility. Like Jesus who lived a holy life but was betrayed by Judas, David was also betrayed by a friend. The betrayal of a friend is worse than that of an enemy. We expect enemies to betray us. When a trusted friend betrays with a kiss or by pretending to be for you while actually speaking or feeling ill against you, it hurts. The only place to find solace, when reconciliation of the wrong is not plausible, is to go to God. We can cast our burden on God (v.22). To trust in God means to trust in His timing to deal with our adversaries. He can be trusted to do what is right and best.

In life we will all get hurt by people we trusted. It is good to know we can always trust God. Are you trusting God with your pain or are you seeking solace in drugs, pornography, work, or something else? Worldly means of escape will only make things worse. Those who trust in the Lord always have a faithful friend in Him and will live with hope.

Numbers 19; Psalms 56–57; <u>Isaiah 8:1–9:7</u>; James 2

There will always be secondhand substitutes the world will offer and the flesh will desire that can be turned to as alternatives for trusting in God. Only those who depend on Jesus will have hope.

Sin will take you further than you intended to go, cost you more than you wanted to pay, and give you less than it promised. Sin is deceptive. It makes us think we are in control. It makes us feel important. Sin soothes our egos in the beginning. Those feelings do not last. Sooner or later the consequences of trusting in something other than God will set in and cause suffering. There were many great people in the Bible who were deceived, just as Israel was during the days of Isaiah's ministry. Isaiah 8:1–9:7 reveals the emptiness of godlessness and the fullness of life in Christ.

Isaiah's ministry was anything but enjoyable. He was responsible for prophesying the Assyrian attack that was coming, and he had it attested to by two trusted witnesses (v.1-2). His poor wife became a prophetess by giving birth to a son whose name spoke of the coming invasion. God's judgment was coming (v.3-4). The people had chosen to trust Assyria rather than God, and now they would pay for it. The way they trusted Assyria is the way we are tempted to trust in sin instead of God. The consequences are catastrophic.

Sin always takes us further than we wanted to go. The Assyrians would not stop where the people of Judah wanted them to. No, the Assyrians would flood the land and swell up to their necks (v.5-10). This is what sin does. It does not stop when we want it to. Sin always has a ripple effect. It contaminates everything. The sad part is that our sin does not just impact our lives. It impacts the lives of those who love us.

Sin always costs you more. The Assyrians seemed like a safe bet, but they were, like all sin is, a dangerous snare. God is a trusted sanctuary. God ordered Isaiah not to support the Assyrian treaty, but rather to speak of the safety of God. Rather than seeing God for who He is, the people perceived God to be offensive and a cause for stumbling (v.11-15). Sin tarnishes our view of God.

Sin gives less than it promises. The Assyrians seemed like people who could be trusted. In reality they were treacherous barbarians. Sin is too. The Assyrians were promising safety, but they were going to plunge the people into darkness. The pain of their circumstances would cause the people to turn on the king of Judah and on God (v.16-22). Sin deceives.

God saves people out of sin. The land of Zebulun, Naphtali, and Galilee, located in the north, were the first to suffer the Assyrian attack. When Christ came, He came among them. Emmanuel was raised there (9:1). He brought light (v.2). He brought joy and gladness (v.3). He brought freedom (v.4). He brought provision (v.5). Jesus is the promised savior of the world (v.6-7).

Each person must choose between what sin gives and what God gives. What are you depending on to get you through life and death? Have you made a treaty with sin? All who repent, that is turn away from sin and turn to and believe in Jesus, will be saved. Those who depend on Jesus have hope.

Numbers 20; Psalms 58–59; Isaiah 9:8–10:4; James 3

When death took hold of Christ, it released us and we were made free by grace through faith in Christ alone. The redeemed of God can now live in Jesus' love. Those who enjoy a genuine passion for Jesus live with hope.

Genuine love is revealed by words, attitudes, and actions. Love does not exist because a person says they love or because they demonstrate some of the characteristics of love. When a person genuinely loves Jesus, their lives will reflect that love, and the consequences of their love will yield the qualities that God commands in His law. James 3 provides a collection of some of the qualities that are made manifest in the lives of those who take delight in the person of Jesus Christ.

There will be a language used that reflects the sweetness and purity of Jesus (v.1-12). Harsh and crude words originate from a proud or angry heart. The vocabulary and character of our conversations are determined by the condition of our heart. If we have a heart for God and have a deep care for Christ, it will be revealed in the way we talk. Those who struggle with using foul language, with gossiping, or with being critical of other people will often attempt to overcome their behavior by stifling their words. This only works so long as they are in control. The moment they are faced with a circumstance that unsettles them or knocks them off balance, the muzzle gets removed and the profanity and evil flies out of their hearts through their lips and into the world.

There will be delight in giving God praise. When God becomes the focal point of our lives, it changes the orientation of our affections. Rather than living for our own glory and honor, we enjoy seeing our God and Master receive praise and His purposes accomplished. A life that is centered on self and that is seeking to gain power, pleasure, popularity, and possessions will be filled with greed and corruption. It is inevitable. This is a dark and destructive way (v.13-16).

There will be wisdom in attitudes and actions. Whatever is in us will sooner or later come out. When Christ is in us, His purity, peace, gentleness, reasonableness, and mercy will be seen in our actions and heard in our words (v.17). The end result will be a life that lives in and pursues peace with others (v.18). This is the life that is sustained by grace and mercy. It experiences genuine joy in the best and worst circumstances in life.

What we love will have a huge impact on how we live. If we love the things of this world, then we will think, feel, and act like people of the world who are separated from God. A life without God is lost and broken. It exists in darkness and pursues what cannot be kept. What are you pursuing with your life? Are you living with a genuine love for God? The person who chooses to love God in response to God's love revealed in the cross will have a strong sense of satisfied delight. By focusing on Jesus and His goodness, our words and deeds will reflect His goodness. This attitude of gratitude and words of grace will come naturally from redeemed Spirit-filled hearts. The presence of Christ changes everything. Those who receive God's love by grace through faith in Jesus alone will live with hope.

Numbers 21; Psalms 60–61; Isaiah 10:5–34; James 4

The Way of the Lord is not always an easy way, but it is the Way of life, and it is along this Way where God guides and provides for His people. We will face trials and temptations along the Way, but God has a plan for everything we must endure. Those who remain humble and grateful will live with hope on the Way.

Israel's journey from Egypt to the Promised Land provides insight for all of God's people for how to remain in God's will and overcome the challenges that must be faced. In Numbers 21, God's people had to deal with both external and internal issues. We need to learn from their choices and experiences. We also need to understand what God did on their behalf and gain a greater sense of who God is and how it is He will be at work in the lives of His people today.

Israel was being led by God, but that did not keep the king of Arad from attacking them and taking some of the people hostage (v.1). The Lord ultimately provided the victory through His people, but it was still a battle (v.2-3). God is with us, but Satan is on the prowl. Our Good Shepherd is leading us through difficulties and dangers. We must always be ready for the attacks that are bound to come and stay close to Jesus, who saves us.

Through the battles and challenges, we must fight against having a negative attitude. The children of Israel chose to focus their attention on the negative (v.4-5). As a consequence for their disrespect, God sent poisonous snakes that bit the people and many died (v.6). Once the people confessed their sin (v.7), God provided grace. The Lord had Moses lift up a bronze snake, and all who looked upon it by faith were healed (v.8-9). Jesus later used this story to explain the salvation He had come to bring (John 3:14-15). Salvation now comes to all who will look to Jesus to be saved by faith from the consequence of their sin.

Before we are aware of our need, God already has the plan for how to provide for us. God knew the children of Israel would need water and He provided it for them (v.10-20). In response to His faithfulness, the people sang praise. So today, God's people are to gather in their local church and celebrate God's provision by singing praise to Him for His spiritual, mental, emotional, and physical provisions.

We must stay on the path God calls us to. While it may seem easier to go another way, it is not wise. Along the way, Israel had to deal with attacks from Arad, and later, from the Amorites and Bashan (v.21-35). The people may have wondered if they were going the wrong way, considering they had so much resistance. Resistance is to be expected. God's enemy does not want God's people to accomplish God's will. God also wants us to bring Him glory by living by faith and trusting in His power, as we face trials and challenges of many kinds. This is the Way of God.

We will often be tempted to get frustrated and be afraid. God wants us to trust Him. Are you walking the narrow way trusting Jesus? Do you praise Him for His provision? The Way is not easy, but those who walk it live with hope.

Numbers 22; Psalms 62–63; Isaiah 11–12; James 5

While spiritual warfare may be one of the most overlooked but most consequential challenges in life, in reality, all of life is difficult and dangerous on this fallen planet. Thanks to God, the children of God can rest assured the Lord will provide for His people. Those who look to God for help live with hope.

David was a man who always seemed to be dealing with difficulties and danger. As a child, he was facing bears and lions to protect his flocks. As a young man, he was fighting giants, Philistines, and running from a crazy king. As an older man, he was battling sin and its consequences. As an old man, he had family issues. He was always under duress. His thoughts and prayers in Psalm 62–63 give hope to us all. If this man with these problems could have confidence in this God in the midst of his circumstances, we can too. David found hope in God's salvation (Psalm 62) and in the satisfaction that God alone can give to a soul (Psalm 63).

God provides when the time is right (62:1). The enemies of life will always be present and appear to threaten us (v.3-4). Life is short and no earthly thing gained by good or evil can save (v.9-10). God alone can provide what is needed. David described God as his rock and salvation (v.2). God alone can sustain us and hold us and will not be moved. He is salvation. David also described God as his fortress and refuge (v.6-7). The Lord is a place of hiding and safety. There is nothing that can overcome God. All that comes at His people comes with His permission and for His purpose. We can know God can and will step in and provide what is best at just the right time. We are not alone. We are loved. God cares for us, and we are saved through obedient faith (v.11-12).

Those who seek God discover His goodness and kindness (63:1). We seek Him because he alone can satisfy the soul (v.1). God has given every human being an eternal soul. That soul is heavy and spacious. Eternity is weighty and unending. No created thing can carry the burden or fill the space of an eternal soul. The only way an eternal soul can be sustained and fully supplied is with an eternal source. God alone can gratify the great need of humanity. This occurs when we worship God by faith and see Him as He is in His glory and greatness (v.2-4). This occurs when we meditate upon God by faith and remember how He has provided in the past and kept His promises (v.5-8). This occurs when we consider the justice of God and see Him as the righteous King over all (v.9-11). The grace of God makes it possible for the children of God to be made right with God and be given the Spirit of God who fills the soul of a believer.

It is not hard to get overwhelmed with the realities of life. Those who trust in Jesus have been given the ultimate gift of God – Himself. God alone is what we long for and need. Do you trust in God to be your strength and salvation? Do you truly worship Him, delight in Him, and stand in awe of Him? Those who look to God for help live with hope.

Numbers 23; Psalms 64–65; Isaiah 13; 1 Peter 1

While God loves and is tender toward His redeemed people, those outside of His grace will be subject to His justice. It is a horrible thing to stand guilty before God. His love is everlasting. His grace is unending. His mercy knows no boundaries. His peace is permanent. His light does not go out. His comfort is perfect. But His wrath is also everlasting. His condemnation does not end. His justice is boundless. His curse is catastrophic. The darkness of hell is all-consuming. Those who walk with God by grace live with hope.

It is no surprise that the world makes light of God and sin. In the pride of sin, humanity has come up with phrases like "the man upstairs" to minimize the terror of who God is. The God of the Bible is dangerous. Yes, He is loving and benevolent, but He is holy. God's holiness demands justice. No one will escape Him.

The people of the world and the nations all go about their business seeking to do what is seemingly in their own best interest. The nation of Babylon is an example of all nations. Like all nations, God had a plan for it. Babylon was to be the tool that God used to discipline His people (Jeremiah 51:20-23). This nation and each of its rulers and all of its inhabitants were responsible for their own decisions. It is not that God made them do anything. In His providence God chose them, but in their own hearts they made decisions that they were held accountable for (Jeremiah 51:24). Isaiah 13 gives details concerning the judgment that would befall this nation. God's judgment on them is like the judgment that comes to all who live and die in sin.

Interestingly, Babylon was not even a world power when Isaiah's prophecy was made. The nation, its rulers, and its people had not yet accomplished the evil that would be done. God is all-knowing. He is timeless. He sees what cannot be seen by finite creatures living in sequential time. He speaks of what is and what will be by His infinite knowledge. This is what makes His judgment perfect. All of the evidence is known by Him before it comes to be. He is also fair. God gives warnings. God told Adam and Eve of the consequences of eating the fruit. God announced the coming flood through Noah for 100 years. The Bible tells of the second coming of Christ and His judgment. God made known His judgment of Babylon before their actions were done. Isaiah 13 tells of the judgment that is to befall the sinful nation and people.

When it comes to the judgment of God, we have to make one of three decisions. One, we can dismiss it as false. Two, we can accept the judgment that is to come, and with pride and disrespect, we can defy God. We can stand in judgment on Him for His judgment of us. Third, we can humble ourselves and cry out for mercy. We can seek grace and find it in Jesus Christ. We can be rescued from our sin. We can be given new eternal life.

God is gracious and just. What is your stance toward God? You can be foolish, arrogant, or humble. Judgment is coming! Have you received forgiveness through Jesus? Those who walk with God by grace through faith in Jesus live with hope.

Numbers 24; Psalms 66–67; Isaiah 14; 1 Peter 2

Each person on the planet has a calling and destiny. God has placed each of us in the world in a specific place for a specific purpose. Those who live in the presence of God through the grace of Jesus in the power of the Holy Spirit face life's challenges with hope.

Writing to a people that were facing challenges of many kinds, Peter explained how the people needed to view themselves and their life from the perspective of Jesus Christ in 1 Peter 2. He did not downplay the hardship each person would face. He wrote in view of their hardships and gave God's people the truth needed in order for them to see beyond what was happening to them to what God had called them to be.

Peter used different metaphors to help God's people understand their unique place in His grace. While we are all living in a specific moment in history, we are also living out an eternal plan that is bigger than our solitary life. Christians are children of the King of heaven, members of His holy dwelling, and citizens of a nation that will never end. As God's children, we are to put away the ways of the world and consume the richness of the goodness of God's truth (v.1-3). Each Christian is a stone in the spiritual house of God. We are now building our lives in connection with other redeemed people and living as a single reality that houses the hope of the world (v.4-8). As a set apart people, we are a nation under the headship of Jesus (v.9-12).

The calling of God is for every Christian to live in the world, but not as the world. This means we subject ourselves to the authorities given to rule us in this life while maintaining our ultimate devotion to God. Our devotion to God will actually make us more effective participants in the world (v.13-20). We are not to make excuses and use our faith as a means to get out of the hard work associated with our place in the world. Instead, as God's redeemed and grace empowered people, we are to serve in the Spirit of Christ. Jesus chose to suffer in order to accomplish the eternal purpose of His life. He did not complain or make excuses. He laid down His life to save us. His life and death made the way for all who believe to be healed and come under the Shepherd of our souls (v.21-24). Christians are to serve others and show our genuine faith in our attitudes and actions. This makes us like Christ.

Negativity and a victim's attitude have no place in the Christian life. God is in control. We are where we are for a divine purpose. Whether in wealth or poverty, in a free nation or under oppression, living with health or sickness, we each are to display the confidence that Christ gives. By showing respect to those in power over us and doing our work with excellence, we please our Master, Jesus Christ.

We will always be tempted to care more for our comfort than our calling in Christ. We must work hard to keep a Christ-centered focus. Are you living each day to pursue your purpose in Christ? Are you revealing the character of a redeemed saint who is a citizen of heaven? The people of Christ face challenges with confident hope.

Numbers 25; Psalm 68; Isaiah 15; 1 Peter 3

What we do with our lives is a reflection of what we long for and desire. Decisions are rarely completely cognitive. What we allow to impact our affections will have a dramatic impact on our behavior. The person who loves God and wants to know Him, please Him, and participate in life with Him will obey Him with hope.

In Numbers 25, there are two men making decisions based upon their desires. One was Zimri and the other was Phinehas. Although they were from different tribes that served different purposes in the life of the nation of Israel, both of them were Israelites. Both had access to the truth of the Gospel. Both knew the story of God's redemptive plan. Both could see the Tabernacle and the cloud by day and fire by night. Both were fed by the manna from heaven. Both drank from the water that was provided in the desert. Both were without excuse before God and expected to honor the Lord and join Him on the journey to the Promised Land and worship Him alone.

Zimri saw the miraculous hand of God, but he was seduced, like many others, by the detestable religious activity of the Moabites. Their deity was Baal. It was a fertility god, and the worship experience involved all kinds of sexual immorality. Israel was being tempted to pursue the desires of the flesh rather than devotion to God. Many were seduced (v.1-2). This rightly angered God, and in His wrath God released a plague upon the people and ordered those who were practicing this evil to be killed (v.3-5). As this order was being given and the plague was in progress, Zimri brought Cozbi, a Midianite woman, among the Israelite people to his home (v.6). This is how sin works. First, we are drawn to it. Next, we go to it. Finally, we bring it home to us and the sin impacts not only our lives, but the lives of everyone in our family.

Phinehas was a righteous man. He had a passion for God and His glory. When he saw Zimri and the woman in the midst of the camp, he obeyed God's order to enact justice. He killed both Zimri and Cozbi (v.7-8). This was a just act. By the time Zimri was killed, some twenty-four thousand people had died from the plague (v.9). This sin, like all sin, was serious. What we see Phinehas do is what we are to do with sin. We are to kill it. We are not to tolerate it in our lives. Using the Word of God as a sword, we are to stab it with truth.

God blessed Phinehas for his faith (v.10-15). He also ordered the Israelites to act with the same zeal as Phinehas. They were to attack the Midianites and learn to despise them (v.16-18). Phinehas was like Christ. He saved the people through His works. Like Christ is to us, Phinehas became the model of behavior for the people. Christ is our model. Followers of Jesus are to fight against sin. It is a spiritual battle that can only be won with faith, zeal, passion for God, and dedication to the Lord.

We all make decisions based upon our desires. What is feeding your desire? Are you focused on the things of God revealed in His Word? Those who learn to hate sin and love Jesus will live with hope.

Numbers 26; Psalm 69; Isaiah 16; 1 Peter 4

One of the greatest comforts in life is to know that God cares about us and will be with us. We do not have a God that is unacquainted with our sorrows. God understands what it is to be human. Those who trust in Jesus will suffer with hope.

The Old Testament is filled with promises, pictures, and prophecies about the coming of Jesus. Many of the Psalms are Messianic. They either provide a prophecy or a veiled reference to Jesus Christ. Psalm 69 gives insight into the trauma of the Messiah in the circumstances surrounding His giving of His life as the atoning sacrifice for sin. It pictures the physical, emotional, and spiritual situation that Jesus was in as He showed His eternal love (John 15:13). While His death gives the redeemed of God healing, the process of His death also gives us hope because His very real human experience lets us know that He understands what we are going through.

God understands and empathizes with our physical pain. David, the writer of Psalm 69, experienced many harsh seasons in his life. He was a hunted man, although He was the king of Israel. What he went through in his body foreshadowed what Christ would endure (v.1-4, 21), minus the sin (v.5). Jesus was overwhelmed with pain. His body was devastated with physical blows. As He died on the cross, His pain was excruciating.

God understands and empathizes with our emotional pain. David was abandoned by those he loved and chastised by those who hated him (v.6-12). The zeal for God's dwelling was overwhelming to David (v.9). Jesus was abandoned by His disciples on the night of His passion. His enemies gloated over Him as He died. Although His zeal was for the dwelling of God (John 2:13-22), none understood His words until after He had been raised. God's children will endure hatred. Those who should love us will turn on us. We can face this heartbreaking experience with hope because Christ did and He is with us.

God understands and empathizes with our spiritual pain. David called out to God and found comfort in his prayers (v.13-29). On the night of His betrayal, Jesus prayed alone. In that garden He was comforted by angels but not human friends. Jesus cried out in anguish when the Father turned away from Him (Matthew 27:46). We cry out in confidence because God looks upon us with compassion and mercy.

David was able to praise the Lord in His day of suffering (v.30-36). All God's children can too. God hears us and does not despise us. He does not turn away from us in our hour of need. We are imprisoned by fallen flesh and a broken world, but our God cares for us (v.33).

There will be difficult days for the children of God. God will be there. Are you growing in your faith so in your day of trial you can look confidently to God? Do you believe that God loves and understands you? Can you articulate the victory of Christ and how it pertains to your darkest days? Jesus has been through the worst life can offer. Those who rely on Him have hope in the worst of times.

Numbers 27; Psalms 70–71; Isaiah 17–18; 1 Peter 5

While it is true that every age and every life is given by God to exist in a special time and place, the same challenges exist in every age. It is the spiritual condition of a society or a life that really matters. Rather than trying to change the way of the world or our lives through physical means, God calls us to look to Him. Those who keep their eyes on Jesus and look to His provision and purpose have hope.

Israel, during Isaiah's day, thought it was impervious to the penalties of sin. They had lived a long time without showing God the proper respect that He was due. Life was seemingly good and the people were lulled into a false assurance based upon their misinterpretation of the promises of God. God's promises come with conditions. When those conditions are not met, God withholds His hand and allows those who want to go forward without Him to do just that. Israel forgot their God.

They continued to be religious. Israel had their temple, their religious ceremonies and seasons, and a leadership structure that gave lip service to the will of God. The problem was that their hearts were far from God. They had come to depend on their strength, their treaties with foreign nations, and their assumed position of necessity to God. In Isaiah 17–18 the penalty for Israel's pride was being explained. Assyria would soon overcome the Northern Kingdom (v.1-3). These ten northern tribes would be stripped down to almost nothing (v.4-7). In that day they would recall their faithlessness and realize that they had become like the nations that God drove out before them in the days of Joshua (v.8-14). God is gracious, but He will not be patronized. Those who want to live without God can, but they will also face the consequences for it.

While God wants and loves all of us, He does not need any of us. God has made a promise to bless the whole world (Genesis 12:1-3). The greatest and smallest will see the greatness of God. Even a small nation like Cush would see and know that the Lord Almighty is God (Isaiah 18). He is to be worshipped and praised. The Lord calls the entire world, every large and small nation and every great and unknown person, to look at what He is doing (v.3). God is at work in the world among the wealthy and poor, the known and unknown, and the big and small nations. One glorious day, God will return and make all things as they were meant to be (v.7).

Until the final victory of God over sin and darkness, He will be at work in the world calling people to trust in Him. Rather than looking to the physical world to answer our ultimate problems or meet our greatest needs, we are called to look to God. We are to seek a spiritual means to deal with our physical circumstances. What or who are you depending on to provide for your needs? Have you grown complacent in your spiritual life by wrongly believing that God is optional for you? Are you pursuing the ultimate plan of God or have you become entangled in your temporary pursuits at the expense of God's Kingdom cause? Israel became spiritually complacent and prideful. It is easy to do. Those who delight in the Lord and rely on Him live with hope.

Numbers 28; Psalm 72; Isaiah 19–20; 2 Peter 1

It is a distinct privilege to be counted among the redeemed of God. It is miraculous to be alive to God, pardoned from sin, and a part of the eternal family of God. Those who know Jesus as Savior and recognize that their standing with God is a big deal live with hope.

In 2 Peter 1, the Apostle Peter wrote to a people that he said had "obtained a faith of equal standing with ours by the righteousness of our God and Savior Jesus Christ." This is indeed a unique honor. They had a relationship with God that provided grace and peace. Grace and peace are meant to multiply in those who believe as their knowledge of God and Jesus grows (v.2). This knowledge is an experiential knowledge. It is a way of knowing that occurs through experience. The Christian life is not a theory. It is a holy way of living.

Through Christ, disciples of Jesus are provided with everything necessary for life and godliness (v.3). Through faith, the precious promises of God are granted to those who are made partakers of God's divine nature (v.4). This does not mean that God's people are made into gods. It means that the character of God resides in them. They are made holy, and that holiness is marked in their activities. Distinct qualities are listed that can and should be pursued (v.5-7). These qualities keep God's people from being ineffective in their pursuit of God (v.8). Sin causes the redeemed to lose sight of God and become forgetful of the redemption provided through Christ (v.9). Those who live in God's presence and with God's promises gain an assurance of salvation and are able to avoid falling and stumbling in their faith (v.10-11). It is the responsibility of every Christian to live a life that affirms their holy standing with God.

When a person lives in light of God's grace, they will be stirred by the truth that establishes them in the power of the Gospel (v.12). Knowing that his death was imminent, Peter reiterated his confidence in the plan of God and his willingness to serve the body of believers by calling them to pursue the way of life that has been given through faith in Christ (v13-15). His desire was that all of God's people would emulate his way of life. It was his unique experience of actually hearing the voice of God when Jesus was transfigured (Mark 9) that provided Peter with such strong convictions (v.16-18). The arguments Peter makes for the faith are not based upon myths. The Christian faith is based upon the Bible. The Bible is the ultimate source of God's truth. It was given by the Spirit of God through the appointed servants of God to enable the people of God to know the truth of God (v.19-21). There is nothing like the Bible. It is a miraculous gift given so those who believe in Jesus can know the truth, live in the truth, and be emotionally affirmed in the truth.

To know Christ and to be counted as a Christian is a unique opportunity and honor. Are you truly a Christian? Do you know the truth of the Gospel, and are you living in that truth and being emotionally stirred and assured by that truth? God has given us all we need for life and godliness. Those who live in His truth live with hope.

Numbers 29; Psalm 73; Isaiah 21; 2 Peter 2

God understands how quickly we can get swept away in the mundane or serious issues of life. That is why He orders us to keep special days for worship. Those who follow God's rhythm for life and take sacred time to rest and reflect on the goodness of God live with hope.

God provides order. In the beginning God created order out of chaos. Each of the six days in creation had a distinct purpose. After the work was done, the Lord set aside a day for rest. God was not tired. He did not need a break. Having made an image-bearer that was responsible for the care of His creation, God set a precedent for Adam to follow. Adam was to work six days, and on the seventh day Adam was to rest. There was order.

After the fall, life became messy. The standard week and the day of rest were still in play, but sin complicated the process. Once God established a people for Himself, He instituted holy days that would provide reminders and a rhythm for life. Numbers 29 gives an overview of some of the most significant celebrations God commanded Israel to keep. They took place in the seventh month, the month of Tishri, which correlates to our months of October and September. These rituals were instituted so the people would commemorate God's goodness. One was the Feast of Trumpets, which took place on the first day of the month (v.1-6). This was a summoning ceremony. It called the people to a divine awareness and drew attention to God. Another was the Day of Atonement, which occurred on the tenth day of the month (v.7-11). It was the day the people fasted and repented of their sin and were established in their holy standing with God. The Feast of Booths occurred on the fifteenth day (v.12-38). The people would live in temporary housing and remember the Exodus and how God provided for them in their desert wanderings.

Each of these events included sacrifices and special offerings. These were to be given along with the regular sacrifices and offerings that were established for the other months of the year (v.39-40). These special celebrations were to be executed in addition to and not in substitution of the regular instituted activities.

Because we are prone to get swept away with the demands and temptations of the moment, God commands us to take sacred time to remember and reflect on His grace. Under Jesus, the Lord has prescribed one day a week and two special ordinances to commemorate His grace. God's people are to gather on the Lord's Day and worship. During those gatherings, God's people are to keep two ordinances: baptism and the Lord's Supper. Through the daily study of God's Word and prayer, along with the worship gatherings of the church, God's people are called to walk in obedience to God. God's way is an orderly way of living.

Given the complexity of life, it is crucial that God's people live lives with a holy rhythm. Are you worshipping God with other believers at least one day a week? Have you been baptized? Do you regularly receive the Lord's Supper? Those who follow God's plan and take sacred time daily and weekly to reflect and remember God's love live with hope.

Numbers 30; <u>Psalm 74</u>; Isaiah 22; 2 Peter 3

Rather than allow us to have what is warranted, God is merciful to us all. In His mercy and for His purpose, God allows evil to exist and sinful people to make a mess of things. Even in dark times, God always has a remnant – a people for Himself who remain faithful to Him. Those who live as light in dark times live with hope.

When Babylon destroyed the temple in Jerusalem in 586 BC, chaos reigned. There was great darkness and despair among God's people. Psalm 74 records the feelings of the people (v.1-11), the faith of the remnant (v.12-17), and a plea for mercy (v.18-23). Of the faithful remnant there were those with a rooted faith that enabled them to remember and reflect on the power of God. That deep-seated faith gave some the strength to pray. It was a prayer that was based on the covenant promises of God.

Desert experiences are bound to come in life. Some enter the desert to be strengthened and prepared for their journey ahead. This was the case with Jesus (Matthew 4). For some, the desert experience is a result of their sin. This was the situation when Babylon destroyed the temple. The people refused to trust in God. In desert experiences, people are forced to learn to depend on God or to die.

The Psalmist was shocked at the extent of the judgment of God. The desert experience seemed too much. It seemed wrong. The people that had sacked the city were making a mockery of God. The Israelites were aghast because they did not receive a word from God concerning their petition. The fact is, God had spoken through many prophets, but the people did not repent. The time for talk was over. They were in the time of reckoning. There would be no escape.

God's power seems to have come to the mind of the Psalmist, and in the midst of the chaos of destruction, the writer remembered a time when God transformed chaos into clarity. At creation, God established the structure of the world. God has the power to take disorder and bring order. He can take what is dead and bring it to life. He can end what was and provide a new beginning.

Having remembered the greatness of God, the Psalmist turned to prayer. He called out to God. The promises of the covenant were the theme of the prayer. By standing on the promises of God the people of God can rightly ask God for His intervention. The requests were offered from the perspective of what is best for the name of God and His Kingdom. The Kingdom of God is an upside-down Kingdom. The powerful in it are weak. The rulers are servants. The wise are foolish in the eyes of the world. The closing prayer of the Psalm is a prayer that all of God's faithful people can pray with good conscience and be confident that God will respond favorably.

We all have to make choices about our lives and where our loyalties will be. Are you living faithfully to God? In the midst of this broken world, are you part of God's remnant? Are you shining as light in the darkness? God blesses those who live for Him. Those who live as the light of Christ during dark times live with hope.

Numbers 31; Psalms 75–76; Isaiah 23; 1 John 1

We should never underestimate the importance of our engagements in the world and how other people will be impacted by what we do. Those who live to fulfill their divine purpose in life will serve others well and live with great hope.

The Phoenician seaport on the Mediterranean Sea known as Tyre was an influential part of the world. It provided the lumber needed for King Solomon's temple (1 Kings 5:1, 7–12) and also the sailors for his navy (1 Kings 9:26, 27). Another Phoenician seaport was Sidon. Those two ports shared the same destiny, according to the oracle given in Isaiah 23. Those two ports, which were once places of respite, were destined for destruction.

While every life is important, there are certain lives that have a greater influence than others. Those who are gifted and called by God to serve as pastors and spiritual leaders within the church play a vital role in the well-being of many. When those leaders fail, it impacts more than just the leader and those in the church. It impacts the city and the people of that area that would look to that person and place as a beacon of hope.

The cause of almost every fall is pride. Tyre and Sidon came to believe they were too big to fail. There had been wars for centuries, but they had always survived. It seemed to them and to the rest of the world that regardless of their faults, they were too vital to ever be destroyed (v.9). Many spiritual leaders have their sins overlooked by others because they appear to be too important to remove or discipline. These leaders become arrogant, and the height from which they fall is significant. The impact of their fall is substantial.

God's discipline, although devastating, is always appropriate. If we will not discipline ourselves, God steps in and does it. Tyre and Sidon were destroyed (v.10-14). Leaders who lose their ability to serve others in the cause of Christ are like broken vessels of fine pottery. They were once so cherished, but have become unnecessary and are soon replaced.

Tyre was down for a while (v.15-17), but it found its footing again. It became a major trading port and regained its riches, but its practices remained ungodly. This is sometimes the case with fallen leaders. They find a way to get back up, but they do not regain a Godly life. Somehow, God had a plan to make them holy to the Lord (v.18). Those who repent and are blessed with spiritual restoration through the guidance of Biblically sound and divinely called counselors can enjoy a renewal of life. These blessed individuals do more than find a way back into ministry. By the grace of God and for His glory, these men and women are given the privilege to serve God's people and Kingdom purpose. Unfortunately, some return to spiritual work as peace-fakers. They have not been rightly restored through repentance and realigned priorities.

It is wise to take seriously the impact your life has on other people. It is a joy and honor to impact others, but it is primarily a responsibility. Are you guarding your life? Are you walking in humble obedience to God? Are there other trusted leaders keeping you accountable and humble? Those who serve others with holy lives have hope.

Jesus Christ came into the world to save sinners. Those who repent of their sin and believe in Jesus will be saved. Their sin will be pardoned. They will be given a righteous standing with God. They will be given a new life. This is the Gospel. Those who live in the power of the Gospel live with hope.

Writing to his beloved church at Ephesus, John sought to combat false teaching. His letter provides fundamental facts of the Christian faith. It also gives great assurance to God's people and teaches them how to live with confidence in the faith. In 1 John 2, there is an overview of the Gospel and an explanation for how saints can be certain of their right standing with God (v.1-6). There is a challenge to God's people to love one another (v.7-14). There is a call to the church to overcome the darkness in the world.

Those who have been pardoned of sin will continue to struggle with sin so long as they are living in this broken world. The grace of God covers all of the sin of the saints and enables those who have been pardoned to pursue a holy life (v.1-2). This is a life that is driven not by willpower, but by a commitment to obey Jesus (v.3). Those who have no desire to obey Jesus are deceived and do not have an assurance of saving faith (v.4). Those who desire to obey Jesus are those who abide in Him (v.5-6). The life of faith comes down to loyalty. Those who are loyal to God and choose to love Him will obey Him.

Being a part of God's family provides not only a vertical relationship with God, but also a horizontal relationship with other believers. The command of God to love God and love other people is nothing new (v.7). God's light has entered the world and God has filled His followers with His love (v.8). The person who claims to be a child of God but hates the rest of the family of God is in darkness (v.9-14). The lack of love is a symptom of a lack of salvation.

The lure of the flesh is strong, even in the heart of a person made righteous by grace. Each of God's people must fight against the temptations of the world. Those things that feel good, look good, and create a sense of pride are dangerous (v.15-16). The wise way of life is to pursue Godliness (v.17). The evil one is always at work attempting to draw God's people away from the truth, and some are deceived (v.18-19). By the grace of God the people of God are able to know the truth of God. That truth sets God's people free (v.20-27). The facts of the faith do not change. While clarity can be gained by greater study of the Word of God, the Gospel truth remains the same. Disciples of Jesus are changed by God's Word. By living in and sustaining focus on the truth, a person of faith can avoid deception.

The Gospel is the hope of the world. What Christ has done and continues to do in those who believe is merciful and gracious. Are you living in the truth of the Gospel? Is there a real love for God and His people in your life? Are you walking in obedience to God's Word? Those who live assured of salvation live with hope.

Numbers 33; Psalm 78:1-39; Isaiah 25; 1 John 3

The Christian life is a journey. Jesus said that the road which leads to eternal life is along a narrow, hard way (Matthew 7:14). God has promised to journey with His people. Those who walk with God live with hope.

In Numbers 33, Moses recorded the stages of the journey of Israel from their bondage in Egypt to Canaan (v.1-49). The journey was a hard one that required divine intervention. The people had to fight to survive. Those who inhabited the land that God had given to Israel did not want to leave. They were pagans. They had no regard for the one true God. Their commitment to idolatry and sin was serious. They would have to be forcibly removed (v.50-56). They were a strong people and their locations were fortified. These enemies of God knew that God's people were coming. The Israelites did not have the element of surprise. Victory came through faith, obedience, and the miraculous hand of God.

The direction the people went after leaving Egypt was curious. Rather than heading northeast, God led the people south. The Lord knew what the people needed. Instead of leading them north, Exodus 13:18 says, "God led the people around by the way of the wilderness toward the Red Sea. And the people of Israel went up out of the land of Egypt equipped for battle." The people were equipped for battle, but not ready for battle, so God led them south into the wilderness.

When a child of God begins the journey toward heaven, God provides all that is needed for the journey. Those who are born again have the Spirit of God to bless them, the blood of Christ to justify and sanctify them, the Word of God to teach them, the family of God to walk with them, and the sovereign plan of God to direct them. Israel was saved by the blood of the lamb, was given the law of God to know how to live, and was guided to the Promised Land. Every Christian is saved by Jesus – the Lamb of God – given the law of God in their hearts to live by, and made ready for heaven by a spiritual journey, under God's guidance. It is a blessed journey.

God allows trials and temptations to strengthen the faith of the saints. The Israelites were given the land of Canaan. It was theirs by decree. It is like the salvation of a Christian. It is given to those who believe. Israel had to root out the enemies that were in Canaan. Likewise, Christians must root out sin. It is a battle that those who believe must fight. God told Israel that if they did not drive out the inhabitants, "then those of them whom you let remain shall be as barbs in your eyes and thorns in your sides, and they shall trouble you in the land where you dwell" (v.55). Those who do not root out the sin in their flesh will face consequences for allowing sin to remain. That sin will always be a burden that frustrates their journey (Hebrews 12:1).

The saints of God are blessed by the plan of God. God's way is not always easy, but it is always best. Are you walking the narrow, hard way of faith? Do you trust God's plan? Are you rooting out sin in your life? Those who walk faithfully with God and are headed for heaven live with hope.

Numbers 34; Psalm 78:40-72; Isaiah 26; 1 John 4

God is faithful. He never struggles to keep His promises or His Word. Those who trust in Jesus have a rock that will not move. Those who have Jesus as the redeemer and the leader of their life have a hope that does not fail.

The story of the Bible is the story of reality. It explains how the world came into existence and what has, is, and will take place in the world. God created out of nothing all that is and made everything to be in harmony. Humanity sinned against God and destroyed that harmony. Rather than abandon us, God promised salvation. He kept that promise and came to rescue His people and will one day return to restore all things. Until that time, the church is to be active in telling others the Good News of Jesus.

In Psalm 78:40-72, we read the story of Israel after the Exodus. Their experience is the experience of all those who know God. The people struggled to remain faithful to God (v.40-41). They forgot the goodness and greatness of God, who had overcome their enemies and freed them from slavery in Egypt (v.42-53). God led the people to a place where they could thrive. They lived in tents along the way and then in houses they had not built and enjoyed peace over enemies that God miraculously defeated through them (v.54-55). And yet they still struggled with sin. They rebelled against God (v.56-58). The consequence of their sin was serious. Many died. Many lost faith (v.59-64). Then God did what He always does. He kept His promise. With a humble servant, God provided salvation for His people. He raised up David to lead the people. He called David to be the head of the family that God would use to fulfill the promise He had made to Abraham (Genesis 12:1-3). David provided freedom for Israel from their enemies by being a good shepherd to God's flock (v.65-72). He also pictured the ultimate Shepherd who would come and redeem a people from every tribe and tongue to the praise of God's great name. Jesus came through the line of David, as promised.

Disciples of Jesus, like the children of Israel, have been set free. We are no longer condemned but have been given salvation from sin and death and provided the Spirit of God. God's love will never leave us (Romans 8). We will struggle with sin, but it will be a struggle. There will be days when we fail, but God is faithful. When we sin, we are not to simply give in and give up and continue in sin. We are to repent. We are to turn away from sin and find renewed forgiveness in Christ. We can turn to Christ for restoration.

A true believer can never lose salvation in Jesus. God sustains His people. The Gospel is the good news that even when we are faithless, God is faithful. His faithfulness is not dependent upon our commitment, but upon His. The Lord promised to save His people. Those who believe are saved and sustained by His grace. Are you living a life devoted to Jesus? Are you dealing with sin by repenting and regularly renewing your faith in Jesus? There is a great blessing that comes with humble faith. Those who have Jesus as the redeemer and leader of their life have a hope that does not fail.

Numbers 35; Psalm 79; Isaiah 27; 1 John 5

Life is hard, but God has a plan. What makes life so hard is the fact that the world is not as it should be. God made the world to be in harmony, but the sin of humanity allowed darkness the authority to reign over the world. The image bearers of God were given dominion over what God had made. Our treason and faith in self and sin have made a mess of the world, but God still has a great plan. He has a plan for every life, every nation, and for everything in creation. He also has the power to accomplish His plan. The person who joins God in what He is doing to accomplish His plan will live with hope.

It is easy to get off course in life. It is also possible to get back on course. In Isaiah 27, the prophet provides a picture of what it looks like when a life gets back on course. This is not the first time Isaiah used the analogy of a vineyard (5:1-7). This time, though, the vineyard pleases the Lord. This vineyard will be one that accomplishes the will and work of God. By His power and for His glory, God will destroy the evil that has overcome His people (v.1).

A healthy life is one that is under the authority of God the Father and is nurtured by Him (v.2-4). It is cleared of sin. The thorns and weeds of this world no longer have the power to overcome it. A life that is under the authority of God has peace because of Jesus Christ (v.5). It is through Christ alone that the justice of God is completely satisfied. Having been forgiven and made righteous by the blood of Christ, a person is born again into a living hope that will never spoil or fade.

In this new life a redeemed saint is able, through the power of the Holy Spirit dwelling in them and at work through them, to accomplish God's original plan (v.6). God placed Adam and Eve in a garden. It was a geographical location shut off from the rest of the world. Their task was to manage it and make it grow. Through their efforts and procreation, they were to fill the whole earth with people made in the image of God in a garden that covered the world. They failed. God's plan and purpose still stands. Through the redeemed, God will get the Gospel to the ends of the earth and one day make all things new and fill the earth with His glory.

Until the Lord returns, there will be tough times, but God will use them to train His people to be righteous. For God's people, the pain is discipline. This discipline brings about change, according to God's plan (v.7-9). Those who do not love God experience God's disdain differently. It is crushing. It overwhelms. It leads to an existence where there is no peace (v.10-11).

The day the Lord brought His people back to Jerusalem was a glorious time (v.12-13). One day the trumpet of heaven will sound and Jesus will return and make all things new and glorious. Are you ready for that day? Are you now living to fill the world with God's Good News? Are you living in the grace of God? Those who join God in what He is doing to accomplish His plan will live with hope.

False unity is unsustainable and dangerous. In the beginning, the enemy came to Adam and Eve in the form of a serpent, seemingly on their side. It wasn't, but it was allowed to remain in their safe circle of relational bliss. Adam should have cut off its head. Instead, he allowed that ancient foe to deceive him and his wife. The world is a broken place because of it. There have been many friendship circles and churches divided and decimated because of a deceiver that was allowed to enter and remain in their midst. Those who can discern false unity and remove it will live with hope in their solid and safe relationships.

Hospitality is crucial to Christianity. The fear of demonic or human deception must not keep God's children from pursuing kindness and compassion through genuine friendship. Thank God for hospitable Christians! God uses the friendship of Godly people to make disciples of those who are lost in sin.

God's people must be hospitable, but also discerning. In 2 John, the beloved Apostle wrote to a precious church to remind them of the necessity of sound doctrine, the danger of friendship with deceived and deceptive people, and the means by which God's family can share their lives, their faith, and their hope most effectively. The abiding love that God gives His people is grace and truth (v.1-3). This is what Jesus came to earth full of (John 1:14, 17). It is truth that reveals the need for the grace of God.

This church was walking in truth and living out the greatest commandments, which are to love God and people (v.4-6). John's concern was that they be aware of the deceivers who had gone out into the world saying that Jesus had not come in the flesh. This deceptive doctrine is Gnosticism, a false teaching of the deceiver, the antichrist (v.7). John warned this church to watch and protect the way they lived (v.8), to watch and protect their doctrine (v.9), and to watch and protect their fellowship (v.10-11). A healthy church is a discerning church protected by wise elders.

To veer from the truth for the sake of false unity is to veer into sin. It is to accept what is false. This is not an option for God's people. We are to love everyone and lovingly expose deception in order to protect the faith and the flock. The doctrinal purity of a congregation serves as a strong wall against the enemy and a penetrating light in the darkness of the world. The church that holds to the truth will be both safe and influential.

John finished the letter by speaking of the desire to see this church and make their joy complete (v.12). A church with sound doctrine and loving friendships will always welcome faithful leaders. Their joy is to not only show their love to those God has called to serve His church, but to enjoy the sound teaching they bring. There is a sincere bond between sister churches and a meaningful exchange and partnership between them (v.13). This kind of unity is crucial. Are you protecting your life and doctrine? Is your church able to discern error and reject heresy? It takes both grace and truth. The Lord Jesus must be the model followed. The Spirit must be at work too. Those who live in grace and truth live with hope.

Deuteronomy 1; Psalms 81–82; Isaiah 29; 3 John

When the lessons of the previous generation are forgotten, the same mistakes are often made by the generation that follows. Those who trust in the Lord and learn from those who have gone before them will live in obedience to God and experience the power of hope.

Moses was not perfect, but he was exceptional. Having lived a long life filled with failure and success, he sought to provide direction for the generation that would follow him. As Israel prepared to finally enter into the land of Canaan, it was clear he would not make the trip and would soon be dead. He was over one hundred twenty years old. According to God's plan, Joshua would be the new leader after Moses. The people would be tempted to follow the ways of the pagans. To bless them and prepare them, Moses was led by God to preach a series of sermons that were written down so they could be kept. This written compilation of messages is known as the book of Deuteronomy.

Much is made of the name of the book and how it was later found in Josiah's day and used by God to bring about a great revival in the latter part of the seventh century BC (2 Kings 22:8-13). It is also quoted in the New Testament, most notably by Jesus, during His wilderness temptations (Matthew 4:1-11). Its importance to the original readers should not be underestimated. It was to the second generation of Israelites that were freed from Egypt. Their parents had failed to trust God and were made to wander in the desert for forty years. Now it was time for this next generation to follow God and conquer Canaan. They would soon face raging rivers that would have to be divided for the people to walk through, strong people that would have to be defeated by divine intervention, and huge walls protecting cities that would have to fall by faith and not by human engineering. This new generation would need to be motivated by the book of Deuteronomy.

Moses began the book by reminding the people where they were geographically (v.1-2), spiritually (v.3-8), politically (v.9-18), and emotionally (v.19-46). The people were on the precipice of their new home. They were about to enter into the place God had promised them. The nation had been in this position before. It was crucial that they remember their past so they would not repeat it. God was speaking to them. Although they had disobeyed Him, God did not abandon Israel. Their last defining moment ended in their defeat (v.45). In many ways the people were coming out of a ditch where they had been stuck for a full generation.

It is important to always remember that goodness of God when we fail. The Apostle Paul spoke of his own moral failures in Romans 7 but never forgot the victory that is in Christ Jesus in Romans 8. In Christ there is no condemnation. All of God's children are now in a spiritual battle en route to heaven. Along the way, we will face temptation. Are you living as the light of Christ? Are you being motivated daily by the truth of God's Word? The truth liberates us to go forward with Jesus. Those who trust in the Lord and learn from those who have gone before them will live with hope.

Deuteronomy 2; Psalms 83–84; Isaiah 30; Jude

There are only two kinds of people in the world. We are divided, as human beings, not by our geography, skin tones, or political systems, but by our faith. There are those who have God's eternal grace through faith in Christ alone and those who don't. Those who believe in Jesus and live under His leadership live with hope.

Psalm 83 and 84 reveal the contrast between the rescued and the perishing. While Psalm 83 pictures what the perishing lives like, Psalm 84 reveals the desires of a rescued child of God. The person separated from God is at war with God. Some are intentional in their defiance of the Holy One, while others are simply delusional in their disobedience. Whether out of a determination to defy God or as simply confused, those who are unable to yield to God's will are at odds with God. Those who are saved by grace have a heart surrendered to God that delights in His goodness and desires to be in His presence.

Psalm 83 is a national lament. The people of God were asking God to act against their foes. This is an imprecatory Psalm. It calls down curses on the enemies of God's people (v.1). The justification for the imprecation is Israel's enemies' desire to destroy and overcome God's purpose (v.2-8). The prayer is for God to obliterate them, as He did the previous enemies of God (v.9-18). There is a touch of grace in this Psalm. Knowing the heart of God and His love for all people, Asaph, the writer of Psalm 83, offered a redemptive inclination to God's action (v.16). The prayer is that the pain of God's punishment will cause the people to repent and turn to seek God. God's love for all people endures forever. Even the condemned are loved by their Maker. That is part of the suffering and torment of hell. While they were sinners, God loved them and will love them forever, even as they suffer eternal punishment, as justice demands.

Psalm 84 is a Psalm that celebrates the presence of God. Those under the Old Covenant would use it as a song that inspired their devotion as they went to the Temple to worship. Those under the New Covenant look to Jesus as they journey to the eternal temple (Revelation 21:22). Both believe in the same God. Both are saved by grace through faith in Christ alone. One looked forward to the coming Messiah to take away the sin of the world, while the other looks back to the cross and resurrection. Both love God and long to be in His presence (v.1-2). Both understand that a blessed life is one that dwells in the strength, presence, and protection of the Most High (v.3-9). Both know that it would be better to have a short life with God rather than a long life without Him. Both know that it would be better to have no earthly goods and have God rather than be rich in the things of earth but not have God (v.10). Both know God provides for His people according to His wisdom and power (v.11). Both know God blesses those who trust in Him.

There are two kinds of people on this planet. What kind of person are you? Is Jesus your savior? There is no in-between place. We are either with God or we are against Him. Those who trust in Jesus and seek Him have hope.

Deuteronomy 3; Psalm 85; Isaiah 31; Revelation 1

There is a big difference between the wise person of faith and the unwise person of foolishness. The wise person of faith looks to the Gospel of God and the promises that ever-standing edifice supplies. Those who find their wisdom and strength in Christ alone will always have hope.

The people of God that Isaiah prophesied to had every reason to place their confidence in the Jehovah-Jireh (Provider God). He had rescued them from Egypt, brought them safely into Canaan, established the Israelite Kingdom, defended them from enemies, and cared for their souls. And yet, they disavowed Him. They turned to others for hope. In Isaiah 31, the prophet called the people from their dismal decision of depending on Egypt. The people were being foolish. They were working off of a wrong assumption with questionable aspirations, using a plan that was void of reason. God reached out to them, but they were choosing to cling to the faltering power of Egypt.

The prophet condemned the foolishness of Israel for trusting in the seemingly powerful army of Egypt (v.1). He pointed to God's unchanging commitment (v.2). God is a promise-keeping God. There is no limit to His power (v.3). The hand of God cannot be stopped. Anything in His way will falter and be destroyed. Those who are not acting in concert with Him will be overcome.

The prophet mocked the power of Egypt and compared it to ineffective shepherds dealing with a lion. God alone can protect His flock (v.4). The Lord is the Good Shepherd. He is a present help. He is always there. He will deliver His people (v.5). God promised that Abraham would be the conduit through which the world would be blessed (Genesis 12:1-3). Abraham's descendants would produce the avior of the world. The Messiah would come through the line of David (2 Samuel 7:16-17). Jesus Christ came and rescued His people as promised.

God is gracious. All who repent and look to Him by faith will be saved (v.6-7). The way God dealt with Assyria is the way God will deal with all evil (v.8-9). Victory will come through supernatural means. The Assyrians were defeated by divine intervention, just as Isaiah prophesied (2 Kings 19:35-37). One day, the evil of this world will be vanquished. God will make a new heaven and new earth, and all who trusted in Him will reside in peace forever (Revelation 21). This is the promise of God.

It is easy to be misled and to think that a created temporary thing can provide what is needed in life. This is foolishness. The world offers help that it cannot sustain. Those who trust in that which they cannot keep rather than have faith in what cannot be lost are foolish. God calls His people to believe in Him, to trust in His promises, and to live by His might. God has proven both capable and faithful to save. Do you trust in God to meet the needs of your life? Are you living a life that is faithful to God or are you living foolishly? Only God can be trusted. Those who look to the power of God and trust in Him will live with hope.

Deuteronomy 4; Psalms 86–87; Isaiah 32; Revelation 2

What we need to go through is often what we do not want to go through. The Lord uses our trials to transform us into the image of His Son. Those who are daily being transformed by the Gospel have hope.

The churches listed in Revelation 2–3 were real people in real places in the first century, but they represent the realities of all God's people for all time. The challenges they went through are the challenges that believers in every age go through. In Revelation 2, the difficulties of the churches of Ephesus, Smyrna, Pergamum, and Thyatira are revealed. God allowed these churches to go through trials in order to gain what is best.

Ephesus (v.1-7) was a church that had been well-trained by the Apostle Paul, the Apostle John, and their apprentices. This church knew the truth and maintained sound doctrine. Their problem was one of affections. Jesus told them to return to their first love, God (v.4). Love of God produces a genuine love for others. Faith without love is dead orthodoxy. It has the skeletal system and muscles, but no life. Love is the life of genuine faith.

Smyrna (v.8-11) was a well-resourced port city. Its emblem was the phoenix, the mythical creature that rose from the ashes of death to live. It is no coincidence that Jesus identified Himself to this church as the eternal one who died and was raised. Those faithful saints were about to be persecuted. They were promised eternal life as a result of their faithfulness unto death. This promise has given hope to many martyrs over the centuries.

Pergamum (v.12-17) was the capital of the Roman province. It housed many places of worship to Roman gods. The worship of the emperor was also prevalent. Jesus referred to this place as being "where the throne of Satan is" for good reason (v.13). The people had remained faithful to the truth of the Gospel, but they were not being faithful in their fidelity to Christ alone. Some were participating in idol worship and sexual immorality (v.14-15). They were warned to repent or they would be disciplined (v.16). Compromise is easy but unacceptable to God. He demands singular devotion. Those who allow idols and immorality in their life miss out on the best God gives.

Thyatira (v.18-29) was a city of merchants and craftsmen that had formed into guilds. These guilds were bound by a god that they worshipped as a means to create unity. The church of this city was loving, faithful, and served the Lord well (v.19). Their problem was that they were also participating in the guilds and their idol worship, which involved sexual immorality (v.20-21). Sexually transmitted disease would soon be widespread among those who committed this sin (v.22- 23). Those who were faithful would not suffer this consequence (v.24). Sin seems so pleasant, but it comes at such a great cost. God calls His people to the best way of life.

Every generation has its challenges. Temptation will always be an issue, but faithfulness is the right choice for God's children. Are you faithful to Christ? Can you see yourself in any of these churches? Take heed to the words of Jesus. He is for you. Those who live faithfully in Jesus have hope in life and death.

Deuteronomy 5; Psalm 88; Isaiah 33; Revelation 3

God gives boundaries to free people to pursue what is best. Those who live by the law of God live with hope.

God provided the law to Israel so they would know how to live. In Deuteronomy 5, Moses described how God had given them the law. It was a unique gift. God spoke directly to them, through Moses. It was by grace. God is holy. He is a consuming fire (v.1-5). God was very clear in what He wanted the people to do, why He wanted them to do it, and was appreciative of how the people responded to Him.

Jesus said that the greatest commandment is to love God and the second is to love people (Matthew 22:37-40). The first four commandments provide the way a person shows their love for God. Love for God is revealed through faithfulness to Him and refusing to worship anyone or anything else (v.6-7), through refusing to reduce God into a man-made image (v.8-10), through refusing to misuse the name of God and empty it of its holiness and greatness (v.11), and through setting aside a day to rest and be renewed in the goodness of God (v.12-15). The last six commandments provide the way a person is to show their love for other people. By honoring parents (v.16), refusing to murder (v.17), refusing to be adulterous (v.18), refusing to steal (v.19), refusing to lie about another person (v.20), and refusing to covet what belongs to someone else (v.21), love for others is revealed. Loving God and honoring Him provides the foundation for loving people.

God gave the law because He wanted the people to have the life they were made for. These laws were the means for living well and with longevity (v.33). The Lord is the maker and sustainer of all things. He designed humanity with dignity and for a purpose. Sin corrupted that design but did not destroy it. Those who will choose to love God and people the way God designed them to love are the people who will enjoy blessings (v.32). Love blesses the giver and receiver.

The response of the people pleased God. Rather than being presumptuous and proud, the people were humbled and fearful of God. They recognized the distinction between divinity and humanity. Their suggestion was simple and came from an appropriate concern. Rather than remaining accessible to the voice of God, they asked that Moses be their mediator (v.22-27). This showed wisdom and an appropriate respect for God and Moses. The Lord heard these words and they pleased Him (v.28). God loves a humble heart. When those who have been made stand in awe of the Maker, it brings glory and honor to Him and blessings to them (v.29-31).

What the people of Israel experienced is similar to what all who receive the Gospel of Jesus experience. Having been freed, those who are saved begin a journey toward heaven. God provides His law through the indwelling Holy Spirit and the Word of God. As a community of saints, the redeemed gather in local churches to be reminded of their hope and the privilege of knowing and living for God. Are you grateful to God? Are you living in obedience to Him? Those who live a life of love live with hope.

Deuteronomy 6; <u>Psalm 89</u>; Isaiah 34; Revelation 4

Providence is a mystery, but it is marvelous. A general reading of the Bible reveals that God is at work in the world achieving glory for Himself in the outworking of His plans. Those who delight in the will of God live with hope.

God's plan from before creation was to enter into the world and rescue His people from sin and death. He revealed His plan and made promises about how He would accomplish His will in the Old Testament. King David would be the line through which the Savior would come. Psalm 89 reveals the providence of God in the choosing of David and the plan of God to establish an eternal Kingdom, through David's family line.

The Psalm begins by praising God for His steadfast love and faithfulness and how it was manifested in His establishing an eternal covenant with David (v.1-4). David did not deserve to be chosen. The people of Israel did not deserve to be God's people. None of us deserves to be loved by God. We have all sinned. We have all chosen to go our own way and committed treason against the King of Glory. And yet God is gracious. He redeems people and transforms them by His might. God promised David He would accomplish His redemptive plan through His family.

The reason God could make the promises He did to David is because of His power. There is no end to the might of God (v.5-18). He has power over the spiritual powers and the physical realities of the world. The Lord overcame the carnal enemies that stood against Him, enemies like Egypt. He also established nations for His purpose. God has power over the seas and seasons. There is nothing in heaven or earth that can stand against Him. Thankfully, God is a righteous and just God. His power and might are leveraged for what is good, pure, and loving. Those who rest under the grace of God have a divine shield. God protects them.

God did not keep His plan a secret but clearly communicated it in His Word (v.19-37). He had David anointed (1 Samuel 16:1–13) and then made His oath to David public (2 Samuel 7:4–17). What a glorious God who takes the youngest son, forgotten by his dad and disrespected by his brothers, and makes him king! What a mighty Lord who promotes a plan and then accomplishes it, despite the failings and shortcomings of His people (v.38-51)! God deals with the sins of His people and allows consequences and suffering to make them obedient. In the end, God always does what He has said He would do. He did with David. He did with Israel. In the end, those who trust in the Lord will gladly say, "Blessed be the Lord forever! Amen and Amen" (v.52).

God does not change. He is the same God who freed Israel from Egypt. He made David a king and the line through which Jesus would come. He raised Jesus from the dead. That same God is at work in the world today. He is providentially accomplishing His purpose. Are you working with God? Are you walking in faithfulness to Him and seeking to accomplish His purpose in the world? Nothing can stop the Lord. What He is doing is right and best. Those who live to honor and build His Kingdom live with hope.

Deuteronomy 7; Psalm 90; Isaiah 35; Revelation 5

God has not kept His intentions a secret. The great and mighty God of heaven, who created all things and by His might sustains all things, has spoken of what will be. In Isaiah 35, the Lord provided one of the most powerful pictures of the ministry of Jesus, almost seven centuries before it came to be. Jesus Christ is the Messiah! He is the Way! He is God in flesh and has come to rescue us. Those who receive Him live with hope.

Because Christ has come, we have every reason to be glad, to rejoice, and to sing (v.1-2). What was broken will be mended. The world that was made in harmony, but cursed by sin, will be restored. This will happen at the second coming of Jesus (Revelation 21). The fact that Jesus has come to rescue us, as promised, gives us complete confidence that He will come again, as promised. It is wise and best to live in light of the coming of Jesus and His eternal judgment. God will help us. Hebrews 12:12, quoting Isaiah 35:3, calls the redeemed of God to receive the Lord's discipline and use it to get spiritually stronger. This is not easy. It takes intentional effort, but God is willing to save and strengthen those who believe (v.4). We must be willing to set aside our desires, and instead, choose to obey God.

When Jesus came, He performed many miracles, proving He was God (v.5-7). The lame were made able to walk. The blind were made able to see. Those who were dead were made alive. The apostles were anointed to continue that miraculous work in order to substantiate the claims of the Gospel. There was and there now is no doubt that Christ has come to provide the "Way of Holiness," and all who walk in this Way by faith will be transformed and governed by the protective hand of God (v.8-10). The Way itself is the protection. The devil is pictured in 1 Peter 5:8 as a lion looking for those it can devour. Those who walk in paths of righteousness with Jesus cannot be touched by the beast (v.9). Darkness must flee the light. So those walking in the light need not fear the evil of this world. Darkness cannot overcome light.

This "Way of Holiness" leads to Zion, the abode of God. This is the ultimate Promised Land. This is the place where sin cannot be. This is the place where there is no more sickness and death. This is the place of harmony, peace, joy, and love eternal. Heaven is what it is because God is who He is. God is holy. God is love. God is peace. God is whole. Heaven is filled with God. Those who walk in the "Way of Holiness" in this life are walking in a blessed way. It is the way to gain what cannot be taken and always satisfies.

We all must choose the path we will take in life. Jesus is the "way, the truth, and the life" (John 14:6). Those who walk in His way will be saved, not only from hell, but from a meaningless, hopeless, and sinful life. Are you walking by faith in the love of Jesus? Have you repented of your sin and chosen to submit your life to the authority of Jesus? Those who live a life of love for Jesus will live with the hope of heaven.

Deuteronomy 8; Psalm 91; Isaiah 36; Revelation 6

The Bible is not a fantasy book written about a fantasy world concerning a fantasy god. The Bible is the story of the world. It explains how the real world came to be, how real people were made, what went wrong, and what God has done, is doing, and will do. It is written by authors who wrote as the Spirit led them. Their writings were for their original readers, but also for future generations. The book of Revelation with all of its symbols was written to real people in the real world to explain how the real God of the universe was at work and would be at work to rescue and restore His world. Those who believe and are rescued from sin and anticipate the restoration of God's rule on earth live with hope.

In Revelation 6, the unveiling of God's plan is revealed through the opening of the seven seals of the scroll that only Jesus can open (Revelation 5). Six of the seven seals are opened in Revelation 6. While the fifth seal provides the justification for what God is doing, the other five seals reveal the justice that God will wield against His enemies.

The first seal unleashes leadership for the world that creates a system of peace that is not sustainable (v.1-2). There have been and will be leaders that will rise up and create great cultures and political systems, but none can survive the brokenness of humanity. Sooner or later, all human systems fail. The second seal reveals what always happens to man-made peace. It ends in war (v.3-4). Selfish pride and a desire for personal gain always lead to destruction. The third seal releases poverty. People left to themselves create cultures with rich and poor, and the poor get poorer, while the rich get richer (v.5-6). The fourth seal releases disease and famine, consequences of war and poverty (v.7-8). The fifth seal reveals the saints who are martyred for the faith. Our dark world hates the light and under the authority of the evil one, God's people are persecuted and killed (v.9-11). The sixth seal releases a cosmological cataclysmic event that will begin God's ultimate restoration (v.12-17). The old earth in its fallen state will pass away, and all humanity will be judged. Those who are not of the Kingdom of heaven will desire to be hidden from the wrath of God. None will escape.

This chapter reveals the way of and the trajectory of the world. The redeemed of God need not fear the things that happen in and to the world. This world is not our home. This world is our mission field. Just as Christ came to us, leaving the comforts of heaven, God calls His people to leave the comforts of silence and speak the Gospel truth to the people of this planet. We are to act as ambassadors and seek to show people the way to be reconciled to God (2 Corinthians 5:13-18). This is our high calling and blessing, although it will often cause conflict with darkness and may cost us our lives.

God is at work in the world and has revealed what is happening and what will happen. Are you living in light of the coming of Christ? Are you living confident in the will of God in this world? Those who refuse to rely on the broken ways of man, but instead trust in Jesus, live with hope.

Deuteronomy 9; Psalms 92–93; Isaiah 37; Revelation 7

God is a gracious and loving God. He is also holy and just. His name is to be honored. When we pray, Jesus said the first thing we need to do is to acknowledge God's otherness, His highness, and His perfection, and say, "Our Father in Heaven, hallowed be your name" (Matthew 6:9). As we live, we must live wisely and live to honor His name. Those who believe in the gracious, just, and glorious name of Jesus and honor Him as Lord and Savior live with hope.

The journey of the Israelites to the promised land from Egypt has many things to teach new covenant Christians about how to live and what we should avoid. In Deuteronomy 9, Moses offered an explanation for why God provided for His people and how gracious God had been to them. What Moses said about God and how the people responded speaks to the person God is and the trials, temptations, and tribulation that believers in Jesus must be aware of and by faith overcome.

When God called Israel to go in and possess the land, He promised He would go before them as a consuming fire. He made it clear they were going to battle people who were very strong, but He promised He would win the victory and they would be able to drive them out (v.1-3). So it is with God's people today. Jesus has won the victory over sin and death. God's redeemed children can now walk with the Lord and overcome the sin that is at work in their flesh. The battle is real. It is a spiritual battle, but the victory has been won in Christ. The means of victory is love for God and faith in His promises.

The Lord blesses and cares for His people because of His grace. It was not because Israel was so obedient that they received God's blessing. The Lord was driving out the Canaanite people because of the Canaanites' sin (v.4-6). The Israelites were sinful people. They had failed over and over again. From the day Moses went to get the law on Mount Sinai until the day they were supposed to enter into the land the first time, they had rebelled against God (v.7-24). Everyone continues to sin, even after they receive God's grace. The Lord disciplines us, as He did Israel, to train us to trust Him, to love Him, and to obey Him.

Moses was a great gift to Israel. He constantly served as a mediator for them, before God. He trusted in the promises of God and prayed them back to God. Moses knew it was by grace these people had been saved and their salvation was for the glory of God. It was not because Israel was so good or so they could make a great name for themselves (v.25-29). Jesus Christ is the mediator for new covenant Christians. It is by His grace we are saved, and it is for His glory that we remain in Him.

Each of us is called to live out God's plan for our life. God's will is that we be holy. Are you living a life that honors God? Are you truly grateful for the grace He has given to you and the provision of the presence of Jesus? Those who live with God and for God's glory in the love and grace of God live with hope.

Deuteronomy 10; <u>Psalm 94</u>; Isaiah 38; Revelation 8

God made the world to be in peace. The world is full of conflict and injustice. The world is broken because humanity has sinned and become allies with Satan. God has not forgotten His people or His world. He is at work in His world and will one day restore this planet into a place of peace. Until then, those who choose to trust God and seek His blessing will live with hope.

In Psalm 94, the writer seems to be sick of having to see suffering and sin (v.1-7). This frustration is healthy. It is a bad sign when a person stops caring about the plight of the victims of wickedness. Those who can ignore the pain of others do not have the heart of God driving their affections. God loves people and hates sin, pride, and those who dishonor His great name. Sinners often imagine their sin to be beyond the sight of God and choose to sin because they do not seek God. No one sins when their focus is on the gracious, holy, and mighty God. The Psalmist made a strong case for God to act and bring about change. Every prayer should do this.

To those who think the Lord does not see their sinful acts, the Psalmist speaks of the omniscience of the Almighty. The writer reminds them that the God who created the ear and eye can surely see and hear (v.8-9). God disciplines the nations. He knows the thoughts of every person (v.10-11). Not only does God perceive the words and deeds of people, but He knows their thoughts. What power!

The Psalmist made a strong argument for God's intervention. The discipline of God is a good thing. Those who are disciplined and repent are blessed. Those who learn God's law and live in God's love will avoid the just wrath of God (v.12-13). Those who repent and look to God in faith will never be forsaken. They will seek God's justice, as members of His heritage, and fulfill God's will.

The hope of humanity is the mediation of God in Jesus Christ. History proves the inability of humanity to govern itself. Empires rise and fall. They rise when they serve the good of humanity and bring glory to God. They fall when sin takes root and selfishness leads to injustice (v.14-23). The people of faith must focus on the presence of God provided in the promised Holy Spirit and recall God's steadfast love. The person who knows and loves Jesus has a stronghold to stand with, a rock to stand on, and refuge to stand under. When the Lord returns, the righteous will reign with Him and the wicked will be no more.

It is not difficult to get discouraged in this world and become negative and hard hearted. The only salvation is the Lord Jesus. He knows what it is to suffer injustice. He knows what it is to live under wicked rulers who frame injustice as lawful to accomplish their evil ends. Christ will overcome in the hearts of His people and one day, in the entire world. Is your heart tender toward God and the hurting people of the world? Are you living for and praying for justice? The Lord loves the righteous and blesses those who humbly seek justice. Hope is found in the hearts of those who have a heart for God.

Deuteronomy 11; Psalms 95–96; Isaiah 39; Revelation 9

What we talk about and delight in communicates who we are, what truly matters to us, and where we are focusing our attention. The world is filled with confusion and darkness. What a blessing the people of God would be if we intentionally kept our focus on our Lord and what He has made us to be – righteous, forgiven, and eternally loved. What a blessing we would enjoy if we often spoke of the goodness of our God. Our conversations would be inspiring and helpful. Those around us would be blessed, the Lord would be honored, and our hearts would be encouraged with hope.

Hezekiah had every reason to speak well of God. He had been miraculously healed by grace and given an additional fifteen years to live (Isaiah 38). He shared his testimony and gave praise to God, but the gratitude did not remain. In Isaiah 39, Hezekiah was given the opportunity to share the good news of God and what God had done for him with the envoys who had come from Babylon (v.1). Rather than speak of what the Lord had done and tell of God's Kingdom, Hezekiah focused his conversation around what he had acquired and his personal kingdom (v.2). God gives us opportunities to share what He has done for us. There is so much to say and so many events to celebrate. If we would only focus on Christ, rather than ourselves, we would have much more interesting conversations. Our words would be filled with life and light and give hope.

When Isaiah heard that the envoys had come, he asked Hezekiah what he had said to them. What a disappointment Hezekiah was (v.3-4). The Lord had provided life where there was certain death. By His grace and for His glory, God had given Hezekiah new life. That is not what Hezekiah shared and showed these ambassadors. He did not show them the temple. He did not speak of the need for forgiveness for their sin. He did not speak of the power of God that had rescued Israel from Egypt and the other nations over the centuries. He did not tell of God's grace in His own life. He boasted of his riches.

Hezekiah could have been a blessing, but instead, he received a curse. These Babylonians appeared to be allies, but were like all nations and people. They were interested in gaining what others had. World conquest was on their minds, and Hezekiah became a target. The consequences for his actions would impact future generations (v.5-8). Rather than repent and seek the welfare of his family, Hezekiah was happy that the difficult days would not impact him. We can only imagine what might have been if Hezekiah had boasted in the Lord. It might have changed the lives of those envoys and the lives of his children. It might have changed world history.

The topics of our conversations are crucial. People need to hear about the love of God, and it is our job to share it. The next generation needs to know of God's goodness and believe in His promises. What do you usually talk about? Is the Gospel of Jesus Christ a regular topic you talk about with friends and family? Our words reveal what we value. Those who value the Lord speak of Him freely and rejoice in sharing their hope in Him.

Deuteronomy 12; Psalms 97–98; Isaiah 40; <u>Revelation 9</u>

We have so little control. The decisions we make are important and our responsibility to God is huge, but in the grand scheme of things, humans are just not that powerful. The angelic hosts are not either. The person with all of the power is God. He is in control. The person who trusts in Him and looks to His authority and power with gladness and confidence lives with hope.

Revelation 9 reveals the unlimited power of God and the limited power of the devil. At the sound of the trumpet of the fifth angel, what is probably Satan falls from the sky to release its demonic army from the pit of hell (v.1-2). It is important to note that the fallen star is given a key. That means what it is doing is permitted by God. It is not free to release and rule this evil army on its own accord. The words "given" (v.3), "told" (v.4), and "allowed" (v.5) need to be a great comfort to the redeemed of God. This unholy hoard was under the control of the Almighty. God allows darkness to reign for divine purposes. Although there will be circumstances and problems that are overwhelming, like the suffering under this intimidating mob and their leader (v.6-11), there is no reason for God's children to fear. God is faithful, even when the sky falls, the demons attack, and destruction is unleased on earth. The time for hell to reign is limited. This woe passed, as all woes do (v.12). Difficulties come and go. God is in charge of the timetable (2 Thessalonians 2:6).

The judgment of death is awful. When the sixth angel blew its horn, four evil angels that had been bound were released to wreak havoc, having been given two hundred million warriors at their disposal. They would kill vast numbers of people (v.13-19). Physical death is awful, but spiritual death is worse. Physical death ends. Spiritual death lasts forever. God is so good and revealed His love for us by sending His Son to die for us so that we would not have to face a spiritual death (John 3:16-18). He tasted death (Hebrews 2:9). He drank the cup of the wrath of God (Matthew 20:22). Those who believe in Him are made righteous and given eternal life. What a Savior!

The hard-heartedness of humanity is as horrifying as anything from hell. A hard human heart can withstand the love of God, reject the authority of God, and ignore the judgment of God. The only hope of hard-hearted humans is the grace of God. Despite their suffering the consequences of sin, those who lived through the attack of the fifth and sixth trumpet would not repent (v.20-21). While we may not be able to control what happens to us, we do control how we respond. Our response to God has an eternal consequence.

God has revealed His grace through His Son and has made His righteousness available to all who believe (2 Corinthians 5:21). Have you been made righteous by repenting of your sin and trusting in the grace given in Jesus? Are you living a grateful, Godly life in Jesus? We cannot control what we go through, but we can control who we go through trials with. Jesus has come to live with, in, and through us. The person who lives under the authority and loving power of Jesus lives with hope.

Deuteronomy 13–14; Psalms 99–101; Isaiah 41; Revelation 11

The life of a follower of Jesus belongs to God. The Lord has purchased His people by the blood of His Son. Those who are God's are to live as God's. Salvation is transformational. If there is no transformation, there is no salvation. The grace God gives to redeem His people is a grace that changes people's lives. Those who live out their calling to be a unique people set apart by God live with hope.

In Deuteronomy 13–14, Moses provided stiff laws with strong demands that applied to those under the theocracy of Israel. Those laws do not apply to Christians in the same way or in the same sense, but there are principles that can be drawn from these laws that provide clear direction for Christians. By applying the principles of these laws, believers in Jesus can honor Jesus and produce hope and confidence.

The battle against sin is real. We must fight against sin or sin will take control of our lives. The person who does not take sin seriously is the person who will live a sinful life. Sin is an unloving act of treason toward God. Those who see sin for what it is will hate sin. A true hatred of sin will lead followers of Jesus to be ruthless in their attitudes toward sin. They will listen intently to those who claim to be spokespersons for God. If in any way a speaker deviates from the Biblical faith delivered to the saints (Jude 3), a wise believer will reject any influence that speaker has in their spiritual life (v.1-5). If any family or friends attempt to entice a believer to stop being devoted to God, that believer will reject their influence from driving what that believer understands to be right and true (v.6-11). If there are places where people are prone to reject God and influence the faithful to turn away from God, then the faithful are to avoid those places and people and reduce the influence they have on the faithful's spiritual life (v.12-18).

The lifestyle of those who claim to know and love God by grace through faith in Christ alone is to be one that is distinct from those who do not know and love God. While the dietary laws no longer serve as a guide for God's people (Acts 10:9-16), the principle of being set apart still stands (14:1-21). A child of God is to delight and find comfort in the Lord and not in food and drink. Food and drink are to be received with gratitude and consumed in a way that brings glory to God (1 Corinthians 10:31). While the tithe offering to the Levites is no longer in effect, the principle of generosity and tithing to the local church stands (v.22-29). Generosity and faithful giving set God's people apart and enable God's children to be renewed regularly as they choose to put God first. By giving to God the first ten percent earned, believers reveal their commitment to God.

The law of God stands. It is summed up in loving God and loving people (Matthew 22:37-40). Does your lifestyle reflect a deep commitment to Jesus? Are you being transformed by the life of Christ in you? Salvation that does not change the way we live is worthless (James 2:14-26). Those who kill sin out of an obedient love for Jesus live with hope.

Deuteronomy 15; Psalm 102; Isaiah 42: Revelation 12

Everybody hurts, but not everybody hurts in the same way. Life is full of pain. We are broken people living in a broken world because of the sin of humanity. The way we suffer and struggle through this difficult place depends entirely on the object of our faith. If we are trusting in anything that originates in this broken world, our faith is misplaced and in time we will despair. If, however, our faith is in the One that is beyond this broken world, our faith will free us to hope, even in the worst of times. Those who depend on God through faith in Jesus by the power of the Holy Spirit live with hope.

In Psalm 102, someone afflicted poured out the sentiments that come when humans suffer. This writer spoke from the perspective of an individual who was part of a community of people who trusted in God. Looking to God in faith, the lament offered rings true. This is no ritualistic rote language here. This was a soul in anguish needing help. There was a cry for help, a request for audience with God, the realization of death, the pain of rejection, and the feeling of being thrown aside (v.1-11). These feelings are normal for sinners. Although God redeems and makes saints of Christ's disciples, we continue to sin. Sin causes suffering.

The good news is that God is good and looks down from heaven on those doomed to die and has chosen to rescue a people for Himself (12-22). God saves for His namesake. The Lord does not save His people because they deserve it. God chooses to love traitors and turn them into servants by grace. This undeserved favor comes from a gracious God. We cannot fully understand God, but what can be grasped of God is enough to cause praise to emit from the lips of the redeemed. The redeemed praise the name that is above every name, the name of Jesus (Philippians 2:9) They rally around Him to delight in Him and to devote their lives to Him.

Death is the consequence of sin. Everybody will die at some point. Although life is brief, the fact that we have life at all is because of the grace God has given. The desire to avoid death is universal among people (v.23-24). No one wants to die, but neither do we want to continue in the state of things. What is longed for is redemption. What is needed is a new kind of life in a new world where sin is vanquished, suffering is ended, and God is praised in every square inch of creation (v.25-28). There will be a new heaven and new earth (Revelation 21). All who are God's people and loyal to His Kingdom will live forever in it and rejoice in the life that never ends. It is life that is secure and established by Christ forever.

Life is not easy. Life is very hard. The more relational connections and earthly capital we have, the greater our sorrow will be. Emotional independence through privatized living may appear preferable. It is not. God has called us to be in community and to love Him and the people of the world. Have you chosen to trust in Jesus? Are you active in His church? Is your hope in the Kingdom to come? Those who look beyond this world for hope find it in Christ.

Deuteronomy 16; Psalm 103; Isaiah 43; Revelation 13

The Story of God is a romance, an adventure, a mystery, and a drama. The Bible is a single story about a King who provided for a people that turned on Him. Rather than completely destroy them, He chose to redeem them at great cost to Himself. Even though He had destroyed the power of the evil that enslaved them, that evil remained. God's redeemed people still struggle with sin. One day, sin will be vanquished and God's people will be completely free. Until then, the people that choose to follow the leadership of the King face trials and tribulations, but live with hope because the King is with them.

Isaiah 43 gives the bullet points of The Story of God. Writing to a people about to be exiled for their sin, the prophet, inspired by God, tells them of God's promise to redeem them. The redemption of God is a result of the everlasting love of God (v.1-7). Despite their rebellion and unfaithfulness, God loves His people. Like a man with a cheating wife, who cannot help but love her even though he faces heartache and disappointment, so God has loved and been disappointed by His people. He still loves them. It is a great romance.

The rescue of God required sacrifice. God was determined to save His people (v.8-13). Those He would save had eyes but could not see. They had ears but could not hear. God is able to do what no others can do. If they searched the nations, they would not find one who could accomplish what He can do. He called His shot. He revealed His plan long before He accomplished it. Just as He promised to rescue His people from Egypt, after 400 years of bondage (Genesis 15:13-14), so through Isaiah, He again promised to save. He is the Lord, and there is none who can save except Him. God's rescue operation is an adventure.

God has a plan for these exiles. Cyrus would come and conquer Babylon and send God's people back to Palestine to build the second temple (Isaiah 44:28). How this would happen was known only by God. What was and is always certain is that God will call His people home. The restoration of Israel is a picture of the ultimate restoration (v.14-21). God is going to do a new thing. There will be a new heaven and new earth and a new way of life, where there will again be harmony. How will this happen? It is a mystery.

Despite God's love, provision, and promises, God's people have struggled to be faithful to Him (v.22-28). There will be many ups and downs in the life of God's people. The one thing that does not change is God. Life will be complicated by our sin and our inability to trust and obey God. God's plan will all work out in the end, but the process will be messy. It is a drama.

The Story of God is clear. The Lord will save all who come to Him by faith. He will lead and bless those who follow His leadership. None can accomplish in life what God demands without the presence and power of God at work in them. Do you trust God? Are you pursuing Him diligently? Do you love Him and desire to honor Him? Those who submit to God will live with soul-satisfying hope.

Deuteronomy 17; Psalm 104; Isaiah 44; Revelation 14

The questions we ask are important. They tell us where our thoughts are. They also direct what and how we process. They guide the trajectory of our ideas. Humans are self-absorbed creatures. Most of the questions we ponder have to do what we want. God made us to be God-centered. We are never more satisfied and at peace than when God is at the center of our thoughts and affections. Those who focus on Christ live with hope.

Revelation 14 reveals the power and purpose of God. He has chosen to save a people for Himself and to guide them in His might. God stands with His people and His people stand in Him (v.1). King Jesus is on the move. He is not seated. He is getting ready to get His Kingdom coming. In preparation for this, the people were singing (v.2-3). It was a song that only they could sing. It is the song of the redeemed. The enemies of God would never sing this song. These saints, seen in the vision, were morally pure and faithful to their King and the ways of His Kingdom (v.4-5). Their love for Him was manifest, as all love for God is, through their obedience (1 John 5:3). The people of God are a great multitude. They are set apart and identified by the way they stand for God, sing to God, and live for God. This is, has always been, and will always be the case.

The Gospel is seen going out simultaneously as this throng is amassing with the Messiah (v.6-7). The people of the world who make the powers of this fallen world their hope are called to repent and turn to the One who can save them and satisfy their souls. Those who ask, "What's in it for me?" would be wise to see what the world can offer and compare it to what Christ offers. The world is fallen. It will not stand (v.8). The things of the world are not liberating. They enslave. They control us, mark us, and lead to destruction (v.9-11). Those who see the world for what it is, a passing broken trash heap, and the grace of God for what it is, a privileged way of life that leads to holiness and happiness, will be wise and rewarded if they choose Christ (v.12-13).

The most crucial question any person can ask is, "Where is the world headed?" The Bible tells of God and of His world and creatures. Every story has an ending. The Bible ends with judgment. This is the destiny of every person on the planet. None will escape the judgment of God. The reapers of heaven will come and the wrath of God will be revealed against all sin and injustice (v.14-20). To understand the wrath of God we need only look to the cross of Christ. The cross reveals what it is to be rejected by God, which causes suffering to the eternal soul. The cross reveals the destructiveness of sin, which dements the mind. The faithful will be saved from this.

What we focus on has everything to do with what we become. God calls us to focus on Him. Are you standing with Jesus? Are you serving His purpose? Is His reward in your future, or will you receive His wrath? We all have to choose. Those who make Jesus the center of their lives live with hope.

Deuteronomy 18; Psalm 105; Isaiah 45; Revelation 15

There are two kinds of people in the world. There are those who love God and are in pursuit of His glory and Kingdom purpose and those who love created things and are in pursuit of temporary happiness and a kingdom that cannot last. God provides for both with common grace. Both are given access to basic human needs. Both are given the power of choice. Those who choose to pursue God and delight in doing what He commands out of love for Him live with hope.

In Deuteronomy 18, Moses wrote of the realities of God's people, the realities of the world, and the realities of God's Kingdom. Living under the Old Covenant, under the theocratic rule of God, Moses and the Israelites were given a special way of life. It was a life that provided them with the opportunity to know and honor God. The world they were in was harsh and evil. Despite God's goodness, they were tempted to desert God and pursue the idolatry around them. Part of their hope, which inspired their obedience, was the certainty of God's plan to send the Messiah, after Moses, who would lead God's people into truth.

Under the Old Covenant, God set aside the Levites to serve as priests (v.1-8). They served as ministers to the people. They did not receive a portion of land. Their calling was to care for the spiritual needs of the nation. In return for their service, the people of Israel were to provide for the Levites' needs. Something similar occurs in the New Covenant. God calls specific individuals to serve His people. They use their gifts and abilities to lead, instruct, and to take the Gospel to the ends of the earth. They are sponsored by God's people in local churches to do this work. They are not paid to do a job. They are cared for by God's people to accomplish God's will.

While God had promised to give Israel the land of Canaan, the land would still have to be taken. This land was filled with evil people who were to be driven out (v.9-14). The Israelites would be tempted to join in the evil practices of those inhabitants. It is amazing how we are tempted. We rarely think of ourselves as being as susceptible to sin as we truly are. God calls us away from sin. He calls us to submit part of our life to Him. Just as the land had been given and yet had to be taken, so salvation is given but also must be worked out.

God's ultimate plan was not lived out by Moses. God had more in mind than simply setting up a theocratic nation among pagan nations. God's plan is to bring salvation and transformation to the world (Genesis 12:1-3). He promised to send a leader, like Moses, who would lead people into truth. Those of us on the other side of the cross know this to be Jesus (Acts 3:22, 23; 7:37). Jesus came, as promised!

God's plan is unfolding before us. Do you see it? Are you joining God in what He is doing in the world? There are many things we can give our lives to. There are things that will last forever and things that will come to an end. It is wise to invest in what we can never lose. Those who live to honor God and build His Kingdom live with hope.

Deuteronomy 19; <u>Psalm 106</u>; Isaiah 46; Revelation 16

Joy is powerful. Those who have joy have hope because they can see beyond the worst of moments and keep sight of what is important in the best of moments. Pure joy is ignited by something beyond the physical. Its source is supernatural. Its application is personal. Its power comes from ideas and beliefs grounded in God's goodness. There is a hope that rises in the hearts of those who have joy.

The writer of Psalm 106 understood the source of joy. It is in God's goodness. God is many things. He is all-knowing, all-powerful, omnipresent, and the maker and sustainer of all things. How awful would it be if He were those things, but not good? What a treacherous, disheartening divine being God would be if He was not good. But He is good (v.1a). His love, like Him, endures forever (v.1b). The only right response to God's goodness and love is gratitude. When we suffer, face trials, and deal with loss, we can know God is good and His love will not fail. We can know God is doing more than we can see (v.2). We can know the best life we can live is one that is like God, full of justice and righteous acts (v.3).

The joy of God's people is personal. Knowing the world is headed into a specific direction and that a blessed outcome is coming provides inspiration. God has a plan for His people and this world. Things may appear to be spinning out of control, but they aren't. Chaos is the work of the evil one, but clarity comes to those who understand and believe God's Word. From the beginning, God has had a plan. Despite our failures and treason, God's Kingdom stands. The writer asks that he be allowed to join in the exuberance of being a part of God's great gathering of blessedness that will come upon His people and the world (v.4-5). Knowing that such a day is coming fills a heart with joy.

The writer is confident of God's plan because of what God has done in the past. The knowledge of the work and will of God in the past reveals the goodness of God to the heart of those who believe. Looking back at the Exodus, the writer is reminded of how God was faithful to His promise. The promise God made on the day the world fell into sin was that a Savior would come and crush the head of the devil (Genesis 3:15). His promise to Abraham was that the whole world would be blessed by his family (Genesis 12:1-3). His promise to Moses was that He would deliver Israel into the Promised Land and guide them to live an abundant life (Exodus 3:8). The writer recalls the faithfulness of God throughout the Exodus and beyond (v.6-46). The people were faithless, but God was faithful to keep His promise.

The Psalm ends with a plea for God's mercy (v.47-48). It is the plea of all of God's people in every age. Today, the church cries, "Come, Lord Jesus!" Is your hope in the coming of the Lord? Is your joy in the victory of God? Is your confidence in the goodness of God? Can you see beyond the bad times and through the times of comfort to the God of the universe who is fulfilling His plan? Those who rejoice in God live with hope.

Deuteronomy 20; Psalm 107; Isaiah 47; Revelation 17

The kingdoms of this world come and go. There is only one Kingdom that will prevail. The Kingdom of God will remain for all time. Just as there is no end to God, so there is no end to His Kingdom. The Lord allows His people to be disciplined. In those moments, when it appears darkness has won, it hasn't. God is still in control. The Lord of hosts will have His way. Those who remain faithful to the King of Glory in tough and tempting times will always have hope.

When God sent His people into exile for their sin, He used the Babylonians. The "Chaldeans" were not righteous. They were not right in their actions. God simply allowed them to rule for a season in order to accomplish His will. Isaiah the prophet, inspired by the Holy Spirit, wrote chapter 47 to explain what God was about to do and why. Any kingdom, company, political party, or individual that stands against God Almighty will face what the Babylonians faced and now face for eternity. Those who stand against God will surely fall.

Proverbs 16:18 has proven true generation after generation: "Pride goes before destruction, and a haughty spirit before a fall." God allows people and nations to rise and enjoy success. It is not because these individuals or countries are so great and good. It is by God's divine will. So often, we humans assume that the good we have done is a result of our own abilities. There is no doubt that success comes through wisdom and hard work. The thing that is often forgotten is the source of the wisdom to act effectively and the source of the strength that enables the hard work. When those who are blessed take credit for their success, a fall is sure to come. It is God who gives the knowledge to do what is best and God that provides the hands that do the work.

Babylon, which became the Biblical symbol of all that is arrogant and opposed to God in the world, had enjoyed a trouble-free existence. Like a virgin never touched, so Babylon had enjoyed complete control over their world, but that was going to change (v.1-3). God was about to act (v.4). The Lord had raised them up for His purpose. He had given the Babylonians power, but also prophets like Daniel to inform the nation of the greatness of God. Instead of turning to God, the Babylonians trusted in their abilities and their gods. Rather than humble themselves and turn to God, they prided themselves in their accomplishments (v.5-15). There was no one to save them. Their redemption and that of those who did business with them could not come through human hands. They needed divine help, but in their pride, they would not pursue God.

Learn the lesson of the Babylonians. Do not follow in their footsteps. A better way has been offered. Jesus Christ has come. He alone can save. He is the maker and sustainer of all things. By His might and for His glory the world exists. Those who worship Him will never be put to shame. Are you making the mistake of Babylon? Is your hope in your power and prestige? Do you give God credit for every good thing in your life? If not, you will fall in your pride. Those who humbly rejoice in God rest in His grace and live with hope.

Deuteronomy 21; Psalms 108–109; Isaiah 48; Revelation 18

While the characters may change and the geography may be different, the same spiritual battle continues to be fought generation after generation. God's Kingdom stands. Until the Lord comes and removes all sin and evil and brings about universal restoration, there will be evil kingdoms that live in conflict with God. The outcome is always the same. God wins. Those who choose to walk with God will live and die with hope.

In Revelation 18, Babylon is again being destroyed. The ancient city's name is a symbol of sin and satanic activity. This narration of the destruction of Babylon is telling (v.1-2). It describes the systemic sin within the network of nations and people that oppose God. It also speaks of the call of God for His people to align their lives under the Lord's direction.

People left to themselves will act on their sin nature and create cultures that dishonor God and destroy the souls of many. These systems typically include political, economic, and sensual activities that disobey God's law and inspire evil among people. Power systems engineered and directed by human beings will always be corrupt. Rather than use power to serve, those outside of God's Kingdom use power for personal pleasure. Without God's love and light, apathy and darkness reign. One nation rises to power and all the others join in its depravity (v.3). When God's judgment comes, those who participated in the revelry will weep, and all they hoped for and delighted in will be destroyed (v.9-19). Destruction is always the result for those who reject God.

Everything that happens is under the ultimate authority of God. For His glory and eternal purpose, God allows demons and sin to work in the world for now. As with those who built the Tower of Babel, the Canaanites, the Egyptians, the Philistines, the ancient Babylonians, and the Sanballats of the world, those who delight in their personal corrupt desires rather than the goodness of God will experience decimation. God has decreed it (v.4-8). Those without God in their life are blinded by pride, which keeps them from seeing their faults. Those faults create misery for many and sadness in their own souls. Their sin rouses the judgment of God.

Revealing the darkness and promising the future devastation of all that is not of God's Kingdom, the Lord calls His beloved people to be unencumbered by sin and to avoid being led astray by those who reject God's loving authority (v.4). When the devastating judgment of God occurs, God's people are to rejoice (v.20-23). Divine judgment is not only an affirmation of God's character, but also of the character of God's people. Judgment reveals the holiness of God. Those who delight in the holiness of God will rejoice with God in the annihilation of evil. Evil has, is, and will cause the martyrdom of many (v.24).

Given the facts of history and God's promises for the future, allegiance to Christ and His holy way of life is the only wise choice. Is your lifestyle God honoring? Is there a distinction between you and the fallen ways of the world? God is just. He will deal with His enemies and their supporters. Those who live for God will live and die with hope.

Deuteronomy 22; Psalms 110–111; Isaiah 49; Revelation 19

One of the great blessings and great challenges of the Christian life is living in accordance with the will and purpose of God. With our limited perspective and our inclination toward disobedience, we will often need to be reminded and encouraged to do what God commands. We may not always understand the reasoning behind God's commands. That does not matter. It is enough that God has spoken and loves us. Those who heed the Word of God and pursue His will and purpose live with hope.

God provided Moses with a litany of commands that were to be lived out by the people. The list in Deuteronomy 22 gave the people some directives, and many were so obvious that even a pagan would know to do them. Some were not as easily understood in terms of why they were necessary and important. Others had to do with sexuality and the Lord's design. In each instance the people were expected to do what God said simply because God said it and because they were His people.

Jesus said if we would love God with all we are and love our neighbor as ourselves, we would be in compliance with the entire law of God (Matthew 22:37-40). While loving God will lead to loving others, we might be tempted to love out of convenience rather than sacrifice. Knowing our capacity to excuse ourselves from submission to God's will, the Lord further simplified His command with "the golden rule" found in Matthew 5:17. We are to treat people the way we would want them to treat us. This is the heart behind the laws pertaining to neighborly kindness (v.1-4), conservation of nature (v.6-7, 9), and public safety (v.8). People with no knowledge of God would know to keep these laws. Those laws that pertain to clothing, farming, and fashion (v.10-12) apply only to the Israelite nation. The point is God expects His people to be distinguished from the rest of the world.

Living within the order of God's design is crucial to human flourishing. Human sexuality is fundamental to life. It is through a man and a woman that life is created and best cared for. The Lord made us male and female. Having been created in the image of God, every human being has the same value to Him. God's love for men and woman of all races and in all places is the same. God loves men and women the same and died to redeem both (John 3:16), but He made them differently. He also made them to relate uniquely. A man is to leave his home and be united to his wife and the two become one flesh and remain loyal to one another, under God, in the covenant of marriage, until death parts them (Matthew 19:4-5). Any sexual activity outside of the covenant of marriage between a man and woman is sin (v.5, 13-30). God's will is clear.

As our Maker and the great lover of our souls, God knows what is best for us. God instructs those He made in His image to comply with His commands with gladness. Is your life marked by a love for other people because of the distinct love you have for God? Is your way of life notably Godly? Are your sexual thoughts and actions holy? Hope comes to those who simply obey God.

Deuteronomy 23; Psalms 112–113; Isaiah 50; Revelation 20

There are so many dynamics taking place within a person who is transformed by the grace of Jesus. When a person is given a new mind, a new heart, a new purpose, and a new direction to pursue by divine benevolence, the implications are limitless. Through the righteous life that comes by obeying Jesus, there are blessings to the mind, soul, and body. The person who looks to Christ is given a blessed life that finds hope in any and every circumstance.

Psalms 112-113 point to the giver of grace and to some of the results of Jesus' redemption.

Those who are truly blessed are blessed by the "blessed man," Jesus Christ. There is no one like Jesus. He is the Holy and Righteous One who was rejected (Acts 3:14), but was vindicated through His resurrection from the dead. Those who love Him and fear Him are truly blessed (112:1). Those who follow Jesus will be blessed in the inheritance of the Almighty (112:2). The families that follow in the path of faith will enjoy the best of what God gives (112:3). What God does in the hearts of His children is reflected in their lifestyle (112:4). They, like their Master, are full of grace, mercy, and righteousness. They are generous and just (112:5); they are eternally secure (112:6); they are unafraid of bad days or difficult seasons (112:7) or opposition (112:8); and they trust God enough to give to others because God has given so much to them (112:9). The life of a saint is strange to the secularist not just because of the way they live, but why. Those who find their hope in the things of the world need credit for their prominence, possessions, and power. Those who find their hope in Jesus are glad to give Him the credit for everything and they "Praise the Lord!" (112:1).

Praise to God is a natural response of the redeemed of God. Psalm 113 is the first of six Psalms (113-118) known as the "Egyptian Hallel." "Hallel" means praise in Hebrew. They were typically sung during the High Holy Days of Passover, Pentecost, and Tabernacles. Psalm 113 was typically sung before the Passover meal. It is appropriate for those who have been rescued by grace to sing them. Like the Israelites of old, the Christians of today have every reason to praise the Lord all day every day for now and forever more (v.1-3). We are to praise Him because He is above us and all things. He is transcendent (v.4-6). He is governing heaven and earth. He is sovereign over all, accomplishing His good will. We are also to praise Him because He is with us. He is immanent (v.7-9). He raises us from the dead and gives us new life in His Spirit out of the ashes. He adopts us into His eternal family, making us heirs of His Kingdom. He remakes us to join Him in His life-giving work and enables us to make disciples, which gives us joy, like that of a new mother.

God is so good to those who love Him. He changes our lives and the trajectory of our eternity. Has God changed your life? Is heaven in your future? Do you delight to praise God and join Him in His Kingdom work on earth as they do in heaven? The blessed life found in and through Christ is the best life and it gives hope.

171

Deuteronomy 24; Psalms 114–115; Isaiah 51; Revelation 21

Great strength comes to those who can look backward and see where the hand of God has moved. God has been, is, and will be at work in this fallen world. His plan is pure and perfect. By His power and might and for His glory, God will do what He has said He will do. Those who doubt (most people have doubts from time to time) can look back and see how God has kept His promises before and have confidence God will continue to keep them in the future. Those who know what God has done in the past can look forward by faith and live in the present with hope.

Writing to a people that could look back and see how God had been at work in the world, according to His will, Isaiah calls on them in Isaiah 51 to persevere in their faith. The prophet provides three distinct incentives to motivate their faith (v.1-8), a practical prayer to offer to God in faith (v.9-11), and a call to live dependent upon God by faith (v.12-23). The prophet pointed to a pivotal truth. God does not change. He is the same God with the same love, the same power, and the same purpose.

Israel had the luxury of the written Word of God. It was delivered to them by Moses and the prophets. It is God's Word. This Word is as true today as it was then. This luxury should not be taken for granted. God's Word told those in Isaiah's day and tells those who will read God's Word today to look back and remember how God raised up Abraham and made a great nation through him and his once barren wife Sarah. It is a call to remember God promised the light of the world would come and now has come to save. It is a call to remember God's promise was not a temporary, but an eternal salvation that would come and now has come. The Lord has done what He said He would do.

In light of what God has done, the right response of God's people is grateful faith-filled prayer. Effective prayer is based upon the Word of God. Believers need only to tell God what He has done and promised to do and, based on those facts, ask Him to accomplish what He alone can do. He has saved! He is saving! He will save!

God's people need never fear. God is our comfort. Fearing people and things that will pass away makes no sense. We are to remember God and what He has done, is doing, and will do. God has revealed Himself in His Word and shown Himself faithful to those who trust in Him. We have all sinned, but by grace have been redeemed and given new life. We must awaken ourselves every day to the grace of God and the purpose of His love. It is there that we will discover our hope.

Who God is, is who God has always been. What God has done is what God always does. God reveals Himself to people and calls them to live under His rule of light in this dark world. Do you know the Bible well enough to be comforted by what God has done and promised? Are you praying and living in those promises? Those who look backward and forward in faith live with hope in the present.

Deuteronomy 25; Psalm 116; Isaiah 52; <u>Revelation 22</u>

The Christian life is not a sprint; it is a marathon. It is a long journey in a hostile land. What is needed for God's pilgrims on their way to their eternal home is faithful endurance. There will be many temptations and opportunities to quit. There will also be many markers to look back on and look forward to for hope. Those who can readily explain why they believe are most likely to endure to the end. The redeemed saints who know why they are on the narrow way filled with persecution, trials, and tribulations can faithfully endure with hope.

Revelation 22 provides the best reason why God's people faithfully endure. This world is not as it should be, and it is not the home of God's family. We are just passing through. Those who know this are looking forward to the home that promotes and provides life and not death (v.1-2). We are looking for the home where Jesus is and where the curse is gone (v.3-4). We are looking for the place where the light of hope shines and the darkness of suffering is gone (v.5). We are looking for the place just for us, where we are wanted and where those who do not love Jesus are not admitted (v.6-17). We are looking for the place that has been promised in God's Word that tells us Jesus is coming and we will not be abandoned (v.18-21). We are looking for the new heaven and earth.

What makes the new heaven and earth so great is the life that flows from the throne. The inhabitants of the city of God will drink from the river of life and eat from the tree of life. These two symbolic elements call to mind the Garden of Eden, where life was meant to be. In the new creation, God's people will not only live forever, but will be nourished by the therapeutic fruit that lines the river. Life will be filled with ultimate health and vitality. What makes the new heaven and earth so great is that we will be with Jesus. We will worship Him as King and Lord with all the strength given to us by the river and tree of life. There will be no more signs of the curse. We will see His face and we will be finally free. What makes the new heaven and earth so great is there will be no more night. There will be no more suffering or pain. The Son will reign. All that is dark and evil will be vanquished. The light of life will shine all around so bright that no other illumination will be needed. What makes the new heaven and earth so great is that the great promise of God to restore His people and all things will have taken place. The Story will have reached its end. The bride, which is the church, and the groom, who is Jesus, will live happily ever after. The promise will have been fully kept. Jesus will have come!

The restoration of God is the hope of God's people. Those who believe and are looking forward to the coming of Jesus have the hope to faithfully endure. Are you living in light of the coming of Jesus? Have you been saved by grace through faith in Christ? Saints of God saved by grace have a living hope that is looking forward to being with Jesus in heaven.

Deuteronomy 26; Psalms 117–118; Isaiah 53; Matthew 1

God needs nothing. He is completely satisfied within His triune being, but God graciously commands His people to give financial gifts to His Kingdom purpose. It is not because God needs the money or resources of His people. It is because His people are designed to give and are the happiest when they do so. By giving to God, the children of God learn to put God first in their life. The most important thing a person can do is to make God their first and greatest priority. The person who gives to God lives with hope.

In Deuteronomy 26, God concluded His list of commands to Israel. His last instructions dealt with tithing. This command on giving informed the people of the amount they were to give, where and when they were to give it, and who the money was to be given to (v.1-4, 12-15). God also told the people what they are to say when they gave their gift (v.5-11). The process of giving is intended to bring glory to God, perspective to the giver, and blessings from heaven.

There are two gifts described in this chapter. The first gift of ten percent was to be given when the people first entered the land. The people would soon be leaving behind a nomadic life and would become an agrarian people settled in a land provided by God's blessing. This gift was different from the yearly Feast of First Fruits (Leviticus 23:9–14), which was celebrated in conjunction with the Passover. God commanded Israel to begin their new life by acknowledging the Lord as their provider. They were to present their gift at the Tabernacle to the priest serving at that time. It was a statement of faith. They were to announce what God had done to save them and what they had become by His grace. When a person under the New Covenant is saved, they end an old life and begin a new one situated on the solid rock of Jesus Christ. The first thing a new believer is to do is to make a public profession of faith through baptism, acknowledging the grace and authority of Jesus over their life.

The second gift to be given by Israel was to be given locally. It was to be presented to the Levites, and the purpose was to provide for the poor and sojourners in each community. This gift was a reminder of how God provided for them when they were poor sojourners, and how God met their needs. Their act of benevolence not only glorified God, but also announced their faith to those in need. The generosity and compassion of God's people is a functional aspect of evangelism. We share God's love well when we show it practically.

This chapter ends with a concluding statement concerning the commands of God (v.16-19). By blessing others and obeying God, the people could anticipate the blessing of God in their lives. It is only in a state of obedience God's blessing can be expected. God is glorified in providing for His people. God provides for His people when they glorify Him.

God is gracious to command us to give financial gifts. Obedient benevolence and holy living are blessings to us that bring blessings from God. Do you have a story of personal salvation? Are you generous to God's work and hurting people? Those who have been saved by grace and give financially to God's work live with hope.

Deuteronomy 27:1–28:19; Psalm 119:1-24; Isaiah 54; Matthew 2

In the world there are some who have talent in a particular field. There are also some who may not be the most talented, but because of training and tenacity, they succeed in their given field. In the field of life, there is not a single person who can rely on talent. We all must rely on training and divine intervention. The person who receives new life in Christ and divine lessons in how to live will be sustained forever with hope.

Psalm 119 is the longest chapter in the Bible, and it has one central theme: the wisdom of the Word of God. The chapter is best studied and meditated upon in pieces. The first twenty-four verses provide a foundation for the entire chapter. These verses speak of the blessedness of God's Word (v.1-8), a function of God's Word (v.9-16), and the need of God's Word (v.17-24).

Those who are saved by grace are given new life in Christ. Through this covenant of grace, a child of God is given forgiveness, the righteousness of Christ, and a new nature. This new life must be nurtured in the truth of God's Word. Blessings come to those who obey the commands of God and walk in the way of the Lord. This way of life is known through the testimonies of God, which inspire the heart already transformed by the love of Jesus. By living under and in obedience to the Word of God, people of faith are free of shame. Rather than regretting what has been, the children of God can look back and praise God for His faithfulness. He does not forsake His own. He pursues us. We will fail, but God does not give up on His children.

To be redeemed is to be made righteous and to receive the call to live a pure life in Christ. The only way purity can be understood and pursued is according to the Word of God. The heart is easily manipulated, but God's Word can protect it. That is a primary function of the Word. When the Word of God is sown in the heart of a person through memorization and meditation, the inclinations of the heart with the help of the Spirit become God honoring. The truth of the Word and the challenges of the flesh will cause God's people to pray. The wisest thing anyone can ever pray to God is "help!" We need God's help to know and obey His Word.

We cannot know what we do not know. The wise person is one who knows they do not know all they need to know and can seek what is needed from the right source. The author of truth is God. God has revealed Himself and His expectations in His Word. Those who see themselves as sojourners in enemy territory and seek God's help because they know they need instruction will find a trustworthy resource in the Word of God. Life is hard and challenges abound, but God's Word shows us how to live and honor our Maker.

Without the Word of God we would be forced to depend on our own broken devices. We would have to trust our broken hearts and deceived minds. Do you know and love Jesus? Are you a student of His Word? The instructions for blessedness are found in the Bible, and those who seek to know and obey them live with hope.

Deuteronomy 28:20-68; Psalm 119:25-48; Isaiah 55; Matthew 3

The Gospel is the good news that God entered our broken world, took on flesh, lived a holy lived, and died an atoning death. Jesus was raised and is coming again to restore heaven and earth and reign with His people forever. The invitation to receive God's great grace now stands. Those who receive salvation by grace through faith in Christ alone are justified and throughout life will be sanctified and live with hope.

Isaiah 55 is a wonderful presentation of the Gospel. It reveals God's call and the command to respond to God's call. It also provides reasons why a person would be wise to respond in faith to God's call. God's call is to both the unbeliever and the believer. God's call to unbelievers is the call to a new life, through faith, that will bless them and honor God. God's call to believers is the call to abide in the life that comes through Jesus.

What a mysterious and glorious joy to know God wants us. He does not need us, but God desires us to be with Him. God's invitation is to "Come!" (v.1). God's invitation is to receive free access to the Almighty and eternal life with Him. God's invitation is to come and enjoy. God does not want us to waste our lives (v.2). God wants us to come to Him and live under His eternal covenant of grace (v.3). God has sent His Son to lead us (v.4) and has formed a new nation of saints (v.5). The unbeliever who will come and be saved will be satisfied in the goodness of God. The believer who continues in faith will be sustained with hope.

Those who hear the Gospel are to seek the Lord. God seeks sinners and will buy their redemption with the blood of His Son (1 Corinthians 6:20). Those whom God has bought are called to glorify Him in their bodies. The Lord is to be sought while He may be found (v.6). To seek the Lord is to repent (v.7). Repentance is a turning away from sin and choosing to trust and obey God. The unbeliever is to begin the new life of faith by repenting and believing in Jesus. The believer will continue a life of repentance and grow in faith day by day.

The reasons for responding in faith to God's call are many. God's knowledge and ways are higher than the ways of fallen humanity (v.8-9). God knows what is best and how to obtain what is best, and His purpose will be accomplished (v.10-11). The unbeliever will find God has provided for the longing of their soul in the Gospel. The believer will enjoy the benefits of grace growing within and rejoice in peace (v.12). Where there was once a dry and broken life, there will be a new fruitful life. God's fame will be great! The everlasting covenant of God revealed in Christ will never come to an end (v.13).

The Lord offers life. Those who will seek Him will find hope and life and peace and joy. The reasons are clear why we should trust in the Lord. The Gospel is real and true. It will do what God promised. Have you repented of your sin and believed in Jesus? Are you being transformed daily by the power of the Gospel? Those who know God's salvation revealed in His Word live with hope.

Deuteronomy 29; Psalm 119:49-72; Isaiah 56; <u>Matthew 4</u>

Jesus undid what humanity had done. Where we failed, He succeeded. Now we can know God and be in a right standing with Him. This is true because of the great exchange that took place at Calvary. "For our sake he made him to be sin who knew no sin, so that in him we might become the righteousness of God" (2 Corinthians 5:21). Jesus took our sin, and by faith we receive His righteousness. Those who have been made righteous by grace Jesus have hope.

Hope is only possible because of the righteousness of Jesus. Were He not holy, His death would have no merit for humanity. Without Jesus' merited righteousness, He could not impute righteousness to us and give us a blameless standing before God. Matthew 4 shows one of the battles Jesus won over sin and reveals the love and plan of God for the world.

Jesus overcame temptation and defeated the Devil. Unlike us, Jesus was able not to sin. Unlike Adam and Eve, who were able to sin or not sin, Jesus was God and able not to sin, although genuinely tempted. Having been baptized and led by the Spirit in the desert, Jesus fasted for forty days (v.1-2). While He was hungry, the devil came to tempt Him (v.3). The first temptation was to trust in physical might rather than divine truth. Jesus overcame by pointing to the sustaining power of the Word of God (v.3-4). The second temptation was to be the participant in a great miracle that forced the hand of God. Jesus overcame by honoring the glory of God and refusing to cheapen it with circus tricks (v.5-7). The third temptation was to bypass the cross and gain world peace without God's glory. Jesus overcame by delighting in the worthiness of God alone to be worshipped and served (v.8-10). The devil left Jesus after the temptations, and the angels ministered to the Lord (v.11).

From that desert experience, Jesus went and called the disciples, who would be the first leaders of His church (v.12-22). He began His ministry in the regions where Isaiah said He would. It was in Galilee that Jesus began to preach of the need for repentance in light of the coming of the Kingdom of God. To help in His crusade, Jesus gathered disciples. These men became authors of Scripture, martyrs of the faith, and proclaimers and witnesses of the hope of glory.

To show His love and prove His divinity, Jesus not only spoke the truth, but brought physical healing to the people of Galilee (v.23-25). The paradigm of Jesus' ministry is needed today. It is not enough to simply tell people that God loves them. We must show them. It also is not enough to show love. We must tell people of the Gospel of Jesus. Jesus preached the Gospel and provided for physical needs. This is the way the Gospel needs to be shared today by God's people.

Jesus did what no one else could do. He defeated sin and lived a holy life. The righteousness of Christ provides the viability of the Gospel. Jesus calls disciples to serve God's purpose. The Gospel is made known through disciples sharing and showing God's love. Have you received the righteousness of Christ by faith? Are you sharing your hope? Those who follow Jesus have hope.

Deuteronomy 30; Psalm 119:73-96; Isaiah 57; Matthew 5

It is marvelous that God has chosen to be gracious. How He has chosen to be gracious is majestic. Why He has chosen to be gracious is mysterious. The Story of God, the Bible, tells of God's amazing grace. While we were in treason, Romans 5:8 tells us it was then Jesus redeemed us. God's grace turns traitors into faithful soldiers; it turns orphans into children; it turns broken lives into holy temples. Those who repent of self-dependence and trust in Jesus will receive God's grace and live with hope.

Deuteronomy 30 provides a powerful picture of the person of God who gives the grace we need. God is all-knowing. God is love. God is sovereign. God is powerful. God is willing to do what humanity cannot do – save sinners. In all that He does, God reveals His glory. God was preparing Israel to enter the Promised Land. He was graciously instructing them, through Moses, who was wrapping up his sermon and providing his last words to the people before his death. As God's spokesman, Moses communicated the truth of God, the will of God, and the grace of God.

God knew the people would fail Him, and so He gave them instructions for what to do when they felt the pain of His curse. If the people would not love and obey God, they would be forced out of the land into slavery in a foreign land (v.1-2). Just as Adam and Eve were forced out of the Garden of Eden for their sin, so the Israelites would be banished if they disobeyed God. God promised the people if they would repent and believe and look to Him, He would save them and transform them (v.1-6). More than that, God would put on their enemies the curses that had been on the Israelites, while He made Israel to prosper (v.7-10). Just as the return of Christ will change the fortunes of the faithful and God's enemies will be cursed eternally, so the Israelites would be given God's blessing if they obeyed God.

A life of faithfulness is possible because of the Word of God. The Word of God reveals the will and way of God. Without the Word of God, humanity has no hope. Because God had given His Word and His covenant, the Israelites could choose to seek God's blessing (v.11-20). The people would still sin, but as they sought grace through the sacrificial system, they would honor God and He would forgive their transgressions. Those under the new covenant of Christ still sin. Even with the power of the Holy Spirit living within, Christ followers still struggle with sin, but God is faithful and just to forgive us (1 John 1:9). What sustains the relationship between God and man is grace. It is by grace we are saved. It is by grace we endure. It is by grace we pursue God.

God is glorious and words fall short to explain Him fully. We experience His glory by grace, through His act of grace. God chose to be gracious and sacrificed His Son so we could be saved. Those who believe are made saints and live in God and God abides in them. Have you accepted the grace of God and been saved by believing in Jesus for forgiveness and given new life? Are you living in the will of God? Only those who look to Jesus can experience grace and have eternal hope.

Deuteronomy 31; Psalm 119:97-120; Isaiah 58; Matthew 6

It is not hard to lose hope. The wealthy and the poor, the healthy and the sick, the influential and the forgotten all have hearts that can be deceived. Our circumstances are never the deciding factor when it comes to the state of our souls. Our spiritual health and the hope of our hearts are dependent upon our capacity to sustain our faith in Jesus. The primary source for understanding Jesus is Scripture. Those who seek Jesus live with hope.

Psalm 119:97-120 provides many of the benefits of God's Word. The goal of any Christ follower is not simply to know truth but to live it. Love for Jesus is revealed in our obedience to Him. Those who know Jesus are in love with Him, and out of love for Jesus, they obey Him. Like a jealous enemy, the world, the flesh, and the devil conspire to keep God's people from delighting in Jesus. If we are to enjoy the blessing that is to know, love, and obey Jesus, we must have the wisdom to discern, the light to see, and the faith to protect.

The Bible gives wisdom. Wisdom is the ability to do what is best in any given circumstance. The psalmist speaks of having wisdom that surpasses that of His enemies (v.98). The greatest enemy of humanity is the deceit of the devil. Rather than worship God and enjoy Him forever, the devil wanted to be worshipped. Many angels fell and became demons. These fallen angels, who were originally made for truth and love, are now filled with lies and hate. They now seek to sack societies through deception. Disciples that meditate on the Scriptures gain compelling truth that confounds lies (v.97, 99-100). Bible students can keep from evil, maintain obedience, delight in truth, and learn to hate what is evil (v.101-104).

The Bible gives light to guide and protect. Those who adhere to God's Word find their path in life illuminated (v.105). It is easy to get tripped up with indiscretions, negative emotions, and selfishness. God's Word shows the devastation of disobedience and inspires fidelity to Jesus, confidence in Jesus, and praise to Jesus (v.106-108). A life centered on Jesus will remember and keep God's rules, discern treachery, build a Godly heritage, and remain strong to the end (v.109-112).

The Bible reveals the faith that saves. Describing the armor needed in spiritual warfare, Paul speaks of "the shield of faith, with which you can extinguish all the flaming darts of the evil one" (Ephesians 6:16). Faith in the Gospel of Jesus not only saves a soul, but sanctifies a life by protecting it from sin. Those who rest in Christ hate deception and are protected by truth (v.113-114). By faith, a child of God can reject what is wrong and hold to what gives real hope, Jesus (v.115-116). Jesus holds up His saints so they are able to transcend the dangers of darkness, find favor in humility, be sustained in trials, and enjoy wisdom that respects God's power (v.117-120).

Without the Bible we would not know the greatness of God or the blessing of His ways. By God's grace and in His truth, sinners are made saints. Do you love Jesus? Has He redeemed you from sin? Do you love and obey His Word? Those who seek to know and obey Jesus live with hope.

Deuteronomy 32; Psalm 119:121-144; Isaiah 59; Matthew 7

God is in complete control and every person is completely responsible for their actions. How these two interwoven realities work together is a mystery. What is not a mystery is the greatness of God. What is not a mystery is the brokenness of humanity. God has made all things and by His might sustains all things for His glory. Humanity was placed over creation but failed to do God's will. The only hope for humanity now is God's grace and mercy. Those who look to the Redeemer will always have hope.

Isaiah 59 paints a very real and very bleak picture of humanity, but it also gives hope. Like the Gospel itself, this chapter points to three distinct realities. The first is the greatness and goodness of God. The second is the sad state of humanity. The third is the redeeming plan of God.

God is glorious and there is no end to His might. There is nothing that God cannot do, and He is fully aware of everything that happens in the universe (v.1). What an awesome God! He is the God who uttered the words that created the world and universe. He is the God who knows all things and for His glory accomplishes His will. Nothing can keep God from accomplishing what He has determined to do. The oceans, the earth, the planets, and all the galaxies are like tools in His hand He uses for His glory.

And yet, because of His holiness and goodness, God is cut off from humanity (v.2). God could and would bless His image bearers, but rather than honor Him, humanity committed treason against the King of heaven. To bless those who stand in opposition to all that is good would be wrong. God does not do what is wrong. God is always right, and so He does not bless injustice, crooked and perverse ways, or evil (v.3-8). Apart from God humanity is blind, broken, and destructive (v.9-13).

Rather than desert us, God promised He would step in and undo what humanity has done. The world is not as it should be. In our world, justice, righteousness, truth, and uprightness are in short supply, and God is not happy about it (v.14-15). Humanity had no hero that could save, and so God stepped in and by His own hand brought redemption (v.16). Like a warrior, He came to do battle and God was victorious! Jesus is the promised Redeemer (v.17-20). He was promised from the beginning (Genesis 3:16; 12:1-3). Isaiah affirmed it. The goal of God, the glory of His goodness in the redemption of His people, would happen! This Savior would do more than change the circumstances of humanity. This glorious God would send His Spirit and He would give life, truth, and hope forever (v.21).

The Gospel is the only hope of humanity. Having turned against God, there was no way the people of this planet could recover from their fall. God sent His Son to overcome sin and death. God sent His Spirit to give life and reveal truth. Now all who believe are saved by the covenant of grace in Jesus Christ. Have you received this pardoning and empowering grace? Is your life marked by the presence of God's Spirit? Do you have a desire to see the glory of God spread throughout the earth? Those who look to Jesus for salvation live with hope.

Deuteronomy 33–34; Psalm 119:145-176; Isaiah 60; Matthew 8

Everyone lives by faith, but not everyone lives with hope. Being finite creatures with eternal souls living in an infinite world, we are incapable of living self-sustained and self-satisfying lives. God made us to trust in Him and live by faith in Him. By divine design, human beings live by faith. Everyone places their faith in something or someone. What we hope in and for is the object of our faith. Those who live by faith in Jesus Christ live with a living hope that does not disappoint.

In Matthew 8, there are people from all different walks of life expressing faith. Each person faces a different circumstance, but Jesus and His love, grace, and power are who and what is needed in every situation in life. Whether our need is physical, spiritual, emotional, or a mixture of all three, Jesus is the answer.

Having preached the Sermon on the Mount and come down to do what was next, a leper approached Jesus (v.1-4). He called Jesus "Lord," which showed his faith in who Jesus is. He recognized the divinity of Jesus. The laws for lepers and those they came in proximity to were very clear (Leviticus 13:45-46; Numbers 5:2-4). People with leprosy were not to be touched. Jesus touched him and healed him, according to the man's faith. Jesus instructed him to go and do as the law commanded, which is the right response of a redeemed person.

Coming into Capernaum, a centurion came to Jesus and showed great faith (v.5-13). He sought the healing of a servant, but told Jesus he knew He did not need to go to where his servant was, based upon his understanding of how leadership works. This showed wise faith. The servant was healed immediately. Those who seek the healing power of Jesus on behalf of others provide a great service in faith.

Jesus also healed Peter's mom (v.14-15) and many others (v.16-17), which fulfilled the prophecies concerning the Messiah. There was a scribe and another disciple who spoke of following Jesus (v.18-22). Jesus made it clear that to follow Him is to leave the comforts of life in pursuit of the Kingdom of God. Real faith will always make real sacrifices, which result in a changed lifestyle. That includes living without fear in the midst of the storms of life (v.23-27). When Jesus is with us and in us, we need not fear circumstances.

There is a big difference in understanding facts and living by faith. Demons understand the facts of Jesus, just like many raised in church know the stories of Jesus. Saving faith changes a person's life. When Jesus was approached by the demon-possessed man, the demons knew who Jesus was, but their knowledge did not change them. The men were saved by grace (v.28-32). The demons were sent into pigs, which ran into the sea and died. Rather than believe in Jesus, the people of that place sent Jesus away (v.33-34). We all have to choose between Jesus and the things of this world.

is only active faith, which results in transformation and love that saves. Do you have saving faith in Jesus? Is His presence changing you? It is impossible to be with Jesus and not be changed. Those who believe in Jesus live with hope.

Joshua 1; Psalms 120–122; Isaiah 61; Matthew 9

Change is often difficult, but change is a part of life. If someone or something is not changing, it is probably dying or dead. God does not call His people to live in a stagnant existence. We are meant to always be growing and going. The Lord will allow us to face challenges that cause us to change. The person who can embrace change, as a means of accomplishing God's plan, will live with hope.

In Joshua 1, there were major changes taking place in the life of Israel. A new leader, Joshua, was being installed. The people were entering a new geographical region. The nature of the community was about to go from being defensive and nomadic to offensive and settled. Change was coming. They had been told of it for years, but now they would have to experience it. Change can bring many blessings and opportunities if we have the faith and courage to trust God. When God is leading a person's life, there are promises, plans, and ultimate purposes that inspire the faith and courage needed to successfully negotiate changes.

God's promise to lead His people to reside in Canaan was about to be fulfilled (v.1-4). Even though Moses was dead and would not lead the people to enter the land, God's promise still stood. God's plan is bigger than any one person. Joshua would now lead them. Strength and courage in the Lord along with faith in God's Word is a must to accomplish God's plan during seasons of change (v.5-9).

God's plan is not complicated. God's plan is to accomplish His will in and through His people. We often make things complicated by getting sidetracked with our doubts, demands, and wanting to control the details. The people were told what to do (v.10-15). There were probably all kinds of issues in people's lives at that time like family events, business deals, and personal conflict. Some probably just did not feel like packing up and going that day. We must never allow our temporary problems or preferences to keep us from accomplishing God's eternal plan.

God's purpose is good. God's purpose is to make His glory known by accomplishing His eternal will in and through His people. The people understood God's purpose, which had been communicated to them by Moses (v.16-18). Their devotion was based on their faith in the Lord. The only thing they needed from their new leader was fidelity to God. Those who lead best, lead from a faithful heart with a clear conscience and in a state of humble submission to God.

Change is inevitable. We are all either about to enter into or are in the midst of or are coming out of a season of change. How we experience change will determine whether that season is a time of blessing and fulfilled opportunities or a time of frustration and failure. Is your faith strong? Are you willing to act courageously for the sake of God's purpose? Are you trusting and obeying God? Change is to be expected. Those who embrace God's promise, plan, and purpose during seasons of change live with hope.

Joshua 2; Psalms 123–125; Isaiah 62; Matthew 10

One of the great comforts enjoyed by the children of God is knowing they are never alone. God is with us. He is accessible to us. He cares for us. He is the ultimate Good Shepherd. Jesus said in John 10:14-15, "I am the good shepherd. I know my own and my own know me, just as the Father knows me and I know the Father." Time in worship helps establish the relationship between the sheep and the Shepherd. Those who gather with members of their church each week and look to the Lord each day in a time of worship live with hope.

Psalms 123–125 are "Psalms of Ascents." They were sung by the Jews in preparation for worship. There is evidence they were sung as the people would make their way to the temple and also when the exiles were coming back from Babylon to Jerusalem. These Psalms would be sung to help people focus their affections on God. He is a God of mercy. He is a God who rescues. He is a God who protects.

Life is rarely easy. Even for those who have resources, healthcare, education, and general safety, life is still difficult. The human condition is such that no matter how comfortable life may be, the heart remains unsettled. There is an insatiable desire for eternal fulfillment. In our sin and brokenness we cannot attain or produce what we ultimately long for. Those who worship the Lord find what the soul needs (Psalm 123:1-2). In His mercy, God gives us mercy. He does not give us what we deserve. Even as we struggle in life, we can worship God for who He is and for what He has done and be contented (v.3-4).

Like a damsel in distress, a sheep in the desert, or a candle in the wind, we are in need of a rescue. Those who repent of self-sufficiency and the ways of self-autonomy and choose to delight in the Lord are helped by Him (Psalm 124). The spiritual powers of darkness are always on the attack. The deceived people that side with the darkness are corrupt in their practices and intentions. Darkness hates the light. Those who worship Jesus live in His light but are hated by the darkness. It is only by grace the people of God are saved and the light of life enables them to worship Christ.

One glorious day, the enemies of Jesus will be vanquished. All those who sided against God and His Kingdom will be judged and destroyed. Until that time, the Lord protects His people while they live in enemy territory. God is like the mountain range around Jerusalem, and His people are like the holy city (Psalm 125:1-2). Those who truly worship Christ will never be ruled by sin or have to live in fear of death (v.3-5). The protection of God is on those who worship Him. They will live and die in peace and find favor forevermore.

There are two kinds of people in the world: those who worship God and those who stand against God. God is with His people. He cares for their needs. Are you a true worshipper of God? Do you worship God, as a way of life? The only way a person can worship God is by grace through faith in Jesus alone. Those who know and love Jesus live under His authority. They worship Him and He gives them hope.

Joshua 3; Psalms 126–128; Isaiah 63; Matthew 11

God is dangerous. Thankfully, He is merciful. Without His mercy, we would have no hope. God's power and holiness make Him dangerous. Were He not all-powerful, His holiness would be nice, but not terrifyingly just. Were He not holy, His power would be awesome, but capable of being manipulated. God's power and holiness make him hazardous to sinful humanity. Because of His mercy, all who trust in Jesus have hope.

Isaiah 63 reveals the serious consequences that come with God's power and holiness. The holiness of God demands justice, and by His power God promises to decimate His enemies. How and why that will happen is clear (v.1-6). God gives mercy to those who will look to Him and honor Him by faith. He gives steadfast love for His namesake (v.7-14). This mercy makes His people mindful of their need for divine intervention in their own hearts (v.15-19). It is by the mercy of God that God's people are saved, sustained, and strengthened in the power and holiness of God.

The disturbing description of how God's wrath destroys His enemies reveals a significant, but often overlooked or forgotten aspect of God. So many people want a safe god they need not take seriously. The ideal god for some is one that has enough power and goodness to provide for what they want, but not enough power and holiness to demand devotion. God is to be feared with good reason. God is to be sought with awe and reverence.

Were it not for God's mercy, humanity would have no hope. Thankfully, God is merciful. He has revealed His benevolent kindness over and over. When He saved Israel from the bondage of Egypt, God exhibited His steadfast love. It was by God's sovereign will Jacob's progeny were rescued. It was for God's namesake Israel was loved and guided to the Promised Land. God is the only true God. All other gods are fakes. They cannot redeem humanity. God alone is worthy of glory. God redeems for the sake of His glory. It is God's glory to be merciful and to save a people for His namesake.

Those who are His people cannot, even though they are saved, sustain their devotion to God on their own and in their own power. Israel rejected God, and God gave them over to their sin and allowed Babylon to destroy the temple and take the nation captive. Even after their redemption from that exile, the people were incapable of keeping their hearts delighted in God. The redeemed of God need the Spirit of God to reveal sin and create delight in their hearts for the Lord. Without the Lord's work in His people, the hearts of the people grow cold and discontented. They ignore God and His power and holiness. The flesh does not die easily. The flesh desires to be its own god and receive the glory God deserves. It is by God's mercy His people are made aware of their sin and are able to cry out for revival.

God is so good! He does not need us, but He wants His redeemed people to know Him and love Him. Do you fear the Lord? Do you live in awe of Him? Do you need Him to restore your heart for Him? Ask Him to. Those who truly live in awe of God and bring Him the glory due His name live with hope.

Joshua 4; Psalms 129–131; Isaiah 64; Matthew 12

Religion and true life in Christ are not synonymous. Religion is an institutional approach to life where rules and systems are assumed to please God, but ultimately produce despair or pride. True life in Christ is realized by God's grace through a person's faith and produces love for God and people. Those who have true life in Christ have a hope that lives and lasts forever.

Matthew 12 shows the little patience Jesus had for religion. Jesus loves people and appreciates the affection that results in merciful kindness. During His earthly journey, Jesus epitomized the love and mercy that He delighted in and taught. The merciful and loving life is what Jesus calls His followers to. It is a result of the work of the Holy Spirit. It is a life that produces the "fruit of the Spirit" (Galatians 5:22).

The religious leaders of Jesus' day sought to project power to gain pleasure, possessions, and popularity at the expense of other people. They made their own laws that exceeded God's laws. Human endeavors that depart from God's will cause suffering. Jesus revealed what God desires. God desires people to give mercy to others. God despises religious theatrics (v.7-14).

The compassion of Jesus reveals the heart of God. He not only protected the weak and healed the sick, but He did not crush the spirits of the struggling (v.15-21). Jesus masterfully and beautifully fulfilled the prophecies made about Him by the prophet Isaiah. He is gracious and "a bruised reed he will not break, and a smoldering wick he will not quench" (Matthew 12:20). Jesus appreciates the efforts of the weak and cares for them, protects them, and even uses them.

The religious leaders of Jesus' day did not delight in Jesus and make Him the object of their worship and affection. Jesus does not fit in the mold that sinful people often want Him to be in. He is self-sufficient and needs nothing. He is not in league with the devil (v.22-27). He is in communion with the Holy Spirit and has been for eternity. He did His work and accomplishes His work now in the hearts of humanity through the Holy Spirit (v.28-30). Every sin can be forgiven, except for the rejection of the work of the Holy Spirit. Without the Spirit there is no life or power to know and live for God.

Those who walk in the grace of Jesus to the glory of God by the power of the Spirit produce the fruit of the Spirit (v.33-37). The redeemed of God do the work of the Spirit and are affirmed in their faith by their works. Jesus promised He would die and three days later be raised (v.38-42). And He was! Those who trust in empty religion will never be filled. They may kill one personal demon, but a hoard will always return to haunt them (v.43-45). Only those who truly delight in God, live for His Kingdom, and make the family of God their highest priority, as Jesus did (v.46-50), will know the freedom of genuine faith.

God does not delight in perfunctory religious practices. God delights in devotion. Religious people pretend to be Godly. Those devoted to Jesus live a life of love delighted in who God is and refuse to reduce God to anything less. Are you like Jesus or the religious leaders of His day? Those who honor Christ and live in the Spirit have hope.

Joshua 5; Psalms 132–134; Isaiah 65; Matthew 13

Service is fundamental to being a follower of Jesus. Through service, God transforms the character of His people. God does not need His people's assistance. God is all-powerful. God wants His people to be a part of what He is doing in the world. Service is a means to bring glory to God when the service rendered is done rightly for the praise of God and not for the praise of people. Those who serve the Lord with the motive to honor Him live with hope.

In order to serve in a way that honors God rightly, God's people must be set apart, humble, and submitted to God. Those who serve God motivated by a desire to gain power, pleasure, popularity, or possessions do not truly serve God. They serve themselves. It is a holy act to serve God. Only those who have been made holy by grace can appropriately accomplish God's will. Joshua 5 shows how God prepared Israel to serve His purpose. Israel had crossed the Jordon on dry ground, and it terrified the enemies of God (v.1). Their terror gave Israel time to prepare themselves spiritually for the mission God had for them.

The first order of business was to get the fighting men within the covenant statutes by circumcising them (v.2-9). Hebrew boys were to be circumcised at eight days old (Genesis 17:10–14). This was a sign of the Abrahamic Covenant. By circumcising the men age forty and under, Joshua was pointing them to the promise of God and positioning these fighting men under the authority of the Almighty. During the forty years of desert wanderings, these men had not been circumcised. Now circumcision set the men apart from the reproach of Egypt. This step of obedience allowed these men to be recognized as God's men.

While they were there at Gilgal, the time came to celebrate the Passover (v.10). This meal reminded them of the grace of God. This meal reminded them that God had intervened by sending them a leader, Moses, and provided the means for their salvation. It was the blood of the lamb that had saved them. Humbled by the reminder, the people discovered they no longer needed to live off of manna (v.11-12). From that point on the people ate of the fruit of the land, as God said they would.

In preparation for the battle, Jesus came and met with Joshua. This "Christophany," a pre-incarnate appearance of Jesus Christ, prepared Joshua (v.13-15). Joshua was worried about the battle, but all he needed to be concerned with was his faith. Joshua wanted God's allegiance and to know God was on His side. God made it clear this mission was not about Joshua gaining victory. The mission was about giving God glory, which is always the primary purpose of God's people. Joshua was worried about the wrong thing. God's children need never worry about anything, except honoring God. Once we are submitted to Christ, everything else is just details.

The Lord is jealous for His glory and rightly so. He is the holy one. Those who know Jesus are to serve Him with lives that are obedient, humble, and submitted to Him. Are you ready and able to serve God? Have you given your life and allegiance to Jesus? Those who serve in the name of Jesus serve a purpose that gives them hope.

Joshua 6; <u>Psalms 135–136</u>; Isaiah 66; Matthew 14

The grace of God the Father revealed through His Son, Jesus Christ, in the power of the Spirit, is glorious. God's grace produces humility, confidence, and gratitude. Without the grace of God, humanity would have no hope. It is because God has loved us and provided salvation by grace and given His people the gift of faith that hope is possible. The only right response to God's goodness to us is praise and gratitude. Those who know God's grace through faith and live a life of praise and gratitude live with hope.

Praise and gratitude are consistent themes in the Psalms. Psalm 135 calls the redeemed of God to praise the Lord. Psalm 136 calls God's people to give thanks to God. The Old Covenant saints were able to praise and give thanks to God for the promises of God. The New Covenant saints can praise God for the promises He has kept in Christ. These Psalms call us to cry out to God with praise and gratitude.

The Old Covenant saints could read Psalm 135 and praise God for choosing them, for being mighty, for saving them, and for being their great provider. Those who know Jesus can praise Him even more! Those who have been grafted in and made members of the eternal Kingdom of God can praise Him for His choosing and calling them. The followers of Jesus can see the mighty hand of God moving throughout history in miraculous ways to accomplish His purpose in and through His church. As those who have been saved by grace through faith in Christ alone, the saints of God can live in awe of the redemption that continues to transform lives. The one true God is not like the idols of the world. He remains. He does not fail. His purpose is built upon His promises and He is a promise-keeping God. He is worthy of praise!

The Old Covenant saints could read Psalm 136 and give thanks to God for His goodness and greatness, His creation, His saving power, His provision, and His mercy. The Lord made heaven and earth and gave life. He intervened in creation and provided miraculously for His people. Today, Christians can celebrate God's creation and give thanks for His wisdom and providential care. Those who trust in Jesus can see how God brought about circumstances that provided and led to their personal salvation. They can see God's provision in the past and His promises for the future. They can see how the Lord has been merciful to them by not giving them what they deserve. Seeing the blessings and benefits of God produces gratitude in the hearts of God's people. This gratitude makes it easy to say over and over His "steadfast love endures forever."

There has never been one millisecond when God was not in control. The Lord has made and sustained all things and intervened in creation according to His will. It was God's will to choose and save a people for Himself who would live to bring Him glory. The world is now full of saints. There are still many more who will be saved. Do you daily give God the praise and thanks He is due? Do you live in a constant state of humility, confidence, and gratitude because of the greatness and mercy of God? Those who praise Him and are grateful to Him have hope.

Joshua 7; Psalms 137–138; Jeremiah 1; Matthew 15

There are some who claim to speak for God but lie to people by teaching that physical comfort comes with Godliness. The apostles and Jesus did not teach this. There is peace and joy in obedience and sometimes ease, but not always. Those who find strength in God's presence and love live with hope.

Jeremiah 1 describes the calling of Jeremiah to ministry. Jeremiah was an outsider. His priestly line was not favored. His message was not appreciated. His purpose was divine, which put him at odds with the devil. He began preaching during the revival period of Josiah, but then had to endure the reigns of Jehoiakim and Zedekiah (v.1-3). He saw Judah fall to Babylon. Jeremiah did what God commanded and suffered for it. It is no small thing to be called "the weeping prophet."

Every Christian is called to ministry. Some are called to full-time service and are supported by the church, but all are called to serve. It is a great comfort to Christians to minister knowing that God has called them. Ministry is rarely easy or comfortable. Knowing they are living out God's will and design for their life strengthens them as they serve God in leadership. Like Jeremiah, all God's ministers are known, formed, and consecrated by God (v.4-5). They, like Jeremiah, are told to serve and are blessed by God to accomplish His purpose, according to His Word (v.6-9). There is power in God's Word to tear down and to build up. God does the work. Ministers simply obey God's commands (v.10).

One of the ways Christians gain confidence in their calling is through trials and testing. Like Jeremiah, they must be affirmed by their capacity to discern the Word of God. God's first question to Jeremiah was about the vision of an almond branch (v.11-12). Interestingly, the almond trees were said to "watch for spring." God said He would watch over His Word to accomplish it. It is not the servants' words, but God's Word that does the work. The second question of God to Jeremiah was about his vision of the boiling pot (v.13-16). God promised destruction to Judah for disobedience. This is what happens when God's people refuse to follow the Godly leadership God provides. Leadership is only as good as the followership of the people.

Like Jeremiah, servants are not to concern themselves with their personal preferences. They are to serve. That means that every day they are to prepare themselves properly through prayer and meditation on the Word of God and then get on with the task they have been called to, regardless of how people respond to their work (v.17). Those who are faithful are defended by the Almighty (v.18-19). Those who fight against the will and Word of God fight against God Himself. God is the King. No one can overcome the King of heaven!

All of God's people are ministers and are to serve God where God calls them. Are you serving your Kingdom purpose? If not, why not? God does not accept excuses. We may not like our calling, but God's will is always right. Those who position themselves to hear from God and then obey His call live with great hope, even in harsh conditions.

It is not a complicated thing to follow Jesus. It is not easy, but it is not complicated. True knowledge of Jesus will produce a love of Jesus, and a love for Jesus will always be made manifest through obedience. Those who have faith in Jesus and follow Him live with hope.

In Matthew 16, Jesus makes several powerful statements about Himself and what it means to be His disciple. Jesus' words are clear and unmistakable. Those who have been exposed to the Gospel can certainly deny Jesus their allegiance, but it is not for a lack of knowledge. The Gospel is simple. A lack of devotion to God is a result of a lack of faith in Jesus.

The religious leaders of Jesus' day did not believe in Jesus. Their interaction with Him was meant to cause others to doubt Him and trust them instead (v.1). They wanted miracles on demand. Even if He had performed miracles, it would appear that Jesus was submitting to them and the signs were by the religious leaders' command. Jesus made it clear these leaders were blind guides, and the only miracles they would see would be "the sign of Jonah" – Jesus' death, burial, and resurrection three days later (v.2-4). Jesus was not pleased with the religious leaders and told His disciples to be on their guard against their teachings (v.5-12). Religious and spiritual instruction without the Gospel at its core is powerless and poisonous.

Realizing the religious leaders did not understand Him, Jesus questioned the disciples to see what the masses were saying and what the disciples actually believed about Him (v.13). Many were confused (v.14). Having asked who they believed He was (v.15), Peter provided a perfect explanation (v.16) and received a blessing (v.17-20). Peter said Jesus was the promised Messiah, and he was right. Jesus told the disciples to tell no one. He did not want more confusion to be created. His identity would be revealed in God's time.

There were various views about Israel's Messiah. Having confessed that He was the Christ, Jesus explained His mission (v.21). Peter did not agree and actually rebuked Jesus (v.22). Jesus then rebuked Peter (v.23). The same guy that had just been called "the Rock" was being called "Satan," which shows how wrong it is to remove the cross and resurrection from an understanding of Jesus' identity and purpose. To know Jesus is to know His sacrifice and to join Him in it. To be a disciple of Jesus is to stop obeying fleshly desire, to choose to die to a worldly way of living, and to live a life of love modeled by Jesus (v.24-26). The only way to gain eternal life is to turn over our temporary lives to Christ in order to be pardoned and made righteous by His power. Jesus promised He would return to judge the world, and some of them – Peter, James, and John – would get to see Him transformed in the presence of Moses and Elijah, as proof of His power (v.27-28).

Jesus revealed His identity and mission clearly. Only those who believe in Him will be saved. Those who are saved will live lives modeled after Jesus. Do you believe in Jesus? Do you live like Jesus? Those who believe in Jesus and follow Him live with hope.

Joshua 9; Psalms 140–141; Jeremiah 3; Matthew 17

One of the great strategies of the enemy of God is deception. If that monster, the devil, were to provide its real intentions and show what it desired for humanity and the world, no one would sin. As it is, we all sin. We are all deceived. By grace we can overcome sin through faith in Jesus. By choosing to look to Jesus for direction and in decision making, disciples of Jesus overcome sin and live with hope.

In Joshua 9, the way the enemy works is revealed. The devil already knows it is defeated. It knows that it is only a matter of time until its kingdom of darkness is vanquished. Rather than hide in hate, the devil has decided to deceive as many as possible. It is compelled to. The only way it can deceive people is to get them to take their focus off of God and trust in themselves. This is what the Gibeonites did. They made God's people think they were no threat (v.1-13). This lack of concern led Joshua and the people to fail to seek God in prayer (v.14). Having no fear or thought of being in violation of God's will, Joshua and the people made a covenant with the Gibeonites and formed a trusting relationship (v.15). It was only after the relationship had been formed that Joshua and the people discovered their mistake (v.16-26). Because of their covenant, the Gibeonites were allowed to live among God's people and influence Israel with their false religions (v.27). While the Gibeonites were only servants doing menial labor, their presence influenced Israel's faith.

The Gibeonite deception is similar to the devil's deception. The devil works to make us believe it is not a threat. It pretends to be our friend and to provide us with good things. This is not its intent. "The thief comes only to steal and kill and destroy" (John 10:10). The redeemed of God must be wise to be faithful to Jesus and reject friendship with darkness.

Once the enemy gets us feeling safe, we often cease to pray faithfully. Prayer needs to be more than a defensive strategy, but it at least needs to be that. Once the Gibeonites made the Israelites believe they were safe, the Israelites saw no need to pursue God in prayer. We are never safe from sin on this fallen planet. We must always be in prayer.

James 4:4 says, "You adulterous people! Do you not know that friendship with the world is enmity with God? Therefore whoever wishes to be a friend of the world makes himself an enemy of God." When Israel formed a covenant with the Gibeonites, they let the devil into the house. Once it is there, it is hard to get it to leave. Habits get formed along with new ideas, attitudes, and beliefs. Over time, sin that was once inconceivable becomes a regular way of life. This is the devil's strategy.

Spiritual warfare is real. Those who are victorious are wise, prayerful, and inhospitable to darkness. Are you allowing yourself to be susceptible to sin? Are you praying for wisdom and discernment? Can you spot the temptation and deception of the devil and by faith look to Jesus for deliverance? The devil has been deceiving people for a long time. He is out to get you and me. Looking to Jesus provides victory over sin and gives us eternal hope.

Joshua 10; Psalms 142–143; Jeremiah 4; Matthew 18

Those who place their hope in other people, things, or circumstances are always disappointed. People are not perfect and their sin causes harm. Things will break, get old, or get lost or stolen. Circumstances always change. Like the weather, life has seasons, and those seasons are always changing. The only true hope in life is in the Almighty and His perfect permanence. Those who look to God for help live with hope.

Psalms 142–143 were written by David. These laments came from a man stuck in a difficult situation. His enemies wanted to destroy him. He felt alone. His emotional strength was failing. Looking to God, David told God his troubles. He confessed his faith. He asked for God's strength. He sought God's glory. These are the actions of a child of faith. This is what worship looks like.

There is a difference between whining and lamenting. When we whine, we want people to feel sorry for us. When we lament, we want people to understand us. Whining is a way to manipulate other's emotions. Lamenting is a way to enable people to connect with our emotions. David lamented his life circumstance. He wanted God to connect with his heart and understand his pain. If there is anyone who can understand what it means to be to be alone and surrounded by those who mean to cause harm, it is Jesus. David believed that God cared about him and understood his pain. Turning to God in times of trouble brings God glory because it calls attention to God's loving, merciful nature.

David did more than tell of his woes. He also asked God to intervene. This is a primary function of prayer. Along with praise, confession, and thanksgiving, a child of God brings glory to God by asking God for help. When we go to God humbly and ask for help, we bring Him glory and honor. The basis for David's request for divine intervention was His confidence in God. He had faith in God's power and providence. He had faith God loved him and had a plan for his life and pain. His request was bold because he dared to believe in the greatness of God. Believing in the greatness of God gives God glory.

David also asked God to do something in his life. David asked God to "Teach me to do your will, for you are my God! Let your good Spirit lead me on level ground!" (Psalm 143:10). God's will is for His people to obey Him in all circumstances. It is in difficult circumstances we learn to depend on God's strength. David did not just seek an escape from his trial. David asked God to do a work in him that would allow him to do God's will. His request was for the Holy Spirit to lead him to live on the path of righteousness, which is the only level ground. This request brings glory to God by acknowledging God's will and depending on God's provision to do it.

Bringing glory to God through prayer is wise. The Lord hears His people and cares for them. Are you looking to God for divine intervention? Are you confident in God's care for you? The Lord Almighty is a merciful savior. He will not abandon you in your time of need. Those who look to God in faith and seek to find their strength in Him live with hope.

Joshua 11; Psalm 144; <u>Jeremiah 5</u>; Matthew 19

The sin of humanity has left the world in a broken condition. Without the Word of God there is no hope to know the truth. Without the Spirit of God there is no hope to understand the truth. Without the mercy and grace of God there is no hope to obey the truth. God has given His Word, His Spirit, and His grace and mercy. We must receive His gifts. Those who receive the gifts of God and live by faith in Him will live with hope.

Jeremiah 5 paints a bleak picture. It is the picture of a people with religious institutions but with no heart for God. There is an awareness of God but no fear of God (v.1-5), which results in the judgment of God (v.6-17; 20-29). But there is hope! So long as God's plan stands, there is a hope for the world (v.18-19). God will accomplish His purpose. He calls us to consider the end of our lives and what we will want then as opposed to what our flesh desires now. The flesh deceives, but the Word of God can be trusted. Those who see God's coming judgment are blessed if they choose to live to trust in God.

Without the Spirit of God the heart of humanity is lost. Those whom Jeremiah ministered to possessed the Word of God. Under Josiah's reign, there had been a great revival. Jeremiah looked among the poor and the rich and saw the same thing: a refusal to repent. Whether housed in a mansion or a cardboard box, those who refuse to turn from sin and obey God have nothing. Those with much are like those with little, when Christ is not present. Those who reject God are yoked with Satan and will be treated as such.

God will not be mocked. Judgment will come and it will be just. God gives people what they want. If they do not want to be under the authority of God, God will allow them to fight for themselves. This is devastating! The devil's armies, like a lion, will prevail over the sheep. If they want to depend on idols, God will allow them to be dependent upon those false gods, which produce emptiness in the soul.

God is gracious! He will have a remnant. God will always have a people who look to Him (v.18). Sadly, they will often be unappreciated and attacked. Those who stand on the Word of God and have an allegiance to Jesus will be sought for answers. Those in darkness will inquire of the light, but because darkness hates light, the truth will be of no use to those in darkness because they do not want the truth. They want to be their own gods that live for their own glory. God will only glorify His great name. He calls all to consider their end and the end of times. What will be left for those who reject Jesus? Nothing! What will be given to those who trust in Jesus and live for His Kingdom? Everything!

We all must choose who and what we will serve. We can serve our flesh and our earthly kingdoms, or we can serve Christ and His eternal Kingdom. Who are you serving? Who do you worship? What is your purpose and why? Those who live to delight in the Word of God by the Spirit of God live with hope.

Joshua 12–13; Psalm 145; Jeremiah 6; <u>Matthew 20</u>

God is exactly what we need. His perfections and plans are always right. Those who look to Him will never be disappointed. There are many secondhand substitutes, but nothing and no one can be to us what God is. Those who look to Jesus in faith will be saved and their souls will have hope.

In Matthew 20, we see some of God's best qualities on display in Jesus Christ. Jesus is God in the flesh (John 1:1-4). God had revealed Himself in many ways throughout history, but it was in Jesus that humanity received a full and final view of God (Hebrews 1:1-4). God is generous in grace (v.1-16), He is sacrificial in love (v.17-28), and His mercy heals (v.29-34).

Jesus came to establish His Kingdom on earth. The Kingdom of God has come, but not yet fully. God's Kingdom is not like the kingdoms of earth. The kingdoms of earth are based and built on merit. The Kingdom of God is based and built on grace. In the way of the world, the person who works earns an agreed-upon wage. The Kingdom of God is different. Jesus said His Kingdom was like that of a man who owned property and hired workers. Some worked all day, some worked half of the day, and some worked only about an hour, but all were given the same wage. The story ends with the landowner asking the upset all-day and half-day workers, "Do you begrudge my generosity?" In the Kingdom of Jesus "the last will be first, and the first last" (v.15-16). In Jesus' Kingdom, the worth of a person is not based upon what they have done, but on what Jesus has done.

Jesus provided sacrificial love. In order for God's people to live in His Kingdom, Jesus had to pay their sin debt by dying and being raised (v.17-19). The cost of sin is death (Romans 6:23). So Jesus came to pay that debt with the shedding of His blood (Hebrews 9:22). The disciples did not understand God's plan. They thought His Kingdom was going to be like that of the world and those closest to Him would gain power in their lifetime on earth. Jesus explained that the greatest in His Kingdom were the servants (v.26-28). Those who put others first, as Jesus put us before Himself sacrificially, will be great in Jesus' Kingdom.

Jesus' Kingdom is built on mercy. Mercy is not getting what is deserved. When Jesus was leaving Jericho, two blind men called out to Him for mercy (v.30). They called Him by His redemptive title "Son of David." This showed they had faith He was the Messiah. Despite being rebuked, the men continued to cry out for mercy. Jesus asked what they wanted, and they requested their sight. By faith they believed in His power, and by His mercy Jesus healed them. This is the way of the Kingdom of Jesus. Gifts are given by faith according to the mercy of God. God does not give us what we deserve. God shows mercy to those who believe.

We are all like the workers, the disciples, and the blind men. We are in a world built on merit, led by dictators, and blinded by sin. Jesus has come to mercifully heal those who believe. Do you believe in Jesus? Those who base their lives on Him live with hope.

Joshua 14–15; Psalms 146–147; Jeremiah 7; Matthew 21

God has come! The Lord Jesus has brought the Kingdom of God into the world through His life, death, and resurrection. He is now at work in the world through His church. His Kingdom has come, but not fully. His Kingdom is still coming. Those who serve God's Kingdom live with hope.

Joshua 14–15 explains the distribution of the land given to the tribe of Judah. The giving of the land and the possessing of the land were not the same thing. These tribes were given the land, but they would have to defeat the inhabitants in order to possess it. God's people were in the land of promise, but now they would have to fight to be free of all the foreign people who did not know the one true God or worship Him. Christians today have been given eternal life in Christ. The spiritual battle of Christ with sin and death has been fought and Jesus has won. The Kingdom has come! Now His people must fight the spiritual fight to make disciples and to vanquish the sin that wars against their souls. This daily battle for Christ must be fought with God's help, with vigor, and with wisdom.

The Levites were not given any land (14:1-5). Their role in the kingdom was to serve as ministers of the people. They were scattered throughout the tribes to provide the ministry of the Word and to point the people to their covenantal responsibilities (Deuteronomy 33:8-11; 2 Chronicles 17:7-9). The other tribes were to care for the Levites' needs through tithes, offerings, and other provisions. In His Church, the Lord Jesus has raised up ministers and pastors who are to serve the people through the ministry of the Word. The people of God are to honor those who serve them and teach them. They are to care for their needs by giving tithes, offerings, and other provisions.

The tribe of Judah was the first to receive land. Caleb, one of the twelve spies who were sent by Moses into the land, was like Joshua. He believed God would provide what He promised and give Israel the land. He was still alive. He was eighty-five but still strong. He requested the privilege to take the hill country of Hebron, and it was given to him to conquer (14:6-15). He is an example to believers today to be faithful to God and remain willing and able to serve all the days of life God gives. Never stop trusting and serving God, even in old age.

To conquer the land that Judah was given, the people would have to be faithful and wise. Caleb provided the incentive of his daughter to the one who could conquer Debir (15:16). Caleb provided a measurable goal and a clear blessing. Othniel won the day and was blessed with Caleb's daughter, who later went to her father and also received springs of water (v.17-19). Those who pursue God's will must be wise and plan accordingly and seek replenishment through the Spirit. We are to live by faith, which is truly wise.

God is not finished yet! The Kingdom has come, but it is still coming. There is more to do. Are you fighting the good fight of faith? Are you removing sin from your life? Are you being wise? Those who work with God to war against sin and darkness live with hope.

Those who know God and understand His greatness have every reason to praise Him. Those who do not know Him are forced to give praise to something lesser: Mother Nature, chance, self, etc. Humanity is designed to praise. There is none more worthy of praise than God. When people praise God, they engage in the fundamental act of their design. Those who praise Him live with hope.

Psalm 148 commands every person, angel, and created thing in the universe to praise the Lord. It is only right that everyone and everything in the universe praise Him. God commands this not because He is an egomaniac, but because He truly is God. God commands the world to praise Him because He alone is worthy of praise and in His praise, the world finds its meaning. Psalm 148 provides at least four reasons to praise the Lord.

One, He created everything by His Word (v.5). God spoke into existence all that is. It was not difficult for Him. Jesus, the second person of the trinity, is given credit for the act (John 1:1-4; Colossians 1:16-17). God was before anything else. In His divine power, God created the universe and all that is in it. Genesis 1 has a repeating line: "And God said…" and what He said happened. The universe was made to display His glory so all that is could exist and bring delight and glory to God.

Two, God ordered everything in nature and regulates it by His might (v.6). Scientist, psychologist, and philosophers study what has been made, but none can understand why. There is no secular answer to the question of why. There is no good pagan answer either. Why do the cells divide and the DNA strands form to make a human being? Why do the birds migrate and mate? Why does the moon circle the earth and the earth circle the sun? God knows. It is for His glory. God determined all that is to be the way it is for His glory.

Three, God sovereignly works to accomplish His will in all things according to His Word (v.7-8). There is no such thing as chance or coincidence. How do fire and hail, snow and mist, and stormy winds fulfill God's Word? Only God knows, but God does know. He knows how to work all things according to His purpose (Genesis 50:20; Romans 8:28). His Word will fulfill its purpose (Isaiah 55:11).

Four, God has chosen to bring salvation to His people (v.14). He has raised up a "horn," a King to save and lead His people in His Kingdom. Jesus has come! His Kingdom is established for all of eternity. God entered creation, as a man, to save all humanity. He became one of us to save all of us who believe. He lived a holy life to fulfill the law. He conquered sin and death. His atoning death satisfied the just requirements of a holy God. Now all who believe in the name of Jesus are saved.

God is to be praised! The command is good and right. When we acknowledge God for who He is and what He has done, we are being honest, honoring, and honored. It is true that He is worthy. It is both honoring and an honor to praise the one true God. Are you living a life that praises the Lord? Is praise normal for you? Those who live to praise the Lord live with hope.

Joshua 18–19; Psalms 149–150; Jeremiah 9; Matthew 23

God has revealed Himself. He has done this with a general revelation of Himself in creation, and with a specific revelation through the Bible. Where there is a lack of admiration, appreciation, and humility toward God, there is devastation, pain, and suffering. God works to restrain the work of sin. Those who push off God's restraint suffer the consequences for it. The consequences for a culture that lacks God's restraint are intense. Those who appreciate and adhere to God's restraining love live with hope.

Jeremiah 9 provides a divine perspective on human suffering. God does not delight to see His people in sin. More than anyone else, God knows how good life can be. When people reject God and His Word and refuse to take Him and His commands seriously, the penalty for this sinful pride produces pain. That pain is felt personally, communally, and divinely.

Jeremiah was known as "the weeping prophet" for a good reason. He was saddened by what he saw God's people doing. He desired to have enough tears to fill the ocean so that his tears could flow like a fountain (v.1). He wanted to flee the presence of the people (v.2). The trajectory of the nation was evil (v.3). Jeremiah's response was the right response. God's people are to tell the truth and call people and nations to repent, but to do so from a broken, humble heart. The pain of sin should break God's children's hearts.

The people of God were at this point a lost cause. They were lost in lies (v.4-11). No one could believe a word anyone else said. When there is no means of trusted dialogue, healthy relationships are impossible. Without collaborate communication people will look only to their preferences and be at war with all others who are viewed as competitors to their personal agenda. Even God was viewed as a tool to be used for personal gain and was not respected (v.12-14). Hearts unhinged by sin will fall into a pit of fury where there is no hope, because each is so isolated from others and God. In that state, there is nothing to hold on to. There is only anger, anxiety, and angst. It is hell.

God will not be mocked. Sinners will reap what they sow (Galatians 6:7). God does not delight in destruction but will devastate sinners with holy justice (v.15-26). The wise who wake up to the reality of God's divine judgment will seek His mercy and grace. Those who delight in the Lord will delight in the things that delight Him. God says in verse 24, "I am the Lord who practices steadfast love, justice, and righteousness in the earth. For in these things I delight, declares the Lord." God desires to bless people, but they must desire that blessing and be found worthy. God makes people worthy of His blessing by grace through faith in Jesus.

We cannot always choose the culture we live in, but we can choose how we live. The Lord will one day bring His perfect Kingdom fully into the world. Until that time, nations will rise and fall in sin. It is vital that the redeemed remain loyal to God. Do you delight in God and in what He delights in? Do you weep over your sin and that of the world? Those who have a heart for God may weep but still have hope.

Joshua 20–21; Acts 1; Jeremiah 10; <u>Matthew 24</u>

We must be careful not to misappropriate or to discount the promises of God. The Lord has promised good things and also warned of trials, thorns, and temptations. The difficulties of life must not discourage us from our hope and the blessings must not be allowed to make us apathetic. Those who endure to the end will be saved and find hope even in the darkest times.

The disciples of Jesus had a distinct view of an earthly Messiah. They, like most of the leaders that taught them, anticipated the Messiah coming and restoring David's Old Covenant kingdom. Jesus came to do more than bring a temporary result with an earthly kingdom that would one day pass away. He came to make eternal changes. His plan was from before time began, and it called for His Kingdom to come, but not fully, until His second coming. Those who endure will have to live by faith. Matthew 24 outlines the coming conditions of the world before Jesus returns to make all things new.

There will be birth pains that come before the second coming of Christ (v.1-14). Jesus said the temple would be destroyed, and it was in 70 AD. There will be war and the constant threat of more war and natural disasters. The redeemed of God will be persecuted and the Gospel will spread to every people group on the planet. Although Christ has come and salvation is at hand, the world is still broken. Until Jesus returns to make all things new, the children of God must endure the suffering that is a part of a world gone mad with sin and that is still hostile to God.

There will be spiritual warfare of every kind, but the coming of Christ will overwhelm the world (v.15-35). History is filled with evil that has manifested itself in many ways. It is no coincidence that it is Christians and Jews who have and will suffer the most. Both the Old and New Covenant people point to the hope of Christ. The world hates Christ and will always be against any that mark the hope and reality of Christ. When Christ returns, the world will weep. The redeemed will rejoice. It is crucial that God's people stay focused and remember when they are living: we are in the days before the final restoration. We must not be surprised by what happens. It will be awful at times.

Normal life will be occurring when Christ returns (v. 36-51). Only the Father knows when Christ will come. Clothed in humanity, Christ was limited by the capacity of a human knowledge, but He knew the plan. Things on earth will continue as they have for millennia and then suddenly Christ will come. The redeemed will rejoice. Those dead in sin will be damned. There will be justice and those saved by grace will experience all of the promises of God. There will be no more sickness, dying, or pain (Revelation 21).

Until Christ returns, God's people should anticipate suffering in many ways. God will give the grace to endure. The victory that is to come gives hope. Those saved by grace must remember this world is not our home and must find peace in Christ, because in this world, we will have pain. Are you looking to the coming of Christ? Are you serving, praying, giving, and sharing in light of the coming Kingdom? Those who endure suffering by faith live with hope.

Joshua 22; Acts 2; Jeremiah 11; Matthew 25

In Matthew 25, Jesus tells the story of a master and three servants. Two of them hear the master say, "Well done, good and faithful servant." There is nothing greater a child of God can hope to hear from the Master of heaven, Jesus Christ, than, "You did it! You did it right! I am pleased with you!" Pursing God's praise by bringing Him praise leads to a life filled with hope.

In Joshua 22, Joshua summoned the eastern tribes of Israel: the Reubenites and the Gadites and the half-tribe of Manasseh, after they had fulfilled their vow to help the other tribes obtain their inheritance of land. Joshua released them from duty and sent them home. He in essence said, "Well done, good and faithful servants! Go home and enjoy your rest." They were able to go home with the blessing of God and God's people. Joshua 22 provides a picture of what a successful life looks like and how God's people can gain the blessing of hearing God say, "Well done, good and faithful servant."

To gain God's blessing the people had to enter into God's covenant and pursue God's Kingdom purpose. The eastern tribes were given land on the other side of the Jordan, as they had requested. Once their position was established, they still had to go into the land and help their brothers conquer the Canaanites. These tribes entered into God's covenant and received God's promise. By faith, they obeyed God and accomplished His purpose (v.1-9). They did not look out just for their interests, but that of God's Kingdom and that of their brothers. Serving the good of others reveals the heart of Christ (Philippians 2:3-8).

These eastern tribes had proven their faith by showing fidelity to the cause of God and His people. Sadly, their brothers misunderstood an action they took that almost caused a war as they were leaving for their home (v.10-29). They had built a copy of the altar as a remembrance. The other tribes thought they were abandoning the true faith for a false faith. Had these eastern tribes turned against God, the other tribes would have been acting in faith to fight them. Sin must be dealt with. Those who want to receive God's blessing must not tolerate sin in any way.

Thankfully, there was a peaceful resolution (v.30-34). Conflict is inevitable. People are not always going to agree, understand, or be kind to one another. When there is conflict, God's people are commanded to resolve it properly. Jesus explains how to resolve conflict in Matthew 18. It takes faith, humility, and grace to make peace. Those who honor God in the process of conflict resolution are able to gain the peace that is desired and please God. Peace is one of the great blessings of God. Those who have peace obtain it through a process of humble God-honoring peacemaking. Everyone has conflict, but God can bring peace.

The eastern tribes entered their rest having been faithful to God. When conflict came, they were humble and steadfast in their faith. Are you seeking to root out the sin in your life? Are you at peace with those you know? The life God blesses is one that seeks the joy of heaven, the victory over sin, and the peace of God. Those who pursue God's blessings live with hope.

Joshua 23; Acts 3; Jeremiah 12; Matthew 26

Jesus changes lives. By the power of His grace, God can take what was dead and bring it to life. He can take what was dirty and make it clean. He can take what was filled with darkness and fill it with light. The salvation of Jesus is a great gift. It changes a person from within and makes a sinner a saint. A redeemed saint is given a new life in Christ filled with love, meaning, and purpose. This new life is filled with hope.

The Apostle Peter was a changed man. Having been redeemed by grace and given forgiveness by the resurrected Christ (John 21), Peter was never the same. Before the resurrection, Peter was proud, self-centered, and easily intimidated. Having experienced the power of the Holy Spirit and received grace from His resurrected Lord, Peter became a shepherd of God's flock, stood for the truth of the Gospel, and pursued the promises of God. Acts 3 shows how Peter lived as an example for all who believe.

All who believe are to care for the broken and forgotten people of the world (v.1-10). When faced with a beggar, Peter did not overlook him. He very easily could have expected the church to provide for the man's needs. After all, the people were giving financial gifts to support the poor among themselves (Acts 2:42-47). Peter could have looked to the institution of the church or government, but instead, Peter gave the man what he had. He had the name of Jesus and the power to heal. We don't all have the same gifts and abilities, but we have the same heart of God in us. Rather than looking to the church organization or government subsidies, God's people are called to give what they have and love those the world tends to ignore.

All who believe are to proclaim the Gospel clearly, confidently, and courageously (v.11-21). When Peter addressed the people about their need for salvation, he did not hold back the truth. He was clear with them about their sin and how they had released a murderer, rather than the Holy One of God, Jesus. Jesus was killed, but Peter makes it clear this was the plan of God. God's people must tell the whole truth. We are all sinners in need of the Savior of the world, Jesus.

All who believe are to know and stand on the promises of God (v.22-26). The Christian faith is founded upon the prophecies and promises of the Old Testament. God promised Abraham he would be the father of a great nation. Through Moses, God promised a prophet would come to save. Through the prophets, God promised that Jesus would overcome sin and death. These prophecies and promises are dear to those who believe. It is vital God's people know God's Word, and be able to gain hope and confidence in the truth of the Bible. That Biblical hope is to be shared with the entire world.

Jesus saves! He saves to put to use a people for His purpose. Are you doing all you can to help the hurting people around you? Are you telling people about the salvation of Jesus? Are you growing in your knowledge of the truth of God's Word? We must avoid making excuses for ourselves. God gives hope to those who accomplish His will and do His work in the world.

Joshua 24; Acts 4; Jeremiah 13; Matthew 27

We will either be killing sin or sin will be killing us. It is the grace of God that makes a relationship with Jesus possible. It is also grace that enables us to kill sin. Those who kill sin live with hope.

Jeremiah 24 reveals the destructiveness of sin. For those who can understand it, this text needs to be a clarion call to fidelity to Jesus. Sin always leads to pride (v.1-11), senseless living (v.12-14), and destruction (v.15-27). Sin always takes us further in degradation than we intended to go, costs us more than we wanted to pay, and gives us less than it promised. Grace always gets us further in holiness than we thought we could go, comes free by faith, and gives us more than we could hope or imagine.

Jeremiah had an interesting preaching style. He was often called to act out his sermons. On this occasion, he took a loincloth, buried it, and brought it back. The loincloth was a very intimate piece of apparel. This speaks of the nature of the relationship God's people are meant to have with God. The children of God are to be directly connected to Jesus in the closest of ways. Sin spoils that relationship and makes what was meant to be a blessing into something useless. If we are not going to walk closely with God, then we will fall into sin, and God's provision of intimate presence is useless. Not only do we miss out on the privilege of glorifying God, but God is robbed of the glory He is due. In our pride, we will make our own gods, and they will fail us and lead us into dark places of depression, anxiety, and anger. We will have dirty and useless lives, incapable of performing the purpose we were made and redeemed for.

Jeremiah's second sermon was about bottles of wine. Sin is intoxicating but short lived. Like drunkenness, sin feels good in the moment, but then fades and leaves us hung over and in a worse condition. Drunkenness, like sin, leaves people in a dangerous condition. Relationships become volatile, harm is caused, and consequences reverberate beyond the individual. Drunks will hurt those they love along with themselves. Sin does this too. Sin does not stay tucked away in a category of our life. It always seeps into other areas of life, causing harm.

The harm of sin is rarely seen until it is too late. Satan is smart. He did not let Adam and Eve see the consequences of their rebellion, and that devil, the flesh, and the world will keep concealed the consequences of our sin. Sin always leads to destruction. God warns us, just as he warned Israel about the coming invasion of Babylon through Jeremiah. God has revealed the seriousness of sin through His Word. Those who will not heed the warning of God will be destroyed by sin.

There is in all of us a tendency to belittle our sin and make a big deal about everyone else's. We like to think of ourselves as above the fray. Regardless of our deceived perspective, sin makes us dirty and useless; it creates devastation; it leads to destruction. Are you taking sin serious? Are you killing sin so you can live in Jesus? The grace of God has the power to redeem and restore us. Those who love Jesus live holy lives filled with hope.

Judges 1; Acts 5; Jeremiah 14; Matthew 28

God has made us to be practical beings. In a state of emotional and mental health, we will always act according to what we believe is best. Those who know that Jesus died to atone for sin, was raised, is now reigning, and will one day return, live like it. Those who live their lives in light of the facts of Jesus live with hope.

The resurrection of Jesus is a crucial piece of information that will determine not only what a person feels in their heart, but what they do with their hands. In Matthew 28, we see different reactions to the reality of the resurrection. What we do with the monumental historical fact of the resurrection of Jesus will determine how we think and feel about everything else, and determine the trajectory of our lives for eternity.

On that eternally significant Sunday morning, after the death of Jesus, when the two Marys went to the tomb where Jesus was laid, they discovered the miracle of miracles (v.1). Jesus had been raised from the dead. The angel of the Lord told them what had happened, showed them the empty tomb, and told them what to do (v.2-7). They felt both fear and joy, and they did what the angel said (v.8). Their faith was rewarded with the presence of Jesus (v.9-10). If we want to receive Jesus' affirmation, we must believe in the fact of the resurrection and live in obedience to His commands. Jesus rewards those who are obedient to Him.

The religious leaders of Jesus' day responded differently to the news of the resurrection (v.11-12). Their hearts were not filled with joyous fear and awe for God. They felt threatened. They felt the need to protect their power with a lie and a bribe (v.13-15). Did they believe that the resurrection had occurred, or did they actually believe that the disciples of Jesus had stolen His body? We cannot know the thoughts and beliefs of others. Their actions indicate a lack of faith in Jesus. Their rejection of Jesus caused them to act treacherously. Rather than rejoicing and giving glory to God, they huddled up and hammered out a false narrative that deceived many. What they did with the fact of the resurrection created negative emotions and dishonest and spiritually destructive outcomes.

The disciples of Jesus believed the resurrection. We do not know their emotional state from this text, but the other Gospel writers indicate they felt the same way the women, who first found the tomb empty, felt. The beliefs and feelings of the eleven disciples led them to obedience (v.16). Their obedience was rewarded by Jesus. He showed up and they worshipped Him (v.17). Having given them the facts of the resurrection, Jesus commanded them to go into the world and make disciples (v.18-20). Worshipping Jesus and sharing the hope of Jesus are practical responses to His resurrection.

What you believe will determine your affections and actions. Do you believe Jesus died for your sin and has been raised? Are you in awe of Jesus? Do your actions reveal your deep conviction that Jesus is the Christ and will come again to judge you? Those who believe in the resurrection of Jesus live in awe of Him and obey Him and have hope.

Judges 2; Acts 6; Jeremiah 15; Mark 1

Sin is always looking to destroy, but sin is no match for the grace of God received through faith in Jesus by the power of the Holy Spirit. God's redeeming power is released through faith, and those who live by faith and choose to trust in the goodness of God live with hope.

Judges 2 depicts the condition of a Christian who is defeated by sin. The people had been given the Promised Land, but they did not drive out the inhabitants, as God had commanded. These Canaanites were pagans who served false gods. Although the Lord had done miracles for His people, provided blessed leadership through Joshua and the elders, and kept His promises, His people turned from Him and faced the terrible consequences for their sin. Believers are enticed by sin when they stop listening to their spiritual leaders, abandon the hope of God, and refuse to be grateful to God.

While no human leader is perfect, God provides good leadership through His servants. Moses, Joshua, and the elders were not perfect, but they were good leaders. The people obeyed the Word of God and were blessed when they were attentive to their leaders. When they disregarded those God selected to serve them in truth, the results were awful (v.1-10). The impact was felt not only by the generation of Joshua, but also by the generations after him. Christians who will not abide in Christ and connect in a local church and train their children to be faithful to God's Word will suffer for it.

When believers lose their spiritual footing, they slip quickly and devastatingly into sin. The generation that came after Joshua and the elders were unable to overcome the temptation of the pagan religions around them. The religions of man always corrupt natural human desires and turn those desires into demands that lead to behaviors outside of God's good law. Those who lived after Joshua committed spiritual adultery and lived for pagan sensuality (v.11-15). Sinful sensuality leaves a child of God defenseless and incapable of fighting off sin. Once sin has taken root in a person's life, it will take a miracle for liberation to take place.

God is gracious and will provide freedom. Although the people, after Joshua, were morally corrupt and incapable and unwilling to honor the goodness of God and live for the glory of God, the Lord raised up leaders, judges, who were able to miraculously lead the people back to God and in victory over their sin (v.16-23). Jesus is the ultimate Judge. He completely defeated the power of sin and overcame the punishment of sin through His life, death, and resurrection. Like the people in Judges, Christians will continue to struggle with sin. These temptations are allowed by God to train the redeemed of God to fight sin and live for the glory of God.

Until Christ returns, the battle against sin will rage on. There is no such thing as a tie in spiritual warfare. Either believers defeat sin or sin defeats them. Are you winning the battle over sin? Do you delight in the goodness of God and live for the glory of God? Those who are victorious over sin live with hope.

The Gospel, when preached and shared rightly, will be offensive to some. While the children of God find their greatest hope in the Gospel, those lost in sin find it offensive. By comparing their lives to the vast numbers of sinful people in the world instead of God, many find no need for a savior. Only sinners need a savior. Those who tell the truth of the Gospel will not always be appreciated, but they will always have hope in the affirmation of the Savior.

Stephen is one of the great martyrs in church history. Although his ministry was brief, it was sincere. Stephen believed Jesus was the Messiah. The sermon he preached in Acts 7 was thoroughly Biblical. He was hated by the religious leaders for it, but he was dearly loved and acknowledged by Jesus for His faith and courage. Jesus was with Him.

Having been brought before the high priest and charged with blasphemy, Stephen bypassed the question asked him and rather than defend himself, he preached the Gospel. His text was the Old Testament. From those familiar stories Stephen revealed the will of God: to come and save a people for His glory. He concluded the sermon by calling the religious leaders to repent of their sin (v.51-53). It takes courage, conviction, and a calling from God to tell people the truth about the fallen condition of their soul. Harsh truth is a kindness to those who are willing to repent and believe in Jesus.

The religious leaders did not believe in Jesus. Stephen's words were like fuel to a flame. They were already prepared to act against him. Stephen's words caused them to explode. Their stoning of Stephen was less of an obedient act based upon the law (Leviticus 24:16) and more like an act of mob violence against a fellow human being they did not agree with. The human condition is so broken that there is no end to the violence a person is capable of doing. Given the right motive and moment, a good person can become a murderous monster, and a group of religious leaders can become a homicidal horde.

In that horrible moment, Stephen was able to see into heaven. He saw Jesus standing and not sitting, as Scripture typically describes Him. Jesus was there giving strength and approval to His redeemed saint. There were two watching and giving approval that day. Saul was also there. He was giving approval to the mob. With his last breath, Stephen – like his Master, Jesus, in His final moments – asked that God not hold this sin against them. In that moment, Stephen "fell asleep." What a glorious picture of death for a saint. Christians are freed from their bodily labor and allowed to rest in the presence of God. It must seem like a dream to be with Jesus.

All God's people are responsible to share the Gospel. The world will not always appreciate it. We must choose whose approval we prefer: that of Jesus or people like Saul. Are you sharing the Gospel with those you know need it? Can you explain the Gospel from the pages of the Bible? Are you willing to suffer for the cause of Christ? Jesus is with His people. Those who stand with and for Jesus live with hope, as Jesus stands for them.

Judges 4; Acts 8; <u>Jeremiah 17</u>; Mark 3

There is little good that comes from pleasure and comfort. The best things in life come through sacrifice, hard work, and trials that require faith in Jesus. Faith in Christ is the means to blessedness. Those who learn from Jesus and trust His plan live with hope.

What we pursue in life will have an impact on what we experience in life and in death. Jeremiah 17 reveals what it looks like when people abandon God and have to pay the price for it. Jeremiah's words to Israel are words the church needs to hear today. God promises blessings to those who root their lives in Jesus. Those who turn away from Jesus will discover that gains are losses and the consequences for sin are serious. Jesus is a wonderful friend and a terrible enemy.

The people in Jeremiah's day claimed to be God's people but did not honor Him as God. Rather than worship, serve, and trust in God for provision, the people looked to the ways of the pagans, the strength of their flesh, and their wealth (v.1-3). The cost of their sin would be the loss of the promises of God and a legacy of darkness. They would be cursed (v.4-6). God's blessings go to the faithful (v.7-8). The heart of humanity wants many things, but only God can satisfy the eternal longing in people's souls (v.9-13). God's people must be mindful of the deceitfulness of the heart and the emptiness of sin.

Those who will turn to Jesus will find grace. God's Word stands. Those who will listen and respond in faith will be saved (v.14-18). God gives good things to those who honor Him. Those who honor Jesus will often be dishonored by those who reject the Word of God. The Word of God is foolishness to them. Rather than rely on the foundation of God's Word, worldly people rely on their own feelings and desires. Dependence on the flesh leads to pride, which is always followed by a fall. Dependence on the flesh also leads to despondency because sooner or later the grass withers and the flower fades. Only God and His Word stand forever.

It is crucial that those who depend on God rest in Him. This rest is pictured in the Sabbath rest of the Old Covenant. The people were to do no work, as a means of showing their trust in God alone (v.19-27). Those who worked on the Sabbath showed dishonor to God and distrust in His provision. Today, the children of God are to trust in Jesus and rest in His provision. By keeping the Lord's Day and living a life of faith, they show their dependence on God, which glorifies Him. Those who want to make their own way in life on their own terms will face the same life and death as the people in Jeremiah's day. Not only will the hopelessness and worldly hazards overwhelm them in life, but they will suffer for eternity in hell for their treason and treachery.

God is to be taken seriously. God has provided salvation at a great cost. To look past God's grace is to invite destruction. It is wise to worship, trust in, and delight in Jesus. Do you worship Jesus as a way of life? Do you trust God to provide for you? Those who build their lives on God's provision live with a hope that will never fail.

Everyone has faith, but not everyone has faith in the best object. Humanity was made by God to glorify God and to enjoy Him forever. It is impossible to enjoy God without faith – to believe that God exists and that He blesses those who trust in Him. While all people have the capacity to look to an object in faith, only the redeemed of God look to Jesus as the object of their faith. Those who live with faith in Jesus live with hope.

In Mark 4, Jesus provides practical insight into what faith produces, what it is supposed to accomplish, and how it works in the real world. Faith that does not change the agent of faith and give honor to the object of faith is useless. The faith God gives actually works. It accomplishes God's purpose in a person, through a person, and provides blessings to a person.

Seeing comes from faith. This sight must be received and then cultivated. Without the right mindset and tenderness of heart, the seed of faith will never take root. Each soul, like soil, must be prepared by God to receive the seed of the Gospel (v.1-20). There are different kinds of soils, which are different circumstances. God orchestrates all things according to His will, and those who are blessed enjoy God's blessing by grace. No one deserves new life. God gives it for His glory. It is received and lived by faith alone.

Jesus came into the world to reveal who God is. He is like a light that entered a dark room (v.21-23). Some cannot see Him. They are blinded by sin. All who see the light of life will be healed by the supernatural power of God. Once they see, the redeemed of God will pursue the light. Those who have the light and delight in it will be given more (v.24-25). Those who hide in the dark corners of their sin will miss out.

The faith that God gives grows supernaturally (v.26-29). The means to cultivate and grow faith are simple activities: prayer, corporate worship, Bible study, evangelism, etc. Those who live in obedience to God's will get to enjoy the fruit of their labors and harvest the blessings of God. It does not take a lot of faith. The smallest bit of faith can do great things (v.30-34). This is because the object of the Christian's faith is great. God is great and those who believe and follow Him grow in faith.

God does not simply give faith. He also tests it with trials (James 1:2-4). Storms are allowed to enter into our lives for the purpose of strengthening our faith (v.35-41). Untested faith is weak faith. God is good to make us go through difficulty so that our faith can be revealed and His Name can be honored. We should never be surprised by storms. We must learn to have faith in life's storms and rest in the God who loves us and has plans for us.

Everyone has faith. What is the object of your faith? Do you believe that God the Father sent His only Son, Jesus Christ, to die for your sin? Do you live in the power of the Holy Spirit of God? Is your faith growing? Is your life changing because of your faith? Those who have faith in Jesus live with hope and their faith is changing them and the world.

Judges 6; Acts 10; Jeremiah 19; Mark 5

Everyone suffers, but not everyone suffers for the right reason. The world is a fallen place. There will always be pain on our planet. The problem is not the pain, but the heart of humanity. Those who have a heart for God will suffer, but they will suffer with hope. Those who live without Christ will suffer, but without hope. Only Christ can give hope in the midst of suffering.

In Judges 6, the people of God were suffering, but not for God. They were suffering because of sin. There is a difference in suffering for the sake of Christ and suffering for sin. Those who suffer for Christ will hide in Christ and in His love; they will experience pruning, but not destruction; they will be brought low, but not further from Christ. God does not abandon His people in sin. He calls the redeemed to repentance in order to gain the life only God can give.

When Israel sinned, the Midianites came in and decimated them for seven years (v.1). The people were forced to hide. They were not hidden in the hand of God, but in the darkness of the world (v.2). When the people turned from God, they were left to fend for themselves. The result of their sin was darkness and fear. Like animals, they hid in caves without hope.

God removed the good things of their labors because the people had removed Him as the source of their hope and joy. When their crops and fields were taken from them, it was a punishment and not a pruning (v.3-5). When God prunes His people, it is painful, but it is also productive. The Israelites were not being pruned. They were being punished. Punishment is a result of sin. Pruning is a result of obedience.

The people were brought low (v.6). This was not a blessed humbling. This was a humiliation. They had humiliated God by rejecting Him. They had made worthless idols the object of their worship. God humiliated them by making them depend on the strength of their idols. Idols do not have the power to provide what we need in life. They defile us and make us weak. Remembering their promise-keeping God, the people cried out to God, and God called them to repentance (v.7-10). Repentance is less about being sorry for the wrongs done and more about taking responsibility and turning back to God in obedient faith. God blesses obedient faith.

In order to restore His people, God raised up a savior – Gideon (v.11-40). Like Jesus, he was born in a lowly estate. His strength was not from the halls of human power, but from divine gifting. By grace Gideon was able to understand God's will and submit to the plan of God. Jesus was willing and able to submit to the Father's will. God turned away from Jesus so that we could turn to God. This is the Gospel!

Our decisions in life have consequences. Choosing to honor God does not keep us from pain. It does keep us from punishment. God allows pain to prune us and make us fruitful. God punishes sin to call us to repentance. Are you suffering out of punishment or is God pruning you? What do you need to repent of in order to live rightly in, with, and for Christ? Those who suffer in Christ are sustained with hope.

Judges 7; Acts 11; Jeremiah 20; Mark 6

The Kingdom of God is on the move in the world. There are those who are joining in the work, those who are criticizing it, and those who are oblivious to it. The workers are few, but their reward is great. Those who are critical may make the work more difficult, but they cannot stop it. Those who are oblivious to it miss the blessing and wander hopelessly. Hope grows and lives in those who choose to join God in His Kingdom work.

In Acts 11, the work of God and the complications that accompany it are on display. God calls every single child in His family to serve in the family business. The family business of God is the Kingdom expansion of the Lord Jesus Christ. Each calling is crucial. Each child's dedication is demanded. Each new follower is forever linked with all of the others. The line of progression from one disciple to the next is meant to go on and on until Jesus returns. Those who have been faithful to plant with the seed of the Gospel and water it with love and prayer will hear God say, "Well done, good and faithful servant!"

The Apostle Peter was faithful. Although raised to avoid Gentiles, he went among them when God called, and God saved many people (v.1). There were those who were critical of the work (v.2-3). It seems that with every good work in the family business, there will be those who criticize. Peter was confident in his calling and stayed true by relaying the Word of God to the church (v.4-17). His faithfulness silenced the critics and brought glory to God (v.18). Critics must not be allowed to keep God's people from fulfilling God's calling on their lives.

It was not only Peter who was faithful to take the message beyond the Jews, according to the will of God. Those from Cyprus and Cyrene were faithful to share the hope of Jesus with Hellenists (v.19-20). God's hand was with them and many believed (v.21). Having heard of the family business expanding, Barnabas was sent to investigate it and discovered it was a true work of God (v.22-24). Barnabas was recognized as "good," meaning he was "full of the Holy Spirit and of faith." Nothing better can be said of a person than that. There is no greater pursuit than to live a Spirit-filled life of faith.

Given the need of the people of Antioch, Barnabas went and recruited Saul to come and invest in the people there (v.25-26). There is no indication the Spirit ordered him. Having been given the Spirit of God, the children of God can think strategically and pursue plans that accomplish the purpose of God without having to be told every detail of what to do. When the church discovered that a famine was coming, they knew to prepare to provide for the needs of Judea (v.27-28). Faith fueled by love will enable appropriate decisions to be made by God's people.

The family business of the Kingdom of Jesus is in full operation. Are you joining in on the work? Some are sitting out and some are being critical. Those who join in on what God is doing in the world will get to see lives changed by grace. Are you being used by God? Hope grows in and around those who share their hope.

Judges 8; Acts 12; <u>Jeremiah 21</u>; Mark 7

There is no escaping the consequences of our decisions. Every action has a reaction. What we choose to do today will have a direct bearing on tomorrow. God has a plan. It includes all people in every generation. Both the redeemed and unredeemed will face earthly and eternal consequences for their choices. Those who live by faith under the leadership of the Lord will live and die with hope.

Jeremiah 21 is a terrifying picture of the consequences of sin. Israel had turned their backs on God, even though they had been warned not to. Now the king of Babylon was about to invade and destroy Jerusalem and take into exile those who were left. In the midst of the destruction and carnage, God held out hope. There was still a way to be saved. This is the wondrous mercy and grace of God. Even when we are faithless, He is faithful. God is patient and kind and willing to bless.

Desperate people have no shame. The king of Israel and the people had rejected God and made a joke of Him, but when they were in dire straits, they wanted God to intervene and provide for them, so they could go on sinning (v.1-2). The Lord had been patient and called the people to faithfulness, but they refused. God calls His redeemed saints to live for Him, in Him, and by Him. If we refuse, we will know what it is to be on our own.

Jeremiah let the king of Israel know that it was too late. The consequences of their sin demanded righteous correction. Just as they had turned against the Lord, the Lord was now turning against them. There was no undoing what the people had done. They would be exiled (v.3-7), but there was still hope. God offered them life. He called them to accept their punishment and surrender to this correction and trust in the Lord (v.8-10). Pride is a poison to the soul and keeps many from finding any true peace. The only peace that can be found on this planet is in the will and hand of God. God offers, even in the worst of consequences, grace and peace to survive and then thrive in His love and kindness.

Living in God's hands comes with specific demands (v.11-14). Those who are given grace and mercy and chosen by God to proclaim His greatness to the world are responsible to be gracious and merciful and to be a blessing, through the power of God. Those who will not submit to the demands of grace will not receive the benefits. Grace is not cheap. It comes at the price of Jesus' life. God gave His life so we could have grace. God demands we give our lives in order to receive grace. A grace-bought life lives in the will and love of God in the world.

Israel was meant to be a blessing to the world (Genesis 12:1-3). They chose instead to mock God and His mercy. Their choice came with grave consequences. We must choose what life we will live and either be with God or be against Him. Those who are with God will obey God. Those who are against Him will disobey God. Are you living in obedience to God? Is your life in His hands? It is only under the leadership of the Lord Jesus that a person can have hope.

Judges 9; Acts 13; Jeremiah 22; Mark 8

Sin has impaired the thinking of humanity. We naturally look to satisfy our eternal souls with temporary things. We make gods out of gold and take comfort in positions of power we cannot keep. We make pleasure our purpose and the opinions of others our joy. Only God can satisfy the longing of the human soul. The Word of God often seems unrealistic and out of touch to us, but that is only because we are so out of touch with God. Those who discern their spiritual need and look to Jesus by faith to provide live with hope.

The disciples of Jesus struggled to see beyond the temporal to the eternal supernatural reality of their Master. The events and conversations of Mark 8 provide insight into the hearts and minds of these ordinary men who were called to extraordinary lives. Their challenges give us comfort. Their failures provide us lessons. Their Master gave them the hope they needed, and He gives it to us today.

According to the teaching of their day, it is not surprising that the disciples believed Jesus was coming to establish an earthly kingdom and just throw off Roman rule so Israel could be a dominant world power again. God had bigger plans and was fighting a stronger enemy. The eternal plan of God was to do more than provide for temporary needs. Jesus came to feed the souls of all nations and defeat the lies of the devil. The disciples did not understand God's eternal plan and failed to see the lesson behind the feeding of the four thousand (v.1-10) and the evil of the Pharisees that Jesus described (v.11-21). God's people often get caught up in social causes, politics, and academic arguments and miss the real battle that is waging for the souls of billions.

The blind man at Bethsaida is a picture of all humanity. We are all born blind to God, but by miraculous grace, we can be healed and freed to believe and obey Jesus (v.22-26). Like Peter, we can understand Jesus is the Christ, the Son of God, and not just a prophet, as Islam and other false religions teach (v.27-30). Unlike Peter, we must understand the implication of Christ being the Savior of the world. To save, Jesus had to die. He had to live a holy life and then give that holy life as the substitutionary atoning sacrifice for the sin of the world (2 Corinthians 5:21). Death is the cost of sin, but life is available by faith in Jesus (Romans 6:23).

The flesh desires world domination now. Christ came to give eternal life and to make all things new. Peter rebuked Jesus because he wanted the temporary and not the eternal victory (v.31-33). Like Satan, the flesh wants to be satisfied in brokenness and to alter the redemptive plan of God. God came to die to give eternal life. Only those who die to the old blind broken life in the flesh can live to the new eternal blessed life in Christ (v.34-38). The world mocks the Godly, but one day the mockery of the earthly will be the glory of the redeemed.

Without grace we are blind. Do you see the grace of Jesus and the purpose of His Kingdom? Are you pursuing Christ and His cause? Jesus came for an eternal purpose. Those who see beyond the temporal and accept the eternal life of Christ have hope.

Judges 10; Acts 14; Jeremiah 23; Mark 9

One of the characteristics of God is celebrated in Psalm 136, where the phrase "for His steadfast love endures forever" is repeated twenty-six times. God's love is eternal and never faltering. That Psalm tells us that God creates, God delivers, and God cares. Thankfully, God is who He is. He is gracious to us. We are broken, foolish, and self-seeking. Without His steadfast love, there would be no hope. Those who trust in His steadfast love live with hope.

In Judges 10, the ongoing struggle of humanity is played out. God had provided and given His people a new life. He had created a covenant. The people continued to vacillate between faithfulness and unfaithfulness. When they were unfaithful, the consequences of their sin reaped suffering and they would cry out to God. When they cried out to God, His steadfast love would provide a deliverer. Once the people felt secure, they would turn from God and pursue the desires of the flesh.

As all God's children know to do, these people trusted God, but they were not consistent in their trust. When trouble came, they knew who to turn to. God was faithful to raise up leaders who would save them. Leaders like Tola and Jair (v.1-5). God has been faithful in every generation to have His people provided for and led. The likes of the apostles, the early church fathers, Augustine, Luther, Calvin, Whitefield, the Wesleys, Edwards, Spurgeon, Moody, and Graham, have come according to God's will and plan to call the church to renewal. Sadly, every new beginning, sooner or later, comes to an end. After the dust settles, disobedience often finds its way back into the lives of God's people.

There is a point at which God turns people over to their sin (Romans 1:21-32). It appeared that God was done with Israel after the days of Jair. The people turned away, and once they were again attacked, they turned back to God (v.6-10). God's response was to recount the favor He had shown them and then He called on them to trust in the gods they had been worshipping (v.11-14). By faith the people repented and put themselves into God's hands saying, "We have sinned; do to us whatever seems good to you. Only please deliver us this day" (v.15). This confession showed their faith in God's steadfast love. They turned from their sin, waited on the Lord, and began looking for the leader God would provide (v.16-18). Their faith was well placed.

In Christ, the redeemed of God have been given the power of the Holy Spirit, the Bible, and the church. There are still many who turn away and give up on God and pursue the things of the world. In their brokenness, many cry out to God and discover He never left them, although they left Him. This is the wondrous, mysterious grace of God. It heals what is broken. It restores what is lost. It remains, even when we leave.

God is willing to renew, deliver, and be present in the life of any who repent and trust in Him. Have you turned away from God? Is your life or your nation in need of revival? Are you willing to be the one to cry out to God and ask for His steadfast love to bring revival? God has shown His grace over and over. Those who trust in Him live with hope, even in dark times.

Judges 11; <u>Acts 15</u>; Jeremiah 24; Mark 10

There are two equally dangerous, but different forces at work among God's people. One is legalism and the other is lawlessness. Legalism occurs when people make up rules intended to help, but ultimately keep people from God. Lawlessness occurs when people ignore God's commands in favor of doing what the flesh desires. Those who obey Jesus out of love live with hope.

In Acts 15, the church was dealing with legalism. God had done a great work. Paul and Barnabas had made disciples of many Gentiles, as Christ had commanded (Matthew 28:18-20). Having been sent on mission by the church at Antioch, Paul and Barnabas returned to celebrate. A group of leaders from Judea attempted to correct Paul and Barnabas concerning the salvation in Jesus they had preached. These leaders were legalists and the debate that ensued between them and Paul and Barnabas was an important one.

Some Judeans believed that in order for a person to truly be saved, they first had to become adherents of the Old Covenant (v.1). Paul and Barnabas disagreed with them and debated these legalists. Paul and Barnabas were sent by the church at Antioch with other leaders to Jerusalem to deal with this issue (v.2). Every church needs leaders who are affirmed to speak for and serve the needs of the church. These leaders must be willing and able to articulate the truth of the Gospel, especially against false teachers.

Paul and Barnabas and their posse of apologists traveled to Jerusalem through cities where the Gospel had been preached and where believers had formed local churches. This delegation from Antioch encouraged those churches (v.3). Gospel-centered people always encourage joy among the Godly. Once in Jerusalem, the delegation from Antioch was received by the leaders of Jerusalem, but the legalists there wanted to augment their doctrine and teaching to include their legalistic rules (v.4-5). The leaders in Jerusalem took up the issue and Peter, Paul, and Barnabas were able to articulate the doctrine of salvation clearly (v.6-18). They explained the Gospel must be proclaimed and those disciples should be taught the law so they can obey God rightly, but not to obey in order to become disciples (v.19-21). The distinction was clear. The redeemed are saved by grace through faith, and their love for Jesus enables them to obey the law. James and the leaders of Jerusalem agreed with Paul and the others. The leaders at Jerusalem sent the delegation from Antioch back home with a delegation from Jerusalem to affirm their Gospel work (v.22-35).

Jesus intended the Gospel to be taken to the world. It is no surprise that once the church had settled the question of what the Gospel is, the church would be led to send missionaries to the world. Paul and Barnabas were again set aside by the church to go (v.36). As sometimes happens, leaders that agree on doctrine do not always agree on method. Paul and Barnabas parted ways over policy, but God's will was done, even in this disagreement (v.37-41).

The Gospel is the power of God. Can you clearly articulate the Gospel? Can you defend it? Are you sending missionaries and living on mission where you live? Those who understand and believe the Gospel have hope.

Judges 12; Acts 16; Jeremiah 25; Mark 11

God is in control. It can sometimes seem that the world is out of control, but it is not. God is at work in every generation, and He is ruling over every tribe and nation. The rule of Christ is now through His providence. The world is not as it should be. Evil is afoot, and yet God is working all things for good. Those who look to God with faith and trust in His perfect plan live with hope.

The prophet Jeremiah had a tough ministry. He was called to preach to people who would not listen to God's Word. To make matters worse, the people were in terrible danger. God was about to discipline them. The nations God intended to use to discipline Israel would ultimately be judged as well. Jeremiah 25 reveals God as the sovereign ruler of all. He acts in accordance with His good and sometimes terrifying will.

God's good and terrifying will was to exile the nation of Israel from the land of promise. The temple would be destroyed. The cities would lie in ruin. There would be complete devastation. This was to take place because of the sinful pride of the people (v.1-14). This action by God was intentional. This exile would last the specific time God determined. What a comfort to know God is in control and His actions are measured. God's sovereign care gives peace to God's children. Although humanity and nations seem strong, they are just created things. God is at work in His creation to accomplish His purpose. He will bring glory to His name among the nations.

God's control of all things does not minimize the real pain, sorrow, and horror that come as a consequence for sin. Pain still hurts, even though there is purpose in it. The nations of the world will come and go. They will rise in power and then fade into history. The nations of the world, under human authority, will fail sooner or later because sin always takes its toll. When sin climaxes into consequences, nations fall. The process of their fall is staggering (v.15-38). There is nothing more terrifying than the wrath of God, as a result of sin.

The hope of the redeemed is found in the mercy and grace of God. Jeremiah knew all that was coming and he was horrified and grieved by it, but he also knew the promises of God. He knew in time, God would restore all things and provide for His people. Even in his life, as he endured the pain of living amongst a fallen people and a nation under the discipline of God, he still had hope. So it is for all of God's people. While we will certainly suffer and face consequences, God will not abandon us. He will work to accomplish good, even in the worst of situations.

Every person on the planet is given life by God. That life may be in the best of times or the worst of times. While we cannot control the times we live in, we can look to God in faith and find hope in His grace and mercy. What kind of world do you find yourself in today? Is your faith in God greater than the challenges you face? Those who can see beyond the moment, to the hand of God that is in control of all things, will live with hope.

Judges 13; Acts 17; Jeremiah 26; Mark 12

God does not remove natural challenges for believers but uses them to reveal Himself and develop the faith of His children. Followers of Jesus should never be surprised by the difficulties they face. Those who see the world for what it is, and God for who He is, live with hope.

God was so gracious to become one of us to provide the means for us to know and love God and to show us how to live in the real world. Mark 12 gives several examples for how disciples of Jesus are to view, live, and struggle through life in this fallen world as redeemed, heaven-bound saints.

Those who follow Jesus will not be appreciated by those who don't. It is not just the secularists that cause disciples of Jesus to struggle, but it is also other religious people who deny Jesus. Almost everyone who is not a disciple of Jesus can appreciate certain aspects of Jesus, but they reject His primary function: Lordship. God made the world and everything in it. His image-bearers rejected Him (v.1). Over the years, God has sent servants to call the people of the world to love and honor God (v.2-6). God sent His Son, but they hated him and killed Him (v.7-12). Servants of Jesus should expect to be treated the way Jesus was treated by the world.

The world will call Jesus' authority into question. Worldly people cannot apprehend the relationship they are meant to enjoy with God under His loving leadership. Without Jesus, people cannot understand how governments and God are to both be honored (v.13-17), how God is present and alive (v.18-27), and how loving God and loving people is what life is all about (v.28-34). Secularists and those involved in other world religions look to structures, ideologies, and laws to make sense of life. Disciples of Jesus understand that life makes sense and has meaning when God is loved and they choose to love other people with the sacrificial love God gave them.

Until Jesus is rightly understood, religion will be life-taking rather than life-giving. Christ came to give new life, as promised by God (v.35-37). God promised that a man from the line of David, who was God, would come and save the world. Those who reject Jesus reject life. The life of a disciple of Jesus seeks to bring attention and praise to God. A disciple never finds fulfillment in receiving the praise of man, although we are tempted to (v.38-40). Disciples of Jesus find strength in weakness and not in positions of power.

By trusting in Jesus and delighting in His generous grace, children of God delight in being generous. Their offerings are given out of a desire to honor God, show their love for God, and to grow their faith in God. How much we give is not nearly as important as the heart we give with. God blesses generous disciples (v.41-44). God's blessing may be more resources or just the great joy that comes from living in dependence on God.

There are disciples of Jesus, secularists, and people of other world religions. Are you a disciple of Jesus? Are you suffering for and with Him by living as Jesus did and giving generously to God's work? Disciples of Jesus who live in the world for the glory of Christ live with hope.

Judges 14; Acts 18; Jeremiah 27; Mark 13

Power is a glorious thing. It can also be a destructive. When people seek power for themselves, they seek something dangerous. Power has a way of corrupting the soul and tempting people to believe they do not need God. Power has a way of tearing apart what God meant to stay together. Those who trust in God and glorify Him in His Gospel power live with hope.

Sampson was a miserable man. He was gifted with great power, but the very power that could have been used for good was often used by him selfishly with destructive results. In Judges 14, we see how power without God's purpose will always end in misery.

Parents are intended to be blessings of God to their children. Children who obey their parents are promised God's blessing (Ephesians 6:1-3). Sampson was unwilling to submit to his parents (v.1-3). Parents are not perfect, but God's design provides parents with a protective love for their children. That love leads parents to want what they perceive is best for their offspring. Their perceptions are not always right. In Sampson's case, his parents were leading him to honor the Lord, but he wanted the power to decide his own direction and gain what he desired. Those who want the power to satisfy their desires rather than the Lord will fall into sin.

God has the power to work all things for good for His people according to His purpose (Genesis 50:20, Romans 8:28, Jeremiah 29:11). Sampson's parents must have been heartbroken to see their son pursue what they knew was outside of God's will. What they did not know was that God had a plan (v.4). God works in mysterious ways, and people of faith can rest in His providence.

When a person is undisciplined in one area, that lack of discipline will often impact other areas of that person's life. Sampson was dishonoring God by pursuing a Canaanite wife, and so it was nothing for him to eat honey from a dead animal and not tell his parents (v.5-9). One sin makes another sin easier, and gaining just a little power makes a person long for more. Sampson not only wanted this wife, but the resources of her people, so he created a riddle they could not answer (v.10-14). The people wanted power, so they threatened Sampson's wife and forced her to discover the answer to the riddle (v.15-18). In the end, destruction came to people that had nothing to do with the whole affair (v.19). The pursuit of power often has ripple effects that cause devastation in many directions.

Once a person gains some power, an attitude of entitlement often follows. Sampson did not get the clothes he expected and so he pouted and lost the wife he wanted (v.20). Power can create an attitude of entitlement, which keeps people from being humble.

Power can be a destructive force. Are you seeking to be in control of your life and other's lives? Do you find it difficult to be grateful and God-honoring? It may be because power has corrupted your heart and mind. The only hope is repentance and faith in the Gospel. Those who glorify God and are grateful to Him live with hope.

Judges 15; <u>Acts 19</u>; Jeremiah 28; Mark 14

Everyone needs a purpose. God in His common grace gives every person on the planet a purpose. Those who receive saving grace are given a divine purpose, and it has eternal significance. While God's children find their identity and sense of self in the cross of Jesus, they find their destiny in taking up their own cross and following Jesus in sacrificial service (Luke 9:23). Those who serve the Father in the power of the Spirit in the name of Jesus live with hope.

Paul served God and fulfilled his divine purpose in Christ (Acts 9:16). He was a missionary to the Gentiles, although he typically began his work in a city by ministering to Jews. What made Paul's ministry so effective was not what Paul did, but who Paul served. In Acts 19, the power behind Paul's work is revealed.

When Paul came to Ephesus, he met twelve men who claimed to be disciples (v.1-7). They had repented and believed in John's message about the coming Messiah, but they had not yet been saved. They had not heard the Good News that Jesus had come. They had not heard of the promise of the Holy Spirit and of His coming into the world. They had missed two big historic events. Paul preached the Gospel to them and they believed. They were baptized and experienced a Pentecost moment. Paul preached that same Gospel to other Jews, but they would not believe (v.8-10). The power of Paul's ministry was the Holy Spirit. Only those who believe are able to experience God's blessing, and only the Holy Spirit can enable belief.

Compared to Paul, the seven sons of Sceva were a joke. Miraculous power was being manifested through Paul (v.11-12), and so these seven sons sought to dabble in a battle they had no business being in (v.13-16). Presuming to have power, these men were beaten naked by a demonic man and everyone heard about it. These seven men had no chance in the spiritual battle they tried to engage in. Only those, like Paul, with the power of Jesus, who defeated sin and death, can stand against the evil of demons. Many understood this and gave up their magic and witchcraft in order to experience the power of Jesus (v.17-20). This same power is now at work among those who are being saved because it is the same God, the same Gospel, and the same purpose at work.

When the power of God is at work, the Gospel changes individual lives and inevitably, entire cultures. This was happening in Ephesus (21-41). The idol worship of the local deity of Ephesus had lost its influence and the financial power that came with it because of the work of Paul. Those who had lost that power wanted it back. Stirring up a riot, they made their plea for the people to reject Paul's message and return to the financial power of their idol. Many were swept up in the emotion of it. This is the mistake many make. Buying into the idolatry of their time, they miss the experience of the power of Jesus.

Paul served God's purpose with God's power. Are you serving God's purpose with your life? Is your life built on the Gospel of Jesus? Without Jesus there is no power and no way to fulfill God's purpose. Serving in the power of God, a person is able to live with hope.

Judges 16; Acts 20; Jeremiah 29; Mark 15

Knowing God is in control and has a plan for the life of His people is a great comfort. God's plan is not absent of pain. It is also not absent of comfort. Just as God used the cross to accomplish the greatest good, He also uses pain in His people's lives for good. It is a great comfort to know God is at work in every circumstance and those who believe in Him can turn to Him and find help. Those who trust God and discern His love in every circumstance will live with hope.

After Israel had been exiled, false prophets were lying to the people and telling them their exile would be short and the blessing of God would soon be found in Jerusalem. This was not the plan of God. In Jeremiah 29, God laid out His plan for His people. This plan provides insight into how the Lord works among those who trust Him and love Him and find their hope in Him today.

The people had sinned against God and their exile was the consequence for their sin. Jeremiah was not taken with the exiles. He was able to watch the events unfold. Having heard of the lie the people were told, God called Jeremiah to write a letter to the leaders in exile (v.1-4). What God told the exiles to do is what God's people are to do today (v.5-9). They were to build a life in the place God had sent them and be faithful to the true Word of God and reject the teaching of deceptive prophets. As a sent people living in exile away from heaven (John 20:21), the redeemed of God are to live like Jesus. Jesus was sent by the Father into our human existence, which had been exiled from the Garden (Genesis 2-3). He came to bless the world. God's people are exiles sent to bless the world in which they live.

It can sometimes appear we are all just victims of circumstance. God's Word says otherwise. God told Israel His timetable and plan (v.10-15). We may not know God's timetable, but we can know it is His will that we pursue Him and His purpose, and trust the Lord will provide for us and in time take us home to heaven.

Until the time of the Lord's return, we must be faithful. God called Israel to be faithful to His Word and to reject the lies of the false prophets, who told the people the real blessing was back in Jerusalem and not in Babylon (v.16-32). The Lord promised to deal with these liars. It may have appeared to the people that they were lambs without a shepherd. They weren't. God made it clear He had sent them to where they were (v.20), and He would bring them back at His determined time.

God's timing is perfect. While we would prefer to have what we want, when we want it, the fact of the matter is God knows what is best. He knows how to discipline us and to comfort us. Both His discipline and comfort are blessings. Both are part of His plan. Do you trust God's plan for your life? Do you believe God's Word? Are you rejecting the lies of false prophets of today? Those who trust in the Lord and abide in His leadership live with hope.

The resurrection of Jesus is the confirmation of His claim to be the Savior of the world. His being raised reveals that He is God. He is worthy to be worshipped. Humanity is made to worship. There are some who worship things, some who worship others, and some who worship self, but all worship. Those who worship the one true God live with hope.

How a person worships is important. God not only designed us to worship, but also provided the means. In Mark 16, we see some of the women in Jesus' earthly ministry coming to worship Him. It was the Lord's Day. It was the first day of the week. They came with a heart of love, they brought their concerns and questions, and they found a miracle happening.

These ladies loved Jesus and desired to honor him. After the Sabbath had ended that Saturday evening at sunset, the ladies went and purchased spices. Early in the morning, they went to the tomb. It was an urgent task that needed to be done. They went to show their love. Anointing a dead body with spices was an act of love (v.1-2). When believers come to worship, it is vital they come with love. God has loved us, which allows us to love Him in return (1 John 4:19). Love is more than a feeling. It is a choice followed by actions. When we worship rightly, we bring offerings of praise, prayer, costly gifts, and service to God.

These ladies had questions and concerns. Their first and most formidable problem was the stone that had been placed in front of the tomb. How they would get to Jesus had not been determined (v3). What they found is what all who long to worship Jesus find. The way had been made. The stone had been rolled away. It was a very large stone, and they could not have rolled it away on their own (v.4). So it is with all who come to worship Jesus. The way must be made for us. We will have questions and concerns in life, but we can bring them to Jesus. He can move those stones and allow us to find more than we were looking for.

These ladies found more than they were looking for that morning. They found themselves in the midst of a miracle. When they entered the tomb, they did not find the body of Jesus. They found an angel proclaiming the Good News of the power of God (v.5-6). There are miracles all around us, if we will just see them. The other Gospel writers reported confusion in the heart of Mary at the empty tomb. We may not understand all that God is doing, but we can know it is good and we can praise Him at all times. Having seen the miracle, these women discovered they were to proclaim it (v.7-8). Worship begins with the gathered church and then continues in our lives as we go and share the miracle of the Gospel.

Those ladies left that day and did as they were told. They lived a life of worship. Do you have a deep love and dedication to Jesus? Do you seek Jesus in worship each week? Are you in awe of the miracles of God? Those who truly seek Jesus live with hope because He is alive and at work in the world.

Judges 18; Acts 22; Jeremiah 32; Psalms 1–2

Intentionality is necessary for God's people. When we live focused on Christ and His purpose on earth, we discover our destiny. Each of us must pursue our destiny to find it and fulfill it. Those who pursue their divine calling and live deliberately for God live with hope.

During the days of the Judges, the people had no king to rally around. They were not without access to God, but they lacked the faith and passion to pursue the Lord appropriately. The tribe of Dan never accomplished their purpose. Rather than taking the land that had been allotted to them, they waited and wandered. In Judges 18, we see what it looks like to live without purpose and to halfheartedly pursue the plan of God.

Those not intentional about accomplishing God's purpose live with a minimalist mindset. The tribe of Dan had been given the land east of Ephraim and north of Judah along the coast of the Mediterranean. And yet they were in the far north of Israel looking for land (v.1). They recruited five men to go looking for a deal (v.2). Rather than trusting God for what He promised, they settled for what they could accomplish. When the Maker of heaven and earth is your God, there is no excuse for failing to pursue His purpose; God demands and rewards faith.

Those not intentional about accomplishing God's purpose live a parasitic life. These Danites were on the run looking for what they could get rather than pursuing what God had promised. Coming upon a helpless person, Micah, and a helpless city, Laish, they took what they could get (v.3-29). Rather than trusting God and pursuing His plan, these people squandered their opportunities and were made to suffer for it. Their suffering led to the suffering of others. There is always a trickle-down effect in human suffering. God saves a people for Himself to bless them so they can be a blessing. How sad it is to see children of the King of heaven live with so little hope and to rob rather than supply blessings to others.

Those not intentional about accomplishing God's purpose live an idolatrous life. God designed humanity to worship and draw their identity from something outside of themselves. God alone is able to be self-defining and self-satisfied in Himself. Humans, being finite creatures, require something beyond themselves to gain meaning and a sense of self. The Danites did not have a healthy, fulfilling relationship with God and so they filled that vacuum in their soul with the idols of Micah. Without a passionate pursuit of God to satisfy the longing of their soul, people will adopt whatever gods are available to attempt to meet their spiritual needs with them. Idols made by human hands can never satisfy the infinite soul within human beings.

The Danites are a sad study in human depravity. Without God and His divine guidance, they got lost. Are you passionately pursuing God's purpose? Are you seeking to fulfill your destiny? Have you foolishly replaced God's will for your life and accepted a life that is void of faith in Jesus and that does not please God? Only those who live intentionally with and for God live with hope.

Judges 19; Acts 23; Jeremiah 33; Psalms 3–4

There will be days of peace and times of trouble. The same God allows both and has a plan and purpose for each. It is the child of God's duty to determine the will of God in every season and situation and accomplish it for God's glory. Those who seek and serve God in all circumstances live with hope.

The Apostle Paul was a man of hope. In Acts 23, he was being deposed by the religious leaders that cared neither for God nor the people they were to minister to. Given his new life in Christ, Paul stood his ground with confidence, respect, wisdom, and faith. What Paul possessed in this trial is what all believers have been given in order to live with hope in all circumstances.

Paul had confidence in his good conscience (v.1). There are always consequences to actions. Paul had stood for Christ and abandoned the way of the religious leaders in Jerusalem. Having met Jesus and been transformed by His grace and used to plant churches, Paul was confident of his calling. The religious leaders in Jerusalem perceived Paul to be a threat. Paul was not concerned about their opinion of him. He was secure in his standing with God. A clear conscience provides peace in tough times.

Paul showed respect for the authorities (v.2-5). Paul knew these religious leaders were bogus, but out of respect for God's Word, he honored those in power. Calling those lost leaders out for their false, dead religion resulted in his being abused. Rather than rail against the high priest, Paul showed respect for the position and God's Word and quoted Scripture. Being able to quote Scripture serves the soul of a saint.

Paul showed wisdom in his words and actions (v.6-10). Seeing the enemies of God united against him, Paul utilized an existing theological divide to his advantage. He put Jesus' words in Matthew 10:16 to work: "be wise as serpents and innocent as doves." His conscience was clear. His allegiance to God and His Word was strong. Paul took advantage of his knowledge and acted wisely. God's children are to be holy and humble, but also wise and use tools to divide the enemy in order to give opportunity for the Gospel.

Paul showed faith in his resilience (v.11-35). Jesus spoke to Paul and revealed His plan to have Paul journey to Rome to testify there. Knowing this, Paul was able to face a death threat and his deportation with confidence. Knowing God is in control of our destinies enables those who believe in Jesus to have hope, even when our lives are in danger. Paul knew his mission. When God's people live on mission for Jesus, they can be confident the Lord is working in and through and around them.

There is always reason to have hope when Christ is the Lord of your life. Paul walked with the Lord and pursued His purpose. Circumstances did not get him down. Are you walking faithfully with the Lord? Is your faithfulness to Christ resulting in your working out your salvation and calling? The mission of God stays the same no matter what our circumstances may be. Are you fulfilling the Great Commission of Jesus? Those who keep their eyes on Jesus and obey His commands live with hope, despite difficulties.

Judges 20; Acts 24; <u>Jeremiah 34</u>; Psalms 5–6

God often gives a glimpse into the broader reality of what is happening in the world through a simple event in the Bible. God made the world to be a place of harmony, but when sin entered the world, through the sin of humanity, the fall occurred. In our fallen world, there is now suffering and death. Thankfully, Jesus has come to rescue us. God's rescued people live with hope now in the peace of God.

When Jerusalem was in its last days and Babylon was about to completely destroy the city, God spoke through His prophet Jeremiah to Zedekiah, the king of Israel (Jeremiah 24:1). Jerusalem was to be a place of peace, but sin had made it a place of death. God chose to rescue His people, although they would have to live in exile. God's salvation was available then and now. God will save any person who will trust Him through faith in Jesus's atoning sacrifice. God will save from sin and eternal death, although those who are saved must live in exile in this fallen world until He returns and makes all things new.

Jeremiah's message was a pronouncement of grace (v.2-5) and judgment (v.6-22). Grace is God's unearned blessing. It is getting what is not deserved. Judgment is God's righteous justice. It is getting the full measure of what is deserved. We must choose what we get from God. We can choose to repent of our sin and receive God's forgiveness or we can choose to live in sin and reject God's loving pardon.

If we choose grace, we will have to live by faith in the Word of God. Doubt is never difficult. It is easy to understand why Zedekiah may have found it difficult to believe that he could be saved. The army besieging him was vast. But he believed. God did not promise to remove Zedekiah from his circumstances, but God promised to save him in the midst of the war and give him peace. God does not remove the redeemed from the spiritual war of this planet, but He promises His blessings and peace to endure.

If we choose justice, we will receive what we deserve. Sin is easy. The people had originally chosen to act wisely and to honor God by keeping God's law concerning slaves. Slavery in Israel was meant to be temporary. After seven years, slaves were to be freed (Deuteronomy 15:12–18). The people freed the slaves, but then turned back and enslaved them again. This faithless act of injustice earned them God's justice. The people broke the covenant bond they had made. Now they would be cut up, according to the covenant they made (v.18-20). This is reminiscent of the covenant God made with Abraham, when God passed through the cut-up animals (Genesis 15:17). These leaders of Jerusalem died for their sin. Years later in that same city, Jesus would die for the sins of the world. Any who look to Him now in faith will be forgiven. Jesus has met the just demands of the law and suffered the punishment for the sin of others to give peace to all who believe.

The story of God is simple: creation, fall, rescue, and restoration. Those who receive God's grace will be saved. Have you trusted Jesus? Are you obeying Him? Those who live in and under God's grace live with hope.

Judges 21; Acts 25; Jeremiah 35; <u>Psalms 7–8</u>

When we are in a right standing with God, we have hope. That hope transcends our highest highs and our lowest lows. Knowing that the Lord is for us and with us and in us and is working a plan that provides what is best, holy, and right is satisfying to the soul. The greatness of God matched with His holiness makes Him trustworthy. Those who trust in the Lord live with hope.

In Psalms 7–8, David revealed His confidence in the Lord. In Psalm 7, David revealed his confidence in the justice of God. In Psalm 8, David revealed his confidence in the grace and mercy of God. These two realities are often at odds in the minds of people. The question is often asked why bad is allowed to harm those who are seemingly good. The difficulty is in understanding how a gracious God would allow any evil or bad to befall helpless people.

Psalm 7 establishes the fact that there are no helpless people. People either help themselves or they look to God for help. Both are helped. David was being pursued by enemies. David knew he was not without sin, but he also knew he had been made right with God by faith. His confidence to call out to God came from the life he had lived under God's leadership. Some would question the heart of God for allowing David to suffer, when it appeared he had done nothing to deserve it. We must remember that in this fallen world it is not pain that will harm us, but worldliness and wantonness. God allows suffering to sanctify His saints and to teach His children to stay close to their Father and reside under the shield of His help.

While God helps those who trust in Him, He judges those who trust in themselves. All humans, left to themselves, become hard-hearted toward God. Their empty souls rot in the barrenness of their dark hearts. Those who will not repent of self-sufficiency will remain in sin and God will judge them for their actions. Only those who seek God's grace will survive God's judgment.

This grace, when understood properly, overwhelms the heart. In Psalm 8, David declares what those who have faith declare: "O Lord, our Lord, how majestic is your name in all the earth!" God is above all things. This not only speaks to His transcendence, but also to His holiness. There is none like God, and it is a wonder that He would concern Himself with the lowly humans that turned their backs on Him. And yet God does care for us. He created all things for His glory, and by His sustaining mercy the world is maintained. For His glory and by his grace and mercy, God entered this broken world to save sinners. This is the Gospel. Those who look to Jesus will be saved and will live with hope.

The choice is ours. Either we will look to God for help and by faith receive God's forgiveness and provision in Jesus, or we will look to ourselves and fall deeper into sin. Do you trust in the grace of Jesus? Do you look to God for help? Are you regularly amazed with the care and concern that God has for you? God has gone to great lengths to love and care for you. Those who look to Him in faith live with hope.

Ruth 1; Acts 26; Jeremiah 36, 45; Psalm 9

It is so easy to get caught up in the outcome and forget that the real blessing is in the process. Outcomes come and go. Processes continue. The action is in the process. As we make decisions and walk by faith, we experience the power and presence of God. Those who delight in God in the process rather than focusing only on the outcomes live with hope.

The book of Ruth is all about a process. In terms of world-changing outcomes, the characters accomplished very little. They did not defeat a great foe, overcome an awful evil, or build a grand edifice. The characters simply walked through their broken world with God. They went through a process that led to a son that led to the line of Jesse, which produced David, who became the one through whom Christ would come. But Ruth, her mother-in-law, and her husband did not do much. They simply lived by faith. Ruth 1 reminds us of the brokenness of the world, the faithfulness of God, and the importance of focusing on Jesus.

The first paragraph is so sad (v.1-5). This husband sought to provide for his family. He turned from God. He left to find provision from a pagan people and place. In the process, he died. And then, his sons died, leaving his wife, Naomi, without the protective care of her husband and sons (v.5). Naomi was not abandoned by God, although she felt like she was. It is vital that the people of God always look beyond their circumstance to find the face of God seeking them. Like Peter, we must walk among the waves and winds of this world, without losing sight of Jesus (Matthew 14:30). In the process of life, there will be many distractions, but the redeemed of God can know the Lord is with them (Hebrews 13:5).

While the desires of the heart can certainly lead to confusion and corruption (Jeremiah 17:9), it is unwise to ignore the desires of the heart completely because God made us with specific desires for His purpose. So many wrongly assume if they want something, it must be wrong and contrary to God's will. We must remember that where we were born, raised, and taught leads us to have specific desires. This is by God's design. Naomi decided to return home and kindly released her daughters to pursue a new life (v.6-14). Ruth's desire to go with Naomi seemed unwise, but her desire was of God (v.15-18). We must not be afraid to pursue the desires of our hearts.

Naomi returned to her home bitter. She wanted to be called Mara, which means bitter (v.19-21). She felt the Lord was against her. Graciously and wisely, the people continued to refer to her as Naomi (v.22), which means my delight. When we are in the process of a trial or tragedy, we need friends who can remind us of the truth of God's love and goodness. Although her life was hard, she was still God's delight. God delights in all of His children, even as He allows them to suffer for His reasons.

We are all in a process right now. Are you honoring God with your decisions? Are you taking the time to seek the face of Jesus in the storm? Those who keep their eyes on Jesus will always have hope, even when life is hard.

Even when we cannot see or understand the purpose of God, we can trust His heart. Even when we do not know what to do, we can know God is at work accomplishing what is best. The child of God can always have hope.

The Apostle Paul was not a sailor, but he knew enough to avoid traveling in the stormy season. The story of Paul's journey by sea to Rome is detailed in Acts 27. There was a centurion and a captain anxious to get home. The pride and impatience of humanity is often our downfall. Being a prisoner, Paul had to abide by their disastrous decision. During this trying moment, Paul displayed the spiritual leadership needed today. He shared the truth without quarreling. He kept his hope in the midst of difficulty. He blessed others with his faith and helped them in their time of need.

It did not take a seafaring genius to know that traveling in the late fall and winter was unwise (v.1-9). Paul sensed that disaster was ahead and spoke up (v.10). We do not know how he had come by this information, whether it was supernatural or just common sense. The leadership decided to go, given that the harbor they were in was unsuitable to remain for the winter (v.11-12). When given a decision and no good answer is available, it is wise to wait. If providence pushes another course of action, then so be it. If not, humbly remaining still until another option comes available is prudent.

As Paul predicted, disaster struck and the men were placed in grave danger by the weather conditions (v.13-17). Having no alternative but to lighten the boat, they threw over the cargo and the tackle (v.18-19). They lost hope when clear skies never came (v.20). It was then Paul stepped up. Reminding them that they did not listen to him before, Paul encouraged them to hear him in that moment (v.21). He gave them hope. Having heard from the Lord, Paul encouraged them to eat and prepare to run aground (v.22-26). Those who walk with God trust in God's provision. We need not worry, and we can comfort those who do.

As Paul predicted, the ship was destroyed, but all of the people survived (v.27-38). In the midst of the calamity, Paul provided peace through his confidence in God. Although he was not the most competent sailor, he became the leader. He was able to point out the need for the crew to stay together and to eat. When tragedy strikes, God's people will find peace by looking to God with grateful hearts.

Paul won the favor of the captain. Rather than killing the prisoners, which was the prudent thing for a Roman soldier to do, the centurion decided against it for Paul's sake. The ship was lost, but all the people were saved (v.39-44). Humbled and left with nothing, these men tasted ultimate reality. In the end, we can take nothing with us. In the end, we will all have nothing, except our souls, and we will stand before God to give an account for our lives.

The children of God can live lives free from worry. We can know that the Lord will provide. Do you trust God? Can others see your confidence in God? The faithful live with hope in any circumstance.

Ruth 3–4; Acts 28; <u>Jeremiah 38</u>; Psalms 11–12

The Lord Jesus Christ came into the world. Truth became flesh. He lived as a man but was fully God. He came bringing Good News. He is the only means by which any person can be saved. God spoke of His Son in the Old Testament. Jesus came in the New Testament. He reigns now from the right hand of God. Those who speak for Jesus live with hope, although they are not always appreciated for their ministry.

Jeremiah is a picture of Jesus. His ministry was not appreciated. His life was in danger from the rulers of the people. He spoke the truth and was persecuted for it. He did not live to give honor to human authorities. He lived to honor His God. In Jeremiah 28, the work of Christ is revealed in the life of Jeremiah.

Like Jesus, Jeremiah was hated and accused of being an enemy to the people (v.1-4). Jeremiah did not follow the party line of the prophets and leaders of his day. They were saying God would deliver the people from the Babylonians, but Jeremiah knew different. Jeremiah knew Jerusalem would be destroyed and the inhabitants suffer and be taken hostage. His message was to surrender. This did not sit well with the leaders. They believed he was being treasonous. The religious leaders of Jesus' day thought the same of Him.

Like Jesus, Jeremiah was sentenced to death (v.5-6). The leaders sought to put him to death. Zedekiah, the king, did not stand with him. Instead of protecting him and by faith trusting the one God had sent, he turned Jeremiah over to be put to death. It appears he had no choice. The leaders lowered Jeremiah into a cistern to die a slow, dirty death. The disciples abandoned Jesus, and Pilate put Jesus on the cross to die.

Like Jesus, Jeremiah was raised from death to life (v.7-13). Jeremiah did not die in that pit. Instead he was raised to life. Jesus did die. He died to pay for the sins of the world. He was lowered from the cross and laid in a tomb. That tomb could not hold Him. Three days after His death, Jesus was raised to life!

Like Jesus, Jeremiah was gracious to those who rejected him and sought to call them to faith (v.14-28). Zedekiah met privately with Jeremiah, after He was raised, and heard the truth again of what was to happen. Jeremiah called Zedekiah to submit to the will and work of God. This was a gracious act on Jeremiah's part. He did not hold a grudge. After He was raised, Jesus spoke with Peter, who had abandoned and denied Him three times. Jesus called Peter to repentance and to a life of service. He did not hold a grudge against Peter or any of those who abandoned Him or sought His harm. He was gracious and called them to faithfulness.

The Gospel is the power of God to save sinners from eternal death and to new life. This life comes by faith in the Son of God. The will of God has, is, and will be done. The promises of God will come to pass. The judgment of God is coming. Do you trust Jesus with your life? Are you loyal to Him with genuine love? Those who trust in the Lord Jesus will live in fellowship with God and have living hope.

Every worldview has a specific view of God, of humanity, and of the natural world. Those who look to the Bible to define these realities have the ability to understand and put into proper context and perspective things like happiness, pain, purpose, and power. Without a Biblical worldview people are left to their feelings and imaginations, which are tainted with sin. Those who know the Gospel look at and live in the world with hope.

King David was a man with a Biblical worldview. In Psalms 13–14, David's way of dealing with and coping with life at its best and worst is revealed. His hope is the hope of all who believe in Jesus. His hope came from a realistic perspective. His hope came through the grace of God. His hope came with an understanding of his own sin and his desperate need for divine intervention.

King David did not look at the world through rose-colored glasses. He was not a fool and he did not pretend to be happy when he was sad. In Psalm 13, he made it clear that his life was not how he wanted it to be. He felt forgotten by God (v.1). And yet, he prayed. He spoke with God. He prayed a simple prayer (v.2). He knew God was sovereign over the world. He knew that God loved Him and could care for him. Those who know God's love, through Christ Jesus, can always pray and know God hears them and cares. We may not feel God's presence or blessing, but we can know that He is with us and for us in Christ, and we can pray to Him.

King David was aware of the brokenness and danger of the world and the power of God to protect His people (v.3). Hurting people hurt people. There is no limit to the evil and destructiveness that humanity is capable of. Given the wrong circumstances and pain, a human being can do monstrous and terrible things. It is vital the children of God pray on behalf of the saints and for the protection of God's people.

King David was aware of God's plan for the world and those who are against Him and those who are for Him (Psalm 14). There are no human beings that are by nature for God (v.1-4). They know there is a God by general revelation (Romans 1:21-23). They know there is a God, but they do not honor Him. Those who honor God with their lives do not have to live in terror, as do those who do not know God (v.5). Those who know God, through Christ, in the life-giving faith-building power of the Spirit, live under the mighty refuge of God. They look to the Lord's appearing and are confident that His Kingdom will come (v.6).

Those who are blessed to know the truth of God's Word and have a relationship with the living God through faith in Jesus by the power of the Holy Spirit have great hope. Do you see the world through the lens of the Word of God? Are you studying the Word of God each day to better understand God, your life, and your world? Those who know the Word of God can understand the will of God and trust the plans of God. Those who trust in God can see the world in all its troubles, and still have hope.

God is who He is whether we acknowledge Him or not. The whole world is full of His glory. There are more stars than there are human sounds to distinguish each one. There are billions of image-bearers walking on earth with miraculous systems all working together to give thought, movement, and vitality to each person. God made all things and all things are sustained by Him. Those who acknowledge and honor God live with hope.

In 1 Samuel 2, there are two types of people revealed. There are those, like Hannah and Samuel, who love the Lord and delight in His greatness and there are people like Hophni and Phinehas, who despise the Lord and treat God with disdain. There are consequences to actions and none more serious than the consequences that come as a result of our response to God Almighty.

The way of this world is not the way of God. This world is fallen, but God is in control and is accomplishing His purpose for His glory. Hannah believed in the purpose of God. Her prayer reflected her faith (v.1-11). Having had a son, Samuel, and given him to the service of God, she celebrated the goodness of God. She had come to see how God raises up the humble, and in time, overwhelms the proud. The way of God is not the way of the world. The way of God is to bless the weak who look to Him for strength, and to break to pieces those who will not yield to His gracious leadership.

Those who look to themselves for authority and leadership are like the sons of Eli (v.12-17). They must depend upon their own capacities to gain what they want and need in life. Rather than faithfully serving the Lord to give Him glory and accomplish His will, they made a mockery of God's glory and dominion. Rather than serve the people, they hustled and intimidated them. Rather than love the Lord, they despised God. They had no respect for the holiness of God's sacrifices. Without God, people cause great harm to others and to their own hearts. These two men were blasphemous and famous for it. They had sick, sad souls. Their father warned them, but it was too late (v.22-36). God is gracious to those who honor Him, but those who reject Him will receive their just punishment.

The best way of life is the humble, confident way of faith. Samuel was a child of faith, and his way of life was not like the way of Eli's sons (v.18). Samuel served the Lord. Samuel was blessed with Godly parents. He had a praying mother who provided him with the tools needed to stand before the Lord and serve God (v.19). Samuel's family was blessed by God (v.20-21). They gave Samuel to God and God blessed them. The contrast between Eli's and Hannah's faith was evident in their parenting.

The Godly life is a simple life. Those who trust in God pray, obey, and wait on the Lord. Life without God is complicated. Those who trust in their own abilities must prey on others, deny God, and thrust their will upon other people and circumstances. We all choose our path. God blesses the way of the faithful. What path are you on? What consequences can you anticipate in light of your choices? Those who acknowledge and honor God live with hope.

1 Samuel 3; Romans 3; Jeremiah 41; Psalm 17

God is in control of the smallest details (Proverbs 16:33 and Matthew 10:30), but every person is responsible for their decisions (Hebrews 9:27). Not one person on this planet chose their parents, the place they were born and raised, or the genetics they received. God is sovereign over the details of every person's life and their destiny (Psalm 139:16). Yet each person is responsible for what they do and must choose the kind of person they will be (Psalm 1). The person who walks with Christ is blessed with hope.

Writing to a church of Gentiles and Jews in his letter to the Romans, Paul sought to affirm what God was doing in their church and to establish the theological reasoning for his missionary efforts. Paul affirmed the Jews in their heritage in Romans 2 and then called both the Jews and Gentiles to live by faith in Romans 3.

The Jews had great advantages in their heritage (v.1). Like those who are now raised in a Christian home, the Jews were given the Scriptures (v.2). They knew the Old Testament. They understood the faith from the perspective of God's work in the world. Admittedly, not all were faithful to the truth, but God was faithful and His truth stands (v.3-4). God brought glory to Himself, despite the unfaithfulness of the Jews, but this is not grounds for disobedience (v.5-9). Those raised in a home that instructs its members in the truth of God's Word are raised with a great blessing, and that blessing comes with a responsibility – faithfulness.

Although the Roman Jews were blessed with a Godly heritage, all Jews are like all people of the world. They are sinners by nature in need of salvation (v.10-18). Every person in the world is accountable to God. Every person in the world is trapped in their sin and separated from God. None is capable of earning their salvation. The law is not the means of salvation, but the means to become aware of our need for salvation (v.19-20). The law reveals the need for justification. It does not make anyone righteous.

Righteousness comes by grace through faith in Christ alone! The righteousness of God has been revealed in Jesus Christ. This gift is for all who believe. There is no distinction. All have sinned and cannot attain the perfection that God demands, but Jesus has come to provide a righteous standing with God. This holy life is a gift that is received by faith. No one can earn this gift. It can only be received by faith (v.21-26). This humbles us and at the same times fills us with confidence. Both Gentiles and Jews can look to Christ and find forgiveness. None can find justification in the law. It is by faith we are saved. This does not mean the law is not valuable. The law reveals our need and Christ meets that need. It is grace upon grace!

All humans have the same problem – sin. All humans have the same need – salvation. All who are saved are saved the same way – by grace through faith in Christ alone. Have you been given a strong Biblical heritage? If so, be thankful. If not, be aware that God's grace is all you need. Are you saved by grace through faith in Christ? Recipients of grace by faith live with hope.

1 Samuel 4; Romans 4; Jeremiah 42; Psalm 18

The pain of trials and tribulations will often lead to an understanding of the greatest truth – God knows what is best. The very thing that brings God glory, our obedience, is the very thing that brings us blessing. When we look to God and trust His will and do what He commands, we live with hope.

The people left in Jerusalem, after the leaders and a majority of the people were exiled into Babylon, were in dire straits. Their common sense was telling them to flee to Egypt. Their supernatural sense told them to go to their prophet and receive a word from God. Jeremiah 42 is God's Word to all who live in a fallen world. It is a call to trust in God's provision and to live faithfully to God in all circumstances rather than trying to find a fix in a new circumstance. No matter where we are, if we are not in God's will, we have no way of having hope.

The people wanted God to affirm their decision to go to Egypt (Jeremiah 41:17). We cannot know if their faith was genuine or not when they asked Jeremiah to seek the Lord's will on their behalf (v.1-5). Their commitment was to obey, whether they perceived it to be good or bad (v.6). God's will is always good. The human perspective is limited, and we need not worry with labeling our conditions. It is enough to know we are in God's will and to know God's will is always right and best.

It appeared the people of Judah were expecting God to bless their decision to go to Egypt (v.7-22). Their primary mistake was in making a decision before seeking the Lord. Like the people of Israel, who made a treaty with the Gibeonites before seeking God in prayer (Judges 9), these Israelites looked to their common sense rather than divine guidance. Going to Egypt may have seemed practical, but without God's blessing, no circumstance is blessed. It is unwise and it is not Godly to make determinations and then check with God. When we check with God first and then simply do what He tells us to do, we enjoy God's blessing.

God made it perfectly clear what would happen if the Israelites stayed in Palestine and what would happen if they went to Egypt. If they stayed in Palestine, as God commanded, they would be cared for. The Lord would look after them and they would not have to fear their enemies. If the people went to Egypt and trusted in the protection of their neighbors in the south, then they would face calamity. We will always be tempted to trust in manmade provisions. People often seem so strong and capable. They aren't. God alone is able to provide. He never grows weary. He never sleeps. His steadfast love endures forever. When we trust in God for hope, we will always find it.

The Israelites were in a tough place, but God had not abandoned them. God's children will go through difficult days, but God is faithful. Do you trust God? Are you walking in His will? Are you praying through your decisions and waiting on God's answer? We cannot know God's will outside of prayer and Bible study. God speaks through His Word and answers His people's prayers. Those who obey God's Word and walk in His will live with hope.

1 Samuel 5–6; Romans 5; Jeremiah 43; Psalm 19

God has graciously revealed Himself in creation and through His Word. This general revelation and special revelation require a response. Either we look to the universe and celebrate the God who made it or we create a false narrative that removes glory from God. The Word has become flesh. Through Jesus, we can understand God. The Bible tells the story of how God is at work in the world. Jesus is the hero of God's story and of the world. Those who receive the message of creation and the Bible live with hope.

In Psalm19, the revelation of God is explained poetically. Those who read this Psalm with eyes opened by the Spirit of God will be in awe of God. His creation stirs the imagination and inspires the heart. His Word delights the mind and helps decision-making in the real world. His grace demands obedience and produces a desire to honor God in all things. The head, the heart, and the hands of a person are all called to action in this Psalm.

God created all that is out of nothing (Genesis 1:1). This creation is a masterpiece. It reveals the greatness of God (v.1-6). Creation is not God. The universe is God's handiwork and it reveals His majesty. It communicates the significance of God and His goodness. Those who can see creation for what it is – God's message to humanity that God is awesome – will bow down and worship Christ alone. Jesus is the one who made and sustains all that is by His Word and for His glory (Colossians 1:16).

The Word of God is holy, and it ministers to the souls of those who believe (v.7-11). The Bible reveals God's will and what He expects of His people. Without the Bible, we would know there is a God by His creation, but we could not know the expectations that He has of us. God warns us to avoid sin and calls us to live in righteousness. These instructions provide the way of life God intends for humanity.

Without a right understanding of creation and the Bible, a person is left to his or her own devices. With broken hearts and sin-stained souls, humans are incapable of seeing their own sins and the sources of their misery (v.12). Those who understand the heart of God can be confident of His will and by grace approach His throne and request His will to be done in their life. God's will is a righteous life free from sin (v.13). The only way to live a righteous life is to receive Jesus' life by faith. Those who repent and believe are born again (John 3:1-18).

Those who are born again gain a new heart and spirit in Christ (Ezekiel 36:26). This new life is free to know God and obey Him. When a person is born again, they are raised to walk in a new life. This life has a new way of thinking. Those who are redeemed are free to process life and speak truth in ways that please God and bless others (v.14). This is a life of worship (Romans 12:1-2).

God has revealed Himself to the world. Are you in awe of God? Do you delight to study God's Word? Have you received new life in Christ? Are your thoughts and words pleasing to God? Those who understand God through creation and His Bible have great hope.

1 Samuel 7–8; Romans 6; Jeremiah 44; Psalms 20–21

Without divine intervention, humanity will falter and fall deeper and deeper into sin. Life without God's leadership causes rationalizations for falling into sin to mount and disobedience of God to be acceptable. The only hope of humanity is the divine grace of Jesus that redeems and renews day by day. Those who look to the Lord each day discover His faithful grace at work through their repentance and faith and live with hope.

In 1 Samuel 7–8, the battle that every child of God must fight daily is revealed. Each day we must decide if we will serve and trust in the Lord or if we will serve and trust in human endeavors. What we choose will have significant consequences on our souls and the lives of others. God is willing to lead us, but we must be willing to follow Him.

The children of God had experienced a miracle, and their response to it in 1 Samuel 7 is sadly typical. Having received back the Ark of the Covenant and experienced the dangerous power of God, they called for the priestly authorities to confiscate it and place it in a safe place (v.1-2). This temptation to keep God at a safe distance, rather than at the center of our lives, is a bad decision. With God at the center of our lives, we will live by faith and honor Him. Without God at the center of our lives, we will fall into sin. The children of Israel wasted away spiritually for twenty years because they chose to keep God at a distance.

The Lord was gracious to them and caused the people to repent. Their right response in faith caused them to be attacked by the Philistines (v.3-7). Quite often, doing the right thing will cause a negative reaction by the world. This should not discourage believers. It should be an affirmation. Coming under attack led the Israelites to rely on God (v.8-11). Temptations, trials, and thorns are meant to drive us to dependence upon God. Dependence upon God leads to victory, ultimately. God's provision led Samuel to set up a reminder of God's goodness to them (v.12-14). Once a victory is won, it is crucial to set up new structures that enable the Lord to be the focus of our lives. Samuel's visits and leadership were a blessing to the people (v.15-17).

The temptation after a great spiritual victory is always to fall back into trusting in human capacities rather than trusting in God's provision. Human provision will always be limited. 1 Samuel 8 shows how Samuel was limited and how his sons were incapable of sustaining Godly leadership for the people (v.1-3). While we must respect leaders, we cannot follow them blindly. When leaders prove to be Godless, they must be removed from positions of authority. The elders gathered to deal with the leadership issue, but rather than ask God for direction, they had predetermined to go in the way of the world. They wanted an earthly human king to lead them rather than God (v.4-22). Thankfully, we have the ultimate King in Jesus to rule us and lead us now!

The world is a tough place. Without God's intervention, we have no hope. Are you depending upon God? Is Jesus the center of your life? Are you obeying your King? Those who gladly live under the authority of Jesus will prosper spiritually and overcome with hope.

1 Samuel 9; <u>Romans 7</u>; Jeremiah 46; Psalm 22

Every person is responsible for their decisions in life. We choose what we want. What we want is not always best. Without Christ and the Gospel, we are slaves to sin. Thankfully, Christ has come. We are free to obey Him, as a result of our love for Him. Our love is not pure. It is tainted. We still live in the flesh and struggle with sin. Those who love Jesus fight sin and find hope in the process.

The Apostle Paul was a very thoughtful man. In Romans 7, he outlined his personal sanctification process. By sharing his personal experience and how the truth was at work in him, Paul provided believers for all time an insight into the struggle of living a redeemed life. Inspired by the Spirit, Paul wrote of the reality of the law, sin, and grace.

The law of God was given so the will of God could be known. Adam and Eve plunged the human race and the world into sin by disobeying God's law. Their progeny now suffer with a sin nature. Humans by nature desire to do what is in opposition to God's law. Thankfully, Christ came to give new life to those who believe. Those who die to their old life in the flesh are free to enter into the New Covenant of Christ (v.1-6). In Christ a disciple of Jesus is able to live by the Spirit and obey the law. Obedience is a result of God's grace, the Holy Spirit's empowerment, and the choice of the redeemed to love Jesus.

The law is still at work. The work of the law is good, but in people with a tendency for sin, it produces a bad result. The law reveals the demands and desire of God. The law is intended to reveal what is best and right. By nature, humanity wants power and control. Although the law is good, people break the law out of a desire to be in control. The law, meant for good, provides an opportunity to rebel. Sin at work in the flesh will inspire people to rebel out of their flesh's natural inclination (v.7-23). Sinning is not what saved saints want to do, but saints do sin. They sin out of a fleshly decision to reject God's authority.

While we are trapped in a fallen world with a tendency toward sin, we still have hope. Jesus has come to save us not only from the punishment of sin, but from the power of sin (v.24-25). God's grace provides the better way of life. This life is free from the power of the law. In Christ a person is free to love Jesus and obey Him out of deep, growing affections. The flesh is still tainted with sin. The soul is rescued, but the body still works in rebellion. Because of this, believers will want to honor God but still choose to sin until the Lord comes back. When Jesus returns, there will be no more sin and no more rebellion.

Every decision we make is our decision. The Gospel of Jesus frees His disciples to make decisions that honor God. Without Jesus people are trapped in sin and cannot honor God. In Christ we can obey God. Have you been freed from the punishment and power of sin by faith in Jesus? Do you desire to honor Jesus? Those who fight sin through the power of Christ live with hope.

1 Samuel 10; Romans 8; <u>Jeremiah 47</u>; Psalms 23–24

People and nations stand against God's commands and cause great harm and destruction, and it can sometimes appear heaven is disinterested. Perception is not always reality. The God of heaven is a just God and His judgments are perfect. They come in God's timing and accomplish His purpose. Those who trust in the Lord will rest in God's just decisions and timing with hope.

Jeremiah 47 seems out of place. God is carrying out judgment on the Philistines, Israel's ancient foes. I can almost hear the people of Israel at that time asking, "Who cares?" The Philistines had already been conquered by Egypt. The complete destruction of the Philistines by the Babylonians would have been insignificant to the people of Israel, who were facing bigger problems at that time. It is important to understand that God's justice has to do with His character. God acts when it is most appropriate and not before.

The justice of God is a horrifying judgment. The description of God's wrath is overwhelming. Time and distance can sometimes buffer the blow of the significance of the suffering that comes to the enemies of God, but not if we will not take it seriously. This text elicits disturbing thoughts of terrifying sights and sounds (v.1-2), of parents unable to help their children (v.3), and of agony without end (v.5-7). All who stand against God will suffer anguish unlike anything the world has known. The damned will be overwhelmed with hopelessness and pain. No parent will be able to help their child or friend. Each one will give an account and be dealt with by God on their own (Hebrews 9:27). The souls of the condemned will suffer day after day, year after year, and millennia after millennia. There is no end to God, and so there will be no end to the suffering of those who stand in opposition to Him.

God's plan is bigger and more awesome than one generation can ascertain. God made it clear He would deal with the Philistines' treachery (Isaiah 14:29-32; Ezekiel 25:15-17; Amos 1:6-8; Zephaniah 2:4-7). Those who had been most impacted by the Philistines' actions would probably have liked to have seen God's just response in their own lifetime, but that was not God's will. While people are certainly impacted by others' sin, all sin is first and foremost against God. The Lord does not forget. The Lord delays judgment according to His purpose. The Lord always does what is right and best. The Lord determined to bring justice to the Philistines in the day of His choosing. In His time, God will bring justice to the world. God's dealings with the Philistines foreshadows final judgment (Revelation 20:11–15). Taken seriously, there is nothing more terrifying than the great white throne judgment of God.

In our lifetimes, we may see injustices go unpunished. In the end, justice will be served. Those who trust in Jesus will be rescued from God's judgment. Because Christ took the punishment for sin, those who trust in Him will not be condemned. Have you trusted Jesus with your life? Do you trust in God's ultimate plan for the world? Are you at work to let others know about God's grace? Those who live by faith in Jesus can have hope in life and death, knowing God's justice is coming and they are forgiven.

1 Samuel 11; Romans 9; Jeremiah 48; Psalm 25

Doubts are an important part of faith. If we have no doubts, then we are probably not being challenged in our beliefs. The Lord is great and mighty, but He is also mysterious. God has often brought glory to His name by allowing His children to have no other hope or comfort other than His promises. Moses, the prophets, John the Baptist, and the Apostle Paul faced challenging times when all seemed lost, except God's Word. Those who count on God and believe in His Word live with hope.

David went through many difficult days. In Psalm 25, he showed his doubt. He was being attacked by those who did not place their trust in God. It seemed God was failing him and so David cried out for the Lord's help. David found hope in God's mercy and steadfast love, God's instruction, and God's protection, according to the promises of His Word.

It was not that David was second-guessing himself as much as it was he was worried that God was not going to provide. David had determined he would trust God (v.1). It looked as though his enemies, who had not placed their trust in God, had the upper hand (v.2-3). David found hope in the truth of God's Word. He knew God had a path and a plan. David knew he just needed to wait in faith and God would provide (v.4-5). It is through obedience to God's Word that faith becomes strong. If we will be faithful each day, we will compile confidence in God and find strength in our times of need.

None deserve God's provision. Like David, we can count on God because of God's mercy and steadfast love (v.6). Having repented of sin, David knew he was under God's covenant of grace and his sin would not be held against him (v.7). In difficult days it is good to know we are right with God. If not, we will and maybe should assume our suffering is a consequence of our sin. Holy living gives hope.

David needed more than a right standing. He needed to know what to do. Knowing the heart of God through the Word of God, David knew that God instructs sinners in the way to go (v.8). Those who are humble and dependent upon Him are not just told what to do, but they are led by God (v.9). The Lord's path leads to blessings (v.10). The path of God is not easy in this fallen world, but it is always best.

God promises His protection to those who walk in His way, truth, and life. Although disciples of Jesus are redeemed, we all still struggle with sin. God is faithful and just to pardon us and provide protection for us (v.11-22). The Lord protects our hearts from being overwhelmed with sorrow. He protects our minds from being overwhelmed with lies. He protects our lives from being overwhelmed with loneliness. God is with us to redeem us and bring glory to His name, through our victory over sin, doubt, and sadness.

Life is filled with difficult days. God has a plan for these moments. His grace is sufficient for every trial we will face. Do you believe in Jesus? Do you trust that His love for you is real? Have you developed a confident faith? Those who learn to count on God and believe His promises live with hope.

1 Samuel 12; Romans 10; Jeremiah 49; Psalms 26–27

Those who have lived faithfully to God have the confidence to call others to repentance. It is a joy to help others know the Lord and trust in Him. Those who claim to walk with Christ but show no fruit of faith can have little influence on others' coming to Christ. It is the faithful who have influence and hope.

Samuel was a faithful prophet. The Lord blessed him with integrity, and God was able to continue to use him into his later years in life. There have been saints over the centuries who were able to have a good run at serving God, but many others burned out, faded out, or sold out. Samuel was faithful into his old age and was able to help God's people see God, trust God, and honor God.

By living a bold faith, Samuel was able to make a bold stand for God in 1 Samuel 12. His life was not perfect, but he harmed no one. His testimony was one of fairness. He had treated all justly, even though the people had not honored him (v.1-11). The Lord had called him to lead them under God, but the people wanted a king (v.12-13). We cannot determine how people will respond to God. Our job is simply to do what we are called to do as well as we can do it.

Even when we go down a road that does not please the Lord, God can work it out for good. Samuel showed the people their wickedness in rejecting God as their king, but gave them hope (v.14-18). Hope comes through faithfulness. Samuel called the people to find hope by trusting in the Lord. They had a king, but no person or human institution can provide what humanity needs. The people of the world need the Lord. Without the Lord there is no hope.

The people wisely confessed their sin and asked Samuel to pray for them (v.19). Samuel consented and revealed the two secrets to his spiritual success. One, Samuel was confident in the Lord, who is merciful and gracious for His own name's sake (v.20-22). God is whole. He needs nothing. He is full and dense with goodness. Those who look to worldly things will discover those things are empty. Worldly people are empty people and become like chaff that the wind blows away (Psalm 1:4). Two, Samuel's calling was to the Lord, who is faithful. God chooses to be good to people, even though they do not deserve it (v.23). Samuel understood God's grace and lived to serve His good God. Those who know the greatness and goodness of God and live to serve Him alone will find strength in difficult days and hope to continue, when others quit.

Samuel's concluding remarks are worth returning to over and over again (v.24-25). This is the call of God to every disciple of Jesus. Remember what Jesus has done for you and delight in that grace. Fear the judgment of Jesus and flee foolishness. The cross is either a symbol of joy or terror. It is either the joy of our salvation or the terror of judgment that is coming. Have you trusted in Jesus by repenting of your sin? Have you given Him complete leadership of your life? Are you serving Him faithfully? Those who walk in the way of Jesus have integrity and a blessed ministry that gives hope.

1 Samuel 13; Romans 11; Jeremiah 50; Psalms 28–29

It is easy to get caught up in issues and miss "the issue" of the Gospel. There are many good things that Christians must do: vote, serve, pray, and care for the culture (Jeremiah 29:7). We are to do what good we can, but we must not lose sight of what is best. The best thing any Christian can do is to live in and share the Gospel. Gospel-oriented people have hope.

The Jewish people were chosen by God to bring hope to the world. God chose Abraham (Genesis 12:1-3) and through Him came David and through David came Jesus Christ, the Savior of the world. The Jews had every opportunity to be the beneficiaries of God's great grace. In Romans 11, Paul explained that God's will for His chosen people had not changed, but that many were not the beneficiaries of grace.

The Israelites became blind to the will of God (v.1-10). The Israelites were blinded by their own agendas. Throughout the centuries, as revealed in the Old Testament, the people would be saved by God and then they would fall away. It was a messy cycle of deliverance to disobedience to disillusionment to destruction and back to deliverance. Fortunately, there was always a remnant. God always had a faithful few. Unfortunately, those who chose dead religion over the living God in order to gain power and prestige became the leaders of Israel. When the light of the world came, they could not stand the light. It was like going from a dark room into bright desert sunlight. It was too much. They preferred the darkness and stumbled in it.

The Israelites were broken off so the Gentiles could be grafted in (v.11-24). God used the faithlessness of the Jews to open the door to the Gentiles. Having been rooted with God's Story of the Gospel that begins in creation and leads to Christ, the Jews had the basis for faith. The Jews who rejected Jesus were cut off from God's Story. Those branches, still connected to the tree that is rooted in God's Story, were used to graft in the Gentiles. The hope was the Jews would be jealous and desire to reconnect with God and rejoin in God's redemptive work.

While every person is responsible for their individual decision, God's sovereign plan is at work (v.25-36). The sovereignty of God and the responsibility of humanity are compatible and at work to accomplish God's eternal purpose. All things are His. God made all things, works all things, and causes all things to fulfill His purpose. How God works and accomplishes His will is mysterious and glorious. Those who are blessed to believe are blessed beyond what they can understand or imagine.

It is easy to lose sight of what is best and most important in life. We all have personal agendas and an affinity to take sides on good, important things that are not meant to be the ultimate thing. God calls His believing saints to see their lives and activities in light of the Gospel and remain faithful to His eternal purpose to save. Is God your priority? Do you allow politics, business, or personal plans to keep you from serving Jesus? Gospel-oriented people keep God first in their lives. The Gospel gives them hope.

1 Samuel 14; Romans 12; Jeremiah 51; Psalm 30

There are two kingdoms in this world: the kingdom of darkness and the kingdom of light. After the fall, these two kingdoms are seen in the children of Eve. These two kingdoms are seen throughout all of Scripture. There is the Kingdom of God with all of the redeemed and the kingdom of the devil with fallen humanity. Those who are citizens of God's Kingdom live and die with hope.

In Jeremiah 51, the Kingdom of God is revealed in glory by bringing judgment to the kingdom of the devil and fallen humanity, Babylon. The might and mystery of God is seen in the promised destruction of this broken behemoth. The Babylonians sacked the city of Jerusalem and brought low the nation of Israel. God's work in, through, and over this evil kingdom reveals His power, justice, and glory.

While Babylon and its rulers acted in complete freedom of will, God was in control. It was not as if God was biting His divine fingernails as Israel was toppled. The Lord chose Babylon to be Israel's captor and punisher. The Lord works through the choices of evil to accomplish His eternal good. Just as God used the cross to bring about salvation, so He used Babylon to sanctify His people. Babylon, like all who live contrary to God's commands, felt strong but was never safe. None who stand against God are ever safe. The power of God is too great a force to overcome.

God chose Babylon to be an instrument in His hand, but its ruler and people were responsible for their decisions. This is a mystery. How does God hold those responsible that He chose to act with evil intent? Like Judas, all of those of the kingdom of the devil and fallen humanity act according to their will, but God is just. In His time, God's justice will overtake all that delight in darkness and do what is contrary to God's law. Justice is the way of God. God will judge the world. All who are found faithful to Him will be saved. All those who stand on the side of the enemy will be condemned (John 3:17-18).

God's power and justice revealed in His judgment bring God glory. It was for His glory that God chose and disciplined Israel. Babylon, like all who oppose God, thought it was their glory and their might that was to be praised. No! All that has been, that is, and will be is for the glory of God! God's glory is in the justification of His saints and in the condemnation of His enemies. It is best to stand with God. Those who trust in the Lord will flee the kingdom of the devil and fallen humanity and seek the Lord while He may be found.

The grace of God is truly amazing. None deserves the kindness of God. By His might and holiness and for His glory, God redeems His saints. The Lord uses the kingdom of the devil and fallen humanity to accomplish His redemptive work, but all who sin will receive the recompense of their sin. The work of Jesus is the hope of the redeemed. By His life, death, and resurrection, God's people are saved. Are you saved by grace through faith in Jesus? Do you serve God's Kingdom? Those who are citizens of God's Kingdom live and die with hope.

1 Samuel 15; Romans 13; Jeremiah 52; Psalm 31

The Christian life is filled with hope but is bombarded with emotions, ideas, and circumstances that can feel overwhelming. The hope of the Christian life is the center from which all of God's people live. This holy center holds the key to life, love, and the power to live for the glory of God. It is this holy center that distinguishes God's people from all others. Those who live a submitted life filled with God's holy presence live with hope.

The last words of Jesus were a quotation of Psalm 31:5. There was never a darker hour than that sixth hour on the day of the Lord's death. Even in that dark day, there was hope. It was for the joy that was set before Him that Christ endured the cross (Hebrews 12:2). We can now look to Him, the author and perfecter of our faith, to guide us through the malaise of feelings, thoughts, and situations that conspire to destroy our hope. Psalm 31 provides prayers, conclusions, and confessions all Christians need in order to sustain hope.

Hope comes through faith in God's redemptive power (v.1-5). God has the power needed for every challenge His children will ever face. When God is our refuge and fortress, nothing can overcome us. When we hide ourselves in the Lord Almighty, we are sheltered in the salvation of God. This position is acquired through faith. It is through submitting to God through faith in Christ that the Spirit of God takes up residence in us. That holy centering covers us and serves as a guide for our decision making.

Hope comes through trusting in God's redemptive plan (v.6-13). Everyone lives by faith. Not everyone has the same object of faith. The psalmist speaks of a hate for idolaters. This is strong language, but appropriate for those who love God. Those who worship anything except God are robbing God of glory that is rightly His. Like their Father, children of God "hate" anything that stands in opposition to God (Psalms 5:5; 11:5), and at the same time are gracious, loving, and merciful (145:9). Those who love idols will hate and persecute those with a holy center. This should be no surprise, and it is a blessing (Matthew 5:10-12). This is God's plan.

Hope comes through confidence in God's redemptive purpose (v.14-24). What a joy to trust in the Lord! Circumstances are not meant to be the final word on God's affections for the redeemed. Those who trust in the Lord can confess their feelings and misgivings and find healing in the steadfast love of God. In looking to God, the redeemed of God bring glory to God. Finding hope in God's redemptive purpose provides the motivation to love God in all circumstances. With hope, the redeemed of God can be strong and courageous. Strength and courage come to those who wait on the Lord and depend on Him.

Life will rarely be easy in this fallen world. Those who live by faith in Jesus Christ will suffer, as He did. God the Father expects His people to submit to Him and glorify Him through obedient faith. This only happens in those who live out of a holy center provided by God's indwelling Spirit. Do you have faith in Jesus? Do you trust in God's plan? Are you confident in God's purpose? A life submitted to God in Christ is filled with hope.

1 Samuel 16; Romans 14; Lamentations 1; Psalm 32

The Lord is at work in His creation. Although He could have easily abandoned us to rot on this rock, God chose instead to seek and to save that which was lost. Humanity is now being sought and saved by God. It is the joy of the redeemed to be able to join the Lord in this work. This work is not easy. The world, the flesh, and the devil conspire against us, but God is greater. Those who work with God live with hope.

The blessing of spiritual growth is a result of serving God. Although there are many obstacles to accomplishing God's work, they are all trivial to God. The Lord allows these obstacles to increase our faith. The more our faith grows the more glory God receives. The more we bring glory to God, the more delight we experience. Delight in God inspires hope to pursue the Lord in greater service. In 1 Samuel 16, the challenges and blessings of serving God are seen.

Service to God is a result of God's calling. Samuel did not come up with the idea to get a replacement for Saul. God called him to it (v.1). The calling of each saint is a supernatural experience. This miracle takes place through the teaching of God's Word and in the affirmation of God's people. In order to know God's will, we must know God's Word. To know God's Word, we must humble ourselves and listen. Many well-intentioned children of God have wasted resources pursuing their plans. God has the plan. We need only pursue Him, and in His time, God will make the call.

Just because God calls us to do it does not mean it is safe. Samuel knew if Saul heard about his mission, Saul would seek to kill him (v.2). God told Samuel to tell Saul he was serving God's purpose. God works through us where we are. Samuel was a priest. His faithful daily service made him ready for a unique service.

Success in service is defined by God. Samuel had a vision in mind of what the next king would be like, but God had other plans. While Samuel was looking for the biggest and oldest, God was looking for the smallest and youngest (v.3-13). The Lord's work is first and foremost a work of the heart. God is love and He is working to transform hearts to love Him and serve Him. David had God's heart (1 Samuel 13:14).

God's timing is an important aspect of God's calling. While David was already king according to God, he was not ready to function as king. He needed to be trained, so God placed David in Saul's service with the most unusual task – making music. We never know how God will use our gifts for His glory. David and his family and friends probably assumed David's love for music and his ability was just a hobby. God knew it was the door through which David would walk to begin His training to be king (v.14-23).

God is at work in the world. Each saint has a unique calling to serve God. The Lord's ultimate plan is fulfilled through the cumulative work of His saints. Are you serving God? Can you define your calling? What gifts has God given to you? How has God worked through you in the past? Those who serve God live with hope.

1 Samuel 17; Romans 15; Lamentations 2; Psalm 33

There is nothing like the local church. It is among redeemed people living in covenant with Christ and one another that God's mission is accomplished. It is vital that every believer find and fulfill their responsibility to God in a local church family. Those who live for the glory of God in the name of Jesus by the power of the Holy Spirit in a local church family live with hope.

Paul wrote to the church at Rome during a difficult time in that church's life. There were two groups of people in that church that were raised and trained to distrust and dislike each other. The Jews were taught to think of Gentiles as dogs. The Gentiles were taught to think of Jews as a pestilence. God rescued them both to be adopted members of His family. In Romans 15, Paul, inspired by the Spirit of God, revealed how to make a local church a God-honoring home, a Spirit-powered training ground, and a Christ-driven mission.

The people of a local church are called by God to live in harmony with one another by bearing with, pleasing, and welcoming one another (v.1-7). Those who know the grace of Jesus do not find this too difficult a task. The Gospel of Jesus reminds all believers that God has borne our sin, pleased us with loving kindness, and welcomed us into His eternal family. We are to do for others what Christ has done for us. The love of God is to shine brightest in the local church. Through the lives of the saints, a city should be blessed by the presence of every local church.

God's plan was to work through the Jews in order to reach the Gentiles and build a Kingdom of saints for His glory. God gave His promise to and through the Jews so the Gentiles could be instructed in the hope of the Gospel (v.8-13). Those who believe in these promises, primarily the promise of eternal life given to all who believe in Jesus, will live with lasting joy and peace. They will know a hope that does not end. The local church is to be a hope factory. Hope is the fruit of faith built on the truth that inspires love.

Within the local church, God's people are able to be affirmed and confirmed in the faith. Paul was confident of the work God was doing in that church at Rome. He was confident they were not only able to instruct one another in truth, but to be an example to all the saints of what a local church family is to be (v.14-15). Paul was proud of the work God had done through Him and was confident this church would join Him in it (v.16-33). Every local church is not only to reach their community and city with the Gospel, but to help reach the world with a global vision. It is through the local church that missionaries are to be sent and resourced.

Every church has its problems. It is filled with people who are saved but still struggling with sin. It is in the local church that God's mission is unfurled. God has chosen to work through His church to accomplish His mission. Are you an active member of a local church? Are you a blessing to your church and community? Saints that fulfill their responsibility to Jesus in a local church live with hope.

1 Samuel 18; Romans 16; <u>Lamentations 3</u>; Psalm 34

This world is a hard, hurting place. On this side of heaven, the redeemed will suffer. The curse of sin is formidable and foreboding. Through all of our difficulties, God is with His people. He is the Good Shepherd (Psalm 23). He blesses His people (Psalm 1). Those who live in this dark, difficult world in light of the goodness of God live with hope.

It is believed that the "weeping prophet," Jeremiah, wrote Lamentations. In chapter 3 there is a remarkable confession revealing the personal experience that all of God's children go through to some degree. There will be days of pain and God's provision in it (v.1-24). There will be days when God's sovereign goodness is seen (v.25-39). There will be days of praying for provision (v.40-48). There will be days of trusting in God's plan to provide (v.48-66). Life is filled with losses, but God's steadfast love is never lost. God's love is our hope.

In the midst of extreme suffering, there is still hope! Even if the demons of hell with their deceptions and fiery darts were to leave us, life would still be hard. Were the pain caused by people removed, life would still be hard. Were the internal struggles of sin gone, life would still be hard. Even though the power of hell, the actions of others, and our own actions harm us, God is still God and He is good. His mercy and love sustain the righteous.

In the midst of the curse of sin, there is still hope! God is not surprised by our trespasses. Before the world was made, His plan to redeem was settled. Sin is serious. The consequences for disobedience are real, but so is the grace and mercy of God. The Lord is at work in all things to bring glory to His name and to redeem and restore His people.

In spiritually empty and emotionally trying times, there is still hope! The Lord desires to bring success and to see His people experience peace. The Lord wants more for His children than comfort. Character formation through spiritual renewal is God's primary purpose. To seek spiritual renewal is to seek an internal transformation that is exhibited in external obedience. When we are in sin, we can always repent and find God ready to restore. When we are down, God is there to lift us up.

In dark days of desperation and deep hurt, there is still hope! The Lord hears His children's prayers. The Lord sees His children's hardships. The Lord is aware of what is needed. It is in the act of praying that God's children give voice to what has been and is, and they can ask for what can be. In His timing, God will restore all things. Evil will be vanquished, harmony will be restored, and life will be good. Until the Lord's return, the faithful can live with hope, knowing God's not finished yet! God will soon make all things new!

We should never be surprised by adversity. Life is hard. It hurts. God knows. He has walked in this world and suffered. He is victorious over our great enemies: sin and death. He is our hope! Do you live with hope in troubled times? Are you seeking God's face? Do you trust God's ultimate plan to accomplish good? Those who live in this dark, difficult world confident of the goodness of God live with hope.

1 Samuel 19; 1 Corinthians 1; Lamentations 4; Psalm 35

Jesus had to deal with injustice and so will every person on this planet. Thankfully, just as God was with Jesus during His earthly ministry, He is now with His saints. God has given His Spirit (John 14), and by His power His saints can overcome (Romans 8). It will not be by their might, but by the Lord's. Those who live in the power of God live with hope.

King David foreshadowed the life of Christ. His experiences were under the sovereign care of God. As He was challenged and vexed, the Spirit of God gave Him God's Word. The Psalms written by David are the Word of God and provide God's people with insight into the heart of Jesus. In Psalm 35, we are reminded of the challenges we face in a fallen world, but also where our hope comes from.

God's people, like Jesus and David, are free to call upon the Lord for help (v.1-2). It is a great comfort to know that nothing we face is greater than God. We can know God is at work accomplishing His great purpose for our life and His Kingdom with every challenge we face. The Lord loves to see His children match fear with faith and look to their God for help. Those who look to God gain great assurance in their salvation (v.3). Of all the gifts of God, prayer provides the greatest intimate experience of delight.

It is a comfort and a disgrace that Jesus knows what it is to have enemies coming for Him (v.4-10). He knows what it is to have people say false things about Him (v.11-12). He knows what it is to have friends betray Him (v. 13-16). He knows what it is to have those who would prefer to see Him hanging on a cross gasping for air and dying in disgrace and in seething pain (v.17-26). The Lord knows the plight of the martyr. God knows the plight of the brokenhearted. God knows the plight of the victim. God knows and cares and comforts those who come to Him in faith and seek His healing and life-changing Gospel.

The Gospel of God required Jesus to live a holy life among those who hated Him. The Gospel of God demanded Jesus be betrayed by His friends. The Gospel of God demanded Jesus suffer and die the atoning death that satisfied the just demands of God's law (Romans 6:23). Now those who die to self, repent of sin, and believe in Jesus in the hope of the Gospel will be saved (v.27). They will delight in God and trust that He will provide for their welfare. Those who are saved by grace through faith in Christ alone can face any circumstance and with hope sing praise to their God and King, who understands their plight and cares for them.

The life of a saint is simple, but it can be difficult. A saint only needs to look to Jesus to find hope and help in times of need. Jesus cares for His people. He died to redeem them. He will not forget them. The Father will work to accomplish His purpose and the Spirit will empower the faith needed to endure. Do you trust in Jesus? Are you simply living by faith? Are you comforted by His empathy and concern for you? The Lord is near. Those who rely on Him live with great hope.

1 Samuel 20; 1 Corinthians 2; Lamentations 5; Psalm 36

Living for God is not easy. There are enemies all around and within. If it is not our own selfishness that is killing our hope and life in Christ, then it is someone in the church. If it is not siblings in Christ, then it's the world that is seeking our downfall. God is not caught off guard by the battles we face, and His children should not be surprised either. Those who can identify the enemy and remain faithful to Jesus live with hope.

Our example of faithfulness is Christ. He was able to remain steadfast in His mission, despite the strategy of the enemy. In 1 Samuel 20, the plight of David foreshadows the plight of Christ. From this sad season in David's life, the saints of Christ can learn to discern the will of God and follow closely after Jesus.

David knew his life was in danger. He was a threat to King Saul's dynasty. David knew it. Saul knew it. The only person who seemed to have not known it was Jonathan, David's best friend and Saul's son (v.1-11). Jesus knew it was the plan of the religious leaders of His day to put Him to death. They knew it. He knew it. The disciples did not seem to get it. Jesus was a threat to their power. The Gospel is a threat to all religious systems because it liberates people to love. There is nothing that matches Gospel power. Rather than yield to the loving and gracious will of God, Saul, in his day, and the religious leaders of Jesus' day fought against the Lord. In so doing, they turned against God's anointed ones and inadvertently accomplished God's will.

Jonathan loved David and made a covenant with him (v.12-17). Jonathan was glad for David to be king. His allegiance was supernaturally inspired. The natural man would not delight to give up his birthright of power, popularity, and possessions. Jonathan was glad to do it. All disciples of Jesus must also have that same heart. Through the New Covenant in Christ's blood, Jesus calls His disciples to give up their old lives in order to make Jesus their Lord and King. Apart from Christ there is no hope.

The revelation of Saul's contempt and desire to kill David was shocking to Jonathan (v.18-34). We are often blinded by love and cannot see the faults of those we care for the most. Jonathan loved his dad, but was grieved over his sin. The disciples of Jesus loved the religion of their day and the faith that they had been given by their families. In the end, everyone must decide between the love of Jesus and anything else.

While Jonathan was upset, David was devastated by the reality of his situation (v.35-42). David knew he would now have to go away. He would return a conquering king, but his departure was devastating. So Christ, on the night of his betrayal, was devastated. He took comfort in the joy that was set before Him (Hebrews 12:2). Jesus knew that He would depart, but later return, as a conquering King to make all things new (Revelation 21).

The world is a tough place for the redeemed, but God has shown us the way. Have you chosen to follow Jesus? Are you willing to pay the price to be faithful to Him? Those who live faithful to Jesus live with hope.

1 Samuel 21–22; 1 Corinthians 3; Ezekiel 1; Psalm 37

Learning to live in the presence of God and trust in His guiding hand is vital to the Christian life. Like Israel, in the days of Samuel, we often desire a person to lead us rather than God. The Lord provides servants to help us in the journey, but the Lord alone is our Lord. Those who live under the leadership of God live with hope.

People are limited. God is unlimited. People have a purpose. Every single person conceived has a purpose given by God. God works His will mysteriously through people's lives to accomplish what is best. It is vital that the children of God learn to discern God's authority, their place in God's Kingdom, and their responsibility to build the life God has designed for them. In 1 Corinthians 3, Paul speaks to these great needs.

The children of God must learn to see leaders for what they are (v.1-9). The church at Corinth had several superstar leaders to serve them in their spiritual journey. Each one had a unique calling. The Lord never intends His people to place their allegiance in a specific servant. The people of God are to follow the servant leaders God provides but understand they are all under God's authority. There is only one Lord and all others are servants with a purpose.

The children of God must learn to see themselves and others within the design of God's will (v.10-11). Paul was a master builder. He had laid the foundation of salvation. God had sent other leaders to build on that foundation. All that God would provide for the church at Corinth, after Paul, would allow the people to build on the foundation already provided. The Gospel is the foundation for life in Christ. It is the Gospel that saves and sanctifies. The Gospel is the foundation of God's design for His people.

The children of God must learn to take responsibility for what they become in Christ (v.12-17). The Lord gives His Word, His Spirit, His servant leaders, and His church to make each person what He wills them to be. To build with flesh and worldly ways is to build with flammable materials that will not survive judgment. Every child of God is a temple. God dwells in them. What we become is determined by what we build our lives with and how we build our lives. We will all give an account for what we have made of our life. Judgment will reveal the real quality of our souls.

The children of God must learn to trust God alone (v.18-23). Living by faith rather than by sight in worldly wisdom is strange to the flesh, but not to the soul. The soul longs for and needs divine guidance. The saints of God appear foolish to the world. The wise child of God gladly becomes a fool in the eyes of the world in order to obtain the wisdom of God. This wisdom looks past the people who serve the King to see the King of glory in His grace accomplishing His will. The wise delight to live for Jesus and live in Jesus.

The Lord is at work in the world to grow His people into eternal edifices that bring Him glory. Do you trust in Jesus alone? Are you building a life that God will reward? Are you being spiritually wise? Those who live under the leadership of God live with hope.

1 Samuel 23; 1 Corinthians 4; Ezekiel 2; Psalm 38

Obeying God is never wrong. Disobeying God is never right. When we live in obedience to God, we do not have to worry about the outcome of our life or the consequences of our decisions. Surrendering to God's will, according to His Word, sets us free from having to worry about the future. Disobedience leaves us vulnerable. When we disobey God, we are responsible for our actions and the consequences of those actions. Those who live in obedience to God have hope in their freedom.

God will often allow His people to face difficult situations, where there is no seemingly good outcome. There are times when the only choices we have all appear to lead to bad repercussions. Ezekiel was placed in a tough predicament by God. God called him to preach to Israel, which was at that time living in rebellion to God. The message he would bring would probably not be well received, but God was not asking Ezekiel. God told Ezekiel to go and preach the message he was given.

The Lord spoke to Ezekiel. As a prophet under the Old Covenant, Ezekiel was provided a unique encounter with God (v.1-4). The Word of God was clear. Ezekiel was to go to Israel on God's behalf and say what the Lord had given him to say. This message was not in written form, but it was from God to Ezekiel and it was the Word of God. God spoke to Ezekiel. Some say they would like to hear God's Word delivered to them audibly. All they need to do is read the Bible out loud. It is God's Word. What is important is not how we hear God's Word, but how we respond to it.

Those who obey God's Word are not responsible for what comes about by their obedience. Once a person decides to obey God, they are free. The person who disobeys God is guilty of sin and the consequences of their sin. God told Ezekiel to simply obey (v.5-7). What the people chose to do in response to the message was not on him. Ezekiel was assured that if he obeyed, the people would know he was a prophet of God.

Like all of God's commands, it is easy to question them and then justify our own disobedience. God commanded Ezekiel to be obedient and to not be like Israel (v.8). The Lord then revealed what it was Ezekiel was going to have to say. It was not pretty (v.9-10). Serving God is not always comfortable. Thankfully, what we are to do is always clear. Under God, the ends do not justify the means. The means are all that matter, because God is sovereign over the ends. Seeking to determine what will or won't happen, depending on what we do, is a waste of time. All any disciple of Jesus needs to do is obey God's Word. God will take care of the rest.

Choices have consequences. What we choose will impact not only our lives, but the lives of others. When we obey God, we need not worry with what happens after. We can trust that by obeying God's Word, we will accomplish God's will. Are you living in obedience to God's Word? Do you find it easy to justify rebellion? Those who live in obedience to God have hope in their freedom.

1 Samuel 25; 1 Corinthians 6; Ezekiel 4; Psalms 40–41

Throughout life, God will allow us to experience broken hearts and fresh starts. The Gospel of God provides fresh starts in the face of broken hearts. Those who find new life in life's endings will always have hope.

Life goes on. People die. Relationships end. New beginnings come. The Lord does not expect His people to understand the reasoning behind every event. God expects His people to trust His provision and plan. In 1 Samuel 25, there are endings that bring about new beginnings. God was at work in them all, although David and Israel could not have known all the Lord was doing. They, like us, had to live by faith.

God had provided what was needed for Israel's flourishing. Rather than trust in the Lord, the Israelites unwisely sought to govern themselves in the ways of the world. God had provided prophets and priests to guide His people, but they wanted a king. Samuel was an answer to the prayer of a desperate mother, and he became a blessing beyond what she could have imagined. At his death, the leadership of Israel fell completely to the king of Israel (v.1a). Samuel's death signaled a new beginning for a Christlike king.

While Samuel was dying and being buried, the true king of Israel, David, was on the run from the rejected king of Israel, Saul (v.1b). God had not abandoned David. Those desert days were training days. While it would have been easier to have received positional authority, God led David to gain personal authority. Those who lead out of a sense of personal calling and with a personal connection to those they lead, lead with great authority and effectiveness. Desert times teach and provide leaders with the opportunity to gain personal authority. (Other examples are Moses, Jesus, and Paul.) While in the desert, David learned many lessons. In the situation with Nabal and Abigail, he learned the importance of gratitude, generosity, and wisdom (v.2-44).

Wisdom and wealth do not always reside in the same person. Nabal's ignorance almost cost him his life, but Abigail's wisdom saved it. The wise person honors culturally understood agreements. What we do when we don't have to do anything says a lot about the kind of person we truly are.

Blessings often come from discouraging circumstances. David could have never known what God had planned for him. David could have never seen the good that would come from Nabal's ignorance. In that moment, David could only see the need to cause destruction in light of Nabal's disrespect. God intervened. David had lost his wife, and through this situation, Abigail lost her husband. In death, there was new life, as there is in the Gospel. Jesus' death provides new life. Under God's grace, sad endings lead to new life and new beginnings.

God has a plan for this season in each of our lives. We can trust Him. He will work all things for good. Do you trust God? Are you willing to learn the lessons He has for you, during this time in your life? Loss and death are sure to come, but God is faithful. Those who find new life in life's endings will always have hope.

1 Samuel 26; 1 Corinthians 7; Ezekiel 5; Psalms 42–43

Every life has real opportunities and challenges. Learning how to take advantage of the opportunities and negotiate the challenges requires wisdom. God's Word is filled with wisdom for how to live. Those who live in Christ have access to wisdom that gives hope.

Under the inspiration of the Holy Spirit, the Apostle Paul wrote to the Corinthian church to answer specific questions they had. The first six chapters of 1 Corinthians give instructions on issues Paul was aware of. In chapter seven, the apostle begins to deal with questions the church had. These were questions concerning marriage, personal pursuits, and future plans.

Concerning marriage, Paul was clear that those who can live celibate single lives should do so (v.1-7). This is not a command, but a strong suggestion. Corinth was a sex-crazed culture. This command to remain celibate was extremely countercultural. Looking to the teaching of Scripture, Paul makes clear that marriage is good and that sex within the confines of that covenant is a blessing. Those who desire to have a spouse should marry, rather than burn with desire and make themselves miserable (v.8-9). Married couples are to remain married. God's plan is for one man to be with one woman for life. Those who were married to unbelievers before they became believers were to remain married to their unbelieving spouse (v.10-16). This union would give their unbelieving spouse and their children an opportunity to be exposed to the power and blessing of the Gospel.

Concerning life situations, Paul was clear that those who have become disciples of Jesus are to focus on their faith development and not on a social change in their situation (v.17). The Lord is sovereign over every person's station in life and each person is to be faithful to pursue what God designed them for (v.18-20). This does not mean that believers avoid promotions. If possible, believers should always seek to be successful and gain greater freedom and responsibility in life (v.21). The goal is to be faithful to Christ, wherever the Lord has you or leads you (v.22-24).

Concerning future plans, those who are looking to get married are fine to do so, but should understand the consequences (v.25-35). Those who marry are responsible for the well-being of their spouse. This burden can cause anxious feelings. Paul's desire for each person was that they be free from as much worldly concern as possible, so they could focus on Kingdom living. Those who desire to be married should marry, but those who could remain single, Paul suggested they remain single (v.36-40). The reality of the difficulties of the Christian life will provide greater flexibility for a single person..

Knowing the right thing to do in a specific situation is wisdom. Every situation is nuanced with particular challenges, opportunities, temptations, and ministry moments. God's Spirit will guide God's people to understand and apply God's Word to their lives. Are you acting wisely? Is Christ first in your life? Are you pursuing God's plan for you? In Christ there is Spirit-inspired wisdom that gives hope.

1 Samuel 27; 1 Corinthians 8; Ezekiel 6; Psalm 44

Like Adam and Eve, every human being has a natural tendency to desire to be their own god and define what is good and evil in their own terms. What fallen people forget is that we were made to worship and live lives dependent on God. Only those who seek to be disciples of Jesus will honor God rightly and live with hope.

In Ezekiel 6, the prophet addressed the mountains, but what he was actually addressing were the "high places," where people went to worship. These places were pagan. Some went to worship the one true God on these mountainous sanctuaries, but at their own peril. God designed not only that people worship, but how they worship. Those who turn away from God to go their own way destroy not only their own souls, but incite the justice of God and suffer the consequences of His judgment.

It is not enough to do the right thing. God demands that we do the right thing the right way. Many of the Israelites were religious. They were faithful to attend places of worship. The problem was they attended the wrong places, relied on the wrong resources, and pursued their spirituality with the wrong motivation. God was not pleased and promised to bring about justice (v.1-4). It is not enough to simply attend worship services and be religious people. God demands we worship properly. Proper worship is done to the glory of the Father, in the power of the Spirit, and in the name of the Son, Jesus Christ.

Many will fail to pursue God properly. Rather than look to Christ alone, masses will seek to make their own way to God and fail. Their lack of faith in the grace of God will lead them to suffer under God's wrath (v.5-7). Despite that many fall away, God always has a remnant. Although most Israel fell into sin, there were some who remained faithful (v.8-10). It is through the faithful that God fulfills His purpose. The blessing of God is given to those who follow Jesus and live to love Him in obedience and delight.

God is not a subjective reality. He is who He says He is. The God of the Bible is the one true God. He is terrifying! He is awesome! He is uncontrollable! Many reject God on the basis of His glory and authority. This is unwise. The penalty for turning against God is extreme (v.11-14). Even in his judgments, He is glorious. In all that He does, God works to reveal His glory. Over and over God says, "Then they will know that I am the Lord." He is the Lord. Look to Him now! The Psalmist's call is for all: "Kiss the Son, lest he be angry, and you perish in the way, for his wrath is quickly kindled. Blessed are all who take refuge in him" (Psalm 2:12).

God made humanity to worship Him alone. He sent His Son to rescue sinners. It is only through the Son of God by the power of the Holy Spirit that a person can gain a right standing with God. Have you trusted in Jesus? Are you delighting in God through your obedience to His Word? Can you discern the difference between being religious or spiritual and being righteous and saved by grace? Only those who seek to be disciples of Jesus will honor God rightly and live with hope.

1 Samuel 28; 1 Corinthians 9; Ezekiel 7; Psalm 44

One glorious day, Jesus will return from heaven and make all things new. The bride of Christ, the church, will be presented to Him. They will live happily ever after. It is the stuff of storybook myth for a reason. It is the deep desire of every human being. One day the redeemed of God will be with the Lord forever. This is the hope of God's people.

Psalm 45 is celebrating that coming royal wedding. It is a Messianic Psalm. It tells of the coming of Christ. This love song is a celebration of God's consummation of history, when He will make all things new and bring His beloved bride to be with Him forever.

The voice is that of a great orator speaking of the King of Glory (v.1). The appearing of Jesus to the world will be in splendor. All will bow in wonder and awe. The grace He will speak to His church will be out of the blessing the Father has bestowed upon Him (v.2). His Word will be at His side, and the majesty of His glory will overwhelm the senses (v.3). This is why God's people worship Christ alone. He alone has eternal beauty in His dignity. His grace is beyond explanation and is based upon the truth of His Word.

God reveals His righteousness through His deeds, bringing justice to His enemies (v.4-5). The beginning of new life for the Church is the end of life for the unredeemed. Their just punishment is eternal death. The righteous bride of Christ will abide with Jesus forever. The reign of Jesus on earth will delight every sensory capacity of His people (v.6-9). He alone can satisfy the infinite thirst of an eternal soul.

Those who come to Christ gladly leave all else to cling to Him. He is the great treasure and costly pearl that all else is abandoned for (Matthew 13:44-46). Salvation is both a death and a birth. Those who believe leave all else and begin a new life in Jesus (v.10-15). It is a life filled with awe and wonder. It is a holy life. It is a life that blesses others. It is a life that will never end. It will multiply in splendor, as each new moment and day reveals more of the goodness and glory of God.

While disciples of Jesus give up much, it is all replaced with heavenly gifts (v.16-17). Yes, God's people will give up old ways but will gain a new family in exchange. Within the love of Christ, disciples of Jesus will make more disciples of Jesus, and the great name of Jesus will fill the earth. On the last day, all the saints will be gathered in, and faith will become sight, hope will be realized, and joy will be unending.

God could have left us dirty and dead in our sin. Instead, He sent His Son to rescue us. Those who believe gain a new life. This new life will culminate into a great wedding with Christ. The return of Jesus will establish a new Kingdom on earth, and the saints of God will rejoice. Do you live with the coming of Jesus in mind? Do you gladly give up your old life of sin in order to serve Christ in the new life He gives? Those who look for and delight in the return of Christ live with hope.

1 Samuel 29–30; 1 Corinthians 10; Ezekiel 8; Psalms 46–47

The place from which we draw our strength determines not only the capacity of our strength, but also the very source of our identity. As creatures in a fallen world, we will always look for something to provide for us and define us. What we look to in faith defines the life we lead, the strength we have, and the hope that fuels us. Those who depend on the Lord live with hope.

King David was a strong man. He had defeated giants, pagan armies, and dealt with the crushing blow of being rejected and hated by a father figure, King Saul. His life was rarely easy. In 1 Samuel 29-30, David was faced with three different foes. His enemies had captured his family, his friends were turning on him, and he was frustrated with himself. The latter being the greatest of all his threats. And yet he endured and recovered.

There will be situations in life when there is not a good choice. In 1 Samuel 29, David was in a situation where he did not have a good choice. He was at the disposal of the Philistines, where he had gone to hide from Saul. The Philistines were about to attack Israel. Turning against the Philistines would put him in a position where both Saul and the Philistines would seek to kill him, but attacking Israel was not right. He was their rightful king. When there is no easy choice, the child of God must simply take one step at a time and trust God to provide. Thankfully, God stepped in and spared David from having to put himself in a no-win situation. God will provide for his people. He is faithful!

Having returned from the battle front, David and his men found their families and possessions had been stolen. In 1 Samuel 30, the wisdom and courage of David is revealed. David was already upset and heartbroken, along with his men. It did not help that David's men blamed David and were considering killing him (v.1-6a). In that moment, David looked to God for strength (v.6b). When we find our strength in the Lord, we not only gain the power we need, but also the living hope that comes from a renewed faith.

Having been strengthened, David sought to know the Lord's will (v.7-8). God said go, but not all of David's men had the strength to go. David trusted God and went forward with what he had (v.9-20). God provided direction, provision, and victory. This victory was a miracle of God that required great effort on the part of David and his men. God never calls His people to passivity, but to join Him in His work for His glory.

Even in victory, there was still conflict. Those who went forward did not think those who had stayed behind should enjoy the spoils of victory (v.21-25). David showed the grace God had given to him. He also was generous with those who had been kind to him (v.26-31). He did not make the mistake of Nabal (1 Samuel 25). Faith provides strength, hope, and wisdom.

Life is complicated. Trusting God is simple. God gives strength and blessings to those who believe in Him. Do you draw your strength from God? Can others see God's grace in you? Those who draw strength from the Lord live with hope.

1 Samuel 31; 1 Corinthians 11; Ezekiel 9; Psalm 49

The question "What am I getting out of this?" is not wrong, but the question "What am I contributing to this?" also needs to be asked by every believer concerning their engagement in their local church. Those who connect with other believers in Christ in their local church live with hope.

Paul loved the church at Corinth. The supernatural manifestation of God's blessing on this precious people was obvious. Paul loved them, and although some struggled with Paul's authority, the people seemed to have loved Paul too. The letter we know as 1 Corinthians had many corrective and encouraging words. Chapter 11 had both. Inspired by the Spirit, Paul shared his gratitude and spoke to changes that needed to be implemented in that local church. The principles for those changes are for every church in every age.

The goal of God's people is Christlikeness. Paul's words were not intended to be boastful, but practical (v.1). Like any good leader, Paul understood his actions were as influential as his words. Calling the people to imitate him, as he imitated Christ, was an act of shepherding and not a petition to seek sycophants. Christ is the Lord. Those who lead in His name are to live as Christ and encourage others to do the same.

To live in Christ is to live a teachable life. The people were faithful to Paul's instructions. He had taught them the apostolic "traditions" that were to be for every church in every generation (v.2). Paul praised them for being faithful to the orthodox faith. Every church in every generation will have to fight to maintain the faith passed down to the saints (Jude 3). Faithful churches are made up of faithful disciples of Jesus and His Word.

To live in Christ is to live as a servant. Corinth was a pagan city with the temple of Aphrodite looking over it. As God saved some of the temple prostitutes with shaved heads, it impacted the culture of the church. Having come to faith, these women would let their hair grow. In the process, they might have the appearance of a man. God's design calls for a distinction to be recognized between men and women, and so women were to cover their heads (v.3-16) so these former prostitutes would not stand out. This was an activity specific to Corinth, but the principal of serving what is best for the church is true for every church and disciple of Jesus.

To live in Christ is to live for the benefit of others. Some at Corinth were making the Lord's Supper about their individual interest and not making it what it should be, a time to unify and build the body. Paul spoke to their inappropriate behavior and demanded changes be made (v.17-34). The Lord's Supper is to be about the Lord and provide an opportunity for the church to celebrate Jesus together and renew their commitment to Him.

Every disciple of Jesus is to be a member of a local church. They are to live in Christ and look to the interests of others by putting the church body before their personal preferences. Are you a disciple of Jesus? As a disciple of Jesus, are you growing in Christlikeness? Are you a blessing to your church family? Living in Christ in a community of believers gives hope.

2 Samuel 1; 1 Corinthians 12; <u>Ezekiel 10</u>; Psalm 49

God is gracious and loving. He is also just. It is the justice of God that makes His grace and love amazing. If God were not just, His grace and love would be cheap. In His grace and love, the Lord is patient, but His patience is not eternal. There is a point, when sin reaches its fulfillment, that God demands justice. Those who delight in the justice of God find hope in Jesus.

Ezekiel 10 is a terrifying text. What is pictured is God's justice being poured out. While God's grace was given to the faithful (Ezekiel 9:4), His wrath was poured out on the rest. God has revealed Himself in creation so that none are with excuse for their sin (Romans 1:18-23). Rejection of God and acceptance of idolatry and sin always leads to punishment. The greatest punishment a human can experience is to be "given over" to their sin and left to live and die in opposition to God (Romans 1:24-32). Ezekiel saw what happens to those who are overcome with a debased mind and lifestyle.

Those who reject God will suffer in the cleansing power of God. The angel was ordered to take the coals and use them against Israel (v.1-3). These angelic coals were capable of purifying repentant sinners (Isaiah 6). Those who refuse to repent but instead choose to be idolaters, who live for their own glory in their sin, will suffer under the righteous judgment of God. The Lord's holy power is a double-edged sword. It can heal or inflict suffering. The redeemed are healed by God's holy power, but sinners are condemned by it.

Those who reject God will be unable to enjoy the presence of God. The Lord was present in the temple, and His glory was radiating through that place (v.4-5). Those made pure by the mercy of God delight in the glory of God. Those trapped in sin are horrified by His splendor. It is a terrible thing for sinners to be in God's presence. Though it is magnificent, it is undesirable to them because of their shame, guilt, and sin.

Those who reject God live in opposition to Him. The angelic servants of the Almighty work in perfect tandem with the providential machine of God's power (v.6-17). With the power of God the angels of God bring about the will of God. They exercise their dominion in exact accordance with God and bring His justice to bear on those who stand against Him.

Those who reject God will lose the capacity to know God. Once a sinner has been turned over to their sin, the glory of the Lord departs (v.18-22). Their capacity to know God is lost because the desire to know God is replaced with apathy toward God. Left to their own devices, sinful humans will act on their carnal passions to be a god and reject and despise the one true God. Once the Lord turns away from a sinner, that person has no hope. They are lost.

Every person gets what they want, but not all want what they get. Sinners are left to suffer in sin. Saints are granted grace and access to God's glory. Sinners are lost in darkness and despair. Saints are saved and filled with hope. Do you desire God? Have you been made righteous by the grace of God? Those who choose the God as their God live with eternal hope.

2 Samuel 2; 1 Corinthians 13; Ezekiel 11; Psalm 50

Finding a healthy rhythm in life is wise. Allowing the way we approach God to fall into a loveless routine is destructive. Disciples of Jesus have been given directives for how to live in a right relationship with God. We are to gather with the saints for worship, serve God's cause in disciple making, and find renewal through prayer and Bible meditation. The devil is always lurking and seeking to find a way to get us to stop being faithful in our walk with God. If he can't keep us from the faithful activities of devotion to Jesus, the devil will work to get us to go through the motions without true affections. Those who seek the Lord with genuine love live with hope.

The goal of authentic faith is genuine love. Without love, life becomes empty and void of motivation. The devil delights in loveless and lifeless religion because it dishonors God. In Psalm 50, God speaks to three kinds of people. There are those who had forgotten the greatness of God, those who had fallen into sin, and those who remained faithful. That remnant, and there is always a faithful few, are the ones who enjoy God's blessing.

God is completely self-sufficient and self-satisfied. He needs nothing (v.1-14). Unlike the creatures He has made, God does not need food, energy, or affections from outside of Himself. In His being, God is complete, all-powerful, and loved. As Father, Son, and Spirit, God is whole. He is truly awesome. To perceive God is to see perfection. To know God is to be in awe. Those who delight in the Lord love Him, and God cares for those who delight in Him for His glory (v.15).

Those who love God are compelled to love people. The Scripture is clear that those who do not love the people they can see cannot love the God they cannot see (1 John 2:20). Without a love for God, people will be incapable and undesirous of loving other people (v.16-22). A lack of love for God is the origin of sin. Evil contaminates and controls the heart of those who do not love God. They lie, deceive, and do harm to themselves and others. They are like their father, the devil (John 8:44). If God is not our loving Father, the devil is.

For His glory and according to His promise, God always has a people He provides for (v.23). The people of God are easy to spot. They are grateful. In the best of times, they praise God for His goodness. In the worst of times, they praise God for His compassion. In all times, the people of God praise the Lord with genuine affection. Their love comes from His love (1 John 2:19). God's love and grace orders the rhythms of His people's lives. In His salvation, there is peace, joy, contentment, and great affection for God.

Humanity is incapable of living without something or someone outside of themselves guiding the motivation behind their existence. What we love determines what we are. Those who love God are children of God by grace through faith in Christ alone. Those who love the world are children of the devil by nature through dependence on fallen flesh. How do you relate to God on a personal level? What drives your affections? Where do you find meaning? Only those who seek the Lord with genuine love live with hope.

2 Samuel 3; 1 Corinthians 14; Ezekiel 12; Psalm 51

When a person comes to saving faith in Jesus Christ, the spiritual battle is not over. It simply changes. The Holy Spirit provides new life, and the atoning power of Jesus cleanses the saint from unrighteousness. The resurrected power of Jesus gives strength to a believer to fight sin and to live for the glory of God. And yet sin still lingers. God's people will battle sin their entire life. As faith is strengthened and the roots of sin are pulled out, God's people become more like Jesus. Those who become more like Jesus live with hope.

Hope has the power to inspire. The Lord has promised to finish the work of making His people like Jesus (Philippians 1:6). This is the hope of God's people. God does the work of sanctifying His people, and His people join Him in that holy work. In 2 Samuel 3, the civil war between the house of David and the house of Saul provides an illustration for how God works to overcome sin in His people. God strengthens His saints to become what Jesus died for us to be – pleasing to God.

Once Saul and his son, Jonathan, were killed, Israel did not immediately come under the authority of David. Instead, there was a civil war between the two houses. David was already anointed the king of Israel (1 Samuel 16:13). He was king, but of a divided nation. Saul hunted David until his death. After his death, the family of Saul continued to fight against the family of David, but the family of David became stronger and stronger (v.1). This is the experience of all disciples of Jesus. Jesus is our King, but we are divided because of the sinful desires in our flesh. Over time sin loses its power over us as we submit to Jesus.

Sin has a terminal problem. It is parasitic. It cannot exist on its own or be defined other than by what it's not. By definition, it is *not* holy. It is missing the mark. In Christ, sin loses its power. It still fights and it fights dirty, but God has the power to overcome. God reveals the treachery of sin to His people. Just as Abner's treachery was revealed, so sin is revealed by God's Word (v.2-25). Disciples of Jesus have the supernatural blessing of God at work in them, enabling them to see sin for what it is and to reject it.

The Christian life is messy. Being holy is not easy. There are always complications. Joab wrongly killed Abner (v.26-27). This was not the desire of David (v.28-30). David could not control all the servants of his kingdom. Christians cannot control all of their desires and will often do what they do not want to do. Christians sin. David grieved over Abner's death, and it pleased the people because they saw it was not David's will for Joab to be murdered (v.31-39). Disciples of Jesus grieve over sin, and it pleases God to see that His people do not want to do the evil they do (Romans 7).

The Christian life is a battle. It is a civil war in the life of ever believer. Have you been born again and received God's grace? Are you fighting the good fight of faith to become more like Jesus every day? Those who are becoming more like Jesus every day live with hope.

253

2 Samuel 4–5; 1 Corinthians 15; Ezekiel 13; Psalms 52–54

Among Christians there are different ideas pertaining to doctrinal "issues" that are not primary. In true Biblical Christianity, there are no differences in belief when it comes to the fundamental doctrine of the Christian faith, the Gospel. The Gospel is the good news of salvation to all who believe. If and when the Gospel is lost, faith loses its power and purpose. Those who believe in, can hold to, and defend the Gospel live with hope.

The Apostle Paul believed and preached the Gospel. In 1 Corinthians 15, Paul outlined his belief and his ministry of the Gospel, describing the benefits that the Gospel provides to those who believe. This chapter explains the fundamental facts of the Gospel and how faith in it transforms lives.

The Gospel is the object of saving faith. It was the focus of Paul's ministry to the church at Corinth. Of all of the things Paul could have taught this church, he made the Gospel the "first importance" and reminded them of the priority of the Gospel (v.1-3). His great fear, as is the fear of all faithful preachers and shepherds, was that any would believe in vain. That is, they would believe only as the demons do (James 2:19), by recognizing the facts of the Gospel, but not being transformed by it.

The Gospel is built on facts. It is proven with Scripture and the verifiable accounts of many different people, who come from different ways of life (v.3-9). It is also proven by the undeniable changes that have taken place and that take place in people's lives who believe (v.10-11). Paul was changed by the Gospel and was called, like many others, to live in and preach the Gospel.

The Gospel is the power of God to liberate humanity. All people are born slaves to sin and are under the condemnation of God's wrath. The Gospel frees people from the power of sin (v.12-34). The Gospel not only frees humanity from the power of sin, but also from the punishment of sin. Death came through Adam, but life has come through Christ. Christ has been raised from the dead (v.35-49). All believers in the Gospel are free from eternal death by the resurrection power of Jesus.

The Gospel is the victory of God. Having freed His people from the control of sin and the fear of death, God empowers each disciple of Jesus to serve His will. Once the power of sin and the fear of the future are removed, people are free to focus on the work of God (v.50-58). Death is now the final victory for those who believe. Having been liberated, God's people are able to serve God's purpose with passion because they know their service is not in vain. The steadfast, immovable faith of the servants of God is not a result of the work of the flesh. It is the work of God's Spirit in God's people to accomplish God's eternal plan.

It is easy to get distracted with secondary "issues" of the faith. It is also easy to lose sight of the truth, the power, and the goal of the Gospel. Have you believed in the Gospel? Has it changed your life? Are you serving God in the grace the Gospel gives? Can you defend the Gospel with your words and deeds? Those who believe and are transformed by the Gospel live with hope.

2 Samuel 6; 1 Corinthians 16; Ezekiel 14; Psalm 55

Syncretism is the combination of two or more differing ideas into one. Christianity is often wrongly combined with non-Biblical cultural norms, false religions, or personal agendas that are not in line with God's purpose. What is dangerous about syncretism is it often feels right. Being in step with cultural preferences, identifying with people of other faiths, and allowing individuals' desires to be considered acceptable is often more comfortable than standing for truth. Syncretism always leads to confusion and negative consequences. It may make other people happy and give us comfort, but it displeases God. Those who avoid syncretism and are faithful and true to the Gospel live with hope.

In Ezekiel 14, God was dealing with a group of people suffering from the effects of syncretism. Ezekiel's ministry was to call the people to faithfulness in God alone. There is a consistent pattern among God's people in the Old Testament. God calls out and rescues a people by His grace. The people are faithful for a while but then fall into sin. God brings judgment but then raises up a leader to rescue the people back into His grace. Ezekiel lived during the exile. The people were being judged. Through Ezekiel, God called the people back to faithfulness, but it was complicated.

There were leaders who had faith in God but also practiced cultural, idolatrous, and personal pursuits in connection with their faith. The syncretism of these leaders was offensive to God. Through Ezekiel, God warned them that they must repent. They were told to only trust the Lord and to get rid of the other influences in their lives (v.1-8). God promised not only would He judge the person with a divided faith, but He would also judge the prophet who did not call the divided person to repent (v.9-11). The goal was complete faithfulness to God. God does not share space in people's hearts. He is either the Lord of a person or He is the enemy of a person.

God will always have a faithful people who look to Him alone in faith. They will usually go through the pain that comes with living in a fallen, idolatrous culture, but they will be saved (v.12-23). This is always the way of God. Societies that live in opposition to God's law, sooner or later, face the consequences for their sin. Within those difficult times, God will still bless His faithful people. Those who live by grace through faith in Christ alone will be sustained and provided for, even in a depraved society. Each person must make their own choice. The children and friends of the faithful will not be natural beneficiaries of God's grace. Each person will be held accountable for their own faith choices.

In our fallen world, it is easy to become influenced with cultural sins, false religions, and personal agendas. It is easy to get captivated with the half-truths of other faith systems. It is often perceived as practical to pursue personal agendas and act as though they are of God. Are you making these mistakes? Are you claiming Christ, but at the same time pursuing the sin of culture, the lies of false teaching, and your personal kingdom? Those who avoid syncretism and are faithful and true to Christ alone live with hope.

2 Samuel 7; 2 Corinthians 1; Ezekiel 15; Psalms 56–57

Disciples of Jesus will always have enemies. Jesus said it would be this way (John 15:18-19). Having been set apart by the Lord, followers of Jesus will find the inhabitants of this planet, who are lost in darkness, to be hostile toward their life and faith. The good news is God is not only with His people, but empathizes with their suffering and provides for their needs. Those who find rest and strength in Christ alone will live with eternal hope.

The Psalms often picture the life and ministry of Christ. Psalms 56–57 are examples of Psalms that are not exactly about Jesus, but reveal the thoughts, feelings, and experiences of Jesus. David prefigures Jesus. What David experienced in his wilderness wanderings away from his home in Israel are like the journey of Jesus in this world away from His heavenly home. In these Psalms, disciples of Jesus get a glimpse of the greatness of God, the goodness of God, the provision of God, and the pleasure of God.

God is greater than any physical challenge His people will ever have to face. Jesus knows what it is to be hated. He knows what it is to have people wanting to kill Him. He knows what it is to be misunderstood and lied about. He knows what it is to have friends turn against Him. He knows what it is to have friends abandon Him in a time of need. Jesus knows the worst pain that life can give, and He has overcome. Jesus is the victor! He has defeated every human challenge. That is why those who trust in Him always have hope. The greatness of God revealed in the grace of God gives the peace of God to those who believe.

God is good. The world is filled with darkness and hate, but Jesus is the light and love of the world. He cares about His people. He understands each person's challenges. He has walked in this world and He gets how hard it can be. He is good to His people. He does not always spare them the pain, but He always goes through it with them. He is closer than a brother. He is a faithful friend.

God is able to meet every need the human heart, mind, and body will encounter. There is nothing He has not seen and experienced to the worst degree. Do you suffer emotionally, physically, spiritually, mentally, and socially? Jesus has too. He overcame every challenge, and now He can provide for those who trust in Him.

God is not bothered by the requests and needs of His people. It is His pleasure to be the provider for His children. It actually dishonors God when His people look to other created things to find their peace. It robs Him of honor. It also limits the help the people receive. Created things are temporary. The human soul is infinite. Only something of infinite power can provide for what humanity needs. It gives Jesus pleasure to be the eternal provider for His people.

Jesus has come to save His people. Do you trust Him? When life is hard and the pain is intense, is it your instinct to turn to Jesus? Christ alone can meet our needs. Those who look to Jesus find all they need to live with hope in life and death.

2 Samuel 8–9; 2 Corinthians 2; Ezekiel 16; Psalms 58–59

If a person is completely shut off and in isolation, there are no opportunities for conflict, but there are also no opportunities for fellowship. So it is with the Christian life. God calls us to position ourselves in life in such a way that we do not willingly open ourselves to spiritual attack, but at the same time we are not to lived closed off to other saints. The person positioned to protect and be generous toward God's people lives with hope.

David was a wise king. He was ruthless with his enemies and generous to his friends. He did not take risks when it came to military conquest or national defense, but he did not miss opportunities to show kindness either. In 2 Samuel 8–9, both aspects of David's life and leadership are on display. His actions picture how Jesus deals with His enemies and His covenant people.

When it came to his enemies, David did not mess around. In 2 Samuel 8, David's actions were intense. Someone unfamiliar with ancient military tactics might see David's actions as cruel and unnecessary. David lived in a very different and dangerous world. To slaughter his enemies, to minimize their capacity for war, and to intimidate them into submission provided peace in the region (v.1-14). The soldiers were destroyed, but the civilians and the land were allowed to flourish. Wisely organizing leadership structures ensured future success and provisions (v.15-18). Jesus, like David, defeated His enemies: sin and death, and positioned His people to live in peace and to be organized to help in human flourishing in societies and cultures all over the world.

When it came to his friends, David was generous. In 2 Samuel 9, David shows what grace looks like in practical ways. Having been established in his kingdom, he recalls his covenant with his best friend, Jonathan (1 Samuel 20:42). David wanted to show kindness to any in Jonathan's family, but his servants downplayed the venture (v.1-5). This sometimes happens in Jesus' Kingdom. He has servants who know the demands of the covenant and the call to share hope with the world, but dissuade themselves and disobey the Lord by ignoring His purpose. Like Ziba, many in God's family would prefer to relax in comfort rather than go and share God's favor with the world.

David was steadfast in his loving commitment to Jonathan (v.6-13). Mephibosheth was brought from Lo-Debar, a place of death, to Jerusalem, the city of God. Mephibosheth was a cripple. As a child, his legs were crushed when the house of Saul fell, and he was required to flee. He had nothing to offer David in terms of military might or governmental ingenuity. David showed him grace for Jonathan's sake. This is true for all who are saved by grace through faith in Christ alone. We have nothing to offer God, but for Christ's sake, God the Father shows us mercy and grace.

God is generous in giving grace and mercy. In His grace, God's people are to be wise and to limit the influence of the world, the flesh, and the devil that war against the soul. They are also to share God's grace generously with the world. Are you protecting your soul wisely? Are you sharing the Gospel generously? People who are wise and generous live with hope.

2 Samuel 10; 2 Corinthians 3; Ezekiel 17; Psalms 60–61

There is a great confidence that comes to any person who can speak specifically of their calling in life. The term "calling" is one that has been lost on many people. Most people talk of a career or job. Every child of God is a masterpiece made for a specific work God has prepared for them to do (Ephesians 2:10). God gifts, provides, and prepares His people to accomplish their calling. Those who fulfill God's calling live with great hope.

Paul was confident. Some wanted to say he was cocky, but he wasn't. He was sure of what he knew and he knew God had called him to be an apostle and a minister to the Gentiles. In 2 Corinthians 3, Paul, writing to a proud people being deceived by arrogant ministers, outlined his calling in Christ. Paul was consistently attacked. Those inside and outside of the church targeted him and his ministry. Paul's confidence to stand and continue in his service came from the fruit of his labors, the greatness of the Gospel, and the glory of God.

Those who attacked Paul were seemingly credentialed. They had letters from churches or individuals with standing that established their training and authority. Paul reminded the people of Corinth that *they* were his letters of recommendation (v.1-6). He asked rhetorical questions intended to highlight the nonsensical concept of his needing letters. God had used Paul to establish the church at Corinth. The Lord had provided miraculously to redeem people and establish a vibrant church. The fruit of God's blessing in the form of lives being changed by the Gospel is the greatest proof of a calling a person can have.

The transformation in the lives of the people of Corinth was not because of Paul, but because of the Gospel. Paul makes it abundantly clear in all of his communications with the church at Corinth that all glory is to go to God and not to any person. The glory is to God because it was He who came and established a new covenant and provided intimate access to the presence of God. What Moses provided was good, but what God has done through Jesus is better (v.7-16). Those who turn to the Lord are able to see God's glory. Those stuck in the ways of sinful flesh without the power of the Gospel cannot see the greatness and goodness of God.

Those who see God's glory are changed by it (v.17-18). The Spirit of God gives new life to those who believe. This faith in Jesus provides the means by which a person is transformed from one degree of glory to another. This change is known as sanctification. Sanctification is the process by which God makes His people more and more like Jesus. Paul had been changed, and he saw this same Gospel transformation take place in Corinth. This is why he was so confident in his calling. Paul believed God was glorified best in sanctified lives.

Every person in the Kingdom of God has a calling. Are you living your life out of a sense of God's calling for you? Can you see the fruit of God's blessing in your life and work? Are you being changed, and are those you serve being changed into the image of Jesus? Those who are confident in their calling because of the results of God's hand at work through them live with hope.

2 Samuel 11; 2 Corinthians 4; Ezekiel 18; Psalms 62–63

Taking responsibility and avoiding the mistake of accepting a victim mentality is crucial for a child of God. Human beings do not like to take responsibility for sin. Adam blamed Eve, and Eve blamed the snake. The fact is all three were guilty. The goodness of the Gospel is liberating, but only for those who can humble themselves and repent and believe in grace. Hope is found in the heart of the repentant sinner who trusts in Jesus.

In Ezekiel 18, the prophet was instructed by God to deal with an erroneous proverb that was being taught. The devil delights in taking what is true and turning it into a lie. By manipulating true words and concepts, the evil one has created some of its best distortions of reality and left many people in a corrupted, broken state. With His true Word, God calls His people to spot the misguided ideas of societal wisdom, to believe in the power of the Gospel, and to delight in the goodness of God's love for humanity.

If something is said enough times in interesting and compelling ways, it can become an axiom for a culture, even though it is a lie. The best way to make a lie seem true is to get it into a song, a story, or a catchy saying. The children of Israel, during the Babylonian exile, had come to the conclusion they were fated for failure because of their parents. The popular saying of their day was: "The fathers have eaten sour grapes, and the children's teeth are set on edge." It meant the children would have to pay for the sins of the parents. God clarified this was a lie and called Ezekiel to teach the truth (v.1-20). The truth is that every person is responsible for their actions and will be blessed or cursed based on their decisions.

God has graciously provided the object of faith that saves sinners. Those who repent, turn away from their sin, and pursue God by faith in His atoning power will be saved (v.21-29). We are never more like the devil than when we call God a liar and claim ourselves to be right. This is a damnable offense. Those who acknowledge their sin and refuse to make excuses for it, but instead, turn to God's grace will be saved. This requires humble faith in the redeeming power of God.

Humble faith is not hard when the love of God is understood. God revealed He has no pleasure in death (v.32). He is the maker and giver of life. Death is a result of sin. Life is the result of grace. Those who turn from sin and trust in Jesus gain what God alone can give – new life (v.30-31). The Lord has gone to great lengths to show His goodness. God is so good to give us the gift of creation, His Word, and His Son. To benefit from God's gifts, we must humble ourselves, repent of our sin, and believe in Jesus.

God has made His truth, His love, and His life available through Jesus. To receive Christ's benefits, we must take responsibility for our actions and repent of them. We must turn to Jesus and trust Him. Can you spot the lies of the devil? Do you have humble faith in Jesus? Do you believe in God's love? Those who repent and trust in Jesus live with hope.

2 Samuel 12; 2 Corinthians 5; Ezekiel 19; <u>Psalms 64–65</u>

How sweet it is for the saints of God to be able to cry out to God in prayer. Like a child, loved by her parents, can call out in the darkest night knowing she will be heard and cared for, so the child of God can cry out to God. A child only sees a few things a parent supplies. In reality, a parent is always doing dozens of things, and a child may only be aware of one or two of them. A child of God may only be aware of a few things God is doing, but in reality God is doing millions of things that work together for good. Those who can trust in God and turn to Him in prayer live with hope.

David shares his prayer journal in Psalms 64–65. What a glorious gift the prayers of the previous generations are to the saints of each new age. One of the enemy's tricks is to deceive a child of God to think, "It is only me that struggles with these thoughts and problems." Through prayer, God's children realize the realities of life, the power of God, and the reasons to rejoice.

In life God's children are always going to have enemies, and some of them will be flesh and blood. It is vital for every human being to know our primary enemy is this present darkness alluded to in Ephesians 6:12. Paul tells us, "...we do not wrestle against flesh and blood, but against the rulers, against the authorities, against the cosmic powers over this present darkness, against the spiritual forces of evil in the heavenly places." When David speaks of the throngs of evildoers and the plots of the wicked, he may have had in mind other people (64:1-6), but behind all hate, strife, lies, and destruction are the spiritual forces of evil at work in this world. Thankfully, Jesus has defeated them with His arrows (64:7-9), His death and resurrection.

In the victory of Jesus, we can approach God with confidence (Hebrews 4:16). The God of grace has a plan and purpose for every single one of His children. The Lord provides for the whole earth, and He will not forget his own children. Jesus tells us not to worry (Matthew 10:26-33). He cares more for us than anything in creation and knows the numbers of the hairs on our heads. This mighty God answers our prayers (65:5-13). Even in our failures, the Lord provides and brings us near for the praise of His name (65:1-4).

Because of the greatness and goodness of God, the children of God can rejoice (64:10). Those who have been redeemed by grace are comforted by the righteousness and power of God. Knowing His steadfast covenantal love has been bestowed upon them by grace through faith in Christ alone, every child of God can turn to the Almighty in prayer and find peace. In the best and worst of times, God does not change. He is always there and is always at work; He is ready to commune with His saints.

Prayer is a great gift from God. We were made to be with God. Sin has destroyed that relationship, but grace restores it. Do you talk with God continually? Do you have confidence in your prayers? Those who can trust in God and turn to Him like a child through prayer live with hope.

2 Samuel 13; 2 Corinthians 6; Ezekiel 20; Psalms 66–67

Sin is a lying, thieving, destructive force that always takes us further than we intended to go, costs us more than we wanted to pay, and gives us less than it promised. God warns the world to avoid sin. Every divine image-bearing person on the planet has some residue of God's hatred for sin in their soul. Sadly, the sin that so easily entangles us takes the desires God intended to be used for good and turns them against us. Those who find freedom from the power and punishment of sin live with hope.

The story of 2 Samuel 13 is a sad tale that gets lived out over and over in every generation. It is a story that tells The Story. The Story is about a king who had a son who came to love a woman. Rather than honor and protect her, the evil one tempted him to act on unholy desires, which left them both broken and ashamed and lost in sin. Adam's sin led to the sins of the world, and his sin is the source of the problems the world has today.

Amnon was a selfish and spoiled boy who believed if he wanted something, he should be able to have it. Rather than see the freedom in the limitation God had placed on his desires, he only saw the limitation as bondage and it made him heartsick (v.1-4). His friend encouraged him to throw off restraint and provided him with a plan for how (v.5-14). The devil seems like a friend in our times of temptation, but when temptation turns into sin, the devil proves to be a traitor.

Sin never satisfies. The result of sin is hate. Gluttons hate how they feel and look after they gorge themselves. Greedy people hate their isolation after they put money before relationships. The lustful hate their shame after they act on their sensual desire. Sin makes a heart sour after the realization that a sin act cannot gratify the eternal appetite of the immortal soul. Amnon hated his sister after he raped her. He sent her away in shame (v.15-19). That is what sin acts do. They create hate, brokenness, shame, and guilt.

Amnon's sin did more than hurt him and Tamar. It impacted his family (v.20-39). It turned Absalom into a murderer. It turned his dad into a grieving man. Sin never stays inside of an individual's life. Sin always impacts the loved ones of the sinner. David hated what Amnon did, and he wept for what Absalom did. He could not restore Amnon, but he could reclaim Absalom and he desired to (v.39). God has the power to redeem and restore broken sinners. It comes at a great price.

The Story tells of how the Lord of heaven took on flesh to die in the place of sinners. Jesus died and was raised. One day, Jesus will return and make all things new. Until that time, those who believe are welcomed back into the Father's Kingdom. Jesus has come to free us from sin. We must choose to trust in Him. We all live by faith. We either live by faith in the flesh and hope that it will satisfy or by faith in Jesus. Do you trust Jesus? Are you free to obey God? Those wo find freedom from the power and punishment of sin live with hope.

2 Samuel 14; 2 Corinthians 7; Ezekiel 21; Psalm 68

God promised to dwell among His people through the power of the resurrected Lord and the presence of the Holy Spirit. This is an individual experience that is shared corporately. The body of Christ is one in Jesus and enjoys a unique relationship to one another in Christ. Within this family there are both good and tough times, but when Christ is honored, there is always hope.

Paul experienced a wide range of emotions during the writing of 2 Corinthians 7. It had been a year since his last letter to Corinth. He had just finished ministering in Ephesus and was looking to reconnect with Titus, who had been to Corinth. Having met him in Macedonia and received word about what was happening in Corinth, Paul, under the inspiration of the Holy Spirit, wrote to Corinth again. In 2 Corinthians 7, Paul speaks to the call of God, the need for peace, and the importance of edification in the family of Jesus.

God calls all of His adopted children to live holy lives. Purity does not come from the willpower of people. The ability to be holy comes from the provision of God in the Gospel (v.1). God has come. Jesus took on flesh and defeated sin and death. It is through the cross and resurrection of Jesus that the saints of God can be made holy in standing and practice. Holiness is a result of faith in the promises of God. We will always do what we believe. Believing in Jesus will result in obeying Jesus in holy living. The varieties of emotions that motivate obedience vary from fear to deep affection. God is dangerous, but He is good.

Paul had every reason to be upset with the church at Corinth. They had rejected him and believed the negative news that the false teachers who had come to them had spread about Paul. Thankfully, Paul was a mature disciple of Jesus. With confidence he could say he had wronged no one (v.2), he was not condemning them (v.3), and he was proud of them (v.4). Although exhausted from the last year of ministry, Paul found comfort in Titus' testimony about them (v.5-9). He was glad the Corinthians still cared for him. Relationships are messy and peacemaking will be a normal part of the Christian life. It is the wise, mature believer who learns to care not only for their own emotions, but also for the emotional welfare of others.

Peacemaking always requires repentance. Those who edify others will discover they are able to speak the truth in love and restore the most devastated relationships. Paul had been grieved and he grieved those at Corinth. It was a Godly grief that produced repentance and renewal (v.10-15). Having spoken to their restored relationship, Paul was able to affirm his confidence in them (v.16). Relationships that go through conflict and are resolved in peacemaking always become stronger in the end.

Being family in Christ is not easy. It requires holiness, confidence in Christ, and a humble, willing heart. Those who live in the presence and power of Jesus have the ability to produce the life and love God commands. Are you living a holy life? Are you at peace with everyone? Those who honor Jesus with love live with hope.

2 Samuel 15; 2 Corinthians 8; Ezekiel 22; Psalm 69

There are natural consequences to sin. There are also supernatural consequences. When a person tells a lie and is caught, it harms their credibility. God may also be at work. The Lord may cause greater consequences than mere social stigma. This power of God is something to fear. The person who fears God and looks to Jesus lives with hope.

The natural human condition is filled with such pride that it struggles to honor God. Many choose to ignore God's existence and some completely deny His reality. This is a mistake. Ezekiel 22 reveals what happens to people, when God is ignored and denied. It's not good for the individual and it devastates a society. The natural consequences cripple a culture, but the supernatural consequences can crush a nation.

After years of idolatry and murder, God allowed the Babylonians to wipe out the Southern Kingdom. God pointed His finger at Jerusalem, the hub of the people, and revealed their blame. This was a culture of death and idolatry (v.1-5). Nations that kill their own children in order to provide an idolatrous lifestyle will not only become selfish and numb to sin, but will experience divine disfavor and be debilitated spiritually, socially, and politically.

Socially, the nation was a wreck. There was gross injustice and immorality (v.6-22). People were being killed by government officials. Those who needed the most help were being cheated and devoured. Families were in disarray with children disrespecting their parents and with parents committing adultery. God was ignored and made a joke of and people gave their time and energy to personal idolatrous pleasures. God removed the people from the land as a craftsman would remove dross from metal. Sooner or later, God washes away those who will not honor Him. It may be through natural or supernatural means.

Not only did Israel have a spiritual and a social problem, they also had a leadership problem. Those who were supposed to be leading the nation were deceiving the people (v.23-29). When the truth is replaced with lies, God becomes hidden from the hearts of the people. Once people stop fearing God and respecting spiritual leaders, a culture has nowhere to go for sure footing.

God is gracious. He can redeem, but it requires a faithful servant. In the days before Jerusalem's destruction, there was not a single man found who could stand in the breach and stop the bursting of God's judgment on the people (v.30-31). There has never been a mere human who could completely save. Humanity and the world needed a man who was God. The only savior that could save was one who was holy and willing to sacrifice His life so others could live. Thankfully, Jesus came. He was God and man. He stood in the breach. He provided the way. Salvation has come. All who look to Him in faith will be saved, sanctified, and one day glorified.

Those who ignore God's laws will be judged and destroyed. This judgment is in life and death. This should produce fear and awe of God. Do you fear God? Do you know you need a savior? Do you look to Jesus for hope? The person who fears God and looks to Jesus lives with hope.

2 Samuel 16; 2 Corinthians 9; Ezekiel 23; Psalms 70–71

The promises of God apply individually and communally. God does not change. He is always the God of the Bible that is to be feared, loved, and adored. God's plan does not change. He is always redeeming and sanctifying a people for Himself. He is always with, for, and in those who look to Him for salvation. Those who cling to Christ and hold to His promises live with hope.

Psalms 70–71 tell of the personal and communal hope that comes from the promises of God. These prayers are from a person who was feeling the pressure of his enemies. Like the devil, these enemies wanted to kill. Like sin, these enemies are always conspiring to overcome a child of God. While there is great stress and strain in these verses, there are also words of hope. These two Psalms point God's people to find victory through the power of God, the promises of God, and the praise of God.

God has the power to save. Sometimes He saves us from our circumstance, but sometimes He saves us through our circumstance. In Psalm 70 David acknowledged God was his provider. He called on God to supply his needs and overcome his enemies (v.1-3). What David dealt with physically is what all of God's people deal with spiritually. There is a real devil that wants to destroy. The Lord is victorious over the power of darkness and can confuse and confound the evil that desires to destroy.

David's confidence to ask for God's divine intervention came from the promises of God (v.4-5). All who seek the Lord can rejoice. The Apostle Paul wrote to the church at Philippi in chains and yet, over and over, he called them to rejoice. All who trust in Jesus have a reason to rejoice. There is a confidence that comes from knowing we are weak, but He is strong. In His strength God is a help and deliverer to those who acknowledge their need of him. It is the proud that fall, but the humble are strengthened by God's grace (James 4:6).

When God is seen as He truly is, praise is the natural outflow. God is truly great. He is greater than all of our sin. He is greater than our biggest problem. He is greater than our most evident need. He is mighty to save. Those who call out to God to be their rock and refuge, as the psalmist did, will delight to praise God. There is a great confidence that exists in the heart of a believer because of God's promises. The command for Jesus to save has already been given by the Father (v.3). When we know God is not only aware, but working out His plan to provide for us, we will worship Him with gladness. We will rejoice knowing God not only allowed for the calamity, but will revive us in His time (v.20-21). It is to His glory that the overwhelmed saints of the world live with hope in Him.

The world is broken and hard. We will all face physical, emotional, mental, and spiritual challenges. We can know God is with us, for us, and in us to accomplish His purpose with His power according to His promises. Do you know the promises of God? Do you trust Jesus to provide for you? Those who cling to Christ will live with hope.

2 Samuel 17; 2 Corinthians 10; Ezekiel 24; Psalm 72

Discernment, wisdom, and humility are crucial abilities needed for success in the spiritual battle that every believer must fight. It is crucial that every child of God have trusted friends and be able to identify those who give unwise advice. Every believer has spiritual gifts, but not all the gifts. In order to be a healthy disciple of Jesus, a believer must have a circle of Godly friends where wise choices can be sought and determined together, using all of their gifts collectively. Those with wisdom, discernment, and humility live with hope.

David was not a good father, but he was a good friend. He had spent his life forging alliances with people from different backgrounds and moral standards. What he was able to do as a monarch, he failed to do as a dad. In 2 Samuel 17, the fruit of his success and failure is seen. His son, having taken the kingdom of Israel, wanted to kill him, but his friends helped him.

David was a wise man and knew who to trust when it came to organizational decisions. Through providential design, David had learned to be a great leader. From the pasturelands where he killed bears and wolves, to the battlefields where he slew giants, to the inner-circle of Saul's kingdom and family, to the desert lands of the Philistines, and then as the king who overcame all regional threats, David learned to be a wise leader. Even when he blew it, he had people like the prophet Nathan help him see his sin (2 Samuel 12), so he could repent (Psalm 51). Absalom had not learned these lessons. The strong follower of Jesus is one who learns wisely through experiences with trusted friends.

David was a man of discernment. He understood the motives of men and how to work with them and around them. He did not like or agree with many he had in places of leadership, but he knew how to deal with them properly at the right time and in the right way. Absalom could not discern the motives of men and it left him incapable of knowing what to do. The strong follower of Jesus learns to see humanity from a Biblical perspective and measure each person's motives in order to know how to handle them.

David was a humble man. He listened to his advisers. He did not do what he wanted to do. He did what was right. He had a true north that drove his decisions. Not all of the advice David received was good. He did not kill Saul when he had the chance and his friends advised him to (1 Samuel 24). He did listen when he was told to flee (v.21-22). Humility allowed David to see what was best and to do it. The strong follower of Jesus is open to hear from others and to be led by God to do what is right.

Life is filled with decisions in our spiritual battles. Our circumstances can often feel and seem overwhelming. When a follower of Jesus can seek wisdom, be discerning, and act humbly, according to the advice of good friends, then success is sure. Do you have trusted, Godly friends? Can you see past the words to the motives of people? Are you able to humble yourself and learn and listen to others? Those with wisdom, discernment, and humility live with hope.

2 Samuel 18; 2 Corinthians 11; Ezekiel 25; Psalm 73

It is easy to get enthralled with positions of power and to find meaning in mere popularity. God calls His people to a deeper life. God calls His people to live for a divine purpose, which is founded in the Gospel of Jesus. To do this, God's people must have a strong sense of their calling in Christ. Those who know what they are supposed to do and why live with great hope.

The Apostle Paul knew what he was supposed to do. His greatest challenges came with those who attacked his authority, which made it difficult for him to serve God's people. In 2 Corinthians 11, Paul established his credentials to be the authoritative voice in the Corinthian church. Many false teachers had visited the city and sought to undermine Paul's credibility. Paul was able to prove his place in their lives and the Kingdom of God by focusing on his love for the people, the power of the Gospel he preached, the sacrifices he had made, and the miraculous ways God had provided for him.

Paul loved the church at Corinth and took on the position of a father figure in their lives (v.1-2). What a powerful picture of love! Paul felt like a daddy who had protected his daughter, the church at Corinth, to present her to Christ. This is how every pastor and leader should feel about those they influence. Leaders for the Lord are to love their people and present them to Christ, holy and ready to serve.

The foundation of Paul's ministry was the Gospel. Paul's greatest concern was that the church would abandon the only hope they had – salvation in Christ alone (v.2-6). There is only one way to God and that is Christ Jesus. Others came to the church and preached things that were not true. Paul pleaded with them to remember the Gospel and look past the lack of his oratory skills to the truth of his message. The power of the Gospel is what changes lives and not the entertaining words of public orators.

The way Paul came to the church was not the way those false teachers came. He came free of charge to the church and did not burden them with his financial needs (v.7-15). The false teachers would fleece the flock. Paul had others support him, which made it possible for him to serve them freely. He also came with scars. Paul had been beaten for his faith. His faith cost him (v.16-31). The popular public speakers that sought to deceive the people had not sacrificed like Paul. Christlike leaders will often suffer and serve out of their weakness.

God had been with Paul throughout his ministry. Over and over, Paul was saved from death so he could continue to preach Christ. One example is how God provided a way out of Damascus (v.32-33). It was not a glorious picture of Paul, but it revealed God's glory. Those God calls, He preserves. The preserving power of God gives a called person confidence to stand for Christ.

Paul knew who he was in Christ. In order to be effective in his role, he had to help others understand God's calling on his life. Do you honor those who serve you in Christ? Do you pray for and encourage them? Those who know what they are supposed to do and why live with great hope. Follow them!

2 Samuel 19; 2 Corinthians 12; <u>Ezekiel 26</u>; Psalm 74

It is impossible to fully understand the sovereign power of God. He knows all things and works all things according to His good purpose, and yet human beings and angels make their choices. All things are done by the will of God, and every volitional creature is responsible for their decisions. Those who choose to submit to Jesus live with hope.

There are many different sources of influence among human beings. There is military might, economic impact, popularity, and the enticement of pleasure. The city-state of Tyre had great economic power. The city was established in 2700 BC. It had seen many leaders and nations come and go and it had survived them all. Ezekiel 26 outlines its destruction, which would have seemed impossible at that time.

The prophecy, as promised, did not happen under the impact of a single nation. This nation, like that powerful fallen angel Satan, arrogantly stood in opposition to God and His people. This city delighted in the destruction of Jerusalem. For their arrogance and lack of alignment with God, God cursed it (v.1-7). Its destruction would come in phases, just as Satan's defeat has and will.

Many nations would bring down Tyre (v.3). The Babylonians, Alexander the Great, and others participated in its destruction over the years. The city was razed, as promised, in AD 1291. The final devastation came after its wealth had been plundered and its prestige lost. Satan will finally fall, just like Tyre. Satan has been defeated many times. God has been victorious over him through Abraham, Moses, and David. Now through Jesus, the church is victorious over Satan. One day, Satan will be completely vanquished, just as God promised. Like Tyre, Satan will be destroyed for its pride. All those who will not submit to Jesus will receive, with Satan, God's divine judgment.

Tyre would first be decimated by Nebuchadnezzar (v.7-18). This destruction not only impacted Tyre, but all those who interacted with the city economically and otherwise. Those connected with Tyre would grieve over the loss of this economic partner. So it will be with those who are partnered with Satan and live at odds with Jesus. They will hate to see the destruction of the world. They will hate to see the dominion of darkness, under the devil, come to an end. This world is their hope and desire. Like Tyre, Satan will be crushed.

Tyre would later be damned to hell, like Satan will be. This world is temporary. The eternal reality of heaven and hell will never end. God proclaimed, through Ezekiel, that Tyre would be condemned to hell with Satan (v.19-21). While they are tormented forever and ever, God will make all things new and "set beauty in the land of the living" (v.20). Those who trust in Jesus will experience God's restoration and rejoice (Revelation 21). Satan, and all those like Tyre, will be lost in darkness and judgment.

Every person makes choices. The ultimate choice of allegiance to God or to the world, under Satan along with the other fallen angels, is the biggest choice a person makes. Is Jesus your Savior? Are you living under His leadership? Those who choose to submit to Jesus live with hope.

2 Samuel 20; 2 Corinthians 13; Ezekiel 27; Psalms 75–76

God does not need anything from humanity, but He is due our praise and gratitude. God is merciful. He does not give us what we deserve. God is gracious. He gives us what we do not deserve. In His all-sufficient being, He is holy and loving. There is nothing wrong in or with God. He is perfect. He makes no mistakes in His dealings. Those who accept His mercy, grace, and love by faith in Jesus are made holy and live with hope.

Asaph provides a powerful and practical picture of the nature of humanity's relational options with God in Psalms 75–76. There are two ways a person can relate to God. We can either be blessed or cursed. Those who are blessed by God are grateful, humble, trusting, and bring God praise. Those who are cursed by God are thankless, boastful, self-centered, and rebellious.

The faithful are grateful and enjoy God's presence and deeds (75:1). With gladness, they recount the wondrous works of God (75:2-8). There is no pride in their praise, but rather a happy self-forgetfulness that stands in awe of God (75:9). Their faith is in Jesus, and by His might they dare to trust Him and join Him in what He is doing in the world (75:10). It is Christ who has overcome sin and death. It is Christ who will vanquish evil. It is Christ who will reign forever and ever. It is His people who join Him and pray His will to be done (Matthew 6:10).

The wicked are not like the faithful, but "are like the chaff that the wind drives away" (Psalm 1:4). Unlike the righteous who rejoice in the peace of God (76:1-3), they are the ones broken by God. They are not grateful for the peace of God. In their arrogance, those who reject God live in pride, but they fall (76:4-6). They and what they depend on for power will fail. In refusing to bow before God, the wicked stand on their own against God and are crushed for it (76:7-9). The railings of the enemies of God become a source of praise to God because it shows His wrath is just (76:10). In the condemnation of the unrepentant, God is revealed as glorious and receives the gifts of honor that bring Him the glory He is due (76:11-12).

There is no in-between place when it comes to God. Either a person stands justified before God in an everlasting covenant of love or a person stands in sin and is guilty before God under His eternal wrath of holy justice. While those who are made righteous by Christ do not live sinless in this world, their faith justifies them and sustains them. Without Christ, people are left to their own devices, and in their silly pride they refuse to find a place for God in their life, except to dishonor Him.

Because of Jesus there is hope. The grace of God has come. The Rescuer of souls has entered the world and defeated God's foes. Have you accepted the forgiveness of God in Christ? Do you stand in a right relationship with God? Are you grateful, humble, trusting of God, and bringing praise to Him with your life, lips, and longings? God is not a tool to be used. He is a Master to be obeyed. Those who live under Christ live with hope.

There is no fate. Coincidence is not real. There is only providence and human responsibility. God is at work in the world. Every person is responsible to God for each decision they make. The law of the Lord is good and right. Consequences come as a result of people's decisions. Those who know the law and live to honor Jesus are blessed with hope.

In 2 Samuel 21, there is a powerful portrayal of life. In life, there are agreements to keep, grace to receive, and wars to fight. Life is not easy. The difference between the heathen and the saved is perspective. God's people know God, His expectations, His grace, and His provision. The heathen do not. God's people know there are consequences and that peace can only be found in Christ. The heathen suffer, not knowing why.

During this time, there was a famine in Israel for three years because Saul, dead at the time of the famine, had broken the covenant Joshua had made with the Gibeonites (v.1-2). This Gibeonite covenant goes back four hundred years. David, king at the time of the famine, had to act on behalf of the nation to atone for Saul's sin. The Gibeonites wanted blood, and David had to give seven of Saul's sons to be put to death (v.3-6). Mephibosheth, Jonathan's son, was spared because of the covenant David made with Jonathan (v.7). Ultimate reality is revealed in this. The death of the sons of Saul (v.8-10) is like the death of all Adam's progeny that do not have God's grace. Mephibosheth is like the children of God saved by the covenant of grace. The only difference between Mephibosheth and his brothers is grace. This is true of all the redeemed, under God's grace, and all the unredeemed, who live and die without grace.

The sacrifice of Saul's seven sons provided the payment necessary to atone for the sin against the Gibeonites. Here again, we see the Gospel. These men were like Christ. They died to save others (v.14). Having satisfied the just demands of the covenant, the land was healed. After their death, a woman, Rizpah, cared for their bodies (v.11-13). Like the women on that first Easter morning who went to care for the body of Jesus, so this woman sought to honor those who died to atone for sin. Her sadness, like those who loved Jesus, was real. These were not actors on a stage. Saul's sons were loved, and like Christ, they died for sin they had not committed to save others.

Meanwhile, the world still raged with war. Israel and the Philistines continued their ancient hostilities and David was almost killed (v.15-22). Two certainties are seen in this. One, until Christ returns, there will be no lasting peace. The hearts of humanity and the work of the devil will make lasting peace impossible. Two, only Christ can save. As great as David was, he was only a man. Humanity needed a man who was God to save. Jesus has come!

The world is a hard place. God expects justice, but humanity is incapable of being just. While dealing with sin, people keep hurting each other. God's law bears down on all, but Jesus can save. Have you been saved by grace through faith in Jesus? Only those saved by the Gospel of God can make sense of the world and live with hope.

2 Samuel 22; Galatians 2; Ezekiel 29; Psalm 78:1-39

The Gospel is offensive to sinners. It tells people they are lost in guilt and in need of a Savior. The Gospel is no respecter of persons. There are many moral and nice people in the world who need the Gospel, just as there are many grossly immoral and mean people who need the Gospel. Every person born on this planet has a sin problem. We all want to be our own god. Those who receive new life and forgiveness in Christ live with hope.

In Galatians 2, the Apostle Paul provided clarity concerning the Gospel by sharing his personal experience, a conflict with Peter, and the impact the Gospel had on his life and future. Writing to the church at Galatia, which was being inundated with false teachers from the Jewish tradition, Paul pointed to the power and prestige of the Gospel. The Gospel is able to do what nothing else can do, and as a unique gift from God, it provides forgiveness and a new life for all who believe.

God was gracious to the Apostle Paul to give him the confidence to hold to the Gospel. Paul was no stranger to Jerusalem or to intellectual disputes. When he went to defend the Gospel from those who would have weakened it with human effort (Acts 15), Paul stood before the influential leaders of the church with his friends Barnabas and Titus (v.1). He went to have the Gospel he taught affirmed (v.2). He had been commanded by Jesus to take the Gospel to the Gentiles, but some insisted that the Gentiles first become Jews (v.3-10). The Gospel and Paul's calling was affirmed. The Gospel alone saves, and those who proclaim the Gospel must be faithful to teach the exclusivity of the Gospel.

Having established his calling and message, Paul ventured to stand on the truth of the Gospel and to fellowship with others who believed. Peter was a fellow believer but was not consistent in his faith practice. When he was with Gentiles, he lived one way, but when Jews showed up, he lived another way. Paul called him out for his hypocrisy (v.11-14). That's what believers do for each other. The fellowship of the redeemed must put Christ first and lovingly call all who believe to fidelity to the true faith.

There is a natural desire in all people to want to justify themselves before God. This sounds devout, but it isn't. Those who are saved are saved entirely by grace. There is nothing that a person can do to make their relationship with God right or better. Faith in Jesus is the only way a person can be justified and gain a right standing with God (v.15-16). This faith creates a new life in a person. It is a life of holiness made possible by Christ, who is alive in all who believe (v.17-19). Those who live in Christ live by faith. That faith is in the atoning work of Jesus and His resurrection (v.20-21). It is that faith alone that saves.

The Gospel tells all people they are not right with God and they can never do anything to make themselves right with God. That is offensive. The good news of God is that all who trust in Jesus will be saved. Do you trust in Jesus alone and not in anything you can do? Those who receive new life and forgiveness in Christ alone live with hope.

2 Samuel 23; Galatians 3; Ezekiel 30; Psalm 78:40-72

All creatures are dependent. God alone is self-sufficient. God alone has no beginning and end. It is by His power that all things have been made and hold together. Human beings, although made in the image of God and given immortal souls, live dependent lives. Without basic physical provisions, people die. The question each person must answer is: who will I trust to provide for my needs? Those who look to the Lord as their provider live with hope.

God's people have always struggled to depend completely on God. Abraham and his offspring had a tendency to look to Egypt in their times of need. This not only limited the capacity of God's people, but it robbed God of His honor. It gave honor to Egypt. God has proven trustworthy. He is always faithful. People and things, like the Egyptians and their wealth and armies, appear to be strong, but they are not. People and things will always fail. God chose to destroy Egypt, His rival for the hearts of His people. In Ezekiel 30, the prophet provided an outline of God's intent.

When God's judgment comes against a people, it is a terrible thing (v.1-5). This storm is unlike anything else. It has a very physical demeanor, but there is far more happening. The Lord brings an overwhelming horrifying sense. There is anguish. Emotionally, the people are overwhelmed. There is embarrassment. Psychologically, the people are put down. There is destruction. Physically, the things that were once so intimidating are leveled. When the Lord returns, there will be nothing like it. This act against Egypt is a foretaste of the coming of the Lord. God will desecrate those who robbed Him of glory.

Sin is never limited to the one who acts, but also impacts those closest to the person. So it is with God's judgment. The righteous judgment of God has ripple effects in the world. Not only would Egypt be destroyed, but so would their allies (v.6-9). It is crucial that Christians be careful with their friend selections. Those who are of Christ are to align their lives with other believers who will point them to depend on God. Egypt pointed people away from God and suffered for it, and all those who were connected with them suffered too.

The most dishonorable act a human being can do is to worship that which is not God. The Egyptians were known for their idols and their pride. God destroyed them for both (v.10-26). They were religious people, but they did not bow to God. They bowed to gods of their own creation and found strength within themselves. Idols fall and human strength fails. God never falls and His strength never fails. He is the Almighty! It is crucial the people of God look to God alone for all their needs spiritually, emotionally, and physically and praise God alone for His grace and goodness. This dependence is an act of worship.

None of us is capable of sustaining ourselves. We are dependent creatures. If we do not look to God to be our provider and object of praise, we will be left to look to fallen people, false gods, and limited physical resources. Where do you place your trust? Do you truly live dependent on God? Those who live dependent on God honor Him and worship Him. Those who look to God for provision live with hope.

2 Samuel 24; Galatians 4; Ezekiel 31; Psalm 79

God is glorious! For God to deny His honor would be dishonest. To ignore the ingratitude and pride that stands against His goodness would make Him complicit in the sin of blasphemy. God is holy and just. He will only do what is right. It is only right that He be honest about His glory and bring justice on those who lie, deceive, and reject Him and refuse to worship Him alone. Those who believe in the greatness of God and glorify Him with their life and love live with hope.

The children of Israel, like all people on the planet, had a serious sin issue. Rather than honor God and worship Him, they turned their backs on Him. God was patient. He brought discipline upon them time and time again. He sent judges and prophets to call them back to fidelity. Over and over they turned away, until finally, God abandoned them in their sin and the Babylonians swept them away. Psalm 79 is assumed to be the prayer of those who had seen the devastation of the Babylonians and were lamenting and looking to God for hope.

Having been wrecked by nations that did not know God, the children of God turned back to God for mercy (v.1-7). Their motivation was their suffering, but what drove their prayer was vengeance. They wanted their God, which they had not been faithful to, to turn against the nations that had harmed them. Their argument was simple. They were His children. As the children of the promise (Genesis 12:1-3), they spoke to God from a familial position and sought the help of the Lord in their distress. All who look to Jesus by faith become children of God and can call to Him for help (1 John).

Help comes to those who repent and by faith trust in the goodness of God for His glory. When people turn to God, they recognize they have done what is wrong. They request compassion. The result is humility (v.8). This is the first step in spiritual healing. Those who turn to God have a confidence God will save for the glory of His name. They have an understanding of His atoning power that gives His name honor (v.9). God's glory and the grace He gives to His repentant children is a blessing to those who believe. Those who do not believe receive justice for their actions (v.10-12). The redeemed benefit from the blessing and the Lord is vindicated in His judgment of the unrepentant.

Even before the blessings come, the children of God can praise the Lord (v.13). The praise of God's children in times of suffering comes from the hope of knowing whose we are and who it is we trust to save us. The hope of the redeemed is not that life will be perfect now. The hope of the redeemed is that, even when we are being disciplined or when life in this fallen world is just simply hard, our God is good and worthy of praise.

God is always good! God is always worthy to be honored and praised. Have you repented of your sin and turned to Jesus for redemption? Are you honoring God with your way of life? In your difficulties, can you delight in the goodness of God and trust that His grace is sufficient? Those who trust in Jesus to the praise of God's glory live with hope.

1 Kings 1; Galatians 5; Ezekiel 32; Psalm 80

God is the perfect Father. In this life there will be many men who will be a great blessing to their children. Their legacy will linger for generations. They will be remembered for their wisdom, love, and confidence. Even among the best of earthly dads, none can compare to God the Father. Those who look to God as their Father live with hope.

King David was great in many ways, but one of his great failings was as a father. He did not seem to have the courage to correct, the discipline to deny, or the vision to instill Godly values. Among his children were rapists, murderers, and arrogant usurpers. In 1 Kings 1, David's incompetence, as a parent, is on full display. When compared to the paternal patterns of God, David's failure is easily recognizable.

David was temporal and his strength was limited (v.1-4). David grew old and could not keep himself warm. His servants had to arrange for a beautiful woman to be with him in bed. David's weakness gave rise to his son Adonijah's plan to take control of the kingdom. God the Father is eternal and there is no limit to His power. He needs nothing. He is able to give life and sustain it for His glory forever. His eternal power inspires faithfulness in His people and fear in His enemies.

David was unwilling to say and do the hard things necessary to train his children to be humble and wise (v.5-10). Correction is a gift that buffets those who misbehave and provides a buffer from the natural inclinations of the flesh that lead to sin. Those who act on impulse rather than informed decisions create disunity and confusion. God the Father is wise and gracious. He corrects His children in love. Through His Word and by His Spirit, God calls His children to humble themselves and choose to be servants rather than self-seeking parasites. God's guidance brings about good results for those children who obey His Word.

David had to be forced through manipulation to keep his word (v.11-53). David had promised Bathsheba that their son Solomon would sit on the throne after him. Because of David's passivity, Adonijah felt comfortable and confident he could simply take the crown and rule as king without his father's blessing. This put Bathsheba's life and Solomon's life in danger. David provided for Solomon's coronation just in time and Solomon proved to be both wise and gracious. God the Father kept His Word and sent His Son, Jesus, to reign. Before the foundation of the world, God determined His Son would come to earth and sacrifice His life to bring about an eternal Kingdom that would reign forever and ever. The children of God enjoy the peace of God that reigns in their hearts and will one day reign over all of the earth.

God the Father is the best dad there has ever been or will ever be. All earthly fathers fall short. God the Father is perfect in all of His actions toward and for His children. It is a wise father who looks to the example of God. Do you love God the Father? Do you delight to obey Him? Have you accepted the grace of Jesus? Those who trust God as their Father live with hope.

1 Kings 2; Galatians 6; Ezekiel 33; Psalms 81–82

A minister once said, "If it wasn't for all of the people, I would love my church." Of course, the church is made up of the redeemed people of God. People are complicated. We are made in the image of God and desire to love and be loved, but sin keeps us from being and gaining what we desire. Desire can lead to desperation, and a desperate person is dangerous. The world is filled with desperate people doing destructive things hoping to gain happiness. Those who look to Christ are able to love and be loved; they live with hope.

Writing to the church at Galatia, Paul sought to uplift the people and to undermine the work of the evil one. The people were struggling with all of the usual stuff of sin. They were also being wrongly taught that they needed to be good Jews to be real Christians. In chapter six Paul concludes his letter and reminds them of the importance of caring for others, standing strong in Christ, and refusing to submit to unorthodox teaching.

Sooner or later, everyone sins. Within the body of Christ, God has provided the blessing of authentic renewal through repentance. By repenting and confessing to Christ (1 John 1:9) and to one another (James 5:16) sin can be overcome. There are times when a person needs to be restored from a lifestyle of sin. The task of restoration must be handled by a mature leader. That leader must be wise to guard against falling into sin in the process (v.1). By bearing the burden of caring for the broken, the law of Christ is kept (v.2). It is one of the great difficulties and blessings of a church to help restore a sibling out of sinful patterns.

Those who are blessed to live devoted to Christ must always be on guard through self-awareness (v.3). There may be no greater strength in the Christian life than the capacity to see ourselves rightly and to test our real motives and actions. We find confident joy that boasts in the Lord when we live in harmony with God and His people (v.4). Those who walk in the Spirit are taught to do so and must bless their teachers with the blessings God has given to them and remain faithful to do the good God commands (v.5-10). The self-aware, confident, and generous Christian will discover his or her desire to love and be loved is always met.

There will be those who wrongly teach the Word of God. Disciples of Jesus must be on guard. Like the Judaizers of Paul's day, there are religious leaders today who teach error (v.11-18). Their motivation is often pride and their desire is to gain followers to "their way." The love they want to give and receive is right, but the way they seek to gain and give it is wrong. The wise person will follow the way of the cross of Christ, as Paul commanded, and find the strength to endure and withstand the attacks of the evil one.

People are broken. It is crucial that Christians follow Christ and not allow the desire to love or be loved to lead them to deceive or be deceived. Do you have a mature faith built on the true Gospel? Are you walking in the Spirit and living a faithful, generous life? Those who follow the way of the cross of Christ live with hope.

1 Kings 3; Ephesians 1; Ezekiel 34; Psalms 83–84

Human beings are like sheep. We have no capacity to fend for ourselves against the spiritual forces that seek to devour us. We are incapable of fighting them off in our own strength. We are easily frightened. We do not know what to feed our souls and will consume just about anything, even if it is bad for us. We need a shepherd. We need the Good Shepherd of Psalm 23. We need the One who will fight for us, give us peace, and feed us truth. Those who follow the Good Shepherd, Jesus Christ, live with hope.

In Ezekiel 34, God condemns the shepherds who were supposed to care for His flock. The term shepherd is usually a pastoral term, but in the ancient near east, kings were often called shepherds. The shepherds that were condemned by God through Ezekiel were given the responsibility to lead and care for the people, but they, like all human-driven institutions, failed. There is only one who can truly care for and lead humanity into a place of security. This chapter points to the coming of the Messiah, who is the Good Shepherd and Savior of souls.

The core issue that had brought about God's wrath was injustice (v.1-10). Those called by God to serve the people slaughtered them instead. Rather than caring for them, they took advantage of them in order to get personal gain. The task of a shepherd was to keep the sheep healthy, protected, united, and fed. These shepherds allowed the sheep to get sick, scattered, and scared. Sheep only flourish when they are healed up, held together, and helped. The people of Israel were scattered throughout Assyria and Babylon, and God placed the blame on the civic and spiritual leaders of Israel. For their failure, they lost their own place of privilege. The good of all the people must always be the goal of a leader. A blessed people bless society.

Recognizing the desperation of the situation, God decided to step in and do something. Rather than depend on fallen people to lead His flock, God promised He would come and shepherd His flock (v.11-24). The Lord promised to do what no one else could do. The promise of God is He will call His people back to Himself, heal them, strengthen them, and bring about justice. Only the Lord has the love and power necessary for such an endeavor. Only One pure in heart, eternal in love, and infinite in power could accomplish this task.

God's promise went beyond the temporal. The hope of God transcends this life and it extends into the eternal. While God did come in flesh and save a people on this broken planet, He also promised He would one day change the world in which His people lived. He promised to make their world into a heaven (v.25-31). In this new reality, there will be no more threats. The Lord will be with His people and dwell with them. The people of God will be with their God and He will reign among them forever and ever.

Human governments will always fail. The capacity of human leadership is limited because of sin. Only a holy, loving, and powerful person of divine essence can save and restore the human race. Is Jesus your Shepherd? Do you follow Him? Those who are led by Jesus Christ live with hope.

1 Kings 4–5; Ephesians 2; Ezekiel 35; <u>Psalm 85</u>

Those who fall into sin rarely intend to fall as low as they do. It can happen not only to a person, but also to a church, a community, and even a nation. Each step toward sin and away from God can seem insignificant, but if enough steps are taken in a dishonorable direction, the destination brings God's discipline or wrath. God is gracious to those who repent. He is able to restore. Those who look to Jesus for grace find hope.

Psalm 85 is a communal lament. The people had fallen away from God. By His grace and for His glory, God awakened the people to their situation and they sought His favor. To become aware of sin and to be willing to turn from it is a miracle. In our natural selves, sin never seems as bad as it truly is. Repentance requires a supernatural influence by the work of the Holy Spirit. When a person or people are awakened by God, they will recognize God's grace, God's holiness, and God's transforming power at work.

Once the people realized how far they had fallen away from God and their need of restoration, they recalled God's grace in former days (v.1-3). When God's grace is at work among people, the Lord does three things. One, He is favorable toward His people and restores His relationship with them. Two, He forgives their sin and covers it in His righteousness. Three, He withdraws His wrath and turns His anger into compassion. This is the work of Christ in a true believer's life.

Coming into a transformational relationship with God allows a person and a people to see God for who He is and realize their desperate need of grace (v.4-9). God would be completely just to remain indignant over the sin of people because He is so holy. There would be nothing wrong with God being judicious in His anger and rejecting those who rejected Him. In His Word, the Lord provides gracious truth. The righteous will listen and refuse to return to their folly. This obedience comes not from will power, but divine delight in God.

Those who receive God's grace by faith are changed and continue to change throughout their life. God's work of grace begins a work that brings steadfast love and faithfulness along with righteousness and peace into perfect harmony (v.10). The result is faithfulness coming out of the life of the saint, as the righteousness of God shines down as a guiding light (v.11). The promises of God become facts of life rather than mysteries of supposition. The goodness of God will be seen, and the people will follow in the righteous way of God. This begins in salvation, but all the promises of God will be realized eternally in the final restoration at the second coming of Christ.

It is wise and best for an individual, a community of faith, and even a nation to remain faithful to God. If, however, there is ever a turning away from God, it is good to know that God is gracious and has the power to restore those who repent and return to Him. Are you walking faithfully with Jesus? Are you experiencing the promises of God and becoming more and more like Jesus? The way of Christ is not easy, but it is blessed, and those who walk with Jesus live with hope.

1 Kings 6; Ephesians 3; Ezekiel 36; Psalm 86

God is at work in the world overcoming the brokenness and despair caused by sin. Those who receive God's favor and find the Way that leads to life, through faith in Jesus Christ, are commanded to join God in His work to fill the world with His glory, goodness, and grace. It is because of love that God did not leave humanity in a fallen state. It is by love the redeemed are saved. It is in love the saints can serve God's purpose. Those who join God in His work in the world live with hope.

Solomon was selected by God to be the builder of the temple. God gives every one of His children a specific task to accomplish for His Kingdom (Ephesians 2:10). The Lord transforms His saints into the image of Christ so that they can serve the eternal purpose of His Kingdom. Every task done for the glory of God in the strength of God with the love of God is an honor and blessing. In 1 Kings 6, the building of the temple is described and the provision of God's grace is seen.

God provided the people and the place for His work to be done. David wanted to build the temple for God, but the Lord did not allow him to (1 Chronicles 28:3). It was the Lord's will to have David's son, Solomon, build the temple. It is important to note Solomon was the son of Bathsheba, and his life was the result of an act of adultery (2 Samuel 11). The place where the temple was built was Mount Moriah. This is the piece of property David had purchased to build an altar to the Lord, after the Lord had disciplined him for taking a census of the people. God's grace is greater than our sin. God can transform what was evil into what is holy and useful.

God provided the plan for His work that was done. The tabernacle that had been built by Moses was built specifically, as God commanded (Exodus 26). Each area had a precise purpose. When Solomon constructed the temple, he did it in accordance with the tabernacle by providing spaces for God's purpose. The most important thing was not the spaces themselves, but the spiritual experiences the spaces were to provide (v.11-13). The temple of God would be a means by which the people of God could recall the grace and goodness of God and seek God and be made right with Him in order to live with Him.

God provided consecrated beauty. The temple was a sacred space built in a sacred way. There was no hammering or any sound of tools being used on the site of the temple (v.7). This space was hallowed and the way it was built was in worshipful awe. Everything about the temple was beautiful. Every room had a unique state of beauty. God's work is to be done with sacred awe. It is to be beautiful. There is nothing more sacred than God's name, and there is nothing more beautiful than divine love. Those who serve in God's name with God's love serve in consecrated beauty.

God has a great plan for your life. Are you fulfilling God's plan for your life? Are you living in sacred awe of God? Are your actions motivated and accomplished in love? Those who do God's work God's way live with hope.

1 Kings 7; Ephesians 4; Ezekiel 37; Psalms 87–88

In these last days, God has spoken directly to humanity through His Son. Jesus, the Messiah, the Promised One, the Rock of Ages, the Ancient of Days, the Son of Man, the King of Kings, the Lord of Lords, the Mighty One, has come to rescue His people. Jesus Christ is God! God took on flesh to sanctify a people for His eternal purpose. Those who submit to Jesus live with hope.

Although we may not always understand or appreciate it, God's plan is always right and best. From before the foundation of the world, God determined to send His Son to overcome the power and punishment of sin and to vanquish evil. In Ephesians 4, Paul provides the practical results that are realized in the lives of all who look to Jesus in faith. The body of Christ now has a shared walk of life, a united work in life, and a unique way of life.

Disciples of Jesus are commanded to walk, that is live, in a manner that is worthy of the One who has redeemed them (v.1-6). Because it is by grace the saints have been saved, there is no place for pride, harshness, or frustration. As Christ loved them, so the disciples of Jesus are to love others and to maintain the unique bond of peace that is made possible by the Spirit of God who lives in each one. It is the Spirit of God who awakens each to the hope, the ordinances, and the doctrines of the orthodox faith. The Christian life is not complicated, unless we get away from walking with Jesus.

Disciples of Jesus are gifted to serve in the work of God (v.7-16). Jesus came to provide the means and blessing of grace. Through His holy life, atoning death, and miraculous resurrection, Jesus has delivered His people from death into life. In this new life, there is a great work that is to be done. To accomplish this great work, God gifts and chooses leaders to equip the saints to do the work. The world is a challenging place, but when God's people are doing God's work the way God commands, there is growth and the people are strengthened.

Disciples of Jesus are liberated to live in a way that is different than the world (v.17-32). The very Gospel that saves the saints also works to sanctify and make them to live like Jesus. The world is calloused to the will of God and lives in impurity. The saints of God are transformed by the love of God and strengthened to live holy lives that please God. This way of life deals with difficulties differently than the world; it speaks words of truth and encouragement; it gladly listens to the Holy Spirit and pleases Him.

Disciples of Jesus, those who have been saved by grace through faith in Christ alone, enjoy the blessing that comes with the sanctifying power of Jesus. What a privilege it is to be a disciple of Jesus! Not only are saints pardoned from sin, but they are commissioned to accomplish a great purpose in life with a God-honoring way of life. Are you a disciple of Jesus? Are you serving His eternal purpose? Does your way of life provide you with an assurance of your salvation and act as an announcement of the grace of God? Those who live in Christ live with hope.

1 Kings 8; Ephesians 5; Ezekiel 38; Psalm 89

One of the great mistakes, if not the greatest mistake mankind makes in life is in thinking God exists for their glory rather than for His glory. From the beginning, Satan was able to deceive humanity into thinking God should exist for their glory rather than for His own. Adam and Eve's sin was aroused by the desire to be independent and glorified. That same desire exists today in every human heart. Only those who live to glorify God live with hope.

God is a jealous God. He is jealous for His glory. He is not like a person fishing for a compliment who gets angry when ignored. God is holy, greatest in power, ultimate in love, and supreme in wisdom and goodness. It is only right that He would be glorified. God's glory is the highest good a person can know and express. A life that is lived ignoring and unmoved by God's glory is cursed. Ezekiel 38 reveals the magnitude of this curse and the level of deception and destruction that a life without Christ is destined to suffer.

Scholars do not agree on when this war will take place. Given the lack of evidence for one verifiable view, it is wise to move past the timing of the battle and look to the reason for the battle. This terrible loss of life and destruction will come about because God's holiness was not honored. The Lord takes full responsibility for the raid against the land of promise. He said He would lead this hoard of Godless people against His people for two reasons. One, "that the nations may know me" and two, that God would "vindicate (his) holiness before their eyes" (v.16). This is God's plan. God's will is that the world would know Him and His holiness, and He would be honored by all people to the praise of His great name.

The offense that caused God to act against His people was their apathy toward Him. The people who would be attacked were said to be dwelling in security (v.1-15). This is one of the fatal flaws of people of faith. No sooner have they been freed from desperation and gain comfort than they remove from their lives their focus and devotion to God. God consistently warned Israel about this (Deuteronomy 4:9-10). Comfort can become a snare to the undisciplined soul. Every believer must take care to keep God in view and to honor Him rightly.

The Lord will accomplish His eternal plan. All the world will know He is the one true God and alone is worthy to be worshipped and honored (v.17-23). He will use the evil of this world to accomplish His purpose, just as He used the cross. The cross was evil, but God used it to bring salvation and hope. This is the power of God.

The grand purpose of God is not to glorify humanity and enjoy them forever. The purpose of God is to bring glory to what is the most glorious, namely, Himself. That is why the main objective of humanity is to glorify God and to delight in His magnanimous perfection forever. Do you live to honor and glorify God? Can you see how God has used hardship to draw you back to Himself? Can you remain faithful to God and glorify Him in your comfort? Those who glorify God live with hope.

1 Kings 9; Ephesians 6; Ezekiel 39; <u>Psalm 90</u>

The difficulty of life and the hardship of living in a fallen human existence is frustrating. No wise person blessed to go through a season of relative bliss ever expects it to last. Those who walk with Jesus have a constant comfort: this world is not our home; God is with us in this fallen world; our eternal God has a plan for redemption. Those who can rest in God's eternal provision live with hope.

Moses was called by God to do a difficult task: lead Israel home. Not only did he have his own doubts to deal with, but God had him lead a million people with scars from abuse and generations of bondage with only a newly founded faith. The first generation failed to follow God, under Moses, into the Promised Land. Psalm 90 appears to be a prayer offered by Moses as this first generation was dying off and a second chance to enter the land approached. This prayer provides perspective on God, ascribes power to God, and humbly pleas for God to act on their behalf.

God never changes, and for all who believe, He is a shelter from the storms of life (v.1-2). Every generation faces a unique set of circumstances that require faith. The Israelites had suffered as slaves for four hundred years in Egypt. They journeyed through the Red Sea, to Mount Sinai, and in lands surrounded by enemies. God led them through it all. Now they were about to enter into a land filled with strong people who would have to be overcome. Their hope and the hope of all who believe is the everlasting God, who was with them.

Those who believe have hope because God shelters them and is eternally powerful (3-12). While humanity dies and returns to the dust, God remains and a thousand years is like a single night to Him. Not only is God eternal, but He is holy. Humanity is sinful and cannot hide anything from God. The brief life of humanity is filled with struggle, but those who can understand and appreciate the brevity of life and the grace of God can live in wisdom and thrive because God will see them through.

The faithful find hope in the pity of God and through faith call on God to act on their behalf (v.13-17). By faith the saints of God can plea for God to satisfy their souls each morning with His steadfast love, to enable them to rejoice, to make them glad, to reveal His power to His servants so their children and later generations can marvel at His greatness and goodness, and to show them favor by blessing the work of their hands He had called them to do. The assumption of Israel was God pursued them and revealed Himself to them for His purpose. Their plea was humble because they were in desperate need. Their plea was also bold because they were confident in the power and mercy of God. Every plea of a redeemed saint should be humble and bold.

Those who expect life to be easy simply because they have trusted God and are doing what He commands will be disappointed. The life of a saint is not easy, but it is significant and satisfying. Are you looking to God from the right perspective, trusting His power, and pleading for provision? Humble, bold saints live with hope.

1 Kings 10; Philippians 1; Ezekiel 40; Psalm 91

The blessing of being a blessing is a great one. It is a sad thing when those who are gifted and called by God to be a blessing miss the blessing of God for themselves. At every level of leadership, from being a parent to a CEO, there is an opportunity to bless others with wisdom, faith, and success-bearing structures, but if Christ is not the delight of a person's soul, nothing else a person does or has will ultimately matter. Only those who delight in Christ live with hope.

Solomon was a wise and powerful king. He asked God for wisdom and received it (1 Kings 3-4). He wanted to build on what his father, David, had been able to accomplish. In 1 Kings 10, Solomon's wisdom was put on display and his wealth was made manifest before the queen of Sheba and her officials. It was an impressive sight that took her breath away (v.5). What must not be forgotten is despite all of the external signs of success, Solomon said of all that he owned and had done, "Vanity of vanities, says the Preacher, vanity of vanities! All is vanity" (Ecclesiastes 1:2).

Solomon was a blessing to his people. When the queen of Sheba visited, her response in 1 Kings 10:8 was flattering: "Happy are your men! Happy are your servants, who continually stand before you and hear your wisdom!" There is a happiness that comes to those who are led well. A great leader can communicate a vision, move the hearts of others to believe and follow, and provide systems that allow for human, financial, and informational resources to be used to their greatest capacity. This is what Solomon did. 1 Kings 10 is a picture of what happens when great leadership is applied.

Solomon not only possessed the genius to shape the structure of his government into an effective machine, but he also was a churchgoing man. It is interesting to note that Solomon also shared his nation's faith with the queen of Sheba. She attended a worship gathering with Solomon. She saw "his burnt offerings that he offered at the house of the Lord" (v.5). Solomon was not the first, nor will he be the last person to appear to have it all on the outside, but feel empty inside and think everything about life is vanity.

The only way to experience true happiness is to delight in what is eternally gratifying and valuable. All created things pass away. All created things can only yield temporary happiness. The weight of an eternal soul cannot be sustained by a created thing. Only God Almighty in His eternal power and love can satisfy the longing of an eternal soul and carry the weight of infinite desire. Solomon knew God had "put eternity into man's heart" (Ecclesiastes 3:11). What a day of blessed peace it must have been when Solomon realized the truth of Proverbs 15:16: "Better is a little with the fear of the Lord than great treasure and trouble with it." That is true wisdom.

True wisdom and blessedness is found in the Lord. Do you delight in the Lord? Is God the great provider of your soul, or are you making created things your goal, strength, and desire? Is your faith truly satisfying, or is it just a charade? Only those who genuinely delight in Christ live with hope.

1 Kings 11; <u>Philippians 2</u>; Ezekiel 41; Psalms 92–93

The Christian life is never meant to be lived alone, and it is always supposed to create selflessness. One of the greatest temptations any disciple of Jesus must fight against is self-centeredness. The fall of humanity was motivated by selfishness and conceit. Those who learn to live and love like Jesus will always have and promote hope.

Paul loved all of the churches, where God had sent him to minister. Each one had different needs and provided different trials and blessings. The church at Philippi was a strong missionary church, but like any church, the members were tempted to be selfish and forget what life in Christ is to be about: loving God and others. In Philippians 2, Paul speaks to three different kinds of Christians: those learning to live in the church, those learning to live in the world, and those learning to live as missionaries.

Churches can get divided over silly and serious things. What will protect the life of any church, regardless of the problems it may face, is having a servant spirit among the members. Paul wrote to Philippi and challenged them to have a humble mindset that joyfully chooses to put others first (v.1-5). The good news for all believers is that we have the perfect example in Jesus Christ. He was willing to serve unto death. He was God, and yet He chose to serve the needs of others and received the glory and praise due His name for it (v.6-11). All who trust in Christ are to live with a servant's heart.

Not only are disciples of Jesus to live as Christ among the members of their local church, but also in the world (v.12-18). It is in the real world, where trials and temptations are consistently pressing upon us, that the children of God work out their salvation with fear and trembling. Salvation is received by grace through faith in Christ alone. Christ then works in those He saves to accomplish His will in them. Christians are to hold to the Word of God and rejoice, as Paul did. They are to avoid being negative, and instead, live as lights in their dark world.

There is to be in every church a missional instinct. Jesus commanded His disciples to go into the world and make disciples (Matthew 28:19-20). He sends His saints into the world just as the Father sent Him (John 20:21). Healthy churches will always be sending and supporting missionaries. Some will send short-term folks from their midst to help those who are called to live full-time on the field. Paul and Timothy were lifelong missionaries (v.19-24), and Epaphroditus was sent on a short-term mission trip to help them (v.25-30). Paul and Timothy were supported by the church at Philippi. Epaphroditus was sent by the church to take the church's provision and to be of help to Paul. This is normal for every local church.

Disciples of Jesus are to serve each other, their world, and to partner together to get the Gospel message to the ends of the earth. Are you a selfless church member? Are you helping share Christ with the world? Are you sending missionaries and willing to be sent? Those who selflessly join God in His work live with and promote hope.

1 Kings 12; Philippians 3; Ezekiel 42; Psalm 94

God is very particular. He has established very clear boundaries for how He is to be approached. Those who pursue religion in ways that suit them will never experience the true God. The true God is known and experienced on His terms, and those who come to Him by grace through faith in Christ live with hope.

There are many chapters in the Bible that seem to have academic, but no real spiritual nourishment for the soul. For some, Ezekiel 42 might be considered in that category. It is filled with architectural designs and priestly designations. Among those designs and designations, there is a Gospel reality to be understood. God provides hope in a particular structure, through a particular person, along with a particular reminder of His goodness and grace that all God's people can celebrate.

The temple design was not something that human beings came up with. God determined how His temple was to be constructed and how it was to function. It was through this edifice the grace of God would be offered and the ultimate sacrifice of Jesus would be pictured. Salvation is found in Christ alone. Old Testament saints looked forward to His coming, and the New Testament saints look back to His incarnation, death, and resurrection. The New Testament saints do not have a building. They are the building (1 Peter 2:5). It is through the church, God's "spiritual house," that the message of the Gospel is now proclaimed and grace is offered.

The plan of God was to produce a nation of priests (Exodus 19:6). This never came to be under the Old Covenant. Under the New Covenant, all believers now make up a "royal priesthood" under the authority and grace of Jesus Christ (1 Peter 2:9). The priests of the Old Testament wore one set of garments when they were in the "Holy Place" (v.14a), and they wore another set of garments when they were in the world, among people (v.14b). There was a separation between the two. In Jesus Christ the two came together. The divine was made human. God took on flesh and made the way for all who believe to enter into the Holy Place (Hebrews 6:19-20). Christ has gone into heaven, and all who follow Him have access to God.

It was in the Holy Place that the priests would eat the "holy offerings" (v.13). These holy foods prefigure the Lord's Supper that celebrates God becoming human. Jesus commanded His disciples to receive the bread and drink from the cup to celebrate His sacrifice until He returns in glory (1 Corinthians 11:17-34). This holy meal not only provides spiritual renewal to the souls of the redeemed, but it also pictures and promotes the unity of the "spiritual house," the church God has built and is building for His glory.

God has made known the particular way of salvation. It is by grace through faith in Christ alone. There is no other name or way that human beings can be saved (Acts 4:12). Have you been made righteous through faith in Christ? Are you a holy stone that is part of a local church? All who live in Christ live with and give hope.

1 Kings 13; Philippians 4; Ezekiel 43; Psalms 95–96

The great invitation of God inspires a hope that is always hopeful and a faith that endures the most hostile environments. The goal of God is to have His glory spread throughout all of the earth. Adam and Eve and Israel failed in this task. The church is now called to carry the hope of glory into the world so the nations can know and be made glad. When the task is done, the result will be exaltation to the Almighty. Those who accept God's glorious invitation and serve God's paramount purpose live with hope.

The Psalms communicate with powerful poetic language the best and worst in life. Psalms 95–96 submit an invitation to serve and savor the glory of God. Participation in the grand adventure of God demands delight, which results in singing. It also demands love, which results in obedient faith. When a saint is singing God's praise and walking in the way of Christ, there is momentum in missional activity. Psalms 95–96 are a call to God's people to live in the love of God and to make His grace known.

The first invitation of Psalm 95 is to sing praise to God (v.1-6). Music is mysteriously powerful. It has a unique influence on humanity. Songs help us remember. Songs move us to feel deeply. Songs incite us to imagine what is often unintelligible but deeply sensed. These verses provide options for what to sing of and to God. Given the glory of God and all He is and can do, there will never be an end to the songs that can be sung of and to Him. The words of this music incite praise for God's goodness, majesty, and power.

The second invitation of Psalm 95 is to be faithfully obedient to God (v.7-11). Despite God's deliverance, the children of Israel refused to trust Him and enter the Promised Land. This rejection led God to keep them from His rest. The rest found in the Promised Land of Palestine was a picture of the rest that is now promised in Christ. There is an eternal rest given to those who will, by faith, enter it and obey Jesus (Hebrews 4).

The result of authentic worship and faithful obedience is evangelistic activity (Psalm 96). Those who know the Lord cannot help but marvel at His holiness and power. In their awe, the saints of God are compelled to proclaim the Good News that God can be known, lived in, and loved. The blessing for believing is gladness of heart. The curse for rejecting is soul sadness and separation from all that is good and right. God offers His splendor and salvation through the saints who sing and magnify His name in all of the earth. Those who receive this grace by faith become members of God's righteous nation of priests.

The Gospel of God is mysterious and marvelous. Those who are given eyes that can see the glory of God and ears that can hear the Good News of salvation will worship and obey the Lord. The redeemed of God are driven by love to sing praise to God and to obey His holy Word. Do you sing the songs of salvation? Are you walking in obedience to God in love? Are you sharing your faith? Those who savor the Savior sing about Him, trust in Him, and tell of Him with hope.

1 Kings 14; Colossians 1; Ezekiel 44; Psalms 97–98

In a God-honoring culture, there will be some who will be unfaithful to God. In a God-forgetting culture, there will be a few who will remain faithful to God. A God-honoring culture is a great blessing to those who believe and those who do not. A God-forgetting culture is not a blessing to either. In times of despair and brokenness, the wicked suffer in hopelessness and idolatry, but the righteous will always have hope, no matter what.

The Bible is filled with stories of how God's people were blessed and then, despite God's blessing, turned against God and chose idolatry. Israel was just a few weeks into their salvation journey from Egypt when they turned against God and made golden calves as idols. The times of the judges were dark times because the people refused to be faithful to God. The days of the kings were no better. In 1 Kings 14, the reigns of Jeroboam in the Northern Kingdom and Rehoboam in the Southern Kingdom reveal how God's people can be deceived, can get self-confident, and can be impacted by the consequences of their sin.

Jeroboam was an amazing man. He was hardworking, motivational, and cunning. He provided a great service to Solomon and the nation of Israel. Solomon's idolatry led to the dividing of Israel, and God gave ten of the twelve tribes, the Northern Kingdom, to Jeroboam. Jeroboam was not satisfied with that. He wanted it all. Rather than trust God, he turned against God and had the nation worship golden calves, as they did when they left Egypt. God had promised David it would be through his lineage that the eternal Kingdom of Christ would come. God's promises stand. Each generation is responsible for their decisions, but God's will, according to His Word, will always be done.

Not only did Jeroboam refuse to submit to God and to be thankful, he actually tried to trick God (v.1-20). His sin led to sickness in his home and devastation in the land. When a people called by God turn against God, sooner or later, pain and suffering follow. As a result of his sin, Jeroboam's family and nation suffered. Sin always has a cost. It may not always be physical at the start, but it always leads to a spiritual sickness, which ends in judgment and destruction.

Under Rehoboam, the Southern Kingdom did not do any better (v.21-31). When darkness begins to take hold, it grows in boldness. Sin never stays the same. It increases in intensity and filthiness. When God is dishonored, there is both a natural and a supernatural consequence. Sin always leads to more sin. The more sin there is in a life and culture, the more there is sickness and pain, as relational structures crumble. When God is dishonored, He will often turn away from and remove His hand of protection and provision. In those moments, lives and nations fall apart and what was once blessed and honorable becomes cursed and embarrassing.

God is going to accomplish His will. The end has already been written and God wins! Every person, nation, and generation must choose to honor God or turn away from Him. Do you trust in Jesus? Are you living in obedience to God's Word? The righteous live by faith and are blessed with hope.

1 Kings 15; Colossians 2; Ezekiel 45; Psalms 99–101

The Christian life is a battle. In Ephesians 6, the Apostle Paul explains the spiritual war that is waging and how disciples of Jesus are able to fight in and with the armor of God. Many smart and kindhearted disciples have fallen. Many have lost their ministries, their marriages, their friendships, and their influence for Christ. They are still the Lord's children, but in their sin, they destroyed relationships. Those who walk in the way of the life of Jesus can overcome with hope.

Writing to a church he did not start and a people he had never met, Paul challenged the church at Colossae to be faithful in their walk in Christ. In chapter two, Paul speaks of his personal battle, the means of spiritual success, and the threat that exists to the souls of all the saints. Believers should never be surprised at the toll it takes on them to follow Jesus; they should never be surprised at the mental fortitude required to remain faithful; they should never be surprised at the intimidation that is used to try to get them to relinquish their faith in Christ.

Paul was no stranger to suffering. When he was saved, the Lord said of him, "For I will show him how much he must suffer" (Acts 9:16). Writing to the church at Corinth, Paul recounted the ways he had been hurt for the faith (2 Corinthians 11:23–28). He also suffered for his love for the church at Colossae (v.1-5). His great concern was they would fall away from the true faith, through deceptive influences that were not of Christ. Every disciple of Jesus must be mindful of the capacity to be deceived with plausible arguments that deny the miraculous reality of Jesus Christ.

The only way to survive the onslaught of the lies and deceit of the world is to walk in Christ and to be "rooted and built up in him and established in the faith, just as you were taught, abounding in thanksgiving" (v.6-7). It is not enough to receive Christ. The disciple of Jesus must walk in His living presence, His grace, His strength, His love, and in all that He is. That only happens when a person is rooted in Christ, like a tree planted by streams of living water (Psalm 1), like a spiritual house built on a firm foundation (Luke 6:47-48), or like a blessed boat anchored in truth (Ephesians 4:14). Those who live this blessed life were taught it by those who lived it. Those who live it are genuinely grateful.

When disciples of Jesus are grounded in the faith and rejoicing in the truth of the Gospel, they are less likely to be intimidated by well-intended, but misinformed people who take Biblical concepts and twist them to get others to adapt to their preferences. Legalistic people often mean well. They do not want people to sin. Their plan is to get people to keep away from things they deem dangerous (v.8-23). The problem is their doctrine and practice robs Christ of glory and His followers of faith.

Every battle is different. Thankfully, the same Lord with the same power is at work and is all that disciples of Jesus need to overcome. Are you able to suffer for Jesus with joy? Is your faith rooted and established in Christ? Those who walk in Jesus live with hope.

1 Kings 16; Colossians 3; Ezekiel 46; Psalm 102

The Old Testament consistently points to the coming of the Messiah and the grace that would change the world. Jesus Christ came, as promised, and fulfilled the prophecies and the pictures of the Old Testament. Jesus fulfilled all that was prophesied about Him. Through His coming, dying, and being raised, He gives new life to all who believe. Those who rest in the finished work of Jesus live with hope.

Ezekiel 46 reveals the real problem of the Old Covenant. Everyone involved in that worship description was imperfect. This chapter provides a helpful picture that highlights the four distinct groups that made up the characters of the Old Testament. There were the people. There were the priests. There was the prince. There was the prophet, Ezekiel. Jesus Christ came to save people by becoming one of us, by being the perfect provider, and by mediating God's grace to us. People are saved by the One who is prophet, priest, and prince/king. He dwelled among us to redeem us from our sin.

God is orderly. His creation is filled with systems that work together in a particular way for a particular purpose. In the Old Testament, God ordered the people's lives with a succinct rhythm. There was a Sabbath and then special feasts that took place. Ezekiel's vision speaks of the Sabbath and the new moon (v.1). On these days the prince would come among the people and provide the offerings prescribed (v.2-7). Jesus Christ came among us to live a perfect life. He lived, as a man, to provide the perfect sacrifice that fulfilled all of the sacrifices made in the Old Testament. They all pointed to Him.

The temple worship along with the sacrificial system was never meant to be the final answer to humanity's sin problem. The plan from before the creation of the world was for Jesus to come and redeem His church. In Ezekiel's vision, the people with the prince passed through the temple (v.8-10). This was not the permanent answer. The offerings were of the highest quality, but they were never enough. They had to be presented over and over (v.11-24). They met the requirements of God and supplied the priests and servants with food, but were never eternally sufficient. Christ alone is sufficient to cancel the sin debt of those who believe.

When God's promise was actualized and the grace of God was given finally and perfectly, it was through the perfect prince, priest, and prophet. Jesus is perfect in every way. He is the perfect leader. All the human kings of the Old Testament could never suffice. He is the perfect priest who offered the final sacrifice and has now entered into the presence of God to mediate for the redeemed. He is the perfect prophet who personified truth and revealed God in human form.

The miracle of Jesus must not be missed. Many will minimize Him and present Him as a mere man who died an unfortunate death. He is God in the flesh who gave His life to atone for sin! Is Jesus the leader of your life? Is Jesus your personal savior? Is Jesus your truth? Those who submit to Jesus enjoy His guidance, grace, and goodness and live with hope.

1 Kings 17; Colossians 4; Ezekiel 47; <u>Psalm 103</u>

In life, dark and difficult days are bound to come. They may come in short spurts or in long days, but it is particularly difficult when there is a season of suffering or soul sadness. It should never surprise a saint to feel the heaviness of gloom. It is not a sin. It is not a lack of faith. Many of God's most faithful servants suffered through seasons of dejection. The world is not as it should be, but God is with us. Those who can keep their eyes on Jesus live with hope.

In Jesus, there is always a reason to "bless the Lord!" The body may not feel like it at times. The mind may not desire to engage in the practice. The emotions may not feel the impulse to praise, but those who have been saved by grace through faith in Christ alone will find strength and hope for their souls when they do. Psalm 103 is a practical place to go during dark, difficult days. In this Psalm, God's benefits are called to remembrance.

Someone may say, "I do not feel I have the strength of heart to look to God." That happens. It sometimes happens because of sin that has hardened the heart. It sometimes happens because the world has come down hard upon a heart. It sometimes happens because God is training a soul and allowing trials to impact a heart. Regardless of the reason, the children of God must preach to their souls. The Psalmist commanded his soul to "bless the Lord" (v.1). He commanded his soul to remember God's benefits: forgiveness, healings, redemption, love and mercy, satisfaction, and strength (v.2-5). All these are benefits of grace!

Someone may say, "I do not feel these benefits." That happens. It is then a child of God must look to the facts of the faith (v.6-19). God has been good to His people the same way He was good to Moses. The Lord did not deal with him and God does not deal with any of His people according to their sin. Because Jesus paid the sin debt of all the saints, the Lord now deals with His people with compassion. He knows we are weak and will pass away like the grass. He made us from the dust and is intimately aware of our inability. Having lived like us in the flesh, the Lord knows we are dependent upon His steadfast love, which He has established in His blood, just as He has established His authority over all things.

Someone may say, "I do not feel God's power." That happens. It is important to remember humanity's place in the plan of God. We are a little lower than the angels but crowned with glory (Psalm 8:5). From this position, the saints of God get help from the angels of God to accomplish God's will (v.20-21), which is revealed in all creation and in the providence of God (v.22a). The redeemed of God are empowered by God to join the heavenly hosts and all of creation to bless God's holy name (v.22b).

We will not always feel strong in the faith. In those moments we must preach to ourselves the sermon of Psalm 103. Are you choosing to bless the Lord? Are you affirming your favored position? Those who look past themselves to Jesus will live with hope, even in difficult days.

1 Kings 18; 1 Thessalonians 1; Ezekiel 48; Psalm 104

Prayer is more than speaking with God. Prayer is listening to God. The Lord speaks through His Word, His creation, His saints, and the circumstances of His people. The Lord will sometimes speak audibly in a supernatural way. Those who know how to pray rightly will pray for great things and see God do great things. They will live with great hope.

The prophet Elijah was called by God to live during difficult days. The nation of Israel was led by a spineless and godless king. His wife was not a believer. The nation was being pulled away from God. Baal worship was in vogue, and there was a drought because of it. In that season of suffering, God called Elijah forward to accomplish God's purpose and overcome the evil of Elijah's day. 1 Kings 18 explains how he did it. He listened to God. He obeyed God. He prayed to God.

Before the battle on Mount Carmel began, the victory was already won. When the Lord determines to do something, nothing can stop Him. He is the Almighty! The Lord has chosen to bring glory to His Name by using weak human vessels to overcome the powerful forces of darkness in the world. Elijah walked with God and was able to discern God's voice (v.1). He was in a position of humility to listen, and God was gracious to allow him the faith to hear the Word of God. The Lord works through those who listen to Him.

Having heard from God, Elijah obeyed (v.2-40). The victory was made possible by Elijah's genuine faith that produced the works God commanded. Elijah did not come up with a great strategy to overcome the Baals on his own. Elijah listened to God and did what God commanded. The result of Elijah's faith caused others to act in faith and believe. Obadiah had to live by faith and approach Ahab. The people had to act in faith and kill the prophets of Baal. The faithfulness of one will influence others to accomplish the work of God. God was doing more than defeating the evil of Baal worship. He was strengthening the faith of His servants and blessing them with hope.

Having seen the people turn to God in faith, Elijah anticipated God's blessing. Elijah knew God's Word. God told Solomon if the people ever turned against Him, there would be a drought, but if they repented, rain would come (2 Chronicles 7:12-14). Knowing this truth, Elijah prayed expectantly and specifically. His prayer was so expectant that he told Ahab to go home, before the rain started (v.41). It was not a general prayer. His prayer was so specific he could send his servant to see if the Lord had answered (v.42-43). At the first sight of an answer, Elijah quit praying and went and celebrated God's victory (v.44-46). Those who know God's Word can discern His will and pray rightly. They see miracles!

Those who see miracles know God's Word and obey Him; they pray with hope by listening to and asking for what God has said He will do; they see God do great things. Do you know and obey God's Word? Are you listening to God? Are you praying expectantly and specifically? Those who trust and obey God, according to His Word, act and pray in faith and live with hope.

1 Kings 19; 1 Thessalonians 2; Daniel 1; Psalm 105

Jesus left the comforts of heaven to come to earth to rescue sinners. He gave His life as the atoning sacrifice for sin and was raised on the third day. This is the Gospel. Just as God sent His Son to the world to save sinners, so now He sends His adopted children to tell the Good News, the Gospel, to the world. Like Jesus, God's children must give up their comforts and connect with lost people. Like Jesus, God's children must make sacrifices. Like Jesus, God's children will live with hope.

The Apostle Paul was a child of God by grace through faith in Christ alone. Having redeemed Paul from sin and changed his life, God called him to share the Gospel with Gentiles. This calling came at a great personal cost to Paul. He had to leave the world he knew in Palestine. He had to venture into the heart of the Roman world. He had to sacrifice family and friendships. Out of his love for Christ and His obedience to Him, Paul went to where he was not wanted to share a hope that can only be spiritually discerned. Writing to the church at Thessalonica, Paul explained his calling in 1 Thessalonians 2. His calling, like the calling of every believer comes from God, is empowered by God, and experiences resistance from the world.

Paul had confidence in his message and ministry because he knew it was not something he had made up or come up with on his own. He knew it was God's message and it was God who had called him to the ministry. He was not treated well (v.1), and yet, he had boldness (v.2). This boldness came from the confidence that what he was revealing was of God (v.3-6). As God had been kind and loving toward him, Paul was able to be kind and loving toward those he served (v.7-8). The children of God can always serve with the assurance they are doing what God told them to do. There is freedom and confidence in simple obedience.

The work Paul did was empowered by God. Paul and his companions had to work night and day in order to have resources for the ministry and to provide for their own needs (v.9). They were able to remain blameless and above reproach and simply teach the Word of God (v.10-13). The work of teaching the Word is a God-empowered work. Not only does God provide the ability and resources for those who teach it, but the Word of God is empowered by the Spirit of God. God promises to work through His Word (Isaiah 55:11).

Those who believe will always be hindered by the forces of darkness. Just as the Jews attempted to silence the Gospel in Judah, so they sought to do the same in Thessalonica (v.14-16). This is the way of the world. It is in opposition to God. Paul was being buffeted from being able to care for them as he wanted (v.17-20), but he still had hope and the Thessalonians' faith gave him joy. Joy comes from faithful service.

The work of God will always be empowered by God and opposed by darkness. God is greater than the darkness! Are you sharing the Gospel? Do you love people as God has loved you? Like Jesus, God's children will struggle and suffer, but they will live with hope.

1 Kings 20; 1 Thessalonians 3; Daniel 2; Psalm 106

It is easy to become overwhelmed with the dangers of the world. While there is certainly a place for loving concern, it is vital the children of God avoid fixating and obsessing over issues, circumstances, and tragedies. God is in control. He is working out a master plan that provides what is best not only for God's glory, but also for all who believe. This does not mean that in this life we will live trouble-free. What it means is God has overcome the world and those who trust in Him will live with hope.

So how are we to live in a world fraught with danger and destruction? Daniel 2 illuminates the irrefutable power of God and the primacy of faith in the life of a disciple of Jesus. In this section of Scripture, the children of God were exiled in Babylonian captivity. Daniel and his companions had been trained and elevated to the office of "wise men." While this place of power provided many comforts, it was also dangerous. Daniel's faith instructs believers in how to live in our dangerous world.

First, realize that the problem of the world is too big for humanity to handle. The king of Babylon was troubled over a dream, and so he called together all of the wise men and asked for its interpretation (v.1-4). His servants were happy to interpret it, but the king wanted more. He expected them to not only interpret the dream, but also to tell him what he had dreamed (v.5-9). The wise men's response was accurate: "There is not a man on earth who can meet the king's demand" (v.10-11). No person on the planet is capable of overcoming the greatest problem of our world. Brokenhearted humanity cannot heal itself. Only God can do that.

Second, realize God has made provision and all who look to Him in faith will be saved. Daniel and his companions were sought and their faith was able to shine (v.12-30). This national emergency was no accident. God was revealing His eternal plan. This trying time revealed the one true God to the world. Daniel and his friends prayed. Having sought God's face and trusted in His power, Daniel received God's blessing. He told the king his dream, but first made it clear that this miraculous act was thanks to divine intervention and not by Daniel's ability (v.28). Daniel's revelation and interpretation saved him and all the wise men of his day.

Third, realize God has big plans and all who join with Him will be saved. The king's dream was a prophecy. In it, God revealed His eternal plan (v.31-45). There would be other kingdoms that would come and go, but finally an eternal Kingdom would be established. This is the Kingdom of God under the leadership of Jesus Christ (v.44-45). All who accept Jesus' forgiveness and new life by faith and gladly surrender to His reign will be saved. Daniel's service made known the greatness of God (v.46-49). This is the work of God's people now. We are to make known the Good News of our great, gracious God.

Our fallen world is a dangerous place. God has not abandoned us in it. Do you trust Jesus? Do you seek His help? Are you sharing with others the hope you have? Those who trust in Jesus have a hope that can heal the world.

1 Kings 21; 1 Thessalonians 4; Daniel 3; <u>Psalm 107</u>

The most trying occasions can be filled with the goodness of God. The start of a strenuous situation can be brought into perspective with a simple prayer of praise and thanks. God has saved many from varied difficult circumstances and because of His grace the redeemed can always have hope.

There is an overview of God's salvific power in Psalm 107. The Lord has saved billions of people from their sin. Each situation was unique, just as each person is. The redeemed of God can look back at what God has done in the past and praise Him. Because God does not change and His steadfast love endures forever along with His eternal purpose, the redeemed can anticipate seeing the miraculous in the days ahead. God is gloriously gracious and gives the redeemed reason to say so (v.1-2).

God is gloriously gracious and the redeemed who have been gathered from every corner of the earth can say so (v.3-4). The Lord is not finished yet. There are still more to be saved, but many have already been saved. What God has done, He will do again. Sinners from all over the planet will be saved, and God's people get to partner in making this plan a reality.

God is gloriously gracious and the redeemed who have been adopted into God's eternal family can say so (v.5-9). Every person conceived on this planet begins as a spiritual orphan and wanders the world longing for a place of shelter and provision. Born with the fallen nature of Adam, humanity has no claim to heaven's goodness. Those who receive the grace of the Father through faith in the Son in the power of the Spirit are made children of God and become heirs of His Kingdom.

God is gloriously gracious and the redeemed who have been freed from the bondage of sin and foolishness can say so (v.10-22). Every person is born a slave to sin, but with every act of ignorant disobedience, the bonds of defiance increase. Were it not for the power of Christ to set prisoners free from the bondage of sin, all would die heavy-laden performing oppressive labor to gain dust. Jesus sets the captives free!

God is gloriously gracious and the redeemed who have been called to the great service of the King of Glory can say so (v.23-43). Without a greater purpose than their own pleasure, popularity, possessions and power, many people have lost their eternal soul to the despair of indignity by living for a creaturely cause. God made humanity in His own image with eternal value and miraculous design. Rather than serve their Maker, many have sought to serve themselves and have shipwrecked their lives. God provides for the helpless, and by faith many have found safe harbor.

God is gloriously gracious and the redeemed who have been enlightened to His grace can say so. They can think on the power of God and give Him praise (v.44). Not only does this remembrance produce hope in the heart of the redeemed, it also provides God the glory He is due. Is God your hope? Is Jesus your salvation? Does the Word of God by the power of the Spirit incite praise from your lips? God is gloriously gracious and His redemption gives hope.

1 Kings 22; 1 Thessalonians 5; Daniel 4; Psalms 108–109

The human mind is masterful at creating justifications for the decisions of the sinful heart. What the sinful heart wants, the mind can typically justify. One big stumbling block to the heart's sinful desires is truth. Those who will hear from and honor God will not always have what they want, but they will gain what is best. Those who listen to and obey God live with hope.

With positions of authority and comfort, a sense of entitlement often sets in. What was once a privilege will often become an expected right in the heart of a person who only listens to their own desires and to people who tell them what they want to hear. This was the plight of the kings of Israel in 1 Kings 22. Rather than honor God and listen to His truth, these kings dishonored God and listened to their own sinful hearts' desires.

Ahab was king of Israel. He had defeated Syria, under the reign of Ben-Hadad, and the cities that Syria had taken from Israel were to be returned (1 Kings 20:34). Ahab had not been responsible, and after three years of peace with Syria, the city of Ramoth-gilead had not been returned to Israel. Ahab asked Jehoshaphat, the king of Judah to join with him in a war against Syria to recover it. Given the previous success, it should have been a sure victory, and Jehoshaphat agreed to join Ahab (v.1-4). Hubris is one of the great causes of human failure.

Jehoshaphat did have one condition for joining Ahab in the war and that was to seek the counsel of a prophet of God (v.5). Ahab gathered false prophets who told him what he wanted to hear, but Jehoshaphat insisted on hearing from the Lord (v.6-12). Micaiah was summoned and was told by the messenger what to say, and so Micaiah at first told the king what he wanted to hear, but then under oath told the truth (v.13-18). Micaiah went on to tell of a troubling conversation in heaven. A fallen angel was allowed to tell Ahab what he wanted to hear so that his sin would lead to destruction (v.19-23). The worst situation in the world is when the Lord gives a person or nation over to their sin and to the lies of Satan.

Ahab thought, as many do, that he could outsmart God. He failed. Syria was victorious, as Micaiah prophesied, and Ahab was killed (v.24-40). Jehoshaphat was spared in the battle. He wisely returned home and sought the Lord, as his father Asa had (v.41-50). While Jehoshaphat honored God, Ahaziah, Ahab's son, ruled in Israel and he rejected God, as his father had (v. 51-54). Ahaziah asked Jehoshaphat to go into business with him, but Jehoshaphat refused (v. 49). Jehoshaphat learned from his mistake. Rather than partner with a proud king who refused to listen to God, he sought God and pursued the Lord's will for his life. His legacy was one of faithfulness.

It is easy to be like the kings of Israel and ignore God. It is easy to make the mistake of Jehoshaphat and to just go with the crowd. The wise choice is always to honor God. Are you being faithful to Jesus? Are you able to reject the offerings of godless people and remain faithful to God? Those who listen to and obey God live with hope.

2 Kings 1; 2 Thessalonians 1; Daniel 5; Psalms 110–111

Encouragement is a crucial aspect of the Christian life. Discouragement is all around us. This broken world is not our home. We are aliens and exiles under duress by the Devil and the world. Our flesh is corrupted and our feelings cannot be trusted. And yet in the midst of all of these difficulties, there is one great truth: the Lord is with us. As the body of Christ, we are to be an encouragement to one another. Our confidence in the midst of our pain is a witness to the world. Although we suffer, those who help others in the Lord live with hope.

The church at Thessalonica was a miracle. The Apostle Paul was grateful for them, and he often bragged about how Jesus had transformed them and was at work in them. In 2 Thessalonians 1, Paul encourages these new believers and challenges them in their faith. What Paul did for them with this first chapter of this letter is what all believers are to do for one another and all the more as the Day of the Lord approaches.

Paul encouraged the church with a blessing (v.1-2). This encouragement is for every local church blessed with a set of leaders that minister to them. Paul wrote to this church, and Silvanus and Timothy were with him. These three men were trusted leaders in their lives. This local family of faith was, as are all local churches, in God the Father and in Christ the Son. This blessed position was made possible by the Gospel. Those believers were now the beneficiaries of God's blessing of grace and peace. All the saints of God in Christ Jesus are given grace and peace. They are the standard gifts of salvation.

Paul encouraged the church with the awareness of the blessing they were to the churches of the world (v.3-4). In the midst of the battle, it is sometimes hard to know if our lives are of any use to God. Paul made it abundantly clear these saints were a source of strength to all of the believers Paul served. He spoke of their growing faith and love and explained how others had heard of their growth, despite the persecution they faced. Faith that is tested is made strong and provides inspiration to other believers who face difficult days.

Paul encouraged the church with the promise of the coming of Jesus and His justice (v.5-12). So often, God's people want justice in this broken world. There are times, when things go as they should, but often they don't. Often, God's people suffer for their faith. Jesus said in this world we would have trouble (John 16:33). Jesus comforts His disciples with the fact He was hated too and the reason the redeemed are hated is because they are one with Him (John 15:18). The good news is Jesus is coming back and the saints will be justified and justice will come to those who rejected the Lord.

It is easy to get overwhelmed by the way the world is going. God calls us to look past the difficulties we face and focus on Jesus and His grace and receive and give encouragement. Is your faith an encouragement to others? Can you trust Jesus in your suffering? In our pain we can help others and live with hope.

2 Kings 2; 2 Thessalonians 2; Daniel 6; Psalms 112–113

Just because God blesses us does not mean life will be easy. More is demanded of those who have received more from God. The people who are strong in themselves are actually weak. Those who feel weak and depend on God are strong. The strongest will often feel the weakest and will often be found in situations that are overwhelming. Those who learn to discipline their lives and look to God in faith will live with hope.

Daniel was a disciplined man. He learned at an early age to depend on God and obey Him, no matter the cost. There is no doubt he was gifted. The Lord was with him and provided supernatural abilities and favor, but Daniel did his part too. Daniel was a faithful man who refused to dishonor God. He lived a life of devotion and was known as a man of prayer. In Daniel 6, his faithfulness is seen and the power of prayer is revealed.

A disciple of Jesus must never forget that every blessing and trial is for God's glory and our good. We may never know on this side of heaven why we had it so good or so hard. There are divine reasons for everything. What the disciple of Jesus must do is live with thanks and do the work God has given with steadfast love and disciplined faith. Daniel was blessed with leadership abilities, which made him a threat to those who wanted power (v.1-4). Those who hated him knew the only way they could find fault with him would be in his faithfulness to God (v.5). God calls His people to be so faithful that even when the world hates us, they find it impossible to find fault with us, except for our hope in the exclusive claims of Christ (1 Peter 3:14-17).

The devil is strong but not very creative. He tends to depend on the same tricks. One of his favorites is to make the worship of God illegal in government systems. The satraps of Babylon wanted to usurp Daniel's authority and gain his seat of influence, so they duped the king into creating a governmental system that was hostile to Daniel's faith by making it illegal to pray to any except the king (v.6-9). Disciples of Jesus must always be good citizens of the nation God has placed them in, but they must always put Christ's Kingdom first.

Once the law was in place, Daniel went public with his prayer in defiance of the law. In great distress the king was forced to put him in a lions' den (v.10-18). In the pit of death, Daniel did what he had always done. He was steadfast in faith and prayer. When the king found Daniel safe the next morning, Daniel witnessed to him and shared how God had delivered him (v.19-23). The king had those who had sought Daniel's destruction to be placed with their families in the lions' den, and they were devoured (v.24). The king decreed favor on the faith of Daniel (v.25-27). God always works all things for good. In the end, all who are without Christ will be destroyed.

We are all responsible with what we have and the positions we possess. Are you disciplined in your faith? Do you honor God in all circumstances? Those who learn to trust God and live a life of devotion at all times will live with hope.

2 Kings 3; 2 Thessalonians 3; Daniel 7; <u>Psalms 114–115</u>

There is a desire in the heart of humanity, even in well-intentioned Christians, to want to be the hero of their story. There is only one true hero: Jesus. There are smaller triumphs by people worthy of noting and celebrating. In truth, many pay a terrible toll to serve others. In the end, all human rescues become history. God's work is eternal. It is repeated in every generation. Those who are rescued by God and make Him the hero of their story live with hope.

In Psalms 114–115, God is honored as the ultimate hero of the redeemed of God. He is mighty to save. He is the sovereign King of the universe. He is all-sufficient in Himself and needs nothing from creation to satisfy His eternal being. In the Godhead – the Father, the Son, and the Holy Spirit – there is complete love, life, happiness, and delight. In His grace, God saves sinners and fills them with His wonder. Psalm 114 speaks to the power of God to do this. Psalm 115 speaks of His glory in doing this.

God is bigger than anything any person will ever face. Everything is small to God. It is a big deal that God saved such small, sinful, unimportant people. Israel was no different than any other people group, except for His glory and purpose, God chose to rescue them and be their God. He rescued them out of Egypt (114:1-2). He led them through the Red Sea and the Jordan (114:3, 5). He violently revealed His law to Moses on Mount Sinai (v.114:4, 6). He provided miraculously for the people and gave them water in a dry land (114:7-8). God was the hero of Israel. He is the hero for all who trust in Him. He is bigger than our greatest enemies: sin and death. He has overcome. He is the victor!

God is glorious in His triumph over the darkness of the world. It was not because humanity deserved it, but because of His glory and steadfast love that the Lord intervened to rescue sinners (115:1). People in darkness create their own gods in their own image and according to their own liking (115:2-8). These so-called gods are idols and have no eternal power. They may satisfy the flesh or ego needs of a person for a while, but sooner or later, like all created things, they fail. The Lord never fails! He is the perfect hero (115:9-13). He is the blessing that is true and good in every generation (115:14-15). The heavens are His and the earth is humanity's. Humanity ruined the world so God became man to save it. He has brought new life, and all who turn to Him enter eternal life at death (115:16). Those who die in the Lord enter into glory, which honors God and delights the immortal soul of every saint (115:17-18).

Just as Israel did not deserve God's provision, so every person on this planet does not deserve salvation in Christ. God chose Israel for His honor and provided a new life for them. Christ has come to give new life to all who believe. It is a heroic act of grace by which God saves. Have you trusted Jesus Christ as your Savior? Is He the hero of your story? Do you delight to tell of His grace? Those who look to Jesus, as their hero, live with hope.

2 Kings 4; 1 Timothy 1; Daniel 8; Psalm 116

Faith in God is powerful because God is powerful. Faith is only as strong as its object. Whatever is believed, no matter how strong or consistent the belief may be, is only as potent as the power of the object of that belief. The power of God to save and secure sinners is in Jesus. There is no other name by which people can be saved. Those who have faith in the power of God live with hope.

In 2 Kings 4, the power of faith is seen in several dramatic events surrounding Elisha the prophet. All of the events reveal the power of God through the faith of people. God can do all things but often chooses to limit His actions to the faith revealed in the hearts of those who love Him. God's will is always done. The degree and joy in which it is done usually depends on the faith of His people.

God provides for His people who have faith in Him. A prophet had died, leaving his wife and sons in dire straits financially. In desperation this widow called on Elisha for help (v.1). Elisha asked what she wanted and what she had (v.2). God works through us. We do not need to be anyone else with anything else to accomplish God's purpose. She had a jar of oil. Elisha instructed her to go and borrow empty vessels from her friends (v.3). Believers are never meant to be in isolation. The Lord blesses through His people. She got the vessels and was able supernaturally to fill them all with the oil from the jar (v.3-6). She went and sold the oil to provide for her needs (v.7). Her blessing came by faith through her willingness to act on what she was told. Faith is always lived out in obedience.

God provides for His people, even in ways we do not ask. A wealthy, childless woman and her husband showed kindness to Elisha (v.8-10). Generosity is an act of faith. God gave this woman a son (v.11-17). God knows the desires of our hearts, and when we desire to honor Him, it positions us to be blessed. For a purpose hidden in God, this son died (v.18-28). We can never know for certain God's ultimate plans. Miraculously, the boy was brought back to life (v.29-37). This is a picture of the Gospel. The son came and died but was raised to bring God's blessing.

God provides for the brokenness of the world. There was a famine. A group of prophets were accidently poisoned because one added a wild vine to their stew, but God provided healing (v.38-41). Humanity has been poisoned with sin, but God can heal and restore. In our world, there are limited resources. Elisha was provided food, but there was not enough for the hundred other men. God blessed and there was more than enough (v.42-44). What may seem like too little is always enough in the hands of God.

God has a plan and He does what He pleases. Graciously, God has given us His Son and His Spirit to provide salvation and blessings. It takes faith to be saved and faith to trust God to provide the blessings we need. This is God's will. Do you trust God to provide? Are you living a life God can bless? Those who live by faith in God live with hope.

2 Kings 5; 1 Timothy 2; Daniel 9; Psalms 117–118

There is a special bond and privilege that exists between a mentor and a student. Jesus Christ is the example all Christians are to follow. Jesus did not serve God in   isolation. He poured His knowledge and life into others who would take the baton of truth He gave and pass it on to others. Those who participate in this activity, both as mentor and student, are blessed. The relationships, instruction that is passed down, and personal development that takes place is powerful. Those who mentor and are mentored in Jesus live with hope.

The Apostle Paul was Timothy's mentor. As Paul continued forward in his calling in Christ, he trained men like Timothy to develop the churches he planted and the people he loved. After being released from his first Roman imprisonment (AD 60-62) and engaging in his fourth missionary journey not recorded in Scripture, Paul wrote to his young apprentice to equip, to challenge, and to encourage him in his calling, as a young pastor in Ephesus. In 1 Timothy 2, Paul provided general instructions to Timothy. These instructions apply to all disciples of Jesus in all churches in every generation.

The church is to be a people of prayer who represent their Lord Jesus Christ (v.1-8). God's people are to be known as a praying people. Their prayers are to be for one another and the government leaders they live under. The goal of their prayer is a blessed life that allows the church to live in peace. The outcomes of their prayer are Jesus to be honored and people to be saved. It is God's will to save sinners. Paul was called to preach this Good News and Timothy, his apprentice, was called to do the same and strengthen God's people. By exalting Jesus through prayer in holiness, God's people bless those inside and outside the church.

Disciples of Jesus are to live unique lives that fulfill God's design for human flourishing (v.9-15). God has made men and women with a unique design. While men are to take responsibility for their families and provide sacrificial service to their local church, women are to help by serving their families and their church. This help is seen through women's modesty. Rather than drawing attention to their feminine beauty, women are to draw attention to God's grace, through good deeds, and to support the men who teach and lead their family and their church. By happily helping and allowing God's design in creation to be exhibited in their behavior, the women, their families, and their communities are blessed. Those who are blessed to have children and care for them are given a ministry that fulfills God's design for them and enables them to bless the next generation.

The life of a disciple of Jesus is meant to be simple. The world is a complicated place. In their desire to satisfy their flesh and allow for others to do as they please, humanity corrupts God's purpose and rejects God's original design for the sexes, families, and society. Disciples of Jesus are to be a countercultural movement that fulfills God's will. Are you a person of prayer at peace in Jesus? Are you living out your role as a man or woman of God? Those who live for Christ and help others to be Jesus' disciples live with hope.

2 Kings 6; 1 Timothy 3; Daniel 10; Psalm 119:1-24

Every person on the planet has both a general and a specific purpose. Only God knows the particular details of each person's life. Not all walk with God or know and love Him, but God loves every person. The redeemed have a unique redemptive love and purpose. Some of the redeemed are called to carry burdens others don't. Those who trust in God's triumphant plan serve Him in peace. It is in serving Christ in all things and at all times a saint finds hope.

Daniel never made it back to Jerusalem. At about the age of fifteen, he came to live in Babylon and he never left. He was in his eighties when he received the vision of Daniel 10. By then he was entrenched in his place in the life of the foreign nation he served and in the life of the people of his Holy God. His citizenship was in heaven and his priority was always the Lord. He was burdened. The Lord called him to serve others by seeing the ultimate plan of God in all things.

No matter what circumstance a person may be in, there will always be challenges that vex the heart and soul. Daniel was a man many would assume was happy. He had served God and experienced great miracles. He was honored by the king and respected by his people. God loved him and entrusted to him a service that would be remembered for eternity, and yet he stood on the bank of the Tigris, having been in mourning for three weeks (v.1-4). The wise mourn and are blessed. Their hope is in heaven and they mourn until they enter that celestial rest.

Daniel was given a grand vision (v.5-12). The experience brought him to his knees and left him trembling. The messenger assured him of his favored position in the heart of God. The messenger also explained the reality of the spiritual battle that is always raging until Christ returns (v.13). God was going to let Daniel know the rest of the story (v.14). Daniel knew God's promises, but did not know how everything would be handled. Again, Daniel was overwhelmed and no strength was left in his body. He had to be touched and supernaturally strengthened (v.15-19). The work of spiritual warfare seems easy: praying, listening, and believing. These don't seem to take effort like digging a ditch, but they are the hardest things a human can do.

Having been strengthened, Daniel was prepared to receive the prophecy. The messenger explained what was about to happen and what the next step in Israel's future would be. Babylon would be overcome and the Greeks would come next (v.20). The archangel Michael would be contending with the demons of both to protect the people of Israel. As the plan of God unfolds through the pages of time, there are spiritual forces at work. God is sovereign and the victory is sure, but God's people must pray and fight with faith, knowing that angels are all around engaged in a celestial battle.

It is easy to get wrapped up in earthly things and miss the eternal realities unfolding around us. Are you seeking God? Do you long for heaven? Are you gladly serving God in your particular circumstance with your unique life? Those who look to God and serve Him live with hope.

2 Kings 7; 1 Timothy 4; Daniel 11; <u>Psalm 119:25-48</u>

What we put in our heads stirs our hearts. Those thoughts and feelings drive our actions. Wise people feed their minds on what is true, honorable, pure, and commendable (Philippians 4:8). Those who think on such things are able to guard their hearts from evil and misguided affections, which helps keep them from foolish and unrighteous actions (Proverbs 4:23). Those who fill their minds with truth inspire their emotions to do what is best, which gives them hope.

In Psalm 119:25-48, the Psalmist pleads with God to encourage and inspire him with truth. His desire is to honor God and enjoy the blessings that come with a life that has hope. It is clear he understood the reality of God and the problem of sin. Knowing he was a sinner in a fallen world, he did what a wise person does: he looked to God for hope.

Hope is often found in the lowest places. This person was emotionally distressed. In the ancient near east people would often cover themselves in dust as a sign of being sad and distraught. Heartache comes to everyone. Those who enjoy deep relationships will suffer sadness. Those without deep relationships suffer from loneliness. Feeling low is a common ailment of humanity. A broken or empty heart often feels lifeless and without strength. In his troubled time this writer looked to God for life and vitality through God's Word.

Hope is found in the Word of God. This person was spiritually competent. Rather than looking to something, someone, or some experience to deal with his symptoms, he went to God to find a cure for the core issue he was facing. Life does not make sense without God. Without God's Word we cannot understand God. This writer was looking in the right place to find and receive the anecdote for what ailed him. God's Word is a light that reveals what we cannot perceive. Knowing there are answers and seeking them gives hope.

Hope is found in obedience to God. This person was aware of his natural inclination to sin. Sin makes suckers of us all. It lies and deceives and then destroys and dishonors. The writer wanted to avoid feeling ashamed. He wanted to avoid the misery of selfish gain. He wanted to do what was best. Doing what is bad is easy. Doing what is good is not hard. Doing what is best requires inspiration and a strong belief in the promises of God. The Psalmist wanted to do what God demands. He wanted what is best.

Hope is found in righteous affections. This person understood the power of feelings. His were low, but he knew they could be lifted up if he could find inspiration in ultimate truth. His desire was to know God and to live his life in light of God's promises. Thinking rightly leads to feeling rightly, which leads to living rightly. This writer wanted the blessing of God, and he went looking in the right place.

None of us can escape the emotional brokenness that comes from living in our fallen world. Through Christ and the gift of the Spirit, we can be saved. We can be made right with God and walk with Him in the light of His Word. Do you turn to God's Word or worldly things to find hope in difficult times? Those who believe the Bible and are inspired by the Spirit have hope.

2 Kings 8; 1 Timothy 5; Daniel 12; Psalm 119:49-72

Is God really at work in the world accomplishing a purpose that brings praise to His name and peace in His people? Can Christians trust God to provide for their seemingly insignificant lives for His glory and their good? Is there really hope in a world filled with so much sadness and suffering? These are the questions people of faith must answer. Like Daniel's friends, we all enter the fire in life at different times and in different ways. Disciples of Jesus never endure the fire alone. God is with us. Those who trust God in all circumstances live with hope.

The world is broken but not hopeless. In 2 Kings 8, the sad, sobering reality of what sin has done and is doing in the world is seen, but so is God's righteousness and sovereign care. People of faith cannot always control the catastrophes of life that befall them, but God has spoken a word of hope to His people. Jesus said in John 16:33, "I have said these things to you, that in me you may have peace. In the world you will have tribulation. But take heart; I have overcome the world." There will often be times of trouble in life, but the children of God can rest in the loving care of the Father. People of faith can ask the hard questions and rest in God's promises.

People of faith can ask: "Is God sovereign over and in the natural catastrophes of the world?" Elisha was aware of a coming famine and instructed the widow, whose son he had raised, to leave the land (v.1-3). God was not caught by surprise and provided for this woman and her family. When she returned, she sought the king to recover ownership of her land. The king happened to be inquiring about the miracle of her son being raised from the dead when she approached him, and the king restored her land back to her (v.4-6). This was providential.

People of faith can ask, "Is God sovereign, even in war and injustice?" Having been approached by the servant of the king of Syria, Elisha wept. He saw the coming disaster that would come through this man who would soon be king of Syria (v.7-15). God has the power to know and reveal to His servants the future. God allows sin to reign in the world now. He is not distant, though. He knows our tears (Psalm 56:1). His Son was mercilessly tortured and killed. He knows our pain and cares for His people.

People of faith can ask, "Is God sovereign over the nations?" Kings came and went. Their decisions had an indelible impact on the people they ruled. The rejection of God by the kings led to sin in the nations (v.16-29). Even though those nations turned against God and faced the consequences for the sin, God still had faithful people in their midst. The faithful suffered too, but God's promise to David never diminished (v.19). No matter how sinful societies become, God's will is done.

It can often seem the world is out of control. While natural catastrophes and sin may be rampant, God is still in control. Do you trust the power and goodness of God? Do you know the promises of God and count on them? Those who know God and trust in Him in all times through all things live with hope.

2 Kings 9; 1 Timothy 6; Hosea 1; Psalm 119:73-96

The only right response of redeemed saints as to who God is and what God has done in their lives, through Jesus Christ and the Holy Spirit, is humility. There is no place for pride in a child of God. We were all once orphans lost in a world of sin, but God loved us and gave us new life. Those who live humbly in the grace of God live with hope.

In 1 Timothy 6, Paul provided his concluding remarks to his apprentice, Timothy. These were words of instruction that Timothy was to pass on to the people he was pastoring. These practical insights not only give God's people a vision for how they should live, but are defining marks that all pastors, like Timothy, need to develop in their people. These qualities will come through a life that is humbled by grace and has sought them through discipline.

Humble saints will always be the best kinds of workers (v.1-2). A Christian should always be an employer's first choice. They are to be the kind of people who are honest and do what they are asked without complaining. They are to be the kind of people who give proper respect to those over them. They are to be thoughtful and never seek to take advantage of others.

Humble saints will always be content to give attention to God and seek to benefit others with His truth rather than gain popularity, power, or possessions for themselves (v.3-10). The world tells us we need others to think highly of our appearance, performance, and ideas. The world also tells us we need an excess of temporal things. God's Word tells us we need more of Christ and His Word in us so we can rightly share it with others. Getting involved in nonessential arguments to show off our intellect or pursuing gain at the cost of our spiritual life is foolish. God calls His people to a humble life of contentment and to find joy in serving others.

Humble saints will pursue what is best and resolutely reject the ease of a godless and empty life (v.11-21). It is easy to go with the crowd. It is easy to follow the wide path that leads to destruction. It is hard to maintain fidelity to Jesus. It is hard to fight against the flesh and the value system of the world and hold to the commands of Christ. No one becomes Godly without intentionality. The discipline required for Godliness comes from a humble heart that acknowledges the greatness of God and the personal need that exists within every human heart to pursue what cannot be earned in the grace of Jesus. It is by grace that a saint is made a saint. It is by grace a saint becomes a stronger saint. Grace humbles. In a state of surrender, children of God are free to pursue the treasure of heaven with the promises of God and find hope for their souls.

The world calls people to a proud life lived under the delusion they are powerful and in control. Jesus frees people to see their life as it is and to see God as He is. Jesus provides a blessed life that comes through humble intentionality. Are you keeping your focus on Jesus? Are you humbled by His grace? Are you pursuing His life in you? Humble saints live with holy hope.

2 Kings 10–11; 2 Timothy 1; Hosea 2; Psalm 119:97-120

The love of God is an inextinguishable fire that can warm the coldest of hearts and bring light into the deepest darkness. The fire of God's love is bright and is meant to woo strangers into the security of Jesus and the communion of the saints. God's love is powerful. Those who accept it will never be separated from it. There is nothing on earth or in the spiritual realm that can overcome God's love (Romans 8:38-39). Those who receive God's love and love Him in return live with eternal hope.

God's love is steadfast, but the hearts of humanity are fickle. Like Israel, God's children are blessed, but not all remain loyal to Him. Some are like the wife of Hosea. Hosea was the last prophet to proclaim truth to the northern tribes before Assyria crushed them. His ministry was not only of words, but was also an enactment of God's love. He married a prostitute and had children: a son, Jezreel, which means "God sows"; a daughter, "No Mercy"; and a son, "Not My People." The heart-wrenching story of this man is the story of God. In Hosea 2, the call of God goes out and the character of His love is seen.

Israel was unfaithful to God. She did not honor Him as her husband, although the Lord had blessed her with every good gift from heaven (v.1-13). Israel, like some saints, wanted the best of both worlds. She wanted to be able to live in sin and dishonor God while receiving the benefits of God. Israel's relationship and the relationship of the church with Christ (Ephesians 5) are both presented as a marriage. God's benefits come to those who are faithful to God.

God is faithful and He promised to call Israel back to faithfulness (v.14-20). This faithful life would be one of intense blessing. This life would be based upon a new covenant. There will be blessings of provision. The people will call upon the Lord and honor Him. In return, He will bless them, and there will be a harvest and great peace. The people will be made right with God and they will live happily ever after. The prophets, looking forward, did not always provide a progression or timeline. Hosea looked forward and saw past the cross and the days of the New Testament church to the consummation of Christ.

The prophet could see the benefit of the cross and resurrection of Christ (v.21-23). He could see the people would call out to God and that God would give grace. Under the New Covenant, the people will gain a new identity and experience a new reality. "No Mercy" will receive mercy. "Not My People" will become God's people. The Lord promised to plant a new seed that produces an eternal harvest of new life by His grace and mercy. In this new life, the people of God will live under the protective care of the Almighty in eternal love.

God's love is unlike anything else in the world. It does not fail. It is everlasting. Those who choose to pursue the loves of the world will be disappointed. God is willing to take back the unfaithful and ungrateful. Have you returned to God? Do you trust in Christ for salvation? Is God's love the driving force behind your decisions? Those who are loved by God and love God in return live with hope.

2 Kings 12; 2 Timothy 2; Hosea 3–4; <u>Psalm 119:121-144</u>

The Gospel changes the identity and experience of every person who believes. While the world does not change and will not change until the Lord Jesus returns, the redeemed of God can live hopeful in the world. The redeemed of God see the world through a different lens. Pain, happiness, sickness, health, wealth, and poverty are viewed through the filter of God's sovereign care. Those who know the truth of God's Word can see what is happening in the world and still live with hope.

Psalm 119 is a song of praise to God for the greatness of His Word. In verses 121-144, the writer laments the circumstances of the world and looks to God for help and hope. The ideal situation for any saint is to be in a place where God can be freely worshipped and the good deeds of the righteous can be rewarded. This is not always the case. When the world is not fond of the faithful, the faithful must learn to rest in God's grace and stand on His Word.

The Psalmist saw himself as having lived a righteous life and was looking to God for the benefits of his good deeds (v.121). Instead, it appears those who were not loyal to God were oppressing this saint (v.122). The writer asked for divine intervention (v.123). He knew the promises of God found in the Word of God. He was looking for redemption. Ultimate redemption will come at Christ's return. Until then, the saints of God will often struggle as the Savior did. We will, like Jesus, pray for vindication and for the cup of suffering to be removed, but God will call on us to endure with hope.

That hope is possible because of the steadfast love of God (v.124). Those who know the standards of God will always benefit from the peace that comes with standing in a right relationship with God. It is in living the commands of God and not just knowing them that understanding and faith grows (v.125-128). Those who walk with God hate what is false and can look to the hand of God to act on their behalf. Sometimes God changes the world, but He usually uses the world to change the saint.

The transformation God is causing in His people comes through His Word (v.129-131). Those who experience the blessing of right living rejoice in the understanding of, the illumination with, and the desire for truth. Those who know the Word can count on God to make their steps steady, make their hearts tender, make their faith zealous, and make their understanding sure (v.132-144). Like Jesus, His disciples will have to walk a difficult road. Along the way, they will find God is faithful. In the end, the promises of God will all be fulfilled. Until then, the Gospel will be the fuel, the Word will be the guide, and heaven will be the hope.

Never allow self-pity to take hold. Everyone suffers to some extent. The saints of God suffer for a purpose. In this real world with real challenges, disappointments, and enemies there is a real hope that flourishes in Christ. Do you hope in Christ? Is God's Word making your faith strong? Is your eye on the ultimate prize or have you limited your goals to this life? The Word of God enables us to live with hope.

2 Kings 13; 2 Timothy 3; Hosea 5–6; Psalm 119:145-176

God works in both mysterious and straightforward ways. Living in a fallen world with a limited knowledge of reality, even the Godliest of saints will sometimes struggle to understand God's purposes. The Lord sometimes will only give enough light for the next step. That's where faith comes in. There are secret things that only God can know, and there are revealed things that all can know. "The secret things belong to the Lord our God, but the things that are revealed belong to us and to our children forever, that we may do all the words of this law" (Deuteronomy 29:29). Those who can trust God with the secret things and obey God in the revealed things live with hope.

During the days of the kings, both Israel and Judah struggled to remain faithful to God. It was not for lack of knowledge. They had been given the Word of God and they knew the will of God, but they did not have faith in Him or a love for Him that empowered them to obey Him, and so they suffered. Even in their sin, God was gracious and provided in miraculous ways. In 2 Kings 13, there are examples of both the natural ways of God that are easily understood and the miraculous ways of God that are hard to comprehend.

God called the people of Israel to obedience, but their kings typically led the people away from God. This was true of Jehoahaz and Jehoash (v.1-13). The formula is easy enough to figure out. Those who are faithful to God enjoy God's divine blessing. Those who turn away from God do not enjoy the provision of God. All of God's children struggle with sin. Those who struggle against sin find God faithful to be strong in their weakness. Those who choose to go their own way and pursue sin find God to be just and they are easily overcome and defeated in their weakness. While the faithful find God to be more than sufficient for their soul's needs, the faithless never have peace.

When the defiant children of God repent, God is faithful and just to forgive them. When Jehoahaz sought the favor of the Lord, he was sustained (v.4-5). The consequences of his sin were not completely removed, but divine provision was made. One blessing was that his son saw that act of faith. As king of Israel, Joash or Jehoash, sought out Elisha (v.14-19). Elisha was dying but was able to give the king hope. The king's faith was small and because of his limited faith, he received a limited blessing. God's blessing is often in proportion to our faith. This part of God's purpose is mysterious.

How God blesses in grace with His power is also mysterious. After Elisha died and was buried, another person was buried in his cave and when the dead body touched Elisha's bones, the dead man was raised (v.20-21). This is the mysterious power of God. God has the power to raise the dead. His covenant of grace stands (v.22-25). The Gospel power of God is at work, mysteriously.

Who and how God blesses is both mysterious and practical. Are you living a life God can bless? Is the mysterious power of God at work in your life? Those who obey what is known often experience the mysterious blessings of God and live with hope.

2 Kings 14; 2 Timothy 4; Hosea 7; Psalms 120–122

Godly leaders and those they lead have a unique relationship that is like a dance. Both have to be active. One has to guide and the other must follow. Both provide support and flow in the movement. A blessed congregation is one that has humble Spirit-guided leadership and willing Spirit-powered followers. Those who dance to the divine beat of God live with authentic hope.

Writing to Timothy, Paul instructed the young man in his responsibilities, as a pastor and also in the dangers of his work. Leadership can be a blessing or a curse, but it is always hard. Those who lead must be on the lookout for themselves and those they are responsible for. Those who follow must be wise to engage in the ministry of God and encourage and work with their leaders. In 2 Timothy 4, Paul outlines steps to take to remain faithful as a leader, what to look for in followers, and what Christian leadership development is to look like.

There are all kinds of missteps that a pastor can make in the dance of leadership. Laziness and unpreparedness are mistakes many make (v.1-2). Fear of being rejected and unappreciated will cause a pastor to get out of sync with the beat of Jesus (v.3-6). Unwillingness to suffer for the sake of the call in the same way Jesus did will make a pastor lose his place in the routine of the dance and move in the wrong direction (v.7-8). It is only by faith and discipline that pastors can remain faithful to their calling and be able to finish the dance God has designed. Internal and external pressures will provide temptation. Leaders must remain loyal to God.

There are all kinds of missteps a congregation can make in the dance of leadership. Creating personal expectations of care by the pastor that make appropriate time for study, prayer, and rest impossible keeps many teachers of the Word incapable of being prepared to rightly handle the Word of truth (v.1-2). Desiring and expecting a preacher to say what they want to hear rather than what is true gets everyone off balance (v.3-6). Failing to encourage and appreciate leadership creates disconnections between followers and their leaders (v.7-8). Each member must be mindful of their responsibility to stay in rhythm with their leadership.

There are all kinds of missteps that can happen in pastoral and congregational development in the dance of leadership. Every leader needs to be developed and have someone that is guiding them, as Timothy had Paul. And every leader needs to be developing leaders, as Paul did with Timothy. And every leader needs other leaders that come alongside and help in the work and decision making of ministry (v.9-22). There will be wolves that seek to cause harm. There will be challenging circumstances in culture. There will be hard choices that must be made. Leaders need other leaders to master the leadership dance, and congregations need to encourage this training and provide for it.

Each person in God's Kingdom has a purpose. Leaders and congregants must work together to accomplish God's will. It is a dance. How are you doing in your role? Is the church being blessed by you or are you causing problems? Those who help the leadership dance to go well live with hope.

2 Kings 15; Titus 1; Hosea 8; Psalms 123–125

God gives His people what they need. Sadly, God's people often need discipline. Humanity is easily deceived. Generation after generation falls into the same traps by seeking money, sex, power, and popularity to get satisfaction. Temporary things never satisfy the soul. They will often please sinful flesh, but only for a while. The sin of the flesh will sooner or later return void. In His grace, God calls His people back to sanity through discipline. Those who can see God's gift of hardship will live with hope.

Hosea prophesied to a people with great physical prosperity who were spiritually sick. God loved these people. They were part of His eternal plan, but they rejected Him. Rather than honor Him as God, they chose to honor themselves and create gods more to their liking and control. With their free time, they engaged in sloth and sexual misconduct. With their extra money, they made idols and worshiped things that had no power. With their power, they took advantage of others. In love and for His glory, God warned, instructed, and disciplined them. He did this to call them back to faithfulness.

In His love, God warned the people (v.1-3). The horn was to be blown in Israel when there was a call to a special occasion, to war, or to a warning. God warned the people that they were in trouble. The vulture of Assyria was coming for them. Although Israel would claim God, they had not and would not honor God. To reject God is to be removed from His provision and protection. The Lord of love is willing to redeem those who repent and return to Him. Those who reject Him have no hope.

In His wisdom God taught the people (v.4-10). Rather than seeking God and discerning His will in choosing leaders, the people went their own way. Their leaders did not know God. The people became corrupt. They were led far from God. The physical realities were to be instructional. When the natural blessings of fruitfulness and the cultural blessings of morality are lost, it is meant to make people aware of their need for God. Those who heed the voice of God find hope.

In His justice God judged the people (v.11-14). Once sin has taken root and the heart becomes hard, sin multiples. People ceased to be able to hear from God. They were blind even to the facts of general revelation. Although religious participation and activity remained, there was no power in it. When worship is done out of habit and without honor to God, it causes more harm than good. Hypocrisy has a double curse. It numbs the soul and angers God. Hard-hearted humans who have no awe or appreciation for God build homes for themselves and altars for their ambitions. Being limited in mental, physical, and emotional capacity, people cannot maintain their lives and over time lose all hope.

God is a loving, wise, and just God. His desire is to redeem. His will is to bring His Kingdom in heaven to earth through His saints. His people must first be faithful to Christ before God can bless them or their world. Are you listening to God? Do you trust in Jesus? God is at work in the world and those who heed Him live with hope.

2 Kings 16; Titus 2; Hosea 9; Psalms 126–128

When God is gracious to a person, whether it is on the day of their salvation or in a season of spiritual renewal, there are blessings and opportunities that come with that grace. The purpose of God is His glory. Those who receive God's grace are provided the good things of God for His glory. Those who pursue the promises of God and reap the benefits of His grace are to glorify God. Those who glorify God live with hope.

Salvation is a restoration. Those who are brought to life by the Spirit and saved by grace through faith in Christ alone are restored in a right relationship with God. What sin robs, grace restores. In Psalms 126–128, the good things of life that come to those who are restored to God are listed. This section of praise in the psalter speaks to how the Gospel of God changes the lives of the redeemed, how God provides for His people, and how God works in and through His saints.

When God restores a life in any measure, there is a change that begins in the heart (126:1-2a). It can seem surreal, almost like a dream. There is a gladness of heart that produces thoughts and feelings that become vocalized in praise. This praise impacts the rest of the world that is still in darkness (126:2b). In response to the amazement of those lost in sin, the redeemed testify to the salvation of God (126:3). It is the responsibility of every saint to tell the world lost in sin what the Lord has done for them. Every disciple of Jesus can speak of the harvest of hope that has come to their life because they mourned over their sin and repented (126:4-6). It is with aching hearts that souls are revived and lives are changed.

Lives that are changed by God's grace are brought under the leadership and protective care of Jesus (127:1-2). The Gospel of John is filled with the promises of the Lord concerning how He will keep His people and how the Helper, the Holy Spirit, will guide His disciples into all truth. A child of God can do nothing without God's strength. Work in the flesh is always in vain. Those who serve in the strength God gives are blessed to see a next generation rise up behind them to live in hope (127:3-5). As a home filled with children is a blessing, so is a life filled with saints who have come to saving faith through disciple-making efforts.

When God is at work in His people's lives producing hope in their hearts, there is an appropriate fear and devotion to Christ (128:1-2). Aware that every good gift comes from God, disciples of Jesus work hard knowing it is the Lord who is working in and through them and producing the blessed outcome. A happy family is a picture of the blessings the redeemed get to enjoy on this side of heaven (128:3-4). The prosperity of God is a life filled with love in Christ, in family, and in the communion of the saints (128:5-6).

It is all to the praise and glory of God who gives these gifts through grace. Do you delight to praise God? Do those far from God see God's grace in your life? Are you making disciples? Living out God's purpose gives hope to the hearts of the faithful.

2 Kings 17; Titus 3; Hosea 10; Psalms 129–131

One of the most rewarding and at the same time most difficult tasks in the world is being a parent. God is the ultimate Father. He does no wrong. He makes no mistakes, and yet, He has wayward children. One of the most challenging aspects of being a parent is to have to watch children make bad decisions and suffer the consequences for their decisions. His love overcomes sin, and the best thing a person can do is to obey the Father. Those who rest in God's love and submit to His gracious care live with hope.

God loved the children of Israel, but they refused to honor Him as God. In 2 Kings 17, the children of Israel were scattered into exile into Assyria. This was not the desire of God. The Lord longs to have His children under His protective care. God's children must make their own choices and will receive the benefits or the punishment their actions demand. When God's children are disobedient, bad things happen in their lives and in the world.

When God's children live in disobedience, the Lord's umbrella of protection is removed (v.1-5). Those who refuse to trust in God must trust in themselves, which is trust in what is fallible, weak, and sinful. Human beings are made by God to live by faith in Him. If people will not live by faith in Jesus, they must live by faith in created things. Israel thought they were capable of outsmarting God, Assyria, and Egypt. They failed. The truth always comes out. Without God's protective care, people will sooner or later get caught in their sin and pay the penalty.

When God's children live in disobedience, their sin carries them away from the Father and His rest (v.6). People are always in a state of spiritual motion. Either we are getting closer to God, or we are growing further away from Him. Those who choose to live in sin are driven by their sin further and further away from God and His rest. Israel had been given rest by God in the Promised Land. Their sin caused them to forfeit that gift and forced them into exile. This is what sin does. It drives people away from God's rest.

When God's children live in disobedience, those near and far from God are influenced toward darkness (v.7-41). Our sin never just impacts us. It always has an effect on those we know. Israel influenced Judah, the Southern Kingdom, to turn from God. God's children must help wayward siblings and lost people without falling into their sin. Judah should have known better, but the nations could not have known the truth. While claiming to worship the true God and pursuing sinful lifestyles, the Israelites created confusion among the nations. These nations had their own gods and sinful ways of life. By not being the light, Israel caused the nations to remain in darkness.

Sin not only grieves the heart of God, who is willing to care for the faithful, it also leads to serious consequences. The longer a person lives in sin, the harder their heart gets toward God. In the process, they encourage the children of the light and people of darkness to pursue darkness. Are you a faithful child of God? Are you helping or hurting God's cause? Those who live under the authority of the Father live with hope.

2 Kings 18; Philemon; Hosea 11; Psalms 132–134

Disciples of Jesus are called to forgive. There is no place for grudges in the hearts of God's people. The Lord has forgiven us of all of our sin. Our sin against Him was eternal in valuation, and our pardon cost the life of Jesus. The forgiveness Jesus has given to us is the forgiveness He commands that we give to others. Jesus said there is a great blessing in being peacemakers. They shall be called the children of God (Matthew 5:9). Those who receive forgiveness in Christ and make peace with others live with hope.

The story of conflict found in Philemon is a familiar tale. One man sinned against another, causing a rift in their relationship. This story takes a providential turn when Onesimus, the one who caused the conflict, meets the Apostle Paul and is saved. Having come to saving faith, it became necessary that Onesimus return to make peace with Philemon. The book of Philemon is Paul's letter concerning the peace that was needed between these men. Paul, serving as a peacemaker, worked to see these men restored, as brothers in Christ.

There is a grace and power that exists within the redeemed of God to make peace (v.1-7). Philemon was a blessing. Paul was not writing to a wayward believer who was unwilling to serve the cause of Christ. He was writing to a believer who inspired joy because of his faithful service. Those who walk in the power of the Spirit have a supernatural ability and responsibility to offer love, forgiveness, and compassion. Onesimus, needing to be reconciled to Philemon, was blessed because he was going back to a man of peace to make peace. Disciples of Jesus, having been given the heart of Christ, have the ability and responsibility to give and receive grace that those outside of Christ cannot give.

Peacemaking is a necessity and a priority for those in Christ (v.8-22). Paul could have commanded Philemon to receive Onesimus, but instead, he chose to point out why he should do this in Christ. It is always best to obey out of love of Christ rather than begrudgingly to please people. Paul made a very strong case for why Philemon should give mercy and welcome Onesimus back with love and not hold anything against him. The motivation that Paul spoke to is the same motivation for all believers today. We have every reason to forgive others and to live as siblings in our Savior, bringing glory to God, as we love one another.

Those who serve well and seek peace belong to a select group of saints (v.23-25). In his greeting, Paul recognizes Philemon, as a worker. In his closing, Paul recognizes another group of leaders, as workers. Those who serve the cause of Christ are provided a unique and privileged role in the Kingdom of God. Paul reminded Philemon of the other workers who were suffering for Christ. Paul's challenge to Philemon was to be the man of faith God had called him to be and that the Kingdom of God needed him to be. This is a call to all of God's people.

Peacemaking is rarely easy. Those who have experienced the Gospel have a unique capacity and responsibility to forgive and live in restored relationships. Are you a peacemaker? Do you need to seek or give forgiveness? Those who make peace live with hope.

2 Kings 19; Hebrews 1; Hosea 12; Psalms 135–136

Fear can be a dangerous thing or a blessing. Fear can drive people to do the worst things. Fear can also lead people to act in the most benevolent and beneficial ways. God gave fear as a gift. Sin takes all of God's gifts and turns them into curses. The way to be blessed by God's gifts is to use them in the way God intended. God intended fear to drive us to Jesus. Those who fear the Lord and pursue Him in all situations live with hope.

The people of God, during the time of the kings, did not fare well. They did not fear God. In Hosea 12, God explained why Ephraim (the Northern Kingdom, Israel) and Judah (the Southern Kingdom) would be disciplined by God. Both were given gifts from God, but neither honored Him. Both sought to find hope in things that cannot give eternal hope. They were stuck with a limited hope and the limits of their idols and political maneuvering were about to run out. God still extended grace, but to receive it, they would have to repent and trust Him.

Ephraim pursued a life without God and paid for it (v.1). Rather than consuming the good things God offered, they ate what was empty. They chased what could not be caught. They trusted in earthly powers and made a deal with Egypt. Rather than fearing the loss of the things of God, they feared missing out on the things of earth. What they needed and wanted was found in God, but those things can only be received by faith. They chose to live by their flesh. This is the constant temptation that must be overcome by fearing the loss of God's blessings. Look to the promises of God!

The outcome of fleshly pursuits is pride. Ephraim was proud (v.8). They thought they had fooled not only the world, but God. Their practices were oppressive, and they thought they could get away with injustice (v.7). God made it clear they would suffer for their sin (v.9). This chosen race was given the gifts of God, but they chose not to honor Him, trust Him, fear Him, or glorify Him (v.10-14). Rather than receive grace, Ephraim received justice. Those who fear God and live by faith receive grace. Those who fear man and live in the flesh receive justice. Fear living and dying without grace!

While Judah had some faith, they also failed to fear God (v.2-6). This was a people who were sinful from birth, and yet God loved them. In His grace, God met with them and called them to live by faith in His promises. Although they had failed God and chose to live in fear of the loss of earthly things, there was still opportunity to repent. Like believers today who struggle to trust God and overcome their fears by faith in Jesus, Judah was called to repent and rely on God (v.6). Rely on God and fear Him only!

Fear can either turn us toward God or away from God. God's will is that we turn to Him in faith and enjoy His gracious favor in Jesus. Jesus alone can save us and soothe our souls in this broken world. Do you fear the loss of God more than the loss of earthly things? Do you trust Christ alone? Those who trust in Jesus live with hope.

2 Kings 20; Hebrews 2; Hosea 13; <u>Psalms 137–138</u>

Despite the destructiveness and evil of this fallen world, the children of God have reason to live with hope. The Lord is never far from His people. Even in the worst of times, God is there to give care. In the battle between the forces of darkness and the Almighty God of light, there are many levels of devastation. Things as small and petty as personal grievances, and things as huge and inhumane as the smashing of infants against rocks are spiritual war realities pouring out into the physical world. Those who hope in Christ can endure devastation and comfort and live with hope.

Psalms 137–138 come from different perspectives. Psalm 137 looks at life from a defeated perspective, while Psalm 138 looks at life from a victorious perspective. Psalm 137 is a communal lament. The Psalmist is looking back to the terrible events of the Babylonian exile and offering up an imprecatory prayer, a curse. In times of great suffering and inhumane activity, the request for divine wrath is often sought.

In times of victory, as in Psalm 128, there is reason to rejoice. Closeness to God and comfort in His calling leads to jubilation and the desire to pursue God's purpose. The Psalmist rejoices in the providence of God and prays for the privilege of accomplishing God's divine destiny for His life.

It is wise to never a judge a person's prayers or emotional state. Behind every evil thought, foul word, and enraged spirit is a story. The stories of those who went through the Babylonian exile were horrific (Psalm 137). Their faith was taunted (v.1-3). The captors wanted to hear the songs of the saints, but they hung up their instruments and refused. Their faith was challenged (v.4-6). The saints knew they would be tempted to forget their God and His promises. They knew they would need accountability to remain faithful. Their hearts were enraged (v.7-9). Whether this was righteous indignation or human frailty, I cannot say. Image-bearers of God were not made to mercilessly kill babies or approve of it. It is best for God's people to look after their own faith and trust God to act justly, according to His will, and to trust His decisions.

In times of jubilation, God's people must be good stewards. It is easy to waste time, energy, and resources when circumstances are pleasant and songs of praise are easily sung (Psalm 138). It is in these moments that disciples of Jesus must discipline themselves to give thanks to God (v.1-3), to seek the honor and glory of God through humble adoration (v.4-6), and to pursue the personal will of God for their lives (v.7-8). There will never be a set of perfect circumstances on this side of heaven. Rather than waiting for things to be as we want them to be, the faithful must learn to trust God in the best of times and pursue His plan in the worst of times.

We live in difficult days, when darkness brings about suffering and harsh realities. God is still God. The wise seek Him and the redeemed trust Him. Can you trust Jesus in the worst of times? He knows suffering and injustice and the path to take through them. Can you seek Jesus in the best of times? Those who look past the world to Jesus live with hope.

2 Kings 21; Hebrews 3; Hosea 14; Psalm 139

What we believe will ultimately drive our affections and determine our actions. It is one thing to know the truth of God and another to believe it. Those who believe in Jesus live a life of love for Him. They obey Him. To know Jesus is to love Jesus and to love Jesus is to obey Jesus. Those who live in disobedience to God may know facts about God, like Satan, but have no true faith. Those with genuine faith in Jesus obey Him and enjoy lasting hope.

Manasseh was the worst of all of the kings of Judah. Having been raised by a Godly father, it is difficult, in worldly terms, to explain his treacherous life. In spiritual terms, it is easy to explain. This man had no true personal relational knowledge with God. He knew facts, but he did not believe in the God of his father or of the prophets, priests, and kings before him. His reign and that of his son, Amon, is described in 2 Kings 21. Not only did these men destroy their own souls, but they brought about the curse of God through their influence. The legacy of these two monarchs reveals the symptoms of hearts that are broken and far from God.

Those who are far from God and live with broken hearts cause devastation (v.1-18). Manasseh was destructive to himself and to his country. He dishonored God. He killed his son. He sought the help of demons. He ignored the teaching of his father and the message of the anonymous prophet who warned him of God's displeasure. He caused the people to stray from God. This is what the Godless do. They not only hurt themselves, but they wreak havoc on their families and all they influence. Sin does not remain still. It works through a life into the lives of others and destroys the souls and the society it infects.

Those who are far from God and live with broken hearts create strife (v.19-26). Amon lived in the same way as his father. For whatever reason, the servants of his house conspired against him and killed him. Either out of loyalty to the king or out of a sense of legal responsibility, the people of the land killed those servants for their crime. This is the way of sin. It always turns on its host. Like a cancer, sin kills the very life that provides its existence. Death is always the end of sin.

God is sovereign and He is able to bring life out of death. God is able to bring hope out of despair. Amon was replaced by his son, Josiah (v.24). Like the Lord Jesus, Josiah brought about a revolution that transformed society. The law of God was restored to its proper place, and the honor of God was again realized within the nation. Josiah was used by God to provide renewal in a dark time.

Knowledge is interesting, but beliefs produce results. Beliefs drive behaviors and behaviors have consequences. Manasseh and Amon cursed not only their own souls, but motivated the defilement of many other's souls. Josiah brought about hope and renewal. Is your life like Manasseh's and Amon's or like Josiah's? Do you have a genuine belief in Jesus? Can your faith be seen through the heartfelt obedience you have in Jesus? Disciples of Jesus obey Jesus and offer and enjoy living hope.

2 Kings 22; Hebrews 4; Joel 1; Psalms 140–141

The Old Covenant was a shadow of the New Covenant. Under the Old Covenant, a priest had to offer up sacrifices year after year. Under the New Covenant, the Great High Priest, Jesus Christ, has offered up His life once and for all and has fully met the just demands of God. Under the Old Covenant, the people of God entered into a partial rest in the Promised Land. Under the New Covenant, the people of God have entered into an eternal rest in the grace of Jesus. Those who live under Jesus live with hope.

The Hebrew writer provided an in-depth explanation of the paradigm shift provided in Christ Jesus. Hebrews 4 maps out the provision of God offered through Jesus Christ alone. There is no other means by which humans may enter into eternal peace, life, and hope than through salvation by grace through faith in Christ alone. This salvation is one that must be entered into by faith, sustained by grace, and pursued by prayer.

By grace, the saints of God act in faith. The object of their faith is Jesus Christ. To receive Christ as Savior and Lord is to enter into God's rest (v.1-11). The Old Covenant provisions were pictures of the New Covenant power. Those before Christ entered into a relationship with God, but by means that were limited. Those means were not the final answer to humanity's need. Those means pointed to Jesus. Now that Christ has come and satisfied the just demands of God, any who trust in Christ will be saved. Any who will not are condemned (John 3:18). Christ's salvation is full and free!

It is by grace a person is saved, and it is by grace a saint is sustained in that great salvation. God has given His Word, and by the power of the Holy Spirit, God's truth cuts into a believer's life and brings about healing. This sanctifying work is spiritual surgery (v.14). It is a gracious act of God. Rather than simply save us and leave us as we were, God saves us and frees us from sin. The Word works to convict and call God's people to repentance and greater faith. God sees all (v.15). Those who are saved and are being sanctified draw comfort in God's grace and look forward to giving an account for what His grace has accomplished.

Justification is a single experience that secures eternal salvation. Sanctification is the lifelong process that makes a saint more and more like Jesus. This happens through the work of God's Word and Spirit. The same Jesus who died for sin has been raised and is now the living mediator for the redeemed in heaven. Those who are saved and being sanctified can go to God in prayer with confidence (v.16-18). Jesus has lived in human flesh and sympathizes with us. The Good News is that He overcame sin through His obedience and defeated its power through His death and resurrection. All who are saved can find strength in Jesus, through prayer.

Salvation is free in Christ but must be received by faith. Those who are saved will be transformed into the image of Christ over time. you have faith in Jesus and are you becoming more like Him? Is Jesus your help, through prayer? Those who trust in Jesus live with hope.

2 Kings 23; Hebrews 5; <u>Joel 2</u>; Psalm 142

Apocalyptic themes continue to show up in the entertainment industry. There is a strong sense within the hearts of humanity that the world is in the midst of a calamity and at any moment a devastating war or epidemic could envelop the entire earth bringing death and suffering. God's Word indicates this as well. The greatest threat of all is God. God will not suffer sinners long before He brings justice. Those who hope in Christ and trust His plan live with hope.

The prophet Joel had a stirring vision from God. Given the descriptions and the underlying theme, it would be easy to assume that without the hope of God's love and sovereign care, Joel would lose sleep and maybe his sanity. The grand story of the Bible is seen in Joel 2. The people had turned against God, just as Adam and Eve had. Death and darkness was the consequence, just as it is now for the human race. God was willing to be merciful to those who repent, as now Jesus is to those who turn to Him. One day, God will restore all things. This will be a blessing to the faithful and a curse to those living in darkness.

The greatest threat to humanity and the greatest gift to humanity is God. God is holy and humans are sinful. Those who stand against God will be overwhelmed by His Kingdom (v.1-11). No one and nothing can stop the Almighty. His power is eternal. His justice is undeniable. The world will be overrun with His greatness, and all who stand against Him will be ruined. He is the Lord!

God is gracious and merciful, and any who repent and turn to Him in faith will find forgiveness and new life (v.12-27). The Lord promised to redeem His people. The Israelites had only clues of the Christ. Their experience of salvation was far more nationalistic than spiritual. Being jealous for His glory, the Lord looked on His people with compassion, just as Christ looks on sinners. Jesus will redeem all who repent and believe in Him. Through God's grace in Christ, new life comes.

The life Jesus gives is completely new. This is a supernatural life filled with wonder and ends in triumph (v.28-32). This prophecy of Joel came to be at Pentecost. The people of God saved by grace through faith in Christ alone were given the Spirit of God. In the power of the Holy Spirit, the church has been able to impact the world with hope. The apostles were able to do miracles in the power of the Holy Spirit. The New Testament was given through the power of the Holy Spirit. Conviction and rebirth were manifest in the power of the Holy Spirit. The Lord began a new work in the New Covenant, and it will culminate in His second coming. The return of Christ will bring restoration. The saints will be saved; sinners will be damned; the Lord will be worshipped.

The world is in the midst of a spiritual battle. Each person must choose their side. Those who align their lives under the authority of Christ will live and die with hope and one day reign with Jesus. Have you repented of sin and believed on Jesus for salvation? Do you delight in the promises and the coming of the Lord? Those who trust in Jesus live with hope.

2 Kings 24; Hebrew 6; Joel 3; <u>Psalm 143</u>

The first step in making something right is to acknowledge that something is wrong. The easiest, but more costly thing to do is to pretend that nothing is wrong. The hardest, but the most rewarding thing to do is to acknowledge there is a problem and pursue reconciliation. Rather than getting caught up in trying to make up for a wrong, the blessed person sees the truth, acknowledges the need for change, and pursues a restorative course of action. Those who work to make peace live with hope.

The Psalms contain seven "penitential Psalms," which express sorrow over sin. They seek to find hope through reconciliation with God. Psalm 143 is a penitential Psalm. The circumstances under which David wrote this Psalm are not known. What is clear is that David saw the need for God's mercy. He did not want what he deserved. In his repentance, he asked for forgiveness, renewal, and freedom from the bondage of his enemies.

David did not come to God with a sense of entitlement. He came humbly before God, asking the Lord not to judge him (v.1). The basis for his request is that none are righteous before God. His reasoning is that it would be better for God to have some of the fallen race who know and serve Him (v.2). There is confidence in his request. He asks on the basis of God's faithfulness and righteousness. The Lord is faithful to His promises, and His righteousness gives sinners the confidence to approach God with hope.

Surrounded by enemies and feeling the desperation that the darkness of sin always causes (v.3-4), David called to mind the faithfulness of God in the past and the ways in which God had graciously dealt with him (v.5-6). The confidence of any saint is the sovereign grace of God. David was the most unlikely of all of Jesse's sons to be made the king, but God chose him. God provided for David's life and leadership. God worked out His plan in David's life. The redeemed always have hope in knowing that God is working all things for good, and they can look back and see the sovereign grace of God that drew them to and sustained them in the Lord.

Having sought grace, David looked to the provision of God (v.7-12). He looked by faith to the answer of God. He even expected it by morning. He looked by faith to the direction of God. He believed not only that God knew the best way for Him to live, but would reveal it. He looked by faith to the deliverance of God. He believed God had the power to overcome and guide him. It is by faith a person looks to God. It is not blind faith. It is faith in truth. Jesus is the truth made flesh. Those who look to Jesus, trusting in His grace, mercy, and purpose, live with hope by faith.

None of us is perfect. All of us live with great enemies that conspire against us: the world, the flesh, and the devil. Left to ourselves, we would all be lost. In His mercy and grace and for His glory and purpose, God provides for His people. Do you understand your need for a savior? Do you trust in Christ? Are you experiencing victory or defeat in your spiritual life? Those who seek redemption and restoration in Christ alone live with hope.

2 Kings 25; Hebrews 7; Amos 1; Psalm 144

While there are many things to fear losing in this world, the greatest loss a person can experience is the loss of hope in God. If the grace, mercy, love, and power of God are not the strength and confidence of a person's heart, there is no protection for the soul. Those who reject God and live on their own suffer great loss. This loss is to be feared. Those who fear the loss of God's blessing and foster a relationship with Jesus live with hope.

The Bible is filled with examples of what to avoid if we want to live with hope. In 2 Kings 25, the people of Israel were suffering under the consequences of their sin. This chapter provides a picture of what happens to those who live without Jesus. Like the last remnants of Judah, before the final fall of Jerusalem, people without Jesus will be chased down and defeated by sin and see their families hurt. They will see God dishonored and their access to God lost. Strife and conflict will abound, but God will accomplish His will.

When the king of Babylon laid siege to Jerusalem, the walls came down and the people were exiled; the king and some of his soldiers tried to escape, but they were caught. The king of Judah watched his sons killed by the marauders and then his eyes were mercilessly removed (v.1-7). The remaining leaders were exiled (v. 8-11). After the exile, the poor were left to care for the land (v.12). This is what happens to those lost in sin. They are overcome by temptation. They lose their capacity to fight against sin. Even those who flee temptation are soon caught in pride or despair. They lose sight of reality. Their loved ones suffer. Sin always reaps destruction in the one who sins and in the lives of those that sinner loves.

Having removed the leadership, the king of Babylon applied a crushing blow. The city was completely looted and then destroyed. Nothing was left. The temple was destroyed (v.13-21). There was no way for the people to make sacrifice for sin. There was no place for the high priest to petition for the people. The Old Covenant means to gain access to God was lost. Without Christ there is no salvation or leadership. The king of Babylon installed a leader who was killed by others seeking power. They fled, after the murder (v.22-26). Without Christ there is conflict and no possibility for peace. Without peace with God, there can be no peace within or with others. Anger, fear, and resentment reign in a heart that does not have the leadership of Jesus.

Despite the destruction and brokenness, God's plan remained. The survivor of the house of David was shown kindness (v.27-30). The book of 2 Kings ends with a small glimmer of hope. God's plan to raise up the Savior of the world, through the line of David, was still on track. Nothing can stop the plan of God.

It is in Jesus alone that a soul can be saved. Without Jesus, sin reigns. Sin reaps destruction. It is wise to fear life without Jesus. The loss of the blessing of Jesus is the greatest loss a person can experience. It is an eternal loss. Are you a disciple of Jesus? Are you living under His grace, mercy, love and power? Those who live under Jesus live with hope.

1 Chronicles 1–2; <u>Hebrews 8</u>; Amos 2; Psalm 145

What is good is often the enemy of what is best. It is typically easy to identify what is bad and to identify what is best compared to it. It is sometimes very difficult to differentiate between what is good and what is best. In matters of faith, what is best is to trust in Christ and to work out our salvation with fear and trembling. It is best to be conformed to the image of Christ by the power of the Gospel. Those who live in the power of the Gospel of Jesus Christ live with hope.

The writer of Hebrews had a big job. Writing to Jews, he was tasked with the responsibility of showing how the ministry of Jesus and the blessing of the New Covenant are best. The Old Covenant and the priestly functions were good, but they were just a shadow of Christ. The Old Covenant provided the means to understand the New Covenant. In Hebrews 8, the writer points to the ministry of Jesus, as the finished work of salvation, as the kept promise of God, and as the new reality for life with God.

Jesus Christ, the Son of God, did not come to serve as a continuance of the Old Covenant. Jesus came to fulfill the promise of God. God promised to come and save a people and build a Kingdom from every nation. To do this, Jesus served as the high priest of heaven and gave His life as the atoning sacrifice for sin. Having completed His work, Jesus is now in heaven mediating between God and His people (v.1-7). God has done what man, under the law, could not do. He has made a new, permanent way for sinners to be made right with God. This is the Gospel.

This new way was promised by the prophets. Jeremiah is quoted (v.8-13). This prophecy was the great promise of God that Jesus kept. Jesus came, as God said He would, to establish the New Covenant. Unlike the Old Covenant, the means for salvation was provided by God Himself. By the power of the blood of Jesus, the person who believes in Jesus is redeemed. Those who receive new life in Christ are given a new heart and mind that delights in God and pursues the Lord's will. In Christ, there is purpose and redemption. Disciples of Jesus teach what is true as they stand in a right relationship with God.

While the Old Covenant was good, it was not best. What is best has come. The new way of life that Jesus offers has replaced the Old Covenant system. That system is now obsolete (v.13). There is no other way to be made right with God except by grace through faith in Christ alone. There is nothing left for humanity to do to gain salvation except to believe in Jesus Christ, the Son of God. There is no other option for being right with God. Jesus has provided the only way of salvation. The way of life in Christ is the only and best way.

While the old ways of the earthly priestly system were good, they were not best. What is best is what God has done through Jesus. Have you accepted the grace and mercy of Jesus personally? Do you trust in the finished work of Jesus for salvation? Those with faith in Christ alone have hope.

1 Chronicles 3–4; Hebrews 9; <u>Amos 3</u>; Psalms 146–147

The tendency of humanity is to take what God gives and then seek self-dependence. Pride desires only enough of God that will gain what the flesh wants. This is not the will of God. This is not the way of discipleship. The Lord redeems broken people to make them whole and then works through them to bring help and hope to the world. It is in service of God's purpose that people find meaning. It is only those who gladly yield to Jesus who live with hope.

The prophet Amos was an unlikely spokesman for God. There was nothing in his training or family tradition that would credential him to communicate God's Word. And yet God called him to speak a disturbing message to a disinterested people. The Israelites had blindly fallen into hubris, and the result of their arrogance would soon lead to their destruction. As God warned them and invited them to come back under His care, as He does all of His kids.

The Israelites had turned their backs on God, and they were about to face the consequences for their actions (v.1) God never intends for His people to live independent of Him. The way of God seems foolish to the world. The world wants to be independent, powerful, and greedy. God calls His people to a life of dependence, service, and generosity. Those who rely on God's strength are always strong. Those who serve God's purpose are always significant. Those who give to God's work are always at peace. The blessing of God comes from being like Jesus and living under God's redemptive reign.

The children of Israel did not remain loyal to God, but instead pursued the ways of the world (v.2-8). Like every born-again believer, God chose the people of Israel and saved them from bondage. Rather than walk with God, under His leadership, the people chose to go their own way. The result was idolatry. The human condition is such that it requires an object of worship. Every person on the planet worships. The children of Israel chose to worship in the ways of the world. Those who claim to be disciples of Jesus but pursue the ways of the world will be disciplined in love.

The discipline of God is often public. Amos prophesied that the strongholds of Ashdod and Egypt would be summoned to see the fallen state of Israel (v.9-11). Even these pagan nations would know Israel was under divine condemnation. The discipline of God is always meant to humble and redeem. Only the humble can experience God's goodness, and only the redeemed can live rightly with God. Once Jesus is Lord of a life, there is peace. It is only under God's reign that God's blessings can fall. Amos prophesied of a remnant, a small number that would be saved (v.12). Those who were not faithfully dependent upon God and chose to trust in themselves by seeking wealth at the expense of the poor would be destroyed.

God's judgment is coming. Only those who trust in the grace of God through faith in Jesus will be saved. Disciples of Jesus live loyally to Jesus. Those who seek their own personal pursuits at the expense of genuine faith do not have saving faith. Are you a true disciple of Jesus? Do you live humbly and happily under Christ's commands? Devoted disciples of Jesus live with hope.

1 Chronicles 5–6; Hebrews 10; Amos 4; <u>Psalms 148–150</u>

God did not make human beings to live with anxiety or inner strife. Anxious thoughts and negative feelings exist where praise is absent. Nothing negative can exist in the life of a person who is praising God. Praising God is not just singing. It is not just telling about the good things of God. It is not just acknowledging what is doctrinally accurate. Praise happens when what is true is known in the mind and felt in the heart and expressed with the body. Those who praise the Lord live with hope.

The Psalms end with a dramatic crescendo of commands concerning the way God's people are to live. Praise is to be the driving act of every disciple of Jesus. Psalms 148–150 call Christians to a transcendent existence. The life of a believer is to be a life of praise. Those who know the one true God by grace through faith in Christ alone and are filled and sealed with the Holy Spirit have the ability to exalt the Almighty rightly. Those who know the Lord will join the angels and creation in praising God. They will glorify God in their righteous deeds made possible by grace. They will exalt God for His goodness.

The world was made, along with all the angels and humans, to glorify God (Psalm148). Although the world is now damaged and broken with sin, it is still magnificent. In every crevice of creation the creativity and power of God is manifest. It is right that every angel, sun, planet, moon, mountain, hill, animal, plant, tree, and human being honor God (v.1-12). God is above all things and rules them perfectly (v.13). God promised the Messiah would come. God raised up that "horn" who would save (v.14). All who believe in Him are blessed to praise with redeemed lives.

Those who believe are commanded to gather with the saints each Sunday and celebrate the Savior. Having been inspired by the Word, they are to go and live hopeful and be helpful (Psalm 149). In the gathering of the righteous, the redeemed rally around God (v.1-4). In their beds and in quiet places, they daily renew themselves through prayer and devotion. In their everyday lives, they work out their salvation with fear and trembling as they fulfill their destiny and do the works God has prepared for them (v.5-9).

All the good that the disciples of Jesus do on the earth is in response to the goodness of God (Psalm 150). Goodness does not come naturally from sinful humanity. Anything that is good comes from the Father and is poured into a saint by the Spirit through the grace of Jesus. Those who are saved from sin cannot help but praise the Lord for what He has done (v.1-2). Those who receive by faith the Lordship of Christ will praise their King. They will live in awestruck wonder of His might and compassion. They will praise the Lord.

Anxiety comes easy to a broken heart living in a fallen world. Freedom comes through Christ. Those who receive the blessing of God's redemption gain a new life filled with praise. Godly praise chokes out the fears of the world as the mind and heart of a saint find focus in celebrating the King of glory. Do you live to praise and in praise of God? Those who praise the Lord live with hope.

1 Chronicles 7–8; Hebrews 11; Amos 5; Luke 1:1-38

God does not change. Humanity cannot change without divine intervention. The work of God in the world is as consistent as His character. The challenges of every generation are different, but in every generation, God is there meeting the needs of fallen people in desperate need of a savior. Those who live in the light of the reality of God and seek Him in Christ alone will live with hope.

Throughout the Bible, there are genealogical lists. Most people, looking for a quick uplifting word or theological insight, often skip the lists. The lists are there for a reason. Each name was written under the inspiration of the Holy Spirit. There is a life connected to every name. The list in 1 Chronicles 7–8 provides a healthy reminder that the Bible and God's ultimate plan is not a fable, but is historical fact. The fact of God's work in the world inspires those with life in Christ to look to be a part of God's plan. God's plan is to save fallen people from death and provide them life, love, and leadership.

The history of the world can only be rightly understood through the lens of Scripture. All other scientific, philosophical, and psychological explanations fall short of speaking to the actualities that are at work in the world. While science is helpful and crucial to human life, it cannot explain the spiritual nature of humanity. While philosophy provides fundamental facts for human understanding, it fails to explain the meaning for life and of life. While psychology uncovers some of the brokenness of humanity and provides some help with the hurts and hang-ups of fallen people, it can never heal fully and finally. Only God's Word can provide real answers, real reasons, and real healing for humanity.

Scripture speaks to the human condition and explains the circumstances of the universe. Generations of people have come and gone. Nations have come and gone. In every generation and in every nation there are talented people with amazing abilities. Despite their strength and success, in time, people and their accomplishments are forgotten. In the end, only one thing remains, and that is the reality of God. The writer of Ecclesiastes promotes a sound understanding of life in this fallen world. Wise people are enabled by God to wake up to the emptiness of human achievement and seek divine grace.

It is God's grace that fully and finally meets the need of the human soul. God's plan has always been to save a people for Himself and to make them to live and die with hope. Without God there is no hope. The hope of God comes through new life in Christ. The hope of God comes through the sustaining love of Christ. The hope of God comes through the wise leadership of Christ. Salvation is new life, filled with love, and under the guidance of God. This is the need and ultimate longing of every generation.

People come and people go. This is the way of the world. We are all a link in the human chain of history. God is always good and always able to save. Have you trusted in Jesus for forgiveness? Do you have new life in Him? Is He leading you? God is at work in the world. Those who live in Him live with hope.

1 Chronicles 9–10; Hebrews 12; Amos 6; Luke 1:39-80

The Christian life is a battle. The war is won, but skirmishes continue. The world, the flesh, and the devil have been overcome, but they will not stop deceiving, destroying, and despising until Christ returns. The hope of the redeemed is a battle-hardened life. It is spiritual combat that provides assurance of salvation and that wins the trophies that will be presented at the feet of Christ in heaven. Those who fight well and develop their skill in spiritual warfare will enjoy the benefit of hope.

The Hebrew writer was inspired by the Spirit to provide a manual for how to live at war against sin and the flesh. The overall lesson of the book is to never retreat back into old cold forms or ritual religion. In Hebrews 12, the author provides steps for day-to-day combat. Until Jesus returns, the disciple of Jesus must always be on guard by learning from those who have been successful in the faith, by appreciating the discipline of the Lord, and by living in awe of the Almighty.

One of the great blessings disciples of Jesus have is the benefit of the faithful who have gone before us and show us how to live by faith. Hebrews 11 lists a number of prominent heroes. Those who would join their ranks must learn from them (v.1). Their example inspires obedience and a ruthless approach in killing sin. The greatest example is Jesus. The disciple of Christ must focus on Him (v.2-4). Jesus suffered death for our sakes. Those who would win the battle against sin must be wise and follow the example of Christ and those saints who walked by faith and won their victories.

This takes discipline. Discipline is a gift. It is not comfortable at the time of its administration, but it produces the desired outcome that the soul longs for and needs (v.5-11). It is a blessing that God, our heavenly Father, disciplines us in His love and grace. The mature believer is one who learns the lessons of the Father and with hope begins to exercise personal disciplines. The discipline to endure through fatigue is vital to success (v.12-13). The wise warrior prepares for weariness. The discipline to make peace is vital to success (v.14-15). Sooner or later unresolved conflict will produce problems, unless it is dealt with rightly. The discipline to kill sin is vital to success (v.16-17). Sin of any kind must be killed before it kills hope in the heart.

It is hope that keeps the disciple of Christ in the fight. The hope of every victorious saint is God. It is by living in awe of God and delighting in His holiness, grace, and power that a disciple is emboldened to fight sin (v.18-29). God is both dangerous and delightful. Through Christ, the redeemed are able to approach God. God is deadly holy. By being made holy by grace, the redeemed of God can live in the holiness of God. Only those who have faith in Christ can stand in the consuming fire that is God.

The battle is real! If we are not fighting for God, we are losing to Satan. Our battles can be won. It takes hope. Do you have hope in Christ? Are you disciplining your life? Do you live in awe of God? Those who fight the good fight of faith live with and are empowered by hope.

1 Chronicles 11–12; Hebrews 13; Amos 7; Luke 2

God longs for His people to live righteously. In His goodness, the Lord has provided the right way of life that His people can pursue. In His Word and by His Spirit the Lord guides His people to know what is true so their decisions can bring blessings. Those who live in the way of Christ live with hope.

The way of God is not complicated, but neither is it easy. The way of God requires faith. Faith comes to those the Holy Spirit gives life to. Those who choose to go their own way without God choose the way of darkness, death, and destruction. Amos 7 shows what happens to those who choose their own way. They do not get all they deserve because of God's mercy. They miss out on what God can and will do for those who love Him. They shut out the message of truth and are cursed by the lies they believe and seek.

The Northern Kingdom of Israel was not the promised people. While they knew God's promise and were given prestige in the goodness of God, they were not of the line of Judah. Indifferent to the will and way of God, they lost out on the privileges of walking with God. God was still merciful to them. They were not ravaged by all that their sin deserved (v.1-6). God withheld calamities. Amos prayed for them. Amazingly, few get what they really deserve. Even the worst are often prayed for and unbeknownst to them avoid justified catastrophes their actions earned. The prayers of the saints are powerful.

God is merciful and also just. His character and holiness do not change. His demands for righteousness never relent. Just as darkness cannot exist in light, so sin cannot go unpunished. When God's lines are crossed, judgment ensues. God provided a line and Israel crossed it (v.7-9). No prayer can change God's law. Israel had been desecrated by sin and lost their sense of right. God's justice prevails and impacts people's lives. Once a person or people get out of alignment with God, what they become is inevitable. Amos did not pray for them a third time. Any sin can be atoned for by grace. The consequences still come. Israel's consequences came. All sin has consequences. Grace pardons, but does not always remove the penalties of disobedience. Israel suffered for their unrepentant sin.

A sure sign that a person or people are out of alignment with God is when God's truth is considered intolerable. Amos was told by Amaziah to go away (v.10-13). Amos assured Amaziah that his ministry was not his choosing (v.14-15). Amos revealed the Word of God to those who did not want to hear it. His message was not what any wanted to live by because of their pride. Amos told the truth and the truth was that Israel and Amaziah and his family would soon be dishonored and destroyed because of their sin. The cost of sin is pain, devastation, and humiliation.

The way of God is not difficult to understand, but it is impossible to do without God's Word and His Spirit at work. Are you receiving and obeying God's Word? Are you praying for the perishing? Do you fear God? Do you need to repent of anything? Those who align their lives under Christ, according to the will and Word of God, live with hope.

1 Chronicles 13–14; James 1; Amos 8; Luke 3

The way God has chosen to work in the world is glorious. God had every right to leave us in our sin, but instead, He promised He would come and save us. He not only promised He would come, but He promised how He would come. He promised someone would precede Him and prepare the way. God's will is understood through His promises. Those who believe the promises and pursue the will of God live with hope.

The hope God gives is not determined by circumstances, but by the power of God. Those who know God and are confident their life is in His will have hope. Hope stems from the grace of God, which gives a new righteous life. The life God gives is a life of purpose built on the promises of God, according to the will of God. Luke 3 contributes great insight into the life of John the Baptist and Jesus. John understood His purpose because He trusted in the promises of God, which enabled Him to do the will of God. Jesus is the promise of God. He came into the world through the line of David, the tribe of Judah, and the family of Abraham, just as God promised.

When God is at work in the world, changes happen. Leaders rise up and proclaim the will of God (v.1-6). Those who are raised up by God live with purpose and find meaning in fulfilling their divine destiny. Miraculously, they are called by God and able to do what He wants, which brings God glory and brings blessings to those who can believe. The most unlikely people come to believe because they are convicted of sin and find new life, through the preaching of God's leaders (v.7-18). The message sounds harsh, but it is described as "good news" by those who believe. It is a message of repentance and a call to live justly with compassion and kindness.

Not everyone appreciates the work of God in the world. Herod hated John (v.19-21). Those who look to make their home and hope in this world are troubled by the will of God and stand against those who stand for God. John was blessed to see many lives changed and to get to baptize Jesus. And yet he was imprisoned and suffered for his faithfulness. Those who fulfill their calling in God will often be both hated and loved. They are hated by the world, but loved by the redeemed and by God. As they serve Jesus, they are conformed to the image of Jesus through suffering. Even John had to suffer, as did Paul, Moses, Elijah, and other great Godly leaders, in order to be like Jesus.

The goal of God's will is Jesus. Jesus is the ultimate fulfillment of God's promises. His lineage speaks to the work of God in the world (v.25-38). At the age of thirty, Jesus began His public ministry. His bloodline is littered with Biblical all-stars. His purpose was to fulfill all God had promised. He did it!

God is at work in the world now. Are you joining in what God is doing? Are you leading and being led in God's will? Are you standing with God? There is no middle ground with God. Either we trust in His promises and fulfill His will or we don't. Those who believe God's promises and accomplish God's will live with hope.

1 Chronicles 15; James 2; Amos 9; Luke 4

God is gracious but also particular. Jesus Christ is the only means of salvation. There is no other way for sin to be atoned for and a relationship with God to be established. This unique specificity must be acknowledged or grace cannot be received. Those who gladly look to God's means of grace rather than pursuing their own ideas will enjoy God's blessings and have hope.

David was a man of action. If there was a giant to fight, an army to lead, or a battle to win, David was effective. When it came to particular details of worship, David tended to act first and research later. Having failed miserably at bringing the ark into Jerusalem, so that God could be honored and the people blessed (2 Samuel 6:2-10), David found the instructions and sought to do it right. 1 Chronicles 15 explains David's success in honoring God and bringing the ark into Jerusalem rightly. He obeyed the Word of God, commissioned the leaders of God, and celebrated the glory of God.

God must be approached with awe, honor, and fear (v.1-14). God's holiness is dangerous to humanity. Because of Adam's sin, the entire race is now cursed with a fallen nature. Clothed in sinful flesh, none can approach God except with God's permission and according to God's prescribed means. David and his people had acted foolishly toward God, and death was the result (v.13). Sin is foolishness and the foolishness of sin always leads to death. God is gracious to those who approach Him rightly. Once David and the people honored God's Word, they were able to draw near to God. So it is now for any who would come near the Almighty. It is only through Christ, the atoning sacrifice, that any can approach God and live.

God is a communal God. He is three in one. As a reflection of His being, God's people are to function communally. By each person in the community living out their unique calling and using their gifts, the work and will of God is accomplished rightly. David put different people to work to bring the ark into Jerusalem (v.16-28). Each person served God with their gifts, as best as they could. None are perfect, but by God's grace and for His glory, God accepts the effort of His children when they act with faith in Him. There are different natural gifts and spiritual gifts given by God to each of His children. Those abilities and gifts are used together bring about God's will and blessing.

It was not just the way the ark was to be handled that mattered. The manner of the heart was also important. David had a heart for God. With expressive joy, David danced for the glory of God (v.29). He was genuinely excited and grateful for God's grace. His wife did not share his enthusiasm and despised David for his behavior. Those who do not believe do not always understand those who do. Believers must not allow other's opinions to keep them from enthusiastically delighting in worship of God.

The way to God is through Christ. Those who believe become a part of the community of people who delight in serving God. Have you come to God through Christ? Are you serving Him? Do you honor God enthusiastically? Those who glorify God, according to His Word, live with hope.

1 Chronicles 16; James 3; Obadiah; Luke 5

Words matter because words express ideas and ideas create the realities in which people live. The only way to know what is true is to measure what others say by the Word of God. Those who know the Word of God and teach it faithfully live with hope.

James 3 gives a strong warning and an excellent lesson in the life of hope. Those who live with hope cannot help but share it. The words that are used are crucial. Whether as a parent, friend, family member, or public authority figure, those who tell God's story will be judged. Those who have received God's call and by grace take on the responsibility of teaching the Word of God, as a voice of authority within a church or community, will be judged more harshly. Spiritual leaders must have humble confidence, true wisdom, and peace, which come by being under the authority of Jesus.

Spiritual leaders are to live with humble confidence. Realizing every good gift comes from God (James 1:17) neutralizes hubris in the heart and creates humility. Because God does not change and His Word is always true, spiritual leaders can be confident. It is in this humble confidence that spiritual leaders can teach God's people without being overwhelmed by the stringent judgment they will face (v.1). Spiritual leaders are first and foremost disciples of Jesus who have repented of self-dependence and have gladly trusted in Jesus for salvation. Those who are called to serve as spiritual leaders gladly yield their mouths to Jesus (v.2-4). They know they are not perfect, but still speak, anticipating holy fire to break out (v.5-6). They speak life-giving truth that refreshes the souls of humanity (v.7-12).

Spiritual leaders are to live wisely. Wisdom is a way of life driven by fearful awe of God, which enables a person to make choices God blesses. The way of the world is not wise. A worldly person is driven by fearful awe of people and circumstances. Rather than delighting in the Lord, they fight to get all they can of things they cannot keep (v.13-16). Like the demons, they are glory thieves. They take what belongs to God and seek to gain praise for themselves.

Spiritual leaders are to be at peace and be peacemakers. In our broken world, there will always be conflict. People with hope can see beyond the temporary moment and perceive life through the lens of the grace of Jesus. This grace grows purity, harmony, gentleness, reasonableness, kindness, Godly character, impartiality, and sincerity in the redeemed (v.17). By being at peace with God and enjoying peace within, spiritual leaders can be peacemakers in the world (v.18). The world needs more peacemakers.

It is a blessing to be a disciple of Jesus. It is an even greater blessing to be called by God to serve as a spiritual leader. Yes, spiritual leaders carry a greater burden of responsibility, but in Christ they can voice hope and with their behavior and character influence others. Are you a disciple of Jesus? Are you called to teach and lead others with wisdom and in peace? Those who know the Word of God and teach it rightly live with hope and are a great help to others.

1 Chronicles 17; James 4; <u>Jonah 1</u>; Luke 6

Running from God will only take a person lower and never where they want or need to be. God is good. His plan is prefect. His grace, love, and mercy give life. Without Jesus there is no hope. Human beings are lost in sin and often get confused by their own opinions, feelings and plans. God has come to rescue us. Those who yield to Christ in faith will find the life they long for and the hope they need.

The little book of Jonah is the Bible in miniature. Within these four short chapters the plight of humanity, the power of God, and the purpose of the world are found. Jonah 1 is a picture of the fall. Jonah had been given a grand job, but he did not want it. He ran from God, as Adam and Eve did in the Garden. Rather than finding the life he wanted, Jonah discovered the God he needed and that we all need. His discovery came through difficulty, as is often the case for God's rebellious children. By the end of the chapter, there is good news.

Jonah had his plan. It fostered his feelings and built his kingdom of hate. His commitment was to his nationalistic prejudice, which produced disgust for the enemies of his country. Living for such a temporary and broken purpose led him to defy God. The Lord called Jonah to go to Nineveh and proclaim Good News, but rather than submit his plans, feelings, and kingdom purpose to God, he ran away and his flight took him down (v.1-15). He went down to Joppa, then down into the boat, and then down into the sea. Disobedience to God always takes people down. Sin never leads upward.

In the plight of the storm, we can see something of the doctrine of humanity. Like all people of the world, the sailors were religious. They were simple people looking to make a living. They had specific beliefs about how things worked. They had faith. In the face of that catastrophic storm, they looked to their gods. What we rely on to give comfort and strength reveals where our true faith lies. Trusting in careers, looks, personal strength, other people, government structures, or anything created is idolatry and will lead to destruction.

In Jonah, we can see something of the Gospel of Christ. Jonah knew what was going on. and he knew what needed to happen. Like Adam with humanity, Jonah had thrust these sailors into chaos. His sin led them into a world of desperation. Like Jesus, Jonah knew the only way to rectify the situation was to give his life so the sailors could be saved. Like Jesus, Jonah was sacrificed (v.16). Unlike Jesus, Jonah was not abandoned by God. God turned away from Jesus and placed on Him the eternal curse that justice demanded. Like Jesus in the tomb, Jonah was down in the whale (v.17). The sailors were saved by the sacrifice of Jonah, as we are saved by the sacrifice of Jesus.

Living for anything other than God leads to disaster. Running from God rather than to Him by grace through faith in Jesus leads us down, down, down to destruction. Are you running from God? Are you in the storm? Do you need a Savior? Look to Jesus! Those who trust in Jesus find the life they long for and the hope they need.

1 Chronicles 18; James 5; Jonah 2; Luke 7

Those with a high view of God will have a right view of humanity. To see God, as He is in His holiness, love, and power, is to be changed. No one can experience God and not be changed. That is the blessing of worship. To understand Jesus is to be in awe of Him. Those who live in awe of God live with hope.

In Luke 7, a number of unique people are introduced. Each person had a problem that Jesus intervened in. There were also bystanders who saw what Jesus did and some of them were changed, but some were not. What was the difference? It was not intelligence. It was not accessibility. The difference was faith. Some could believe, and that belief impacted their feelings, which gave them hope. Their hope produced a response that showed their faith.

There were two issues of physical need. There was a centurion who had a servant who was sick (v.1-10) and a widow's son who was dead (v.11-17). The centurion had such faith that Jesus marveled at him. His servant was healed by Jesus' grace and power and the centurion's faith. The widow's son inspired compassion in Jesus. He was healed by the love of God. Our faith and God's love and power are necessary for miraculous change, but all are a mystery. Sometimes, God acts because we act. Sometimes, God acts and we react. The end result in either case is awe of God and devotion to Jesus.

God does not always act in accordance with our desires or expectations. John the Baptist had been set apart by God to be the promised forebearer of Jesus, but his faith was tested (v.18-35). Having been arrested and having not seen the consummation of the Kingdom of God in Jesus, as John seemed to have expected, John had doubts. However, Jesus was gracious to John. He did not condemn him for struggling to believe. Instead, Jesus pointed to the observable data. He sent word concerning the miracles that had been done. After the servants left with that message to John, Jesus praised John to the people. Our doubts do not discourage God, and they do not disqualify us. God understands our struggle, and He is gracious to us.

When we get a glimpse of the character of God, we will understand and be convicted by our lack of character. Isaiah the prophet experienced this (Isaiah 6) and so did Peter (Luke 5:8). There was a woman of sin who came to Jesus in the most unexpected way (v.36-50). When dignitaries, like the Pharisees, had a dinner, it was not unusual for it to be public so others could see. This was to bring honor to the Pharisee. That night, this sinful woman came and worshipped Jesus. Her actions showed faith, hope, awe, and humility. Jesus gave her grace. Those who come to Jesus by faith in awe of His love and power will be humble, and they will find hope in the salvation of Jesus.

In this chapter there are those who did not believe in Jesus (v.30 and 39). They saw God's grace and power, but they refused to believe. There is a human and divine reason for this. What matters is the result. Do you believe in Jesus? Have you been changed by Jesus? Those who believe in Jesus live in awe of Him and with hope.

1 Chronicles 19–20; 1 Peter 1; Jonah 3; Luke 8

In this fallen world, faithful friends are hard to find. Loyal allies are rare. Those who find good friends do well to protect those relationships and insure they remain secure. There will always be battles to fight and foes to face. Having good friends and the strength of the Lord is a must. Those who are blessed with a trusted circle of friends in Christ have a fortified hope.

David was a wise man when it came to friends, foes, and battles. He was fair with his friends, ruthless with his enemies, and passionate about his calling. In 1 Chronicles 19–20, David's relational wisdom is displayed and the foolishness of others is revealed. The importance of discernment, relational support, and the power of divine hope is seen.

David sought to show his friendship to the Ammonites, but it was not well received (19:1-5). The new king had unwise advisors who did not discern David's intentions properly and created an unnecessary war (19:6-9). The world is filled with relationships. Each one has a unique purpose. Wise people appreciate and sustain healthy relationships with those they agree with and can support. Keeping respectful relationships with friends and acquaintances who share similar goals and purposes is an investment that will often reap peace.

Having entered into a war with the Ammonites, which had sought the help of the Syrians, Joab, the commander of Israel's army, sought the support and help of his brother, Abishai (19:10-15). The time to determine who can and cannot be trusted is not in the moment of crisis. Those who get the relational support they need are those who build the relationships with people before they need them. A good principle for relational support is to know people before you need them. Joab had a good relationship with his brother, and in his time of need, Abishai was there as a trusted support.

The Syrians attempted to rally their defeated troops with the support of the rest of their army, but David stepped in and joined Israel, which led to Israel's victory (19:16-19). David was God's anointed king. David wisely put to use the strength of his army under capable men who were qualified to lead. When the time came, Joab knew he had not only the king's support, but also the king's strength to rely on. So it is with all of God's people. All who claim Christ will live daily in the spiritual battle between light and darkness. The saints of God are equipped to fight the battles they face. Those who live in obedience to Jesus know they are fighting under the Lord's banner and the Lord's blessing. They are not being foolish in their obedience, although it may seem so to some. When the battle gets to be too much, the children of God are free to call on their commander, Jesus Christ, for strength and support (Nahum 1:7-8).

Good friends are partners in the mission of God. They are rare. Wise saints always seek to sustain solid relationships with those who are for them and for Christ. Those who are discerning and wise will live lives surrounded with the support of other believers and under the Lordship of Jesus. Do you have a strong relational support structure? Do you rely on Jesus for strength? Those who are blessed with a trusted circle of friends in the Lord have a fortified hope.

1 Chronicles 21; 1 Peter 2; Jonah 4; Luke 9

Those who have blessings often fail to appreciate them and give God praise for them. The flesh, the world, and the devil often lead people astray by corrupting them with the thought that they have earned their blessings and deserve them. Those who live humble, grateful, and content lives live with hope.

Peter had a passion for God's people. During a time of persecution, Peter was inspired by the Holy Spirit to write a letter to the church. This Scripture, which is now 1 Peter, was intended to give God's people hope and to help them understand who they were and what it is God expected them to do and to be. In 1 Peter 2, Peter outlines the people's privileged position, personal responsibility, and powerful example in Jesus.

The church is made up of privileged people. Those who are saved by grace, adopted into the eternal family of God, and formed into the holy priesthood of God have a special place in the universe (v.1-10). Those who have come to saving faith are a people chosen by God to be His dwelling. By the grace of Jesus and the power of the Holy Spirit, disciples of Jesus are given a new life that connects them to Christ and other believers in a holy and eternal way. Those who are saved become the fulfillment of God's purpose for humanity. God made people to be with Him, for Him, and like Him in order to serve Him, love Him, and worship Him. This is the privileged life of a disciple of Jesus.

By being obedient and satisfied in Christ, the people of God are able to represent their Lord (v.11-20). God does not promise His people a painless existence. Those who serve God and take their responsibility in His Kingdom seriously will not live in continual comfort, but will often face personal and circumstantial struggles. Those who follow Jesus should anticipate it being difficult, but rather than complain and give up, God's people are to strive to live the lives that show respect to others and gain the respect of others. God places people where He wants them, according to His purpose. The children of God can live by faith knowing they do not need a certain position to have peace, but can be content in their life in Jesus.

The example of this servant lifestyle is Jesus (v.21-25). Those who follow Jesus should anticipate facing the same challenges as Jesus did and overcoming those challenges as Jesus did. Jesus did not complain. Jesus did not sin. He was disrespected, but He did not despise those who sought His harm. Instead, Jesus entrusted His life to the Father and served His eternal purpose. By dying for our sins, Jesus brought eternal healing to the souls of His followers. Those who believe now have the great Shepherd and Overseer of souls as their master. What a blessing to be saved and to exemplify the life of Christ in the world!

The life of a disciple of Jesus is not easy, but it is blessed. The Lord provides a privileged position to His people and enables them to serve an eternal cause. No earthly position, possession, power, or pleasure can provide what Jesus gives to His disciples. Are you a disciple of Jesus? Do you delight in your life in Him? Those who are grateful for their Godward life live with hope.

1 Chronicles 22; 1 Peter 3; <u>Micah 1</u>; Luke 10

What is most miraculous about God is that He is who He is, holy and powerful, and yet He loves those He made in His image who turned against Him and are trapped in sin and death. The Lord has chosen to be at work in the world. He cares about humanity and His creation. He has a plan. Those who look to the Lord and listen to Him live with hope.

God is speaking, but are we listening? The communication of God is all around in creation. It is in the Bible. It is in the Spirit. The Lord God is calling people to Himself to work in them and through them. God raised up Micah during a time of prosperity. The Word of the Lord came to this ordinary man so that the people of God and the world would know who God is and repent of sin and love Him. Micah 1 tells of God's power, God's prerogative, and God's plan.

The power of God is a terrifying reality (v.1-4). For His glory and in His eternal wisdom, God has designed the world and heaven. God is in heaven, and He does what He pleases in perfect righteousness and justice. There is no limit to His strength. In the beginning, there was harmony in the universe. God was with humanity, and humanity was over the world. Now that humanity has sinned and turned against God, there is disharmony and the power of God in His holiness and justice is dangerous to sinful people. This power is restrained, but when God comes again to right wrongs, the effect will be devastating to people lost in sin.

The Almighty has the right and responsibility to do as He pleases (v.5-14). While God can look away and leave the world in disharmony, He has instead chosen to engage the world and bring correction. Judgment begins with God's people. They must learn to be faithful. If they will not trust in God, their gods will sicken them and be their undoing. Micah's words in the original language were puns. The gist of his message was that whatever created thing the people worshipped and entrusted, their hope would become the means of their destruction. This is what sin and idols do. Sooner or later they turn, like cancer, and kill their host.

The Lord's plan is perfect (v.15-16). Micah believed the Lord would soon bring a "conqueror" to accomplish God's purpose. This curse would cause the destruction of Israel and later destroy Judah. Thankfully, God had promised Abraham, Moses, David, and the prophets He would send a gracious conqueror. This man would be God, and He would live the holy life that humanity failed to live. He would die the atoning death humanity needed to be made whole. He would overcome death, humanity's greatest curse. Jesus is the redeeming conqueror. He is the plan of God.

The Lord is gracious and merciful to have anything to do with us. His engagements are dangerous. With Him being holy and humanity being in sin, His presence will kill those trapped in sin. In Christ, humanity gains a healing and a covering that enables them to be with God and live. Do you live in awe of this God? Have you trusted in Jesus for salvation? Those who look to God and respond in faith to His grace live with hope.

1 Chronicles 23; 1 Peter 4; Micah 2; Luke 11

The Christian life is not theoretical. It is practical. There are many Christians who have some knowledge of the truth, but that knowledge does not always translate into real life. That is not authentic faith. Authentic faith is lived in real life. A relationship with God through faith in Jesus will alter a person's life. If there is no life alteration, then faith is not real. Faith in Jesus Christ gives real hope to real people in the real world.

A disciple of Jesus will pray, fight off sin, and be a light in our dark world. Supernatural life in Christ is not easy. It takes great discipline to be a disciple of Jesus. Authentic faith requires action. Those who want to talk about the faith and simply learn Bible facts, but never put into practice the truth, are not experiencing the life Jesus offers. In Luke 11, Jesus reveals what real faith is like. These are the practices of a disciple of Jesus.

A disciple of Jesus will pray (v.1-13). Jesus modeled a life of prayer. It seems the way Jesus prayed was different than what the disciples were accustomed to. Rather than join in with Jesus in prayer, because of their history and understanding of what to do, the disciples asked Jesus to teach them to pray, as He did. This abbreviation of the Lord's Prayer gives a great outline for prayer: honor God, seek His Kingdom, and ask for God's provision in light of obedience. With an illustration of the importance of prayer, Jesus provided another instructive method for prayer that can be remembered with the acronym ASK: Ask, Seek, and Knock. Pursuing God in prayer is a practical aspect of the life of a disciple of Jesus.

A disciple of Jesus will fight sin (v.14-28). There is a real spiritual battle taking place. The devil and the legions of demons are real. Those who walk with Jesus are saved by grace through faith in Christ alone. This salvation does not make them impervious to sin. Salvation in Christ gives believers the power to overcome sin. Sin is never done attacking. Those who gain victory in Christ through repenting of sin must move on to the next step, which is living righteously. Those who only see the Christian faith as a rejection of sin and not acting in righteousness will find the one sin that was rejected has become a host of sins that are overwhelming them. To defeat sin, a disciple of Jesus must repent and go forward in loving obedience to Jesus.

A disciple of Jesus will be the light in the world of darkness (v.29-54). Jesus is the better and greater Jonah. He was dead for three days and was raised to bring eternal hope. Those who believe in Jesus are the light of the world. They are the proof of the reality of the new life of Christ. The religious leaders of Jesus' day promoted dead religion and Jesus scolded them for it. The life of a disciple of Jesus is one filled with light, love, and hope.

Being a disciple of Jesus is not easy, but it is hopeful. Do you pray faithfully? Are you going beyond just saying no to sin and saying yes to obedience in Jesus? Is your life an uplifting example to the world? Faith in Jesus gives real hope to real people in the real world.

1 Chronicles 24–25; 1 Peter 5; Micah 3; Luke 12

God created all things to be in harmony. Even after the fall, the order of the world still stands. Although tainted by sin, humanity is still structured in families. Healthy societies are made by healthy families. God's system in creation and restored by Christ produces God's blessing. Those who live within God's will live with hope.

When the nation of Israel was ready to begin to worship in the first temple, David provided an organizational structure for the temple leadership. The priests and musicians were a crucial part of God's plan to bring glory to Himself in the worship of Israel. In 1 Chronicles 24–25, the people were organized within forty-eight weeks of a year, according to the lunar calendar, to provide ministry. They were organized primarily around their family origin, their unique gifting and calling, and ultimately, for God's glory.

God places people in a family for a purpose. People displaced from their families for whatever reason struggle. Human beings are made to be in families. Humanity has created orphanages in a desire to provide for children who have no home. God's plan is adoption. So while orphanages are a great good, families are the best way to provide for human flourishing. David organized the priests and singers according to their families to provide a strong structure for the needs of the worship that would take place in the temple. Societies that promote and provide structure around families will be blessed.

God places people in positions according to His purpose. God's purpose is revealed through His calling, which is realized through understanding gifts, abilities, and opportunities. The priests and singers were called by God to serve His purpose. They were each gifted, able, and provided the opportunity to be affirmed and confirmed in their calling. Every member of the body of Christ is called to serve. Each one has a place in the body that the Lord has fitted them for and that the church needs them to do. God's calling is a grace that makes churches healthy. Societies with healthy churches are blessed.

God's purpose is always to bring glory to His name. This is not an ego-driven act. God is holy, glorious, great, and beyond all others. None compares to Him. He alone is worthy of all praise and honor. Those who served the Lord in the first temple were given a significant opportunity to honor God. Those who are now in Christ are the building of God where the Lord dwells (1 Peter 2:5). Disciples of Jesus are now a nation of priests called and redeemed by God to serve the Lord with their lives (1 Peter 2:9-10). All that a saint saved by Jesus does is to glorify God (1 Corinthians 10:31). It is through glorifying God by pursuing righteousness that everything else is able to go forward harmoniously, as God designed it to (Matthew 6:33).

God made all things to be in harmony. Despite the fractured lives, families, and societies that permeate this world, God is still at work bringing hope and healing. Those who walk in Christ are free to fulfill God's will for their life and the world. Are you serving God's purpose for your life? Those who serve God's purpose live with hope.

1 Chronicles 26–27; 2 Peter 1; Micah 4; Luke 13

God is gracious to work in His people's lives and to arrange circumstances and trials that produce character and greater faith. Mature disciples of Jesus must discipline themselves to pursue spiritual depth. The natural way of the world and the natural inclination of the flesh do not delight in spiritual discipline. Spiritual discipline takes faith, character, and dedication. Those who discipline their lives to grow spiritually in Christ live with hope.

Writing to the saints of God before his death, in 2 Peter 1, Peter challenged these disciples of Jesus to be purposeful in their spiritual development. Having lived a life of faithfulness, Peter called these saints along with all the saints for generations to come to engage in the work of personal discipleship. This requires personal faith in Jesus, diligence, and motivation.

Only those who have been born again into the blessed hope of Jesus Christ can grow spiritually. Those who have not repented of their way of sin, believed Jesus is their Savior, and submitted to the power of God cannot develop as disciples of Jesus. Disciples of Jesus have obtained a faith equal to that of the apostles by the righteousness of Jesus (v.1). Disciples of Jesus are saved by faith in the righteousness of Christ and do not trust in their own righteousness. The imputed righteousness of Jesus is made possible only by the grace of God, which produces peace and the capacity to grow in the knowledge of God (v.2). Faith in Christ is a great gift that demands growth in the faith, which produces peace and spiritual knowledge for living.

The redeemed are saved by grace and called in grace to be partakers of the divine nature and to live free of sin (v.3-4). This freedom enables the redeemed to pursue the best things in life: virtue, knowledge, self-control, steadfastness, godliness, brotherly affection, and love. These things make believers effective and successful in their life in Christ (v.5-8). It is easy to forget or to take the blessing of salvation for granted. The saints of God must be diligent and demand fidelity to the calling of Christ (v.9-15). It is in living in and growing in the life of Christ that believers gain assurance of their righteous standing with God, which gives them hope.

The pursuit of God is inspired by the promises of God (v.16-21). The motivation for godliness and Christ-likeness does not come from clever human ideas. The motivation to walk in the hope of Jesus comes from the Word of God. God spoke to Peter, James, and John on the Mount of Transfiguration (Mark 9:2-13). The Lord now speaks through the Bible to His people. The message is the same. The entire Bible tells of Jesus, God's beloved Son, who has come to save sinners and make them His blessed and loved people. God's Word stands and is given by the Spirit to bless the saints.

A disciple of Jesus will exercise spiritual discipline. Are you a disciple of Jesus saved by grace? Are you being transformed into the image of Christ through spiritual activities that are changing your character and growing your faith? Do you know the promises of God and are you being inspired by them? Those who discipline their lives to grow spiritually live with hope.

1 Chronicles 28; 2 Peter 2; Micah 5; Luke 14

The world and our personal lives can often seem out of control. There are broad cultural and global issues that plague humanity, but there are also individual and intimate conflicts that create a sense of chaos. The consequences of sin are overwhelming at times. In the midst of all of the moral failure, frustration, and emotional fatigue, God is there. Those who seek God and trust in His loving plan will live with hope.

Micah prophesied Israel would fall. In Micah 5, he also prophesied the Messiah would come and establish a new reality for the people. Our world and our lives are broken. The consequences for sin are justified. The truth is the world, and our lives could and probably should be worse. God has restrained so much of the evil and the normal outcomes of sin. Ultimately, God is working all things toward His triumphant victory. Those who live with hope will see the power, mercy, and love of God provided for His glory.

The children of Israel had fallen. The Lord had called them back, but they would not listen. When people choose to go their own way apart from God, the outcome is cataclysmic (v.1). Once the Lord withdraws His provision of protection and the enemy is allowed to work without restraint, there is great destruction. Without God there is no defense to the schemes of the evil one. There is only humiliation, harassment, and hopelessness. Life outside of the love and gracious care of God is empty and full of loss.

But God is still gracious. Despite the rejection by Israel of their God, the Lord's eternal plan and promises still stood. Although the children of Abraham would suffer exile and Jerusalem would be destroyed, the salvific work of God would not be stopped. God would soon come to a small place to accomplish a great work (v.2). This is the way of God. He takes what is seemingly insignificant and by His power accomplishes, through the least, what is the greatest. The Messiah would come, as foretold and planned in ancient days. Jesus, the Savior of the world, would come and rescue His people and shepherd them (v.3-4). He would provide peace (v.5a). Those who walk in faith with Christ obtain the grace and mercy that heals their soul.

Sin always has consequences, but God's mercy and grace is redemptive. There will always be a light of hope. There will always be a remnant of people who are faithful to God. Under Jesus, the people would thrive (v.5b-10). God loves holiness too much to allow sin to last long, especially among His people. He allows devastation to wipe out idols and false hopes (v.11-15). There is only one true hope. Jesus is the only hope of humanity. Those who look to Him will dwell securely, even in a world that seems out of control. Even in lives that are far from perfect, Jesus will be gracious and kind and sustain the saints.

On this planet and in our lives, we all live with loss, pain, and false hope, but the Lord reigns. He is able to save. He can sustain. He can strengthen. He has the plan. We must have faith in Christ alone and be faithful to Him. He is the plan. Do you trust Jesus? Are you faithful to Him? Those who trust and obey Jesus live with hope.

1 Chronicles 29; 2 Peter 3; Micah 6; Luke 15

Humanity has a special place in the heart of God. Each person on the planet has been made in the image of God with special care. Each of us is formed and placed in a particular family and country in the world, according to God's purpose. Although every person on the planet is dearly loved by God, but not all of them know it. It is the responsibility of those who intimately know the love of God through Jesus Christ to see to it that the rest of humanity knows God's love. Those who share God's love live with hope.

In Luke 15, there are three similar stories that show the heart of God for lost humanity. The religious leaders of Jesus' day did not like the friendships and the availability that Jesus provided to those lost in sin (v.1-2). These religious leaders were blind. God was standing in front of them, and rather than worship Him, they judged Him. God had come to find His lost sheep, to recover His lost possession, and to bring His children home.

The first story Jesus told was from the farm (v.3-7). He told of a common scenario. The people in that day understood shepherding and sheep. They understood the value each sheep had to a shepherd. It was not just the economic value, although that was great. Good shepherds had an emotional bond with their sheep. Sheep were completely dependent upon shepherds for their survival. For one to get misplaced meant the lost sheep would probably die. When a shepherd found a lost sheep, there was a celebration. Jesus is the Good Shepherd looking to save His sheep. God's people are to join Him in searching for lost sheep and to celebrate each time one is found. Every sheep matters to God.

The second story is economic (v.8-10). A woman had lost some money. This woman did not take a casual glance around to see if she could find it. No, she swept and went over her entire house until the coin was found. When it was located, she called on friends to celebrate with her. God's people are to be like Jesus and to get into the midst of the culture and search for the lost people God loves. They are to prayerfully and practically seek out those who need Jesus and celebrate when they are recovered.

The third story is familial (v.11-32). A father had a son who had dishonored him. He had taken his inheritance while the father was alive. This was shameful and economically costly to the family. And yet the father looked for his son to return. When the son was awakened in his sin and returned home, the father humiliated himself by running to the boy and welcoming him home. The boy knew he did not deserve the reception he received. It was grace. The older brother despised the father for showing grace. The older brother believed he had earned his father's favor. Those who believe they have earned God's blessing don't give grace well. Those who understand the grace they've been given celebrate grace given to others.

The heart of God is easy to understand. He loves sinners and delights to see them saved. Do you love lost sinners? Are you seeking out those who need Jesus? Are you gracious? Those who know and share God's grace with love live with hope.

2 Chronicles 1; 1 John 1; Micah 7; Luke 16

Having the capacity to know what to say, when to say it, and how to say it takes wisdom. Knowing what to do, when to do it, and how to do it takes wisdom. Without wisdom the truth can get lost. The messenger must be able to communicate the message well in order for it to be received. The worker must be able to do the job rightly for there to be success. Those who are wise live with hope.

Solomon is said to be one of the wisest men to ever live and lead. 2 Chronicles 1 gives the story behind Solomon's wisdom. He was blessed with a wise father. He was blessed with a humble heart. He was blessed by a gracious God. He was blessed with resources.

Although David was not the best dad, he was an industrious and successful leader. His priorities were right. David made honoring God his highest priority. When tempted to take matters into his own hands, David refused. He trusted his life to God. He made the worship of God his highest priority. Solomon did the same thing (v.1-6). Parents do well to show their children the importance of God through their personal devotion, church involvement, and prayerful habits.

God blesses humility. When Solomon was asked by God what he wanted, Solomon asked for wisdom (v.7-10). The one prayer God always seems to say yes to is the request for wisdom. We read in James 1:5, "If any of you lacks wisdom, let him ask God, who gives generously to all without reproach, and it will be given him." Solomon recognized the magnitude of the responsibility and opportunity that had been bestowed upon him. He was smart enough to see his need for wisdom. God blessed him. The best thing a person can do is to be humble and ask God for wisdom.

The blessings of God come by grace through faith. Solomon humbled himself and sought to be a blessing to others. This is the greatest blessing. God graciously gave Solomon what he asked for and what he did not ask for. God was gracious to promise provisions for Solomon (v.11-13). This blessing was not deserved. Solomon, like all people, was a sinner. By grace God had placed him in a position of authority. Solomon humbly asked to be given wisdom, which revealed a servant's heart. God graciously gave him more.

The resources that came to Solomon and the city of Jerusalem were significant (v.14-17). Was this hyperbole? Possibly, but the reality is that Jerusalem was blessed by Solomon. His faith in God and his faithful worship inspired the people to have faith in God and to worship the Lord rightly. God's provisions for Solomon were shared by the people. What a glorious time for Israel! The kingdom was under God with wise leadership and blessed with resources that benefited all the people.

Unfortunately, the humility, wisdom, and resources given to Solomon were lost. Solomon turned from God's grace. No human being has the character to provide the leadership needed in the world. God had to come to provide that. Jesus has come. Have you humbled yourself and asked for the grace of Jesus? Are you living wisely under Him? Those who are wise in Christ live with hope.

2 Chronicles 2; 1 John 2; Nahum 1; Luke 17

The world is not in harmony. The saints of God are not yet what they should be. God remade each Christian through new birth to be righteous and in harmony with God. While every saint has a righteous standing with God, none has yet been perfected in Christ, but they are in process. Those who are in the process of being perfected in Christ live with hope.

The process of being perfected in Christ is at times frustrating but is always filled with grace and the hopeful love of Jesus. In 1 John 2, the children of God are given insights into the way of God in this imperfect world. In this chapter the challenges and the ultimate answer to life is found. The ultimate goal of Christ is revealed. The church is inspired and the means of understanding who is and who is not truly saved is clarified.

Following Jesus is not easy. Sin is still at work in our flesh. Thankfully, there is hope. The hope is, although we continue to sin, we have Christ as our propitiation (v.1-2). Jesus has satisfied the wrath of God. In Christ, we are given a new life, and that life is being conformed to the image of Jesus so we can be more faithful to obey God's law (v.3-6). It is through the transforming work of Christ that obedience is enabled and that assurance of salvation is found.

The obedience God demands is what God is and gives: love (v.7-11). The purpose of the Law of Moses was to reveal God's love. This is the purpose of the life of Christ. Love is not a new idea with God. It is the eternal will of God. Those who love, as Christ loves us, live with the confidence they are indeed in Christ.

Those who are in Christ's love are connected with other believers in a loving local church. Within each local body of believers there are directives for every age level and every level of spiritual maturation (v.12-14). Some see these verses addressing people in their physical age and stage of life. Others see them as speaking to people's point of growth in Christ. In any case, the Word reveals the hope of every person in Christ and why they can live a life of love in Christ.

This communal life in Christ is intentional. Each individual is aware of the tendency in humanity to love the things of earth and to drift from God because of "the desires of the flesh and the desires of the eyes and pride of life." (v.15-16). Saints know the world is passing away and the work of antichrist is real (v.17-18). Those who remain steadfast and intentional in Christ and remain faithful to their local body of believers have great hope, and the truth is setting them free (v.19-29). The Christian life is not complicated, but it is challenging. It comes down to faith placement. Either we abide in Christ or we don't. Those who abide in Jesus have hope.

The Lord has not abandoned us in this broken world. Christ has come to set us free. Are you free in Christ? Are your sins paid for by the blood of Jesus? Are you abiding in Christ and living a life of love as a member of a local church? Those who abide in Christ are being changed and they live with hope.

2 Chronicles 3–4; 1 John 3; Nahum 2; Luke 18

Every person and every generation must make their own decision concerning Jesus Christ. Those who are blessed with preceding generations of family or friends who followed Jesus cannot depend on the faith of those who have gone before them. They must pursue the truth of God's Word for themselves and determine to be disciples of Jesus Christ by their own volition. Those who turn away from God's grace will live empty and frustrated lives and have unsatisfied souls. Those who look to Jesus in faith will live with hope.

Nahum was a prophet of Judah. He lived during a sad time in Israel's history. The Northern Kingdom had been destroyed in 722 BC by Assyria. Nahum was from Judah. At the time of his ministry, Judah was under the authority of Assyria, whose capital city was Nineveh. The ministry of Nahum was opposite that of Jonah. Jonah was sent for the blessing of the city. Nahum prophesied the city's destruction. Nahum 2 describes how this city, which once knew the mercy of God, would experience the wrath of God.

Those who will not become friends of God by submitting to Jesus will face serious consequences. The people of Nineveh had forgotten the message of Jonah. They had been steered away from the Lord by their leaders. Cultural norms are hard to overcome. Once a society has turned against God, it can only be saved by a supernatural revival. The Assyrians had been used by God to bring judgment on Israel, but now God would bring judgment on them and save Judah. Judah was nothing in the world at that time. They were just another little nation being tossed about by the then reigning empire. Assyria was Judah's source of suffering during the ministry of Nahum. Soon Babylon would cause them to suffer. Neither empire could overcome the plan of God to bring salvation to the world through the line of Judah and David's family tree.

The judgment of God is a terrifying reality. When God deals with people, as they deserve, there is no escape. No army can stand against Him (v.1-6). The earthly powers of humanity cannot overcome the divine power of God. The best of what the world can offer by way of protection is useless against God. When God comes, the walls fall and the people who stand against God are humiliated (v.7-12). Families, goods, and strength are all lost. There is no source of comfort. When God brings judgment, everything is taken except the soul (v.13). Nothing is left accept the agony of knowing the wrath of God for all of eternity.

The Gospel is the only hope for any soul. Jesus has come to rescue sinners from the wrath of God. Those who will look to Him, as their justice-satisfying sacrifice, will enjoy eternal peace. Those who gladly live under His leadership will enjoy eternal hope. Those who follow His way and find life in Him will be born again and live forever in the love of God.

Each person must decide what they will do with God's love revealed in Jesus Christ. The Assyrians turned away from God and trusted in their own power. We can either trust in Jesus or ourselves. Who do you trust with your soul – you or Jesus? Are you ready to face the judgment of Jesus? Those who look to Jesus in faith live with hope.

2 Chronicles 5:1–6:11; 1 John 4; Nahum 3; <u>Luke 19</u>

When Jesus is at work in a person, there is a visible change. He is like the rising sun. The presence of Jesus changes hearts, minds, and lives. He does not change everyone in the same way. There are those who are drawn to Him and those who are repulsed by Him. Those who ignore or reject the leadership of Jesus suffer for their decision. Those who respond in faith to the blessing of Jesus' presence live with hope.

During His time on earth, Jesus did and said many things. His influence, love, and teaching had a dramatic impact on people. Jesus' work and words were not always well received. Jesus does not just love; He is also acts justly. As a loving and just God, there were times, during His earthly ministry, when His presence brought a blessing and times when it brought judgment. In Luke 19, there are instances and a parable that reveal the grace, the expectations, and the heart of Jesus.

The experience of Zacchaeus is one that many have heard of because of the famous song about this "wee little man." Although small in stature, he was large in reputation and response (v.1-10). Having heard of Jesus, Zacchaeus did all he could to get a glimpse of Him. Jesus, in His grace, looked upon his actions as a work inspired by the Father and sought to reach out to him with hope. Jesus looked for those the Father was drawing. He saves all the Father has chosen. Zacchaeus welcomed the words of Jesus and responded in faith. His repentance was seen in his making restitution. True disciples of Jesus are changed by grace.

The love of Jesus is as perfect and powerful as His justice. Those who want to make Jesus out to be soft and easily ignored do not know Him. Jesus has high expectations. Jesus demands devotion. Jesus demands fruitfulness. In the parable of the ten minas, Jesus revealed what real and false disciples do (v.11-27). True disciples act in faith, as Zacchaeus did. They do what is right. This takes faith. Those who reject Jesus' authority and ignore His zeal for justice do so at the risk of their eternal soul. They will be harshly judged and the judgment of Jesus is eternal.

Yes, Jesus loves all people, but He will not and cannot tolerate sin and disrespect for His Father. When Jesus entered Jerusalem in His triumphal entry, He gladly received the glory due His name (v.28-40). He also wept over the city (v.41-44). He longed to see these people receive His loving care, but He knew the judgment that was coming for them. What was coming was seen in Jesus' response to those who were using God's house for personal profit (v.45-48). He had a heart for people and a heart for God to be honored. Those who refuse to honor God are driven out. True disciples of Jesus have the same love for people and the Father Jesus has.

Life is hard. It is made harder when Jesus' love and leadership is rejected. Have you given your life to Jesus? Are you living in happy obedience to Him? Do you love people and the things of God more than earthly things? Those who delight to live in the presence and under the leadership of Jesus live with hope.

2 Chronicles 6:12-42; 1 John 5; Habakkuk 1; Luke 20

The Gospel produces in a person's life what nothing else can: humble confidence. There are things that humble humanity, but outside of the grace and mercy of God, what should humble and create a heart of worship for God often humiliates and leaves a person ashamed. There are also things that create confidence in God's image-bearing creatures, but without God's glory as the goal, what should inspire and lead to a heart of worship for God often creates pride, which leads to a fall. Those who are saved by grace through faith in Christ alone gain a humble confidence that enables them to live with hope.

At the time of the temple dedication (2 Chronicles 6:12-42), Solomon was a humble, confident man. He was not ashamed. He willingly knelt before God in the assembly of the people and asked great things of His great God. He was not proud. He was aware of God's goodness and gave God glory. His faith was clearly seen in his leadership, his knowledge of the promises of God, and in his prayers for the people.

For all of his faults, Solomon was a good leader. When his heart was loyal to God, his leadership was a blessing. After losing focus on God and falling into idolatry, his leadership was a curse. No matter what Solomon did, he made an impact on people's lives. People followed him, whether it was toward or away from God. When the temple was dedicated, Solomon was walking by faith in God and he set the example for how to pray (v.12-13), for what to pray (v.14-42), and to whom to pray (v.12-42). Solomon humbled himself by going to his knees. This was not a typical posture for a king. He prayed for the people he served and to the Almighty God of grace.

What Solomon prayed was not from human thought. Solomon was praying God's Word. He knew the promises that God had made to His father, David (v.14-17, 42). The prayer he prayed was humble and confident. He prayed with the understanding he was king by God's grace and the people he led were a chosen people blessed by God because of God's steadfast love. His confidence came because of God's grace and love.

Understanding the inclination of the heart of humanity to sin, Solomon prayed for God to be gracious to those who would repent and believe and ask for God's salvation when they sinned and felt the consequences of their sin. Only those who are blessed to feel the pain of sin and know the hope of the Gospel can turn from sin and seek the favor of God. It is grace that convicts and grace that saves. Solomon prayed that, when, not if, but when God's people fell into sin and repented, God would save them (v.22-43).

Solomon was aware of the limited capacity of the temple (v.18). Although he did not know it, one day, God would dwell with man. Emmanuel would come. Jesus, God and man, would be with us to save us. Have you repented of your sin and trusted Jesus? Are you living a humble, confident life? Are you praying the promises of God? Those who trust in Jesus are humble and confident and live with hope.

2 Chronicles 7; 2 John; Habakkuk 2; Luke 21

The way to unity and congregational health is never through theological compromise. What makes a local church distinct and durable is the shared sound doctrine of the membership. Those who belong to a local fellowship are to share a sound Biblical definition of their faith in Jesus Christ. Without a shared Biblical faith, the church cannot hope to accomplish a shared mission. Any who claim Jesus to be less than the man who was God, who lived a holy life and died to pay for sin and was raised to conquer death have a false view of Jesus. Those with sound doctrine live with hope.

In every church in every generation, decisions must be made concerning the doctrine of the church and who is and is not eligible for membership. Writing in the late first century, the Apostle John penned a letter, having been inspired by the Spirit. This inerrant, infallible Word was first presented to a local church that was seeking to obey Christ's command to love, but was being tempted to water down the truth. John lovingly reminded the church what they had, encouraged them to hold to the truth and love of God, and shared his personal desire.

John reminded the church they were a blessed people to have the Gospel (v.1-3). Their love was not found in the misguided emotions of the human heart, but in the truth. It is by the Gospel truth the saints of God are able to love so well. This truth is eternal. Through the Gospel, the children of God are able to know the grace, mercy, and peace of God that is from God the Father and God the Son. There is no greater hope than the truth and love that has come from God.

John encouraged the people to hold to God's truth and love (v.4-11). John rejoiced that some were still walking in the truth. He encouraged them to live the command of God's love but not to be deceived. Hospitality is a hallmark of the Christian faith. Disciples of Jesus open their hearts and lives to all people. In that Christlike activity, they must not abandon the truth. Paul told the Ephesian elders to be on guard against the wolves that would come from within the flock and postulate lies and destroy the flock (Acts 20:28-32). John offered the same warning here.

John shared his desire to gather with the church to talk face to face about the many things on his mind and heart (v.12). Longing to be with a church family in order to enjoy fellowship is a normal desire among disciples of Jesus. John longed to speak to the church about many things. He did not want to write them. There are some issues that demand a conversation. It is vital that God's people not only gather, as a whole, to receive the instruction of the Word of God, but then circle up in groups to discuss the truth to gain the collective wisdom of a few. This is the art of discipleship.

John was not afraid to speak the truth in love. He recognized the danger the church was in and sought to help them. Do you belong to a doctrinally sound church? Do the members stand together in their faith? Is your life and church filled with love and truth? Those with sound doctrine live with hope.

2 Chronicles 8; 3 John; Habakkuk 3; Luke 22

One of the greatest challenges in parenting is getting children to trust what they cannot understand. Children, like all people, want good things. The problem with children and adults is we expect to get what we want, when we want it. Our western culture has wrongly taught us to believe we know what we want and what we want is best. We have forgotten God. God is holy and just and loving. God knows what is best and He does what is right. Those who trust in the Lord live with hope.

The song of Habakkuk 3 is moving. It is the prayer of a man who has come to terms with reality. Habakkuk thought he knew what was best. He had a plan and it did not include the overthrow of Judah that God was promising. The first two chapters of Habakkuk are his complaints about God's plan. In chapter 3, the prophet has come to terms with the perfection of God, the power of God, and the right response to God.

God is to be feared. He is very dangerous to sinful creatures. People are liable to God for their actions. Habakkuk began his prayer by speaking to the reality of God's character and to what He had done. It caused Habakkuk to fear Him (v.2a). God is not safe, but He is good. Habakkuk, trusting in God's goodness, despite the judgment that was coming against Judah because of God's wrath, asked for mercy (v.2b). God is holy and hates sin, but He is merciful to those He loves. He lifts up the humble who acknowledge God's right to be wrathful, but have the faith to seek His mercy.

What makes God's holiness so horrifying is God's power. If God were not all-powerful, His holiness would only be an inspirational idea. Because God is powerful and His holiness demands justice, He is to be feared. Habakkuk harkened back to the Exodus and how God intervened in nature to bring about His plan (v.3-15). Considering God's omnipotence, Habakkuk trembled. His body hurt. His legs shook. He was terrified (v.16). He was right to be in great fear and awe. All who know God will respond as Habakkuk did.

Because of the grace and mercy of God, the fear and trembling produced praise in the prophet. Habakkuk saw what was coming. He knew that what he wanted was not what God was going to do. The nation would be destroyed by pagans. The people would be cursed (v.17). He submitted to God's plan and trusted God knew best. In submission, the prophet rejoiced in the Lord (v.18). Like the apostle Paul, who said in Philippians 4:4, "Rejoice in the Lord always; again I will say, rejoice." Habakkuk was not happy about what was about to happen, but He was happy with God. The Lord was his strength. God enabled him to walk in high places (v.19). This is the gift of God.

God is the best father. He works in ways that accomplish His purpose, which is always right and good. We may not agree with or understand what God is doing, but we can trust Him. Are you in awe of God? Do you trust God to do what is right and best? Can you say in any and every situation: it is well with my soul, and mean it? Those who trust in the Lord live with hope.

343

2 Chronicles 9; Jude; Zephaniah 1; Luke 23

God's grace is not cheap. What Jesus did to save sinners was costly. He did what no one else could do. He lived a holy life. In His righteousness, He was able to give His life as an atoning sacrifice for all who believe in Him. As eternal God, He became man and died to save people from the wrath of God that we deserve. Those who trust in Jesus for salvation live with hope.

Having been betrayed, Jesus prepared the disciples with the Lord's Supper and prayed for God's strength. Then He was arrested. The religious leaders charged Him with crimes, but there was not enough evidence to convict. The only thing they would get Him to do was to tell the truth. The truth was He is the Son of God. This was heresy in their minds and worthy of death. They could not kill Him. They had to turn Jesus over to the secular authorities. Luke 23 reveals the expensive grace of Jesus that is to be exhibited in His disciples. He told the truth and was mocked. He suffered for the sake of God's eternal purpose. He was cared for by loving friends.

Jesus was taken before Pilate and Herod, the secular leadership in Palestine. Pilate found no grounds for executing Jesus (v.1-5). Herod was hoping for some morning entertainment, but when Jesus would not comply, Herod mocked Him (v.6-12). The powers of the world can often seem omnipotent, but they aren't. These two men appeared to have power, but they both stood before Jesus at their death and gave an account for their life. What was judgment like for those sinful, broken men? Disciples of Jesus will often have false accusations made against them and be mocked. Like Jesus, followers of Christ must remain devoted in dark times.

Pilate knew Jesus was not guilty of a crime and was no danger to the government (v.13-16). Rather than do what was right, Pilate did what was politically expedient. He ordered Jesus beaten and then crucified (v.18-33). Although it was Pilate's decision, Jesus' death was the eternal plan of God, and Jesus knew it (Matthew 16:21). As He was dying, He prayed for His enemies (v.34) and offered paradise to a sinner with faith (v.43). He gave up His life to save sinners from eternal death (v.46). Jesus' disciples must trust God's plan, pray for their enemies, offer new life in Christ to sinners, and sacrifice themselves so others can know God.

After His death, Jesus' body was cared for by His friends (v.50-56). Throughout His ministry, Jesus was dependent upon friends to provide for Him. His burial was not different. He was dependent on friends. He was laid in a borrowed tomb. Those who follow Jesus must rely on other disciples of Jesus. This requires humility and trust. We must humble ourselves to receive help and trust God for who we are in Christ. We are never victims of circumstance. Jesus was dearly loved by the Father and so are those who love Jesus (John 15:9).

The life that Jesus lived was not easy. The life of a disciple of Jesus will be hard. Jesus offers grace that came at a great price. Jesus' disciples will have to give up their life to serve God too. Have you given your life to Jesus? Those who trust in Jesus for salvation live with hope.

2 Chronicles 10; Revelation 1; Zephaniah 2; Luke 24

Wisdom is a gift. The blessing of wisdom may or may not be worldly success or a life of comfort. The Kingdom of God is better and bigger than the things of the world. Those who live wisely live for what is eternal, holy, and good. The wise are surrounded with counselors who speak the truth in love and give insights that lead to the best decisions. Wisdom is Jesus Christ. Those who live in wisdom live with hope.

Although Solomon was a wise man, his son, Rehoboam was not. Within a matter of days of his taking leadership of the nation, there was a rebellion. It was a rebellion that could have easily been avoided. The events of 2 Chronicles 10 help disciples of Jesus learn to be wise. The wise understand there is always a lurking enemy ready to cause trouble. The wise are mindful of the dangers of a nemesis and seek wise counsel from mature friends. The wise enjoy peace and blessings.

Once Solomon died and his son, Rehoboam, was made king, Jeroboam returned to Israel (v.1-2). Jeroboam had fled from Solomon to Egypt, having been promised by the prophet Ahijah that he would be made king of ten of the twelve tribes of Israel (1 Kings 11:26-40). This nemesis was God's plan. Although seen as an enemy to Solomon and his family line, he was actually a blessing in disguise. Had Rehoboam been mindful of him, he would have been humble and wiser, as a leader. A nemesis is often the means to humble us, which makes a nemesis a friend to the wise.

But Rehoboam was not wise. When Jeroboam and the nation of Israel approached Rehoboam about his plans as king (v.3-5), Rehoboam did not seek wise counsel. Rather than listen to the older, wiser men (v.6-8a), Rehoboam listened to the younger, inexperienced men he had grown up with (v.8b-14). This foolish act by Rehoboam divided the nation and provided the means for Jeroboam to take leadership of the ten northern tribes of Israel as God had promised (v.15). Foolish people make enemies of those who could be friends.

People will always do what is best for them and those they love. Given the response of Rehoboam, the northern tribes returned to their homeland (v.16). Rather than enjoy the blessing of unity, Rehoboam had created enemies who could have been friends. He was left with only the tribes of Judah and Benjamin loyal to him (v.17), but he did not recognize his new limited authority. Thinking he was still king over all Israel, he sent his taskmaster to do what he said he would do. He made harsh demands of the people, and the people killed his taskmaster. Rehoboam had to escape to Jerusalem (v.18). He could have had peace and shared blessings among the people. Instead, Rehoboam caused strife and division because of his lack of wisdom.

Jesus has come to live in His people. Those who receive Jesus in their lives receive wisdom. Are you being wise and Christlike? Do you have trusted, wise counselors who help you make decisions according to the truth of God's Word? Are you enjoying the peace and blessings that come from wise decisions? Those who live in wisdom live with hope.

2 Chronicles 11–12; Revelation 2; Zephaniah 3; John 1

The battle against sin is not done until the threshold of heaven is crossed and we have entered into our heavenly home. Until then, the children of God will join their heavenly Father in eradicating sin in the power of the Spirit in the name of Jesus. Those who remain faithful to Christ and grow stronger in Him live with hope.

In Revelation 2, Jesus is talking to four of His churches and urging them forward in the faith. Each church was experiencing victory and struggling to overcome evil. Their victories and challenges are not foreign to us today. Their battles are ones that all Christians face. The church at Ephesus was doctrinally sound but lacking in love. The church at Smyrna was about to face great persecution. The church at Pergamum had theological errors. The church at Thyatira was a loving church, but they tolerated sin. Each had blessings to enjoy and challenges to overcome.

The church at Ephesus is like a disciple of Jesus who knows the right facts about God and the Bible and can give a clear explanation and defense of the faith, but does not have a deep love for Jesus (v.1-7). The Christian life is certainly built on facts, and those facts are true. The truth of the love and power of God revealed in Jesus is meant to create love. A genuine love of God will always result in obedience. Those who know Jesus love Jesus. The church at Ephesus had a diminished love for Jesus. Disciples of Jesus must make sure their heart is engaged in their faith.

The church at Smyrna is like a disciple of Jesus living in a tough secular or pagan environment (v.8-11). When children of the light live in dark places, they are often attacked on many levels. They are challenged cognitively and told their beliefs are false. They are challenged emotionally when they are ridiculed. They are challenged physically when they are put in physical or financial danger. God blesses the faithful.

The church at Pergamum is like a disciple surrounded with many world religions who struggles against syncretism, the melding together of different beliefs (v.12-17). Every religious system is exclusive to some extent. Some well-meaning Christians attempt to connect with other religious beliefs and find common ground, but can lose the true Christian faith in the process.

The church at Thyatira is like a disciple of Jesus with little discernment (v.18-29). This is a disciple who finds it easy to love others but struggles to deal with sin appropriately. Rather than enacting discipline and keeping others accountable, these disciples downplay the seriousness of sin and accept it as a normal part of life. God expects His children to stand for truth and lovingly call the redeemed to repentance and faithfulness.

In this fallen world, disciples of Jesus will be tempted in many ways, like these churches in Revelation 2. It takes faith, hope, and love based upon the truth of God's Word and the power of the Holy Spirit to remain faithful to Christ. Are you growing in your personal faith in Jesus? Are you overcoming sin? Those who grow in faithfulness to Jesus live with hope.

2 Chronicles 13; Revelation 3; <u>Haggai 1</u>; John 2

Left to ourselves, we humans will make a mess of our lives and take what God has given to us and waste it on transient, passing things. The Lord has given each of us one life to live for what matters for eternity. Our hearts will never be at rest until they are fully resting in God through faithful submission and service to His Kingdom purpose. Those who live for God with Jesus in the power of the Holy Spirit live with hope.

God had graciously given Israel new life. He had called them from the Babylonian captivity to return to the Promised Land to rebuild the temple and establish a covenant community. This miracle took place after many miracles, as recorded in the books of Daniel and Esther. Cyrus had not only given the Israelites freedom to return but had supplied them with what they needed to rebuild the temple. And yet by the time of Haggai 1, the temple was not built. Haggai was the prophet God used to call the people from a life of self-centered sin to faithful obedience. Through his ministry and that of Zechariah, the Israelites returned to the mission of God and got busy building the temple.

God's mission is to bring sinners into a loving, gracious, and eternal relationship with Him. The Bible is a single story about how God has, is, and will do that. After the Babylonian captivity, the people were given a precious opportunity, just like those who are born again by the power of the Spirit into a saving relationship with Jesus Christ. New life in Christ comes to liberate people to accomplish God's purpose in their life. God gave Israel new life when Cyrus released them to rebuild the temple. Rather than rebuild the temple with the supplies provided by Cyrus, the people built houses for themselves with the wood Cyrus gave. God called them to reconsider their decision (v.1-5). The people had done much, but they still had so little (v.6-11). That is the problem with living contrary to God's will. It never satisfies. It is void of God's blessing. Only a life that is living out God's plan has peace and the fullness the Gospel promises.

God raised up Haggai to call the people back to the mission of God. The leaders and the people were responsive to the call of God and obeyed (v.12a). Obedience is the fruit of a life that loves and fears God. The people knew God had cared for them and now was calling them to what is best. They rightly feared the Lord (v.12b). It is a wise person who understands the power of God and lives in obedient awe of Him. God promised to be with them in the work (v.13). This is where the strength of a believer comes from. In God's strength and by the stirring of the Spirit, the people got to work (v.14-15). The work of God is always done in the power of God, by the will of God, for the glory of God.

God expects His redeemed people to join the mission of God. Are you faithfully serving God and sharing the Gospel in the world? Are you living in obedient awe of God? Are you enjoying the strength and stirring of God in your life? Those who live for God with Jesus in the power of the Holy Spirit live with hope.

2 Chronicles 14–15; Revelation 4; Haggai 2; <u>John 3</u>

The Christian life is both a gift to receive and a choice to make. Those who don't believe in Jesus are often bewildered by those who claim to have a relationship with Him. For Christians, Jesus is God, and He is as real as their next breath. Although they cannot see either, God or the air they breathe, they live because of both. Explaining to those who don't believe is like trying to explain a sunrise to a blind person. The blind don't have the color categories to understand. Those who have life in Christ are truly blessed with hope.

In John 3, Jesus explained the basis of the Christian life to a man seeking to understand, and John the Baptist explained what must happen in the life of every true believer. Jesus explained to Nicodemus how a person is saved, and John explained to his followers what it means to live for Jesus. Those who are saved experience rebirth and through their belief are given eternal life. The life that is given to a believer in Christ is one that gladly submits to the authority and gives glory to Jesus.

Nicodemus was no dummy. He knew there was something significantly different about Jesus. He did things no one else could do (v.1-2). Nicodemus wanted to understand who Jesus was. He was convinced Jesus was from God. Beyond that, Nicodemus did not have categories in his mind that could explain Jesus. In His kindness, Jesus explained what Nicodemus and every person that has ever lived on the planet was looking for. It is a new life that only the Spirit of God can give (v.3-8). This regeneration is a new birth. Those born again understand Jesus to be the Savior of the world. Those who believe in Him are given eternal life. Those who do not believe are left in their sin and condemned (v.9-21).

The new life that is received by grace through faith transforms a person's priorities. Without Jesus, there is a need to justify our existence in order to feel that our life matters. Once Jesus transforms a person's life, there is a great freedom to live for what is best. John knew Jesus was God (v.22-29). John knew Jesus had come to take away the sins of the world (v.31-36). John's disciples did not understand who Jesus was. They wanted John to be "the man!" John explained Jesus was the only Savior. John confessed he would have to become less and Jesus would become more (v.30). This is the heart of every true follower of Jesus. John loved Jesus. He was excited He had come. It was not a sad or bad thing that others were turning to Jesus. It was the hope of John's life. Jesus was John's hope.

For those who have been blessed to be raised in Godly homes and see many come to faith over the years of their life, the Christian life can seem to be little more than a practical choice made by intelligent people. The fact of the matter is new life in Christ is a miracle. Followers of Jesus must never lose their sense of gratitude for and awe of God. Christians are called to think of themselves less and focus more on Jesus. Have you been born again? Is Jesus becoming more influential in your life? Those who live in and for Jesus live with hope.

2 Chronicles 16; Revelation 5; Zechariah 1; John 4

It is not enough to begin well. To honor God and experience the joy and blessing that comes from hearing the Master say, "Well done, good and faithful servant," the disciple of Jesus must remain faithful to the end. Throughout the journey, God does not change. He is the same gracious, powerful, and loving God. Circumstances change. We change. The change that brings blessing to us is the change in us that brings glory to God. This change comes by faith and results in loving obedience. Those who walk by faith and bring God glory live with hope through the end.

Asa was considered one of the good kings. He started so well. God spoke to him through the prophet Azariah and said, "The Lord is with you while you are with him. If you seek him, he will be found by you, but if you forsake him, he will forsake you" (2 Chronicles 15:2). Asa's reforms reflected his faith in this promise. When faced with a challenge from the northern kingdom, Israel, Asa did not trust in the Lord. He sought to find strength by a covenant with Syria. He rejected the Word of God from God's prophet. He refused to seek the Lord for healing. Instead, he sought the limited power of human physicians. He died in disobedience.

God had provided Asa with a great promise. He had no reason to fear when the northern kingdom rose up against him. Rather than trust in the might of God, he trusted in his own clever schemes. Rather than honor God, he took the gold and silver from the temple and used it to buy an ally (v.1-6). God's people should never be surprised when difficulties come. The good news for those who trust in the Lord is that God has a plan for every challenge we will ever face. Not only does He have a plan for our circumstance and all those involved, but He has a plan to bless us and grow us through the challenge. Asa lost that chance to grow, and rather than gain a greater intimacy with God, he became less interested in God.

By being able to change his circumstances with a bride rather than depend on God, Asa became proud and took pleasure in his perceived success. It was no surprise Asa would be angered by the words of the prophet Hanani (v.7-10). Rather than repent, Asa put the prophet in prison. One of the great promises in all of the Bible was told to him in 2 Chronicles 16:9: "For the eyes of the Lord run to and fro throughout the whole earth, to give strong support to those whose heart is blameless toward him." Asa was foolish and rejected the Word and blessing of God. It is easy to do that when we wrongly believe we are strong and smart.

Asa had lost his awe of God. When illness struck, he did not turn to God. He died in his pride. People who look away from God have to find strength in their circumstances. Asa's circumstances ended badly (v.11-14). The life of a faithless disciple does not end well.

God calls His disciples to faithfulness and blessings. God's blessing is not a problem-free life. God's blessing is His provision for every problem. Do you trust in the Lord? Do you have awe of God? The faithful live and die with hope.

2 Chronicles 17; Revelation 6; Zechariah 2; John 5

Since the fall, the world has suffered under the consequences of sin. Humanity has maintained its prominence on the world stage. Having been made to serve but having forfeited the right to serve God, the race has fallen under the dominion of darkness. God has graciously intervened by sending His Son to rescue sinners to make them saints free to serve God. The Holy Spirit has come to bring to life those who were dead so they believe. Those who rest in the Gospel of God will suffer, but will live and die with hope.

The world is in great peril. Revelation 6 reveals how God's divine wrath is being revealed. Disciples of Jesus are not going to suffer the worst of what those who are lost in sin will suffer, but the redeemed will face struggles. Thankfully, God is in control. He ordains what comes to be. The pride and desire of humanity will cause war, which will lead to famine and disease. In the end, the Lord will make all things new, but until then the saints of God must wait hopefully in the steadfast love of the Lord and in the righteousness of Christ.

The Lord Jesus is alive! According to the Word of God, Jesus will execute the divine plan that was prepared before the foundation of the world. Jesus alone has the power to open the seals that release the plans of God (v.1). The first seal releases the hunger for power in humanity. God made His image-bearers to have dominion. That responsibility soaked in sin creates a desire to possess. The white rider releases the desire in the human heart to pursue personal power (v.2). War is what happens when the natural desire for dominion functions under the control of sin. The result is suffering (v.3-4).

The suffering is not only the loss of human life through conflict but also through famine (v.5-6). War destroys resources. The land made by God to produce and provide for life is wasted in war. All suffer in this loss. With limited resources, sickness sets in because of pestilence (v.7-9). The numbers of people who die from these three consequences of sin are astronomical. None of this is new. This has been the way of the world since the fall. As the human population increases, so does the devastation.

The redeemed not only suffer these realities, but also face the hate of the evil one. They are martyred for their faith (v.9-11). They are comforted with the Word of God. They are told to trust in the Lord and wait in peace. They are given the holy standing of Christ, having been clothed in the white robes of the righteousness of Christ. God's timing and plan are both perfect. The saints will suffer, but God is with them. His Word is a great comfort to those who believe.

In the end, the old world will be wiped away (v.12-17). God will make all things new. In His righteous wrath Jesus will bring judgment to the world. The inhabitants of the planet who placed their hope in the transient comforts of the flesh will seek shelter from the divine eye of God, but they will be judged. Are you a follower of Jesus? Will you be counted among the redeemed or the damned? Those who rest in the Gospel will suffer, but they will live and die with hope.

2 Chronicles 18; Revelation 7; Zechariah 3; John 6

People are fallen and foolish. Like sheep, we are easily deceived, prone to wander, and are defenseless. God is all-powerful and benevolent. God's will is to work through humanity. It is by His strength God's will is done. It is through His chosen people God has determined to bring about His will. Those who join God in His work live with hope.

When the remnant of Israel returned from Babylon to Jerusalem, they were seemingly at risk. Not only did they face many physical challenges, but also very serious spiritual challenges. In Zechariah 3, God's grace and sovereignty was on display. He cursed Satan. He cleansed His people. He inspired His people.

The world is in a spiritual battle. The fallen angels, under the leadership of the great accuser, Satan, seek to steal God's glory. The battle is for the hearts of humanity. Satan seems to have the upper hand, having captured humanity in sin. God's grace is greater than all our sin. The accusations Satan makes against Joshua are true of all people (v.1). We are far more sinful than we know, but far more loved than we can imagine. God has plucked us from the fire. Satan is cursed, but those who live by faith in Jesus are saved (v.2). God's salvation is certainly a removal of guilt, shame, and punishment, but it is more.

The salvation of God is also cleansing. Not only does God forgive His people by saving them from the fire of His wrath, but He also imputes His righteousness to His redeemed people. When God saves, it is to make people holy. God doesn't just pull us out of the fire. He covers us in the righteousness of Christ (v.3-5). We are given a righteous standing with God. We are marked by the Holy Spirit and sealed in His holiness (Ephesians 1:13). The turban placed on Joshua was significant because it was traditionally inscribed with the words: "Holiness to the Lord" (Ex. 28:36, 37; 39:30, 31). All who are saved by grace through faith in Christ alone are forgiven and sanctified and set apart by the power of God!

Having been made righteous by sovereign grace, the Lord inspired this remnant with His eternal plan. It was through those Joshua represented that the Savior of the world would come (v.6-10). There were conditions to the blessing, as there always are. God had called this group of people back to Jerusalem to accomplish His plan. Through them, God would bring Jesus, who would take away the sin of the world in a single day. It is by the power of the cross of Christ that sin has been atoned for and people are saved. Those who are saved are the beneficiaries of divine favor and are called and equipped to be the purveyors of God's eternal hope.

God's plan has stood since before the creation of the world (Ephesians 1:3-10). God chose to establish His Kingdom through His redeemed people. One day Jesus will return and make all things new. Are you part of the Kingdom of Heaven by grace through faith in Christ alone? Are you living a holy life? Are you joining in on God's eternal work? Those who join God in His work live with hope.

2 Chronicles 19–20; Revelation 8; Zechariah 4; John 7

Life can often appear to be a mix of random events with lots of decisions in between. That is not true, but life sometimes feels that way. God has a plan for every life. Psalm 139 reveals a great mystery about God and every person's life. Like David, God formed us and gave us the parents and the places we are from. Before any of our days came to be, God already knew each one of them and has determined how to use them. This is not fatalism. The Bible does not teach fate. The Bible teaches destiny. God has given each person a destiny to pursue and discover. Those who live with a sense of God's destined purpose live with hope.

Jesus knew God's purpose for His life. He knew He was the promised Messiah. He was the suffering servant. He was the King of Kings and Lord of Lords. This knowledge gave Jesus hope. In His hope He had the courage to wait on the Lord and to speak His truth in God's time. Jesus never got ahead of the Father. Jesus spoke the truth of the Father. Jesus knew the will of the Father.

God's timing is perfect. We are all tempted to march forward, as we feel. Jesus did not do that. Jesus stayed in step with the Father and lived on God's timetable (v.1-13). It had been several months since Jesus called the people to His "hard teaching," which caused many to stop following Him (John 6:60-71). He had been laying low in Galilee training His disciples. He knew the Jews down south wanted to kill Him. While His half-brothers encouraged Jesus to go public at the Feast of Booths, Jesus waited on the Lord. It is always best to wait on the Lord and act on His timetable.

Jesus went to the Feast later, but He went undercover. He waited on the Lord before He began to teach. He amazed the religious leaders of His day. Not only did Jesus teach objective truth, but was able to speak to their subjective concerns, questions, and evil plans (v.14-24). Jesus was an enigma to the leaders and the people, even though He told them the complete truth (v.25-31). The leaders wanted Him dead for claiming to be from God. The people were unsure of who He was. The same reality persists today. There are those who want the influence of Jesus vanquished. Many people are still confused by His teaching and claims.

Jesus is God. As God, Jesus knew the eternal plan. We are able to look back two millennia later and grasp what Jesus was saying. He was proclaiming the Gospel (v.32-52). He was preaching to people trapped under blind leadership, limited by their knowledge, and incapable of understanding the miracle that was happening before their eyes. Jesus knew what had happened, what was happening, and what would happen. Those blessed with the entire New Testament are strengthened by the life of Jesus.

Christ came at the perfect time (Galatians 4:4). This was the will of God. God's timing is always perfect. It takes faith to know God is working His plan in all things. Do you trust Jesus is the Christ and Savior of the world? Do you trust God's timing for your life? Are you pursuing and fulfilling your destiny? Those who trust in God's timing and purpose live with hope.

2 Chronicles 21; Revelation 9; Zechariah 5; John 8

The world is a tough place. It is a wise person who seeks the help of God to make it through this plagued planet. The Lord has made humanity with the capacity to choose. Those who are lost and stuck in sin are cursed to live without God and without hope in the world. Those who are blessed to choose God by faith live with hope.

Jesus said His disciples could move mountains by faith (Matthew 21:21). What a blessing to know the power that raised Jesus from the dead is at work in those who follow Jesus! In Him there is power to overcome obstacles. Without Him obstacles are formed. While the faithful can move mountains, the faithless create mountains that keep them from God and the blessings of Jesus. 2 Chronicles 21 tells of the life of Jehoram. This traitor turned against God, which resulted in a broken family, a broken kingdom, and a broken life. All would do well to avoid Jehoram's path he chose in life and his place in death.

Jehoram was given the kingdom by his dad, Jehoshaphat, who walked with God (v.1). His father not only blessed him, but also blessed his brothers (v.2-3). In his insecurity and depravity, Jehoram killed his brothers (v.4). He was a broken man who lived separated from God (v.5-6). He was shown grace for the sake of David and for the purpose of God (v.7). Those who will not and cannot walk with God are enemies of God. The Lord is able to maintain His eternal purpose, but those who live outside of His covenant of grace suffer for it.

Because of his sin, God made Judah to lose influence and power (v.8-17). Without the power of God, the work of God cannot prosper. Judah was a work of God. The Lord had protected this people and enabled them to prosper by grace. Jehoram turned against God and by doing so lost the source of strength needed to thrive. He lived like the pagan king of Israel, Ahab. Having married his daughter, he lived a sinful, resentful life, and the Lord removed His hand of blessing.

God's blessing is to be a blessing. Jehoram was cursed and was a curse to others. When he became sick because of his sin and died, the people did not grieve his loss (v.18-20). Beyond the emotional suffering that followed his political and military failures and the physical suffering that came with God's curse, Jehoram died a miserable, spiritually broken man at the age of forty. The people did not regret to see him go and he was not buried in the tombs of the kings. He lived and died apart from God. He was an arrogant, mean-spirited murderer and idolater. He was a failure in every sense that a person can fail. His soul is alive. For all of eternity he will pay for his actions and remember the opportunity he was given and how he used it to curse himself and others. How horrible is hell!

We all choose the life we live. By grace, some are saved. Those who are saved live blessed lives that see mountains move. The damned build mountains of regret in life and suffer for eternity in hell for it. Have you humbly received Christ? Do you walk in obedient faith to Jesus? Those who live by faith in Jesus live with hope.

2 Chronicles 22–23; Revelation 10; Zechariah 6; John 9

In the midst of chaos, God is there. In moments of peace and tranquility, God is there. He is the great I Am. He has always been. He will always be. He has revealed Himself in His creation, in His Bible, and in His Son, Jesus Christ. All who have Jesus will find Him to be faithful. His power is at work for a great purpose that will bring peace on earth and restore all things. Those who trust in Him will live with hope.

Revelation 10 provides an interlude between the sixth and seventh trumpets. God is gracious and merciful to His people. During this detour, God comforts His people. He reminds them He is in complete control, He has not forgotten His beloved bride, and they will be victorious with Him. It can sometimes seem God is so wrapped up in accomplishing the grand scheme of His eternal perfect plan that our individual lives do not matter. God cares for His people. He knows our struggle and will strengthen us. He glorifies His name by blessing His people.

The angel the Lord sent from heaven was unlike the angels sounding the trumpets (v.1). His task was to comfort. He comes covered in a cloud, which points to the transcendence of God. He comes with a rainbow over his head, which points to the promise of God. He comes with a face like the sun and legs of fire, which speaks to the purity of God. The joy and strength of the redeemed of God is the power, promises, and purity of the One who rules over all. He is perfect in every way. He does not change. He will accomplish what He has promised from the beginning.

The angel had a little scroll and he stood on both the sea and the land (v.2-7). The message of this angel was for all of the earth. God was about to finish the work of redemption. This is good news to those who believe, but terrifying to those without Christ. Jesus thundered His message to John, but John was not to write it down. This secret message was only for those who are born again. God's will is mysterious. The world will not accept it. John and all who believe will see God do what He promised.

John was told to eat the scroll, just as Ezekiel and Jeremiah were commanded (Ezekiel 2:9–3:3 and Jeremiah 15:15-17). Like these prophets, John was to receive this truth from God. It was sweet to John, but it was bitter in his stomach (v.8-11). The hope of the Gospel is sweet to those who believe. To the many different people, nations, and languages it is a message of judgment. It is a bitter thing to have to tell the truth of hell to those who are languishing in sin. The sweetness of heaven for the saints of God is a great hope. The horrors of hell for the damned are a hard truth in the stomachs of the redeemed. God is righteous, holy, and just. He is to be feared.

God is a great comfort to His people. In this life we will suffer, but God is with us. He has overcome and will overcome. Do you rest in God's grace? Do you trust His plan? Do you know His truth? Those who have Jesus and believe Him live with hope.

2 Chronicles 24; Revelation 11; <u>Zechariah 7</u>; John 10

God delights in the genuine love of His children. Where there is a genuine love for God, there is consistent obedience to God. The obedience the Lord demands is to be motivated by love. Those who know the Lord by grace through faith in Jesus have a deep love for God. That love results in a life that honors God. Those who live to honor God live with hope.

It is easy to fall into the entanglements of life and to place God in a category of activity of life rather than honor Him as Lord over all of life. When the remnant had returned from Babylon and had begun to build the temple, they also began to settle into their towns. They were tempted to focus on their religious activity rather than delighting in God with authentic affections. Zechariah 7 is a call to love the Lord and to serve Him with sincere devotion. It is a warning against legalism. It is a call to genuine faith.

The people from Bethel had been blessed. Their houses were built and their lives were beginning to take on normalcy again. They wanted to seek the favor of the Lord (v.1-2). The temple was being constructed back in Jerusalem, and the priests and prophets were again serving God's purpose. The people of Bethel sent representatives to inquire of the priests and prophets as to whether they were to participate in the annual fast and weeping over the destruction of the temple by Nebuchadnezzar (v.3). This was a practical question, but it also revealed a tendency toward duty rather than delight.

The Lord graciously responded through the prophet Zechariah (v.4). What a joy and a blessing for the people! The Lord was speaking. There was a real relationship here. Those who know the Lord hear from the Lord. Rather than simply give an answer to their question, the Lord provided a series of probing questions intended to convict the people and to encourage reflection on the condition of their hearts (v.5-7). When God asks a question, it is not so He can get information. He knows all things. God asks questions so His people gain a deeper understanding of His goodness and the needs of their own souls.

The Lord was not interested in their fasting or religiosity. What God wanted from them and for them was a heart committed to loving Him and serving others (v.8-10). This was nothing new. The people blessed in the days before the Babylonian exile knew what God expected, but did not do it (v.11-13). God disciplined them for their disobedience. God expected these new inhabitants of Judea to pursue a deeply devoted life to God and to serve Him out of gratitude and faith (v.14). God was offering them a renewed opportunity to experience His blessing. The blessing of God comes to those who honor God, serve Him in love, and pursue His plan of spiritual renewal, which always results in compassion and kindness toward others.

The Christian life is meant to be a life filled with love. Have you allowed your life in Christ to be a list of things to do rather than a life of delight and devotion to God? Do you truly love God? Can your love be seen in your obedience to His Word and your kindness to people? Those who know, love, and obey God live with hope.

2 Chronicles 25; Revelation 12; Zechariah 8; <u>John 11</u>

God has a plan for His children's pain. Jesus commanded His followers to take heart in the difficulties because He has overcome the world (John 16:33). While the saints of God cannot always understand what God is doing in the world and why, they can always trust His goodness, love, and power to accomplish what is best. Those who count on God to bring about good in all things live with hope.

When Lazarus died in John 11, Jesus was fully aware of what needed to happen. God is never surprised by our calamities. Each one of our days is already written in God's book (Psalm 139:16). We cannot fathom how it is we are completely free and responsible in our decisions, and yet God is completely in control accomplishing His purpose in every event of our lives. What we can know and see in this chapter is God has a plan for our pain. He understands our pain. He has the power to help us in our pain.

John set the stage for the story of the raising of Lazarus by making it clear these people going through this horrifying experience were not just acquaintances of Jesus. These three siblings were dear friends of Jesus and had been through a lot with Him (v.1-3). It would be shocking to the first-time reader to perceive that although Jesus loved Lazarus and presumably had power to heal, He did not immediately go and help this family (v.4-7). The twelve disciples were concerned about theirs and Jesus' safety. Jesus was concerned they learn who He really is (v.8-16). God seeks to strengthen the faith of His saints with unsafe and sad circumstances.

Martha was extremely upset and even disappointed with Jesus. She made it clear she knew Jesus could have kept Lazarus from dying (v.17-21). She still believed Jesus could ask God to do something (v.22). Jesus challenged her faith by speaking of Lazarus being raised (v.23-24). Jesus made it clear He is God with this "I am" statement and identified Himself as the personified power of life (v.25-26). Martha recognized her doubt and confessed her faith in Him (v.27). All, like Martha, who place their faith in Jesus, enter into His life and His life enters them so their old life dies and His new life rises in them.

Jesus wept when He saw the pain of Martha, Mary, and the burial place of Lazarus (v.28-37). God keeps track of our tears (Psalm 56:8). He cares about our suffering. He does not keep us from suffering, but He cares for us when we suffer. He also uses our suffering. Jesus raised Lazarus from the dead to show He was God (v.38-43). Having raised Him, Jesus commanded the grave clothes be removed from him (v.44). Those who Jesus gives new life to are not to parade around like the dead. They are to be alive in the new life He gives.

This miracle made the religious leaders even more afraid of Jesus and more determined to kill Him (v.45-57). This too was the plan of God. Jesus had been promising the religious leaders would put Him to death and that He would be raised three days later. Do you trust God no matter what? Have you seen God make things that have caused you pain to work for good? Those who count on God to accomplish good in all things live with hope.

It is typical story. A person becomes blessed because of divine intervention, but pride sets in and destroys. Pride is powerful and seductive. The proud person rarely knows pride has taken hold until it is too late. Pride places a person outside of the realm of gratitude. Rather than looking to God as the great giver of all good things, proud people view themselves as their own providers. Once pride has set in, it is hard to destroy. Those who live humbly in God's grace and mercy live with hope.

Uzziah was a blessed man. His father was an arrogant man, but Uzziah was discipled by Zechariah. 2 Chronicles 26 depicts his life in both its positive and negative aspects. He was one of those "good kings." It was said of him that he did right in the eyes of the Lord. He was practical in his approach to the world and made provisions for his nation's protection. His biggest flaw was his downfall. Later in life, he became very proud, and his pride led him to sin against God and to die in isolation.

The capacity to know and walk faithfully with God is not a natural gift. It is a spiritual gift. The text does not say, but it is clear, as a young man, Uzziah had a tender heart toward God. He began to rule at the age of sixteen (v.1-3). This may have helped him be humble, but God had given Uzziah a heart for the Lord. This is seen in Uzziah's setting himself to seek God (v5). The work of God is done by the people of God because God has done a work in them. God gives spiritual life so that His followers are free to pursue Him. We are born again to be made into disciples of Jesus through humble obedience.

A life that is disciplined in the spiritual sense will be disciplined in other areas as well. Uzziah was not only a Godly man, but he was a wise and practical man. Understanding the threats that other nations posed, he went to war at the right time in the right way (v.6). The Lord helped him (v.7). A life that obeys God enjoys the blessings of God in day-to-day matters. Uzziah had both an offensive and a defensive strategy (v.8-15). The way Uzziah led provided security for the people.

Unfortunately, Uzziah forgot it was God who made him prosper. He sought to position himself as monarch and priest (v.16-18). It is not clear why he did this. Pride often produces the strangest choices. The penalty for his sin was harsh. Uzziah was plagued with leprosy, which forced him to remain away from the house of the Lord and from having regular interactions with other people (v.19-21a). His son became the leader of the home (v.21b). When he died, Uzziah was not remembered by the people of his day for his faith or leadership. They remembered he was a leper (v.22-23). Sin robs people of a Godly legacy.

We all have choices to make about the life we lead. Those who are blessed to know Jesus must be careful to love and obey Him with gratitude. Do you love and obey Jesus? Is pride seeping into your heart in any way? Have you forgotten the mercy and grace of God? Those who humbly love and obey Jesus live with hope.

2 Chronicles 27–28; Revelation 14; Zechariah 10; John 13

The Christian life is a life of obedience to Jesus. The Great Commission recorded in Matthew 28:19-20 demands the disciples of Jesus make disciples and baptize them and teach them to obey all that Jesus commanded. There are many well-intentioned leaders calling on people to believe and be baptized, but not all are teaching the new disciples to live a life of obedience. It seems that in the minds of some so-called Christians obedience is optional. It is only those who believe and obey Jesus that live and die with hope.

The easy believism that expects so little of the disciples of Jesus, which has become so prevalent in the United States, is not God's Biblical design. Revelation 14 reveals the real choice that lies before every human being. People will either follow Jesus to live a sanctified life that glorifies God or they will be lost in sin and live in opposition to God. Those who are genuine disciples of Jesus will live in purity in order to give glory to God. The unredeemed will live in sin and suffer the wrath of God with all the devils of hell. Only those who obey and keep the faith find rest for their souls.

The redeemed of God are truly blessed (v.1-3). They are the chosen who stand with Jesus as members of His eternal army. They are able to sing the song of the redeemed. It is a song that only the true disciples of Jesus will be able to learn and proclaim. It is a song of victory! It is a song that will be sung in the presence of the Almighty and His heavenly hosts. It will be the ultimate worship experience. Those who sing will be those who were made pure because only the pure in heart will see God (Matthew 5:8). Those who claim Christ, but live a life of sin are deceived. They are not redeemed. The truly redeemed die to sin and live for God (v.4-5).

On the day of God's judgment, everyone's standing will be made clear. Every person on earth will bow before the Almighty and give an account for their life. All will proclaim Jesus is Lord and worship God (v.6-7). Those who lived in opposition to God will be revealed in their fallen condition (v.8). Those who refused to live for Jesus will suffer for it. Their identity and affinity with the beast will be made known. The wrath of God will be experienced by them forever (v.9-11). The misery is inexplicable.

The children of God saved by grace through faith in Christ alone will endure with hope, knowing the day of the Lord is approaching (v.12). They will obey and keep the faith. When Christ returns, they will rest from a long life of fighting sin. Their redemption will be finalized in their glorification. They will be truly blessed and will dwell in the house of the Lord forever (Psalm 23:6). Their deeds of sacrifice by faith will be their legacy in the halls of heaven forever (v.13).

To follow Jesus is to walk the narrow way. It is a hard way. It comes at the price of the blood of Jesus and requires obedience to God's commands. It demands sacrifice and purity. Are you a disciple of Jesus? Do you obey God's Word? Those who love Jesus obey Him and live and die with hope.

2 Chronicles 29; Revelation 15; <u>Zechariah 11</u>; John 14

When God's glory ceases to be the goal and personal success and acclamation become the purpose of a leader, disaster will follow. Those who glorify God and enjoy Him forever live with hope.

God was in the process of bringing judgment against His people in Zechariah 11 because they were not seeking Him. Rather than rejoicing in the benefits of being God's sheep, the leaders and the people had become self-consumed and sought to live for their own glory and desires. When leaders fail, they must be replaced. Sadly, the effects of their leadership can be so malignant that the people become incapable of being led. Zechariah sought to lead the people, but they were too far gone. The only hope was for the "Good Shepherd." This text points directly to the coming of Jesus.

Leaders carry a burden for themselves and their followers. Those who are faithful can influence faithfulness in the people. When the shepherds are faithless, the people usually will be too. God removed the leaders who were leading the people (v.1-6). Many well-intentioned people enter leadership, but few remain. The intensity of the responsibility along with the selflessness required leaves many leaders ravaged in sin and darkness. Only those willing to humble themselves and seek the Lord and the good of His flock in holiness will make it.

Once the wicked shepherds were removed, Zechariah became the shepherd (v.7). He served with the blessing of God's "Favor" and "Union." With these covenantal blessings Zechariah tended this flock. But it was a flock doomed to be slaughtered. The sin introduced through the lack of care by the former shepherds had already contaminated the people. They were without hope. Zechariah became frustrated and resigned. The covenant was broken. He sold them off. God's blessing was removed (v.8-11).

Asking what he was worth to them, Zechariah was paid thirty pieces of sliver (v.12). This is what Jesus was worth to Judas (Matthew 26:15). This was the price of a common slave. It was blood money and so it was thrown back into the temple (v.13-14). It was not only the people who were rejected, but the temple activities as well. These people had lost any hope of redemption. When the Lord turns a person or a people over to their sin, there is no redemptive hope left for them (Romans 1:28-32).

Where Godly leadership is vanquished, sinful leadership gladly steps in and brings overwhelming destruction (v.15-17). This is what happens when people are led by sinful shepherds who live for their own pleasure, popularity, possessions, and power. This is why churches fail. The only hope is Jesus. On this Christmas Eve, all of God's people can rejoice that the Good Shepherd has come to lead His people.

Without Christ there is no hope. Left to themselves, people will always fall into sin, which leads to destruction. Is Jesus the shepherd of your soul? Are you influencing others with your hope in Jesus? Those who humbly and happily love and serve Jesus live with hope.

2 Chronicles 30; Revelation 16; Zechariah 12:1–13:1; John 15

Within every person there is a longing to be someone special, to do something great, and to be part of significant experiences. Unfortunately, we live in a fallen world and in flesh contaminated with sin. In a fallen state, human beings pursue what cannot satisfy their eternal soul or fulfill their ultimate longings. Jesus has come to give new life. The life lived in Him produces what the human heart desires. Those who live in His life will live as light and have great hope.

Jesus is the source of the good life. Without Jesus there is no way to experience what is best. In John 15, Jesus provides an analogy for how human beings can live the best life and offers a warning that His disciples must heed to be wise. The Lord explained He is the vine. He is the source of all life and His people must abide in Him. Jesus also explained that the world hates Him and will hate them. Those who are saved by grace are both blessed and challenged under the authority of the Almighty.

The only way people can find true and lasting fulfillment in life is through new life in Christ. Everything else people can pursue and produce with their lives will ultimately fade and fall apart without Jesus. Jesus is the vine and His disciples are the branches. He gives life to the branches, which produce the fruit of the vine (v.1-5). Everyone will produce something with their life. The branches that don't produce the holiness of God that comes only through faith in Christ will be judged in the wrath of God (v.6). Those who trust in Jesus are friends of God and will enjoy His blessing of fulfillment in God's eternal purpose (v.7-17).

Those who walk with the Lord in the light of His truth will enjoy God's blessings, but will be hated by the world. While those outside of Christ and His grace are accepted by the world and gain earthly enjoyments, they are under the wrath of God. The followers of Jesus are accepted by God and produce holiness, but they are under the wrath of the world (v.18-25). The fallen world hates Jesus and all who claim Him as the source of their life and hope. It is wise to live under the grace of God and the wrath of the world rather than to live under the blessing of the world and the wrath of God.

The life Jesus offers is only possible through the power of the Holy Spirit (John 3:1-18). Jesus came to live a holy life, to die a redeeming death, and to be raised in power. He promised that after He was raised He would send the Holy Spirit. The Helper would bear witness about Jesus and enable the saints of God to bear witness of God's grace revealed through Jesus Christ (v.26-27). There is nothing more special, nothing greater someone can do, and no experience more incredible than to live for Jesus in the power of the Holy Spirit.

The world promises what it cannot give. Jesus offers a life that will satisfy the longings of the eternal desires that reside within the human heart. Do you trust Jesus or the world? Are you producing the fruit of Jesus? Are you living in the power of the Spirit? Those who live in Jesus live with hope.

2 Chronicles 31; Revelation 17; Zechariah 13:2-9; John 16

One of the greatest needs in the Kingdom of God is leadership. Without leadership people fail to focus, function, and live effectively. Like sheep without a shepherd, people will naturally wander into dangerous places and get devoured by the wolves of the world. Godly leadership blesses both believers and nonbelievers. The moral compass, supernatural blessing, and humble confidence that exist in people clearly called by God to lead are a blessing to all. Those who lead in Christ and those who are led by them live with hope.

Hezekiah was a good leader. The people of Israel thrived under his leadership. 2 Chronicles 31 shows what is needed and what happens when a Godly leader shepherds people. There is a clear vision that the people can rally behind. There are opportunities for the people to give their resources to and ways for people to participate in the mission. There is a system and structure that serves and strengthens the cause.

Hezekiah had a heart for God. The Lord had graciously stirred Hezekiah to love God and to want to serve the Lord with all of his heart, soul, and strength. He repaired the temple and restored the proper worship of God (2 Chronicles 29). He had the people celebrate the long-neglected Passover Feast and sought grace for and gave grace to those who were not able to do it exactly as it had been prescribed (2 Chronicles 30). He inspired the people to rejoice in the Lord and to tear down the unholy elements in the temple (2 Chronicles 31:1). All of this came to be because Hezekiah had a vision for the way the nation of God was to function. He called the people to do what was right and best. These activities did not happen by chance. The decisions that made these realities come to be were based upon a clear vision.

This vision included the ongoing establishment of the religious ceremonies that honored the Lord and blessed the people. These ceremonies and practices required the people to give of their most important resources: energy, finances, and time. The people responded generously (v.2-10). When the vision is clear and God is at work, people respond in faith and gladly join in the work of the Lord.

These offerings and activities had to be led and they had to be led well with the right people who were called and prepared to lead. Hezekiah organized the priesthood and commissioned them to function according to the law of God (v.11-19). There was an appropriate lineage necessary to serve as priests. These men were discovered, deployed, and paid for their work. Good leaders do more than get people excited once. They develop systems for the ongoing operation of the work that fulfills the vision.

The result of Hezekiah's leadership was physical and visceral. The king and his people prospered (v.20-21). Prosperity that blesses comes from faithfulness to God. Are you praying for God to bless and raise up Godly leaders? Are you helping Godly leaders accomplish God's work? Are you gladly and generously contributing to the Lord's work? Good leaders need the support and resources of the people. Godly leaders cause God's people to live with hope.

2 Chronicles 32; <u>Revelation 18</u>; Zechariah 14; John 17

When God is understood as He really is and not as some weak, distant, benign old man in the sky, He is awesome. The only response that can be mustered when God is understood rightly is awe. Awe is amazement and fear and delight and wonder all at once. This God is not safe, but thankfully He is good. He gives grace to those who repent of self-centeredness and worldly ways and choose to trust in His Son and obey Him by faith. Those who are saved by grace through faith in Christ alone are citizens of heaven. They belong to the city of God. All those who belong to the city of God live with hope.

There is another city. It is symbolized Biblically as Babylon. While heaven is the city of God, Babylon is the city of man. Revelation 18 provides a stunning narrative of what is happening and will finally happen to these two cities. The city of man will be destroyed along with its occupants and partners with it. Those who belong to the city of God in Christ will be saved. The world will again be the dwelling place of God with humanity, and there will be harmony, as it was in the beginning. It will be even better than at the beginning because the gratitude for God and the awe of God will be greater.

The world offers power, pleasure, popularity, and possessions. Babylon is the source of these gifts. This source of Babylon is evil. Evil works its way in the world and tempts humanity to remain separated from God in sin. The manifestations of the temporal earthly treasures of Babylon are wealth, sexual perversion, and gain at the expense of others through injustice (v.1-3). Many, even some who claim Christ, have partnered with Babylon. Jesus calls humanity to Himself. He asks in Mark 8:36, "For what does it profit a man to gain the whole world and forfeit his soul?" The answer is nothing. In the end all is lost when Babylon is fallen.

The people of the city of God are blessed with God's judgment. Having refused to defile themselves with the things of earth, they find their eternal reward in Christ. While there is nothing evil in having power, pleasure, popularity, and possessions, it is evil to live for them or be defined by them. It is evil to give your soul for them. Jesus calls His disciples away from a worldly lifestyle and promises that one day He will call His people fully and finally home (v.4). In that day the redeemed of God will enjoy the eternal blessing of God. Even in this life the hope of the Gospel and the presence of God in the life of the saints give living hope.

The thing feared and hated by the city of man is the thing most desired and hoped for by the citizens of the city of God. It is justice. God will bring justice to the world (v.5-24). It will come in a single hour (v.17). When the final judgment of God is given, He will give to all, according to their belief. Each city will get what justice demands. Have you repented and believed in Jesus? Are you living as a faithful citizen of heaven? Are you falling into the temptation of Babylon? All those who belong to the city of God live with hope.

Without God, the heart of humanity is empty. Many seek to fill it with earthly, temporal things. Those things cannot satisfy the vast eternal desire that exists within the human heart. Only something of eternal density, purity, and quality can gratify the never-ending appetite of a single human heart. We are empty because we have rejected God. Sin stripped us of God's fullness. God has not abandoned us. He has come to fill us with Himself. That happens through faith, love, and obedience to Jesus. Jesus-filled lives have hope.

While Jesus does fill the heart of a redeemed saint, He has not yet chosen to transform the world. So long as sin is allowed to exist in the world, the disciples of Jesus will never feel at home. We long for a world of excitement, rejoicing, comfort, and satisfaction. It's not yet time for that world to be. The people of God must live by faith and wait patiently for Jesus' return. Malachi wrote to God's people at a time when they were disenchanted. They had returned from the Babylonian exile, but Jesus had not yet come. Their love for God had grown cold. Malachi 1 is a call for the people to respond appropriately to God's calling, God's love, and God's preeminence.

This oracle or burden placed on Malachi was to Israel (v.1). God was not speaking to just the remnant that had returned to Judea. God was speaking to "Israel" – God's covenant people. This message is a reminder of who they were. They were God's chosen people who were to bless the world (Genesis 12:1-3). Malachi spoke on behalf of God. God spoke and now speaks through common grace to all people, but to God's covenant people, this Word of God speaks of redemptive grace. Only those with new life in Christ have the spiritual capacity to understand God's communication (1 Corinthians 2:13-15).

God loves and blesses His redeemed people. We do not always get what we want, but we get all we need to be fulfilled in God's love and to make it through our journey in life. The Lord loves His people (v.2). This love is seen in God's provision of grace. God hates sin and holds sinners, like Edom, responsible (v.3). They may think they can overcome God, but none can (v.3-5). In the end, God will vanquish evil and make all things new (Revelation 21). He does this because of His redeeming love and not based on the merit of those He saves.

Those He loves are expected to love God in return. A lack of love for God reveals a lack of faith. To believe in the God who is holy, powerful, and good is to love this God. A lack of love will lead to disobedience at worst and indifferent empty obedience at best. These exiles had no regard for God and it was seen in their worship (v.6-14). Empty, heartless worship lacking authentic awe is insidious. It insults God. It puffs up people.

It is easy to become self-centered and to see God as a distant idea that has no real value. Those who trust in the Lord will experience lows but will choose to pursue God on High. Do you truly love God? Are you a genuine disciple of Jesus or just going through religious motions? Those filled with the love of Jesus live with hope.

2 Chronicles 34; Revelation 20; Malachi 2; <u>John 19</u>

It is no small thing that God came and took on flesh to rescue people from sin. The distance between God and humanity, heaven and earth, and sin and holiness cannot be calculated by finite beings. God says, "For as the heavens are higher than the earth, so are my ways higher than your ways and my thoughts than your thoughts" (Isaiah 55:9). God's exaltation above creation and humanity is inexpressible. God transcends all things, yet is with us. Those who live by faith in God's oversight and personal care live with hope.

Because God took on flesh, we can hope in Him. What Jesus did was extraordinary. He became sin that we might become righteous (2 Corinthians 5:21). More than that, He has shown us the way to live in this broken world. What Jesus experienced in His death reveals how our victory for life was won. In John 19, we see God's love and how it is He can understand our pain as we sojourn as exiles toward our heavenly home. He knows what it is to suffer physically, emotionally, and spiritually.

When we suffer physical pain, we can know God understands that pain and cares for us and comforts us in it. God does not have a hypothetical understanding of our pain. God knows what it is to hurt (v.1-3). One of the great fears in life is the pain associated with death. Disciples of Jesus do not fear being dead. It's the dying that is scary. Thankfully, we have a high priest in heaven who understands what it feels like and can comfort us and strengthen us when our bodies fail and we suffer.

When we suffer emotional pain, we can know God has felt it too. We can be comforted with His empathy and wisdom (v.4-27). Jesus knows what it is to experience injustice. He knows what it is to be hated by powerful, broken, and bitter people. He knows what it is to see His loved ones despair. His mom, family, and friends could not help Him. It broke His heart to see their hearts break. In His last hours he was looking after His mother and asking a favor of His best friend, John. When we are cheated and hated for no reason and are forced to watch those we love struggle, we can turn to God in prayer and be certain He understands and will show us how to wisely handle this emotional pain.

When we suffer spiritual pain, we can know God felt it far worse than we ever will. He took on the sin of the world. He was rejected by the Father so that the righteous requirement of the law would be met (v.28-42). Jesus knows what it is to experience hell. No redeemed saint will ever have to do that. He knows what it is to pass from this world to the next. He will be there for His people. Jesus will journey with His disciples through life and walk them through the halls of death to lead them to the Father's throne room. There they will worship in ultimate freedom and delight.

This world is broken. God knows it full well. He understands our pain, having been through it. Do you draw strength from Jesus in prayer? Do you have gratitude for God's grace? Those who live by faith in God's oversight and personal care live with hope.

2 Chronicles 35; Revelation 21; Malachi 3; John 20

Human beings are made to worship. Whatever defines us, drives us, and gives us meaning and hope is the object of our worship. Because of our natural sinful nature and our inclination for worship, we are prone to become idolaters. God is the only one truly worthy of worship, but without the Spirit of God and the truth of God, people will seek and make idols. These false gods deceive and destroy. Those who worship God in spirit and truth live with hope.

True worship comes from the grace of God. Without God's grace the human race runs from God, as Adam and Eve did, and attempts to make a way in the world outside of God's will. That is a recipe for disaster. When God moves and transforms lives by His grace and truth, people are free to worship God in spirit and truth. 2 Chronicles 35 records a time in Israel when God was gracious and the people were liberated to worship God. Their worship was according to the Word of God, made available to the people of God, and was done for the glory of God, as all true worship is.

When "the Book of the Law of the Lord given through Moses" was found (2 Chronicles 34:14), Josiah responded rightly (v.19). He had the book read in the midst of the leaders of Israel and commanded the law be obeyed (v.30-33). Josiah led the people to celebrate the Passover (2 Chronicles 35:1-6). Everything they did was according to the law of God. They did not worship according to their whims and desires. They worshipped according to what the law stipulated. True worship is done according to God's Word. Any worship that does not conform to the Word of God is idolatry.

Josiah did not limit the worship to just his family and leaders. He made this celebration available to the masses (v.7-15). It included the elements of the Passover along with the singers of the temple. When the Lord is worshipped according to the Word of God by the power of the Holy Spirit, people are able to worship as Jesus commanded: in spirit and in truth (John 4:24). On this side of the cross, the disciples of Jesus understand worship in a deeply personal and powerful way. Worship is no longer limited to a geographical location.

The worship of the people brought God great glory (v.16-19). It was a long-avoided blessing. The leaders and the people of Jerusalem had gathered, and together they celebrated the grace of God. They remembered His goodness. The spirit among the people was one of gratitude and excitement. True worship will always be done with grateful hearts that are genuinely excited about celebrating God's power and mercy. God is glorified when His people gather and celebrate Him in the right spirit.

The children of God must never assume that rightly worshipping God will keep them from the world's dangers. Josiah acted foolishly and went to war with Egypt (v.20-27). It seemed Josiah was acting in pride. Being right with God should promote humility and a desire for peace. Do you gather with your church family to worship according to the Word of God? Do you encourage others in worship with your spirit? Is your worship humbling you and making you grateful? Those who worship God in spirit and truth live with hope.

2 Chronicles 36; <u>Revelation 22</u>; Malachi 4; John 21

For eternal beings, endings are always and only new beginnings. While our lives on earth will end in death because of the sin that has entered the world, our souls will continue to live. The being of a person never ends. That is an overwhelming consideration. Although our circumstances may change, a person is the person they are wherever they are. Whether in mortal flesh on earth plagued by sin or in a spiritual state, we are who we are. Those who live and die as the redeemed people of God have eternal hope.

A day of reckoning is coming. At the present time there is a heaven where the souls of the saints are with God and His holy angels; there is a hell where the unredeemed are suffering; there is a fallen physical universe. Revelation 22 provides a pointed and powerful promise of God. Jesus is coming again. Those who receive His life will live with Him forever. Those who live and die in sin will receive a just eternal punishment for their actions. The opportunity to gain God's blessing is now. The opportunity to come to Jesus is today!

In the end of the world, as we now know it, there will be a new beginning. There will be a new heaven and a new earth (Revelation 21). The new heaven and earth will be a single entity. In this new world, the life of Christ will flow like a river and the fruit of life will feed the inhabitants of heaven (v.1-2). There will be no more war. Peace and harmony will reign in the cosmos (v.3). The people of God will be with Jesus and there will be no more evil. This is the blessing of God!

This new world is getting closer every day. God has promised. Jesus is coming (v.6-7). God has not kept His plan a secret. He has given His Bible. John was commissioned to make known what is about to happen (v.8-10). People's true identity is revealed in their decisions now (v.11). Jesus is coming to reveal and to judge each person and to repay each accordingly (v.12-13). Those who repent and believe are blessed (v.14-16). The opportunity for salvation is right now. The offer of God and His church is for all to come and receive freely God's provision of grace and mercy (v.17). Any who repent and turn to Jesus will be saved.

The will of God will not change. What has been written is final. Any who attempt to change the message of God's Bible will receive a catastrophic judgment (v.18-19). Jesus is coming! This is the great hope of the redeemed of God (v.20-21). This world is not our home. The Story of God is about to enter the final chapter. Creation and the fall have taken place. The rescue is under way. The restoration is about to happen. The blessed will respond in faith to the offer of God's amazing grace. Today is the day of salvation!

At death, the life of every person is sealed. Their allegiance for or against God determines their eternal reality. When Christ returns, He will make all things new, and the saints of God forever saved by grace will be blessed. Are you a disciple of Jesus? Are you living in light of the return of Jesus? Those who live for Jesus and die in Jesus have eternal hope.

ABOUT THE AUTHOR

Jason Pettus has served as an ordained pastor since August, 1993. His wife, Carrie, led him to saving faith, when he was fifteen. They married six years later and now have three children: Mackenzie, Jackson, and Asher. He has degrees from Belmont University (B.A. in Religion), David Lipscomb University (M.Div.), and Reformed Theological Seminary (D.Min.). His passion is to make disciples who know the Word of God and have a deep love for Jesus.